The Antenicene Pascha

Liturgia condenda 7

1. Gerard Lukken & Mark Searle, *Semiotics and Church Architecture. Applying the Semiotics of A.J. Greimas and the Paris School to the Analysis of Church Buildings*, Kampen, 1993.

2. Gerard Lukken, *Per visibilia ad invisibilia. Anthropological, Theological and Semiotic Studies on the Liturgy and the Sacraments*, edited by Louis van Tongeren & Charles Caspers, Kampen, 1994.

3. *Bread of Heaven. Customs and Practices Surrounding Holy Communion. Essays in the History of Liturgy and Culture*, edited by Charles Caspers, Gerard Lukken & Gerard Rouwhorst, Kampen, 1995.

4. Willem Marie Speelman, *The Generation of Meaning in Liturgical Songs. A Semiotic Analysis of Five Liturgical Songs as Syncretic Discourses*, Kampen, 1995.

5. Susan K. Roll, *Toward the Origins of Christmas*, Kampen, 1995.

6. Maurice B. McNamee, *Vested Angels. Eucharistic Allusions in Early Netherlandish Paintings*, Leuven, 1998.

7. Karl Gerlach, *The Antenicene Pascha. A Rhetorical History*, Leuven, 1998.

Liturgia condenda is published by the Liturgical Institute in Tilburg (NL). The series plans to publish innovative research into the science of liturgy and serves as a forum which will bring together publications produced by researchers of various nationalities. The motto *liturgia condenda* expresses the conviction that research into the various aspects of liturgy can make a critico-normative contribution to the deepening and the renewal of liturgical practice.

The editorial board: Paul Post (Tilburg), Louis van Tongeren (Tilburg), Gerard Rouwhorst (Utrecht), Ton Scheer (Nijmegen), Lambert Leijssen (Louvain), Charles Caspers (secretary – Tilburg)

The advisory board: Paul Bradshaw (Notre Dame IN), Paul De Clerck (Paris), Andreas Heinz (Trier), François Kabasele (Kinshasa), Jan Luth (Groningen), Susan Roll (New York)

Honorary editor: Gerard Lukken (Tilburg)

Liturgisch Instituut
P.O. Box 9130
5000 HC Tilburg
The Netherlands

The Antenicene Pascha

A Rhetorical History

By

Karl Gerlach

PEETERS

© 1998, Uitgeverij Peeters, Bondgenotenlaan 153, 3000 Leuven, Belgium

ISBN 90-429-0570-0
D. 1998/0602/266

TABLE OF CONTENTS

PART TWO: THE RHETORIC OF DISPUTE

SIGLA

AB	Anchor Bible (commentaries), NY.
ACC	Alcuin Club Collection
ACG	Koester, Helmut. Ancient Christian Gospels. Their History and Development. London/Philadelphia 1990.
ACW	Ancient Christian Writers, Westminster, MD.
AGAJU	Arbeiten zur Geschichte des antiken Judentums und des Urchristentums, Leiden.
AGWG^{PH}	Abhandlungen der (königlichen) Gesellschaft der Wissenschaften zu Göttingen. Philosophisch-historische Klasse.
AH	Adversus Haereses
AIPh	Annuaire de l'Institut de Philologie et d'Histoire Orientales, Brussels.
AKG	Arbeiten zur Kirchengeschichte, Berlin.
ALW	Archiv für Liturgiewissenschaft, Münster.
AmUSt	American University Studies, NY, Series VII, Theology and Religion.
AnLit	Analecta Liturgica (=StAn)
ANRW	Aufstieg und Niedergang der römischen Welt. II. Principat. Berlin/New York.
ASNU	Acta Seminarii Neotestamentica Upsalensis, Uppsala, etc.
ATANT	Abhandlungen zur Theologie des Alten und Neuen Testaments, Basel/Zürich.
AThR	Anglican Theological Review, NY.
Aug	Augustianum, Rome.
BA	Biblical Archaeologist, New Haven.
BAR	Biblical Archaeology Review, Washington, DC.
BBB	Bonner biblische Beiträge, Bonn.
BBKg	Bonner Beiträge zur Kirchengeschichte, Bonn.
BEFAR	Bibliothèque des écoles française d'Athènes et de Rome, Paris.
BEL.S	Bibliotheca "Ephemerides Liturgicae" Subsidia, Rome.
BETL	Bibliotheca Ephemeridum theologicarum Lovaniensium, Leuven.
BFchrT	Beiträge zur Förderung der christlichen Theologie, Gütersloh.
BGBE	Beiträge zur Geschichte der biblischen Exegese, Tübingen.
BGBH	Beiträge zur Geschichte der biblischen Hermeneutik, Tübingen.
BHT	Beiträge zur historischen Theologie, Tübingen.
Bib	Biblica, Rome.
BibPatr	Biblica Patristica
BiKi	Bibel und Kirche, Stuttgart.

BKV²	Bibliothek der Kirchenväter. Eine Auswahl patristischer Werke in deutscher Übersetzung. Hrg. O. Bardenhewer, Th. Schermann, K. Weymann. Kempten/ München.
BSO(A)S	British Society of Oriental (and African) Studies, London.
BZ	Biblische Zeitschrift, Paderborn.
BZAW	Beihefte zur Zeitschrift für die alttestamentliche Wissenschaft
BZNW	Beihefte zur Zeitschrift für die neutestamentliche Wissenschaft
CCSL	Corpus Cristianorum Series Latina, Turnholt.
CCWJCW	Cambridge Commentaries on Writings of the Jewish and Christian World.
CHQ	Catholic Historical Quarterly, Washington, DC.
ChrAnt	Christianisme Antique, Paris.
CogFid	Cogito Fidei, Paris.
Conc(D)	Concilium, Eine Internationale Zeitschrift für Theologie, Einsiedeln.
CoptSt	Coptic Studies, Leiden.
CQL	Easter in the Early Church. An Anthology of Jewish and Early Christian Texts. Selected, annotated, and introduced by Raniero Cantalamessa. Revised and Augmented by the Author. Newly Translated from the Sources and Edited with Further Annotations by James M. Quigley, SJ, and Joseph T. Lienhard, SJ. Collegeville, MN (USA) 1993 = ET Cantalamessa, Raniero, La Pasqua nella Chiesa Antica (=Traditio Cristiana), Torino 1978 (dÜ = OAK).
CQR	Church Quarterly Review, London.
CRI	Compendia Rerum Iudaicarum ad Novum Testamentum, Assen.
CrSt	Cristianesimo nella Storia, Bologna.
CSCO	Corpus Scriptorum Cristianorum Orientalia. Louvain, etc.
CSEL	Corpus Scriptorum Ecclesiorum Latina, Vienna.
DOP	Dumbarton Oaks Papers, Wash., DC.
DOS	Dumbarton Oaks Studies, Wash., DC.
dÜ	deutsche Übersetzung (German translation)
EH	ἐκκλεσιαστική ἱστορία, Historia Ecclesiæ, various authors.
EHS	Europäische Hochschulschriften, Reihe 23, Theologie, Bern, etc.
EKK	Evangelisch-Katholischer Kommentar, Neukirchen.
EL	Ephemerides liturgicae, Vatican.
EO	Ecclesia Orans, Rome.
EPhM	Études de philosophie médiévale, Paris.
ESW	Ecumenical Studies in Worship, Richmond, VA.
ET	English Translation
EvTh	Evangelische Theologie, München.
EvQ	Evangelical Quarterly, London.

FC	Fontes Cristiana, Freiburg (D).
FGNK	Forschungen zur Geschichte des neutestamentlichen Kanons und der altkirchlichen Literatur, Erlangen/Leipzig.
FKDg	Forschungen zur Kirchen- und Dogmengeschichte, Göttingen.
FRLANT	Forschungen zur Religion und Literatur des alten und neuen Testaments, Göttingen.
FS	Festschrift (regardless of language)
GCS	Die Griechischen Christlichen Shriftsteller der ersten drei Jahrhunderte, Leipzig 1897-1941; Berlin 1953 ff.
Goodspeed	Goodspeed, Edgar J. Die ältesten Apologeten. Texte mit kurzen Einleitungen. Göttingen 1914.
HDR	Harvard Dissertations in Religion, Minneapolis.
HisTh	History and Theory
HSCP	Harvard Studies in Classical Philology, Cambridge, MA.
HThR	Harvard Theological Review, Cambridge, MA.
HThSt	Hamburger Theologische Studien, Hamburg.
HUCA	Hebrew Union College Annual, Cincinnati.
InThSt	Innsbrücker Theologische Studien, Innsbrück.
JbAC.Eb	Jahrbuch für Antike und Christentum Ergänzungsband
JBL	Journal of Biblical Literature, Philadelphia.
JECL	Journal of Early Christian Literature, Baltimore <SecCent.
JEH	Journal of Ecclesiastical History, London.
JJS	Journal of Jewish Studies, London.
JLW	Jahrbuch für die Liturgiewissenschaft, Münster > ALW.
JLCR	Jordan Lectures in Comparative Religion, London.
JRel	Journal of Religion, Chicago.
JSS.Sup	Journal of Semitic Studies, supplement, Manchester.
JThCh	Journal for Theology and Church, NY.
JThS	Journal of Theological Studies, London.
LCL	Loeb Classical Library, Cambridge, MA/ London.
Lehrbuch	Drobner, Hubertus. Lehrbuch der Patrologie. Freiburg, Basel, Wien, 1994.
Leitourgia	Handbuch des evangelischen Gottesdienstes. Hrsg. Karl Ferdinand Müller und Walter Blankenburg. Kassel
LEW	Brightman, F.E., al. Liturgies Eastern and Western, Vol. I, Eastern Liturgies, Oxford 1896.
LF	Liturgiegeschichtliche Forschungen, Münster.
LitCon	Liturgia Condenda, Kampen (NL).
LJ	Liturgisches Jahrbuch, Münster.
LOrS	London Oriental Studies
LQF	Liturgiegeschichtliche Quellen und Forschungen, Münster.
LThJ	Lutheran Theological Journal, Adelaide.

LThK	Lexikon für Theologie und Kirche.
Mem	Memorial volume (any language)
MPes	Neusner, Jacob. A History of the Mishnaic Law of Appointed Times, Part Two, Erubin, Pesachim, SJLA 34, Leiden 1981.
NAWG[PH]	Nachrichten der Akademie der Wissenschaften zu Göttingen, philosophisch-historische Klasse.
Neotest	Neotestamentica, Pretoria.
NF	neue Folge = new series
NHLE[3]	Nag Hammadi Library in English, third revised edition, James Robinson, ed.
NHMS	Nag Hammadi and Manichaean Studies, ed. J. M. Robinson and H. J. Klimkeit. Leiden <NHS.
NHS	Nag Hammadi Studies, ed. J. M. Robinson. Leiden >NHMS
NS	New series
NovTest	Novum Testamentum, Leiden.
NT	New Testament, neues Testament, etc.
NT.S	Supplements to Novum Testamentum, Leiden.
NTA	Neutestamentliche Abhandlungen. Münster.
NTApo[5]	Neutestamentliche Apokryphen in deutscher Übersetzung. Hg. Wilhelm Schneemelcher, 2 vols. Tübingen, 1987, 1989.
NTApoc	James, Montague Rhodes, trans. The Apocryphal New Testament, being the Apocryphal Gospels, Acts, Epistles, and Apocalypses. with other narratives and fragments. Oxford. 21953.
NTS	New Testament Studies, Cambridge.
OBO	Orbis Biblicus et Orientalis, Freibourg (CH).
OCA	Orientalia Christiana Analecta, Rome.
OECT	Oxford Early Christian Texts.
OkSt	Ostkirchliche Studien, Würzburg.
OLA	Orientalia Lovaniensia Analecta, Leuven.
Origins	Bradshaw, Paul. The Search for Origins of Christian Worship, London 1992.
OrChr	Orientalia Christiana, Rome.
OrSuec	Orientalia Suecana, Uppsala.
OrSyr	L'Orient Syrien, Paris.
OT	Old Testament
OTL	Old Testament Library, London.
OTPseud	Old Testament Pseudepigrapha, 2 vols. Ed. by James Charlesworth, London 1983, 1985.
PEER	Prayers of the Eucharist Early and Reformed. Jasper, R.C. and Luming, G.J., ed., N.Y., 1987.
PG	Patrologiae cursus completus. Series Graeca. Acc. Jacques-Paul Migne, Paris.

PL	Patrologiae cursus completus. Series Latina. Acc. Jacques-Paul Migne, Paris.
PTS	Patristische Texte und Studien. Berlin.
PUCSC	Pubblicazioni dell'Università Cattolica del Sacre Cuore, Milan.
RB	Revue Biblique, Paris.
RevBen	Revue Benedictine, Paris.
RGRW	Religions in the Graeco-Roman World, Leiden.
RHE	Revue d'Histoire Ecclésiastique, Louvain.
RHPhR	Revue d'Histoire et de Philosophie Religieuses. Strasbourg.
Roots	The Roots of Egyptian Christianity. Pearson, Birger A. and James E. Goehring, eds. SAC, 1986.
RQ	Römische Quartalschrift für christliche Altertumskunde und Kirchengeschichte, Freiburg i. Br.
RQH	Revue des Questiones Historiques, Paris.
RSR	Recherches de Science Religieuse, Paris.
Saec	Saeculum. Jahrbuch für Universalgeschichte. München.
SANT	Studien zu Alten und Neuen Testament, München.
SBL	Society of Biblical Literature, Missoula, MT.
SBL.MS	Society of Biblical Literature, Monograph Series.
SBL.SP	Society of Biblical Literature, Seminar Papers.
SC	Sources chrétiennes, Paris.
SecCent	Second Century, Abilene, TX.
SJLA	Studies in Judaism in Late Antiquity, Leiden.
SJT	Scottish Journal of Theology, Edinburgh.
SPAW[PH]	Sitzungsberichte der Preußischen Akademie der Wissenschaften, philosophisch-historische Klasse, Berlin.
SL	Studia Liturgica, Rotterdam.
SNTS.MS	Society for New Testament Studies, Monograph Series
SpicFrib	Spicilegium Friburgensis
SPMed	Studia Patristica Mediolanensia
StAn	Studia Anselmiana, Rome.
STANT	Studien zur Theologie des Alten und Neuen Testaments, München.
StDoc	Studies and Documents, London.
StEv	Studia Evangelica, Berlin, etc.
StJud	Studia Judaica, Berlin.
StPat	Studia Patristica. Papers presented to (Papers of) the International Conference on Patristic Studies.
StPBib	Studia Post Biblica, Leiden.
StTh	Studia Theologica. Scandinavian Journal of Theology. Lund, etc.
SUC 1	Schriften des Urchristentums, erster Teil. Die Apostolischen Väter, eingeleitet, herausgegeben, übertragen und erläutert von Joseph A. Fischer. Darmstadt, 1959.

SUC 2	Schriften des Urchristentums, zweiter Teil. Didache (Apostellehre), Barnabasbrief, zweiter Klemensbrief, Schrift an Diognet. Eingeleitet, herausgegeben, übertragen und erläutert von Klaus Wengst. Darmstadt, 1984.
TANZ	Texte und Arbeiten zum neutestamentlichen Zeitalter, Tübingen.
TEL	Textes et études liturgiques, Louvain.
TF	traducion française (French translation)
THNT	Theologischer Handkommentar zum NT.
Theoph.	Theophaneia. Beiträge zur Religions- und Kirchengeschichte des Altertums, Bonn.
ThStL	Theologische Studien der Leogesellschaft, Vienna.
TrMem	Travaux et mémoires, Centre de Recherche d'histoire et civilisation byzantines, Paris.
TThS	Trierer Theologische Studien, Trier.
ThZ	Theologische Zeitschrift, Basel.
TU	Texte und Untersuchungen zur Geschichte der altchristlichen Literatur, Leipzig, 1882-1950; Berlin 1950 ff.
UALG	Untersuchungen zur antiken Literatur und Geschichte, Berlin.
UCOP	University of Cambridge Oriental Publications.
UTB	Universal Textbibliothek, Darmstadt.
VC	Vetera Christianorum, Bari.
VEGL	Veröffentlichungen der Evangelischen Gesellschaft für Liturgieforschung, Göttingen.
VigChr	Vigilae Christianae, Amsterdam.
VigChrS	Supplements to VigChr, Amsterdam.
VT	Vetus Testamentum, Leiden.
WA	Luther, Martin, Werke, kritische Gesamtausgabe, Weimarer Ausgabe.
WBT	Wiener Beiträge zur Theologie, Vienna.
WSt	Woodbrooke Studies, Christian Documents in Syrian, Arabic, and Garshuni, Cambridge.
Wor	Worship. A review concerned with the problems of liturgical renewal. Collegeville, MN.
WUNT	Wissenschaftliche Untersuchungen zum Neuen Testament, Tübingen.
ZAW	Zeitschrift für die alttestamentliche Wissenschaft, Berlin.
ZBK	Zürcher Bibelkommentare.
ZDPV	Zeitschrift des deutschen Palästina-Vereins, Wiesbaden, etc.
ZKG	Zeitschrift für Kirchengeschichte, Stuttgart.
ZKTh	Zeitschrift für katholische Theologie, Vienna.
ZThK	Zeitschrift für Theologie und Kirche, Tübingen, etc.
ZNW	Zeitschrift für die neutestamentliche Wissenschaft, Berlin, etc.
ZwissTh	Zeitschrift für wissenschaftliche Theologie, Jena.

FOREWORD

These studies end where they first began, with the paschal controversy of the late second century. As in many such endeavors, the road eventually travelled, its map tokened by the chapters that follow, did not take the direction initially planned. There was considerable change of route along the way and far too many interesting sidetrips to leave unexplored. The trip began something like this: to understand early Christian rhetoric about the paschal feast and the rhetoric about the rhetoric, ancient church histories and contemporary scholarship, I began to look more and more at the rhetorical structures Antenicene writers and their commentators used to craft narratives about Christian rite, especially as they incorporated the Hebrew scriptures, the teachings of Jesus, and the story of his birth, death, and resurrection. Certain regional patterns began to emerge, not so much in the texts chosen to interact with Christian ritual, but in the ways in which they were interpreted and translated into ritual action. Though Exodus 12 is a common landmark, paschal traditions in Asia Minor, Egypt, and Syria each create a particular rhetorical landscape, which the first part of this study attempts to describe. The scenery becomes especially rugged in the final chapters, when these traditions collide in the paschal controversies of the second and fourth centuries.

Acknowledgments

As you can see from the bibliography at the end of this particular journey, historical questions about the paschal feast and its rhetoric could, and likely will, continue indefinitely. Here, valuable assistance was rendered by my adviser Dr. Andreas Heinz, whose most prudent counsel, along with frequent access to his consummate knowledge of the Christian liturgy, was a comment often necessary in the beginning stages of this study, "That is a very interesting idea, but when do I get to see something in writing?" Dr. Balthasar Fischer, Professor Emeritus of the Theological Faculty of Trier, who served as second reader for the dissertation as well as the Lizentiat thesis, also accompanied the progress of the current work with interest and encouragement. Dr. Gordon Lathrop of the Lutheran Theological Seminary at Philadelphia also offered valuable advice.

I would also like to thank my friends Dr. Julia and Thomas Shinnick, Austin, TX, and the Rev. Douglas and Monica Ogden, Whitehall, MI, for their letters, their hospitality on my yearly visits back to the United States, and for providing several articles and books unavailable to me in Germany. The need for these, however, was quite rare due to the ample holdings of the library of the Roman Catholic Seminary of Trier, the excellent library of the German Liturgical Institute, and the speed of interlibrary loan service among the theological libraries of Germany. The staffs of these institutions have well earned my gratitude. I am also grateful to the Rev. Mark Herbener, Bishop of the Northern Texas-Northern Louisiana Synod of the Evangelical Lutheran Church in America, the Synod Council, and national judicatories of the ELCA for granting me a graduate study leave from parish service. My friends in Trier, Volker Wienecke and Tanja Paffenholz, originally from Hannover, and Eberhard Driesler, Traunreut, provided necessary distraction as we discovered together the beauties (and delightful beverages) of the Mosel valley.

Since I dislike having to switch linguistic gears within the same work even for languages I know, I have "englished" all but a few citations. Translations from Greek, Latin, and modern languages are mine unless otherwise noted, those from Oriental languages are usually translated from modern versions from the *Corpus Scriptorum Christianorum Orientalium*. I have naturally consulted other modern translations, particularly the French series *Sources Chrétiennes* and the venerable German standard, *Bibliothek der Kirchenväter*, as well as the newer series *Fontes Christiani*.

Many texts dealing with the paschal feast have been gathered and carefully annotated by Raniero Cantalamessa in a sourcebook now available in English translation: *Easter in the Early Church*. Unfortunately, the first act of the translator (or publisher?) was to jettison the original language version of all texts, then fatten the footnotes and march them to the end of the book. This reduces the usefulness of the English version compared with the Italian original as well as French and German translations in the series *Traditio Christiana*. Since page numbers differ, texts taken from this anthology are also given with their number. My indebtedness to Cantalamessa's book will be obvious to anyone who has used it.

A Note on Names and Numbers

The second century equivalent of Easter and the paschal Triduum was called by both Greek and Latin writers "Pascha (πάσχα)," a Greek transliteration of the Aramaic form of the Hebrew פסח, the Passover feast of Ex 12. I have used the term "Pesach" and occasionally "Passover" to distinguish the rituals of the one from the other, even though for these writers "Pascha" means both.

The term "Quartadeciman" ("Fourteener," from *quarta decima*, fourteenth of the moon/month) is a Latin translation of what in English would appear as "Tessaraskaidekatite," a designation with overtones of heresy that lumped together all those who celebrated the Pascha on the Hebrew date of Pesach, 14 Nisan, or some solar equivalent, in opposition to the custom of the majority. As far as we know, neither term was used by the people so labelled, and no second century author used the word to refer to the Asian paschal practice. Needless to say, this Greek "Four-and-ten-ite" would not play lightly on the Anglo-USAmerican tongue, so the Latin has been retained. As Wolfgang Huber[1] points out, there are more occurrences of the spelling "Quart*o*deciman," which has also generally been used in English and USAmerican scholarship. One writer even invented a "Quartodecimatus"[2] who like Montanus for the Montanists, was the founder of a sect, while some copyists understood the word as "quarto decim anni/annus," implying that second century Asian Christians observed a fourteen-year calendrical cycle or, like some sort of liturgical locusts, celebrated Pascha every fourteen years. For the later church, the term had lost all meaning.

If the truth be known, I had begun spelling the term with an "a" after several German scholars before I gave the matter any thought. Yet since my association of the term is with the paschal full moon and its fourteenth day in a lunar calendar, both feminine gender in Latin, I have chosen to retain the more euphonious "Quartadeciman."

The psalter used by virtually all authors treated here was that of the LXX, whose numbering is followed in this work, with the Hebrew in parenthesis.

For dual language or synoptic editions, "f." refers to the next even or odd page; the same for editions with *en face* translations other than English (e.g., *Sources Chrétiennes*), but not for English ones (e.g., *Oxford Early English Texts*), where "f." may include the translation.

---

[1] Huber, Wolfgang, Passa und Ostern. Untersuchungen zur Osterfeier der alten Kirche. BZNW 35, 1969, n. 35, 5 f.

[2] Huber refers to the Spanish epitome of the Council of Laodicea, Ecclesia Occidentalis Monumenta Iuris Antiquissimi, ed. C. H. Turner, 347.

To the People of God
of University Lutheran Church, Philadelphia,
and Good Shepherd Lutheran Church, Marshall, Texas,
who taught me much about the language of rite.

At this feast * was paid
the sin of all * by the Lord of all.
At this feast * the Lord emptied forth
the treasures full * of the symbols of his death.
At this feast * our Lord released
the symbols that had striven * to proclaim him.
Ephrem Syrus, Azyma 12.1-5, CSCO 249, 15.

PART ONE: THE LANGUAGE OF RITE

A. INTRODUCTION

I. Rite and Narrative

With a characteristically Syriac love of parallel, Ephrem transforms reading rite, story, and mystery into rich imagery. As the Pascha proclaims the forgiveness of sins through Christ's death, it reveals yet another mystery, the exegetical treasures of Ex 12, a ritual text embedded in the Exodus saga, the story of origins of the Jewish people. How these "treasures full of symbols" pour forth their riches to Christian writers is intimately linked to the story of the paschal vigil, the sacraments of baptism and eucharist, and indeed the identity of Jesus and the community gathered in his name. It is also the story of a people being exegetically removed, sometimes with considerable rhetorical force, from their own sacred writings, just as the Pascha, a transparently Judaic heritage in Christian liturgy, becomes a major locus of anti-Judaic polemic.

Long before Ephrem could reflect on this process, Christian authors were striving to release the symbolic worth of Christian rite with a diligence only matched by its absence in the NT. Writing in the 130's, "Barnabas" could begin this unfettering exegesis, "Let us investigate whether the Lord strove to say something beforehand about water and the cross." For Barnabas, it is a foregone conclusion that such messages do not elude those gifted and knowledgeable enough to find them. The first step is a decision about genre: the Hebrew scriptures spoke *from the beginning* of Christ, the gathered community, and the rituals that shape it. The results of Barnabas' search are carefully chosen and, in part, carefully rewritten and combined chains of OT citations to mirror baptismal rite and teaching. Similar constructs inform the meal prayers of the *Didache*, where the act of gathering for the meal becomes a central metaphor, and the baptismal narratives of the *Shepherd* of Hermas, for whom getting in and out of water begins to tell a story. As the Hebrew scriptures are "released" to speak in new contexts, they also begin to explain what it means to be baptized, to gather in common worship around the table, and to celebrate the Pascha.

Around the turn of the third century, however, not long after Irenaeus elevates the gospel canon to holy text, bishops and theologians across the Empire are suddenly arguing about details of the passion narrative and how they relate to liturgical action in the paschal night. Jesus could not have eaten the paschal lamb, he *was* the lamb, Hippolytus writes. Tertullian finds a type for paschal baptism in the man carrying water who shows the disciples to the Upper Room. Drawing from both testaments, the Syrian *Didascalia* offers a whole catalogue of aetiologies for the paschal fast to encourage a week-long observance. NT narrative is being incorporated into narratives about rite in new ways, especially as they are attacked and defended. When paschal traditions and the hermeneutic underlying them conflict again at the Council of Nicaea, the "old" method of exegeting liturgical practice is scarcely found, but anti-Judaic polemic, a constant of the Christian paschal tradition, takes on a new twist.

Arguing against those who substitute water for eucharistic wine, Cyprian shows how standard this new language of rite and text had become:

> No one should imagine, dearest Brother, that one should follow the practice of certain people who up to now have thought it proper to offer only water in the chalice of the Lord. Yet one must first ask whom they themselves have followed. For if we are only permitted to follow Christ in the sacrifice that Christ offered, then we must also surely follow and perform what Christ did and commanded...
>
> For if Christ Jesus, our Lord and God, is himself the highest priest of God the Father and offered himself as sacrifice to the Father, commanding that this happen in his remembrance, then only that priest truly represents Christ who imitates what Christ did, and only offers the Father a pure and perfect sacrifice in the Church of God when he does this in the way he sees that Christ himself has offered it.[1]

---

[1] Cyprian, Ep. 63.14, CSEL 3.2, 712.

This acute rubricization of the meal narrative places Cyprian in a somewhat awkward position:

> Of course the Lord did not offer the mixed chalice in the morning, but not until after the evening meal. Should we then perhaps not celebrate the liturgy until after the eucharist, to offer this way the mixed chalice in the celebration of the liturgy? Yet Christ had to offer the chalice in the evening of the day to indicate even by the hour of sacrifice the sunset and evening of the world, as it is written in the Book of Exodus, "And all the people of the congregation of the sons of Israel shall sacrifice it [the paschal lamb] toward evening," [Ex 12.6] and in the psalms, "Let the lifting up of my hands be as an evening sacrifice" [Ψ140 (141)2]. But we celebrate the resurrection of the Lord in the morning.[2]

Cyprian remembers that the eucharist celebrated in his day does not correspond exactly to its founding narrative. In the gospel account, the cup follows the meal, and the meal was held in the evening. To extricate himself from this rhetorical corner, Cyprian performs a code switch, reverting to the "old" style of exegeting used earlier in his letter in a Melchizedek typology. A ritual drawn from the Hebrew scriptures, the slaying of the paschal lamb, and a ritual metaphor, prayer as evening sacrifice, are read as "mysteries": not as rites, but as prophetic actions fulfilled in Christ. Kerygma supersedes rituals, but the result is read strictly in the new fashion as scriptural rubric, ritualizing the texts into the new context of the Christian liturgy. Of course Cyprian could have just as easily weighted these scriptures differently and obtained the opposite result. The point is not where Cyprian arrives, but how he gets there.

Those who demand contemporary relevance for analyzing such constructs and their history should compare the following statement by Hans-Christoph Schmidt-Lauber, as he argues against Luther's reduction of the anaphora to the Words of Institution:

> But in the way it works itself out in the liturgy, there is a quite simple and persuasive argument against Luther's idea. Christ did not command, "Recite my words," but "Do this in remembrance of me." And that means: take the bread and the chalice, say thanks over them – as the Jewish householder does and as Christ did in a special way – break the bread and distribute both elements. For this reason the certainly correct

---

[2] Cyprian, Ep. 63.16, CSEL 3.2, 714.

theological emphasis on the content of the Words of Institution may be combined with a real doing of what Christ commanded his disciples.[3]

The differences between Cyprian and Schmidt-Lauber rest solely in the value given ritual continuity with Judaism and the distance each author removes a particular practice from appropriate Christian ritual. The argument is identical: those who substitute water for wine, or those who recite only the bare Verba, do not completely carry out Christ's command.

In view of such modern rhetoric, it quickly becomes apparent that when ancient Christian texts are read only for their value as "history" of the liturgy, which often reduces to their aetiological value for current or desired practice, a vital piece of the earliest liturgical tradition is lost. There is an entire Medieval/Reformation tradition, still active among European and American Lutherans, with which Schmidt-Lauber is in dialogue, and if this paragraph were one among many ancient fragments, reconstructing this tradition would be impossible without acknowledging what moderns see as a transparent rhetorical agenda.

II. The Pivotal Role of the Second Century Church

In extant literature, the paschal feast does not emerge until a rhetorically charged dispute arises between apostolic sees claiming apostolic origins for apostolic practices through apostolic writings. In other words, Christian identity is being shaped around rite and narrative that predate this new self-definition through the episcopal office and a scriptural canon now including the NT. Yet despite its sudden appearance, this dispute is only part of a much longer conversation between rite and text inevitable in a religious community gathered around holy words and holy actions. Just as ritual action defines community, so do words about rite spoken outside the liturgy. As with Cyprian's diluted eucharist, they do so more acutely in the heat of controversy.

Except for Ignatius of Antioch and the Christian Sibyl, no writer of the early second century Great Church constructs narratives about rite remotely resembling Cyprian's exegesis. Something has radically changed, but this change is no mere byproduct of NT canonical formation. At the

---

[3] Die Bedeutung der "Lima"-Liturgie für die ökumenische Bewegung, LJ 35, 1985, 131-147.

end of the century, the "new" method is generating more and more narratives about rite and story, while the "old" is on its way to a catalogue of scriptural metaphors. The "old" method could still produce works of great beauty like the mosaics on the north wall of Ravenna's San Vitale, where Abel, Melchizedek, and Abraham and Isaac stand as types for the eucharist. This decorative two dimensionality, however, hardly carries the same significance as the Jerusalem Triduum, which combined Holy Story with the Holy Places into a great salvific drama. Once Melchizedek serving bread and wine to Abraham "means" the eucharist, there is little more to do than point to the picture.[4] Yet in the early second century, this connection to a canonical narrative did much more than merely illustrate.

Christian ritual narrative begins as a thoroughly Christian story told through a thoroughly Judaic body of literature, the LXX canon, reconfiguring bits and pieces of these writings around rituals with Judaic roots. Neither the NT nor Christ narrative without OT referents is yet the definitive recension of this story, just as NT authors show almost no interest in founding cult. Instead, Christian authors use the tools of allegory, typology, or simple analogy to creates a "likeness" within the OT canon or basic teachings that may generate narrative about the liturgy or in some cases, even liturgical action. This same interpretive search lies deep within the structure of the gospels. OT motifs are taken from their contexts, either as images or whole narratives, and addressed to the mystery of Christ's life, death, and resurrection. Just as early scriptural exegesis seeks to define and, indeed, prove this mystery, so by the same interpretive means it seeks to define and legitimate Christian rite.

Whatever modern scholarship may term them, when early Christian authors employ such constructs, they usually call it "spiritual" interpretation,[5] which Justin Martyr is fond of contrasting to a Judaic "carnal" understanding of scripture. The blood rite of Ex 12, for instance, becomes a favorite baptismal typology not because of common ritual elements, only found in the most general fashion in the use of liquid (blood,

---

[4] "Pointing" could still produce much discussion. Melchizedek, Pesach lamb, and other OT sacrifices, and Cyprian's letter, figured heavily at the Council of Trent. Pratzner, Ferdinand, Messe und Kreuzesopfer. Die Krise der sakramentalen Idee bei Luther und in der mittelalterlichen Scholastik, WBT 29, 1970, esp. 27-52.

[5] Distinctions between allegory (events) and typology (images) are modern. Mazza, Enrico, Mystagogy. A Theology of Liturgy in the Patristic Age, NY 1989, 7-13.

water, or oil) and a smearing action (daubing on post and lentil, chrismation), but because of their similar contexts: ritual acts in a story of salvation. These motifs are able to carry meaning for Christian exegetes only
because the sacrifice of the paschal lamb was read as a figure for the
sacrificial death of Christ and its efficacy signed in the baptismal rite. It
cannot be stressed enough that when early Christian exegetes read Ex 12
or any other scripture for kerygmatic or ritual content, they are not craft-
ing rhetorically decorative mosaics, but are convinced that their reading is
the only legitimate one in harmony with the will of God.

In this interpretive task, narrative elements may be addressed directly
to ritual or first to a kerygmatic narrative that then transfers its meaning
to rite. The earliest baptismal rites show two ways this can occur.
Anointing with oil was a part of ancient bathing that began to be
viewed as a separate ritual event, then to attract motifs from the anointing of kings to the anointing at Bethany. In contrast, a drink of milk
mixed with honey[6] at the baptismal eucharist is inexplicable except as a
ritual generated by equating baptism with entrance into the Promised
Land.[7] Yet since mothers in Late Antiquity often gave their infants a
drink of water mixed with a bit of honey, milk and honey *together* could
be explicated as signs of new birth. With chrismation, a variety of scriptural narratives attaches to an action ritualized from the general culture;
with the milk and honey, a single scriptural narrative with rich associations produces ritual, which then may be further interpreted with a
metaphor drawn from daily life. Though the direction of development
is exactly opposite, Ephrem's highly imitative "releasing" of symbols is
the necessary link.

Before the end of the second century, this hermeneutical "release"
is particularly acute because only then does a primary marker of community identity, the canon of four gospels and Pauline epistles, begin
to emerge as the authoritative writings around which the Church was

---

[6] The Mithras cult initiated into the "Persian" stage (5 of 7) with milk and honey.
Betz, Johannes, Die Eucharistie als Gottes Milch in frühchristlicher Sicht, ZKTh 106,
1984, (1-26, 167-185), 1-4.

[7] Cf. Barn 6.17: The child is first kept alive with milk and honey. So also us, because
we are kept alive by the promise and word…" Cf. Clem. Alex., Paed 1.25.1-52.2; Tert.,
De cor 3.3, Adv. Marc. 1.14.3, Marcionites still used the drink at the baptismal
eucharist, presumably without the OT connection. ApTrad 21; Odes of Solomon 4.10.
Betz, Milch, and van de Bunt, Annewies, Milk and Honey in the Theology of Clement
of Alexandria, in: Fides Sacramenti, Sacramentum Fidei (FS Smulders), Assen 1981, 27-
39.

gathered. Though he often stresses (and stretches) continuity through Polycarp of Smyrna to the apostolic age, Irenaeus, likely only a child when Polycarp was martyred, was also aware of epochal change in his day.[8] Christianity had spread to every part of the Empire, just as Irenaeus was active in a mission to Celtic "barbarians." In the beginning decades of the century, communities of Jewish Christians may still have been the "mighty minority" Jacob Jervell[9] proposes, but the century's waning years saw their continued marginalization by both Great Church and Jewish groups.[10] With its Judaic roots only dimly remembered, Christianity was becoming a Gentile social phenomenon.[11]

Yet a century or so before Irenaeus' birth, there are far-reaching changes in the way Christian writers speak of Christ. Though the evangelists would take much teaching and place it into narrative frames, Paul uses as little Christ teaching as Christ narrative. Instead, the essential mystery of the faith, the death and resurrection of Jesus, informs Paul's ethical teaching, and only in the meal narrative is there anything approaching a story about Jesus anchored to time and place. The gospels need not make any arguments for authority simply by showing Jesus speaking words to and for the community: they are, in essence, self-canonizing works.[12] The use of narrative material, "canonical" or no, grows steadily from the turn of the first century, spawns numerous gospels and acts around the middle of the second, and in its relationship to the liturgy reaches a manneristic apotheosis in the Syrian *Didascalia* in the early decades of the third, where the first words of the risen Christ criticize the apostles' paschal fast. Stories about Jesus have become an authoritative genre, even if not taken from authoritative writings. This

---

[8] Heretics arose "multo posterius mediantibus iam Ecclesiae temporibus." Irenaeus, AH 3.4.3, SC 210, 52.

[9] Jervell, Jacob, The Mighty Minority, StTh 34, 1980, 13-38.

[10] Katz, Steven T., Issues in the Separation of Judaism and Christianity after 70 CE: A Reconsideration, JBL 103, 1984, 43-76; Joubert, S. J., A Bone of Contention in Recent Scholarship: The 'Birkat Ha-Minim' and the Separation of Church and Synagogue in the First Century AD, Neotest. 27, 1993, 351-363.

[11] According to Melito, Christianity "was awakened in the midst of barbarians," (i.e., Jews) but "came to fruition" among the Gentile peoples of the Roman Empire. EH 4.26.7, GCS 9.1, 384.

[12] Esp. in Jn. "The words of Jesus are essentially 'canonized' by the application of the typical Johannine fulfillment formula to them in John 18.9 (quoting J 17.12) and J 18.32 (J 12.32)." Aune, David Edward, The Cultic Setting of Realized Eschatology in Early Christianity, NT.S 28, 1972, 69.

in turn points to the full ritualization of the passion narrative in the Triduum of late fourth century Jerusalem, where rite and text have merged. Yet there is a great deal of history to tell before this narrative approach to the liturgy becomes the standard language of rite.

III. Rituals are not their narratives...

That rituals define a community, if only for the very moment of their performance, was for some years apparently not quite as obvious to historians of religion as it was to participants and leaders of organized ritual acts. Before Victor Turner unsettled the regnant paradigm of "myth and rituals," most scholars saw rites as dramatizing a mythic narrative according to a "ritual pattern" most often defined not by the celebrating community but by the observer.[13] Instead, Turner proposed "communitas" as the driving force behind organized ritual behavior where rituals may carry a narrative or simply speak for themselves as common experience, the ritual medium being, as it were, the primary message.[14]

Yet regardless of their effectiveness as method, both paradigms point out an equally obvious fact. Outside of *doing* ritual, which has its own significance, speaking *about* ritual, whether by observers or participants, becomes something else – an interpretation, a restatement of its content, a story of origins – a *meaning* conveyed in narrative that may be shaped more by the dialogical moment than rite. This is especially the case if the original dialogue has been submerged in the name of "science."

The universal pattern to which the myth and rituals school of early twentieth century Britain and Scandinavia addressed all rites was "divine kingship," an archetypal narrative abstracted from Mesopotamian sources and applied in blanket fashion to religions in ancient cultures

---

[13] Turner,Victor W., The Ritual Process, London 1974, 15. The African Ndembu people have few "myths and cosmological or cosmogonic narratives" but a rich ritual life.

[14] Ritual "is not simply the dramatization of an event described from a textual praxis ..., but *is* the event itself, true and present, because it is completely and effectually experienced. ... The *credo* bearing it is always simultaneously *proclamation* of that to which one assents." Jacques, Francis, Von den Sprachspielen zu den "Textspielen." Conc(D) 31, 1995, (178-192) 182.

across the Orient and Mediterranean basin, including Judaism and
Christianity:

> Nowhere is this more clearly seen than in the annual celebration of the
> death and resurrection of Christ in the Holy Week and Easter mystery,
> which forms the Christian counterpart of the New Year Festival in the ear-
> lier culture pattern of the Ancient East. As has been shown, it was on this
> occasion that the king renewed his reign for the benefit of the community.
> In other words, he underwent a mimic death and resurrection for the pur-
> pose of ensuring the fruitfulness of the earth, and the increase of man and
> beast. This involved a ritual rebirth – a dying to live – and a reenactment
> of the drama of creation, or of some determining feature in the cultural
> history of the community. Then came a struggle or contest of some kind,
> in course of which the king or hero was slain and restored to life again tri-
> umphant over his adversaries. A marriage typified the union of heaven and
> earth, frequently marked the victory, and the festival concluded with a
> public manifestation of the restored victor, and his proclamation as King
> and Lord of creation and its processes.[15]

This is E. O. James' cultic narrative for the Christian Pascha, a "ritual
pattern" this brand of scholarship reproduced for any ritual it investigated, though the motif of divine marriage often had to be jettisoned in
the face of historical data. James' method is cued by certain key expressions: *counterpart, pattern, mimic, reenactment, drama, typified*, all
informed by a concept already used by Plutarch to speak of the mysteries of Isis – *mimesis*:

> ...nor did she [Isis] allow the contests and struggles which she had under-
> taken, her wanderings and her many deeds of wisdom and bravery, to be
> engulfed in oblivion and silence, but into the most sacred rites she infused
> images, suggestions and imitations of her experiences at that time, [ταῖς
> ἁγιωτάταις ἀναμείξασα τελεταῖς εἰκόνας καὶ ὑπονοίας καὶ μιμήματα τῶν
> τότε παθημάτων] and so she consecrated at once a pattern of piety and an
> encouragement to men and women overtaken by similar misfortune
> [εὐσεβείας ὁμοῦ δίδαγμα καὶ παραμύθιον ἀνδράσι καὶ γυναιξὶν ὑπὸ συμ-
> φορῶν ἐχομένοις ὁμοίων καθωσίωσεν].[16]

Cultic remembrance, *anamnesis*, and its divine institution as mimetic
ritual action is stronger in Plutarch than in James, primarily because it is
crucial to James' theory that ritual continuity take place even when the

---

[15] James, E. O., Christian Myth and Rituals. London 1937, 300.
[16] Plutarch, De Iside et Osiride (27), ed., J. Gwyn Griffiths, Cambridge 1970, 158.

original vegetation myth is forgotten, suppressed, or spiritualized. The accent on *imitation*, however, is the same. Noting certain correspondences between rite and holy story, an observer assumes a *mimetic fit*: the narrative is the story of origins for the rite, which in turn dramatizes the narrative. In other words, the program notes *are* the symphony – the music is only a question of form. This is true on both sides of the equation, even if the celebrating community is not calling the tune. So Plutarch, noting the importance of wine in Jewish Sabbath observances, postulates a connection to the cult of Dionysius,[17] just as Tacitus muses about Dionysian ivy garlands and vines decorating the Jerusalem Temple[18] and the Saturnine origins of the Sabbath.[19] These writers have found a ritual pattern into which they may pour any ritual description, the original mold being, of course, a purely Hellenistic one.[20]

The ultimate source of James' narrative comes closer to the surface when he discusses the medieval Sarum rite, which provides the same motifs addressed to divine kingship as all others:

> In ascending the steps of the altar the priests and their attendants actually, though unconsciously, were reproducing on a higher spiritual plane the solemn moment when Pharaoh beheld the face of his divine father, Amon-Re, and performed upon his image those mysterious rites described in a former chapter. As the Egyptian monarch in his priestly capacity entered the sanctuary, and, after a preliminary burning of incense, broke the seals, opened the doors of the shrine, censed and sprinkled the statue with holy water, so the Christian priest censes the altar and its relics upon his arrival in the holy place.[21]

This remarkable description betrays yet another aspect of imitation. As Jonathan Z. Smith has carefully demonstrated,[22] James and others discussing the origins and nature of Christian ritual are themselves actually, though unconsciously, reproducing on a somewhat higher intellectual plane a polemic narrative crafted in the earliest days of the Protestant

---

[17] Plutarch, Table Talk 4.6, Moralia VIII, LCL 424, 360-367. An initiate of the Dionysian mysteries, the speaker finds "parallels" in Jewish rites.

[18] Cf. Josephus, Bell. 5.210, LCL 210, 264 f.; "…golden vines, from which depended grapeclusters as tall as a man…"

[19] Tacitus, Histories 5.4.3-5.5. Halm, 205 f.

[20] But see Tertullian's theory that Serapis is Joseph in disguise, Ad nat 2.8.16 f.

[21] James, Myth, 147 f.

[22] Smith, Jonathan Z., Drudgery Divine. On the Comparison of Early Christianities and the Religions of Antiquity. JLCR (SOAS), 1988.

Reformation. Smith cites from *A Letter from Rome Shewing an Exact Conformity between Popery and Paganism* by the Englishman Conyers Middleton, who visited Rome in the early decades of the eighteenth century:

> The very first thing that a Stranger must necessarily take Notice of, as soon as He enters their Churches, is the use of Incense or Perfumes in their Religious Offices: The first Step he takes within the Door will be sure to make him sensible of it... A custom received directly from Paganism; and which presently called to my Mind, the Old Descriptions of Heathen Temples and Altars, which are seldom or never mention'd by the Ancients without the Epithet of perfumed or incensed...In the Old Bas-Reliefs, or Pieces of Sculpture, where any Heathen Sacrifice is represented, we never fail to observe a Boy in Sacred Habit, which is always white, with a little Chest or Box in his Hands, in which this Incense is kept for the Use of the Altar. In the same manner still in the Church of Rome, there is always a Boy in Surplice, waiting on the Priest at the Altar...[23]

Modernize the grammar, mingle the aroma of ancient Egypt with the incense of the Tridentine high mass, and the narratives are indistinguishable. Ritual motifs have been addressed to a preconceived narrative, one grossly confessional, the other serenely scientific, but they somehow manage to tell the same story. Smith concludes:

> The pursuit of the origins of the question of Christian origins takes us back, persistently, to the same point: *Protestant anti-Catholic apologetics*...The same presuppositions, the same rhetorical tactics, indeed, in the main, the very same data exhibited in these early efforts underlie much of our present-day research, with one important alteration, that the characteristics attributed to 'Popery' by the Reformation and post-Reformation controversialists, have been transferred, wholesale, to the religions of Late Antiquity.[24]

Mimesis in E. O. James is twofold: with little regard for history, the paradigm assumes an "exact conformity" of rituals from wildly disparate times and places while it imitates a polemic whose forgotten history has been masked by a veneer of scientific objectivity.

Ritual did not suddenly become polemicized in the Reformation, nor were the rhetorical tactics to which Smith alludes invented in the sixteenth century. In confrontation with the religions of Late Antiquity, Christian writers of the first and second centuries could arm themselves

[23] Cited Smith, Drudgery, 23 f. The work was published in London in 1729.
[24] Smith, Drudgery, 34.

with the same arsenal of rhetorical tactics and use them for the same
purpose as early Protestants: to secure a distinct religious identity by
polemicizing the rituals of the "other."

Yet this polemic is only one feature in a larger rhetorical landscape. Hellenic authors find in Christian rituals the same "ritual pattern" – worshipping the head of an ass, cannibalism, ritualized incest, and infanticide –
that had already been used to dehumanize a sizable Jewish minority, presumably far longer than the first literary sources – Tacitus, Philo, and Josephus – would indicate.[25] And when early Christians appropriate Judaic
ritual and scripture, they must rhetorically destroy the Judaic cult to do so,
pitting selected cult-critical passages of the prophets against all ritual prescriptions in the OT. Early apologetic literature also provided later writers
with a similar set of readily applied arguments to attack Hellenic cult and
myth – as demonic "imitations" of true religion.[26] The success of both
anti-Judaic and anti-Hellenic polemic assured their transference to conflicts
about Christian ritual merely by association. James' "scientific" reworking
of the Reformation rehash of such polemic is proof enough that such
constructs long outlive their original rhetorical setting, but rarely their
rhetorical effectiveness.

IV. Mimesis as Liturgical Action and Rhetorical Construct

Following its use in aesthetic criticism, modern liturgical scholarship
appropriates the concept *mimesis* to describe the *historicization* or *dramatization* of the liturgy, especially in the services of Holy Week. Since the
latter fourth century there is a marked tendency for these liturgies not
merely to proclaim or celebrate events in the last week of Christ's life,
but to act them out symbolically.[27] Even here, the relationship between

---

[25] See Seeliger, Hans-Reinhard, Gemeinsamkeiten in der antijüdischen und antichristlichen Polemik in der Antike, in: Christlicher Antijudaismus und jüdischer Antipaganismus, ed., H. Frohnhofen, HThSt 3, 1990, 88-94.

[26] First emerging in Justin: "It has so happened that this [eucharist] has been
imitated and then passed on by evil demons to the cult of Mithras." 1Apol 66.4, Goodspeed 75.

[27] See the collection of essays, Scicolone, Ildebrando, ed., La Celebrazione del Triduo
Pasquale, Anamnesis e Mimesis, StAns 102 (=AnLit 14), Rome 1990. For the more
bizarre side of this type of piety, such as crucifixions of real persons with varying degrees
of verisimilitude, see Daxelmüller, Christoph, Der Untergrund der Frömmigkeit. Zur
Geschichte und Pathologie religiöser Bräuche, Saec 47, 1996, 136-157.

liturgical action and narrative is more subtle than just rubricizing the
NT. Mimesis may accent the differences as much as establish likeness.
This is demonstrated quite nicely by Cyril of Jerusalem, as he explains
the relationship of kerygma to baptismal rite:

> Oh strange and paradoxical act! We did not truly suffer, we were not truly
> buried, we were not truly crucified and raised again, for in a figure is the
> mimesis (ἀλλ᾽ ἐν εἰκόνι ἡ μίμησις), but in truth the salvation. Christ was
> truly crucified and was buried and truly rose, and all these things have
> been given to us, so that imitating his sufferings, we may obtain the truth
> of salvation.[28]

At the cost of the sacramentalism Cyril maintains, the truly dramatic
is reached only in the Middle Ages, both in East and West. Robert Taft
points out a salient example in the Slavonic little compline. The general
character of this timelessly serene nocturnal office is hardly dramatic.
Yet after the Creed on Good Friday, there is a brief dialogue between the
Virgin and Christ:

> "Heal now the wound of my soul, my child," cried the holy Virgin, weep-
> ing. "Rise and still my pain and bitter anguish. For you have power, O
> Master, and can do what you will. Even your burial is voluntary."
> "How is it that you have not seen the depths of my tender love?" said
> the Lord… "Because I wish to save my creation, I have accepted death.
> But I shall rise again, and as God shall magnify you in heaven and on
> earth."[29]

Even if spoken by the same person, this is dramatic dialogue, even
dramatic conflict, with clearly assigned roles. Costumes and gestures
could be supplied by a troupe of actors – or the hearer's imagination.
Such snippets of dialogue, especially the Easter "Quem queritis?",
inspired an entire genre of popular drama that readily moved from the
chancel to the marketplace.[30] What holds these lines within the liturgy

---

[28] Cyril of Jerusalem, Hom 2.5, St. Cyril of Jerusalem's Lectures on the Christian
Sacraments (=Texts for Students 51), ed. F. L. Cross, London 1966, 20.

[29] Trans. Taft, In the Bridegroom's Absence. The Paschal Triduum in the Byzantine
Church, StAns 102 (=AnLit 14), 1990, (71-97) 77. Text: Pitra, SpicSol 4, 492-495.

[30] See Hardison, O.B., Christian Rite and Christian Drama in the Middle Ages.
Essays in the Origins and Early History of Modern Drama, Baltimore 1965; Muir, Lynnette, Biblical Drama of Medieval Europe, Oxford 1995; Bärsch, Jürgen, Das Dramatische im Gottesdienst. Liturgiewissenschaftliche Aspekte zum Phänomen der Osterfeiern und Osterspiele im Mittelalter, LJ 46, 1996, 41-66.

is that on Good Friday, it is an *absent* Christ who speaks, and the message is pure kerygma – to Mary, who takes the role of a mourning community.

In her late fourth century report of Jerusalem liturgies, Egeria, whose admiration for worship "appropriate to time and place" is boundless, does not mention a ritual in which Christ is symbolically buried. Yet as Taft notes,[31] Byzantine Good Friday liturgies have not one such ritual but two, at vespers and Saturday matins, now anticipated Friday night. Their dramatic character is exuberantly advertised in a letter of Athanasius I, twice patriarch of Constantinople at the turn of the fourteenth century, who invites the reader "to assemble to marvel, glorify, venerate, lament, and sing in a holy manner the mysteries of the awesome entombment."[32] This cinematic appeal could not be further from the somber paschal epistles of the patriarch's Alexandrian namesake a millennium before.

Again, there is a deeper connection between two aspects of mimesis. Anyone who has listened to a passion cantata or heard one of the passion narratives read with assigned roles knows how easily these works may move into the dramatic medium. The liturgical and the literary could most easily converge to shape Holy Week rituals because of all the events depicted in the gospels, the passion is the most completely drawn. What was the weather like when Jesus was baptized in the Jordan, or at the wedding at Cana? What an irrelevant question! Yet in the passion narratives, the reader feels the chill of a spring night when Peter warms himself before a charcoal fire.[33]

Mimetic liturgies are not caused by texts, but by reading them, and reading liturgical acts as narratives about Christ reaches a highpoint in the Antiochene school, of which the mystagogical homilies of Cyril of Jerusalem and Theodore of Mopsuestia are the most prominent examples.[34] While this historicism was a particular nemesis for Gregory

---

[31] Taft, Bridegroom, 79 f.

[32] Cited Taft, Bridegroom, 84, from Talbot, Alice-Mary, The Correspondence of Athanasius I Patriarch of Constantinople, DOT 3, 1975.

[33] With its realism and humble characters, the dialogue between Peter and the accusing woman violates Hellenistic conventions of representation. Auerbach, Erich, Mimesis. Dargestellte Wirklichkeit in der abendländischen Literatur, Bern/München [3]1946, 43-49.

[34] Taft sees the synthesis of Antiochene and Alexandrine exegesis in the Jerusalem and Constantinopolitan rites. The Liturgy of the Great Church: An Initial Synthesis of Structure and Interpretation on the Eve of Iconoclasm. DOP 34/35, 1980-81, 45-75.

Dix,[35] Taft argues that such an approach to Christian rite has much deeper roots in the interplay of rite and canonical text.[36] In another article, Taft touches upon this mutuality, at the same time alluding to its rhetorical purpose:

> All healthy liturgical interpretation depends on a ritual symbolism determined not arbitrarily, but by the testimony of tradition rooted in the Bible. Like the scriptures, the rites of the Church await an exegesis and a hermeneutic and a homiletic to expound, interpret, and apply their multiple levels of meaning in each age. Mystagogy is to liturgy what exegesis is to scripture. It is no wonder, then, that the commentators on the liturgy used a method inherited from the older tradition of biblical exegesis.[37]

As Taft suggests, addressing Christian rite to biblical narrative or teaching is a timeless constant. With specific speakers (teachers, presbyters, and bishops) and a specific audience (the gathered assembly or the catechumenate) this is the life setting for a discourse about the liturgy that could challenge even the genius of an Origen:

> Among various observances of the church there are a number of practices that everyone is required to do, but whose reasons are not clear to all. That we bend the knee in prayer, for example, and that our prayers are directed toward the east – though, of course, there are other cardinal directions – is not easy to make apparent to everyone. In the same way, who finds it easy to explain receiving the eucharist or the ordo of eucharistic action? Who finds it easy to explain what happens in baptism, for example, the meaning of the words and gestures, the meaning of the ordo, and the questions and answers?[38]

Origen's less than favorable attitude toward ritual, a philosopher's prejudice against external signs shared with Clement of Alexandria, may have contributed to the difficulty of the mystagogical task. Other writers, however, remain close to the liturgy, combing through the Hebrew canon for prophetic types for Christian rites as diligently as they search for proof texts for the kerygma. Among these proofs are a number of ritual

---

[35] "As the church came to feel at home in the world, so she became reconciled to *time*. The eschatological emphasis in the eucharist inevitably faded…Instead, the eucharist came to be thought of primarily as the representation, the enactment before God, of the historical process of redemption…" Dix, Gregory, Shape of the Liturgy, London ²1945, 305. For a reevaluation of Dix's theory, see Taft's article, next note.

[36] Taft, Robert, Historicism Revisited. SL 14, 1982, 97-109.

[37] Taft, Liturgy, 59.

[38] Num. hom. 5.1, GCS 30, 26.

texts such as Ex 12. It is a curiosity of the earliest liturgical theology that in most provinces of the church, OT rituals *as texts* carry the kerygma long before Christian rituals *as rite* tell the story of Christ. When such narratives emerge, they have been formed in the same mimetic fashion. This suggests that Taft's analogy may be taken even further: mystagogy not only imitates the same rhetorical structures as scriptural exegesis, but establishes a hermeneutic in which ritual and narrative exegete each other.

A major tenet of the present study is that mimesis, whether in Plutarch, E. O. James, or the *Didache*, is a timeless constant of any secondary text about ritual and many primary ones, regardless of rhetorical purpose, because it is the sole generator of language about rite. When any human activity – lighting a lamp, bathing, eating a meal – moves to the realm of communally recognized ritual, an interpretational space is created that demands to be filled with meaning. As Theodore of Mopsuestia explains:

> Every mystery points in sign and symbols to things invisible and ineffable. A manifestation and explanation of these signs and symbols is required if those who present themselves are to experience the power of the mysteries. If all that occurred was these actions, any discourse would be superfluous; the sight of them would be enough to make plain to us each thing that occurs. But since the sacrament contains signs of what will take place or has already taken place, a discourse is needed that will explain the meaning of the signs and mysteries.[39]

Since the ritual medium employs its own symbolic system that cannot be translated without remainder into another, i.e., speech, mimesis enables language about rite both to fill this space and to transform itself through that ubiquitous but scarcely definable process called "tradition." The chief endeavor in restating ritual thus consists of choosing an object for a mimetic construct and establishing the "likeness," whether it is the spiritual process of Origen and the Alexandrians, or the events of salvation history of Theodore and the Antiochenes. Because mimesis can perform this task only imperfectly, mimesis addressed to Christian rite is theoretically capable of generating a virtually infinite number of narratives incorporating images and stories, i.e., *types*, from both testaments and the natural and social world. In practice, however, the

---

[39] Hom. 12.2, Commentary of Theodore of Mopsuestia on the Lord's Prayer and on the Sacraments of Baptism and the Eucharist; ed., trans., A. Mingana, WSt 6, 1933, 325.

field of choice has already been considerably limited by hermeneutical traditions. Mystagogy becomes a kind of improvisation like Baroque coloratura or jazz: great freedom to vary a traditional melody within set parameters.

This requires a certain broadening of the term. As the word *mimesis* will be used here, ritual action need not act out narrative for a mimetic relationship between rite and text to exist. The lavishly dramatic liturgies of the Middle Ages would have been impossible had not an earlier age interpreted Christian rite as signs capable of representing narratives about Christ, seeing in liturgical action a kind of "postfiguring" typology with clear narrative referents. For as Taft infers, this interpretive act, regardless of medium, is rooted in the relationship of one *narrative* to another, which may or may not function as dramatic script.

V. Rhetoric and History

Over the last decades, "rhetoric" and "discourse"[40] have become the juggernauts of post-modern criticism,[41] whether using paradigms from ancient rhetors[42] or modern scholars such as Paul Ricœur or Jacques Derrida. "The tradition of defining rhetoric," Campbell Lyons writes,[43] "begins with the vague, but classic definition of rhetoric as the art of persuasion." Vague though it may be, this definition is as serviceable as any, acknowledging constructs of speech to motivate thought, belief, or action in the listener without placing a philosophical or political value on the art or the speech itself. As Ricœur notes, the art (poetics) and the persuasion (rhetoric) meet in all mimetic literature if only to persuade the reader that its representation of reality is indeed real.[44] The same

[40] For relief, see Henscheid, Eckhard, Dummdeutsch, Stuttgart 1993 (Reclam 8865), 61, defining "discourse" as "*der* Quatsch der akademischen 80er Jahre. Erscheint deshalb meist bei Suhrkamp. Ab 1990 in jedem zweiten Buchtitel oder Untertitel."

[41] See survey: Lyons, Campbell N. D., From Persuasion to Subversion: A Review of Past and Current Trends in Defining Rhetoric, Neotest 28, 1994, 429-456.

[42] Ancient rhetoric is useful, but only "as it makes us conscious … that communication is universal." Cornelius, E. M., The Relevance of Ancient Rhetoric to Rhetorical Criticism, Neotest 28, 1994, (457-467) 466. For contrast, see Tortorelli, Kevin M., The *Ars Poetica* of Horace as a point of reference for reading Irenaeus, VC 27, 1990, 333-338.

[43] Lyons, Persuasion, 432.

[44] Ricœur, Paul, Zeit und Erzählung, Bd. I. Zeit und historische Erzählung, München, 1988, 87 f. (=dÜ, Temps et récit, tome I, Paris 1983).

is the case with narratives about ritual: there is always a relationship between how an author depicts ritual and rhetorical goals.

Yet beyond this theoretical base, the plan is not to filter Early Christian literature through any modern or ancient analytical system, which ultimately would only prove their already demonstrated viability as analytical tools. Instead, I have chosen to move deductively, discovering the object of mimetic constructs addressed to rites of an author's community or those of another. Since all these texts wish for rite to tell a story, the task becomes a matter of listening carefully as they speak.

This method has the salutary advantage of acknowledging both the state of preservation of Early Christian literature and its original rhetorical intent. Virtually all Christian texts selected for analysis occur in classically rhetorical genres, not by choice, but because that is all time and tradition have left us. Other than the "literary" narratives of canonical and extracanonical gospels, letters, apologies, homilies, controversial writings, and church orders comprise the entire Christian literature extant from the first two hundred years.

Attempting to read history out of second century rhetoric is not a recent problem, but one Eusebius faced as he culled the libraries of Caesarea and Jerusalem for materials for his *Ecclesiastical History*. At *Praeparatio Evangelica* 1.3.4, Eusebius describes what he found: "refutations and contradictions of the arguments opposed to us," "the inspired and sacred scriptures in exegetical commentaries and in homilies on particular points," and apologetic works "in a more controversial fashion."[45] How Eusebius read rhetoric for history, and how he engaged in various rhetorical controversies himself, embroils any discussion of the Antenicene Pascha in questions of accuracy, revisionism, or simple ignorance. In turn, these questions have produced a considerable amount of modern rhetoric, to which, for better or worse, this study contributes.

---

[45] Trans., Grant, R. M., Eusebius as Church Historian, Oxford 1980, 42.

B. PASCHA, PASSION, AND BAPTISM:
THE "ASIAN" OR COMMON TRADITION

"Most of the brethren," Origen laments in his paschal treatise, "indeed perhaps all, think that the Pascha takes its name from the passion of the Savior."[1] The death of the Lamb as story of origins for the Christian paschal feast is more than a folk etymology Origen is anxious to correct, but a keystone of liturgical theology that not Origen, but Augustine finally dislodges by bonding it to other traditions, including Origen's own.[2] The great Alexandrian is also aware that this almost universal reading of name, feast, and text is not unique to the Christian communities of Asia Minor. For while it is from Ephesus that Paul writes, "Christ our Pascha has been sacrificed for us," Ephesian Christians were not likely the first to hear that Ex 12 did not speak about the rituals of Pesach, but the death of Jesus of Nazareth.

Even so, like a red thread running through the fabric of early Christian exegesis, the transformation of Ex 12 into a founding narrative for the only annual feast, the sacrament of baptism, and the creation of the Gentile church unfolds with particular richness in Asia Minor. Justin Martyr sojourned in Ephesus; Melito of Sardis and Apollinarios of Hierapolis were bishops of Asian cities. Readily telling anecdotes about Polycarp of Smyrna, Irenaeus owes much to the land of his birth. Unnamed Asian "presbyters"[3] rank highly in Irenaeus' exegetical past, and even the *Epistle of Barnabas* may have first proclaimed its scriptural discoveries to an Asian congregation of the early second century.[4]

At the end of the century, when the Asian practice of celebrating Pascha on 14 Nisan comes under attack from Sunday celebrants in Rome, Alexandria, and Palestine, Ex 12 – as canon and as subtext for the Syn meal narratives and the Joh passion – becomes an exegetical battleground. If this tradition was not Asian in origin, it finds its most

---

[1] Origen, Peri Pascha 1.1-18, Guéraud-Nautin, 154; ACW 54, 27. For discussion, see below, p. 85.
[2] CQL, 17 f.
[3] Two examples: AH 4.31.1, SC 100/2, 786; AH 4.32.1, SC 100/2, 796.
[4] See below, note 173, p. 75.

eloquent proponent in the sexagenarian Polycrates of Ephesus, who defends the paschal practice of his see as a direct tradition from the apostles. There is, of course, no way of knowing whether Polycrates is historically correct. Yet in a rhetorical history of the paschal feast, this is only a side issue for modern scholars. The aged bishop firmly believed in the antiquity of his tradition, and out of this conviction he thought, wrote, and preached.

Long before this controversy, Ex 12 as story of origins and its ritual expression had been firmly fixed in the Christian imagination. Though before the final decades of the second century only accessible as an exegetical tradition, already in the Pauline letters the Exodus saga is deeply involved with the celebration of bath and meal. Even here, this relationship does not suddenly appear, but represents developments in ritual narrative that must have begun at the very inception of the Christian message. Jesus of Nazareth was crucified during Pesach-Mazzot, an event that a new covenant people of Jews and Gentiles saw both as definitive and defining. Rituals also define a religious community. Ex 12 is thus one of the few reliable guides for tracing the synergism among ritual, text, and kerygma before the Council of Nicaea.

Though much is known only from bibliographical notes in Eusebius' history, readings of Ex 12 produce a rich literature well into the fourth century. Cyprian gives a clue for its disappearance. Following the Synoptics where Jesus celebrates the Pesach meal, later tradition transfers an originally paschal theology to the eucharist, a connection made by virtually no author of the second century and still bitterly disputed at Nicaea. Despite this loss, Ex 12 can be traced through evanescent NT allusions to extended interpretations by every extant second and early third century author except Minucius Felix and Theophilus of Antioch. By Polycrates' day, this exegesis is addressed unambiguously to the Christian celebration of Pascha. The power of the Pesach institution narrative to generate literature does not wane until Ex 12 takes its place as one among many lections at the vigil, its siblings obscuring the significance a ritual and christological reading of this text once had for Christian worship and teaching. The purpose now, however, is to trace the beginnings of this tradition as an act of reading – the most basic rhetorical technique of all – before the challenges of other important sees prevailed against the Christian communities of Asia Minor, persuading them to modify how they followed this text in the paschal night.

I. The Making and Reading of a Ritual Text: Ex 12 and Pesach[5]

Another paschal hymn of Ephrem sings of the highly mimetic nature of paschal exegesis at a time and place, fourth century Mesopotamia, where reflection on Ex 12 could still produce new nuances of thought and image:

> [23] The prophets carry * as servants
> the images of Christ, * who became ruler over all.
> [24] Nature and scripture * carry together
> the symbols of his humanity * and his divinity.
> [25] So the People shall be ashamed! * For their Testament
> has become a mirror * for our Testament.
> [26] Glory be to you * O Lord of our Pascha
> For the Pascha in Egypt * proclaimed your symbol.
> [27] Praise be to you * O Lord of the prophets!
> For all the prophets have proclaimed your image [type].
> [28] Thanks be to you* O Lord of Nature!
> For all Nature * adores you completely.[6]

Other than its now stereotyped "shaming" of the Jews, the most lucid feature of Ephrem's mirror is its restoration of a hermeneutic that sees ritual not as ritual, but as allegorical narrative and prophetic action, to a highly ritual image. The procession of image-bearing prophets, followed by Creation and Word as revealers of Christ, parades before the reader that remarkable interpretive process that transformed one of the most important ritual texts of the Hebrew scriptures into the kerygma of the only annual liturgical feast in Early Christianity. Yet Ex 12 could have reflected little for Christian exegetes were it not a highly mimetic text giving a meaning to its rites that could be modified or reassigned.

The canonical text strives to attain a tight fit between these rites and the story of salvation in which it is imbedded. Yet as in all mimetic constructs, correspondence between rite and story is accomplished only imperfectly, leaving other meanings for first century evangelists, second century rabbis, or modern exegetes to discover. Biblical scholars read to

---

[5] See Bokser, Baruch, The Origins of the Seder, Berkeley/Los Angeles 1984. For a "myth and rituals" study, see Segal, J.B., The Hebrew Passover from the Earliest Times to A. D. 70, LOrS 12, 1963.

[6] Ephrem, Azym 4.23-28, CSCO 249 (Syr 109), 8 f.

remove layers of tradition, reaching for the most primitive Pesach rituals. Prompted by the same textual cues, early Christian interpreters craft narratives about the death of Christ, the sacraments of baptism and eucharist, and the Pascha. In each case, the rhetorical strategy of the text, the work not of a single author but of a whole religious tradition, is reversed.

Such a strategy is signaled early in the book of Exodus:

> I declare that I will bring you up out of the misery of Egypt, to the land of the Canaanites, the Hittites, the Amorites, the Perissites, the Hivites, and the Jebusites, a land flowing with milk and honey. They will listen to your voice; and you and the elders of Israel shall go to the king of Egypt and say to him, "The Lord, the God of the Hebrews, has met with us; let us now go a three day's journey into the wilderness, so that we may sacrifice to the Lord our God."

This otherwise unknown pilgrimage sacrifice[7] is the first frame of a festival *inclusio*[8] for the entire Exodus saga. The action pauses for the institution of the first Pesach (Ex 12) and reaches a climax in the Song of Miriam and Moses (15.1-19) and the victorious dance of the women on the banks of the sea[9] (15.20 f.). A second Pesach is celebrated before the tabernacle in the wilderness (Num 9.1-14), just as the saga ends with Joshua's Pesach at Gilgal, when the manna ceases to fall and the wanderers prepare unleavened bread for the first time in the new land (Jos 5.10-12).[10]

Performing a similar framing function, texts originating cultic practices[11] form ritual stations embedded in the narrative stream. Such halachic prescription inserted into haggadic description does more than originate the feasts or historicize them. For the celebrating community,

---

[7] This sacrifice (Ex 3.17 f.) may be the pre-Mosaic Pesach, another rite, or a literary device. Peter Laaf, Die Pascha-Feier Israels, BBB 36, 1970, 121, sees a separate "pilgrimage tradition;" loc. cit., n. 21, for other views. Cf. Schmitt, Rainer, Exodus und Passah. Ihr Zusammenhang im AT, OBO 7, 1975, 25, lit. n. 39.

[8] The first and third Passovers form a great chiasm: Passover-Crossing (Red Sea), Crossing (Jordan)-Passover. van Goudoever, J., Biblical Calendars, Leiden ²1961, 54 f.

[9] One of the oldest traditions. Childs, Brevard, Exodus. A Commentary, OTL, London 1974, 246 f.

[10] This may preserve a local Pesach tradition for the Gilgal shrine, where the Ark of the Covenant was processed across the Jordan. Kraus, Hans-Joachim, Gottesdienst in Israel, München ²1962, 181-187.

[11] These sections are *catechesis*: connection to lamb and Mazzot requires instruction. Maertens, Thierry, Heidnisch-jüdische Wurzeln der christlichen Feste, Mainz 1965, 77-79.

narrative and feast have become an organic whole: the means of appropriating the Exodus story of rescue and creation is a liturgical festival.
This is the rhetorical strategy that Christian exegetes must alter to obtain
their own mimetic reading. Over time, Judaic ritual must alter it as well,
not by changing the signified, but the signifiers.

1. From Text to Rite: the Haggadah

In the home liturgy still in use today, the *Haggadah*, ritual catechesis is
incorporated into the rite, exemplified by *the* Pesach question, which it
is the duty of the youngest to ask, "Why is this night different from
other nights?" The answer is the story of the Exodus remembered
through song, rabbinical texts, and the various dishes of the Seder meal.

A statement attributed to Gamaliel I in the Mishnah tract *Pesachim*
gives a succinct plot summary of both the institution narrative and the
meal celebration of the *Haggadah*:

> Rabban Gamaliel said whoever did not say these three things on Passover
> did not fulfill his obligation:
> Pesach, mazzah, and merorim [פֶּסַח=lamb or festival, unleavened bread,
> מְרוֹרִים=bitter herbs][12]
> Pesach – because the Omnipresent skipped over the houses of our ances-
> tors in Egypt.
> Merorim – because the Egyptians embittered the lives of our ancestors in
> Egypt.
> Mazzah – because they were redeemed.
> *In every generation a person is duty-bound to regard himself as if he personally
> has gone forth from Egypt, since it is said, "And you shall tell your son in that
> day saying, It is because of that which the Lord did for me when I came forth
> out of Egypt* [Ex 13.8].[13]
> Therefore we are duty-bound to thank, praise, glorify, honor, exalt, extol,
> and bless him who did for our forefathers and for us all these miracles. He
> brought us forth from slavery to freedom, anguish to joy, mourning to fes-
> tival, darkness to great light, subjugation to redemption, so we should say
> before him, Hallelujah.[14]

---

[12] Herbs and mazzot now carry the meaning of the lamb. Bokser, Seder, 79 f.

[13] Often cited as if it were a 1 c. text, but not included in the oldest ms. of MPes,
Budapest Mishnah Codex, this text was interpolated from 4-5 c. Gemara. Bokser, Seder,
1-31; Beer, G., Pesachim (Ostern), Mischna II,3. Gießen 1912, 195.

[14] Trans. Neusner MPes, 266, who includes the italicized passage.

The courses of the Pesach meal – Gamaliel reduces them *pars pro toto* to three – with their accompanying rituals and stories become anamnetic stations[15] to bridge the separating centuries to the time, story, and – the most important connection – to the *community* of origins.[16] In passing through these stations, participants fulfill the command of Ex 13.8-10 to pass on the story of the Exodus to their children, this on a course laid out by the *Haggadah*, (Heb. "the telling") with the Pesach plate and its foods as central symbol. Each year, the Pesach festival and its narrative ritually recreates[17] the people of Israel through the remembrance of salvation, punctuated by a resounding "Hallelujah!"

2. From Rite to Text: The Genesis of Exodus 12

The *Haggadah* and the Mishnah tract *Pesachim*, which presumes a form of the *Haggadah* essentially like that in use today,[18] are not ossified liturgical history, but living traditions representing a second century rabbinical Judaism without temple cult and priesthood that has successfully reinterpreted major motifs from the Second Temple period. "Gamaliel" has relocated the paschal lamb to a speech act, and it is not necessary to think of the paschal sacrifice or even eating the lamb at the mention of "skipping over the houses," which recalls the biblical etymology. That Pesach was once a pilgrimage festival where thousands of lambs were sacrificed and their blood offered as Levites chanted psalms has now been rendered irrelevant.

As both Jewish and Christian traditions have moved within these texts for centuries, it is not superfluous to point out that except for the costume prescribed in Ex 12.11 (reminiscent of the desert travelling dress of either nomads or their temporary counterparts, pilgrims[19]), there is nothing *obvious* in any commemorative feature to evoke either a saving passage through water, the miraculous destruction of enemies, or

---

[15] The Samaritan liturgy assigns each of seven Sabbaths before Pentecost the name of an event. Goudoever, Calendars, 130 f.

[16] Bokser, 76 f.

[17] Maertens, 84-86.

[18] Essentially complete by Tannaitic times, if not by the Second Temple Period. Roth, Cecil, Haggadah, London (n.d.) iii-iv; Neusner, Jacob, A History of the Mishnaic Law of Appointed Times, Part Two, Erubin, Pesachim, SJLA 34, Leiden 1981, 134.

[19] This mimetic touch gave Johannes Pedersen (Passahfest und Passahlegende, ZAW 52 [NF 11], 1934, 161-175) proof for the dramatic character of the Exodus saga. See also Engnell, Ivan, Pæsah-Massot and the Problem of 'Patternism,' OrSuec 1, 1952, 39-50.

a prolonged wandering in the desert.[20] The bread left unleavened in the "kneading bowls wrapped up in their cloaks on their shoulders" at a hasty departure (Ex 12.33) is narrative detail, but exposes an aetiological concern to wed rite to text not found in prescriptions for the Mazzot festival.[21] The ritual features of Pesach-Mazzot, not in themselves imitative or dramatic, were not generated directly by mimesis addressed to the mystery of the festival, i.e., salvation and divine rescue, but rather become imitative only in light of its kerygma.

Later practices prescribed by the *Haggadah* have this simpler character, where the mimetic object is the biblical text or themes abstracted from it. Dining while reclining on cushions,[22] for instance, is to suggest the eating habits of free people in the ancient world, just as the hasoret, a delicious relish of minced fruit moistened with wine, is to "symbolize" the mortar for bricks made by Hebrew slaves in Egypt. In the biblical narrative, this type of monovalent, and quite secondary, symbolism is only seminally present in Dt 16: in the unleavened bread memorialized as the "bread of affliction" (16.3) and the sacrifice, now a Temple ritual, to be performed "between the two evenings, the time of day when you departed from Egypt" (16.6). This strongly suggests that the rites described in the institution narrative, and perhaps others whose origins had been suppressed, revalorized, or simply forgotten before reaching written form, are much older and were initially addressed to a different "mystery."

Leonhard Rost[23] argues that the original setting of Pesach was the migration to higher summer pasture signaled by the end of the winter rains. The blood rite was to placate the desert demon(s) to insure safe passage to greener pastures. After being fused with a narrative of rescue, the transition from winter to summer pasture became the ultimate "transition," the Exodus. Othmar Keel offers a modification of Rost's theory, pointing out that

---

[20] The Therapeutæ of Upper Egypt celebrated such rituals every fifty days, including a symbolic meal of bread and salt, antiphonal singing, and a festive dance. Philo De vita cont 8.65, 3.30, 4.36. Eusebius, EH 2.17, knows they are Christians holding a paschal vigil.

[21] Ex 12.15; Lv 23.6, Num 28.17.

[22] One now leans to the left while seated, thus a symbol of an antiquated custom whose original social meaning had already become symbolic. MPes10.1B, 263.

[23] Rost, L., Weidewechsel und altisraelitischer Festkalender. ZDPV 66, 1943, 205-216. An often cited article. Childs, 189: Rost's theory retains "a high level of historical and geographical specificity which differentiates it from the usual patterns of comparative religion, in which all festivals, whether spring or fall, begin to look alike."

the desert is not demonized in the OT, a fear of malevolent spirits being evoked far more by desolate towns and villages.[24] The usual winter pasture-lands are not forbidding landscapes, the summer pastures even less so.[25] Instead, the original "Destroyer" of the Exodus saga might not have been some ephemeral desert spirit, but the quite real danger of the scirocco, the blood rite performed to ward off its early arrival. This extremely dry east[26] wind off the Arabian desert[27] can appear without warning in the early spring, evaporating streams and ponds, withering all vegetation in a matter of hours, and debilitating or fatally dehydrating small animals, infants, the sick and the elderly.[28] The blood of the sacrificial victim was sprinkled on the entrance of the tents, perhaps also on the animals, as a protective measure to insure that the wind would not come earlier than usual and catch the tribe before it could move its herd.

While Rost[29] posits an origin for each of the features of Ex 12, it is hard to imagine that everything from bitter herbs to mazzot was part of two festivals merely taken over by Yawistic religion and furnished with a founding narrative. The separate agrarian origin of the Mazzot festival, for instance, has been contested by several scholars.[30] Unleavened bread, still standard fare for travellers, nomads, and pilgrims in the Middle East, may have been a part of the Pesach meal from the beginning, though initially without ritual significance. With the rise of agriculture, the Mazzot festival could represent an acculturation of the originally nomadic features of Pesach to a now farming community, the first transference of anamnetic charge from one ritual to another in the wake of cultural change.

---

[24] Cf. Berakoth I, i, Goldschmidt 1, 5. Ruins could also be haunted by prostitutes. A delightful bit of rabbinical logic finally allows "two righteous men" in a recent ruin: no danger of architectural or moral collapse.

[25] Keel, Othmar, Erwägungen zum Sitz im Leben des vormosaischen Pascha und zur Etymologie von פסח, ZAW 84, 1972, (414-434) 416.

[26] The wind that parts the sea (Ex. 14.21) also comes from the east.

[27] Arabic 'es-serqije,' (easterly) or 'el-hamasin', a Christian or Jewish survival in Arabic, the 'fiftieth,' because the scirocco is especially strong from Pesach to Pentecost.

[28] Scott, R. B. Y., Meteorological Phenomena and Terminology in the Old Testament, ZAW 64, NF 23, 1952, 11-25.

[29] "Originally, the bitter herbs were probably desert plants eaten with the meal, thus to bid farewell to the winter pasture." Rost, 212.

[30] Halbe, Jörn, Erwägungen zu Ursprung und Wesen des Massotfestes. ZAW 87, 1975, 324-346; Wambacq. B.N., Les Mazzot, Bib 61, 1980, 31-54; Van Seters, John, The Place of the Yahwist in the History of Passover and Massot, ZAW 95, 1983, 167-182. For the traditional agrarian view, see Kutsch, Ernst, Erwägungen zur Geschichte der Passafeier und des Massotfestes. ZThK 55, 1958, 1-35.

This also obtains for the Pesach meal. Was the lamb always eaten after the blood rite, even at the most primitive stage? Joseph Henniger seeks a parallel in a Bedouin practice where an animal sacrifice, now sacred, is buried or burnt whole.[31] The "resurrection" of the animal in new births, a prime motif in such sacrifices, could also be the motivation for not breaking the bones of the victim: wholeness guarantees physical integrity, power, and life in tribe and herd. The mention of a single animal in the earliest texts also suggests that the animal was solely a source of blood, not meat for a festive meal.[32]

In these readings, the first dynamic shift lying beneath Pesach texts comes into view. The most striking feature is that the sacrificial animal has been reduced to the main course of a festive dinner. The blood rite is given a clear aetiology in the "historical" Pesach night, but all the more pressed into the past, just as the "Destroyer" wind becomes a means of salvation recalled as "casting horse and rider into the sea," but no longer feared as a supernatural threat. Rescue from Egypt, the new mystery which Pesach is to appropriate into the present, has pushed the original rite into narrative mimesis, reversing the dynamic of the original rite.[33]

Like virtually all apotropaic rituals, the primitive blood rite locates "mystery" in the performance of a ritual that greater, unseen forces are to imitate, the ultimate in *do ut des*. The animal is a scapegoat whose death bears destructive force on behalf of the community and its livestock. Yet in the biblical account, mystery has been assumed by the saving God of Israel, its kerygma by the Exodus saga. The original mystery has been transformed into a mimetic feature and placed into an entire festival complex. Later, the blood rite is integrated into the Temple sacrifices as part of the festival's centralization at Jerusalem, (Dt 16.2) while other sacrifices, including those for atonement (Num 28.22), are also prescribed. This too minimizes any special meaning the blood of the Pesach animal once had, the meal taking on the full meaning of the festival.[34]

As other dishes in the meal – the herbs, the mazzot, and later the haroset

---

[31] Henniger, Joseph, Les Fêtes de printemps chez les Sémites et la Pâque Israélite, Paris 1975, 454-475, also ibid., Über Frühingsfeste bei den Semiten. In: In Verbo Tuo. Siegburg 1963, 375-398; Stendebach, F. J., Das Verbot des Knochenzerbrechens bei den Semiten, BZ NF 17, 1973, 29-38.

[32] Laaf, 158.

[33] For text-critical implications of this shift, see Bar-On, Shimon, Zur literarkritischen Analyse von Ex 12,21-27, ZAW 107, 1995, 18-31.

[34] Cf. MPes 7.5 (Neusner, 151 f.): "If the meat is made unclean but the fat is clean, one does not toss the blood. The meat is the main thing, because it is eaten."

and wine – become equally commemorative, the Pesach lamb can pass out of the celebration without loss of content. Anamnesis shifts to other objects, but the dynamic remains unchanged.

3. The Christian Connection

The desert sacrifice of Ex 3.18 or some other ritual whose origins fade into the Bronze Age, the Pesach festival of Ex 12, and the *Haggadah* are all stations in a living religious tradition in which the Christian Pascha also fully participates. The Judaism of the late Second Temple period taught the earliest Church a well-developed paschal language that historical circumstance, the death of Jesus of Nazareth in Jerusalem during Pesach-Mazzot, all but forced the new faith to speak. Paschal themes lie close to the heart of Christian proclamation. Without them there would be no language to speak of the sacrifice of the firstborn, no paschal lamb, no dramatic rescue through a passage through water, no festive meal of remembrance and thanksgiving, no creation of a covenant people.

Yet in the worship and preaching of the earliest Church, Ex 12 undergoes a mimetic shift no less radical than shaping a nomadic blood rite warding off the desert wind into anamnesis of the saving acts of God. Christian exegetes place the new faith in the center of paschal texts and rituals and let both speak a new message, the atoning death of Christ, through the very motifs Ex 12 seeks to obscure: paschal themes produced by centuries of celebration shift to mimesis of the cross. The sacrifice of the lamb again becomes holy event as a figure of Christ's death, the blood rite as baptism again fends off the Destroyer, the unbroken bones of the lamb sign resurrection to the Fourth Evangelist. The Pesach of Ex 12 is a meal rite for tribes or families; the Synoptics institute the Christian meal rite in a paschal frame. Early Christian authors return again and again to this text, and they learn much from their reading.

In the same way, mimetic readings of narrative joined to equally mimetic readings of rite enable selective preservation of Judaic ritual. Except for the earliest community in Jerusalem, Christian reconfiguration of both arise in a matrix of domestic rituals of meals, prayer, and the Sabbath. Though the frescoes of the Dura synagogue show that later Judaic liturgy would refer to Temple sacrifice,[35] it did not attain fixed

---

[35] See iconographical study: Weitzmann Kurt, and Herbert L. Kessler, The Frescoes of the Dura Synagogue and Christian Art. DOS 28, Washington DC, 1990.

forms until well after the Temple's destruction.[36] Nor are there witnesses to communal Sabbath *worship*, as opposed to Sabbath *observance*, outside of sectarian Judaism (Qumran, Philo's Essenes) until the late first and second centuries.[37] Even then, Mishnah and Talmud portray the study of Torah, not corporate worship or prayer, as the consummate religious act.

This is why a weekly pattern of worship and fasting, Pascha, the singing of "psalms, hymns, and spiritual songs,"[38] the lighting of lamps, the meal rite, the eucharistic anaphora,[39] daily prayer, and other observances are most rooted in that matrix, while direct lines to synagogue worship are far less easily drawn. Christian worship was at the very beginning doubly "paraliturgical," combining home meal liturgies of thanksgiving and praise – in this case transformed for the entire community – and a service of readings, psalms/hymns with homily, traditionally linked to the synagogue[40] but more likely developed around the reading of scripture, prayer, and song that often accompanied meals.[41]

As all ritual behavior, these practices were learned by direct imitation, the "schools" where they were taught were the first housechurches, the teachers Jewish Christians or those who had learned from them. Even though the process of Christian transformation cannot always be completely traced, transferring these customs primarily to communal rather than familial practice, at the same time addressing them to Christ, then narratives about him, was the chief means of that transformation. Rituals could remain relatively untouched, but they could be founded in a different, or differently understood, story of origins. Mimetic narrative could thus assure, then completely obscure, ritual continuity with Judaism.

[36] See survey in Bradshaw, Origins, 1-29; also Kee, H. C., The Transformation of the Synagogue after 70 CE: Its Import for Early Christianity, NTS 36, 1990, 1-14.

[37] See McKay, Heather A., Sabbath and Synagogue, RGRW 122, 1994.

[38] See Renckens, Han, Le Chant de la Diaspora. Théologie et mélodie. In: Fides Sacramenti, Sacramentum Fidei (FS P. Smulders), Assen 1981, 1-8. The "sacrifice of praise" in song was the functional equivalent of the Temple cult.

[39] Literature here is quite large. See Bradshaw, Origins, 131-160.

[40] Salzman, Jorg Christian, Lehren und Ermahnen. Zur Geschichte des christlichen Wortgottesdienstes in den ersten drei Jahrhunderten, WUNT 2/59, 1994, esp. 450-472.

[41] Bradshaw, Origins, 158.

II. Paul

1. 1 Cor 5.6-8. Celebrate without Old Leaven

Paul's first letter to Corinth confronts the reader with a choice between two types of mimesis: first century Christians *read* Ex 12, but did they also *perform* any of the rituals prescribed there? Less enigmatic is the rhetorical context: Judaic narratives are being drawn into Christian catechesis in a new configuration – around rituals with Judaic roots.

The earliest writing dealing with the meaning of sacraments and the ordering of congregational life, 1Cor already connects Exodus motifs to baptism and eucharist, while the meal is also anchored to the night before Jesus' death. Allegorizing a Jewish paschal ritual into moral example, the letter also shows that the paschal sacrifice and the death of Christ had already been linked by mid-first century. While this typology bears a clear message in Paul's letter, its implication for paschal rituals observed or not observed is a paschal controversy all its own. Liturgiologists like James F. White like to believe, "This passage is the chief evidence for the keeping of Easter by the New Testament church."[42] Biblical scholars are far less convinced.

Calling the Corinthians to task for allowing a man living with his father's widow to remain in fellowship, Paul defines a community boundary by referring to the custom of removing all leaven from the home before Pesach:

> [5.6b]Do you not know that a little yeast leavens the whole batch of dough? [7] Clean out the old yeast so that you may be a new batch, as you really are unleavened. For our paschal lamb [πάσχα], Christ, has been sacrificed. [8] Therefore, let us celebrate (the festival), not with the old yeast, the yeast of malice and evil, but with the unleavened bread of sincerity and truth.

This Pesach-Mazzot typology does not belong to the same genre as second century paschal texts, nor, in all probability, their pre-Pauline source.[43] It is neither an integral part of a passion narrative, an allusion

---

[42] White, James F., Introduction to Christian Worship. Rev. Ed. Nashville 1990, 58.

[43] Joachim Jeremias (Abendmahlsworte Jesu, Göttingen, [4]1967, 53 f) points out "un-Pauline, Semitic" Greek. Adjectives follow the noun in 1 Cor 5.7a, while Paul characteristically employs the opposite order. The article is missing in ἐν ζύμῃ κακίας and εν ἀζύμοις εἰλικρινείας, a use which "only occurs in places with strong Semitic flavor"; ἑορτάζειν + ἐν is nonidiomatic and corresponds to 1 Sam 30.16, הגגב.

to the meal rite, nor an apologetic proof text. And whether actually performed, the ritual removal of leaven is positively valued as a sign of
purity. This is rhetoric transferred, but from where?

That the ritual is not explained means that the Corinthians already
knew something about the custom,[44] all the more surprising, unless
those with Latin names were either "God-fearers" or proselytes. Yet
Paul takes for granted that his hearers knew that the custom meant
renewal, separation, and purity in connection with a religious festival,[45] and that when used alone the word "πάσχα" meant the paschal
sacrifice as well as the paschal feast. The typology *assumes* these meanings as part of the thought world, though not necessarily the ritual life,
of the hearers. This means that there are other dialogues about Ex 12
and the rituals of Pesach, other discussions of Judaic ritual texts and
their new meanings in Christian contexts, in which this brief mention
takes part. The Corinthians have learned to speak paschal language.
Otherwise Paul's point would be lost, the perpetual festival of the
Christian life imaged in a feast no one in Corinth observed or knew
much about.

There is more history to this typology that needs to be explored,
another Christian reconfiguration of Judaic narrative that will continue to
inform paschal discourse well past Nicaea. Without prior tradition, Paul
would only be comparing the Son of God to the main course of a festive
meal, slaughtered on the eve of the feast. While the Temple stood, the
paschal lamb had no salvific or atoning function even as metaphor, a
transfer of meaning further accentuated by the sin offering prescribed for
the day of the festival. The "lamb" only assumes this function long after
it was no longer a part of the Pesach meal and had become one of many
figures for the atonement previously accessible in Temple rites. The first
dynamic shift in the history of the Pesach festival, (blood rite to commemoration, taboo sacrifice to meal) insured that the lamb and its blood
were stripped of their original cultic significance. Why is Paul recovering
this meaning for the Pesach lamb?

At an early stage in the formation of the narrative about the death of
Jesus, the Pesach lamb had been conflated with a similar image:

---

[44] Huber, Passa, 109.

[45] Klaus Berger says that Gentile Corinthians probably had no idea what Paul was
talking about. Manna, Mehl und Sauerteig. Korn und Brot im Alltag der frühen Christen, Stuttgart 1993, 54-56.

⁵³·⁷ He was oppressed, and he was afflicted, yet he did not open his mouth; like a lamb [LXX ἀμνός] that is led to the slaughter, and like a sheep [LXX πρόβατον] that before its shearers is silent, so he did not open his mouth. ⁸ By a perversion of justice he was taken away. Who could have imagined his future? For he was cut off from the land of the living, stricken for the transgressions of my people...¹¹ᵇThe righteous one, my servant, shall make many righteous, and he shall bear their iniquities.

God's vindication of the Servant "by whose stripes we are healed" becomes a gospel simply by assuming the text speaks about Jesus of Nazareth, a view Luke canonizes at Acts 8.26-39. The eunuch is reading the Servant Song before he encounters Philip, and all the soon-to-be-baptized Ethiopian requires is to know about whom this story is told. Lamb and sheep had already become a single hybrid in Paul's typology. They remain inseparable throughout the early paschal tradition.

a) Corinth: The History

By the time Paul writes to the church he founded at Corinth[46] (1 Cor 3.6), this booming city had scarcely seen its first century. A stronghold of mainland Greek resistance to Roman rule, Corinth had been virtually depopulated after its defeat in 146 BCE, but its ideal location for the sea trade led to a Roman refounding in 44 BCE. Latin was the official language, but most of the settlers were freed slaves and the less wealthy, mostly Greek-speaking. There was a synagogue (Acts 18.8), but evidence for the Jewish community is quite slim.[47]

Like similar new settlements across the Empire, Rome settled many veterans there.[48] Given the city's economic importance, Jewish and Syrian tradespeople likely made their way to Corinth, just as the smattering of Greek and Latin names of Corinthian Christians in 1/2 Cor and Rom

[46] See Wiseman, James, Corinth and Rome I: 228 BC-AD 267, ANRW II.7.1, 1979, 438-548.
[47] Synagogue inscription, "of the Hebrews", dates after Paul. Smallwood, E. Mary, The Jews Under Roman Rule. From Pompey to Diocletian, SJLA 20,1976, 121 f. Philo, Legatio ad Gaium 281 f., Opera VI, 207, lists Corinth among Ionian and mainland cities.
[48] See Murphy-O'Connor, Jerome, St. Paul's Corinth. Texts and Archaeology. Good News Studies 6, Wilmington (DE) 1983. Plutarch's Life of Caesar 47:8 (M.-O'C., 107). Strabo (Geography, 23c; M.-O'C., 66) says colonists were mainly freed slaves.

reflects a mixed heritage. Luke relates that Priscilla and Aquila had fled to Corinth after the Edict of Claudius (Acts 18.2); other Jewish Christians had surely found their way there as well. Yet unlike Antioch or Rome, problems between Jew and Gentile do not number among those Paul addresses, nor has any recent commentator tried to reduce the myriad troubles of Corinth to differences between Jewish and Gentile identities.[49] Given the tendency to factiousness along other lines, this is an eloquent silence.

A picture emerges, then, of a quite diverse congregation comprising first, second, or at most third generation immigrants. The newness of the city and the heterogeneity of the congregation in ethnicity, education, and social status likely contributed both to the success of the Christian mission and Paul's concentration on questions of worship and sacraments. Despite the "food for idols" dilemma, there was no entrenched civil cult or "ancestral religion" with deep-seated loyalties in Corinth. The Christian community and its worship could provide a communal identity arching across class and ethnic lines, and through baptism and catechesis, a personal identity for each believer.[50]

b) The Evidence for a Corinthian Pascha

Is Paul's exegesis of unleavened bread the first occurrence of a rhetorical commonplace?[51] The inner logic of the image – comparing one action to another – might suggest that as the congregation performed the one (removing the leaven) they would also perform the other (excommunicating the offender). Could Paul then be interpreting a part of Pesach-Mazzot observance, or given the brief clue in the lamb typology, a festival on its way to becoming a Christian feast *without* the ritual, but with a new narrative attached to its scriptural command? In other words, is "Let us keep the feast" (ἑορτάζωμεν[52] -5.8) rubric or metaphor?

---

[49] Schrage, Wolfgang, 1 Kor 1, EKK 7/1, 1991, 47: "The mention of circumcision without any suggestion of its controversy in 7.18 is a clear indication that in Corinth there had been no judaizing-nomistic agitation and thus no problems resulting from it."

[50] Perkins, Pheme, Gnosticism and the NT, Minneapolis 1993, 34-37; Koester, Helmut, The History-of-Religions School, Gnosis, and Gospel of John, StTh 40, 1986, 115-136.

[51] Bradshaw, Search, 41 f. Cf. Dial. Tryph. 14.1, text and discussion below, p. 55.

[52] This verb occurs only here in the NT, but note the double use in LXX Ex 12.14.

It has been deduced from this notice that 1 Cor was written in the spring, around the time of Pesach, when travel again would be possible after the winter.[53] Paul writes that he plans to stay in Ephesus until Pentecost[54] (16.8), which also assumes that this is a meaningful date. Why is Paul using a Jewish calendar? Probably for the same reason he does not bother to translate "Maranatha" into Greek: both were already known – and used – in Corinth. Since the Roman solar calendar had replaced the Greek lunar calendar Corinth had used before its destruction, these dates would have no parallels without considerable calculation. If the Corinthians could associate Pascha and Pentecost with specific days or weeks, it means at least some of them were observing these feasts, the only reason for keeping the calendar in the first place.

From these considerations, some scholars conjecture that the Corinthians did "keep the feast," employing the lamb typology that plays an important role in Jn and the second century Pascha.[55] Building on the findings of his student Lohse, Jeremias views Paul's typology as based upon an "urchristliche Passahaggada" and provides an "original" eschatological interpretation reaching back to the historical Jesus.[56] In both his more popularly written commentary on 1 Cor and his labyrinthine work on the paschal calendar,[57] August Strobel believes this text is not only proof positive that Corinth celebrated Pascha, but that Paul agrees chronologically with John (and the majority of modern scholars) in dating Jesus' death to 14 Nisan.[58] In his commentary, Strobel even suggests that the removal of leaven was a kind of primitive Lent.[59]

[53] Strobel, ZBK 1Kor, 1989, 156; but this view is often criticized.

[54] The Syro-Western text of Acts 18.21 adds "I must by all means keep the approaching feast in Jerusalem, but [canonical] I will return to you if God wills." (δεῖ με πάντως τὴν ἑορτὴν τὴν ἐρχομένην ποιῆσαι εἰς Ἱεροσόλυμα), which J. M. Ross takes to be the original reading. The phrase was dropped so as not to give Pauline authority for observing Jewish festivals. See ibid., The Extra Words in Acts 18.22, NovTest 34, 1992, 247-249.

[55] Lohse, B., Das Passafest der Quartodezimaner, BFChrT 2/54, 101.

[56] Jeremias, Abendmahlsworte, 53-54.

[57] Strobel, Ursprung und Geschichte des frühchristlichen Osterkalenders, TU 121, 41, holds that the "door which has opened" is the large number preparing for paschal baptism.

[58] Koester (Jesus' Presence in the Early Church. CrSt 15, 1994, 541-557) makes the same assumption, though couching it in the subjunctive.

[59] Strobel, ZBK, 102: "The congregation at Corinth already conducted a 'Christian' Passover, by which we should imagine a night celebration…, as recent liturgical reforms wish to introduce and encourage in the Evangelical Church." Cf. TU 121, 1977, 28, 65.

Staring too deeply into NT texts to find evidence of the second century Pascha is like trying to photograph a moving object with slow film, and a purely cultic reading is using the wrong lens. Looking for those interpretive moves necessary for that shift to take place, however, runs less risk of blurred results. Paul's letter offers two instances of such a process: the identification of Christ with the Pesach lamb and a typological reading of the Red Sea narrative linked to baptism and the meal rite. Another motif, the Last Supper as Pesach meal, is conspicuously absent, but also in the Joh tradition where this typology takes another direction. The Corinthians were fluent in paschal language, even if ritual, Christian or Judaic, cannot be reconstructed from this text.

c) The Locus of Reorigination

Rhetoric versus history is a question this text alone will never definitively answer.[60] Yet dismissing the idea of a paschal observance just because the Corinthian community may have been more Gentile than Jewish errs in the other direction. It would be naive to think that Christians maintaining a Jewish identity, or even those whom they converted to Christianity "Jewish rite," would have ceased celebrating Pesach en masse until it had been properly integrated into the new faith. Festival customs are virtually impossible to eradicate, nor do they simply expire when their founding narratives are forgotten or expunged. As the later church would understand quite well, such feasts could be given new origins by addressing them to christology and scripture. The Corinthian celebration may thus represent the first example of the *interpretatio christiana*.

·For Pesach, the locus of rituals newly interpreted would not be an exercise among the scripturally astute with a flair for typology, but dinner among friends. This might help those scholars who vote only for rhetoric break down their exegetical wall of hostility between Jew and Gentile Christians (or between ritual and ethics) and thus discard the idea that the only unifying feature of the Corinthians was that they did not celebrate a paschal feast.[61]

---

[60] Huber, 102, assumes the Corinthians had never celebrated Pesach. Green, Joel B., The Death of Jesus, WUNT 2.33, 1988, 189, considers this text "neutral" in terms observance, speaking neither for nor against.

[61] Orr, Wm. F., and James Arthur Walther, 1 Cor AB 32, 1976, 187, see a slight eucharistic reference. Howard, J.K., "Christ Our Passover," EvQ 41, 1969, (97-108) 101, n. 8, finds no reference to Passover "especially as most of the Corinthians seem to

Deducing from 1Cor 14.23 that the entire community could meet at least for special occasions in the house of Gaius, Murphy O'Connor notes that the atrium and triclinium (dining room) even of luxurious homes would only have room for 50-60 people.[62] The problems at the meal may have been between the wealthy "strong" who were privileged to dine in the triclinium on choice fare, while the "weak" were relegated to the atrium.[63] Perhaps no one in Corinth felt called upon to enlarge the dining area as was done some generations later in the housechurch at Dura Europos, appropriately enough, by knocking out an interior wall. But the Corinthian community was relatively small, and their division into housechurches with baptismal "mascots" must have only increased their differences.

Pesach in the Diáspora centered as today in a meal ritualized toward a story of salvation, and the Seder was, and will always be, a meal of hospitality.[64] The Jewish Christians of Corinth had broken with the synagogue and like Paul had resolved the question of table fellowship. If circumcised, Gentile "sojourners" in Israel were able to eat the Pesach meal (Ex 12.48). Would the Jewish Christians of Corinth have insisted on this requirement, though otherwise willing to share the weekly common meal? Would the "strong" who thought little of attending the banquets of pagan cults have refused the invitation?

On the night of the full moon of early spring, Jewish Christians who celebrated Pesach had invited their Gentile brothers and sisters to supper, and if Gentiles had not adopted the custom of removing leaven from their homes, they knew people who did. That atmosphere alone would guarantee a new interpretation of both meal and story, the general

have been Gentiles." Schrage EKK, 380 f., provides an extensive "anagogical" reading but denies the "historical." Only Karl Fascher, THbNT VII, I, 1 Kor 1, [4]1988, 162 f. says the lamb typology is drawn from actual observance.

[62] Murphy-O'Connor, Paul's Corinth, 153-161.

[63] Theißen, Gerd, Soziale Schichtung in der korinthischen Gemeinde, Ein Beitrag zur Soziologie des hellenistischen Urchristentums, in: Studien zur Soziologie des Urchristentums, WUNT 19, [3]1989, 231-271 (=ZNW 65, 1974, 232-272); ibid., Die Starken und Schwachen in Korinth, Soziologische Analyse eines theologischen Streites, WUNT 19, 272-289 (=EvTh 35, 1975, 155-172).

[64] Shemot Rabba 18 sees this hospitality in the first Pesach: "Thus through their salvation God occasioned joy for Israel. For God said, 'Whoever loves my children, come and have joy with my children.' The pious Egyptians came and even took part in the Pesach feast with the Israelites and departed with them." Cited by Braulik, Georg, Pascha–von der alttestamentlichen Feier zum neutestamentlichen Fest, BiKi 36, 1981, (159-165) n. 11, 165.

frame of a Jewish festive meal offering easy associations to the eucharist, the other common meal they shared. How many meals before "Christ our Pascha" would arise as the best way to articulate this fellowship in the common language of worship, and for "Christ the Lamb" to have provided grammar and vocabulary? How many dinners in how many homes before a new understanding of the Pesach festival would lead to a meal for the entire congregation at Corinth, perhaps marked by the same problems between wealthy and poor, but *not* between Jewish and Gentile Christians? And how many years of common celebration before the eucharist began to take on *narrative* features of the Pesach meal, especially as told in the story of Jesus' death?[65] What the Corinthians celebrated was not the Pascha of the late second century. Yet if first century rhetoric about observance or non-observance of OT ritual laws is historicized into Jewish-Gentile *apartheid* at the beginnings of Christian origins, then in the second century there would have been no Pascha, and no church to celebrate it.

Corinth was one place this reinterpretation could have occurred, Antioch with its "Hellenists" and their Gentile converts another, perhaps even Rome, but not necessarily everywhere. There was probably a certain ambiguity even after the dynamic shift to Pascha took place. Yet such a shift, fully accomplished at least by mid-second century, presupposes a continued celebration in enough congregations of the first, and that widely spread among Gentile, Jewish Christian, and mixed congregations, to reoriginate the feast.

2. The Hebrew Calendar

a) Galatians

Even without the "Paul" of Acts confusing the issue, ambiguity toward Judaic ritual is unambiguous in Paul's letters, which is probably why many commentators are reluctant to consider paschal observance in a Pauline congregation. In Gal 4, Paul criticizes the Galatians for observing, or contemplating observing,[66] Judaic practices:

---

[65] Brown, Raymond E., The Death of the Messiah, London/NY 1994, 1371. "…Mark has taken over an understanding of the supper as a paschal meal and not attempted to change the basic narrative of the passion … because he thought of the paschal characterization of the meal as liturgical theology and not as history."

[66] The tone of the letter suggests that they are just toying with the idea. Betz, Hans Dieter, Der Galaterbrief, München 1988, 378 (=dÜ Galatians, Phila. 1979).

$^{4.8}$ Formerly, when you did not know God, you were enslaved to beings that by nature are not gods. ^{9} Now, however, that you have come to know God, or rather to be known by God, how can you turn back again to the weak and beggarly elemental spirits? How can you want to be enslaved to them again? ^{10} You are observing special days, and months, and seasons, and years. ^{11} I am afraid that my work for you may have been wasted.

Paul sees his opponents leading Gentiles to observe the features of baseline Jewish identity[67] – circumcision (which bears the major brunt of Paul's polemic), festivals, and days (Sabbaths, New Moons) – as necessary for salvation, to which Paul is soundly opposed *for Gentiles*. Since these observances had been touted as the next and most vital step in Gentile conversion, Paul transfers anti-pagan rhetoric to Judaism: The lunar calendar does not obey the commands of the God of Israel, but the "powers of the world."[68]

For Paul, the OT festival calendar was at issue in Galatia, but not for Corinth, with both Jewish and Gentile members. Thus it would be as inappropriate to assume that Paul would be totally against any celebration of the Passover *anywhere* as it would be to assume that all Pauline congregations were boisterously charismatic or baptized for the dead. As Tertullian would pose the historical question:

> ...if the Apostle abolished each and every observance of times, days, months and years, why do we then celebrate Pascha in the course of the year in the first month (i.e., of spring)? Why do we spend the following fifty days in all exultation?[69]

The calendar dispute in Galatia suggests an answer: for Christianity "Jewish rite," Pesach and other feasts were indispensable to *Christian* identity. Neither were such Christians active just in Galatia, nor was Paul in every place able to stem their influence, nor did they vanish after 70 CE.[70] – So Paul writes to another mixed congregation:

[67] See Grünwaldt, Klaus, Exil und Identität. Beschneidung, Passa und Sabbat in der Priesterschrift, BBB 85, 1992.

[68] See Betz, Galaterbrief, 372-374; Thornton, T. C. G. Jewish New Moon Festivals, Gal 4.3-11 and Col 2.16, JTS NS 40, 1989, 97-100.

[69] Tertullian, De ieiunio 14.2 f. CCSL 2, 1272 f.

[70] Jervell, Minority, 16: "I have always found it peculiar... that the only main group involved in the story of the Jewish war which did not survive should be the Jewish Christians." Cf. Pritz, Ray A., Nazarene Jewish Christianity. From the End of the NT Period until its Disappearance in the Fourth Century, Jerusalem/Leiden 1988; specific to Gal: Martyn, J. Louis, A Law-Observant Mission to Gentiles: The Background of Galatians, SJT 38, 1985, 307-324.

14.5 Some judge one day to be better than another, while others judge all days to be alike. Let all be fully convinced in their own minds. Those who observe the day (ὁ φρονῶν), observe it in honor of the Lord. ⁶ Also those who eat, eat in honor of the Lord, since they give thanks to God; while those who abstain, abstain in honor of the Lord and give thanks to God. ⁷ We do not live to ourselves, and we do not die to ourselves. ⁸ If we live, we live to the Lord, and if we die, we die to the Lord; so then, whether we live or whether we die, we are the Lord's. ⁹ For to this end Christ died and lived again, so that he might be Lord of both the dead and the living.

In one step, the potential for ritual discord becomes a harmonious picture of the central mystery of the faith, as long as the practices are "in honor of the Lord." Perhaps Paul was more successful with this tactic than Irenaeus will be with a similar plea to Rome a century and a half later. Yet if the Corinthians – or the Romans – had already moved toward a paschal observance "in honor of the Lord," Paul would not have objected. Paul does not have a single approach to ritual continuity with Judaism, but he is unambiguous about the narrative all rituals are to tell.

b) Colossians

The deutero-Pauline[71] Col echoes Paul's rhetoric in Gal, but with Paul's characteristic edges smoothed down:

> 2.16Therefore do not let anyone condemn you in matters of food and drink or of observing festivals, new moons, or sabbaths. ¹⁷ These are only a shadow of what is to come, but the substance (σῶμα) belongs to Christ.

While the negative answer to Jewish cultic practices is the same as its Galatian model, the rhetorical strategy of Col is quite different. Paul opposes slavery under the Law to the freedom of the Gospel:[72] observing Judaic feasts is only pagan slavery in a new form. Col opposes prophecy to fulfillment: Judaic cult is the shadow of which Christ is the "body." Paul also argues strictly on kerygmatic grounds, but Col introduces mimesis by addressing, albeit negatively, Jewish feasts to the mystery of Christ.

---

[71] Convincing arguments for dtPl authorship gathered in Schenk, W., Der Kolosserbrief in der neueren Forschung (1945-1985), ANRW 2.25.4, 3327-3364.

[72] George Howard argues Paul meant this stringency only for Gentiles. See Crisis in Galatia, SNTS.MS 35, ²1990, 52-54.

As paschal texts from second century Asia Minor will show, "no" is not the inevitable answer to this shift to a shadow-reality hermeneutic, but the very origins for the feast. The festival that once carried the kerygma of the creation and salvation of Israel becomes a shadow, a type, mimesis of the reality of Christ: Ephrem's mirror in which one sees the cross.   ·

III. Looking Ahead

For the next three hundred years, the Pauline grammar of lamb, Law, and calendar dictates both the language of rite and its polemic twin as Christian authors explain or defend what it means to "keep the feast" – in, through, and often against the rituals of Ex 12. Far from exhausting its meaning, the metaphor "Christ the Lamb" creates a rhetorical matrix that engenders homilies, treatises, and hymns, whole sub-genres of speech that explore the mimetic possibilities of this equation.

As Tertullian has already intimated, the deuteropauline author of Col is not the last to exploit Gal 4.10 to negate cult. It will be transferred to a variety of conflicts where *Christian* "days and months and years" are at issue. Even Origen finds himself cornered by the rhetorical power of this verse, but with characteristic bravura, sees a means of escape – through an extremely literal reading of one word in its Col copy.

Hippolytus is the first to include the whole church in Paul's verb ἑορτάζωμεν. Thereafter 1Cor 5.7 is an unambiguous scriptural rubric to observe the paschal feast – except, that is, for the fourth century schismatic Aerius, as Epiphanius reports:

> Next he says, "What is the Pascha you celebrate? You are giving your allegiance to Jewish fables again (Titus 1.14). We have no business celebrating the Pascha," he says, "Christ was sacrificed for our Pascha."[73]

Second century authors, however, neither rubricize this text nor hurl its kerygma at Christian ritual, but at Judaic rite and narrative: the "myths" of Trito-Paul that stand in the way of "spiritual" interpretation. A letter from the Valentinian teacher Ptolemy garners 1 Cor 5.7 as proof for the classic image/reality hermeneutic:

> Likewise the Pascha and the unleavened bread: Paul the Apostle makes it clear that they are images when he says, "Christ has been sacrificed as our

[73] Epiphanius, Pan 75.3.4, GCS 37, 335; NHMS 36, 492; cf. CQL 67.

paschal lamb," and further, "that you may be unleavened bread, having no share in the leaven" – by leaven he means wickedness – "but that you may be a new dough."[74]

Curiously enough, though its reading of 1 Cor 5.7 is indistinguishable from that of the Great Church, this text is taken to mean that Valentinians did not celebrate a paschal feast. While Cantalamessa entertains thoughts of a Corinthian Pascha,[75] Ptolemy elicits a different response: "Since the orthodox Christians observed the Pascha with fast and vigil on a definite day, Ptolemy and most other Gnostics probably rejected its ritual observance."[76] Valentinians, however, were not "most other Gnostics," and the *Gospel of Philip* testifies both to their self-perceived "spiritual" Christian identity and rich ritual life, two reasons why this group of Gnostic Christians was able to survive into the fourth century. Ptolemy's exegesis is thus as ambiguous about actual rituals as the Pauline original.

Disagreement among modern interpreters about a Pascha celebrated or not celebrated in first century Corinth exemplifies the difficulty of reading highly rhetorical texts for their historical background, an ambiguity exploited by Hippolytus and Aerius – and Cantalamessa. The question whether 1 Cor 5.6-8 is ethical and/or ritual mimesis will never be answered, because this verse is only an echo of a conversation in which modern readers cannot take part. Demonstrating from social patterns operative in the Corinthian congregation that such a celebration is historically plausible does not prove its existence any more than stressing the ethical nature of the text proves the contrary.

The absorption and restatement of one narrative to readdress ritual motifs to another is a technique that will occur in countless second century texts. Yet the connections between the Exodus story of origins and Christian ritual will not take the same route as in the Syn evangelists. The Pesach blood rite as baptism, but virtually never the meal as eucharist, is the paschal sign. The Fourth Gospel provides a cue: the blood and water streaming from the pierced side of Christ as the Pesach lambs are slain. Ex 12 is read by early Christian exegetes not as ritual text, but as prophetic narrative, and that which "dramatizes" the ritual is neither eucharist nor baptism, but the passion of Christ. Both Apollinarios of

---

[74] Ptolemy, Letter to Flora, SC 24 bis (Quispel), 1966, 66.
[75] CQL, 127, n. 'b.'
[76] CQL, 135, n. 'b.'

Hierapolis and Hippolytus eloquently defend this kerygmatic reading against any paschal aetiology read into the Synoptic meal. There can be but one kind of mimesis: Christ cannot *be* the paschal lamb and eat it too.

As Ptolemy's letter shows, Colossians' "image-reality" hermeneutic casts a long shadow in the second century. Gentile authors in an ever more Gentile church take the motif of supercession far beyond its Pauline use, which most often is designed to assure Jewish Christians of the legitimacy of the Gentile mission. Even circumcision, attacked with every weapon in Gal, becomes much more nuanced in Rom, where Paul is writing a congregation with strong Jewish Christian members. This nuance, and any positive value of Jewish cultic practices, disappears when a Gentile church takes over the motif of supercession not as a mark of the gospel, but community identity. In stern instruction to Gentile Christians at Rom 11.13-36, Paul directs a threat to an imagined partner:

> You will say, "Branches were broken off so that I might be grafted in." That is true. They were broken off because of their unbelief, but you stand only through faith. So do not become proud, but stand in awe. For if God did not spare the natural branches, perhaps he will not spare you.

If Gentile Christians had not already begun to define themselves at the expense of Jews, these words would not have been necessary. Yet when Ignatius writes the Magnesians,

> Discard, then, the bad leaven, which has become old and bitter, and turn to the new leaven, Jesus Christ. [3] For it is out of place to say 'Jesus Christ' and live Jewish. For Christianity did not believe in Judaism, but Judaism in Christianity...[77]

Paul's image of leaven is retained, but the terms of Paul's message to the Gentiles in Rom 11 are reversed. For second century Gentile authors, Paul's admonition might well have never been written.[78]

---

[77] IgnMag 10.2 f., SUC 1, 169.

[78] A "presbyter" warns not to be boastful toward *pre-Advent* Jews; the olive tree is metaphor for post-baptismal sin, AH 4.27.2; Tert., Test 5.6: the graft is Christian use of scripture. Otherwise Rom 11.13-36 is treated as a parable free for any interpretation. AH 4.20.12: Rom 11.17 prophesies emergence of Gentile church. AH 5.10.1-2, parable of flesh and spirit against Valentinians. (Cf. Origen, CommRom 8.11: Followers of Valentinus and Basilides read the verses as predestination in their favor.) Clem., Strom 6.117-120: the domesticated olive is Christ, the wild branch is pagan

Given massive confirmation with the destruction of Jerusalem in 135, the triumphalist pride against which Paul warns will often target Jewish ritual, and over and over again, these rituals will tell the story of one people rejected, and another who was never grafted into an existing vine, but all along was the original "pleasant planting" of the Lord.

IV. Shaping the Paschal Narrative

By the second generation Christian communities of Jewish or Gentile origin had appropriated the LXX and would maintain it for almost a century as their only scriptural canon.[79] Yet the rule, i.e. *canon*, by which Paul[80] already measures is a NT hermeneutic. The Christ event is the goal to which all scripture must point. For if the scriptures are of God, and Jesus God's Son, then holy words must also have spoken definitively of his coming, his humiliating death, his glorification, and his coming again. If this is true, then these scriptures must also define Christian identity, speak of Christian rites, and order communal life.

While reading sacred texts as living documents speaking to the immediate present is not unknown in Jewish and Hellenistic exegesis,[81] a number of NT passages invoke its charismatic nature. The Spirit, Paul writes, had removed the veil from Moses' face, revealing the true meaning of the OT to a new community (2 Cor 3.7-17), just as at Emmaus

philosophy grafted onto a more noble tree. A plain reading: "After this, the Apostle teaches us not to be boastful toward the root or the broken branches from Israel and not to insult them; for we do not carry the root, the root carries us." Origen, CommRom 8.11, FC 2/4, 294 f. Chrysostom cites Paul's rhetorical "partner" positively as if the "shadow" were Paul, advJud 1.2, PG 48, 845.

[79] Campenhausen, Hans Frhr. von, Das AT als Bibel der Kirche. Vom Ausgang des Urchristentums bis zur Entstehung des NT.s, in: ibid., Aus der Frühzeit des Christentums. Studien zur Kirchengeschichte des ersten und zweiten Jahrhunderts, Tübingen 1963, 152-196.

[80] Paul "knows only one way which leads from Christ to an understanding of the Scriptures, and its direction cannot be reversed." Campenhausen, Die Entstehung der christlichen Bibel, BHT 39, 1968, 37.

[81] See Reventlow, Epochen der Bibelauslegung, Bd. I. Vom AT bis Origenes, München 1990, 24-51; Fitzmyer, Jos. A., The Use of Explicit OT Quotations in Qumran Literature and the NT, NTS 7, 1960/1, 296-333. Cf. Pesher on Hab, VII, 1-4, Lohse, 234 f.: "When it says, 'He may make haste with what he reads,' it therefore refers to the Teacher of Righteousness, to whom God has revealed all secrets of the words of his servants, the prophets."

the risen Christ opens the Scriptures and instructs the disciples about his suffering and death (Lk 24.44-47). Moses' veil is only a metaphor, but the Emmaus story is a *kerygmatic* aetiology: not only reflecting a particular biblical hermeneutic but providing a dominical example for imitation, a construct the gospels employ toward rite only in the Syn meal narrative, Lord's Prayer, and Joh footwashing.[82] Yet whether the kerygma speaks of Jesus as incarnate Logos, angel, or cosmic revealer, high priest, Messiah or king,[83] the method used to draw such images, whether closer to Hellenistic or Jewish models or a Philonian synthesis of both,[84] was secondary to creating a scripturally based kerygma addressed to the Christ event.

1. The Red Thread

Narrowing the focus to one narrative at first unrelated to the Pascha shows how intricately encoded second century paschal language could become and how easily it could translate other, originally purely keryg-matic narratives into its vocabulary. In Adversus Haereses (AH), Irenaeus refers cryptically to a "red sign" whose interpretation is more assumed than demonstrated:

> So too the prostitute Rehab was condemned as a Gentile and an open sinner, but she nevertheless hid the three who were to scout out the entire land. They are the Father with the Son and the Holy Spirit. And when the entire city where she lived fell to ruin before the sound of the seven trumpets, through faith in the red sign the prostitute Rehab and her whole house were saved at the last moment. Thus the Lord said to those who did not receive his coming and made light of the red sign – which means the Pascha, salvation and the Exodus of the People from Egypt – that is, the Pharisees: "Publicans and prostitutes will go before you in the kingdom of heaven" [Mt 21.31].[85]

What is Pascha doing in Rehab's window as the red sign the Pharisees ridiculed? What does the Trinity have to do with signs that "save at the

---

[82] The Great Commission is a command, not a model. The footwashing is ethical mimesis enacted as rite as narrative. Cultic aetiologies reduce to two.

[83] Grillmeier, Aloys, Christ in Christian Tradition, London ²1975, 33-106.

[84] See Reventlow, Epochen I; Blöningen, Christoph, Der griechische Ursprung der jüdisch-hellenistischen Allegorese und ihre Rezeption in der alexandrinischen Patristik, EHS 14/59, 1992; Goppelt, Leonhard, Typos, Die typologische Deutung des AT.s im Neuen, Gütersloh 1939.

[85] AH 4.20.12, SC 100/2, 674.

last moment" keyed to the Exodus? Some paragraphs later, the red sign appears again, only slightly clarifying the meaning:

> This (i. e., relationship between both testaments) is shown typologically by many other things, especially by Tamar, the daughter-in-law of Judah. For when one of her twins first stretched out its hand and the midwife thought that this one was the firstborn, she tied a red marker (signum) around its hand. Yet when this one afterward had withdrawn its hand, his brother Phares came out first and then as second the one with the red sign, Zara. Thus scripture clearly demonstrates that the People with the red sign, that is faith in the foreskin, was first shown in the patriarchs, and then withdrawn, so that first his brother would be born. Then the first was born in second place and recognized by the red sign. This means the suffering of the Just One. In the beginning it was prefigured in Abel, described by the prophets and fulfilled in the last days in the Son of God.[86]

The twins of Tamar follow a Paul-inspired exegesis characteristically Irenaean: the younger son supplanting the elder is the Gentile Church superseding Israel as the People of God.[87] The "red sign" is suddenly no longer circumcision but the sufferings of Christ, prefigured in the death of Abel: a red thread running through the entire biblical history.

The red thread is still difficult to follow without knowing that previous exegetes saw the color of blood as metonymy for the death of Christ. This first becomes visible in 1 Clem:

> [12.7] And they also advised her to give a sign. She should hang something red from the house; doing this, she revealed that through the blood of the Lord, all who believe in God and hope in him are rescued.[88]

In Barnabas' exegesis of the scapegoat ritual (7.7-11), red wool is placed on the head of the goat banished into the wilderness. Other rituals of stabbing and spitting are keyed to the passion. The wool is also hung on a bush yielding red berries (whose sweetness Barnabas recommends) and becomes the robe placed mockingly upon Christ. The first scapegoat slaughtered on the altar is the cross, the second

---

[86] AH 4.25.2, SC 100/2, 706 f.

[87] Irenaeus applies the allegory of Hagar and Sarah (Gal 4.21-31) to other pairs: Shem-Ham (Epid 21) in AH: Cain-Abel (4.18.3), Jacob-Esau (4.21.2-3). At AH 4.31.1-3, a "presbyter" story, Lot's daughters are "the two Synagogues…who bring forth as fruit from their Father living sons to the living God." The "mighty minority" still has a voice.

[88] 1 Clem 12.7, SUC 1, 40 f.

goat will return from the desert, and the Jews will be shocked "at the similarity to the goat."[89]

In the red heifer ritual (8.1-6), the cow is not *red*, only young, but with a hyssop branch, red wool is hung on a tree. This is meaningless without knowing the Syn passion accounts, and that behind the wool is a sheep, behind the sheep is the Suffering Servant, and behind the color red the blood of the paschal lamb and Jesus. There is sprinkling of ashes for the forgiveness of sins, along with an odd mention of the number twelve for the apostles and their commissioning by Christ. The juice of the hyssop, Barnabas informs his readers, has curative powers.

Chances are good that Barnabas is not only reworking previous traditions about the scapegoat and red heifer, but imitating a paschal sermon he has heard (or delivered)[90] where the sacrifice of the lamb is the story of Christ's death. The construct is evocative of paschal language, even though the object is a different ritual text.

Without admixture from Barn, Justin picks up the red thread from 1 Clem:

> Also the symbol of the red thread, which the spies sent out by Jesus, Son of Nave, gave to the prostitute Rehab instructing her to tie it outside on the window by which she let them escape, reveals the mystery of the blood of Christ, which rescues all Gentiles who once served immorality and injustice, if they have received forgiveness of sins and sin no more (cf. adulteress, now at Jn 8.11).[91]

Justin remembers that Rehab is a Gentile, who, as it were, whored after false gods, so Clement's "all who believe" receives a particular restriction: Rehab gives birth to the Gentile Church. The "also" at the beginning is the exegetical window through which Irenaeus sees a paschal type: just before Justin interprets the red thread, he equates the blood of the Pascha [lamb] with the blood of Christ, which will "save those from death who believe."

Irenaeus ties all these red threads together, but if his readers did not already speak this exegetical vocabulary, he would offer nothing more than tangled tradition. Themes of birth, saving signs, the creation of the Gentile Church, Pascha, and cross focus even more vaguely on baptism

---

[89] Barn 7.11, SUC 2, 158 f.

[90] This led L. W. Barnard to mistake imitation for the genuine article. The Epistle of Barnabas – A Paschal Homily? VigChr 15, 1961, 8-22.

[91] Dial 111.4, Goodspeed, 228.

than in Barnabas, but as cryptic as these passages are, one can recognize paschal language, even if every word cannot be deciphered. This is not just literary tradition, but the product of a specific rhetorical situation in which Gentile Christian exegetes read Judaic texts for kerygmatic value. If none of these authors had ever seen each other's works, similar results would still have been produced. The color red may yield a narrative identical to that of Ex 12 because the act of reading begins with the same knowledge of what will be found.

Not all of these exegetical features would have found their way into a paschal homily in second century Lyon, but since the paschal typology is as automatic as the triune name for the number three, this red thread may still lead to Irenaeus' preaching in the paschal night. One thing is certain. From his homeland in Asia Minor, Irenaeus brought with him a reading of Ex 12 as a story of the passion:

> Without number are the places where Moses points to the Son of God. For he was not ignorant of the day of his suffering and preannounced it figuratively by calling the day Pascha, and on this Pascha, prophesied long ago by Moses, the Lord suffered and fulfilled the Pascha. Yet Moses described not only the day, but also the place, the time frame, (Lat. extremitatem temporum) and the sign of the setting sun. [Dt 16.5 f.][92]

...and as a reading of the creation of the Gentile church:

> For everything God did at the Exodus of the People out of Egypt was a type and image of the church, which would come out of the Gentiles. And so finally he will lead the church from here into its inheritance, which not Moses the servant of God, but Jesus the Son of God will give.[93]

A narrative from the Hebrew scriptures first read as a type of salvation through Christ further transforms into an identifying story of the Gentile church as the "new" Israel. Just as with the rituals and narrative of Ex 12, the surface meaning must be removed before the Gentile Church may find itself reflected there. This is especially the case when ritual – Judaic or Christian – is not on the periphery as in Irenaeus' Rehab story, but at the center, when in the paschal night single threads are woven into a complete narrative of cross, baptism, and the supercession of Israel, all from the founding narrative of a Judaic feast.

---

[92] AH 4.10.1, SC 100/2, 492 f.
[93] AH 4.30.4 SC 100/2, 785.

2. Early Christian Anti-Judaism

Early Christian appropriation of the Hebrew scriptures is accompanied by a total disenfranchisement of the Jewish people from the covenant to which these scriptures bear witness. Far from limited to one province or author, from the evangelists through the Didache, Ignatius, and Barnabas, to Justin, Melito, and the Syro-Western text of Acts,[94] anti-Judaic polemic pervades the entire early literature of the Church. While anti-Judaism may vary in intensity and affect, its content remains curiously monolithic across time and space,[95] this as an already varied Judaism is radically changing from a Temple-centered sacrificial cult to its rabbinical form. Already typecast in the Fourth Gospel as foil for Christian teaching, "the Jews"[96] rarely move beyond this brand of caricature, even though archaeological evidence shows that in many cities, Church and Synagogue were virtual next door neighbors.[97] This paradox suggests that Christian writers are often shadow-boxing a chimeral image with no substantial counterpart in contemporary Jewish thought and practice that may have otherwise been familiar to them. Early Christian anti-Judaism is first and foremost theologically, rather than historically or socially determined.

Taking issue with Marcel Simon's mercantile reconstruction of a contest between two actively proselytizing religions vying for the same

[94] Epp, Eldon Jay, The Theological Tendency of Codex Bezae Catabrigiensis in Acts, SNTS.MS 3, 1966.

[95] The academic version is "Strack-Billerbeck" Judaism, where Judaic texts from divergent times are treated as if they were 1 c. texts familiar to all Christian writers.

[96] Pierre Grelot seeks a way out of this dilemma by universalizing the figure of the "Jews": "... La confrontation qui a lieu entre lui et Dieu dévoile celle qui existe entre Dieu et tous les membres du genre humain." ibid., Les Juifs dans l'Évangile selon Jean, Enquête historique et réflexion théologique. RB 35, 1995, 190 f.

[97] Dura-Europos: synagogue and church along city wall on different sides of main street. Rome: tituli churches in the same areas as Jewish / Syrian settlement; Hopkins, Clark (ed. Goldman, Bernard), The Discovery of Dura-Europos, New Haven/ London 1979; Lampe, Peter, Die stadtrömischen Christen in den ersten beiden Jahrhunderten. Untersuchungen zur Sozialgeschichte, WUNT 2.18, 1987, 36-46. Palestine: Meyers, Eric M., Early Judaism and Christianity in the Light of Archaeology. BA 51/2 (June 1988) 69-79. These conclusions, with those of the Franciscans (Bagatti, et. al.), are not unchallenged. See Taylor, Joan E., Christians and the Holy Places. The myth of Jewish-Christian origins, Oxford 1993. Edessa: Drijvers, Han J. W., Syrian Christianity and Judaism, in: The Jews among Pagans and Christians in the Roman Empire (J. Lieu, J. North, T. Rajak, eds. London/NY 1992, (124-146) 128.

constituency in Late Antiquity,[98] Miriam S. Taylor characterizes the anti-Judaism of the patristic period as

> a tradition which remains constant over centuries, and forms a coherent body of mutually reinforcing arguments. It functions according to an internal logic in which the invalidation of Judaism emerges as a theoretical necessity in the appropriation of the Jewish God and the Jewish Bible for the church…The church's portrayal of Judaism is expressed in terms of a dualism opposing Christians and Jews which is built into the very logic and into the very structure of Christian teaching. Recognizing this, scholars have acknowledged…a theological dimension in the formation of the "Adversus Judaeos" tradition, and they have further linked these theological arguments to the formation of Christian identity.[99]

Some may feel that Taylor has overstated her case. Yet Simon's method[100] cannot account for contradictions arising from such purely "historical" readings. Compare, for instance, the following statements:

> Eusebius reports that Clement wrote a work on the 'Ecclesiastical Rule against Judaizers.' This proves that 'Judaizing' was still a great danger to the church in the beginning of the third century.[101]

And in the same volume of essays,

> By the fourth century, when our documentation begins, the area in question [i.e. the location of an Alexandrian church dedicated to St. Mark] was outside the city, a place for "cow pastures" (βουκόλια). But in the first

---

[98] Promulgated in Verus Israel, Étude sur les relations entre Chretiens et Juifs dans l'Empire romain (135-425). BEFAR 166, Paris 1948. Applied by Hvalvik, Reidar, The Struggle for Scripture and Covenant, The Purpose of the Epistle of Barnabas and Jewish-Christian Competition in the Second Century, WUNT 2.82, 1996: "…both groups fought over the same people among the Gentiles," i.e., wealthy God-fearers (318).

[99] Taylor, Miriam S., Anti-Judaism & Early Christian Identity. A Critique of the Scholarly Consensus, StPBib 46, 1995, 129. See also Gager, John G., The Origins of Anti-Semitism, Attitudes Toward Judaism in Pagan and Christian Antiquity, NY 1985; Ruether, Rosemary Radford, Faith and Fratricide: The Theological Roots of Anti-Semitism, NY 1974.

[100] "C'est dire que le fondement premier de cet antisémitisme chrétien n'est ni social, ni à proprement parler religieux, au sens où l'était celui des païens…le vrai antisémitisme chrétien est théologique." Simon, Verus Israel, 245 f. Simon then creates an historical situation: an actively proselytizing "competing" Judaism. This is like recreating the foreign policy of the Soviet Union solely from the rhetoric of Sen. Joe McCarthy.

[101] Klijn, A. F. J., Jewish Christianity in Egypt, Roots, (161-175) 164.

century this area was the main Jewish neighborhood, described in glowing terms by Josephus. This is a sign of the relative complete destruction/ depopulation of the Jewish community in the early second century.[102]

If "judaizing" has any connection to Judaism, then to fit these facts together, one would have to posit some rather strange population movements in Alexandria or agree with Taylor. An actual Jewish community was as threatening to Clement as a vacant lot.[103]

The often ahistorical nature of early anti-Judaism should also sound a warning against charges of "judaizing" or "sabbatizing" as signifying an unbroken survival of Jewish Christian traditions or rituals – or anything else than the parties hurling these terms about are in disagreement. Just as much anti-Judaic rhetoric is anti-pagan rhetoric with a new address (Gal 4.10), the rhetoric of dispute can assign labels and values almost at will. Already with Ignatius such terms are stock epithets whose meaning is less important than the strong boundaries they create.[104]

The remarkable feature of anti-Judaic rhetoric is that once forged, this weapon can be used in contexts where an historical reading prohibits Jewish involvement. With only slight variation, anti-Judaic rhetoric can serve Valentinians[105] as well as the Montanist Tertullian in attacking the Great Church. In debate at the Nicaean Council, anti-Judaic polemic will be heaped upon the Syrian paschal tradition by supporters of Alexandria and Rome. By the same token, the anti-Judaic polemic occasioned by Ex 12 in Justin's *Dialogue* at mid-second century is identical to that in the paschal *Demonstration* of Aphrahat of 344. Aphrahat even provides a "shadow" rabbi with whom to debate. Certainly there were Jewish communities in Rome and Mesopotamia. But the Jews with whom these two Christian exegetes are debating are those who refuse to give up their rights to the rituals and narrative of Ex 12. These, however, are in the text itself.

---

[102] Pearson, Birger A., Earliest Christianity in Egypt: Some Observations, Roots, (132-157) 153.

[103] For historical background see Tcherikover, V., The Decline of the Jewish Diaspora in Egypt During the Roman Period, JJS 14, 1963, 1-32.

[104] Taylor, Anti-Judaism, 36. See below, p. 55.

[105] See Perkins, Gnosticism, 39 f. For Valentinian accusation that the Great Church only knows "the Passover of the Jews" in their Eucharist, see Pagels, Elaine, A Valentinian Interpretation of Baptism and Eucharist, HThR 65, 1972, 153-169, esp. 162 to end. Also Pagels, The Johannine Gospel in Gnostic Exegesis, SBL.MS 17, 1973, 76-82.

3. Testimonia

Another factor of early Christian proclamation from a Judaic book has a much more practical side: scrolls, then codices, of the complete LXX were expensive and time-consuming to produce. Even if a Christian community could afford such a luxury, there was always the matter of which scriptures to chose and how to interpret them. Both text and meaning could be transmitted orally, but chances are good that some literary transmission took place, especially where the lines of oral communication could be severed by time, space, or circumstance. Such literature could shape texts as much as interpret them: "actualizing"[106] changes occur where the contemporary meaning of the text becomes the text itself. Not surprisingly, such changes were often generated in life settings where texts were excerpted for liturgical, homiletic, or apologetic use. Psalm manuscripts, as well as Barn, Justin, Irenaeus, and Melito, present texts varying considerably from either the Masoretic Hebrew or the majority readings of the three great LXX traditions.[107] *Testimonia*, chains of OT citations accompanied by interpretative passages closely tied to the proclamation of the church, could in this new linkage lead textual lives of their own.

The shape of these testimonia – theories have ranged from a great "Testimonia Book" to florilegia with no commentary to scraps with a few verses – is somewhat controversial, but a theory of literary transmission of early exegetical traditions is still the most economical answer to a lack of full LXX and gospel mss. in the earliest Christian communities, similarities in non-LXX patristic citations, and the recurrence of certain verses in cluster, often with diverging interpretations.[108] These testimonia represent, as it were, the first "preaching helps" with lectionary and exegetical hints already provided – also for Ex 12. From the barest beginnings in

[106] For this type of reading see Decock, Paul B., The Reading of Sacred Texts in the Context of Early Christianity, Neotest 27, 1993, 263-282.

[107] Pre-Origen: Upper Egyptian, Lower Egyptian, and Western. Petraglio, Renzo, Le interpolazioni cristiane del Salterio greco, Aug 28, 1988, (89-109) 90. See this article for examples from Ψ'Ψ'.

[108] Discussion was acute in the 1960's and 70's, but recent scholars are more comfortable with the theory. For the genre, see Audet, Jean-Paul, L'hypothèse des Testimonia, RB 70, 1963, 381-405; and Hodgson, Robert Jr., The Testimony Hypothesis, JBL 98, 1979, 361-378. Earlier lit. see Barnard, L. W., The Use of Testimonies in the Early Church and in the Epistle of Barnabas, in: Studies in the Apostolic Fathers and their Backgrounds, Oxford, 1966, 109-135.

1Cor, early second century exegetes invisible behind the works of Pseudo-Barnabas and Justin Martyr develop paschal language around selected LXX texts – and a few "agrapha" that attain canonical authority simply from a new literary context.

a) The Sprinkled Blood: Barn 5.1

As Rehab's "red thread" runs from Clement to Irenaeus, it connects two genres of speech: *kerygma* to identify Christ and *didache* to identify those who have heard this saving message and believe. Baptismal catechesis could engender both, but is is also a rhetorical setting demanding ritual motifs as medium. As the Pesach narrative is read as Christ narrative, the blood rite, reduced to historical detail in the scriptures, becomes a rite that saves now, the people saved an increasingly Gentile church. The rhetorical matrix of this typology underlies Barn 5.1 f., which anchors once again the Fourth Servant Song to the passion:

> [5.1] For this purpose the Lord submitted to having the flesh given over to destruction, so that we would become pure through the forgiveness of sin, that is, through the *sprinkling of his blood.* [2] For as it is written, partly to Israel, partly to us, as it says, "He was wounded for our transgressions and crushed for our sins. By his *blood* we are healed. As a lamb he let himself be led to slaughter and like a sheep that is silent before its shearers.[109]

There is no sprinkling of blood in the Fourth Servant Song, but wounds and stripes, yet there is sprinkling in the ritual sacrifice of the scapegoat and the red heifer, both favored images in Barn, and smearing of blood in the Pesach rite. The lamb/sheep of Isaiah is conflated with the scapegoat and the paschal victim into one overarching type. Blood for stripes, "αἵματι" instead of the LXX "μώλοπι,"[110] reinforces the connection. "Sprinkling" and "pure through the forgiveness of sin" suggest that Barnabas' source read the blood rite as baptism.[111] Yet Barn does not pause to draw out any paschal significance or make a connection to "water and cross," as he will do later in the epistle.

---

[109] Wengst, SUC 2, 148.

[110] Wengst, SUC 2, 149, n. 67. Ms. L usually harmonizes to LXX; here the reverse.

[111] Skarsaune, Oskar, The Proof from Prophesy. A study in Justin Martyr's Proof-Text Tradition: Text-type, Provenance, Theological Profile, NT.S 61, 1987, 178.

b) Pesach and Baptism in Justin

Scattered through Justin's *Dialogue with Trypho* are paschal typologies likely gleaned from *testimonia*.[112] In Dial 13-14, the lamb typology appears with Is 53.7,[113] with the Servant Song cited in full at Dial 13. Further connecting the baptismal rite to the paschal lamb, water and oil are presented in Dial 86, along with a lengthy catalogue of types, as an anointing with blood. In Dial 14, Justin even adds an allusion to Paul's leaven:

> [14.1.]Therefore through the bath, which effects conversion and the knowledge of God, and which, as Isaiah said, [1.16] was instituted to heal the People of God from sin, we have become believers. We announce to you, that this is the washing which he prophesied and which alone has the power to purify humankind, given that they repent again. This is the "Water of Life." "The cistern which you have dug for yourselves has collapsed" [Jer 2.18] and brings you nothing. What, then, is the use of that washing which cleanses flesh and body alone? [2] Wash your souls clean of anger, greed, envy, hatred, and you will see: the body is clean. For that is the meaning of the unleavened bread: you should not do the old works of bad leaven. Yet you have thought of all things in a carnal way, and consider it to be piety, even though when you do such things, your souls are filled with guile, and, in fact, every evil.[114]

Given the ample arsenal of anti-cultic scriptures at Justin's disposal,[115] the allusion to the unleavened bread of 1 Cor 5.7-8 must have been prompted by the typological equation paschal blood=baptism, which becomes much clearer in the course of his work.[116] But Justin moves beyond Paul's intent, taking his cue from the "cisterns of death" so prominent in Barnabas' exegesis of baptism (11.1 f.) as negative counterpart to the Christian rite. Justin transforms Paul's metaphor into anti-Judaic

---

[112] Paschal lamb typology: Skarsaune, Proof, 42, 282, 296, 299. The following relies upon Skarsaune's textual work, where collation of LXX and non-LXX citations shows shape and content of testimonia sources.

[113] See Skarsaune, Proof, 178.

[114] Dial 14.1 f., Goodspeed, 106.

[115] Cf. Dial 27.2, Goodspeed 120 f., for a salvo of 13 anti-cultic scriptures hurled at his "shadow" Trypho for inquiring why Christians do not observe the Sabbath. "Trypho" cites Isa 58.13 f., the only occurrence of these verses *together*. Isa 58.1-10, however, occurs 31 times, most often to negate Judaic cult. For these, see BibPatr 1, Paris 1975, 157 f.

[116] Skarsaune, Proof, 301 f.

polemic by the same method that splits ethics and cult in numerous OT cult-critical prophesies: Paul's ethical interpretation is the true spiritual meaning of a feast that the Jews only celebrate "carnally." Yet Justin is merely drawing an anti-Judaic polemic into a more narrow focus on ritual differences. Ignatius had already used the same image of leaven to shore up Christian identity in opposition to the Jews.

The connection between "Christ our Pascha" and baptism is more explicit at Dial 40.1-3:

> [40.1] The mysterious celebration of the lamb, which according to God's command was sacrificed as the Pascha, pointed to the Anointed One. For following their faith in him, his believers anointed their houses, that is, themselves with the blood of Christ; for all of you should know that the body from which God formed Adam became the house of God's inbreathed spirit. That that divine commandment was given only for a particular time I will show by the following: [2] God allowed that the paschal lamb would be sacrificed only at that place where his name would be called [Dt 16.5]; but then, as God knew, there would come a time after the sufferings of Christ when even the place Jerusalem would be handed over to your enemies and all sacrifices would cease.
> [3] The command that each lamb must be completely roasted was an allusion to the sufferings on the cross that Christ would undergo. For when the lamb is roasted, it takes on the form of a cross, one of the spits pierces it vertically from the hind legs to the head, while the other, upon which the forelegs of the lamb are attached, pierces it through the shoulders.[117]

The full association comes in a list of types for the cross:

> [111.3.]Also those who in Egypt, who, when the Egyptian firstborn were killed, escaped unharmed, owe their salvation to the blood of the Pascha [lamb], which was smeared on both doorposts and the lentil. For the Pascha was the Christ later sacrificed, as Isaiah said, "Like a lamb he was led to slaughter." That you took him on the day of Pascha and likewise killed him during the Pascha, that is so written (καὶ ὅτι ἐν ἡμέρᾳ τοῦ πάσχα συνελάβετε αὐτὸν καὶ ὁμοίως ἐν τῷ πάσχα ἐσταυρώσατε, γέγραπται) In the same way, however, as the blood of the Pascha saved those in Egypt, so too will the blood of Christ save those from death who believe.[118]

---

[117] Justin may recall how Samaritans prepared the lamb. See Jeremias, Joachim, Die Passahfeier der Samariter und ihre Bedeutung für das Verständnis der alttestamentlichen Passahüberlieferung, BZAW 59, 1932, 55-96; Skarsaune, Proof, 299, n. 128.

[118] Dial 111.2, Goodspeed, 227 f.

Since this passage follows a reading of the outstretched arms of Moses (Ex 17.11-13) as the cross, Justin also sees this sign in the blood on doorposts and lentil of the "house" of the body. This reading is also the one Irenaeus conflates with Rehab's "red sign". Yet Justin draws out the implications of Barnabas' sprinkling into a fuller, more transparent exegesis of both Ex 12 and the Servant Song as passion narratives: even the lamb prepared for roasting images the cross. For both ritual and narrative, the century between Paul and Justin has increased mimesis in descriptive detail and motival correspondence.

This transparence does not immediately extend to Justin's chronology. Since there is no trace of the Fourth Gospel in Justin's works, the time cues "took him" and "killed him" on the Pascha do not harmonize Syn and Joh chronology, but rather use the same vocabulary, mirrored in contemporary Judaic writings, where Pascha designates the entire Pesach-Mazzot complex. Yet Justin is careful enough distinguish the *day* of Pesach (14 Nisan) from the festival period *in which* Jesus was crucified. Though Justin has no interest in the Pesach meal, this is Syn chronology.

Justin's negative mimesis, however, is much easier to see. The sacrifice of the Pascha in Egypt saves the Hebrews from death only because Christ *was* the paschal lamb. The smeared blood brings rescue only as the blood rite prefigured Christian baptism. The Jews have slaughtered the Lamb again, and they neither recognize Christ in the lamb slain in Egypt nor in Jesus of Nazareth whom they "took and killed" on/in the Passover. Now the Temple has been destroyed and no lambs are slain. Ex 12 has supplied a cast of shadow rites performed by shadow Jews to bolster Justin's polemic. If this polemic is bracketed out, the tight mimetic fit between baptism and the Pesach blood rite becomes apparent. If the polemic is left in and augmented with a sense of the rhetorically dramatic, Justin's exegesis becomes the plotline for the paschal homily of Melito of Sardis.

If Justin's paschal texts are viewed synoptically, one will see with Oskar Skarsaune[119] the central place of baptism in Justin's source. As in Paul and other NT texts, these testimonia restore typologically the apotropaic function of the paschal lamb. The continuous use of Ex 12 as "mystery" to be decoded by the Christ event has brought baptism into its thematic orbit, a connection developed with particular drama in

---

[119] Skarsaune, Proof, 282.

the second section of Melito's homily. Paschal language has increased
its vocabulary, and is moving toward the ubiquity of which Origen
complains.

c) Justin, Melito, Cyprian

With the LXX canon and *testimonia* extracts from it, Justin inherits a
dilemma of Christian exegesis: a crisis of authoritative text as well as
authoritative hermeneutic. The divergence between OT traditions in
early Christianity and rabbinical Judaism grew even wider with the
work of the proselyte Aquila of Pontus, who attempted a new translation directly from the Hebrew, a situation engendering much of the
"debate" in Justin's *Dialogue*. In Christian eyes, Aquila was tampering
with a received and inspired text. Yet a number of texts had never
appeared in Christian LXX mss., but in *testimonia* or other exegetical
with equal claims to canonicity.

Another chain of citations in Justin's *Dialogue* speaks the primary
paschal language of Christ's passion and death. After Justin and Trypho
converse about various textual "changes" in the LXX, Trypho conveniently inquires more specifically about verses Justin claims have been
removed:

> 71.4 Trypho said, "Now we would like for you to cite a few passages you
> believe have been totally removed."
>
> 72.1 I responded, "I will do as you wish. Your teachers have removed from
> the explanations of Ezra of the Pascha law the following explanation: 'Ezra
> spoke to the people: This Pascha is our savior and our refuge. When you
> consider and think that we will humiliate him on the sign [of the cross]
> and if we then place our hope on him, then truly will this place not be
> deserted forever; thus speaks the Lord Almighty. Yet if you do not believe
> in him nor listen to his preaching then you will become the laughingstock
> of the Gentiles.' [*This is an agraphon, to put it mildly*]
>
> 2 "They also erased the following from the words of Jeremiah [extant:
> 11.9] 'I have become like an innocent lamb to be slaughtered. They con-
> cocted a scheme against me and said, 'Let us put wood in his bread and
> wipe him out from the land of the living, his name shall truly no longer
> be remembered!' 3 Now this passage is still found in many copies in the
> Jewish synagogues, [*and in all extant mss., regardless of provenance*] for only
> recently did they excise the words mentioned. Thus it is once again pro-
> claimed about Jesus that which was prophesied by Isaiah; for also from
> these words may be deduced that the Jews held counsel about Jesus and
> that they decided to take his life through death on the cross. About the

one who according to Isaiah [53.7] is led to slaughter as a lamb is here revealed that he is an innocent lamb. In your distress you allow your teachers to lead you to blasphemy.

4 Also they struck the following words from Jeremiah: "The Lord, the holy God of Israel, remembered his dead who slept in earthen graves, and he descended to them, to bring them the good news of their salvation."

Paschal language has attained a new accent, foreign to the LXX, but native to the Asian tradition. "Jeremiah" provides a proof text especially crafted for the Descent into Hell, but no verse in either Jer or Lam can be construed as the original to which this is a gloss. Justin, however, cites it in good faith as authoritative scripture. While Melito shows no interest in the descensus motif, this prophecy of Christ preaching to the dead becomes a favored text of Irenaeus,[120] appearing no less than six times at important junctures in both the *Epideixis* and AH.

"Ezra's"[121] shadow Pascha inseparably links the rejection of the true Paschal Lamb to the devastation of Jerusalem, just as Melito will do without pseudepigraphic assistance. While the imagined context of this prediction is the description of the paschal feast at the exiles' return (Ezra 6.19 ff.), this passage cannot be termed an insertion[122] since it does not occur in any extant ms., and there is no pressing reason to assume that it ever did. It did occur in a written source that Justin considers an authoritative rendering of the LXX.[123] The Jewish "rejection" Justin claims for these verses assures their canonicity as much as their content assures divine rejection of the Jews.

With other scriptures, some also deviating from majority readings, prophetic passages are listed again in Melito's *Peri Pascha*, roughly a decade later than Justin's *Dialogue*:

58 (l. 413) But if you look carefully at the model (τύπος),
you will perceive him [Christ] through the final outcome...
60 Look also at the sheep which is slain in the land of Egypt,
which struck Egypt
and saved Israel by its blood.

---

[120] More exactly at Epid 78, AH 3.20.4, 4.22.1, more loosely, at AH 4.33.1,12; 5.31.1. Irenaeus may draw directly from Justin or a common source. Skarsaune, Proof, 452.

[121] Also cited by Lactantius, Div. Inst. 4.18.22, presumably on Justin's authority.

[122] Robert Kraft argues this text need not be a totally Christian insertion. See, "Ezra" Materials in Judaism and Christianity, ARNW 2.19.1, 119-136.

[123] Skarsaune, 371 f.

[61] But the mystery of the Lord is proclaimed by the prophetic voice.
For Moses says to the people: *"And you shall see your life hanging before your eyes night and day; and you will not believe on your life."* [Dt 28.66, not LXX or MT].

[62] And David said, *"Why have the nations raged, and peoples contemplated vain things? The kings of the earth stood by and the rulers assembled together against the Lord and against his Christ."*[124]

[63] And Jeremiah: *"I am like a harmless lamb led to be sacrificed. They devised evil things for me, saying: 'Come on, let us put wood on his bread, and wipe him out from the land of the living; and his name shall not be remembered.'"*[125]

[64] And Isaiah: *As a sheep he was led to slaughter, and as a lamb speechless before him that sheared him, this one opens not his mouth: but his generation who shall tell?*[126]

[65] Many other things have been proclaimed by many prophets
about the mystery of the Pascha,
which is Christ.
To him be glory forever. Amen.[127]

As in Justin, Jer 11.9[128] and Isa 53.7-8 appear together, augmented by the "raging heathen" of Ψ2.1-2 (Acts 4.25-27) and Dt 28.66, also in a slightly divergent reading. But now the psalm provides types for Herod and Pilate as well as the angry crowds in the passion narrative, and the Pascha as mystery – here not just the paschal victim – is equated with Christ himself. There can be no more concise digest of the Asian paschal tradition.

When this exegetical tradition reaches Cyprian, the chain has the following shape:

Is 53.7-9, 12	Fourth Servant Song
Jer 11.18-19	Like a lamb to the slaughter…
Ex 12.3, 5-11	Institution of Pesach, slaughter of lamb
Rev 5.6-10	Heavenly Lamb
Jn 1.29	Behold the Lamb of God[129]

[124] Cf. Acts 4.25-7, 1Apol 40.11; Iren. AH 3.12.5.

[125] Cf. Justin, Dial 72; Tertullian, AdvJud 10.12, AdvMarc 3.19.3, 4.40.3. Some of Melito's divergences from LXX appear also in Justin.

[126] Cf. Acts 8.32-33-3.1; 1 Clem 16.7-8; Dial 72.3. Some divergences from LXX shared by Barn 5.2.

[127] Melito, PP 414 f., 422-450; OECT (Hall), 32-35.

[128] See also IP 48: "A lamb is the sacred victim. For it is written, 'Like a sheep led to the slaughter and like a lamb silent before the one who shears it.' And John: 'Behold the Lamb of God who takes away the sin of the world.'"

[129] Cyprian, Ad Quir (Test) 2.15, CSEL 3.1, 80-82.

Now canonical NT texts have been added, but in an unusual order. Familiar texts from Isaiah and Jeremiah function as predictions of the killing of the Just One, while verses in Ex 12 about the lamb's slaughter are given at length. This is followed by the heavenly lamb of Rev as the apotheosis of Ex 12, only then to be concluded by Jn 1.29. This balanced threefold scheme – humiliation and death, exaltation, affirmation and confession – not only employs many of the same texts as Justin and Melito, but arranges them in a kerygmatic pattern. The affirmation in Jn 1.29 is a rubric: this chain of *testimonia* is also liturgical in shape. The thematic cluster leading to the beholding of the Lamb has become an extended metaphor for the entire paschal mystery, not from one testament to the other, but *through* both, culminating in a christological affirmation: the Pascha is Christ.

Cyprian provides the guidewords for an established paschal lexicon, each scripture and all language they engender growing from the lamb typology Paul briefly mentions some two centuries before. The most obvious setting for this merger is the same Cyprian likely envisions: preaching at the celebration of Pascha with Ex 12 as a primary text about Christ. By the late second century, the complete identification of Christ with the lamb is already so traditional that Melito can even refer to the Virgin, for the first – but not the last time[130] – in early patristic writings, as "a lovely ewe" (PP 71).

V. Melito of Sardis († before 190)

Almost nothing is known of the life of Melito of Sardis, and until the paschal homily was published in 1940 by its discoverer Campbell Bonner,[131] his works were known only in a few fragments tucked away in various catenæ and the EH of Eusebius. Eusebius also gives a list of Melito's works, none of which has survived. While a paschal treatise in two books is mentioned, Περὶ Πάσχα (PP) is not this work, but a homily prepared for publication.[132] By no means textually secure, other

---

[130] Romanos Melodos, Hymn 35.1, SC 128, 1967, 160, which finds its way into the Byzantine Good Friday liturgy, and in a Hymn to the Virgin attributed to Ephrem (S. Ephraemi Hymni et Sermones, ed. Lomy, Mechlin 1886, 2:520-642). OAK 43, n. 1; CQL, 139, note 'b' to text 23.

[131] Bonner, Campbell, The homily on the Passion by Melito Bishop of Sardis and some Fragments of the Apocryphal Ezekiel, StDoc, 1940.

[132] Hall, Stuart G., Melito of Sardis and Fragments, OECT, 1971, xix-xxi.

titles can indicate nothing more than Melito's participation in important theological discussions of his day, including two dealing with liturgical topics: a treatise on the Lord's Day and one on baptism.

1. Paschal Homily (ca. 160-170)

For all its display of rhetorical skill,[133] Melito's paschal homily follows a simple strategy that in the century since Paul has coalesced paschal exegesis into a fixed narrative. Ex 12 is a story of origins for a covenant people. The paschal blood signs baptism as a rite that saves from death, the lamb is Christ, the death that saves the cross. None of these typoi are new to his congregation; they have heard them preached at past vigils. Yet the exegetical task is not easy, for even in a thoroughly christianized book, Ex 12 is still a story of the creation of the Jewish people and must remain so to be a holy story. Salvation must happen in the text, the problem is for whom. With this task in mind, Melito introduces an ambiguity between text and meaning he will later resolve:

> [1] The scripture from the Hebrew Exodus has been read
> and the words of the *mystery* have been plainly stated,
> how the sheep (πρόβατον) is sacrificed
> and how the People is saved
> and how pharaoh is scourged through the *mystery*.
> [2] Understand, therefore, beloved,
> how it is new and old,
> eternal and temporary,
> perishable and imperishable,
> mortal and immortal, this *mystery* of the Pascha...[134]

What is Melito's "mystery"? In a long excurse (33-45), Melito explains how the δύναμις (PP 34.17) of the paschal mystery is revealed through a typological understanding of the scriptures. Yet Melito does not tie method to result until the end of the passage, where the "now worthless" Temple is revealed as type for the "Jerusalem above." Instead, he discusses the preliminary nature of plans, models, types, and images.

---

[133] See Wellesz, E. J., Melito's Homily on the Passion: An Investigation into the Sources of Byzantine Hymnography, JThS 44, 1943, 41-57; and Wifstrand, A., The Homily of Melito on the Passion, VigChr 2, 1948, 201-223.

[134] PP 1-2 (1-10), 4. Stich, (line), p. no. of Greek text. Occasional alterations have been made to Hall's trans.

Addressing his hearers directly, Melito explains that once a plan for a building is finished, "You complete the work; you want that alone, you love that alone, because in it alone you see the pattern and the material and the reality." In a little over 85 lines, Melito constructs an interpretive space for his hearers and directs them there:

> The People then was a model by way of preliminary sketch,
> and the law was the writing of a parable,
> the gospel is the recounting and fulfillment of the Law,
> and the church is the repository of the reality....
> The model then was precious before the reality,
> and the parable was marvelous before the interpretation (πρὸ τῆς ἑρμηνείας):
> that is, the People was precious before the church arose, (ἀνασταθῆναι)
> and the law was marvelous before the gospel was elucidated (φωτισθῆναι).[135]

In retelling the Pesach narrative, Melito draws motifs from baptismal rite and catechesis as well as the language of initiation of the mystery cults.[136] Throughout the homily, however, mystery is not primarily cult, but the hidden meaning of scripture revealed by typological reading. Thus when Melito speaks of the blood rite, he is relating three narratives at once – an historical, christological, and sacramental reading, all the while initiating his hearers into a particular biblical hermeneutic. All four are necessary for Melito's understanding of Christian identity.

[15] τότε Μωυσῆς σφάξας τὸ πρόβατον	[15] Then Moses, when he had slain the sheep,
καὶ νύκτωρ **διατελέσας τὸ μυστήριον** μετὰ τῶν υἱῶν Ἰσραὴλ	and at night performed the mystery with the sons of Israel,
ἐσφράγισεν τὰς τῶν οἰκιῶν θύρας	*signed* the doors of the houses
εἰς φρουρὰν τοῦ λαοῦ καὶ εἰς δυσωπίαν τοῦ ἀγγέλου.	to protect the people and to win the angel's respect.
[16] ὁπότε δὲ τὸ πρόβατον σφάζεται	[16] But while the sheep is being slain
καὶ τὸ πάσχα βιβρώσκεται	and the Pascha is being eaten
καὶ **τὸ μυστήριον τελεῖται**	and the *mystery is being performed*
καὶ ὁ λαὸς εὐφραίνεται	and the People is making merry
καὶ ὁ Ἰσραὴλ **σφραγίζεται**,	and Israel is being *signed*,
τότε ἀφίκετο ὁ ἄγγελος πατάσσειν Αἴγυπτον,	then came the angel to *strike Egypt*,
τὴν **ἀμύητον** τοῦ μυστερίου,	the un*initiated* in the mystery,
τὴν **ἄμοιρον** τοῦ πάσχα,	the non-*participating* in the Pascha
τὴν **ἀσφράγιστον** τοῦ αἵματος,	the un*marked with the blood*,

---

[135] PP 40-41 (262-269), 20.
[136] PP 15-16 (88-104), 8.

τὴν ἀφρούρητον τοῦ **πνεύματος**,	the unguarded by the *Spirit*,
τὴν ἐξθράν,	the hostile,
τὴν **ἄπιστον**…	the faithless…

The paschal blood rite is a mystery just as Justin has outlined. A catalogue of alpha-privatives – *uninitiated, non-participating, unsigned, unguarded, faithless* – all directed toward the "unbaptized" Egyptians, introduces the next section, where Pharaoh becomes not only the victim of death, but its symbol.

Melito now has two choices. To underline the salvific quality of baptism, he could tell the Exodus saga, then draw out the typological significance for the "new" Israel, as Barn does in a Temple-Promised Land baptismal allegory (Barn 6.8-17). This choice, however, would fix the shape of the homily prematurely, leaving Melito nothing to do but place Christian meaning into the narrative structure he would already have built. Combining the two narratives as he does initially in his depiction of the blood rite, or telling them sequentially as Barn, could also lead his hearers to identify with the Jews being saved. This Melito will avoid at all costs. Thus "while the People are making merry" (16.4), Melito tells, at great length (17-30) and with great pathos (or bathos, if you will), the story of the destruction of the Egyptian firstborn, those without the σφράγις of baptism.

"But the strangest and most dreadful thing you have still to hear," he begins:

> In the darkness that could be grasped lurked death that could not be grasped, and the wretched Egyptians were grasping at the darkness, while death was seeking out and grasping the firstborn of the Egyptians at the angel's bidding. If therefore one was grasping at the darkness, he was led to execution by death. And one firstborn, as he clasped dark body in his hand, terrified in soul let out a piteous and dreadful cry: "Whom does my hand hold? Whom does my soul dread? Who is this dark one enveloping my whole body? If it is father, help; if mother, comfort; if brother, speak; if friend, support; if enemy, go away, for I am a firstborn." But before the firstborn grew silent, the long silence of death caught him and addressed him, "You are my first-born; I am your fate, the silence of death."[137]

The "grasping darkness" is not just melodrama, but embraces the delivery of the homily in a dark place where Christians have gathered on

---

[137] PP 23-25 (144-164), 12. Because of the narrative structure of this passage, I have dropped the arrangement in stichoi.

the paschal night with only a few candles or torches for light. Rhetorically, Melito's hearers are being killed off one by one, except for the sign of blood:

> Such was the calamity that encompassed Egypt, and suddenly made her childless. But Israel was *guarded* by the slaughter of the sheep, and was even *illuminated* together by the shed blood, and the death of the sheep became a wall for the people.
>
> O strange and inexpressible mystery! The slaughter of the sheep was found to be Israel's salvation, and the death of the sheep became the People's life, and the blood won the angel's respect.
>
> Tell me, angel, what did you respect: The slaughter of the sheep or the life of the Lord? The death of the sheep or the type of the Lord? The blood of the sheep or the Spirit of the Lord?
>
> It is clear that your respect was won when you saw the mystery of the Lord occurring in the sheep, the life of the Lord in the slaughter of the lamb, the type of the Lord in the death of the sheep; that is why you did not strike Israel, but made only Egypt childless.[138]

Melito now recalls the baptismal images that introduced this section, making his typological equation with particular force. The efficacy of the blood rite is because of the mysterious presence of Christ at the first paschal night in Egypt. Through negative mimesis, the Pesach narrative has become an anamnesis of baptism.

Recounting biblical history from Creation to the Flood, the third section (46-56) matches the drama of the slaying of the firstborn by depicting human sin as violation of every divine and natural law, reaching a gruesome height in a passage about a mother devouring her child:

> But the strangest and most terrible thing occurred on the earth: a mother touched the flesh she had brought forth, and tasted what she had suckled at the breasts; and she buried in her belly the fruit of her belly, and the wretched mother became a terrible grave, gulping, not kissing, the child she had produced.[139]

For once in Late Antiquity, such a tale of cannibalism is not directed at Jews, Christians, or Hellenes by an opposing religious group,[140] but

---

[138] PP 30-33 (194-212), 16. Hall translates τύπος as "model," altered here to make the use of the term more transparent.

[139] PP 52 (366-371) 28.

[140] A sampler: WisSol 14.23-26 rationalized the *Landnahme*. A sin catalogue of complements a Canaanite rituals (12.3-7): child sacrifice, cannibalism, sorcery. Josephus

functions as a simple horror story. Even so, it is still worth taking a look
at Melito's probable source, Josephus, to compare rhetorical purpose.
After relating a tale of maternal cannibalism during the siege of Jerusalem,
the Jewish historian draws the inevitable conclusion:

> The horrible news soon spread to the Romans. Of them some were
> incredulous, others were moved to pity, but the effect on the majority was
> to intensify their hatred of the nation. Caesar declared himself innocent in
> this matter also in the sight of God, protesting that he had offered the
> Jews peace, independence, and an amnesty for all past offenses, while they,
> preferring sedition to concord, war to peace, famine to plenty and pros-
> perity, and having been the first to set fire with their own hands to that
> Temple which he and his army were preserving for them, were indeed
> deserving even of such food as this. He, however would bury this abomi-
> nation of infant-cannibalism beneath the ruins of their country and would
> not leave upon the face of the earth, for the sun to behold, a city in which
> mothers were thus fed.[141]

The Temple is no more coincidental to Josephus' attempt to justify the
destruction of Jerusalem than the Temple's "worthlessness" [PP 44] to
Melito's exegesis. When Josephus depicts the Jewish War in his fifth and
sixth books, the lines of ritual purity are consistently drawn well outside
the Romans earthworks.[142] Roman legions are doing a service to the God
of Israel by exterminating a sub-human evil now raging in what once was

---

relates Apion's tale of a foreigner fattened up for the kill on an annual Jewish festival,
presumably Pesach, accompanied by an oath to hate all Greeks, Contra Apion 2.95,
LCL 186, 330 f. The most complete list, Min. Felix, Oct 9.1-5 may come from the
attack on Christians by Fronto (d. after 175 CE), tutor of M. Aurelius. Apologists return
the accusation by pointing to various myths: Theoph. of Ant., AdAuto 3.3-6, OECL,
102-106 f. There is no cannibalism, but Barn 7.2-11 tells of Jewish priests devouring raw
entrails soaked in vinegar as a Pesach/Yom Kippur rite to match the vinegar and gall (an
intestinal product) at the cross. See ad. loc. SUC 2, 199, n. 117. Mishnah Menahot
11.7: "If it [Day of Atonement] fell on a Friday, the he-goat of the Day of Atonement
was consumed at evening. The Babylonians used to eat it raw, since they were not squea-
mish." Barn may be repeating a slur aimed at Alexandrians by Palestinian rabbis. Cf. the
Gamara to this passage [100a]: "They were not actually priests from Babylon, but
Alexandrians; and the Palestinian Sages called them Babylonians in hatred of them."
Texts after Danby in Skarsaune, Proof, 308.

[141] Josephus, Bell. 6.3.5 (214-218), LCL 210, 438 f. Cf. the entire narrative, Bell.
6.201-220, 434-438. Eusebius also cites this passage at length at EH 3.6.20-28, GCS 9.1,
206-212. For its possible origin, see Dt 28.47-57.

[142] The Temple was "defiled by blood" through no fault of "the Romans, who entered
to purge with fire thy internal pollutions." Josephus. Bell. 5.19, LCL 210, 204 f.

a holy place. The final third of Melito's sermon will see different reasons behind this destruction, but the rhetorical goal is the same: a pronouncement of divine judgment.

The images of human sin Melito ticks off one by one depict the violation of the body, the natural ties of family, and every human norm. This language of the murders of parents and children, cannibalism and sexual depravity is the same language of the demonized "other"[143] used by Josephus, here directed toward Sin itself. Yet unlike Josephus' destroying army, in Melito's history, the Flood does not come.[144] The watery annihilation of this generation, an obvious counterpart to the drowning of the Egyptians, is not told. Instead, this long shadowy *Haustafel* leads to a theological conclusion: the "image of the Father" given humankind at creation had become "desolate"[145] and must be restored: "This, then, is the reason why the mystery of the Pascha has been fulfilled in the body of the Lord." This conclusion leads into the remainder of the section, where Melito arranges typological proof texts from OT narrative and prophesy (57-65) to announce the Lord's coming:

> Just so also the mystery of the Lord, having been prefigured well in advance and having been seen through a model, is today believed in now that it is fulfilled, though considered new by human beings. For the mystery of the Lord is new and old: old according to the Law, but new with reference to the grace.[146]

The mysteries, both ritual and exegetical, have been demonstrated, and the ambiguity between old and new, model and reality, which Melito established from the beginning has now been resolved. Melito reaches for another rhetorical highpoint in perhaps the strongest christological section of the homily (66-72):

> It is he that clothed death with shame
> and stood the devil in grief
> as Moses did Pharaoh.

---

[143] See Girard, René, The Scapegoat, trans. Yvonne Freccero, Baltimore 1986, Chapter Two, Stereotypes of Persecution, 12-23.

[144] Cf. Josephus. Bell 5.566 (Thackeray), 374 f. After temple stores of wine and oil were plundered, Josephus writes, "I believe that, had the Romans delayed to punish these reprobates, either the earth would have opened and swallowed up the city, or it would have been swept away by a flood, or have tasted anew the thunderbolts of Sodom."

[145] PP 56 (395), 30.

[146] PP 57 f. (398-412), 30.

It is he that struck down crime
    and made injustice childless
        as Moses did Egypt.
It is he that delivered us from slavery to liberty,
    from darkness to light,
    from death to life,
    from tyranny to eternal royalty,
    and made us a new priesthood
        and an eternal people personal to him.
He is the Pascha of our salvation.

Melito has reassigned every role in the Pesach drama to Christ. He is not only the sacrificial lamb, but the Destroyer and the saving God who creates a covenant people. A catalogue of OT typologies in a quickened rhythm then sees Christ in patriarchs and kings, concluding with the NT mysteries of incarnation and birth, death, and resurrection:

It is he who in many endured many things:
it is he that was in Abel murdered,
    and in Isaac bound,
    and in Jacob exiled,
    and in Joseph sold,
    and in Moses exposed,
    and in the lamb slain,
    and in David persecuted,
    and in the prophets dishonored.
It is he that was enfleshed in a virgin,
    that was hanged on a tree,
    that was buried in the earth,
    that was raised from the dead,
    that was taken up to the heights of the heavens.[147]

This christological "releasing" of OT types, simply by being strung together with allusions to gospel narratives, unfolds a unified salvation history.[148] It achieves its power in simple repetitions proclaiming the presence of Christ with and in major figures of OT narrative. God's definitive answer to human sin was not the Flood, but the death and resurrection of Christ.

---

[147] PP 68-70 (467-493), 36, 38.

[148] Campenhausen, Hans, Die Entstehung der Heilsgeschichte, in: Urchristliches and Altchristliches, Tübingen 1979, 20-62 (=Saec 21, 1970, 189-212), here 46 f.

All of the most emotionally charged passages in Melito's sermon have now been directed to the victory of the cross and the creation of the (Gentile) church. His hearers are now able to identify with the salvation in the first Pesach in Egypt, but only viewed through the windows of Melito's carefully planned "building." They will only see Christ's passion in the sacrifice of the lamb and baptism in the smearing of blood.

Should there be any doubt, however, that even in the prefigured sign that saved them the "old" Israel was not as doomed as the Egyptians, Melito's christological affirmation flows seamlessly into yet another lengthy, dramatically charged section (72-100), which is nothing more than an impassioned indictment of the Jews for the murder of Jesus:

> What strange crime, Israel, have you committed?
>> You dishonored him that honored you;
>> you disgraced him that glorified you;
>> you denied him that acknowledged you;
>> you disclaimed him that proclaimed you
>> you killed him that made you live.
> What have you done, Israel? Or is it not written for you
> "You shall not shed innocent blood," [Jer 7.6, 22.3]
>>> so that you may not die an evil death?
> "I did," says Israel, "kill the Lord.
>> Why? Because he had to die."
> He had to suffer, but not by you;
>> he had to be dishonored, but not by you;
>> he had to be judged, but not by you,
>> he had to be hung up, but not by you and your right hand.[149]

Melito then contrasts the festivities of the Jews at the Passover with Christ's death:

And you were making merry,	while he was starving;
you had wine to drink and bread to eat,	he had vinegar and gall;
your face was bright,	his was downcast;
you were triumphant,	he was afflicted;
you were making music,	he was being judged;
you were giving the beat,	he was being nailed up;
you were dancing,	he was being buried;
you were reclining on a soft couch,	he in grave and coffin.[150]

[149] PP 73-75 (519-536) 40 f.
[150] PP 80 (566-581) 42 f.

This negative *commercium* is the same contrast drawn in Melito's retelling of Ex 12 as the Egyptians were being slain, now fully revealed as the Jews feasting while Christ is being crucified. Pesach rituals, expanded by music and dancing, become a grim *Totentanz*. The typologies clash, but logic is not at work: the only ones truly saved at the passover in Egypt are Gentile Christians.

In sheer volume, Melito has devoted more space to the most violent anti-Judaic polemic[151] in second century Christian literature than he has to explaining the christological significance of Ex 12. Even the passion narratives a basis for proclamation only as they may be turned into a prophetic oracle against the Jews. The prodigies at the death of Christ – the earthquake, the darkening of the sun, the tearing of the Temple veil – become the shocked grief of nature, who trembles and turns away in horror over the crime of the Jews. "When the People did not tear their clothes, the angel tore his…,"[152] Melito cries, as he alludes to the Temple veil. He then pronounces his oracle:

> Therefore, O Israel,
>   you did not quake in the presence of the Lord,
>   so you quaked at the assault of foes; …
> you did not lament over the Lord,
>   so you lamented over your firstborn;
> you did not tear your clothes when the Lord was hanged,
>   so you tore them over those who were slain;
> you forsook the Lord,
>   you were not found by him;
> you did not accept the Lord,
>   you were not pitied by him;
> you dashed down the Lord,
>   you were dashed to the ground.
> And you lie dead,
>   but he has risen from the dead
>   and gone up to the heights of heaven.[153]

---

[151] See the reaction of Winslow, D. F., Melito of Sardis' Christology, StPatr 17/2, 1982 (765-776) 774: "I cannot avoid the conclusion that the second target for Melito's polemic is, in fact, the whole of the human race." Melito and his anti-Judaism exit Christian tradition, just as for Tacitus, Christians were "enemies of the human race."

[152] PP 97 (727), 54 f.

[153] PP 99-100 (730-747), 54-57.

Here again are the images of grief and mourning Melito had so elaborately drawn at the description of the slaying of the Egyptians. The oracle, of course, had already come to pass a generation before Melito pronounced it: the destruction of Jerusalem at the hands of the Romans, who have taken over the role of the destroying angel. For Josephus, the destruction of Jerusalem was a purification of the Temple because of the ultimate transgression of Jewish rebels. For Melito, its cause is a crime far more horrible than a mother devouring her infant's flesh: the murder of God.

2. History or Rhetoric?

What compelled Melito of Sardis not only to preach this anti-Judaic homily in the same night as "the People were making merry" in homes nearby, but to edit it for publication? Though its content is indistinguishable from Justin or Irenaeus and its affect no more strident than Barn, the "historical" view believed it had the answer in the discovery in Sardis of one of the most splendid synagogues of Late Antiquity. Adjacent to public buildings in the center of town, the synagogue had an attractive courtyard whose marble fountain would have invited passers-by to linger.[154] Inscriptions record a number of benefactors who had also held civic office.[155] This was a wealthy congregation well integrated into the community-at-large.

In Melito's day, the Jewish communities of Asia Minor could look back on nearly five centuries of continuous settlement. Except for more recent immigrants, their forebears were the two thousand Babylonian Jewish families whom, according to Josephus, Antiochus III had invited to settle in Lydia and Phrygia in the third century BCE.[156] In the wake of two wars, the Jewish communities of Asia Minor had not suffered the same disastrous fate of those in Alexandria, Cyrene, or Jerusalem.

---

[154] Kraabel, Alf Thomas, Paganism and Judaism: The Sardis Evidence. In: Paganisme, Judaïsme, Christianisme. Influences et affrontements dans le monde antique. (FS Simon) Paris 1978, 13-33. This theory most recently discounted by Sykes, Alistair Stewart, Melito's Anti-Judaism, JECS 5, 1997, 271-283, who clouds the issue by maintaining that Melito, Polycarpe, and Polycrates were all Jews by birth.

[155] Trebilco, Paul, Jewish Communities in Asia Minor, SNTS.MS 69, 1991, 46-47. Jewish inscriptions stress the status of Jews in the city and in the local and provincial government, rather than simply their status in the Jewish community, as is usually the case elsewhere.

[156] Josephus Ant 12.148-153, LCL 365, 76-78. See Trebilco, Asia, 5-7.

Though they sent their contributions toward the upkeep of the Temple, they did not support the Jewish cause against Rome either in 70,115, or 135 CE.[157] They, too, paid the *fiscus iudaicus* imposed by the Romans after the fall of Jerusalem, but neither were they the victims of major violence, nor were any of their rights and privileges taken away.

In view of this evidence, it seemed a matter of course that in a kind of religious adolescent crisis, Melito was voicing a communal jealousy[158] directed at the wealthier, more numerous, and more socially prominent Jews in Sardis, who, according to Simon's view, were vigorously proselytizing the Gentiles among whom they lived. The only problem is that archaeological evidence points to a third,[159] rather than a second century date for the magnificent synagogue. Then it must be assumed, as R. M. Grant does, that

> [p]resumably the third-century building did not suddenly appear, however, but emerged from an older establishment which Melito may have found oppressive.[160]

Analogous to Melito's rhetorically constructed "building," the luxurious synagogue only the great-great-grandchildren of Melito's congregation would see gracing the cityscape of Sardis is still used to explain the violence of his anti-Judaism. "When it comes down to it," Miriam Taylor writes, "the basis for the theory of 'reactive' anti-Judaism is little more than evidence of Jewish wealth and prominence in Sardis, coupled with a heated denunciation of Israel in Melito's homily. How many conceptual leaps can any interpretive, reconstructive hypothesis demand of us and still retain its credibility?"[161] However many leaps the "historical" theory makes, it moves nowhere. Locating the causes of Melito's anti-Judaism in the Jewish community of Sardis follows perfectly the rhetorical cues of the homily, merely substituting socioeconomic values for exegetical ones: Trypho becomes Shylock.

---

[157] Trebilco, Asia, 32 f.

[158] See Norris, F. W., Melito's Motivation, AThR 68, 1986, 16-24.

[159] See Bonz, Marianne P., Differing Approaches to Religious Benefaction: The Late Third-Century Acquisition of the Sardis Synagogue, HThR 86, 1993, 139-54. An accumulation of many small contributions enabled the Jewish community to purchase the building. For a date, see ibid., The Jewish Community of Ancient Sardis: A Reassessment of its Rise to Prominence, HSCP 93, 1990, 342-259.

[160] Grant, R. M., Greek Apologists of the Second Century, London 1988, 96.

[161] Taylor, Anti-Judaism, 60.

Looking at the same material remains of synagogue, shops, and dwellings, but in their proper chronological setting, John S. Crawford[162] found that the Christian and Jewish symbols displayed in neighboring shops form a narrative not of separation, but of multiculturalism in Sardis. One Jewish shopkeeper did not bother to remove a cross inscribed by a former owner, but let it to stand next to a menorah newly scratched into the stone. The mere juxtaposition of such signs tells nothing of the shopkeeper's motivation – fear of reprisal, a comfort with the cross as magical sign, consideration of his neighbors – but at least there were no Jewish or Christian "quarters" or ghettos in Sardis.

Rather than find historical Jewish communities to match the rhetoric, it might help to look at how other Asian authors spoke of the "Jews."

The homily with the most affinities to PP is an anonymous work, *In sanctum Pascha* (IP), which circulated under the names of Hippolytus and Chrysostom. While Cantalamessa may have erred as to its early date, his arguments for an Asian provenance are sound, if only for its rhetorical geography.[163] Yet Melito's virulent anti-Judaism neither provides rhetorical structure nor, for that matter, much exegetical content. The destruction of Jerusalem only makes an appearance as the explanation of the bitter herbs:

> *Thou shalt eat unleavened bread with bitter herbs* [Ex 12.8, 15]: for herbs are for you the mystery of your sinful works: "Your land deserted, your city devoured by fire, your land will be devastated by foreigners under your very eyes; it will be desolate and overthrown by a foreign people." [Is 1.7][164]

Melito uses the same text for an extended tirade based on the passion narrative:

> [93] Bitter therefore for you is the feast of unleavened bread, as it is written for you: *"You shall eat unleavened bread with bitter flavors."* Bitter for you are the nails you sharpened, bitter for you the tongue you incited, bitter for you the false witnesses you instructed, bitter for you the ropes you got ready, bitter for you the scourges you plaited, bitter for you Judas whom you hired, bitter for you Herod whom you followed, bitter for you Caiaphas

---

[162] Crawford, John S., Multiculturalism at Sardis, BAR 22, no. 5, 1996, 38-47.

[163] Cantalamessa, Raniero, L'Omelia "In S. Pascha" dello Pseudo-Ippolito di Roma. Richerche sulla teologia dell' Asia Minore nella seconda metà del II secolo, PUCSC 3.16, Milan 1967.

[164] IP 25, SC 27, 153.

whom you trusted, bitter for you the gall you prepared, bitter for you the vinegar you produced, bitter for you the thorns you culled, bitter for you the hands you bloodied; you killed your Lord in the middle of Jerusalem, in the city of the Law, in the city of the Hebrews, in the city of the prophets, in the city accounted just.[165]

IP has not chosen to exploit the rhetorical potential of anti-Judaism with the expansiveness of Melito's "bitter" details. In the passage preceding the bitter herbs in IP, however, the homilist mentions Jews of "our own day," a connection between "exegetical Jews" and real ones Melito never makes:

The whole assembled congregation of the sons of Israel shall sacrifice it [12.6]: For the unbelieving people of Israel became guilty of that precious blood, first because they killed him, then, up to our own day, because they continue not to believe. Therefore the divine Spirit testifies against them, crying, "Your hands are filled with blood." [Is 1.15][166]

This is as close as IP gets to Melito's accusation of Israel. Unless all occurrences of the supercession motif are considered anti-Judaic, two other passages dealing with the eucharist as a "pure" paschal observance versus Jewish "carnality"[167] exhaust the anti-Judaic rhetoric of this homily.

Whether IP is contemporary with Melito or fifty to a hundred years later, if real relations between Jews and Christians lie behind anti-Judaic arguments, then this homily is a paragon of restraint. Historically, however, it is closer than Melito to the time of Sardis' beautiful synagogue and other less splendid buildings in major Asian cities.

The theory of "communal jealousy" would be more plausible if first century writings of Asian provenance could set up a solid beginning for its trajectory. Col mentions the Hebrew calendar at 2.16-17, but Christians at Sardis celebrating the Pascha on 14 Nisan obviously had a different slant on a "shadow-substance" hermeneutic than the deutero-Pauline author. Except for Titus 1.10-13, where Judaizing agitators, pointedly slurred as being "liars, vicious brutes, [and] lazy gluttons" from Crete,[168] none of the Past gives any hint of trouble with Jewish

[165] PP 93 f., 51 f.
[166] IP 24, SC 27, 151 f.
[167] IP 50, SC 27, 176. Text, below, p. 228.
[168] "Titus" bypasses the logical paradox intended by the author, the philosopher-poet Epimenides, who came from Crete. See Grant, Apologists, 25 f.

competition or threat. The same goes for 1 Pt, addressed to congregations in Asia Minor, while Eph, wherever it was written, serenely tells
how the "dividing wall of hostility" (Eph 2.14) has been broken down
in Christ. Of course many of these writings predate Melito by several
generations, but so, too, the lavishly appointed synagogue appears in
Sardis years after his death.

There is ample anti-Judaic polemic in the letters of Ignatius, but
directed at most to Jewish *Christians*, or at least at those Christians whose
ideas appear "Jewish" to Ignatius. At Magn 9.1, Ignatius argues against
"sabbatizers," but these are not Jews.[169] At Phild 8.2,[170] Ignatius argues
against a "Judaizing" exegesis current somewhere in Asia,[171] but this is
the *language* of anti-Judaism without a Jewish object. None of these
texts are aimed at Jews,[172] but at the kind of *Christian* biblical exegesis
most accessible in Barn. Ignatius' description characterizes the methods
in Barn so well that Klaus Wengst has made a case for its Asian provenance.[173] After a rhetorical analysis of Phild, Smyrn, and Magn, Jerry
Sumney finds no trace of a dialogue with practicing Jews.[174] With this
lack of supporting evidence, can Melito's anti-Judaism be *historically*
based?

Melito's polemic is aimed at the "Jews"[175] in the passion narrative.[176]
If the shadow Jews who killed Christ are destroyed, then those who
accept him must live. There are no images of luxury or power insinuated

---

[169] Mag 9.1, SUC 1, 166. For discussion, see Rordorf, Willy, Der Sonntag. ATANT 43,
1962, 138 f., 208; Taylor, Anti-Judaism, 36.

[170] Ignatius, Phild 8.2, SUC 1, 200.

[171] See Campenhausen, Entstehung, 86-87; Molland, Einar, The Heretics Combatted by Ignatius of Antioch, JEH, 5, 1954, 1-6.

[172] 'Judaism' und 'Christianity'are modes of life. "In their contexts, both key words
have a rhetorical function. They serve the cogent designation of identifying characteristics and imply a border of separation from those modes which could endanger this identity." Niebuhr, Karl-Wilhelm, 'Judentum' und 'Christentum' bei Paulus und Ignatius
von Antiochien, ZNW 85, 1994, (218-233) 232.

[173] Wengst, Klaus, Tradition und Theologie des Barnabasbriefes, AKG 42, 1971,
105-118.

[174] Sumney, Jerry L., Those Who "Ignorantly Deny Him": The Opponents of
Ignatius of Antioch, JECS 1, 1993, 345-365.

[175] Wilson, S. G., Passover, Easter, and Anti-Judaism: Melito of Sardis and Others,
in: To See Ourselves as Others See Us, Chico 1985, 337-355, says since in PP, "'Israel'
refers indiscriminately to all Jews," contemporary Jews are included.

[176] So Rengstorf, Karl Heinrich and Siegfried von Kortzfleisch, Kirche und Synagoge: Handbuch von Christen und Juden, Stuttgart 1968, vol. 1, 73.

into this two-dimensionality, no hint of hidden meanings. The "soft couch" (PP 80) alludes to the custom of reclining at the dinner. But what of Amos' oracle against the rich "who lie on beds of ivory, and lounge on their couches, and eat lambs from the flock" (Am 6.4), who buy "the poor for silver and the needy for a pair of sandals" (Am 8.6)? Found only a few verses away is the prophecy about the day of the Lord, whose eclipsed sun had already found its way into the passion narrative (Am 8.9-10), where the Lord "will turn your feasts into mourning...like the mourning for an only son." It would be foolish to think that Melito was not intimately familiar with all of these passages.

Directing these images to a powerful and wealthy community allegedly competing for converts would have been irresistible for a Christian bishop assumed to be leading a smaller, poorer congregation seething with jealousy for the proselytizing success of the Jews. Yet there is no sense that Melito is actualizing anti-Judaic polemic against the Jews of Sardis, nor is the destruction of the Temple directed at a synagogue. If Melito can all but invisibly weave the story of Christian baptism into the Pesach narrative, he could just as easily have shown how the feasting ingrates who murdered their Lord are the same people who, like the Christians that very night, are reading Ex 12 as a story of salvation and yet are doomed to the "darkness that could be grasped," the synagogue of the Sardis Jews as destined to rubble as the Temple of old. This is an association Christians in later centuries will presume again and again with disastrous results, but it is one Melito does not make.[177]

The destruction of Jerusalem is incontrovertible proof of God's disfavor toward the Jews and thus God's favor toward the Gentile church. For Melito, this historical event and its interpretation are inseparable from the resurrection: both define one another as history and truth. By making this connection, Melito is moving much further along the same gospel trajectory exonerating the Romans and placing all responsibility for the death of Jesus on the "Jews."[178] The crime, as it were, fits the punishment, a construct that reaches its most absurd form with sixth century Copts, who regard Pilate not only as a fellow countryman, but martyred saint.[179] Neither Melito nor the Copts reflect an historical

[177] Cf. Taylor, Anti-Judaism, 52-57.
[178] A plea against this trajectory by Winter, Paul, On the Trial of Jesus, StJud 1, 1961.
[179] In the 18th c. the martyrdom of Pilate was still read in Coptic churches. Van Den Oudenrijn, Marc-Antonius, OP. Gamaliel. Äthiopische Texte zur Pilatusliteratur,

situation. Both must remove the Jews from the story of the salvation before the may find themselves saved there, and both follow NT cues to do so.

The urgency of this exegetical surgery is no less acute for Melito than Barn or Justin, for whom the gospels have no indepent authority. The difference is one of degree, not kind. The mystery of passion-resurrection, not its gospel narratives, undergirds Melito's homily. He proclaims the revealed truth of the scriptures addressed to that mystery, but not the gospel canon. Thus it is fitting that the first mention of an OT canon by a Christian author comes from none other than Melito of Sardis.[180] The Christ event is tied to the LXX canon as holy word; details of the passion narrative only supply rhetorical power. If Ex 12 is to be an authoritative Christian text fully appropriated toward the Christ event, then the Jews and their salvation must be removed before a Christian meaning may take place. The wrenching affect in Melito's paschal homily is the sound of that meaning being ripped from the text: a rhetorical and exegetical necessity to preserve the meaning of Ex 12 as the story of origins for the "new" Israel.

Similarities to Barnabas' method as well as Justin's more christocentric "proof from prophecy" require no further comment than to suggest them. It is the same desire to find the "new" in the "old" that generates the rich scriptural allusions of the First Gospel, the paschal testimonia, and OT "prophets" who speak far more like Melito of Sardis than their Hebrew models. Only a few decades later, Irenaeus employs other means to achieve the same ends, developing motifs of supercession and salvation history that preserve what is "precious" in the covenant with Israel while guaranteeing its relativity as human history after the coming of Christ. Melito's affect, however, is entirely absent. While for later second century authors, Melito's polemic had been rationalized into the inevitabilities of divine history, part of the relative calm of Irenaeus[181] must also stem from the authoritative role of the NT, just emerged as the

---

SpicFrib 4, 1959. p. LIV. The Lutheran Agende of Electoral Saxony (1771) included with the usual passion harmony the history of the "erbärmlichen Zerstörung der Stadt Jerusalem." Anon., Etwas von der Liturgie, besonders der Chursächsisch-Evangelischen, Halle 1778.

[180] Eusebius, EH 4.26.13-14, GCS 9.1, 386 f.

[181] "Since he recognizes *in its own right* the limited historical period of the OT, he has no difficulty in looking at its events, institutions and doctrines as true history ..." Farkasfalvy, D., Theology of Scripture in St. Irenaeus. RevBen 78, 1968, (319-333) 328.

canon by which Christian identity is measured. The main cause of Melito's anti-Judaic stance is thus the paradoxical result of maintaining the absoluteness of a Judaic text as the canon of the church and the definitive story of the suffering of Christ: Pascha is the Christ and Ex 12 is a gospel. Not long after Melito's death, with Irenaeus attempting a mediary role, the Asian understanding of Ex 12 will come under fire from theologians across the Empire for this very reason.

C. CELESTIAL RITE OF PASSAGE: EGYPT

I. Pascha as Paradigm of Spirituality

The narrative guiding the Egyptian paschal rite of passage is already part of Irenaeus' reading of the Exodus saga:

> Yet in the thornbush, he [the Logos] spoke with Moses and said, "I have observed the misery of my people who are in Egypt, and I have come down to deliver them" (Ex 2.7,8). He came, descending to free the oppressed and tore us away from the power of the Egyptians, that is, from all idolatry and all godlessness. He rescued us from the Red Sea, that is, he freed us from the death-bringing tumult of the pagans; he freed us from the harmful temptation of their sin. For what happened to them was our preparation through the Logos of God. At that time, he showed in advance the future things through a type, but now he tears us away from the oppressive slavery of the pagans. He let a spring gush richly forth from the rock in the desert, and the rock was he himself (1 Cor 10.4).[1]

Reconfiguring motifs of revelation, passage, and freedom, Alexandrian exegetes read Exodus-Wilderness motifs the same way as they were likely read in first century Corinth: not as the story of a whole people, but with the Logos as mystagogue, as the human spirit's solitary journey through the waters of passion and death. Simultaneously moral allegory and eschatological promise, Egyptian paschal rhetoric charts this passage as mimetic process on two vertical levels. Irenaeus' earthward descent of the Logos is mirrored in a heavenly ascension, invariably read – as Origen does here – as paradigm for the believer:

> *Eat it with haste; it is the Lord's Passover*, i.e. the passage (ὑπέρβασις) of the Lord. For the one person who has passed beyond the limits fixed by God because of the disobedience of Adam, this one person is indeed the Lord who has blunted *the sting of death* [1 Cor 15.55] and suppressed its power, giving by his gospel preaching a means of escape *to the spirits imprisoned* in hell [cf. 1 Pt 3.19; 4.6], and also by providing them with a means of ascent into heaven, by means of his own ascent...[2]

---

[1] Epid 46, BKV² 4, 34 (616).

[2] Origen, Peri Pascha 47.32-48.10. Origène. Sur la Pâque, O. Guéraud, P. Nautin, ed., ChrAnt 2, 1979, 246 f. ET: Daly, Robert J. Origen. Treatise on the Passover and

In its various guises, this celestial *transitus* remains virtually constant in Christian literature of Egyptian provenance. Its relationship to rite, however, has a much richer though broken history, chiefly because its main proponents have little interest in liturgical acts. Whether for the Jewish philosopher Philo or the Christians Clement and Origen, paschal and Exodus motifs require neither ritual nor celebrating community, but the power of allegory and a spiritual elite eager for instruction. With disdain for the mediating symbols of rite and suspicious of the joys of common celebration, the Alexandrian Pascha searches for divine access in an *inner* Exodus whose sole medium is rhetoric:

> This Gnosis leads us to the perfect end that itself has no end, and teaches us beforehand the life that we will have according to God's will with the gods, when we are free from every punishment and penalty which, because of our sins, we must bear as healing discipline. After this release, honors and prizes will be given the perfected, for whom now purification – and even every other liturgical usage – has ended, even if it is holy and performed among holy people. And thus, when they have become pure of heart [Mt 5.8], they await the longed-for transition to the eternal vision close to the Lord... Gnosis is a speedy means of purification...
>
> Then Gnosis transmits the human being easily into that divine and holy state that is allied to the soul, and with a light all its own leads him through the mystical steps, until it has brought him to the place of rest superior to everything, and then taught the one who is pure of heart to see God face to face with clear knowledge and full understanding. For the perfection of the Gnostic soul consists of moving beyond all forms of purification and liturgy and uniting with the Lord, where it rests in closest vicinity to him.[3]

Rather than means of divine communion, ritual action is an outward form addressed to an inner process or transcendent idea, whose final unity with its source makes such sacramental forms unnecessary. There are no paschal motifs in Clement's Gnostic journey because they are not necessary for its narration. Thus when he wishes to put the final touch on his attack on Hellenic myth and ritual in *Protreptikos*, Clement can construct the same narrative as a quite serious parody of a mystery rite:

Dialogue of Origen with Heraclides and his Fellow Bishops on the Father, the Son, and the Soul, ACW 54, 1992, 47 f.
[3] Strom 7.56.3-7.57.2. GCS 17, 41 f.

Oh how truly holy are the mysteries, oh, how pure the light! I am illumined by the light of torches [δαδουχοῦμαι] to see the heavens and God. Initiated into the mysteries [μυούμενος], I am made holy, for the Lord is Revealer of sacred signs and seals the myste with enlightenment and gives the one now having believed into the care of the Father to be kept for all ages. These are the Bacchanalia of my mysteries; if you wish, you too may be initiated. And with the angels you will dance about the uncreated and unchanging [τὸ ἀγένητος καὶ ἀνώλεθρος, Plato's Timaeus] and truly one God as the Logos of God sings with us. This eternal Jesus, the High Priest of the one God, who at the same time is Father, prays for humankind and calls to them,… "You, who, though you have all along been images, but not pure likenesses, I will bring you into harmony with the original image, so that you will become like me. I will salve you with the ointment of faith, freeing you from all that is transitory, and will show you uncovered the image of righteousness, in which you may rise to God. *Come to me, all who are heavy-laden…and I will give you rest.*[4]

This is mimesis, even a "ritual pattern," but not ritual. Paschal texts will perform the same function as Bacchanal revels: to clothe ineffable idea in ritual dress and point it toward mimesis of the divine. As in Hellenic mysteries, only the elite few will make this journey through idolatrous passion toward virtue, the sacred vision, and divine rest. The passage through the Red Sea of Ex 15 and an oceanic application of allegory will enable paschal motifs to tell the same story. Thus Clement, arriving at a not quite perfect ten for the human person by adding body, soul, speech, procreation, and thought "or whatever else it might be called" to the five senses, transcends them through a paschal image:

> …the feast of Pascha began with the tenth day, for it means the transition from every passion and every sense perception [παντὸς πάθους καὶ παντὸς αἰσθητοῦ διάβασις]. The Gnostic remains steadfast upon faith, but the one who thinks himself wise does not hold to the truth, but allows himself to be driven by unstable and transitory passions.[5]

Transition (διάβασις) is the catchword that connects the Pascha to the narrative of spiritual perfection, and all of it is a direct borrowing, at times verbatim, from Philo of Alexandria.[6]

---

[4] Protr 120.1-2, 4-5, GCS 58, 84 f.

[5] Strom 2.51.2 f., GCS 52, 140.

[6] Cf. De cong. 102-6; Quæst. et Sol. in Ex. 1.2. For the general topic of Philonic borrowing, see van den Hoek, Annewies, Clement of Alexandria and His Use of Philo in the *Stromateis. An Early Christian reshaping of a Jewish model*, VigChrS 3, 1988.

Though Philo often functions as intermediary, Clement can just as easily go directly to Philo's source to craft ritual narratives even closer to these models than any of Philo's allegories. The path to true Gnosis consistently follows a three-step ascent already described in Plato's *Phaidros* and *Symposium* in language drawn from the Eleusian rites.[7] In the same way, new Platonic impulses would enter the Christian mystical tradition through Pseudo-Dionysius' reworking of Proclus, the fifth century director of the Platonic academy and one of the last pagan revivalists in a more and more christianized Empire. There, the process is also distilled into three stages: purification, enlightenment, and union.[8]

Beginning with the light of Eleusian torches, Clement's Hellenic parody reaches this final stage in beatific vision (ἐποπτεία), the revelation of cultic objects culminating a mystery rite.[9] There is little change when Clement interprets the "flesh and blood of the Logos" of Jn 6, not as sacrament or even proclaimed word, but the Gnostic journey:

> Thus when the Apostle calls "milk" the food of children and "solid food" that of the mature, then one must understand milk as beginning instruction, as first food of the soul, but solid food is the highest, direct vision. For that is flesh and blood of the Logos. "Taste and know that the Lord is good!" For so he communicates himself to those who in a more spiritual fashion partake of such food, for as the soul "already nourishes itself" according to the word of the truth-loving Plato, then to take heavenly teaching as food and drink, that means to know the being of God. Thus Plato also says in the second book of the *Republic*, "One should first sacrifice not something like a suckling pig, but a sacrifice great and difficult to obtain."[10] Yet the Apostle writes, "For Pascha has been sacrificed for us, Christ."

[7] See Riedweg, Christoph, Mysterienterminologie bei Platon, Philon und Klemens von Alexandrien, UALG 26, 1987, 2-21, esp. comparative chart, 21, and 144-147. Riedweg posits Aristotle as the originator of the succinctly outlined three-step process.

[8] See Nygren Anders, Agape and Eros, Chicago 1982 (=repr. Phila. 1953) 566-575.

[9] At Protr 22.4-5 (GCS 58, 17) Clement lists the *realia* of several cults: sesame cake, pyramid cake, rolls, grains of salt, a snake, pomegranates, tree twigs, oregano, lamp, sword, a woman's comb. For survey, see Burkert, Mysterien, Chapter 4, "Verwandelnde Erfahrung," 75-97.

[10] A favored text of Christian apologists. Tales of Chronos devouring his children are not true, but even if they are, they should not "be told thoughtlessly to young unknowing persons, and best not at all. But if it should be necessary to tell it, then only as few as possible in secret fashion, after they had sacrificed not a suckling pig (as in the Eleusian mysteries), but something quite large and difficult to obtain, so that only a few would come to hear it." Rep 377e-378a, 156 f.

The sacrifice pleasing to God [Phil 4.18] consists of renouncing the body and its passions without regret.[11]

Clement describes a cultic meal without food, rite, eating, drinking, or community, and addresses scriptural and catechetical motifs to the mystical process of Gnosis, supported by Plato and the usual Stoic war on the human body. This is the ritual at which Clement presides as mystagogue: "eating the flesh of the Logos" is a speech act.

The most global expression of *transitus* clothed as ritual occurs in Origen's *Against Celsus*. Starting from a Platonic[12] definition of the Deity as common to all, wholly good, and contingent upon nothing,[13] Celsus argues that there should be no harm in participating in the rituals of civil religion. This is illogical, Origen counters, for such rites are not divine institutions but human commemoration of historical events or the natural order. To this standard "Euhemerist" argument, Origen adds the all-purpose cultic eraser Gal 4.10 f., then retreats from its implications:

> If, given these things, someone should reply that we observe our Lord's Days or preparation days (Friday station fast) or Pascha or Pentecost over several days, then to this it must be replied that the fully perfected person (τέλειος), ever within the words, deeds, and thoughts of the Logos of God, by nature Lord, is always in his time and always doing the days of Kyriake. Yet this one also prepares for the true life: abstaining from the pleasures of life that deceive the multitude, not feeding the strivings of the flesh [Rom 8.6 f.] but rather punishing and enslaving the body [an athletic image, 1 Cor 9.27], he ever performs days of preparation. Further, the one who knows that "Pascha has been sacrificed for us, Christ," also knows to keep the feast by eating of the flesh of the Logos, thus never ceases to perform the Pascha, which is interpreted as διαβατήρια: he ever passes over (διαβαίνων) through thought, every word, and every action from the things of earthly life to God, rushing toward his City. Who furthermore may say in truth, "We have been made alive together with Christ" [Eph 2.5], yet also "he raised us up with him and seated us with him in the heavenly places in Christ [Eph 2.6], is ever in the days of Pentecost; yet even more when he also goes up to the "upper room" [Acts 1.13 f.] like the apostles of Jesus and makes room (σχολάζει) for prayers and supplications, so that he becomes worthy of the "mighty rushing wind" [Acts 2.2 f.] from heaven, which

[11] Strom 5.66.2-67.1, GCS 52, 370.
[12] Phaed. 247a, Tim. 29c.
[13] A divine predicate often repeated by Irenaeus.

destroys among humankind all evil and what comes from it, yet worthy also of a certain partaking of the God-given fiery tongue.[14]

Origen has produced the identical twin of Clement's mystic parody, but its shape and content are determined as much by the anti-cultic power of Gal 4.10 as rhetorical context. Origen must refound the Christian cult as reminder of the greater spiritual journey, which in turn, reminds the reader of Plutarch's story of the Isis mysteries:

> Yet the multitude (ὁ πολὺς) only appears to believe, and not being of this magnitude, either not wishing or not able always to keep such days, requires perceptible models to remember (αἰσθητῶν παραδειγμάτων... ὑπομνήσεως), so as not to drift away from the whole. This, I think, is what Paul had in mind when he called a "part" (μέρος) of the feast those feasts fixed on days apart from other days, (Cf. Rom 14.5) hinting somewhat obscurely with this expression that a life always in accord with the Logos of God is not "in the parts" of the feast (i.e., a "partial" feast, ἐν μέρει ἑορτῆς Col 2.16), but in wholeness and perpetuity.[15]

To draw this "ritual pattern," Origen must enliven a metaphor at Col 2.16 that modern translations leave for dead: "ἐν μέρει," meaning quite colorlessly "in matters/affairs of." Colossians' shadow/substance is literally shadow/body, and "μέρος" can also mean a part of the body as well as "part of the whole." Though Origen completes this argument with a reference to various OT rituals, all ascetic in character,[16] he does not infer that these ritual "parts" ever partake of the divine realities they model. This apparent negation of the efficacy of signs may be mitigated by other passages in Origen's works, yet it is equally apparent that for none of these authors – Philo, Clement, Origen, or Proclus – is the performance of ritual acts necessary either for the attainment of the *unio mystica* or for its description.

As it moves from Philo into Christian exegesis, the Alexandrian Pascha does not migrate solidly to *liturgical* theology until Origen's pupils return ritual metaphors to the realities of worship, usually flattening into a moral commonplace what began as a consummate love of the Logos as logoi: scripture. This would not have been possible had not Origen seen a mystical encounter with biblical texts as a paschal meal. "Eating the Lamb/Logos" is exegesis; the sacramental *realia* are words.

---

[14] Contra Celsum 8.22, SC 150, 222 f.
[15] Contra Celsum 8.23, SC 150, 224 f.
[16] Bread of affliction (Dt 16.3), humble your spirits (Lev 16.29), unleavened bread with bitter herbs (Ex 12.8), Contra Celsum 8.23, SC 150, 226.

Until Augustine and often long after him, Asian and Alexandrian paschal motifs move easily in parallel throughout later exegesis, often in the same author.[17] With an eye on Christ's passage to the Father of Jn 13.1, Augustine combines the two into one kerygmatic narrative: *transitus per passionem*, passage by means of passion.[18] This synthesis ends the independent transmission of both Asian and Alexandrian traditions, finally correcting the folk etymology so disturbing to Origen.[19] Yet even after what was originally a paschal motif had been transferred to the eucharist, a millennium later the tradition arrives virtually intact for the young Martin Luther:

> But repeating this memorial is far more necessary now than when the memorial of the passing over of the Lord and the Exodus from Egypt was commanded. For this sacrifice of the New Testament is fulfilled through the head of the Church, which is Christ, and has ceased altogether. Yet the spiritual sacrifice of his body, the Church, is offered day by day, in which it continually dies with Christ and celebrates the mystical Pascha, dying to its fleshly desires and making a transition from this world into the future glory.[20]

Connecting these points strewn across 1500 years of Christian tradition shows the consistent pattern of Alexandrian paschal readings, their initial resistance to liturgy, and their incomparable resilience once that resistance was overcome. They enable a new genre of discourse that moves far beyond the Asian equation of Pascha with passion, because Clement and Origen apply paschal motifs to the faithful as a spiritual allegory. The passage through the Red Sea then makes room in the original typology for resurrection and ascension.

More elusively, a few sources suggest that neither Ambrose, Augustine, nor even Origen's pupils were the first to transfer a Philonian narrative to Christian rite, and these sources point as well to Egypt. The Exodus typology of 1Cor 10 may be the first reception of Philo into Christian liturgical tradition, while the *Epistola Apostolorum* (EpAp), often regarded as Egyptian in provenance, tells much about Clement's rise of the Gnostic soul. For this second century work, neither Philo's influence nor Egyptian origin is a prerequisite. Its purpose is to reclaim

---

[17] OAK XXIII, (CQL 18 f.).
[18] Augustine, Enn. in Ps. 120.6, CCSL 40, 1721 (CQL 126).
[19] Cf. Tract. in ev. Ioh. 55, 1, CCSL 36, 464 f. (CQL 127).
[20] Luther, Martin, Lecture on Hebrews 1517-1518, WA 57, 218, 3 ff.

important motifs from Christian Gnostics more radical than the author, one of which is the eschatological "rest" at the end of Clement's Gnostic quest. Its rhetorical strategy is reminiscent of the Syrian *Didascalia*: the paschal feast is instituted by the Risen One almost immediately after his resurrection. Because this institution has eucharistic overtones – the hallmark of the Syrian tradition – a Syrian provenance should be seriously considered. The same paradigmatic ascension of Christ so crucial to Clement's "mystery", however, gives the work a decided Egyptian flavor.

The few extant Valentinian readings of Ex 12 offer an ironic contrast: target narratives are surprisingly similar, but in the EpAp, paschal motifs are missing. Heavenly ascent is not narrated in the language of Ex 12 or 15. Yet if the paschal liturgy instituted by the EpAp carried the same kerygmatic content as the work itself, then that liturgy celebrated the celestial passage of Christ and believer, whether the first readers of the EpAp lived on the Orontes or the Nile. Thus the EpAp appears in its *rhetorical* geography with other texts directing paschal motifs to the heavenly *transitus* of the believer. The first point on this rhetorical map is Alexander's great founding on the littoral between Lake Mareotis and the Mediterranean, where the many points of this tradition converge upon its origin, Philo of Alexandria.

II. Philo of Alexandria

Urbane but pedantically repetitive, mystical yet conscious of social position and propriety, a thinker proud of his Jewish identity yet equipped with a storehouse of Stoic and Middle Platonic commonplaces, Philo of Alexandria[21] (ca.25/20 BCE-ca. 45 CE) cannot easily be compartmentalized any more than he himself systematized his thought. Philo's influence on Christian exegesis leads to Christian legends about Philo: he is all but baptized in Eusebius, a distinction later excelled by Byzantine catanæ where Philo regularly appears as bishop. The fifth century *Acts of John* tells a conversion story: Philo embraces Christianity on Patmos

---

[21] For intro., see Runia, David T., CRI III, 3, 1993, Philo in Early Christian Literature. A Survey; Sandmel, S. Philo Judaeus: An Introduction to the Man, his Writings, and his Significance ANRW II.21.1, 1984, 3-46, and in same volume, Mack, Burton L., Philo Judaeus and Exegetical Traditions in Alexandria, 227-271.

after John heals Philo's wife of leprosy.[22] Only matched by that of Pilate, this christianizing of Philo contrasts starkly to Judaic sources, for whom Philo does not exist.

On a less legendary front, Philo's influence on early Christianity has yet to be completely investigated. Recent scholarship has also begun to look at Egyptian Gnosticism, suggesting that Philo is a "proto-Gnostic,"[23] supplying important foundations for later Gnosticism, but not a proponent of an early Jewish form of Gnosis. After the more nuanced view of Gnosticism the Nag Hammadi discoveries afford, this prefix exhibits far more reserve than E. R. Goodenough, who through Philo posited a Jewish Gnosticism influenced by Hellenic mystery cults, which that writer saw even in the paintings of the Dura Synagogue.[24]

What then is Philo's paschal mystery? For the Mazzot festival,[25] Philo sings of spring and creation: the season is a divinely instituted memorial to remind humankind of its beginnings, just as unleavened bread is pure and natural food unsullied by human art, recalling the pristine state of Eden (Spec 2.159-160). Mazzot falls in the spring because it is the true New Year (150-151) recalling the harmony of the spheres, a cosmic truth ignored in the autumnal New Year of the Egyptian solar calendar (154).[26] The musical metaphor continues in the significance of the first and last days of the festival, which, as outermost strings of a musical instrument set the tonality of the others, cause the intermediate days to harmonize (157).

For Pesach, Philo reserves two related words that do not occur in Ex 12 (LXX): διάβασις or διαβατήρια, not a *passing over*, but a *passing through* or a *passing over into*.[27] Even the verb 'διαβαῖνω' appears infrequently in other contexts,[28] suggesting that this term had a special meaning Philo

[22] For these and other details, see Runia, CRI III,3, 3-33, "Philo Cristianus." The Christianization of Philo predates Eusebius. Hegessipus, or more likely, Clement of Alexandria may be source.

[23] See Pearson, Birger, Philo and Gnosticism, ANRW II.21.1, 1984, 295-342.

[24] ibid., By Light, Light: The Mystic Gospel of Hellenistic Judaism, New Haven 1935. For Dura paintings, see Gutmann, Joseph, Early Synagogue and Jewish Catacomb Art and its Relation to Christian Art, ANRW II.21.2, 1984, (1313-1342) 1322-1324.

[25] For the following, see Spec Leg 2.145-161, Opera V, 120-125; Werke II, 146-151.

[26] Cf. QuæstEx 1.1, Œvres 34C, 63.

[27] Cf. De cong. 104-106, Opera III, 93, and Mig. 25, Opera II, 273.

[28] Only the verb appears in NT: Abraham can not *cross over* to Lazarus (Lk 16.26), Paul *passes by* Mysia (Acts 16.9), and, signifcantly, "By faith the people *passed through* the Red Sea as if it were dry land..." (Heb 11.29).

does not wish to transfer even to the wanderings of Abraham, which are interpreted in an identical sense. Though he makes no explicit reference to the Greek practice, context and emphasis indicate a comparison between the Pesach lamb and the custom of making an offering before or after a important journey, especially border or river crossings, i.e. quite literally a rite of passage: an imprecation or thanksgiving for safe travel. This is the practice of 'διαβατήρια θυεῖν/θυέσθαι' mentioned in classical sources,[29] where generals offer sacrifice before or during major campaigns. At least a century before Philo, the Alexandrian Jewish philosopher-mathematician Aristobulus also refers to Pesach quite casually as "ἡ τῶν διαβατηρίων ἑορτή."[30] This parallel to Hellenic ritual may have been a part of the Hellenistic Jewish reading of Ex 12 long before Philo draws out its implications.

To achieve the motion and process implied in διαβαῖνω, Philo must transfer the accent from Pesach, that is, from the rites of Ex 12 and the meal, where participants are to remain behind closed doors while the Destroyer passes over, to the passage through the Red Sea. After commenting on the unusual nature of the sacrifice, Philo explains the feast as a rite of passage like the Greek διαβατήρια:

> [146] After the New Moon follows as the fourth feast that of Transition [διαβατήρια] – Pascha it is called by the Hebrews in the language of their fathers – on which the whole people from noon until the breaking of night slaughter many thousands of sacrificial animals, in fact, the whole people, young and old. For on this day all are given the status of priests. For, while otherwise the priests perform the communal and private sacrifices according to the prescripts of the Law, the people themselves for this occasion are given permission to carry out the office of priest and sacrificial service.
>
> [147] The reason for this provision is the following: the festival is dedicated to the thankful remembrance of the greatest migration, [the Exodus] from Egypt, which more than two million persons of both sexes undertook according to the Word of God given them. At that time, then, as they left a land full of hatred and inhospitality – where, beyond this, (which is the worst thing), dumb animals, tame and wild, were given divine honors – they, in an understandable exuberance of joy, performed the sacrifices

---

[29] PE 9, 301. Standard lexica (LSJ, PRP) cite Thucydides (5.54.55), Xenophon (Hist. Gr. 4.7.2), Herodotus 1.205, and a generation after Philo, Plutarch (Luc. 24.2). Lucullus offers a sacrifice before crossing the Euphrates.

[30] Cited by Anatolius of Laodicea, in turn by Eusebius, EH 7.32.17, GCS 9.2, 724.

themselves in their inexpressible haste and desire for as speedy an execution as possible, not waiting for the priests. And as they acted according to the urgings and drives of the heart, as a thankful remembrance the Law allowed them to proceed in the same manner once a year. So it is reported in an old tradition.[31]

This is Philo's summary of Exodus 12 and 15, as well as his view of native Egyptian cults. A muted note of thanksgiving is sounded, but for Philo it is because the people are grateful for a legal loophole: they may function at this one moment in a priestly role.[32] After this quite rational "historical" aetiology for an exception to the immutable Law, Philo then turns to the allegorical meaning, which he would consider its universal significance:

> But according to those who are accustomed to interpreting the written word allegorically, the "Transition" offering (διαβατήρια) means the purification of the soul, for the striving of the disciple of Wisdom is, in their opinion, solely directed toward freeing oneself from the body and its passions,[33] each of which overpowers the human person as a raging stream if one does not stem and subdue their torrents by the fundamentals of virtue. [148] Each house receives at this time the character and consecration of a shrine, for the sacrificed animal is prepared for a solemn meal and the participants in this festive meal have purified themselves with holy water; they have not just come together as for other banquets with wine and food for the sake of their bodies, but to fulfill the customs of their fathers with prayer and song.[34]

The *diabasis* exemplified in the Exodus is the mystery of *anabasis*: the rise of the virtuous soul away from the passions that enslave it,[35] including a healthy appetite for a festive meal that for Philo smacked too much of pagan revels.[36] Pesach is not just another banquet: the Diaspora home is a temple, and all the people priests in a holy liturgy. The deeper meaning, however, is a Platonic rite of passage to a higher plane of existence, in

[31] Spec 2.145 f., Opera V, 120.
[32] The priestly code permits laymen to handle paschal blood, a sign of great antiquity. Segal, Passover 158-162.
[33] In Quæst. in Ex. I.4, where Pesach is always termed διαβατήρια, there is a double διάβασις: the transition from youthful foolishness to maturity and the freeing of the soul from the body and the senses through ecstasy. Philo Werke II, 148, n. 1.
[34] De specialibus legibus 2.147 f., Opera V (Cohn), 120.
[35] Cf. Quis re. div. her. 78;255, Opera III, 283; 50 f.
[36] A distaste Clement shares for agapes "which reek of roasted meat and gravy." Paid 2.4.3, GCS 58, 156.

this text and others, initiated by God, embodied in the Law, and aided by virtue. Philo sees this as the destiny not only of the Jews, but of all humankind. Because they know the true God and God's Law, Jews are uniquely placed to undertake this spiritual ascent, but it is by no means exclusive to them.[37] This is the universal mystery of which the Pesach narrative is but a particular type: Philo has established a "ritual pattern." He has also heightened mystery beyond the particulars of history to such a degree that the anamnetic, even any temporal connection becomes almost nonexistent. This emphasis on type addressed to idea, that is, mimesis addressed to spiritual narrative, as opposed to anamnesis addressed to revelation in history, is the most Hellenistic feature of Philo's analysis.[38]

In a similar vein, Law is not identical to the written Law, as much as Philo notes the "customs of the fathers." Written laws partake of the perceptible world, and thus comprise special, or particular laws[39] that mirror nature and the spiritual, unwritten absolutes that govern the universe. The heroes of the OT – Abraham, Moses, Isaac – are all exemplars of perfection who embody the Law in their lives (νόμοι εμψύχοι).[40] All function for Philo as types of the divine Logos. Philo moves these heroes through a mythic landscape of allegorical persons and places to convey the paschal mystery to his readers. The historical reduces to a minimum, because the target narrative is timeless and immutable.

III. 1 Cor 10.1-6: First Reception of Philo?

In first century Corinth, Exodus-Wilderness narratives have been refitted mimetically into a story of baptism and eucharist. Either mediated through Philo or appropriated directly from wisdom traditions, the Hellenistic Judaism of Alexandria has helped shape a narrative that sweeps the Corinthians to ever greater spiritual heights, but ever further from the central message of sacred history: Christ's life, death, and

---

[37] Sandmel, 26 f.

[38] "[T]he interest which lay behind, and which provoked, their [the Hebrews'] detailed account of the past as a continuum was, of course, a religious one, the story of the unfolding of God's will from the Creation to the final triumph in the future. The Greeks had no such interest, religious or otherwise…" Finley, I. M., Myth, Memory, and History, HisTh 5, 1965, (281-302) 294.

[39] Mig. 3-5. Sandmel, 21.

[40] These figures are models for imitation, Sandmel, 20. See also Winston, David, Philo's Ethical Theory, ANRW II.21.1, (372-416) 387.

resurrection.[41] As in Philo, a ritual narrative based not on Ex 12, but the journey through the Red Sea toward the Promised Land, salvation through water, and a miraculous food may be the first echo of Alexandrian paschal language audible beyond the Nile.

1. Corinth: The Rhetoric

Since Paul's epistle is a responds to a letter (7.1) or oral report ("Chloe's people," 1.11) whose only traces are contained within his own, much exegetical effort has striven to reconstruct the theological views of the various factions within the Corinthian congregation. The danger inherent in this "mirroring" technique is always one of caricature: presenting this community as a gaggle of carping enthusiasts, rabid individualists with a boomtown swagger, or outright Gnostics, their contours distorted in funhouse fashion by Paul's diatribe.

Elisabeth Schüssler Fiorenza tries to avoid such dangers through rhetorical and reader-response criticism:

> That interpreters follow the directives of the implied author to understand the Corinthian Christians as 'other' of Paul or as 'opponents' becomes obvious in all those interpretations that characterize the Corinthians as foolish, immature, arrogant, divisive, unrealistic illusionists, libertine enthusiasts, or boasting spiritualists who misunderstood the preaching of Paul in terms of "realized eschatology."[42]

This should warn against a common technique: paraphrasing a highly rhetorical text does *not* yield historical fact. Paul presents the Corinthians a distorted image of themselves to achieve definite results. Reducing the affect of polemic, then translating it into academic prose merely dilutes the rhetoric and pours it sloppily from one discursive container to another. Rhetoric addresses real problems and situations, but in language designed not to describe, but to *move* people. Paraphrase moves nowhere, often rationalizing distortions that exist only as speech.

Paul takes the Corinthians to task for identifying themselves along baptismal lines under the names of figureheads. Helmut Koester sees these divisions resulting from a Hellenized wisdom theology where the

---

[41] Victor Pfitzner (Cultic Narrative and Eucharistic Proclamation in First Corinthians, LThJ 25, 1991, 15-25) sees a "history versus myth" strategy in cultic passages.

[42] Schüssler Fiorenza, Elisabeth, Rhetorical Situation and Historical Reconstruction in 1 Cor. NTS 33, 1987, 386-403.

rite was seen as initiation into gnosis accompanied by the teaching of a mystagogue.[43] Paul's name and 'wisdom' were being pitted against Apollos', Peter's,[44] or even Christ's, and the basic organization of the Corinthian Christians refracts in modern exegesis far more as tiny, bickering "schools" than a congregation. Given the highly rhetorical nature of the letter, this is likely Paul's fear of where the Corinthians are heading more than where they actually are: "When you come together as a church," Paul writes, "I hear that there are divisions among you; and *to some extent* I believe it" (11.18).

Paul is not just trying to clean up the edges of a fuzzy Corinthian theology, but redefines the community by the central mystery of the faith: "I did not come proclaiming the mystery of God to you in lofty words or wisdom. For I decided to know nothing among you except Jesus Christ, and him crucified." (2.1-2). Though *gnosis* need not be burdened with all its second century weight, spiritual knowledge is so treasured by Paul's correspondents that he must show how inadequately an anthropocentric wisdom can address the mystery of Christ. Yet first Paul must deconstruct this narrative, especially as it relates to bath and meal, before he can supplant it with another.

To define this mystery and its rites, the meal (11.23) "on the night when he was betrayed," acknowledges a narrative and temporal frame around meal and story "proclaiming the Lord's death until he comes."[45] That Paul is 'giving over' (παρέδωκα) the narrative he 'took over' (παρέλαβον) means that it was original neither to him nor the churches he founded, but a part of Christian worship he came to know in Antioch.[46] In the same way 'given over,' the creedal summary (15.3-6) "according to the scriptures…" is both method and result of a christological reading of the LXX original to the first Christian communities from whom Paul learned it.[47] While Paul will plead a special revelation in his dispute with the Galatians, tradition, scripture, and a narrative

---

[43] Koester, ACG 55-62.

[44] Vielhauer, Philip, Paulus und die Kephaspartei in Korinth, NTS 21, 1974-75, 341-352, believes there is enough evidence to suggest Peter's activity in Corinth.

[45] See Koester, Jesus' Presence.

[46] Leon-Dufour, Xavier, Abendmahl und Abschiedsrede im NT, Stuttgart 1983, 113. Anamnetic tradition with command is "Antiochene." See also Chilton, Bruce. A Feast of Meanings, NT.S 72, 1994, 115.

[47] Juel, Donald, Messianic Exegesis. Christological Interpretation of the OT in Early Christianity, Phila. 1988, 5-10.

about Jesus' last meal are the rhetorical means Paul chooses in 1 Cor. Why the difference? In Corinth the privilege of special revelation Paul will invoke against the Galatian "judaizers" – and their scriptural injunctions – has likely been turned against Paul himself.

Yet the Corinthians' story of the saving bath may have first been told by another baptismal "mascot," an Alexandrian whose wisdom traditions and Philonian allegories probably refracted as much in the Corinthian "schools" as Paul's teachings. Paul's letter provides an even greater distortion to reach a rhetorical goal. Since Apollos was "an eloquent man," "spoke with burning enthusiasm," "well-versed in the scriptures" and "taught accurately the things concerning Jesus" (Acts 18.24-25), he appears as a charismatic preacher equipped with traditions about Jesus and a christological interpretation of the scriptures. Luke records the Alexandrian origins of Apollos, the Syro-Western manuscript tradition (D) even asserting that "Apollonios" was taught Christianity "in his native land."[48] Even if this is nothing more than Alexandrian patriotism turned narrative, Apollos as a Jew of some educational and rhetorical ability would have encountered "in his native land" Philo's allegory of the passage through the Red Sea. Did Apollos have his own version of Philo's ascent of the soul that he taught in Corinth?

Returning to the Wisdom literature, it would not be too difficult to reconstruct a typology from the same sources from which Philo drew his image.[49] The Corinthians experienced a baptismal διάβασις[50] sweeping them into a higher state of pneumatic gnosis, manifested by the charismatic gifts they so enjoyed displaying in the assembly. The meal rite is a seal of that perfection, the possession of spiritual manna.

2. Paul's Corrective

If read against this background, Paul's Exodus typology takes on a different coloration:

---

[48] Nestle-Aland, [26]1979, 377, ...κατήντησεν ἐν τῇ πάτριδι τὸν λόγον.

[49] Cf. Prov 1-9, WisSol 10.15-21. In an allied question, see Sterling, Gregory E., Wisdom among the Perfect: Creation Traditions in Alexandrian Judaism and Corinthian Christianity, NovTest 37, 1995, 355-384.

[50] Cf. On Baptism A, Nag Ham. XI 40,30-41 (NHLE[3], 488) for further Valentinian development: "For the interpretation of John is the Aeon, while the interpretation of that which is the Jordan is the descent which is the upward progression, that is, our exodus from the world into the Aeon."

[10.1] I do not want you to be unaware, brothers and sisters, that our ancestors were all under the cloud, and all passed through the sea, [2] and all were baptized into Moses in the cloud and in the sea, [3] and all ate the same spiritual food, [4] and all drank the same spiritual drink. For they drank from the spiritual rock that followed them, and the rock was Christ.[51]

By this point, Paul's loving repetitions and the christological interpretation of the "spiritual rock" have probably lulled his readers into a false sense of security, which is exactly what he destroys in the next verse:

[5] Nevertheless, God was not pleased with most of them, and they were struck down in the wilderness. [6] Now these things occurred as examples [τύποι] for us, so that we might not desire evil as they did.

Paul inverts the terms of the wilderness traditions: the story of judgment is told with the motifs of the story of salvation. This is an *anti*-Exodus, not the story of salvation dryshod through the Red Sea, led by the presence of God in the cloud, nourished by the manna and miraculous water from the rock, but a story about idolaters who cannot abandon the stewpots and idols of Egypt. The Deity again becomes the Destroyer (Ex 12.23), and the blood of the lamb does not save them.[52]

Paul's Exodus is an anti-*mystery*, used to mimic, then deconstruct a wisdom-based, triumphalist typology current in Corinth.[53] In Paul's reversal, the Corinthians are rhetorically destroyed in the wilderness, their spiritual gifts revealed as wholly contingent upon the giver. The *effects* of salvation are moved out of the center to be replaced by the Savior. This deconstruction of the Corinthian myth then allows Paul to "reoriginate" the community in a meal rite anchored to the anamnesis of the cross, in the proclamation of Christ and him crucified, and in the self-giving agape of Christ.

---

[51] Vielhauer, art. cit., sees an allusion to Cephas/Peter. Jeske, Richard, The Rock was Christ: The Ecclesiology of 1 Corinthians 10. in: Kirche. FS Günther Bornkamm 75, Tübingen 1980, 245-255, (248) says the type "refers to the pre-existence of the corporate body of Christ, the church." For OT models, see Knowles, Michael P., "The Rock, His Work is Perfect": Unusual Imagery for God in Dt 32, VT 39, 1989, 307-322.

[52] Koch, Dietrich-Alex, Die Schrift als Zeuge des Evangeliums, BHT 69, 1986, 214 f. assumes a pre-Pl source with adaptation, including the Rock = Christ metaphor.

[53] The 'strong' "are the modern wilderness generation who, like the latter, are free from the dangers posed by the demons, because they are sustained by the πνευματικὸν βρῶμα and πόμα provided them in the one body of Christ." Jeske, 253.

IV. Pascha and Gnosis: Epistola Apostolorum

"But you celebrate the memorial day of my death," the risen Lord tells his disciples, "that is the Pascha." With this command to remember, the second century *Epistola Apostolorum* (EpAp) institutes the paschal feast until the Lord's return. Yet any similarity to Paul's story of Jesus' last meal or even the Asian reading of Ex 12 vanishes as soon as the risen Lord begins to explain what these words mean. Lacking both Asian and Egyptian vocabulary, the *Epistola's* paschal language speaks neither of Pesach rites nor the passage through the Red Sea; nor are passion and cross the objects of this memorial. Instead, the command to celebrate is surrounded by motifs of release, resurrection, and heavenly rest, all configured toward the *transitus* of the believer. As in Clement, this narrative does not require paschal motifs, but for the EpAp, the paschal vigil and its story of origins are not forms to be transcended, but ritual paradigms.

1. The Work and its Rhetorical Strategy

In the EpAp, salvation occurs through *revelation*, which the two most recent studies take be the actual title. Julian Hills translates EpAp 1.1: "The Book of the Revelation of Jesus Christ to his disciples: The Book of what Jesus Christ revealed through the council of the apostles, the disciples of Jesus Christ, for all people."[54] A curious amalgam of anti-Gnostic polemic, revelation dialogue, resurrection treatise, apocalypse, and church order – all nominally introduced as an epistle, the work includes every text type considered authoritative in the second century except Sibylline hexameters. Even a christological exegesis of Ψ3.1-8,[55] cited in full, is given the risen Lord to speak:[56] "If all the words spoken through the prophets have been fulfilled through me – for I myself was in them," the Lord tells the disciples after explaining the psalm, "how

---

[54] See Hills, Julian, Tradition and Composition in the Epistola Apostolorum, HDR 24, 12; Vanovermeier, Pedro. Livre que Jésus-Christ a révélé à ses disciples, Diss., Institute catholique de Paris, 1962.

[55] EpAp 19(30)12-13. Schmidt, Carl, and Isaak Wajnberg. Gespräche Jesu mit seinen Jüngern nach der Auferstehung. TU 43B, 1919, 66-71. A favorite proof text, cf. 1Clem 26.2; Justin, Apol 1.38.5, Dial 97; Iren., Epid 73, Clem. Alex., Strom 5.14.105.

[56] EpAp is more enamored of the *act* of citation than citation of authoritative text. Except for the psalm, citations do not exist. See Hills, Julian, Proverbs as Sayings of Jesus in the Epistola Apostolorum, Semeia 49, 1990, 7-34.

much more will that which I say to you come to pass so that the one
who sent me may be glorified by you and by those who believe in me."[57]
With this *a fortiori* argument the author canonizes his work, claiming it
as a foundational document for a worshipping community.

Cast as a dialogue immediately after the resurrection, the EpAp has
adopted the favored genre of Gnostic works.[58] The author condemns the
heresiarchs Simon Magus and Cerinthus[59], then adapts Gnostic narrative
to reclaim important motifs denied or differently understood by Gnostic
groups: incarnation, resurrection of the flesh, and the one Creator God.
The Gnostic, particularly Valentinian, *transitus* remains intact, but it
must carry not only the spirit, but also the body toward salvation.

Julian Hills, the latest scholar after a lengthy hiatus to treat the work
extensively, characterizes its revelatory nature:

> First, in light of the inclusive time frame (from resurrection to ascension),
> the record of the Lord's post-resurrection words in the EpAp 13-51 (*i.e., the
> dialogue*) is complete. There is no implied gap, in narrative or discourse,
> which might have allowed additional conversation to go unrecorded. The
> Epistola claims to offer not merely a selection of teachings but the full record
> of them, as testified by the disciples as a united group. Secondly, this body of
> teaching is not only complete, it is also uniquely saving. Its content is
> new…, what is taught is "revealed"…; and the revelation is hailed as fully
> salvific…. The saving event par excellence is therefore declared to be the
> transmission of a final revelation in the presence of the leaders of the first
> Christian community. Its medium and its content are the words of the risen
> one, who has chosen to deliver his saving gospel only after the resurrection.[60]

The identity of Jesus' teaching with that of the apostles, given eight
commissionings as stories of origins for the teaching office, is the greatest
assurance of salvation the EpAp can give.[61] This teaching is the identifying

[57] EpAp 29(36)13, TU 43B 68-71.

[58] Köster, Helmut, Dialog und Spruchüberlieferung in den gnostischen Texten von
Nag Hammadi, EvTh 39, 1979, 532-556.

[59] EpAp 1,TU 43B, 25, and 8(19), 32f: "Cerinthus and Simon have come to tra-
verse the world. These, however, are enemies of our Lord Jesus Christ, for they pervert
the words and the object (Eth. word and deed), that is, Jesus Christ."

[60] Hills, Proverbs, 9.

[61] 19, 46, with the command to teach; 30, 41, like the Great Commission; Peter
released from prison (EpAp 15) is to preach; Paul mission is also preaching (EpAp 31).
[I]t is in imitation of the Lord that the disciples are to preach. Indeed, the Epistola
claims that it is the very preaching ministry of the disciples … that generates the continued parousia, or presence, of the risen Lord." Hills, Tradition, 128.

mark of the community, and it is to this teaching and narrative that the EpAp addresses Christian rite.

2. The Paschal Command

Though no NT texts explicitly originate the Christian Pascha, the author of EpAp finds an aetiology neither in Ex 12 nor the Syn meal narrative, but in a somewhat unlikely place:

> [12.1] About that time King Herod laid violent hands upon some who belonged to the church. [2] He had James, the brother of John, killed with the sword. [3] After he saw that it pleased the Jews, he proceeded to arrest Peter also. (This was during the festival of Unleavened Bread.) [4] When he had seized him, he put him in prison and handed him over to four squads of soldiers to guard him, intending to bring him out to the people after the Passover [Pascha].[62]

While this is the story of James' death during Pesach-Mazzot, it also tells of Peter's freedom from prison,[63] themes often commingled in martyr narratives. The story continues with an angelophany, the miraculous freeing of Peter, and the faithful gathered at the house of John Mark's mother, where the servant Rhoda is reluctant to admit what she thinks is a ghost. The motifs are martyrdom, paschal time, epiphany, freedom from prison, a nocturnal prayer vigil, a brief recognition scene, and restoration to community. In the EpAp, all but one of these motifs (recognition) recombine to form a story of origins for the Pascha, while the motif of martyrdom and death is transferred back to Christ:

COPTIC	ETHIOPIAN
After my return to the Father, remember my death. When Pascha takes place, then one of you will be thrown into prison for my name's sake, and he will be in sadness and worry that you celebrate the Pascha while he is in prison and away from you, for he will mourn that he does not celebrate the	But you celebrate the memorial day of my death, that is the Pascha. Then they will take one of you who stands before me and throw him into prison for my name's sake. And he will worry and mourn bitterly, because while you celebrate the Pascha, he will be in prison and will not do the

---

[62] James' martyrdom may imitate passion chronology. Prison epiphanies are also a common feature. Cf. Buschmann, Gerd, Martyrium Polycarpi, Eine formkritische Studie, BZNW 70, 1994, foldout at end.

[63] In the frequent prison scenes of ATh, the prison is the world from which Christians are to be freed to go to their true home. See ibid., ATh 160-162, NT.S 5, 282 f.

Pascha with you. But I will send my power (δύναμις) in the form of the angel Gabriel and the doors of the prison will open. He will go out and come to you; he will spend a night-watch with you and remain with you until the cock crows. But when you have completed the memorial which takes place in reference to me and the Agape, then he will again be thrown into prison as a witness until he comes out from there and preaches that which I have given (commanded) you.

feast with you. And I will send my power in the form of my angel and the gate of the prison will open and he will come to you, to watch and to rest. And when the cock crows and you have completed my agape and have sufficiently performed my memorial, they will again take him away and as a witness bring him back to the prison, until he goes free and again preaches what I have commanded you.[64]

The anamnetic command is quite explicit, and the form of the paschal nightwatch is outlined: a vigil until cockcrow (ca. 3 am) culminating in a meal rite. The author of EpAp reads the time references and the prayer watch at the home of Mark's mother as a paschal vigil, originating the Pascha in a word of Jesus and as a prophetic word fulfilled.[65]

The EpAp is not reading the chronology of Acts 12 haphazardly. Peter is imprisoned *during* Azyma (ἦσαν δὲ αἱ ἡμέραι τῶν ἀζύμων-12.3) and Herod plans a post-holiday execution. Pesach and Mazzot are equated, but only the week-long observance can be meant by "after the Passover" (μετὰ τὸ πάσχα-12.4). As Luke tells it, the vigil was held *after* the Pesach night of 14/15 Nisan with Peter freed on or shortly before 21 Nisan. Since paschal chronology is the primary cue for this reading, the author envisions a Sunday celebration of Pascha within the Feast of Unleavened Bread. A provenance in Quartadeciman Asia Minor is eliminated, but not Egypt or Syria.

3. The Christological Context

Beyond its chronology, the miraculous freeing of Peter was especially attractive for its angelophany. With Christ as angel/heavenly messenger, the EpAp is steeped in a Logos/Sophia christology with no distinction

---

[64] TU 43B, 52-55, Ethiopian, even; Coptic, odd, where both extant.

[65] Strobel reads Acts 12 as a paschal text at the NT level, seeing belt and sandals as Pesach costume. Ibid., Passa-Symbolik und Passa-Wunder in Act. XII. 3ff., NTS 4, 1957-58, 210-215. For a balanced view, see Radl, Walter, Befreiung aus dem Gefängnis. Die Darstellung eines biblischen Grundthemas in Apg 12, BZ NF 27, 1983, 81-96.

between ontology and function.[66] Yet this angelic Christ is archaic typology, not a tradition of Jewish Christian angel christology[67] (cf. Heb) or even the angelic speculation of Herm. Justin sees Christ in every OT theophany,[68] and an extreme "appearance" christology has Jesus all but the latest avatar of the Logos. The EpAp applies this hermeneutic of epiphany to NT narratives, which accounts for the unusual juxtaposition of large amounts of NT material and a christology more primitive than the narratives EpAp incorporates.

As the EpAp envisions the Christ event as freeing kerygma, not saving deed, the Christ narrative is the descent and ascent of the Heavenly Revealer,[69] not resurrection of the crucified Messiah. The story of suffering and death reduces to a creedal minimum:

> ...concerning whom we testify that the Lord is he who was crucified by Pontius Pilate and Archelaus between the two thieves (and with them he was taken down from the tree of the cross, Eth.) and was buried in a place which is called the place of a skull (Cranion, Eth.).[70]

Other than the paschal command, this is the sole mention of the death of Christ, and the deposition from the "tree of the cross" may stem entirely from the Ethiopian translator or an Arabic archetype. Christ's death is testimony to his full humanity and the first station of his ascent to the Father, but not saving event, all the more striking given how much the author has internalized Joh language. The EpAp bears no trace[71] of a theology of the cross, even though it includes Paul in the circle of apostles and eloquently defends the Gentile mission (31, 33). The EpAp has no place for the Asian reading of Ex 12, the death of the lamb, or the blood as a sign of baptism.

Thus the injunction, "commemorate my death," is not self-explanatory; it cannot be the same as the command to remember in 1Cor or Lk. In this community Pascha was focused neither toward the salvific

---

[66] See Schmidt, TU 43B, 264-304; Hornschuh, Manfred, Studien zur Epistola Apostolorum, PTS 5, 1965, 60 f., for more detailed discussion of EpAp christology.

[67] Barbel, Josef, Christos Angelos, Theoph. 3, 1941, 235-241, 261 f.; Stuckenbruck Loren T., Angel Veneration and Christology, A Study in Early Judaism and in the Christology of the Apocalypse of John, WUNT 2.70, 1995. (EpAp not included.)

[68] See esp. Dial 75.4. For discussion of Justin's christology, see Grillmeier, Christ, 89-94.

[69] "Every christological moment in the *Epistola* involves vertical movement, expressed or implied." Hills, Tradition, 97.

[70] TU 43B, 36 f.

meaning of the cross nor anamnesis of the passion, but celebrated the death of Christ as paradigmatic for the heavenly ascent of the believer. The first words of the risen Lord speak of such a journey:

> Rise and I will reveal to you that which is above the heaven and that which is in heaven and your rest (ἀνάπαυσις) in the Kingdom of Heaven. For my father has given me the power (ἐξουσία) to lead you there and those who believe in me.[72]

The purpose of the resurrection mystery is to lead the believer heavenward: "rest" (ἀνάπαυσις, Copt. M̄TAN) is both current and future gift, as in Clement, the very goal of salvation.

4. Catechetical Context

After quickly abandoning the epistolary form, EpAp presents the first of two lengthy creedal narratives, both used as framing devices:

> 3(14) This we know: our Lord and our Savior is Jesus Christ, God, Son of God, sent by God, the Ruler of the whole world …, who through his word commanded the heavens to be, created the earth and what is in it, and determined the limits of the seas so they would not overstep them, … who created humankind according to his image and form and spoke to the ancient fathers and prophets in parables and in truth; of which the apostles preached and the disciples touched. God, the Lord, the Son of God, we believe that he is the Word made flesh, bore a body in Mary the holy Virgin, and was born not of fleshly desire, but through the will of God, was wrapped [in swaddling clothes] in Bethlehem and was revealed, raised and matured, as we saw it.[73]

The simpler *regula fidei* of Irenaeus and Tertullian[74] is troped with narrative and poetic elements, much like the section this passage begins. After verses interwoven from the Joh prologue, the first six chapters comprise an aretology of miracles stories, some in summary form, five others – the "alphabet story" (cf. *Gospel of Thomas* 6.13), Wedding at Cana, the Gerasene demoniac, stilling of the sea, fish with coin – narrated in greater detail. The creedal frame closes with an allegory of the Feeding of the Five Thousand:

---

[71] Hornschuh, Studien, 19.
[72] EpAp 12(23)-4 f., TU 43B, 42-45.
[73] TU 43B, 27 f.
[74] Countryman, L. Wm., Tertullian and the Regula Fidei, SecCent 2, 1982, 208-227.

What do these five loaves signify? They are the picture of our faith in "great" (i.e. full, baptized) Christianity, even in the Father, the Lord Almighty, and in Jesus Christ our redeemer, and the Holy Spirit, the comforter, in the holy church, and in the remission of sins.[75]

Revelation and teaching are again linked, just as the miracles are all framed as epiphanies. The reason for this revelation: "This our Lord and Savior revealed to us and taught us. But we do as he, so you may take part in the grace of our Lord, in our worship and our songs of praise."[76] This *traditio*, exemplified in miracle stories and baptismal teaching,[77] initiates the reader into a community of grace and worship.

Against this narrative background, one story is conspicuously absent: the theophany at the Jordan. The suppression of a narrative otherwise irresistible to the *Epistula's* theological stance is a strong witness to the work's anti-Gnosticism.[78] Instead, the EpAp links baptism to the descensus as well as the baptism of the disciples and their commissioning as baptizers,[79] that is, to narratives showing Christ as active baptizer[80] rather than passive recipient. Christ descends, not the Spirit as a dove:

ETHIOPIAN	COPTIC
27(38) For that reason I descended and spoke to Abraham, Isaac and Jacob, your Fathers, the prophets, so that they may bring the rest from beneath into heaven, and I have offered them the right hand, baptism of life, and pardon and forgiveness of all evil, as to you, and also from now on to all of those who believe in me.	21. For that reason I descended to the place of Lazarus [Lk 16.22] and preached to the righteous and the prophets, so that they may come out of the rest beneath and go up to that above. 22. and I poured out? with? my right hand over them <...> of life and forgiveness and salvation from all evil, as I have done for you and for those who believe in me.[81]

[75] EpAp 5(16), TU 43B, 32. See Hills, Tradition, 61-64, for translations.
[76] EpAp 6(17), TU 43B, 32 f.
[77] Kelly, J. N. D., Early Christian Creeds, London ²1960, 82: "...a three-clause formulary, modelled on the baptismal interrogations, which has been expanded to five clauses by the tacking on of additional articles at the end."
[78] See Segelberg, E., The Baptismal Rite according to some of the Coptic-Gnostic Texts of Nag-Hammadi, StPatr 5, 1962, 117-128; Bertrand, Daniel Alain, Le baptême de Jésus, BGBE 14, 1973. Gnostic interpretations, 56-82.
[79] See discussion, Hills, Tradition, 126-145.
[80] For discussion of Jesus' baptizing or not (Jn 4.1 f.), see Berger, Klaus, Theologiegeschichte des Urchristentums, UTB, 1994, §50, 110.
[81] EpAp 27(38)21.12-22.4, TU 43B, 86 f.

A few lines later, a parallel to the "Peter in chains" narrative describes the benefits of baptism:

> 28(39) (Eth.) But to you I have granted to be children of the light, free from every evil and from every power of punishment (Copt.: power of the archons),[82] and so I will also do for those who through you believe in me. As I told you and promised you, that the one (Copt.: who believes in me will be) freed from prison, loosed from the chains and saved from the sword and terrible fire. And we said to him, "Lord, in all things you have brought us joy and promised rest..."[83]

The story of baptism is virtually identical to that of the Pascha because this is the *Epistola's* story of salvation, reinforced with two mimetic narratives about rite.

5. Narrative Context

The author embeds the paschal command and its founding story to culminate a series of christophanies and to introduce another. The first revelation of the Risen One is the mystery of the heavenly descent:

> It came to pass, as I was about to come here from the Father of the Universe and passed through the heavens, I put on the Sophia of the Father and I put on the strength (δύναμις) of his power. I found myself in heaven, and I passed by the archangels and the angels in the same form as if I were one of them... But the Archistrategos of the angels is Michael and Gabriel and Uriel and Raphael, they, [Cop 6] however, followed me until the fifth heaven, for they thought in their hearts that I was one of them. The Father had given me the strength (δύναμις) of this quality, and on that day, I graced the archangels with a wonderful voice, so that they would go into the altar of the Father and serve and fulfill the service, until I would return to him. Thus through Wisdom I created the likeness. For I have become all in all, so that I <praise?> the Œkonomia of the Father and fulfill the glory of the one who sent me and return to him. For you know that the angel Gabriel brought Mary the message." We ourselves answered: [Cop 7] "Yes, O Lord!" Then he replied and said to us: "Do you not remember that I said to you a little while ago, 'I

---

[82] Cf. GosPhil 70.8-10: "The powers do not see those who are clothed in the perfect light, and consequently are not able to detain them. One will clothe himself in this light sacramentally in the union." NHLE³, 151. Baptism is signed by ascent, but in the EpAp, first by the descent of Christ to Sheol. See also Gospel of Mary 16.19-17.7, TU 60, 75 f.

[83] TU 43B, 88 f.

have become an angel among the angels and I have become all in all?" We said to him, "Yes, O Lord!" then he replied and said to us: "For on that day, when I took on the form of the angel Gabriel, I appeared to Mary and spoke with her. Her heart took me up and she believed; I formed myself and entered her body; I became flesh (σάρξ), for I alone was servant (διάκονος) in terms of Mary in a visible appearance of the form of an angel. Thus will I do after my return to the Father. But remember my death…[*here follows the paschal command*][84]

Without a trace of kenosis, this is a heavenly *transitus*, not an earthward descent that ended on a cross. The "form of a servant," not "slave" (Phil 2.7), is angelic. While "incremental" incarnation could be no more than the Joh prologue as sequential narrative, contemporary Gnostic sources offer the closest parallels:

> [The Archons] thought [that I] was their Christ. Indeed I [dwell in] everyone. Indeed within those in whom [I revealed myself] as Light [I eluded] the Archons. …And among the Angels I revealed myself in their likeness, and among the Powers as if I were one of them, but among the Sons of Man as if I were a Son of Man, even though I am Father of everyone…

This is as far as the parallel reaches, as the Gnostic work continues:

> As for me, I put on Jesus. I bore him from the cursed wood, and established him in the dwelling places of his Father. And those who watch over their dwelling places did not recognize me. For I, I am unrestrainable together with my Seed, and my Seed, which is mine, I shall [place] into the Holy Light within an incomprehensible Silence. Amen.[85]

Narrative elements of a Gnostic myth[86] have defined the structure, but not the content, of the heavenly descent in the EpAp. Through a redefining strategy, the author returns to the kerygma of the Joh prologue. As Paul had done for the Corinthian reading of the Exodus, the EpAp

[84] EpAp 13(24)5.6-14(25)6.14. TU 43B, 44-53. Copt. only is translated. Eth. is almost identical.

[85] Trimorphic Protennoia, NHLE³, 521. Egyptian provenance for Trimorphic Protennoia likely, first quarter or half of 2 c. for final Christianizing recension, 512 f. work as Sethian: Schenke, Gisene (ed., trans.), Die Dreigestaltige Protennoia (Nag-Hammadi-Codex XIII), TU 132, 1984, 20 f.

[86] Cf. this passage in GosPhil:, NHLE³, 144-145: "Jesus took them all by stealth, for he did not appear as he was, but in the manner in which [they would] be able to see him. … He [appeared to the] angels as an angel and to men as a man. Because of this his word hid itself from everyone. … He became great, but he made the disciples great, that they might be able to see him in his greatness."

has imitated a Gnostic narrative and transformed it into what it is not – a proclamation of the true enfleshment of the Logos.[87]

6. Eschatological Context

a) The Date

The command to celebrate the Pascha, linked by a simple contrastive in the Ethiopian to the story of incarnation, is joined temporally in the Coptic to the second Advent. The celebration of Pascha is to continue until Christ returns from the Father with his wounds[88] (Coptic) or his wounded ones,[89] the martyrs (Ethiopian). The announcement of Christ's return elicits questions from the apostles:

COPTIC	ETHIOPIAN
9. ...We said to him, "O Lord, what you have revealed to us before is great. Will you then come in the power of any kind of creature or in a perceptibility of some sort?" He answered us, saying, "Truly I say to you, I will come in the fashion of the sun which is risen, and I am seven times greater more resplendent than it in my glory. As the wings of the clouds <carry> me in glory, and as the sign [σημεῖον] of the cross is before me, I will descend to the earth to judge the living and the dead. But we said to him," O Lord, after how many years will this come to pass? He said to us, "When the hundred-and-twentieth is completed, between Pentekoste and the Feast of Unleavened the Advent of my Father will take place."	16(27) Then we said to him, "O Lord, great is that which you say to us and reveal to us. But with what power and in what form is it determined for you to come?" And he said to us, "Truly I say to you, I will come like the sun in its rising, so I will also shine in glory in sevenfold brightness. Carried on the wings of the clouds in glory, and as my cross marches before me, I will come to the earth to judge the living and the dead. 17(28) And we said to him, "O Lord, how many years?" He said to us, "When 150 years are over, in the days of the Pascha and Pentecost feasts (*only Eth. ms. S, all others*, between the Pentecost and Pascha) the advent of my Father will take place.[90]

[87] The ultimate demythologization of the Gnostic "descensus" is Irenaeus, AH 2.22.4, where Christ sanctifies each human age by maturing – to the age of fifty.

[88] Cf. Barn 7.9, Hippolytus, Com. in Dan. 4.10.4. The original was probably either μετὰ τῶν τραυματῶν μου or μετὰ μῶν τραυματιῶν μου. See Hills, Tradition, 115 f.

[89] Cf. Hippolytus, C. Gaium, frag. 5, Hills, 114: "...when the King comes in glory with his slain."

[90] Schmidt, TU 43B, 56-59.

If Pentecost means "fiftieth day," "between Pentecost and Pascha" comprises a portion of the year that except for the weekly celebration of the Lord's Day carries no liturgical charge in the second century, while "between Pascha and Pentecost" is the sole feature of a liturgical "year." This has elicited a bevy of interpretations, the most reasonable being simple transposition.[91] Ethiopian ms. S attempts a correction, "in the days of the Pascha and Pentecost feasts," which gives the sense, if not the original text. Since all extant mss. of the EpAp date well after the fourth century emergence of incarnation/epiphany festivals, this simple reversal could easily have been preserved. Except for the mention of the *Father's* Advent, for the scribe of the fifth/sixth century Latin palimpsest[92] "inter pentecoste et azyma erit adventus patris mei" would have been a banality of the liturgical calendar.

There is thus no need to narrow the *kairos* of the second parousia to the paschal night. Had the author wanted the Pascha alone to bear the eschatological weight of the season, there would have been no mention of the Fifty Days at all.[93] The second century Pascha – fast and vigil – was a liturgical beginning, not a culmination. The paschal night began the Fifty Days; it did not end a nonexistent Lent or Holy Week, and the highly mimetic *Day* of Pentecost linked to the giving of the Spirit (Acts 2) was unknown. So Tertullian speaks of the Fifty Days as an appropriate time for baptism, "because it was then, when he had been taken back into heaven, that angels told the apostles that he would come exactly as he had gone up to heaven – meaning, of course, during the Pentecost."[94]

This is a translation of Acts 1.11 from space to time: the white-robed figures at the Ascension tell the apostles, "Men of Galilee, why do you stand looking up toward heaven? This Jesus, who has been taken up from you into heaven, will come *in the same way* as you saw him go into heaven." Tertullian's angelic voices also give the simplest reason for similar speculation in EpAp. So the risen Lord of the EpAp declares after

---

[91] So Casel, Art und Sinn, 5. Talley (Origins, 83 f.) claims "between Pentecost and Pascha" was original: EpAp points to an early 2nd c. feast of the incarnation or baptism. What he calls a "misprint" is Eth. ms. S.

[92] For dating and Latin text, see Schmidt, TU 43B, 20 f.

[93] So Lohse, 78-81. See Strobel, Kalender, 33; Quigley, CQL 133. Gry, Louis, La date de la Parousie d'après l'Epistola Apostolorum, RB 49, 1940, 86-97, esp. 89-91, reconstructs a comedy of scribal errors to produce "on the feast of the Pascha."

[94] De bapt. 19.2, CQL 92, 91; CCSL 1, 293 f.

relating the mystery of his incarnation: "Thus will I do after my return to the Father."

The Coptic dates the parousia "after the hundredth part and the twentieth part have been completed," while the Ethiopian predicts the second Advent in 150 years. This has often been taken as internal evidence for the date of the work, a hypothesis rightly discarded by more recent studies.[95] It has also been conjectured that the number fifty in the Ethiopian resulted from the translator reading "Pentecost" twice, once as festival, once as numeral.[96]

In any case, there is a NT text which could have provided the number "120" in the original Greek.[97] At Mt 24.37-39, Jesus accentuates the unpredictability of the Parousia by alluding to the Flood:

> [24.37] For as the days of Noah were, so will be the coming of the Son of Man. [38] For as in those days before the flood they were eating and drinking, marrying and giving in marriage, until the day Noah entered the ark, [39] and they knew nothing until the flood came and swept them all away, so too will be the coming of the Son of Man.

How long are the "days of Noah"? If verse 37 is ripped from its context and used as guide to a specific OT text, then a reader searching for a date would come to a passage at Gen 6.3 numbering the "days of Noah":

> Then the Lord said, "My spirit shall not abide in mortals forever, for they are flesh; their days shall be one hundred twenty years."

Yet if the imminence of the parousia is the message behind the numbers, the disciples do not react one way or another, but ask how it will be the *Father* who will appear:

> But we said to him, "Just now, what you have said to us, 'I will come – and how do you say, 'the one who sent me is the one who will come? And he answered, "I am totally in my Father and my Father is in me." [*Coptic has skipped a few lines because of the repetition of the phrase, Ethiopian continues*] Then we said to him, "Will you then really leave us until your coming? Where will we find a teacher?" He answered us and said, "Do you not know that as I was now here, I was also there with him who sent me?"

---

[95] See summary of views in Hills, Tradition, n. 73, 116 f. Hills correctly follows Hornschuh (Studien, 118-119) in maintaining that dating must be sought outside this chapter.

[96] Lohse, Passafest, 78 f.

[97] Possibility 6 in Hill's list mentioned above.

And we said to him, "O Lord, is it then possible, that you are both here and there?" But he answered us, "I am totally in the Father and the Father in me [*Coptic resumes*] because of the similarity of form (μορφή) and the power (?) and perfection and light, the complete measure and the voice. I am the Logos, to him I have become an entity, that is, <...> the thought, perfected in type (τύπος); I have become the Ogdoas (Eightness), which is the Kyriake [Lord's Day].[98]

The question concerns not the time of the parousia, but only its nature, a response to the question of Christ's presence until the second Advent. The Lord's Day is equated, not temporally as in Barn[99] with the "eighth day" of new creation, but spatially with the eighth and final heaven, and finally, to Christ himself. The aetiological note rings clear. Yet the introduction of the Lord's Day as regularly occurring parousia softens, if not fully negates, the imminent nature of the second Advent.

In a survey of the parousia in every relevant work until Augustine, Kurt Erlemann attempts a taxonomy of three basic types: *revolutionary*: a sudden inbreaking of the kingdom coupled with a pessimistic world-view, *evolutionary*: an incremental revelation of the kingdom with time for repentance (key motifs: perfection, completion), and *revelatory*: an assurance that a heavenly home awaits.[100] Though the EpAp exhibits characteristics of all three, it is hardly surprising that the third predominates. Revolutionary apocalyptic is reserved for a section condemning sinners and the uncharitable rich, while believers will find protection, and if they suffer, inherit the crown of martyrdom (34-40). Yet sudden inbreaking is softened: Judgment Day horrors are depicted to make the apostles intercede for the wicked.[101] The overall picture of the *Epistula's* eschatology hardly suggests it was written with the end of the world but a few years away.

b) Eschatological "Rest" and Valentinian Readings of Pascha

Also speaking against an urgently chiliastic interpretation is the *Epistula's* "vertical" eschatology, realized now in Christ's presence and awaiting

---

[98] Copt. 10.1-10, TU 43B, 59 f. Eth. interpolates a resume of the resurrection.

[99] Barn 15.9: "For this reason we observe to our joy the eighth day, on which Jesus also rose from the dead, and after he had appeared, ascended to heaven."

[100] Erlemann, Kurt, Naherwartung und Parusieverzögerung im NT. TANZ 17, 1995, 393 f.

[101] EpAp 40(51)30.8-14, TU 43B, 128 f.

believers in final union with the Father. Reflecting this presence, the
Ethiopian mentions another aspect of the paschal night that the Coptic
does not: after his miraculous escape through the δύναμις of Christ, the
apostle will watch and *rest*, while in Coptic, he merely remains (ϭⲟⲟⲡ)
for the nightwatch until cockcrow.[102] In other contexts, ἀνάπαυσις,[103] as
transliterated loanword or Coptic ⲘⲦⲀⲚ, used solely in parallel to the
Greek, is the heavenly rest promised by Christ. As emended by Wajnberg, the Ethiopian at 12(23) reads "resurrection"[104] as an equivalent to
ἀνάπαυσις of the Coptic at 5.3. In the Descensus narrative, Christ brings
the OT righteous from the ἀνάπαυσις below to that above, the paschal
aetiology transferred to Sheol.

As the risen Lord speaks his first word of revelation, rest is its content:

> Then our Lord and Savior said to us, "Rise up, and I will reveal to you
> what is above the heaven and in the heaven, and your rest which is in the
> kingdom of heaven. For my Father has given me power (sent me, Eth.) to
> take you up thither, and them also that believe on me."[105]

This promise is repeated:

> Be of good courage and rest (ⲘⲦⲀⲚ) in me. Verily I say unto you, your
> rest (ἀνάπαυσις) shall be above, in the place where is neither eating nor
> drinking, nor care nor sorrow, nor passing way of them that are there, for
> you shall have no part of <...>, but you shall be received in the everlast-
> ingness of my Father. As I am in him, so shall you also be in me.[106]

"Rest" recalls the Joh "abide" (μείνατε ἐν ἐμοί, Jn 15.4), suggesting
that the Greek behind the apostle's "remaining" was either the obvious
μένω, or ἀναπαύω in the sense 'to make station.' Yet given the central
role of ἀνάπαυσις in the EpAp, the Ethiopian may preserve the original
wording and intent: Eusebius, whose image of the paschal *transitus* is a

---

[102] Cited above, p. 68.
[103] See Helderman, Jan, Die Anapausis im Evangelium Veritatis, NHS 18, 1984,
word study, 47-84.
[104] TU 43B, 44, n. 2.
[105] EpAp 12(23)4 f., TU 43B, 42-45.
[106] Coptic 11.9-12.1, TU 43B, 65, 67, Coptic text 7* f. This is not the banquet of
Asian chiliasm. Cf. Iren., AH 5.33.1: wine will be drunk in resurrected flesh. Eusebius
blames similar "carnal" ideas on Papias (whom Iren. cites, AH 5.33.4), whom Eusebius
calls weak-minded, EH 3.39.12-13. Justin shows there was already controversy about
such speculation, Dial 80.2.

direct borrowing from Origen, explains just what such a reading of the Pascha-Pentecost would entail:

> We are thus not to engage in ascetic exercises during the festival [of Pentecost], but rather we are to bear the likeness of the heavenly rest in which we hope (ἐλπιζομένης ἐν οὐρανοῖς ἀναπαύσεως)...
>
> In these days of the holy Pentecost, it is appropriate that, depicting our future rest (τὴν μέλλουσαν ἀνάπαυσιν διαγράφοντες), our spirits rejoice, we give the body a respite (τό σῶμα διαναπαύομεν) as if we were with the Bridegroom and could not fast.[107]

It is neither necessary nor possible that Eusebius stand in a direct line of tradition with the EpAp. But there are earlier writers, Gnostic teachers in second century Egypt or Syria, whose paschal readings may echo in those of the EpAp.

In Nag Hammadi writings, use of the term ἀνάπαυσις concentrates in the *Paraphrase of Shem* (28) and in the Valentinian *Gospel of Truth* (27), where "rest" receives particular stress as salvation realized now in the life of the believer.[108] In his commentary on John, Origen reports that the Valentinian Heracleon also associated the Pascha with rest:

> It would be more opportune to review in another place the problems about the time of the Pascha, held around the spring equinox, and any other problem that demands explanation. At any rate, Heracleon says: "This was the great feast; for it was the figure of the Savior's passion, when the sheep was not only slain, but by being eaten, brought rest (ἀνάπαυσις). By being sacrificed it signified the Savior's suffering in the world; by being eaten, the rest (ἀνάπαυσις) in the wedding."[109]

Though eating the lamb suggests the Synoptic meal narrative and the rite it institutes, Heracleon reads the Pesach frame of the supper as pneumatically as Ex 12. Pesach signs the passion; the eucharist is not anamnesis of the passion, but signs the union of the bridal chamber. The "wedding" in which ἀνάπαυσις is granted, is a major motif of Valentinian narrative. The ascending human spirit is wed to a heavenly opposite: one receives "a male power or a female power, the bridegroom and the bride. One receives them from the mirrored bridal chamber."[110] The

---

[107] Eusebius, Paschal Solemnities 5, PG 24, 700B, C; (=CQL 56).

[108] Helderman, Anapausis, 16, 339.

[109] Origen, Commentary in John, GCS 10, 1903, 190 f., CQL 16.

[110] GosPhil 65.7-12, NHLE³ 149.

Valentinian *unio mystica* is thus not with the divine "other," but with the true self.[111]

Valentinian nuptial imagery speaks so vividly that even a careful reading cannot discern whether the "wedding" in the "bridal chamber" was performed rite[112] or a mimetic mirror for virtually all ritual action, including the kiss of peace.[113] Yet since the bridal chamber is the only ritual concept in GosPhil that remains consistently, though not ultimately, transcendent, the latter is much more likely. Liturgical action is a series of images conveying both the human and the divine into the bridal chamber:

> Truth did not come into the world naked, but it came in types and images. One will not receive truth in any other way. There is a rebirth and an image of rebirth. It is certainly necessary that they should be born again through the image. What is the resurrection? The image must rise again through the image. The <bridegroom> and the image must enter through the image into the truth: this is the restoration.

> The Lord has made everything into a mystery: one baptism and one anointing and one eucharist and one salvation and one bridal chamber.[114]

The "wedding" is the *kerygma* of rite but not its ritual form: ritual action is access to the "bridal chamber," the target narrative of Valentinian catechesis. The paschal meal signs the "rest" in the "wedding" because this is the story of Valentinian salvation. More important to the Valentinian understanding of baptism, however, is the very narrative the EpAp conspicuously omits: Jesus' baptism in the Jordan. The bridal chamber is the place where the (docetic) body of Jesus was generated through the "father of everything" who united "with the virgin (Sophia) who came down, and a fire shone for him that day" at the Jordan:

> He appeared in the great bridal chamber. Therefore, his body came into being on that very day. It left the bridal chamber as one who came into being from the bridegroom and the bride.[115]

---

[111] Helderman, Anapausis, 295 f.

[112] For various views, see Buckley, Jorunn Jacobsen, A Cult-Mystery in the Gospel of Philip, JBL 99, 1980, 569-581; also Pagels, Elaine, Mystery of Marriage in the Gospel of Philip, in: The Future of Early Christianity (FS: Koester) Minneapolis 1991, 442-454.

[113] GosPhil 59.2-6, NHLE[3] 145: "For it is by a kiss that the perfect conceive and give birth .... We receive conception from the grace which is in one another."

[114] GosPhil 67.9-19, 28-30, NHLE[3] 150.

[115] GosPhil 71.1-10, NHLE[3] 152.

The origin and descent of Jesus mirror the ascending *via salutis* to the imageless Pleroma. Though they are eventually discarded (cf. Clement), sacramental images are the necessary means of ascent, repeating in reverse the generation of Jesus, a type of mimesis François Sagnard aptly termed "reverse exemplarism."[116]

If the EpAp is reacting to Valentinian ritual narrative, then it has doubly reversed the Jordan exemplar by transferring the descent to an unusual but orthodox narrative of annunciation and incarnation, then to the descensus. For both Valentinians and the EpAp, "rest" and union through heavenly ascent are major motifs. Both stress the "verticality" of Pascha: Heracleon by reducing the historical element to a symbol of a greater reality, the EpAp simply by accenting the ascension, i.e. Christ's restoration to the Father, as eternal paradigm. The *positive* exemplar in the EpAp, however, is an incarnate Christ who promises a resurrection in the flesh and union with the divine.

Neither Origen nor any other author mentions a Valentinian celebration of the Pascha. There is ample evidence, however, that Valentinians baptized, celebrated a meal rite, read the scriptures in their assemblies,[117] and that they considered themselves Christians, though "pneumatic" rather than "psychic" believers. There is no intrinsic reason why a Valentinian "pneumatic" interpretation could not have extended to the yearly observance.

7. Liturgical Context

Unlike a hypothetical Valentinian Pascha, the externals of the paschal celebration of this community are secure: Pascha is a Saturday night vigil culminating in a meal rite at 3 am Sunday morning. The paschal fast of whatever duration is of no concern. Yet the meaning the paschal night may have had in this community still remains somewhat elusive.

Isolating either eschatological speculation or the command to "commemorate my death," scholars have made far reaching conclusions about the nature and origins of the second century Pascha, universalizing the theology and narratives of this obscure apocryphon into historical data for one or more provinces of the Great Church. Strobel and

---

[116] Sagnard, François Marie-Mattaeus, La Gnose Valentinienne et le Témoignage de Saint Irénée, EPhM 36, 1947, 244-249.

[117] Irenaeus, AH 1.8.1, SC 254, 112.

Lohse[118] see a "highly eschatological"[119] feast ritualizing the watch for the parousia. Lohse is convinced that this was the feast's original content, while Strobel appropriates every "at midnight comes the cry" passage for an observance that ended not at midnight, but near dawn. Such conclusions reveal less about the nature of the earliest paschal celebration than they imitate the "highly eschatological" nature of postwar German Protestant theology.[120]

In contrast, Carl Schmidt and others take the command to "commemorate my death" as the true content of the Pascha,[121] ignoring the context into which EpAp places its command to celebrate. This view limits the kerygma-anamnesis dynamic to fourth century categories, likely filtered through somber Lutheran and Reformed Good Friday liturgies still observed in the twentieth century. At the same time, this view utterly fails to acknowledge the decidedly non-Pauline kerygma the EpAp urges upon its readers.

Attempting to harmonize these findings is reminiscent of Lewis Carroll: jam yesterday, jam tomorrow, but never jam today. Yet as the Pascha celebrates the presence of Christ among the gathered faithful, it inaugurates the Fifty Days, during which the author expects the second Advent. The eschaton is then fused to liturgical time now on the Lord's Day. The author of the EpAp, it seems, has cast a vote soundly for "jam today."

Revelation and presence also govern the choice and sequence of Christ narratives. The apostles summarize miracle stories as revelations of divine power and wisdom, just as the first creedal statement shimmers with OT theophanic language. The apostles recount birth, death, and resurrection, while the risen Lord reveals the "mysteries": the heavenly descent and the annunciation, the parousia, and the descent into Hell. Regardless of narrator, all Christ narrative is *epiphany*, equated with a kerygma the apostles are urged eight times to proclaim. This is the narrative and theological context for the paschal command.

EpAp places this command immediately between the two parousias. Yet the paschal night, caught between remembrance and hope, is founded not in anamnesis, but in a narrative of rescue through Christ appearing in

---

[118] Recently followed by Cacitti, Remo, Grande Sabato. Il contesto pasquale quartodecimano nella formazione della teologia del martirio, SPM 19, 1994.

[119] Strobel, Kalender, title of section I.3.

[120] Succinctly summarized, Erlemann, Naherwartung, 2-19.

[121] Schmidt, TU 43B, 759: "Dort Passah, hier Ostern!"

angelic form. Peter is a figure of the paschal celebrants, and this narrative a celebration of the Christ event: a freeing epiphany contained in the words of the risen Lord, which Peter is then to proclaim. "Commemorate my death" does not mean "meditate upon the passion," but "celebrate my ascent to the Father": Pascha celebrates the *via salutis*, not the *historia salutis*.

Concluding a section on the general resurrection, the risen Lord makes one of the most powerful christological statements in the entire work:

> Truly I say to you, I have obtained the whole power of my Father, that I may bring back into light those who dwell in darkness, those who are in corruption into incorruption, those who are in death into life, and that I may free those who are in captivity. For what is impossible with human beings is possible with the Father. I am the hope of those who despair, the helper of those who have no savior, the wealth of the poor, the physician of the sick, and the resurrection of the dead.[122]

This is the "Peter in chains" narrative cast in Joh language: a series of "I am" statements incorporating the pointed conclusion of the dialogue with Nicodemus.[123] This comes closest to the paschal mystery as this community might have heard it proclaimed at the vigil: Christ has been empowered to save as he has ascended to the Father, but his presence remains with the community. Analogous to the narrative of the heavenly descent of the Redeemer, the heavenly ascent of the believer imitates an essentially Gnostic Christian kerygma and readdresses it to the Great Church Christian mystery.

EpAp has a theological agenda it never ceases to drive home: following the Lord's commandments is constitutive of the community as much as baptism and proper transmission of the kerygma.[124] Paschal

---

[122] EpAp 21(32) Copt. not extant, TU 43B, 74. Parallel in the Liturgy of St. Mark: "...for you our God are the one who sets free those who are bound, who restores the broken, the hope of the hopeless, the helper of those who have no help, the resurrection of the fallen, the harbor of the storm-tossed, the advocate of the oppressed." (Greek text: Brightman, LEW, 127; Hills, 127, n. 1.) Also Hornschuh, Studien, 104. Cf. Melito Frag. 15* (Hall, 84), Iren. Arm. Frg. 2 (Jordan, TU 36/3, 59 f.): He is the repose (anapausis) of the dead, the finder of the lost, the light of those who are in darkness, the redeemer of the captives, the guide of the wanderers, the refuge of the forlorn, the bridegroom of the Church, the charioteer of the cherubim, the chief of the army of angels."

[123] The apostles' questions are solely prompts, but Nicodemus' "How is it possible..." echoes six times. See Hills, Tradition, 30.

[124] Hills, Tradition, 167 f.

celebration is intimately connected to these points. Overstressing either of the paschal passages in the EpAp without acknowledging their contexts can only further distort their interpretation beyond the rhetorical strategy of the work itself.

For the mid-second century, whether in Egypt or Syria, a skeletal outline of a dominical paschal liturgy and its content as feast of presence still provides information of great worth. Yet as little influence as this apocryphon exerts on later tradition, with the addition of a Philonian exegesis of Ex 12, the transition from captivity to freedom of the EpAp is not far from the διάβασις that becomes the hallmark of later Alexandrian paschal theology. As the EpAp, Origen concentrates on the paradigmatic nature of Christ's διάβασις to the Father as the essential paschal mystery, just as he will use a "third level" Gnostic hermeneutic not to move beyond NT kerygma, but to mirror it.

V. Feasting on the Word: Origen

In Origen's relatively late seventh homily on Exodus, there is still a decided "Asian" echo:

> Therefore, now, let us see the various levels of mystery [ordo mysterii] in these prescriptions. The first Pascha is that of the first People, the second Pascha [Ex 16.1] is ours. For we were unclean in soul [cf. Num 9.3], "worshipping wood and stone" [Ezek 20.32] and "in our ignorance of God serving things which were not divine in nature" [Gal 4.8]. We were also sojourners from afar – the apostle says of us that we were "aliens and sojourners to the testaments" of God, "without hope and without a god in this world" [cf. Eph 2.21]. Nevertheless, the manna is not given from heaven on the day on which the first Pascha is kept, but on that of the second [i.e. Sunday]. For the "bread which came down from heaven" [Jn 6.51] did not come to those who kept the first festival but to us who have received the second. "For Christ is sacrificed as our Pascha" [1 Cor 5.7] and he is the "true bread which comes down from heaven."[125]

In this tightly linked catena, the Exodus as creation of the Gentile Church is bolstered by a citation from that chapter crucial to Gentile Christian identity, Gal 4.[126] With Melito, the paschal mystery is the story

---

[125] Origen, Hom. in Ex. 7.4, SC 321, 216 f. Trans. altered CQL 40, 56.
[126] Gal is "foremost against Judaism." Tertullian AdvMarc 5.2, CCSL 1, 665.

of Christ, its ritual expression, and Christ himself. So too the manna of Jn 6 is simultaneously Sunday eucharist and the descent of the heavenly Logos. After this equation, there is nothing more than can be said about these texts, thus the need for a "third" heavenly and spiritual Pascha as Origen delves further into their meaning. This new level, however, may only be reached by applying Origen's new hermeneutic, not the old one.

Raniero Cantalamessa describes Origen's paschal theology as "anthropocentric,"[127] quite correct in the sense that Origen keys paschal texts from both testaments to the human experience of faith. Yet since Origen's readings do not spiritualize ritual as much as ritualize an encounter with scripture, it is more accurate to term his approach "logocentric:"[128]

> If the lamb is Christ and Christ is the Logos, what is the flesh of the divine words if not the divine Scriptures? This is what is to be eaten neither *raw nor cooked with water.* Should, therefore, some cling just to the words themselves, they would eat the flesh of the Savior *raw,* and in partaking of this *raw flesh* would merit death and not life – it is after the manner of beasts and not humans that they are eating his flesh – since the Apostle teaches that *the letter kills, but the Spirit give life* [2 Cor 3.6]. If the Spirit is given us from God and *God is a devouring fire* [Dt 4.24; Heb 12.29], the Spirit is also fire, which is what the Apostle is aware of in exhorting us to *be aglow with the Spirit.* [Rom 12.11]. Therefore the Holy Spirit is rightly called *fire,* which it is necessary for us to receive in order to have converse with the *flesh* of Christ, I mean the divine Scriptures, so that, when we have roasted them with this divine *fire,* we may eat them roasted with fire. For the words are changed by such fire, and we will see that they are sweet and nourishing.[129]

Even more than Clement, Origen exegetes ritual *texts,* not rituals, toward an act of reading: ἀνάγνωσις as γνῶσις. Eating the lamb or the bread of Christ's body is understanding biblical texts, in Origen's image, cooking them in spiritual fire, not eating them raw in their literal sense. Clement's glowing descriptions of perfect Gnosis become for Origen a fascinating struggle for meaning in texts that remain far more transcendent than the rituals they prescribe:

---

[127] Cantalamessa, CQL p. 11 f.; see also Huber, Passa, 155 f.

[128] See Lies, Lothar, Wort und Eucharistie bei Origenes. Zur Spiritualisierungstendenz des Eucharistieverständnisses, InThSt 1, 1978. Lies assumes that Origen is spiritualizing the eucharist.

[129] Origen, PP 26.5-27.5. Guéraud-Nautin, 204 f.; ACW 54, 41 f.

Just as the mysteries of the Passover which are celebrated in the Old Testament are superseded by the truth of the New Testament, so too the mysteries of the New Testament, which we must now celebrate in the same way, will not be necessary in the resurrection, a time signified by the *morning* in which *nothing will be left, and what does remain of it will be burned with fire*[130]

The "flesh" of ritual will leave no residue, but even the gnosis to which Origen directs all paschal motifs is finally burned away:

For our knowledge is imperfect and our prophecy is imperfect, as the same Apostle teaches, but when the perfect comes, the imperfect will pass away, [1 Cor 13.9f], This is what the Scripture says is burned in the morning. The night is taken for the present world [cf. Gal 1.4] and the day for the world to come [cf. Mt 12.32; Eph 1.21] as the same Apostle attests, saying: The night is far gone, the day is at hand. [Rom 12.13]. But only a very few [Mt 22.14] are they who have their faculties trained by practice to distinguish good from evil and who can take solid food [Heb 5.12,14] and who will be capable of not leaving any flesh until the morning, as the Scripture says, perhaps one in a thousand or two in ten thousand [cf. Eccl 7.28; Sir 6.6; Dt 32.30], among whom were the blessed apostles.[131]

A sweeping transcendence that reduces all flesh to ash returns again to the solid food of apostolic writings. The apostles, and especially *the* Apostle Paul, had attained the spiritual perfection to which Origen directs his exegesis. While there is an echo of Philo's patriarchs as νόμοι εμψύχοι, Origen's accent again is on process, not the flatness of Philo's allegory. Thus in his *Commentary on Romans*, Origen shows that in the Corinthian correspondence, Paul had not yet reached the same level of perfection as in the later letter.[132]

As little as it is initially concerned with the liturgy, this exegetical endeavor becomes liturgical theology not only when Origen is ordained presbyter in Caesarea, but also by being read and applied by those who preside at Christian liturgies. With a large debt to Philo and Clement, this teaching is furthered by Athanasius in his paschal epistles and finds

---

[130] Origen, PP 32.20-28, Guéraud-Nautin, 216; ACW 54, 44 f. Reconstructed from Paris Bib. Nat. lat. 12309. See Guéraud-Nautin, 75 f.

[131] Origen, PP 34.10-30, Guéraud-Nautin, 220; ACW 54, 45 f.

[132] Origen, ComRom 1.1, PG 14, 839C. See Heither, Theresia, Translatio Religionis, Die Paulusdeutung des Origenes, BBKg 16, 1990, 31-34.

later proponents in Ambrose,[133] Augustine[134] and the great Cappadocians. Origen's textual exegesis becomes ritual exegesis as it is absorbed by later tradition as a supplemental, but never the primary meaning of rite. This entails a mimetic move not generally made by Origen himself.

An early recipient of this elegantly interpreted Logos-Pascha is the IP homilist, who prepares the reader to hear both the scriptural text and its point-by-point exegesis:

> If we wish then for complete nourishment from the Word, and feasting not on earthly things but on the heavenly reality, we also eat the spiritual Pascha with the same relish with which the Lord wished to eat it with his disciples, when he said, "I have desired to eat the Passover with you" [Lk 22.15].[135]

At the conclusion of an epitome of this sermon (4-8), perhaps a literary feature added for publication,[136] the homily itself is presented as meal:

> These are for us the provisions of the sacred celebration, this the spiritual table, this the immortal enjoyment and food. We who are fed by the bread descended from heaven [Jn 6.31] and who have drunk from the cup which gives joy, that living blood which has received the mark of the heavenly Spirit, taking up again our discourse, we say first of all what the Law is and the œconomia of the Law and thus we will learn by comparison what is the Word and the freedom of the Word.[137]

Origen's exclusivism disappears when an entire community is invited to feast upon the Word. Vigil, lessons, homily, and prayers no longer merely talk *about* the Pascha, but *become* the paschal meal as much as the culminating eucharist. In this author, however, Origen's great exegetical struggle disappears, along with a good deal of content:

---

[133] Baus, Karl, Das Nachwirken des Origenes in der Osterfrömmigkeit des Ambrosius, RQ 49, 1954, 21-55; Huber, Passa, 165-170.

[134] See Cantalamessa, OAK, XX, for later influence.

[135] IP 3.3, SC 27, 121 f. The IP homilist has no use for Origen's construct of the Pascha as *transitus*, but remains firmly within the Asian Pascha=passion typology.

[136] Christine Mohrmann thinks the epitome is a later interpolation, ibid., Note sur l'homélie pascale VI de la collection Pseudo-Chrysostomienne dite "des petites trompettes," in: Mélanges en l'honneur de Mgr. M. Andrieu, Strasbourg 1956, 351-360. For genre questions raised by this section and others, see Visonà, Giuseppe, Pseudo Ippolito, In sanctum Pascha, studio, edizione, commento, SPM 15, 1988, 47-55.

[137] IP 8, SC 27, 133.

The meat shall be eaten at night [Ex 12.8]: For the light of the world set beneath the great body of Christ, "Take, eat, this is my body."

The meat cooked in fire [Ex 12.18] and roasted in reality is the rational body of Christ (λογικὸν σῶμα): "I have come to ignite a fire over the earth and how I wish that it were already kindled!" [Lk 12.49]

The meat is not raw, because the word is well digestible, easy to say, easy and ready to be assimilated; not boiled in water, because the word is not moist, not drowned, not dissolved.[138]

Liturgical context tightens the connection between visible word and audible sacrament, but the homilist does not have the time (or genius) to do much more than point to the eschatological significance so crucial to Origen's reading of the Pascha.

Reading Origen's reading is always fraught with the same ambiguities – and offers the same rich possibilities – as reading the Logos and eucharistic motifs of Jn 6, the ultimate source of these extended metaphors. In the real Origen, this ambiguity usually remains suspended,[139] but it can always be resolved by a reader wishing to increase the mimetic relationship between Origen's exegesis and ritual acts. Sometimes Origen appears to do this himself:

Paschor struck Jeremiah the prophet and threw him into the waterfall which was at the gate of Benjamin, from the upper story [Jer 20.2 LXX] There was an upper story in the house of the Lord, and he threw the prophet into the waterfall. And we urge that we take Jeremiah now and make him go up to the upper story in the house of the Lord.

The upper story is the sublime and elevated sense, as I will show from Scripture, when it testifies that the saints gave hospitality to the prophets in the upper story…Yet when Jesus was about to conduct the festival for whose symbol we celebrate Pascha, he answered their question, "Where do you wish that we prepare the Pascha? Go and you will meet a man carrying a jug of water, follow him; he will show you a large dining room in the upper story furnished with cushions, cleaned and ready." No one who

---

[138] IP 26 f., SC 27, 153.

[139] So in another context, A. Grillmeier writes, "The ambivalent way Origen leaves suspended the difficult problems arising from obviously contradictory passages in Scripture has led… to one-sided solutions in his hearers and readers." ibid., Das "Gebet zu Jesus" und das "Jesus-Gebet": Eine neue Quelle zum "Jesus-Gebet" aus dem Weißen Kloster, in: After Chalcedon. Studies in Theology and Church History (=OLA 18, FS A. Van Roey), 1985, (187-202) 195.

wishes to celebrate the Pascha like Jesus remains in the lower story. Yet when one celebrates the feast with Jesus, he is above in the great dining room, in the clean room, in the decorated and prepared room. When you go up with him to keep the Pascha, he gives you the drink of the new covenant, he gives you also the bread of blessing [τὸν ἄρτον τῆς εὐλογίας], he gives you his body and blood.[140]

The connection with an upper story and water is guaranteed by the LXX of Jer 20.2, which has the prophet not imprisoned in stocks in the upper story of Benjamin's Gate, but tossed from the upper story into a waterfall. This rather indecorous splash, however, only partially explains why Origen does not follow Tertullian's unusual reading of a baptismal reference in the jug of water.[141] For as Origen conducts Jeremiah to the "upper room," he guides both text and his hearers there – to yet another hermeneutical "building."

The upper story as spiritual sense of scripture is a cue that the connection between rite and word is not as simple as it looks. Body and blood, eating and drinking rarely signify for Origen a ritual act: here the rituals are presented as mimesis of the superior "upper room" of allegorical exegesis because they are in the "upper room" in an NT narrative. Mimesis is from *text to text*: Jeremiah is not being conducted to a liturgical, but a hermeneutical space where the "sublime and elevated sense" of scripture, i.e., its christological meaning, is revealed. The paschal frame is also not Judaic rite, but Origen's dining on the flesh of the Logos *in the text*, now signed in the eucharistic meal. The act of cognition inherent in any sacramental action is identical to that conveying the presence of Christ through scripture: the flesh of the Logos is eaten by reading and hearing logoi as the body and blood in the eucharistic meal:

> In the fourth place among the festivals of God is the celebration of Pascha, in which festival the lamb is killed. But look at the true Lamb, the Lamb of God, the lamb who takes away the sin of the world [Jn 1.29] and then say, "Our Pascha has been sacrificed, Christ." [1 Cor 5.7]. The Jews may eat of the lamb's flesh in a carnal way, [cf. Justin] but we eat the flesh of the Logos of God, for he himself said, "Unless you eat my flesh, you will not have life in you" [Jn 6.53]. What we speak of now is the flesh of the Logos of God as long as the food we offer is not like vegetables for the sick or milk for children. If what we say is perfected, robust and strong, then

---

[140] Origen, In Ieremiam homilae 19.3, GCS 6 (Origen 3), 169; =CQL 42.
[141] For text, see below, p. 140.

we offer you the Logos of God to eat. For where there is mystic speech, solid and full of dogmatic and Trinitarian faith [*adjectives presumably thanks to Rufinus*], where the mysteries of the age to come are spread out without the veil of the letter on the spiritual law...all of this is the flesh of the Logos of God. Whoever can feed on them with a perfect mind and a purified heart truly performs the sacrifice of the paschal festival and the feast with God and God's angels.[142]

While other exegetes ancient and modern attempt to resolve the "word versus sacrament" paradox of Jn 6, it is the tension between the two that Origen fills with meaning. As in the IP homilist who followed him, the liturgy leads the homilist Origen to apply his own scriptural hermeneutic to the words proclaimed in the assembly.

1. Peri Pascha

As in Jn 6, any spatial, linguistic, or temporal distinction in the text can become for Origen a guidepost to true Gnosis. This method is far from arbitrary, but employs a classical rhetorical technique known as *diairesis*, where similar but not identical phenomena or concepts are differentiated to penetrate to the highest idea.[143] Modern exegetes note that in Ex 12, God speaks once to Moses and Aaron alone, then instructs them to speak to the entire congregation in similar, but not identical words. "In the scriptures," Origen concludes, "will be found many such things which, to those who read superficially, will seem to be identical, but which, to those who read with care and attention, will reveal their differences."[144] Modern critics[145] address this anomaly to the history of sources; Origen finds a complete transformation after baptism:

> God says to Moses and Aaron that this month is the *beginning of months* and is also *the first month of the year* for them when they leave Egypt. As far as the history goes, this month is indeed the *first month,* and the Jews celebrate this festival each year *on the fourteenth of the first month* by sacrificing a *lamb in each household* according to the law given them through

---

[142] Origen, Num. hom. 23.6, GCS 30, 218; CQL 41.

[143] Christiansen, Irmgard, Die Technik der allegorischen Auslegungswissenschaft bei Philon von Alexandrien, BGBH 7, 1969, sees the origin of Philo's method in this technique coupled with Aristotelian categories.

[144] Origen, PP 12.3-10, Guéraud-Nautin, 176; ACW 54, 34.

[145] Weimar, Peter, Zum Problem der Entstehungsgeschichte von Ex 12.1-14, ZAW 107, 1995, (1-17) 5.

Moses. But when Christ came *not to abolish the law or the prophets but to ful-fill them,* he showed us what the true Passover, is, the true "passage" out of Egypt. And for the one in the passage, *the beginning of months* is when the month of passing over out of Egypt comes around, which is also the beginning of another birth for him – for a new way of life begins for the one who leaves behind *the darkness and comes to the light* [Jn 3.20f] – to speak in a manner proper to the sacrament (σύμβολον) through water given those who have hoped in Christ, which is called *the washing of regeneration* [Tit 3.5] For what does rebirth signify if not the beginning of another birth? ...[146]

Except for a brief appearance in a list of typologies in Tertullian's *De baptismo,*[147] the passage through the Red Sea, the figure for baptism so cherished by the Corinthians, finds no mention in any other writer of the second century. Milk and honey, after all, were tokens of arrival, not food for a journey. Daniélou argues that the Red Sea typology was part of "official catechetical instruction in the earliest Church."[148] Yet this cannot explain why such "official teaching" already found in first century Corinth would disappear, only to surface again when Origen becomes an "official catechete." With Philo as source, the Red Sea typology begins as a literary and philosophical, not a catechetical tra-dition. Its attraction is that it can sign a continuing process. The Destroyer passes over in a single night, but one is awash in the Red Sea until one reaches the distant shore of spiritual perfection.

Even Clement does not find a baptismal type in Ex 15, primarily because he follows Philo more exactly than Origen. For Philo the Red Sea was the passions, "each of which overpowers the human person as a raging stream, if one does not stem and subdue their torrents by the fundamentals of virtue." For Clement, the Red Sea won:

And when it says in the Song of Victory: "For he has triumphed glori-ously, horse and rider he has cast into the sea," then this means that the many-armed and animal and stormy passions, the desires, together with the riders sitting upon them who have given over the reins to lust, he has "cast into the sea," that is, given over to worldly immorality.[149]

[146] Origen, PP 3.37-4.33, Guéraud-Nautin, 158 f.; trans., ACW 54, 29.
[147] Tertullian, De bapt 9.1, CCSL 1, 283 f. See Lundberg, Per, La typologie bap-tismale dans l'ancienne église, ASNU 10, 1942, 116-135, for further use of this image.
[148] Daniélou, J., Traversée de la mer Rouge et baptême aus premiers siècles, RSR 33, 1946, (402-430) 405.
[149] Clement, Strom 5.52.5, GCS 52, 362. Stählin point out parallels to Philo De somn. 2.267, 269 f., De agric. 82 f., Leg alleg 2.99. Rom 1.24-26 also comes to mind.

Philo did not draw a connection to Christian baptism, so neither does Clement. But in Origen, baptism soon evaporates, and the echoes from Philo become more audible:

> One must enter into a perfect state of life and a perfect love in order to be able to hear, while still in this present world, the words: *This month is* for you *the beginning of months.* For this is not said by God to the whole people, but only to Moses and Aaron. For it is not written: "And God said to the people: This month is for you the beginning of months; it is the first month of the year for you." Rather, it is written: *The Lord spoke to Moses and Aaron in the land of Egypt, saying: This month is for you the beginning of months; it is the first month of the year for you.* Then he adds: *Speak to the whole assembly of the sons of Israel and say: On the tenth day of this month they shall each take a lamb.* If he had added: "Speak to the whole assembly of the sons of Israel and say: this month is for you the beginning of months," he would have been saying this without distinction both to Moses and Aaron and the whole people. But since it is *to Moses and Aaron* that it is said: *This month is for you the beginning of months: it is the first month of the year for you,* and since he (Moses) is ordered not to say this, but that *on the tenth day of the month* they should *take a lamb according to their fathers' houses,* it is clear that it is not for the whole people that that month was then *the beginning of months,* but only for Moses and Aaron to whom it was spoken. For it is necessary to have completely renounced creation and this world to understand that one has become almost other than what one was in order to be able to hear: *This month is* for you *the beginning of months: it is for you the first month of the year.*[150]

I have resisted shortening the endless repetitions of this passage to give a sample of both the acribious style to which Origen is given and his obsession with finding two levels of meaning wherever he can. As tiresome as it may be, exegeting this distinction between "beginning" and "first" takes up sixteen of fifty manuscript pages. For Origen's pupils, Moses and Aaron represent a completely different class of Christians to whom a new beginning has been revealed. The rest merely receive ritual instruction. The same is the case with the baser "barley loaves" of Jn 6.9 opposed to the finer "wheat loaves" of Mt 14.19 at the Feeding of the Five Thousand[151] and with the disciples who go into the

---

[150] Origen PP 4.36-5.4, Guéraud-Nautin, 160 f.; ACW 54, 29 f.

[151] Origen, PP 23 f. [II.7 f.]: "Because for some he breaks five loaves of wheat, and for others seven loaves of barley, so that those who cannot partake of Christ as purest bread of wheat because they are of beastly nature and do not yet live spiritually (λογικῶς) will partake of him as barley bread." Guéraud-Nautin, 198 f.; ACW 54, 40.

Upper Room to dine with Christ. There are always two stories in Origen's hermeneutical "building." Where there is no motival polarity to generate "levels of mystery," Origen creates it.

To read the Pascha simutaneously as interactive process with biblical text and as spiritual paradigm, Origen must first remove the established reading of Ex 12 as a keyed passion narrative. This he does at the very beginning of his paschal treatise:

> Before beginning a word-for-word exegesis of the Passover, a few words about the mere name of the Passover are in order. Most of the brethren, indeed perhaps all, think that the Passover takes its name from the passion of the Savior. Among the Hebrews, however, the real name of this feast is not πάσχα but φάς – the three letters of 'φάς' and the rough breathing, which is much stronger with them than it is with us, constituting the name of this feast which means "passage" (διάβασις). For since it is on this feast that the people come out of Egypt, it is thus called 'φάς', that is, "passage."[152]

This semicorrect derivation of פסח dispenses with the folk etymology linking Pascha to Passion, which, as Origen points out, is all but universal in his day. Yet the main function of this philological note is to enable him to adopt wholesale the διάβασις of Philo, who has now travelled with Origen to Caesarea to enter Christian thought in a more decisive way. Later in his treatise, Origen returns to deconstructing the Pascha-Passion equation by pointing out that mimesis in such a reading is inconsistent. Some of the roles have been improperly assigned:

> ...the lamb (πρόβατον) is sacrificed by the saints or the Nazirites, while the Savior is sacrificed by criminals and sinners. And if the Passover lamb is sacrificed by saints, and if the Apostle has said, *For Christ, our paschal lamb, has been sacrificed* [1 Cor 5.7], then Christ is sacrificed according to the type of the Passover, but not by the saints, and thus the Passover is indeed a type of Christ, but not of his passion. It is necessary for us to sacrifice the true lamb – if we have been ordained priests, or like priests have offered sacrifice – and it is necessary for us to cook and eat its flesh. But if this does not take place in the passion of the Savior, then the antitype of the Passover is not his suffering, rather the Passover becomes the type of Christ himself sacrificed for us. For each one of us first *takes* the lamb, then dedicates it, then sacrifices it, and thus after roasting it, eats it and after eating it *leaves nothing until the morning*, and then celebrates the *feast of unleavened bread,*

---

[152] Origen, PP 1.1-18, Guéraud-Nautin, 154; trans. Daly, ACW 54, 27.

after having come out of Egypt. To show that the Passover is something spiritual and not this sensible Passover, he himself says, *Unless you eat my flesh and drink my blood, you have no life in you.* [Jn 6.53] Are we then to eat his flesh and drink his blood in a physical manner? But if this is said spiritually, then the Passover is spiritual, not physical.[153]

Here, the "scandal of the eucharist" in Jn 6 has been resolved as in Clement toward a "logocentric" understanding. Yet the kerygmatic intent of the Fourth Gospel is maintained: the object of "eating" is still profoundly christological, a sacrament whose *realia* are words. As Origen continues, each verse in Ex 12 becomes a paradigm of moral and spiritual perfection, either directly applied to the believer or by first showing such perfection in Christ, as Origen indicates, the antitype of Pascha not being the passion, but Christ himself. The irony here is that Origen interprets Paul's Pascha (lamb) = Christ with strict literalness toward the text of Ex 12, though not its rituals. Each link of imagery is supported by one or more verses to yield a narrative that seems to spin out effortlessly from the scriptures. The narrative is both method and result of that sort of Gnostic reading Barnabas was so delighted to have discovered, now in the hands of a consummate master.

2. The Third Pascha: Commentary on John

Origen's rise of the soul is moral perfection in the present and resurrection in the future, a systematic interpretation more than reminiscent of Heracleon and the *Gospel of Philip*, where the same allegorical tools used by earlier authors to shape OT narrative into kerygmatic and ritual narrative are now applied to NT texts. The only difference lies in the target narrative: Origen does not remythologize ritual texts toward a Valentinian "bridal chamber," but to a narrative of spiritual perfection of his own construction. With Origen, however, the relationship of this narrative to biblical text is never a matter of just attaching motifs from the one to the structure of the other, but always an interaction with the text itself. The most detailed presentation of this hermeneutic occurs in Origen's *Commentary on John*:

> Nevertheless, this aforementioned prophecy about the lamb [Ex 12.3-10] ought to be our nourishment only during the night of the darkness in life. For, of that food which is thus useful to us only in the present, we are not

---

[153] Origen, PP 12.25-13.35, Guéraud-Nautin, 176 f.; trans. Daly, ACW 54, 34 f.

to leave anything over until the dawn of the day that follows this life. For the night having passed and the day after these things having arrived, we have the unleavened bread that is entirely free of the old earthly leaven. We eat this, and it will be useful to us until that is given which comes after the unleavened bread, namely the manna, the food of angels [cf. Ψ77(78).25] rather than of mortals…

This, then, is the way in which we would summarize the meaning of Christ sacrificed as our Pascha [1 Cor 5.7], in harmony with what the gospel says about the lamb.

For it is not to be thought that the historical events are types of historical events nor that corporeal things typify corporeal things; rather the corporeal things are types of spiritual realities and the historical events represent ideal realities.

Raising our minds to the third Pascha, which will be celebrated among myriads of angels in the most perfect festivity [cf. Heb 12.22] and with the happiest exodus, is not necessary at this time, especially since we have spoken more fully and longer than the text required.[154]

Origen embraces Ex 12, 1 Cor 5.7, Jn 6, and the Syn meal accounts into one overarching narrative about encountering the Word through holy words. To accomplish this, however, GPhil's three-phase *image-image-reality* variation of the older two-phase *shadow-reality*, which Origen decidedly negates, has become a single-phase *corporeal-historical/spiritual-ideal* that can be applied to both testaments without distinction. This new construct moves the entire enterprise completely out of the sphere of proof-texting and insures both the inexhaustible transcendence of the texts and the generation of a new set of mimetic narratives.

To reach this new level of interpretation, Origen first makes a distinction between "the Pesach of the Lord" and the "Pascha of the Jews" of Jn 2.13:

It should be stated that in the Law, "your Pascha" [i.e., the Jews] is never said, but rather, in what we have cited, one time "the Pascha" without any other addition, and three times "the Pascha of the Lord."[155]

This is typically Origen. But his next enabling move is the standard tactic for erasing the historical meaning of Ex 12:

---

[154] Origen, Commentary on John 10.18.108-111, SC 157, 446-452. Trans. alt. from CQL 38, 54.
[155] Origen, Comm. in John, 10.73, SC 157, 1970, 428; CQL 38.

In order to admit our explanation of the difference between "the Pascha of the Lord" and "the Pascha of the Jews," we look at what is written in Isaiah: "I cannot endure your new moons, your sabbaths, your Great Day; my spirit hates your fasts, your sabbath rest, your new moons and your feasts." [Isa 1.13-14 LXX]

Removing Judaic rituals and celebrants is the only purpose of these classic Isaian verses, just as Origen removes the typological reading by showing its lack of mimetic fit:

> Concerning the word of the Apostle, "Our Pascha, Christ, has been sacrificed," one meets first of all with the following difficulty: if the lamb of the Jews is the figure for the sacrifice of Christ, it would be necessary that they sacrifice but one single lamb and not many, just as there is one Christ, but since many lambs are sacrificed, one would have to find, according to the figure, many Christs sacrificed.[156]

To argue that "eating the Lamb" and reading scripture are identical actions, Origen has to remove historical, christological, and eucharistic readings of Ex 12. Yet in his later Exodus sermons, this step is no longer taken. A different role and a different geography of both the rhetorical and historical kind – Origen as teacher in Alexandria versus Origen as presbyter in Caesarea – are responsible for the return to more traditional motifs.

3. Commentary on Matthew

When in one of his last commentaries Origen turns unequivocally to paschal rites, the modern reader is immediately confronted with yet another history versus rhetoric dilemma, compounded by the transfer of polemic from one address to another before and after Origen.

> But on the first day of Unleavened Bread the disciples came to Jesus and asked him, "Where do you wish that we prepare the Passover for you? But Jesus said, "Go into the city to someone and say to him, etc." [Mt 26.17-19].

> In Mark, however, it is written thus, "And on the first day of Unleavened Bread, as the Passover lamb was slain, his disciples said to him, 'Where do you wish for us to go to prepare for you, that you may eat the Passover?' [Mk 14.12-15 *cited in full*] ...

---

[156] Origen, Comm. in John, 10.92, SC 157, 439; CQL 38.

Accordingly, someone inexperienced will perhaps fall into Ebionism and, since Jesus of course personally celebrated the Passover according to Jewish custom as well as the first day of Unleavened Bread and the Passover, demand that it is proper that we also, in imitation of Christ, do likewise. This person is not considering that Jesus, who came as "the fullness of time" [Gal 4.4f], was sent, came "from woman," "came under the Law" not to have those who were under the Law remain under the Law, but rather to lead them out of the Law. If he then came to lead those under the Law out of it, how much less fitting is it then for those who were before outside the Law to enter into it?[157]

Unlike many earlier exegetes who ignore the implications of the Pesach frame of the supper, Origen has too much respect for the text to do so. He is also writing a commentary on a canonical gospel where he cannot play the "historicity" of John against Matthew. Yet this is as far as Origen is prepared to go: he acknowledges the "historical" sense *in the text*, but the moment he touches the paschal frame, he must unleash a series of Pauline antinomian phrases to negate any meaning it might have for Christian ritual. Pesach is a "Jewish custom" with only an historic meaning in the gospel accounts, a law negated by grace.

Is Origen's "falling into Ebionism" a purely hypothetical case of literal interpretation, an historical reminiscence of first century conflicts reverberating throughout the NT, or an echo of some current debate over paschal observance? If the latter, then whose reading of Ex 12 and the passion narratives is the target? Unless Origen is being extremely polite and clothing what is usually a naked anti-Judaic argument in an "Ebionite" Jewish Christian disguise, the most "historical" choice would be the Ebionites themselves. A search for this history in writers before and after Nicaea, however, is immediately confronted with more rhetoric, already beginning with the name. For Hippolytus and Tertullian,[158] a non-existent "Ebion" is the founder of the sect. While this may violate modern rules of historiography, writers who choose this strategy are merely transferring a convention of civic rhetoric to religion. "Various authors," Josephus writes, "have attempted to sully the reputations of nations and of the most illustrious cities, and to revile their forms of government."[159]

---

[157] Origen, Comm. Mt. ser. 79, GCS 38, 188 f.
[158] Cf. Hippolytus, Haer. 7.35.1; Tertullian, De carn. Chr. 14; 18.24; De virg. vel 6; Praes 10.33.
[159] Josephus, Contra Apionem 1(24)220, LCL 186, 252 f.

As much as the praise of a city or ruler was a standard exercise for a rhetorician's skill, so too its "shadow," as Quintillian instructs:

> We also hate those who have fathered evil. Founders of cities incur disrepute if they have produced a people pernicious to others, as for example the originator of the Jewish superstition.[160]

Epiphanius enriches the rhetoric against "Ebion" by passing along Irenaeus' story of John's confrontation in the bath, substituting this mythical originator of a Jewish (-Christian) "superstition" for Cerinthus.[161] The lengthy chapter in Epiphanius' *Panarion* does give some concrete information, but it is a composite of Hippolytus, Irenaeus, the Pseudo-Clementine literature and Eusebius as well as legend, hearsay, and personal recollection.[162] The Ebionites observe the Sabbath, circumcision, strict separation from Gentiles, and other Judaic practices, especially water purification rites (Pan 30.2.1-2). The "Ebionites" consider a redaction of Matthew or some Syn-type gospel as canon. This work began with the Jordan narrative, at which a great light appeared (30.13.6 f.). They baptize and celebrate a eucharist with water and unleavened bread (30.16.1). Except for the citation of an "Ebionite" gospel and the detail about diet and sacramental elements, all of this is already contained in Irenaeus' AH at 1.26.2. The shape of an "Ebionite" story was thus long set before it reaches Epiphanius.

Irenaeus also lies behind Origen's statement in *Contra Celsum* that there are Jewish Christians who do not hold to the doctrine of the virgin birth.[163] While Origen does not choose to turn "Ebion" into a sect leader, he does rhetorically exploit the etymology of the name. The "Ebionites" are "poor in spirit," "in faith," and "poor"[164] because of their literal, not spiritual, interpretation of the Law. This is the most important cue for Origen's use of the term in his commentary. What Origen does not tell us anywhere is anything historical about the Ebionites, because anti-Jewish-Christian rhetoric is as conventionalized as its anti-Judaic sibling.

Especially in Epiphanius, much of this rhetoric centers on the Pascha. To refute his own Jewish Christian composite, Epiphanius contrasts

---

[160] Quintillian, Training of an Orator 3.7.21, ET: Whittaker, Molly, Jews and Christians: Graeco-Roman Views, CCWJCW 6, 1984, 120.
[161] Pan 30.24.1-5.
[162] NHMS 36, 119, n. 1.
[163] Contra Celsum 5.61.
[164] Spirit: De princ 4.3.8, GCS 5, 334; faith: In Mat, 11.12, GCS 10, 513.

Ebionite vegetarianism with the Pesach meal celebrated – with lamb – by Jesus and the disciples, a reading from the *Didascalia* Epiphanius now polemicizes. To match their dietary practice, the Ebionite gospel had altered Jesus' desire to eat the Pascha into a surprised question, "Have I desired meat with desire, to eat this Pascha with you?"[165] In the same way, the "Ebionites" hold up Christ's circumcision as a model for their own practice (30.26.1), a type of ritual mimesis Epiphanius deconstructs (30.33.3-34.3). Immediately before the section on the "Ebionites," Epiphanius had used the standard argument from the now impossible pilgrimage feasts enjoined at Ex 23.14-17 (Justin, et. al.) against the "Nazoreans," another Jewish Christian composite, but localized not in southern Palestine like the Ebionites, but Beroea and Pella (29.7.7). These are the Jewish Christians with whom Jerome is familiar (Vir. ill. 11.3). One suspects that hidden among all this transferred rhetoric is some true history, which may, however, ultimately reduce to geographic notes.

While Epiphanius offers no great assistance in historically identifying Jewish Christian group(s) or their paschal practice, his rhetoric does point to a particular kind of mimesis that has transformed Lk 22.15 into an admonition not to eat meat and sees a model for imitation in the Jewish identity, i.e., circumcision, of Jesus of Nazareth. Adopting this hermeneutic is what Origen is calling "falling into Ebionism." This raw (Origen) or carnal (Justin) literalism is compounded by acting out the hermeneutic in a paschal liturgy.

As Nicaean debate will understand Origen's comment, anyone who uses the Syn meal narrative in an aetiological sense – that Jesus ate the Pascha – has not only fallen into "Ebionism," but celebrates Pascha "with the Jews." Though no extant Asian writer uses the meal narrative as story of origins, this passage can be construed to hit both Asian and Syrian targets, denying mimesis of time (14 Nisan) or action (Syrian aetiology). Yet here, Origen is perfectly consistent with his other readings of paschal texts: he is primarily concerned with the text as text, not a mimetic interpretation in the liturgy. This does not mean that others before or after Origen may not find a more specific target. Hippolytus had already used the same Galatians-Romans construct aimed at the Quartadecimans of Asia Minor, while the textual argument appears in an Hippolytan fragment against an unnamed opponent who uses the

---

[165] Pan 30.22.4, GCS 25, 363.

meal narrative as paschal aetiology. Eusebius will use the same "gospel history versus liturgical mimesis" against Syrian readings of the paschal meal.

VI. Observations

The Alexandrian διάβασις provides a vocabulary a variety of authors may speak with or without paschal language as easily as it may be spoken with or without reference to ritual. Only for Origen is this vocabulary antithetical to Asian or Syrian "Ebionite" readings. The Asian reading exhausts the transcendence of Ex 12 as holy text by equating it with historical events; an "Ebionite" reading compounds such literalism by reading either institution narrative – Ex 12 or Syn meal – as paschal rubric. For Origen's pupil's, however, it is a simple matter to combine Alexandrian tropology with Asian typology, though often at considerable loss.

In his interaction with paschal texts, Origen shows an ever increasing reception of a Philonian model, at the same time synthesizing it with an overarching theology of the Word that inspired volumes of painstaking exegetical and textual work. Depending upon rhetorical situation and genre, this development takes two turns: a homily spoken in the liturgy incorporating more traditional motifs, or a biblical commentary meant to reproduce Origen's reading of scripture in and for his readers. As presbyter in Caesarea, Origen is less strident about the tertiary role of liturgy and sacraments than Clement, but both agree that the transcendence of ritual is limited: they point to, but do not reach the divine. The locus of divine διάβασις is not rite, but reading. The paschal meal conveys Origen's encounter with scripture to his readers as sacramental action: partaking of the Logos is the word-sacrament in perfect harmony with the bread-and-wine-sacrament:

> This bread and wine can be interpreted by those who keep to the literal sense as the eucharist is generally understood; for those who have learned to listen more deeply, these words [i.e., "take and eat"] are interpreted according to the more divine promise of the Logos concerning the food of truth.[166]

---

[166] Mat. ser. 85, GCS 38, 196.

Origen's move to preacher and presider signs the same move of the Alexandrian philosophical Pascha to a liturgical one, but only as an auxiliary narrative about rite. Though later mystagogical catechesis elevates this narrative to a canonical standard, its rhetorical value in paschal disputes was minuscule. This is because at its heart, Origen's paschal theology was not designed for conflict, or even for social discourse of any kind, but for the individual reader alone with the Word and Origen's words about it. At Nicaea, Alexandrians will find Philo's cosmic harmony and images of vernal Creation far more conducive to their rhetorical purpose – inculcating the equinoctial rule – than any of Origen's paschal readings.

In first century Corinth, conflict marks the first liturgical appropriation of paschal motifs from Philo and Wisdom traditions. Far from being a catechetical mainstay, the Red Sea typology disappears, except for an oblique reference in Tertullian, until Origen revives it as spiritual process. Though in Corinth the poles between the eternity of the spirit and the kairos of history may have been further apart, the dangers of timeless spiritualization and the inherent elitism of "Gnostic" readings of Pascha and Exodus, both battled by Paul, are a constant of the Alexandrian tradition until its synthesis with the more kerygmatic (but etymologically deficient) Asian reading.

This synthesis is a move not taken in the EpAp, where the content of the paschal feast is the paradigmatic ascension of Christ, but not expressed in the language of Pesach or the passage through the Red Sea. Instead, the paschal liturgy itself becomes a self-fulfilling type. The disciple's miraculous escape through the δύναμις of Christ will lead him to a waiting community, a paschal vigil, and an agape feast, a prediction of the risen Lord that also founds the feast in explicit command. Pascha is to be observed until his return, the Second Advent to take place during the Fifty Days. Pascha is a feast of presence, epiphany, and passage to heavenly rest, but neither baptism nor the death of Christ, and only obliquely the eucharist, are carried by paschal themes. The far more visible line of tradition from Philo through Clement and Origen all the way to Luther thus contrasts to two isolated points where the Alexandrian rite of celestial passage was already firmly attached to ritual acts, but which produce no audible echo in extant literature.

The *Epistula's* creative reading of NT narrative material as liturgical aetiology points first to the Gnostics the author wishes to combat, but it also suggests the hallmark of the Syrian paschal tradition, which reads not Acts 12 as a founding narrative for the paschal feast, but a much more obvious choice, the Syn institution of the supper. This mimetic reading of the NT as it moves from its earliest beginnings in Ignatius of Antioch to the conflict at the Council of Nicaea is the next journey through the rhetorical beginnings of Pascha.

D. Imitating the Narrative:
The Beginnings of the Syrian Tradition

I. Images of Mimesis: Ignatius, Acts of Thomas, Tatian

Writing congregations in Asia Minor on his way to execution in Rome, Ignatius of Antioch pleads for ordered community life in an image drawn from the liturgy – the bishop surrounded by presbyters, deacons, and the faithful around the eucharistic table:

> In a similar way, all should respect the deacons as Jesus Christ, just so the bishop as a type of the Father, the presbyters like the council of God and the college of apostles. Without these there can be no speaking of the church.[1]

Since Ignatius knows his letters will be read in a full assembly, he gives his hearers an immediately accessible symbol of unity: the liturgy *as it is being celebrated* becomes an image of the oneness and the order of the church. From the bishop as head of the local church and its chief sacramental minister to the heretics who exclude themselves from the celebration,[2] Ignatius' entire ecclesiology flows from the same image.

By the time it reaches the Syrian *Didascalia*, the image has lost some of its freshness, but the bishop is still an "imitator of Christ" whose authority Ignatius' letters have helped secure. A more differentiated communal organization must also be drawn into the image:

> [The bishop] is a servant of the word and mediator, but to you a teacher, and your father after God, who has begotten you through the water…But let him be honored by you as God (is), because the bishop sits for you in the place of God Almighty. But the deacon stands in the place of Christ, and you should love him. The deaconess, however, shall be honored by you in the place of the Holy Spirit. But the presbyters shall be to you in the likeness of the apostles, and the orphans and the widows shall be reckoned by you in the likeness of the altar.[3]

---

[1] Tral 3.1. SUC 1, 174 f. Ignatius also receives the bishop as "exemplar" of the community's love. Cf. Eph 5.1, 6.1; Mag 3.1-2, 6.1, 7.1, 13.2; Phild 7.2, Smyr 8.1.

[2] Bishop, Mag 4,7.1; Trall 2.2, 7.2; Smyr 8.1, 9.1; Poly 4.1, "heretics", Mag 4, 7.1; Smyr 7.1.

[3] DA 10, CSCO 408, 100.5-15. The altar receives gifts.

Ignatius is also not beyond borrowing images from Judaic and Hellenic worship. After introducing at IgnEph 9.2 a temple allegory echoing "Paul's" earlier letter to the same community, Ignatius extends it with a catalogue of Hellenic ritual terms[4] and a Christian coining of his own:

> You are all companions on the way (σύνοδοι), God-bearers (θεοφόροι), temple-bearers (ναοφόροι), *Christ-bearers* (χριστοφόροι), bearers of the holy (ἁγιοφοῖοι), in every way made beautiful with the commandments of Jesus Christ.[5]

Underscoring the fellowship inherent in the word σύνοδοι, Ignatius makes a wordplay on his second name *Theophoros*, but he has no words like the later *thurifer, lucifer,* or *crucifer* to draw upon. Christian worship has not yet been permitted an extension into public space, just as the author of Rev writing some of the same communities had had to transfer the liturgy to heavenly visions to explore its breadth.

In his letter to the Romans, Ignatius returns to an image of the Christian liturgy. Concerned that through connections and judicious application of funds[6] the Roman congregation might seek to hinder his execution, he writes:

> [2.1] ...For if you are silent about me, then I will be a word of God; if you, however, love my flesh, I will merely be a sound (φωνή). [2.2] Allow me nothing but to be sacrificed to God, as long as an altar (θυσιαστήριον) has been prepared, so that you may form in love a choir and may praise the Father in Christ Jesus, because God has counted the Bishop of Syria worthy to be in the land of the sun's setting, summoned by rising. It is beautiful to set [as the sun] from this world to God so that I may rise to him.[7]

A few paragraphs later, this image strains the limits of the bearable:

> [4.1]I am writing all the churches and lay it upon them all that I am glad to die for God, if you will otherwise not hinder it. I call to you, do not wish me untimely good will. Let me be fodder for the beasts, through whom it is possible to attain to God (θεοῦ ἐπιτυχεῖν).[8] I am God's wheat, and

---

[4] Perhaps from processions of the Ephesian Artemis cult, so Fischer, SUC 1, 149, n. 37. There were many "-φόροι" named for duties or clothing. Burkert, Mysterien, 39-43.
[5] SUC 1, 148.
[6] Rom 1.1-2.
[7] SUC 1, 184 f.
[8] A favored expression for the goal of martyrdom. Cf. Eph 12.2; Mag 14; Trall 12.2, 13.3; Rom 1.2, 2.1; 4.1, 9.2; Poly 2.3, 7.1

through the teeth of beasts I will be ground up, so that I will be found as pure (or fine) bread for Christ.[9]

In the *Didache* wheat is a figure for the integrity of the assembled body gathered into the Kingdom as scattered grain becomes bread. This is also Ignatius' intention,[10] but first he reverses the metaphor to one of physical disintegration. Yet however drastic the image, Ignatius presents the Romans with the same picture of the liturgy he draws in other letters. Forming a choir, the Romans are to sing praises at Ignatius' death, for which an altar has been prepared. If the Romans attempt to hinder his martyrdom, the bishop whose liturgical role has been a "servant of the word" will become a mere sound. Instead, Ignatius is begging for silence, and for the Romans to offer him up as the eucharistic element in this gruesome, but very real, liturgy. This is so that Ignatius may more deeply become a disciple by imitating the death of Christ:

> [6.3] Allow me to be an imitator of the suffering of my God (μιμητὴν τοῦ πάθους τοῦ θεοῦ μου). If anyone bears him within himself, he will understand what I wish and sympathize with me because he understands my sense of urgency...

> [7.2] ...For I am writing to you as one who lives and yearns in love for death. My love is crucified and there is no fire in me that looks for nourishment in material things. Yet living water that speaks is in me that says to me inwardly: 'Come before the Father.' [7.3] I have no joy in transitory food or the pleasures of this life. I wish for God's bread, that is the flesh of Jesus Christ, who came from the seed of David, and as drink I wish for his blood, that is undying love. (*or both taken together as antecedent,* the undying agape meal.)[11]

In Ignatius' rubrics, this liturgy of the arena will move him beyond earthly fire and water into the realm of the spirit: an apotheosis in imitation of Christ's sufferings[12] and victorious ascension spoken through the meal that remembers.

---

[9] SUC 1, 186 f.

[10] Cf. Iren. AH 5.28.4. Believers (wheat) are gathered, trials thresh and grind them, then they are kneaded with the Word and baked for a royal banquet. Ignatius then cited without name.

[11] IgnRom 6.3, 7.2 f. SUC 1, 189-191.

[12] See Swartley, W. M., The Imitatio Christi in the Ignatian Letters, VigChr 27, 1979, 81-103; and an older study, Preiss, Th., La mystique de l'imitation du Christ et de l'unité chez Ignace d'Antioche, RHPhR 18, 1938, 197-241, with which Swartley takes issue.

Around the turn of the third century, the East Syrian author of the *Acts of Thomas* (ATh) follows earlier martyria in translating Ignatius' mystical imitation into its literary counterpart. After an adventurous mission to the East where Thomas converts and baptizes an Indian king, raises the dead, and wins converts for the celibate life, the imprisoned apostle is about to be martyred. Yet in each of these episodes, the rites of initiation serve as an important element of narrative structure. Prayers are spoken, water blessed, people are anointed, baptized, and fed. Epiphanies of angels, heavenly voices, and even Jesus himself bathe the scenes in supernal light. With major theological motifs expressed in image, ritual event becomes narration:

> And after they had been baptized and had come up, he brought bread and the mingled cup; and spoke a blessing over it and said: Your holy body, crucified for us, we eat, and your blood, poured out for us for salvation, we drink; may your body become for us life and your blood forgiveness of sins. Let your body be to us for life, and your blood for the forgiveness of sins. For the gall, which you drank for us, may the bitterness of the Enemy be taken away from us. For the vinegar that you drank for us, may our weakness be strengthened. For the spittle you received for us, let us receive your perfect life. That you took for us a crown of thorns, let an unfading crown encircle us who loved him. For the linen in which you were wrapped, may we be girded with your victorious strength. And because you were buried in a new sepulcher for our mortality, let us too receive converse with you in heaven. And as you arose, let us be raised, and let us stand before you at the judgment of truth. And he broke the eucharist, and gave to Vizan and Tertia, and to Manashar and Sifur and Mygdonia and to the wife and daughter of Sifur and said, "Let this eucharist be to you for life and rest and joy and health, and for the healing of your souls and bodies." And they said, "Amen." And a voice was heard saying to them "Yea and amen." And when they heard this voice, they fell on their faces. And again the voice was heard saying, "Be not afraid, but only believe."[13]

Unlike four earlier eucharistic prayers little more than extended invocations of the Holy Spirit,[14] this prayer not only proclaims the death of Christ, but narrates the passion in a highly rhetorical *commercium*. This is a clue that the author has more in mind than imitating an anaphora

---

[13] ATh 158. Slightly altered from Klijn, NT.S 5, 149 f.
[14] Cf. ATh 26, 29, 49, 121. Rouwhorst, Gerard, La célébration de l'eucharistie selon les Actes de Thomas, in Omnes Circumadstantes (FS Wegman), Kampen 1990, 51-77.

in common use.[15] Another is the same repetition of opposites that the author uses outside a liturgical setting.[16] With this simple technique, the author has crafted a eucharistic prayer for the final baptismal liturgy before the apostle's death. The object of imitation is the Syn meal rite and the Joh passion: Thomas "the twin" celebrates bath and meal just as Jesus institutes the supper before his crucifixion and washes the feet of his disciples.[17] Even if this final episode is not anchored to a specific time, ATh is speaking paschal language.

Roughly contemporary with ATh, Tatian's lost *Diatessaron* places this same liturgical fullness into the gospel text. The Joh footwashing and farewell discourses are joined with the Syn meal into a single ritual event in the paschal night.[18] In his only extant work, the *Oratio ad Graecos*, Tatian presents a theology of mimesis as baptismal rebirth:

> For as from one torch many fires may be kindled, the light of the first torch not being diminished by lighting many other torches, so the Logos, as it proceeded from the Dynamis of the Father, was not bereft of the Logos. For even I speak and you listen, but as my word goes over to you, I the speaker have not lost the word, but rather when my voice goes forth, it is my intention to order the chaotic substance in you. And in the same way as the Logos begotten in the beginning has himself created our world by fashioning substance, thus I too have been reborn in mimesis of the Logos and made receptive to the truth, improving the disorder of the substance born with me.[19]

Especially in the "twin" motif, H.J.W. Drijvers sees distinct parallels of this mimesis throughout ATh:

> The concept μίμησις means a precise reproduction as the Acts of Thomas says: the born again person and the firstborn of God are twins. The human being becomes immortal and with free will created according to

---

[15] Lietzmann, Hans, Messe und Herrenmahl, AKG 8, ³1955, 247, sees the first line as an actual prayer; Schille, Gottfried, Das Leiden des Herrn, ZThK, 52, 1955, 161-205, sees the prayer as lifted whole from the liturgy.

[16] "That marriage feast you see, how it passed away and is gone; but this marriage feast shall never pass away. That was the marriage feast of corruption; this is the marriage feast of life everlasting. ..." ATh 124, Klijn, 132; also ATh 139, Klijn, 139: "You are the son of Mazdai, this king who passes away; and I am the servant of Jesus, the king who abides for ever..." Both passages continue this simple antithesis for some time.

[17] See Rouwhorst, Célébration, 70, n. 37, for connection to Syrian paschal theology.

[18] See below, p. 118.

[19] Tatian, Or. ad Graecos 5.1-3, Goodspeed, 272.

the image of God, loses immortality as he obeyed the firstborn of the angels, Satan, who since then creates folly in the world. The loss of immortality occurs because the human being loses the stronger or higher Pneuma, the image and likeness of God.[20]

Thomas as Jesus' twin and Jesus' appearing disguised as Thomas at important turns of the plot is this mimetic theology turned to narrative. These images intertwining liturgical action, imitation of the suffering Christ or the immutable image of God suggest that mimesis is a category with many facets in writers from both eastern and western Syrian traditions. Many are shared with other literature of the second and third centuries, especially from Asia Minor. In the *Martyrdom of Polycarp*,[21] the aged Bishop of Smyrna predicts his own passion, he is betrayed and captured on a Friday, an interrogating officer is named "Herod," Polycarp rides toward the arena on a donkey, he stumbles once on the way, etc.[22] At his execution, Polycarp "put his hands behind him and let himself be bound like a ram from a large herd who is designated as a sacrifice, as a pleasing whole offering to God" (14.1). After a prayer of thanksgiving with eucharistic overtones,[23] Polycarp is not killed by the flames, but receives a coup de grâce from a dagger (16.1). In the midst of the flames, however, Polycarp appears "like baking bread, or as gold and silver is purified in the oven" (15). These naive allusions to the passion narrative take Ignatius' understanding of martyrdom and transform it into a *Volksbuch*.

In the same way, restoration of the fallen *imago Dei* is not a motif Tatian has discovered, but already an important concept for Melito, as well as Irenaeus in his recapitulation of creation through the incarnation. Yet as Tatian sees this concept more closely tied to baptismal rebirth, an essential characteristic of Syrian liturgical theology comes

---

[20] NTApo[5] 2, 300.
[21] Comparing the shorter version, Eus. EH 4.15.1-45, Campenhausen (Bearbeitungen und Interpolationen des Polykarpmartyriums, in: Frühzeit, 253-301) and Conzelmann (Bemerkungen zum Martyrdom Polykarps, NAWG[PH], 1978, 41-58) see interpolation. Integrity defended: Barnard, Leslie W., In Defense of Pseudo-Pionius' Account of Saint Polycarp's Martyrdom, in: Kyriakon (FS Quasten) I, 1970,192-204; Dehandschutter, Boudewijn, Martyrium Polycarpi, BETL 52, 1979, and Buschmann, BZNW 70.
[22] See list in Barnard, Defense, 194 f.
[23] Lietzmann sees a lightly edited citation of an anaphora, Ein liturgisches Bruchstück des 2. Jh.s, ZNW 54, 1912, 56-61 (=Kleine Schriften III, TU 47, 43-47).

to light. Addressed to ritual, Drijvers' "precise reproduction" blends rite, mystery, and narrative into a grammar of symbols uniquely Syrian. With narrative material from the NT providing the vocabulary, Tatian's baptismal mimesis of the Logos translates into reading the Jordan baptism as story of origins,[24] while the paschal language of ATh and the *Diatessaron* is still spoken with remarkable fluency by fourth century Syriac writers. When this mimetic language of Christ narrative and Christian rite is spoken more widely as the second century draws to a close, two authors from Syria, Ignatius of Antioch and the Christian Sibyl of Book 7, have long spoken the first words. This new way of speaking about rite, however, does not arise from their influence, but from a direct encounter with the four gospel canon.

II. From Text to Rite: The Beginnings of Mimetic Liturgical Theology

The relationship of Pascha to Ex 12 and the passion narratives is deeply involved in what Hans von Campenhausen calls "the crisis of the OT canon in the third century,"[25] a long standing instability brought to equilibrium only when acceptance of the core NT canon became the identifying mark of the Great Church. As the EpAp has shown, narrative traditions independent or secondary to the Syn-Joh "mainstream" hardly disappear, but in the course of the second century the Christ event gradually becomes fixed into the Christ narrative of the four gospels. The imitation and generous inclusion of NT narrative in the EpAp mark this development as much as obscure it.

While inextricably linked to canon, the relationship between Christian rite and Christ narrative, Christ teaching, or OT typology maintains its own shape throughout the second and third centuries. Authoritatively citing NT narrative as history, doctrine, or moral example moves along one level of canonical formation. Connecting biblical passages to Christian rite – whether as typological proof, anamnesis of specific events in the life of Jesus, or as stories of origins – is quite another. The distinction may be as subtle, and decisive, as the difference between a story that tells of a holy event and a story that in itself is holy.

---

[24] Winkler, Gabriele, Zur frühchristlichen Tauftradition in Syrien und Armenien unter Einbezug der Taufe Jesu. OkSt 27, 1978, 281-306.

[25] Title of third chapter of Entstehung der christlichen Bibel, 76-122.

This distinction could still be felt at the beginning of the third century, but would soon disappear. The NT canon is virtually identical for Irenaeus, Hippolytus, and Tertullian, but the two younger writers ritualize narrative far more readily than the older Irenaeus, for whom NT narrative traditions are rarely interpreted beyond historical event. For the next generation, liturgical mimesis addressed to stories about Jesus is becoming a standard theological language, but one with two dialects: one concerned with aetiology, the other with attaching Christ narrative to rite as proclamation.

Like spoken languages, the lines between these two dialects could be quite fluid, but Tertullian can still contrast them to make rhetorical points. Searching the passion narrative for passages with a mimetic fit for baptism during the paschal season, Tertullian produces the following results:

> The Pascha affords a most solemn day for baptism, since the passion of the Lord, in which we are baptized, was at that time accomplished. And it is not inappropriate to see a figure [Nec incongruenter ad figuram interpretabitur] in the fact that when the Lord was about to keep his last Pascha, he said to the disciples he sent to prepare for it, "You will meet a man carrying water." With the sign of water he showed them the place for celebrating the Pascha.

> After this, the Pentecost is an extremely happy season for conferring baptism, because the Lord's resurrection was celebrated among the disciples, the grace of the Holy Spirit was inaugurated and the hope in the Lord's coming indicated, because it was then, when he had been taken back into heaven, that angels told the apostles that he would come exactly as he had gone up to heaven – meaning, of course, during the Pentecost. Moreover, when Jeremiah says, "And I will gather them from the farthest parts of the earth on the festal day of the Pascha" (Jer 38.8 LXX), he also means to say, "the day of Pentecost," which is properly the festal day. For that matter, every day is the Lord's; every hour and every time is suitable for baptism. If there is a question of solemnity, it has nothing to do with the grace.[26]

Tertullian has found the man bearing water who shows the disciples where to prepare for the meal (Mk 14.13, Lk 22.10). It is appropriate – but not a fixed rule – to inaugurate the festival with the sign of water, chiefly because such "congruence" is capable of generating elegantly

---

[26] De bapt. 19.1-3, CCSL 1, 293 f.

kerygmatic language about rite. Cross, resurrection, and Second Advent are the answers to a simple question of timing, and time itself becomes grace.

Quite inelegant, however, is the "congruence" between the water-bearing man and baptism. Could this hastily found type reflect an innovation requiring a new connection to scripture: a liturgy on Friday focussing on the passion narrative in addition to the older vigil? Since there is no other indication in Tertullian's writings that early third century Carthage liturgically marked the Friday before Pascha other than with a fast, this mimetic reading does not reflect a new liturgy but only the underlying construct that will produce it.[27] All that is needed is to synchronize paschal observance with gospel narrative – more smoothly than Tertullian – while marking the fastday with communal worship.

Tertullian's typology from Jeremiah is of no less interest. This use of Jer 31.8 (LXX 38.8) is a record of sorts: the only case I know where a single OT verse is actualized *twice* toward ritual. The Masoretic text reads:

> See, I am going to bring them from the land of the north, and gather them from the farthest parts of the earth, among them the blind and *the lame*, those with child and those in labor, together; a great company, they shall return here.

LXX reads for "lame," which has the same consonants פסח, "[ἐν ἑορτῇ] φάσεχ," yielding:

> I will bring them together from the ends of the earth on the festival of Pascha. And you will give birth to a great people, and they shall return here.

The thematic cluster in this text of פסח, gathering, and birth formed a Pesach narrative in the minds of the translators, aided by the consonantal text: an almost identical row of consonants, with the common substitution of ר for ד and the transposition of one ו and ע. If this reading first emerged in the LXX, which is strongly suggested by comparison to other early translations,[28] it is further proof of the great power of the Pesach festival to connect the Egyptian Diaspora ritually to Jerusalem.

In Tertullian's reading, not only is he explicit that these verses are "figures," he is equally explicit that they are not founding narratives, i.e.,

---

[27] Huber, Passa, 150-152.
[28] See Füglister, Notker, Die Heilsbedeutung des Pascha, SANT 8, 1963, 33.

scriptural rubrics. The paschal season only adds solemnity; there is no difference in grace. Mimesis is kerygmatic, not aetiological: the church does not baptize *because* in two Syn gospels there was a man carrying water, it is "appropriate" to do so because Tertullian can find a certain "congruence."

Somewhat later, with Montanist practices under attack by the greater church, the real reason behind ritual customs, Tertullian writes in *De corona*, is "tradition":

> When we are going to enter the water, but a little before, in the presence of the congregation and under the hand of the president, we solemnly profess that we disown the devil, and his pomp, and his angels. Then we are thrice immersed, making a somewhat ampler pledge than the Lord has appointed in the gospel. Then, when we are taken up (i.e., as new-born children), we first of all taste of a mixture of milk and honey, and from that day we refrain from the daily bath for a whole week. We take also, in congregations before daybreak, and from the hand of none but the presiders, the sacrament of the eucharist, which the Lord both commanded to be eaten at meal-times[29] and enjoined to be taken by all alike. As often as the anniversary comes around, we make offerings for the dead as birthday honors. We count fasting or kneeling in worship on the Lord's day to be unlawful. We rejoice in the same privilege also from Pascha to the Fiftieth Day. We feel pained should any wine or bread, even though our own,[30] be cast upon the ground. At every forward step and movement, at every going in and out, when we put on our clothes and shoes, when we bathe, when we sit at table, when we light the lamps, on couch or chair, in all the ordinary actions of daily life, we trace upon the forehead the sign. If, for these and other such rules, you insist upon having positive scriptural injunction, you will find none. Tradition will be held forth to you as the originator of them, custom as their strengthener, and faith as their observer. That reason will support tradition, and custom faith, you will either yourself perceive, or learn from someone who has.[31]

The point of Tertullian's detailed description is that none of these practices has scriptural precedence, except for the meal rite and the creed "more ample" than that in the NT, compared with the Great Commission or the already "amplified" Western (D) text of Philip's baptism

---

[29] "…as often as you do this…," i.e., eat.

[30] i.e., brought as offering, from which the elements for the eucharistic meal were chosen.

[31] Tertullian, *De corona* 3.2-4.1, CCSL 2, 1042 f.

of the Ethiopian eunuch.[32] Mimesis of NT narrative is a harmonious kerygma, yielding no stories of origins except for "unamplified" baptism and clearly commanded eucharist. But there were those who did not speak the language of figures, but direct imitation of scriptural models, and some of them had spoken strongly against Montanist liturgical "innovations."[33]

Even though Tertullian employs the same method in his baptismal types, the unbridled ritualization of biblical narrative in the Syrian *Didascalia*, which reduces the passion account to a midrash on prescriptions for the paschal fast, would have given him even greater concern. This recension of an original Greek church order not only fails to make any distinction between "grace" and scriptural rubric, but offers its rather bland proof texts in the identical setting as the EpAp: they are the disciples' report of words of the risen Lord spoken on the very day of resurrection. After appearing to the Magdelene "and the other Mary":

> ...then he appeared also to us ourselves. But he said to us, teaching us, "Are you fasting because of me these days, or do I need it that you should afflict yourselves?"[34]

This immediate application of the cultic eraser Isa 58.3[35] as *ipsissima verba* is a clue that "grace" will not be a major feature of this special revelation. The *Didascalia's* goal is also not to add "solemnity," but to further an innovation of its own: lengthening the paschal fast all the way to Monday.

There is a more fundamental difference between Tertullian and the Syrian tradition of the *Didascalia*, Ephrem, Aphrahat, and Cyrillonas: how the Syn meal story is read toward the Pascha. Only in Syria does the Syn Pesach frame outline the whole picture of paschal theology. For a moment, even Tertullian can invoke the Pesach meal:

---

[32] Acts 8.37: And Philip said, "If you believe with all your heart, you may." And he replied, "I believe that Jesus Christ is the Son of God." With the doxology of the Lord's Prayer, a rare instance where the liturgy had quite early crept into the NT text.

[33] Cf. Tertullian, De ieiunio 10.1, CCSL 2, 1267.

[34] Didascalia 21, CSCO 408 [Syr 180] (Vööbus) Didascalia II,191.4 f. Hereafter cited vol. no., page and line(s).

[35] Cf., for example, Barn 3.1 ff., SUC 2, 143. "Concerning this he speaks again to them: Why are you fasting for me, says the Lord, hoping that your voice will be heard today in your shouting?... To us he says, Behold, this is the fast that I desire..."

Accordingly he also knew when he whose passion the Law prefigured was to suffer. For among all the Jewish feasts he chose the day of Pascha. In view of this mystery [sacramentum] Moses proclaimed, "It is the Pascha of the Lord." Thus he also showed his feeling, "I have desired with a desire to eat this Pascha with you before I suffer." A fine "destroyer of the Law," who even desired to keep the Pascha! Could it be that he was so fond of Jewish lamb's meat? Was it not rather that he, who was going to be led like a sheep to the sacrifice, and who, like a sheep before the shearer who was not going to open his mouth, desired to fulfill the figure of its saving blood?[36]

Marcion's version of Luke and Paul had excised Lk 22.8, 14 f., thus all reference to Pesach, as well as 1 Cor 5.7.[37] The Marcionite challenge to the OT and the God of Israel has forced Tertullian to show Jesus of Nazareth desiring to perform a Judaic ritual, but it leaves a sour taste. Hardly a neutral expression, "Jewish lamb's meat" immediately wraps the idea of Jesus' eating the meal in absurdity, only to cover it again with the "Asian" exegesis of Ex 12-Isa 53. The Synoptic ambiguity between Pesach frame and eucharistic story may be exploited for strategic advantage, but it must be instantly resolved. This means that when Tertullian mentions the Lord's "last Pascha" in his baptismal typologies, he is similarly reading Synoptic chronology, but thinking Johannine types: Christ suffers on "the day of Pascha."

Outside of the Syrian tradition, the almost instinctive move away from the Pesach meal rite takes on the character of a mass exodus. Without the warning of "Ebionism" in his Commentary on Matthew or the anti-Judaic arguments of other authors, Origen's connection of eucharist and Pascha in his Exodus homily is a unique text, but remains exclusively on the textual level. Yet the *Didascalia* not only assumes the meal narrative as story of origins for paschal observance, but rearranges gospel sequence so that the meal is held not on Thursday, but Tuesday night:

> Indeed, while he was yet with us before he suffered, as we were eating the Passover with him, he said to us: "Today, in this night, one of you will betray me." [CSCO 408, 188.21-24]
> Indeed, when we had eaten the Passover on the third day of the week... [189.9 f.]
> "...I ate my Pascha with you, and in the night they seized me." [192.2 f.]

---

[36] Tertullian, Contra Marc. 4.40.1, CCSL 1, 655 f., trans. CQL 95, 92.
[37] Cf. Pan 42.11.6.61 f., 42.11.8.40.13.

For when our Lord and teacher ate the Passover with us, he was delivered up by Judas after that hour, and immediately we began to be grieved because he was taken from us. [196.19-21]

Behind the *Didascalia's* rescheduling of the Pesach meal is the need to recast it as a story of origins for a week of fasting, not the traditional two days. This move would have been unnecessary, even impossible, were the Syn meal story only seen as an aetiology for the eucharist. Part of the tradition the *Didascalia* inherits is not only the narrative link to the betrayal, already witnessed by Paul, but that Jesus *ate* the paschal meal with his disciples.

While Ephrem Syrus maintains the same relationship between OT shadow and NT reality as Tertullian and the "Asian" tradition, the Pesach meal is exactly the moment where the transition from ephemeral type to saving reality occurs:

1 Between Lamb and lamb * the disciples stood.
   They ate the paschal lamb * and the true lamb.
2 The apostles stood * between symbol and reality.
   They saw how the symbol ended * and the reality begin.
3 Blessed are they, * for whom the fulfillment was accomplished
   of the symbol * and the beginning of the reality took place.
4 Our Lord ate the Pascha * with his disciples.
   Through the bread, which he broke, * the Unleavened disappeared.[38]

Like Melito, Ephrem constructs a hermeneutical space for his readers, but the Syriac writer places the disciples at the moment of fulfillment as they stood "between Lamb and lamb." during the meal. The "shadow" Pesach-Mazzot vanishes before their eyes. This disappearance reaches the same rhetorical goal as Tertullian's sarcastic mutton: with no difference in how Judaic ritual is valued, both aim to break ritual continuity with Judaism while maintaining it with Hebrew scripture. Yet unlike Tertullian, Ephrem and other Syrians arrive there through the Syn Pesach meal. As the risen Lord tells his disciples in the *Didascalia*: "...I ate *my* Pascha with you, and in the night *they* seized me."

1. Ignatius and the Ritualization of Christ Narrative

In Tertullian's day, and certainly by Ephrem's, the gospel canon is generally acknowledged and writers have begun to draw Christ narrative into

---

[38] Ephrem, Azyma 6.1-4, CSCO 249, 11.

their discussions of rite, both as kerygmatic "congruence" and "rubric" to be imitated in the liturgy. Yet at the very beginning of canonical formation, Ignatius fuses Christ narrative to Christian rite with interpretive tools unknown in other Christian centers for at least two generations, but actively at work in Syrian literature throughout the second century and beyond. This alone should warn against paralleling too closely the evolutionary, statistical[39] model used to trace canonical formation, but it does invite a geographic one: looking for regional differences in the ways narrative traditions are brought into play as liturgical theology.

Arguing in the first decades of the second century[40] against a kind of hyperbiblicism current in some congregations of Asia Minor,[41] Ignatius gives ample witness to how he believes mystery must control exegesis:

> When I heard that there were some who say that if they do not see it in the archives [i.e. OT], they do not believe in the Gospel, I said to them that it is written, and they answered, 'That is just what we are discussing.' To me the archives are Jesus Christ, the inviolable archives his cross and death and resurrection and the faith that comes from him, and in which, I hope, with your prayers, to be saved.[42]

For Ignatius, "cross-death–resurrection" outlines a narrative with canonical weight,[43] certainly as "measure" if not text. Yet it also points out the meager place Ignatius reserves for the "archives": two lone maxims from the book of Proverbs make up the sum of Ignatius' quotations from the Hebrew scriptures.[44] This vacuum cannot be filled merely by the circumstances under which Ignatius wrote. Had OT proof texts and typology been favored exegetical methods, Ignatius could have used as many of these images as the Pauline, Johannine and Matthean material he cites from memory.

---

[39] See statistical study, Stuhlhofer, Franz, Der Gebrauch der Bibel von Jesus bis Euseb. Wuppertal 1988.

[40] Drobner doubts Eusebius' date (110); may be as late as 135. Lehrbuch, 41.

[41] See Molland, (p. 55, n. 208); Sumney, (p. 55, n.211); Campenhausen, Entstehung, 86-87.

[42] Ignatius, Phild 8.2.

[43] Koester, ACG, 7. Cf. the "Star" passage (Eph 19) immediately following the citation brought below, as well as Mag 9.11 and Trall 9, "creedal summaries."

[44] Prov 3.34=IgnEph 18.7, Prov 18.7=Mag 12. "…deux maximes de sagesse, somme toute assez banales et qui pourraient provenir d'une vague tradition orale…" Blanchard Yves-Marie, Aux sources du canon, le témoignage de'Irénée, CogFid 175, 1993, 28.

Ignatius also refers to specific events in the Christ narrative: at IgnEph 17.1 to the anointing at Bethany (Mk 14.3-9, Mt 26.6-12) and more obliquely to the inbreathing of the Spirit (Jn 20.22):

> The Lord received ointment (μύρον) upon his head for this reason: that he might breathe immortality upon the church. Do not anoint yourselves with the foul odor of the teaching of the Prince of this World, so that he might not lead you away from the life which lies before you.[45]

A few lines later Ignatius links the virgin birth, a great star, the baptism in the Jordan, and the cross in a similarly condensed narrative:

> [18.2] For our God, Jesus the Christ, was carried by Mary in the womb, according to God's Oeconomia from the seed of David yet of the Holy Spirit: he was born and baptized, in order to purify the water through his suffering.

> [19.1] And hidden from the Prince of this World were the virginity of Mary, her giving birth, and the death of the Lord – three loudly shouting mysteries accomplished in the stillness of God (τρία μυστήεια κραυγῆς, ἅτινα ἐν ἡσυχια θεοῦ ἐπράχθη). [2] How were they revealed to the Aeons? A star shone in heaven, brighter than all stars, and its light was ineffable and its newness caused astonishment. But all the other stars with sun and moon formed a choir around the star, but its light was greater than all. [3] The result was the dissolution of all magic and the abolition of every bond of evil...[46]

For Ignatius, mystery is inseparable from both Christ narrative and Christian rite. Jesus was anointed at Bethany in order to breathe immortality upon the church, just as Jesus was baptized in the Jordan to purify the water through his suffering. The close proximity of anointing, spirit, cross, and baptism is not accidental: Ignatius addresses the first narrative to chrismation as much as he does the second to the bath.

Unfortunately broken off at 20.1 with a promise of a second letter Ignatius never had a chance to compose,[47] the polished style of this section has suggested that Ignatius is citing an early hymn about the star at Jesus' birth.[48] Yet such a hymn probably did not sing of the effects

---

[45] Fischer, SUC 1, 154, 156. Anointing and spirit linked in Theophilus, AdAut 1.12, text below, p. 116.

[46] Fischer, SUC 1, 156.

[47] At Poly 8.1, (222 f.) Ignatius writes that he is unable to write all the churches because he must unexpectedly sail from Troas to Naples. The second letter to the Ephesians was probably among those letters planned. Fischer, SUC 1, 159, n. 93.

[48] SUC 1, 159, n. 88.

of salvation, including the abolition of magic and astrology. Instead, several moments in Ignatius' mystagogical preaching have been recalled and placed into a new context. Picture, for instance, the first to hear Ignatius' word about the stench of evil still damp with the smell of chrism about them.

Baptismal mimesis also models Valentinian theology of the "Oriental" (i.e., Syrian/ Mesopotamian) school.[49] Clement of Alexandria preserves an extended baptismal catechesis in his *Excepts from Theodotos*, who taught ca. 160-170:

> For this reason, there came a strange and new star, destroying the ancient order of the stars, shining with a new light not of this world, bearing the new way of salvation, just as the Lord himself, Guide of humankind, descended upon the earth to move those who believe in Christ from Fate [Εἰμαρμένη] into Providence [Πρόνοια]...
>
> Just as the Savior's birth removes us from the process of becoming and from Fate, so too his baptism frees us from the fire, and his suffering [πάθος] from suffering, so that we may follow him in all things. For the one who has been baptized into God has come before God and has received the power "to tread upon scorpions and serpents" [Lk 10.19~Ψ'90(91).13], the evil powers. And he urged the apostles "Go and preach, and baptize those who believe, in the name of the Father, the Son, and the Holy Spirit," [~Mt 28.19] in whom we are reborn, becoming superior to all other powers.[50]

In the Valentinian version, "all authority in heaven and on earth," which before the Great Commission the risen Lord claims as his, has been arrogated to the believer. Yet without this Gnostic twist, the star that breaks the power of Fate shines equally bright in Ignatius' exegesis. The common source must be a Syrian baptismal catechesis whose first witness is the martyred bishop of Antioch.

Ignatius has configured rite, narrative, and mystery into a kind of mutual exegesis found in the NT in only three texts: the Lord's Prayer, the Joh footwashing, and the Syn institution of the supper. Just as Jesus originates the meal rite, so too has Jesus originated baptism – by purifying the waters by his death. This harmonizes with the gospels' apologetic

---

[49] Hippolytus, Ref 7.35.7, lists Bar Daisan as a major proponent.
[50] Clement of Alexandria, Excerpts 74.2,76.1-4, SC 23 (Sagnard), 1948, 197-200. The omitted passage (75) brings a rare moment of philo-Judaism: Christ came to the Jews because they alone among the peoples of the world were known for their piety.

concern to explain Christ's submission to John, just as a moral lesson drawn from the anointing at Bethany is not far from Paul's ethical reading of the Passover leaven. But the extent of Christ narrative distinguishes Ignatius from Paul, just as the link to baptismal rites goes beyond the gospels.[51] Ignatius' letter stands at the beginning of a characteristically Syrian baptismal theology that elevates the beginning of the Christ narrative – birth and baptism – to founding texts[52] by reading them more closely through the mystery of the cross than the gospels.[53]

This view of the Jordan baptism is not an exegetical choice comparable to the eventual Western ritualization of Rom 6, a text that influences Tertullian as he writes, "the passion of the Lord, in which we are baptized," or when he finds the water-bearer as "congruent" type. No amount of rhetoric can ever make a bath look like death by crucifixion and rising from the dead. Liturgical actions that already attract theological motifs in Hermas are addressed to Christ narrative when this becomes standard mystagogical speech. Syrian liturgical theology, however, demands an explicit example to imitate in its rituals: as Jesus was baptized, so too the new believer; as Jesus celebrated the paschal meal, so too the institution of the eucharist will become the story of origins for the annual feast.

Ignatius' early connection of rite to Christ narrative is not the only characteristic that sets him apart from other late first-early second century writers. As signs of the church's unity, baptism and the eucharistic "medicine of immortality"[54] have become as efficacious a means of speaking the Christ event as the kerygma with which these rites are more deeply intertwined. This may well be a further unfolding of a still older Syrian

---

[51] Koester argues that Jn uses sacramental images to elucidate Christ narrative, not the reverse, as Ignatius. History and Cult in the Gospel of John and in Ignatius of Antioch, JThCh 1, 1969, (111-123), 119 = Geschichte und Kultus im Johannesevangelium und bei Ignatius von Antiochien, ZThK 54, 1957, 56-69, here, 64.

[52] Chevallier, Max-Alain, L'apologie du baptême d'eau à la fin du premier siècle: Introduction secondaire de l'étiologie dans les récits du baptême de Jésus, NTS 32, 1986, 528-543, argues that only Mark is free of aetiological concerns.

[53] Koester places not just Mt, but also Mk and Jn in Syria. See Köster, Einführung Mk, 602; Jn, 616. Fitzmeyer, Luke I, AB 28, ²1981, 45-47, thinks Luke might have been an Antiochene. Could this region have produced all four gospels (but not Q) *and* the Diatessaron *and* a corresponding liturgical theology? An intriguing thought…

[54] Eph 20.2; Magn 7.1-2; Phild 4. See Wehr, Lothar, Arznei der Unsterblichkeit. Die Eucharistie bei Ignatius von Antiochien und im Johannesevangelium, NTA, NF 18, 1987.

liturgical theology. If the meal rite fused to the Christ narrative that Paul transmitted to the Corinthians some sixty years before is of Antiochene origin, then there is evidence of narrative material being drawn into the liturgy of that city only a few years after the death of Jesus. This can only hint at the role Antioch may have played in the formation of pre-literary Christ narrative, including the paschal framing of the supper.

2. Baptism of Jesus: Sibylline Oracles, Book 7 (Syria, before 150)[55]

One of the most intriguing examples of Syrian liturgical mimesis pre-scribes a rite never celebrated by an author who did not really exist – except in the guise of a pagan prophetess. This pseudepigraphic mask forces the author to present the Jordan baptism in an equally pagan setting, but the mimetic relationship between rite and story is not a pagan borrowing. The Christian Sibyl of the seventh book begins as if she were going to pronounce an oracle of destruction typical of the genre. Instead, she portrays the baptism of Jesus, then proposes an unusual "sacrifice":

> Ah, Coele-Syria, last possession of the Phoenician men
> where lies the source of Beirut's inland sea,[56]
> wretched one, you did not recognize your God, whom once Jordan washed
> in its streams, and the spirit flew like a dove.
> He, before either earth or starry heaven,
> was sovereign Word, with the Father and Holy Spirit.
> He put on flesh but quickly flew to his Father's home.
> Great heaven established three towers for him
> in which the noble mothers of God now live:
> hope and piety and desirable holiness.
> They do not rejoice in gold or silver but in reverential acts
> of human beings, sacrifices, and most righteous thoughts.
>
> You shall sacrifice to the immortal great noble God,
> not by melting a lump of incense in fire or striking
> a shaggy ram with a sacrificial knife, but with all
> who bear your blood, by taking a wild dove,
> praying, and sending it off, while gazing to heaven.

[55] Syria, first half of 2 c.: J. J. Collins, OTPseud I, 408.
[56] Here translation of Kurfess (Sibyllische Weissagungen, Berlin, 1951, 152 f.) is fol-lowed. Collins' "on whom the brine of Beirut lies belched up" is a line which should never have been generated in any language.

You shall pour a libation of water on pure fire, crying out as follows:
"As the father begot you, the Word, so I have dispatched a bird,
a word which is swift messenger of words, sprinkling
with holy waters your baptism, through which you were revealed out of fire.

You shall not shut the door when some other stranger
comes, begging you to ward off poverty and hunger.
But take the head of this man, sprinkle it with water,
and pray three times. Cry out to your God as follows:
"I do not desire wealth. I am poor and I have received a poor man.
You, Father, Provider, deign to listen to both."
He will give to you when you pray.[57]

The Sibyl has "reoriginated" a rite with a particularly pagan character: a sacrifice of water over fire as a bird is not killed, but freed. The
motifs of water, fire, flight and freedom, however, are not part of a
pagan rite the Sibyl has adopted, but simply invented to maintain the
pseudepigraphic illusion of a pagan prophetess as she narrates the Jordan baptism. Just as early Syrian theology images baptism as mimesis of
Jesus' baptism, so the mystery of that event is told as mimesis of the narrative. Motifs of the Jordan narrative – water, dove, and (extracanonical)
fire[58] – have become the elements of rite telling the story, as it were, in
reverse. Instead of the heavenly voice, an anamnetic prayer interpreting
the action is provided: a remembrance and proclamation of the
epiphany at the Jordan.

The second ritual, no more performed than the first, is ethic as narrated rite not far from the Joh footwashing. The "other" stranger[59] is
another Christian in need of hospitality, the sprinkling ritual dramatizing the recognition of the other's baptism.

If rite as narrative were not already a well developed model of Syrian
liturgical theology at the time the Sibyl composed her oracle, it would

---

[57] Trans. except as noted, Collins, J. J., The Sibylline Oracles, OT Pseud 1, 411-12.

[58] See Drijvers H.J.W., and G. J. Reinink, Taufe und Licht. Tatian, Ebionäerevangelium und Thomasakten, in: Text and Testimony (FS Klijn), Leiden 1988, 91-110.
Fire at the Jordan baptism is attested by Justin, Praedicatio Pauli (cited by psCyprian);
light in the Diatessaron, the Gospel of the Ebionites, and two mss. of the Vetus
Latina.

[59] Cf. paschal fast in Didascalia 21, text, below, p. 186. ATh and Liber Graduum
also inculcate humility and charity to mendicants. See Klijn, ATh, 38, 201 (lit.). The
"other" is ἐπήλυτος rather than the usual πάροικος. See Feldmeier, Reinhard, Die Christen
als Fremde, WUNT 64, 1992.

have been impossible for her to make this elegant configuration of rite, mystery, and kerygma. Depending upon where the dating of the seventh book falls in relation to Ignatius, this may be the first witness to the movement toward ritual mimesis of the Christ narrative apart from NT aetiologies of the Lord's Prayer and the meal.

3. Other Provinces, Other Models

While Ignatius' "loudly shouting mysteries" continue to be proclaimed, particularly in Justin's First *Apology* and Irenaeus' *Epideixis*, Ignatius' ritual link to Christ narrative is not found in the literature of other major centers, where Christ narrative is not ritualized, if at all, beyond familiar aetiologies. Instead, two different models, equally rooted in the NT, are followed to generate narrative about rite: (1) just as the gospels furnish teaching with narrative frames, Christ teaching is brought into liturgical contexts; and (2) OT typology, in the gospels pointed toward Christ events as well as the Christ event, is now directed toward Christian rite. Irenaeus exploits a third model: ritual does not imitate Christ narrative or teaching, but theological motifs distilled from them.

a) Rite as Mimesis of Words of Jesus

Helmut Koester points out that in Corinth, words of Jesus were already being discussed in new contexts to order community life, especially the body of teaching in the Sermon on the Mount/Plain.[60] Faintly echoing this interpretive work, Christ teaching scattered through the earliest literature has been brought into play as liturgical exegesis.

In the *Didache*, daily prayer and the two stational fasts are enjoined:

> [7.1] Let your fasts not coincide with [those of] the hypocrites. They fast on Monday and Thursday; you, though, should fast on Wednesday and Friday. [2.]And do not pray as the hypocrites do; pray instead this way, *as the Lord directed in his gospel...*[61] [the Lord's Prayer]... [3] Pray this way thrice daily.[62]

---

[60] See Koester, ACG 52-54. Words of Jesus in Rom 12-14, 1 Cor 7-14, 1 Thess 5 parallel the church-order material of Mk or Sermon on the Mount/Plain, except for 1 Cor 9.14, a Q saying.

[61] Kurt Niederwimmer sees the italicized words as redactional, Der Didachist und seine Quellen, NT.S 77, 1995, (15-36) 29 f.

[62] SUC 2, 76 f.

The Syrian *Didascalia*[63] and even Tertullian[64] anchor fasting practice to the "Bridegroom's absence," while Clement,[65] taking a tropological approach typical of the Alexandrian school, presents the stations as fasts against the pagan divinities of these days: Hermes (greed, thievery) and Aphrodite (lust), which along with the idolatry these names suggest, are the root of all sin. None of these narratives, of course, are about the *content* of a Christian fast, but the *Didache* also has a narrative identical in function to Clement's anti-Hellenic polemic. It is sufficient that fast days are not coterminous with the Pharisaic models from which they are obviously derived, and those who might continue fasting on Monday and Thursday run the risk of becoming "hypocrites." The mark of the Christian[66] is that he/she does not fast on the same days as the Jews. With no further reasons for the practice, the negative image of Judaism is enough to crystallize Christian identity by defining it by what it is not.

While mimesis addressed to Christ narrative is as conspicuously absent as in the meal prayers, the inclusion of the Lord's Prayer, especially with a dominical command probably the work of secondary redaction,[67] reveals a kind of "institution by analogy" addressed not to Christ narrative, but to authoritative Christ teaching. That teaching did not include a schedule of daily prayer, but does so now by mere proximity.

In similar fashion, the *Shepherd* of Hermas cites a "Johannine" baptismal verse:

> "Why, Lord," I said, "have the stones risen from the depths of the water and been placed into the building [the tower]...?" "They had to rise from the water," he said, "to receive life, for otherwise they would *not be able to enter into the Kingdom of God*, if they had not laid aside the deadness [νεκρώσις] of their earlier life."[68]

An almost identical logion occurs in Jesus' discourse with Nicodemus: "No one can *see* the kingdom of God without being born from above" (Jn 3.3) and "No one can *enter* the kingdom of God without

---

[63] See below, p. 214.

[64] De ieiunio 10, CCSL 2, 1267-9.

[65] Strom 7.75.1-3. GCS 17 (Clemens Alex. 3, Stählin), 54.

[66] See Draper, Jonathan A., Christian Self-Definition against the "Hypocrites" in Didache 9-10, SBL.SP 1992, 362-377.

[67] Niederwimmer, Quellen, 29.

[68] SC 53, 326-329. Cf. Justin, Apol. I, 61.4.

being born of water and Spirit" (Jn 3.5). Since the interplay between
seeing and believing is such an important motif in Jn, this latter verse is
likely more original. Yet the reluctance in Rome to accept the Fourth
Gospel[69] – Justin, despite his ties to Ephesus, does not once cite Jn –
should warn against seeing this tradition merely as quotation. Arthur
Bellinzoni, who has investigated a similar saying in Justin Apol 61.4,
maintains the independence of the logion and proposes the baptismal
liturgy as source.[70] Jn places the logion in a catechetical dialogue, a
more probable setting. This means that Hermas has no use for the Joh
narrative as aetiology even if he knew it, but is framing the logion with
a symbolic narrative of his own. Mimesis is addressed to Christ teaching, not narrative.

The baptism of these "stones," the OT righteous, is a process linked to
liturgical action:

> The seal [σφραγίς] is the water: they descend into the water dead and
> come out again living. Also to them was this seal proclaimed, and they
> accepted it to enter the Kingdom of God.[71]

The act of going down and coming back up from the baptismal waters
occurs after the laying aside of "the deadness of their former lives." But
Herm does not establish a one-to-one correspondence between liturgical
action and theological content: the removal of clothing before immersion
is not the stripping away of sin and death, and the movement in and out
of water is not the burial and resurrection of Christ. The contrary view
would hold that Hermas is operating with a type of baptismal mimesis
not occurring until the fourth century, when the baptismal rite is divided
into component parts and exegeted as an imitation of the greater story of
salvation.[72] In Hermas, baptism is the result of hearing and accepting the
kerygma, but the rite itself does not proclaim or imitate it.

The "congruence" Hermas leaves unspoken is not this later mimesis
but the narrative of the life-giving bath. The stones rising from the

[69] The "Hippolytan school" defended Joh lit. against the "Alogoi." See Brent, Allen,
Hippolytus and the Roman Church in the Third Century, VigChrS 31, 1995, 140-146;
171-177; Streeter, B. H., The Four Gospels, London/NY 2/11 1964, 436-442.
[70] Bellinzoni, A.J., The Sayings of Jesus in the Writings of Justin Martyr, NT.S 17,
1967, 136-138.
[71] Sim 9.16.4 (93.4), GCS 48 (M. Whittaker), Berlin ²1967, 90.
[72] See Stommel, Eduard. "Begraben mit Christus" (Röm 6.4) und der Taufritus. RQ
49, 1954, 1-20.

water demonstrate the response to the life-giving word. The rite itself is the mimetic object: a series of verbs of motion – going down, coming up, entering – connects the action of the baptizands and divine action in the sacrament. Just as the baptizands enter and leave the water, they enter the Kingdom of God. They were dead and now are living stones to build the church.

With its dreamlike discourses with heavenly beings, ShepHerm offers the ideal setting for stories of origins for the liturgy, an opportunity a sixth century writer could not leave unexploited. Having read Eusebius, and probably finding the passages concerning the paschal controversy as opaque as modern scholars, the author of the *Liber Pontificalis* solves the problem once and for all by disclosing that during the bishopric of Pius (ca. 145, immediately before Anicetus!) an angelic vision revealed to Hermas the celebration of the Pascha on the Lord's Day. Unfortunately, Hermas failed to record this helpful revelation anywhere in his work.[73] In fact, at Sim 5.1, Hermas must explain to the Shepherd appearing to him on the mountain why he is fasting: "What is a 'station'?" the Shepherd asks. In later centuries celestial beings will become much more liturgically aware, conveniently revealing practices desired from on high.[74]

While the *Liber Pontificalis* has no difficulty inferring a Quartadeciman practice for early second century Rome, the author also originates a seven week fast before Pascha, the introduction of the Gloria, and the mass on Christmas Eve all during the bishopric of Telesphorus, ca. 130.[75] This is hardly accurate history, but the author does have a sense of the organic growth of the liturgy, and this is the best way of describing its antiquity, authority, and catholicity. Like gospels, liturgies of other sees were eventually assigned to single figures such as Mark, James, Chrysostom, or

---

[73] It might be that the writer was desperate enough to see Hermas' all-night prayer session with the twelve virgins (Sim IX, 8-11) as a paschal vigil.

[74] Reported dreams/visions are a common locus for cultic aetiology. The celebration of the Nativity of the Virgin is revealed in a dream – a popular medieval story. An ecclesial figure hears heavenly music recurring on a particular day each year. The Virgin reveals it is the celestial celebration of her nativity. For one version, see Honorius Augustodunensis, Gemma Animae 3.166, PL 172, 690.

[75] Attribution to Telephorus could rest upon a reading of Irenaeus' letter mentioning ancient differences in fasting practices. For warnings about using the LP as source for liturgical history, see Davis, Raymond, (ed. and trans.), The Book of Pontiffs (Liber Pontificalis), Translated Texts for Historians, Latin Series V, Liverpool 1989, xv-xvii. This warning includes the reference to the birthplace of Victor of Rome as North Africa.

Addai. Instead, the *Liber Pontificalis* gives each bishop a role in shaping the Roman liturgy, much like the legend of the Apostolic Creed, where each of the Twelve contributes a phrase.[76] Though the seven-week quadragesima becomes even more rhetorically "apostolic" because of its lack of historically apostolic roots, Sunday Pascha has long since become a non-issue.

b) Words About Jesus: Irenaeus and the *Regula Fidei*

In his *Epideixis,* Irenaeus employs a construct quite similar to Hermas:

> And for this reason the baptism of our rebirth proceeds through these three points, as God the Father graces us with rebirth by means of his Son through the Holy Spirit. For those who bear within themselves the Spirit of God are led to the Word, that is, the Son; but the Son leads them to the Father, and through the Father they receive immortality.[77]

The only place where baptism could be said to "proceed through three points of faith"[78] is at the scrutinies and the proclamation of the triune name. Irenaeus is exegeting the threefold questions and immersion[79] of the baptismal rite as progress from death to eternal life through the persons of the Trinity. In theological content, this life-giving progression is identical to Hermas: the bath is still telling the same story. The new comes in the object of mimesis: not specific words of Jesus, but *doctrine*: the baptismal formula pronounced over the baptizands as they are immersed also signs the teaching surrounding initiation. Irenaeus may easily make the transition because baptismal teaching has grown organically from the rite into the *regula fidei*.[80] Exegesis has grown along with it, but a shift to incorporate Christ narrative has not occurred.

To combat Valentinian christology, Irenaeus applies a similar model to the eucharist and the mystery of the incarnation. Though Valentini-

---

[76] Cf. Rufinus, Comm. in symb. apost, 2, CCSL 20, 134 f.; twelve articles for twelve apostles appears in PsAugustine, De symb, appendix to PL 5. See Kelly, Creeds, 1-4.

[77] Epid 7, TU 31/1, 7. Cf. Justin Apol 1 215-22, 23.

[78] Epid, loc. cit.

[79] A threefold immersion is a mimetic rubricization of the Trinity. Threefold *infusion* already attested at Didache 7.3; threefold *immersion* by ApTrad 21 and Tertullian De cor. 3.3, Adv. Prax. 26, De bapt. 6.2. See also Kretschmar, Leitourgia 5, 89 f. for synopsis.

[80] See Grossi, V. Regula veritatis e narratio battesimale in sant'Ireneo, Aug 12, 1972, 437-463. The rhetorical form "narratio" with life setting in baptismal catechesis has contributed the basic structure of AH. This structure even more visible in Epid.

ans celebrated a meal rite, Irenaeus deduced that real food and drink nourishing real human flesh would be particularly troublesome to docetic understandings of Jesus. Yet for all of Jesus' meals, Valentinus had an answer:

> Jesus bore everything and was abstinent (ἐγκρατής). He sought to attain divinity. He ate and drank in a way particular to him, for he never eliminated waste. The power of his abstinence was so great that food was not subject in him to decay, for he himself was not subject to decay.[81]

Posterity is fortunate that Irenaeus did not choose to argue directly against this particular *via salutis*. Instead, he returns to the most basic narrative about the rite – people eat. Bread and wine are the stuff of creation, creatures of the one Creator through the Son, who appeared in human flesh. Irenaeus counters docetic christologies not by explaining how the eucharist is as holy as Christ, but how Jesus is as real as bread. This strategy arranges rite and narrative into perfect mirrors of Irenaeus' incarnational theology:

> Therefore, either let them change their opinion or refrain from offering the things (i.e. bread and wine) just mentioned. But our opinion agrees with the eucharist, and the eucharist in turn confirms our opinion.[82]

This strategy is not dictated solely by Irenaeus' anti-Valentinian stance, but a fundamental understanding of the sacrament – informed as much by biblical theology as rites and prayers reaching back to the first century.

At Dial 41, Justin confirms the role already quite prominent in the meal prayers of the *Didache* of thanksgiving for creation, an element transformed, and later considerably elaborated, from Jewish meal prayers.[83] Trypho, of course, is too polite to mention this liturgical history, because Justin is unaware of it. Instead, Justin offers the following typology of a "carnal" Hebrew rite and a story of origins for the Christian rite for which it is the antitype:

---

[81] Strom 3.59.3, GCS 52, 223. Clement only slightly distances himself from this citation from Valentinus, letter to a certain Agathopus. At Strom 6.71.2-3, Clement's super-Stoic Jesus eats only to show that the body was real. See Procter, Everett, Christian Controversy in Alexandria, AmUSt VII/172, 1995, 69 f.

[82] AH 4.18.5, SC 1002, 610.

[83] Primarily by accenting thanksgiving more than praise. See Talley, Thomasn, from Berakah to Eucharistia: A Reopening Question. Wor 50, 1976, 115-137.

The sacrifice of wheat flour, which according to tradition is offered by those cleansed of leprosy, was a type of the bread of the eucharist whose celebration Jesus Christ our Lord commanded as a memorial of the suffering he endured for those who have been cleansed from every sin. For he wished that we would give God thanks not only that *for humankind God created the world with all that is in it,* but also that God has liberated us from the sin in which we lived and that God has completely triumphed over the powers and principalities through the one who, according to God's will, was made to suffer.[84]

Though a natural unfolding of a thanksgiving spoken over food, thanksgiving for creation neither appears in the Syn meal accounts, nor is there any content given for the thanksgivings Jesus spoke over bread and cup. Just as in the thanksgiving for the victory of the cross, Justin is drawing on liturgical tradition, not gospel texts. Thus in describing the origins of the supper Justin maintains that thanksgiving for creation and the Christ event was a content of the meal not only intended, but instituted by Jesus, because this was the content of celebrations known to him. In this sense, Irenaeus is elaborating a motif all but constant in the anaphoræ of the Great Church assumed to reach back to the Last Supper, but one hardly proclaimed in Gnostic eucharists, whose prayers likely extended the thanksgiving for gnosis and revelation also voiced in the *Didache* prayers.[85] In similar fashion, in four extensive exegetical passages in AH, including the institution narrative and the footwashing in Jn, birth and incarnation do not just dominate over passion motifs: not once does Irenaeus explain the meal rite as anamnesis of Christ's death. For Irenaeus, "the eucharist is the *representatio* of the Incarnation,"[86] not cross, but manger.[87]

Other than heightening eucharistic motifs of creation and incarnation, Irenaeus does not find ritual in any NT text where it is not there already. Irenaeus reads the Jordan narrative not as cult aetiology or paradigm, but

---

[84] Dial 41.1, Goodspeed, 138. Emphasis mine.

[85] No mention of creation in in Acts of John 85, NTApo (James) 250. Both this lack and expansion are shared by the anaphora of Sarapion, text in Dix, Shape 163 f., PEER 39 ff.

[86] Betz, Johannes, Die Eucharistie in der Zeit der griechischen Väter, Bd. 1/1, Die Actualpräzenz der Person und des Heilswerkes Jesu im Abendmahl nach der vorephesinischen griechischen Patristik, Freiburg (D), 1955, 273.

[87] For the interplay of incarnational and "paschal" motifs, see Jossua, Jean-Pierre, Le Salut: Incarnation ou Mystère Pascal, Chez les Pères de l'Église de saint Irénée à Léon le Grand, CogFid 28, 1968.

speaks of the gift of the Holy Spirit through baptism.[107] The baptism of the Ethiopian eunuch is also a story about proclamation, not baptism. Philip could depart in such Spirit-assisted haste because the eunuch, with Name and Book, now has all he requires.[108] Thus while Irenaeus is one of the first witnesses to the NT canon, he develops and extends, but never departs from earlier models when he brings rite and narrative together. For a writer who readily acknowledges his debt to Asian exegetes of the generation before, this is a silent tribute to his teachers.

c) The "Archival" Search: OT Typologies

Greatly outnumbering words of Jesus incorporated into ritual narrative are OT typologies such as the paschal blood of the Asian tradition. This method also imitates an NT model: favored texts addressed to the whole Christ event or to specific narratives are not just narrative fabric, but the loom upon which it was woven. When the liturgy is discussed, the same prophesied-fulfilled/hidden-revealed schema, often bolstered by the negative mimesis of anti-Judaism, applies to rite as much as the life of Jesus, spread of the gospel, or Gentile mission.[90] Those rites essential to Christian identity, initiation and the meal, are depicted as both the true object of prophecy and the true subject, now revealed, of selected passages where no prophetic intent can be detected. In this sense, the liturgy is "historicized" from the very beginning, but only by dehistoricizing OT texts in contemporary proclamation. As Ignatius knows, these "archival" texts may not always be transparent to the Christ event.

Lack of transparency easily results from the very nature of typological exegesis: the search for types in the "archives" often reverses the mimetic dynamic found in both OT Pesach texts and the meal narrative of the NT. In these texts, rite originates and is given anamnetic charge in a story of salvation. Typology, however, often ritualizes text instead of historicizing rite. The underlying narrative is actually about ritual action or its benefits, which directs the search for corresponding types. With ritual as starting point, OT texts are then read as prophecies fulfilled just by the existence of Christian rite.

[88] AH 3.17.2, SC 211, 330-334.

[89] AH 4.23.2, SC 1002, 694-698.

[90] Cf. Irenaeus, Epid 30-84, 17-45: types roughly arranged in gospel chronology of life of Jesus; 86-97, 45-51, TU 31/1, for common proof texts addressed to mission and church.

In some instances, this rests with apologetic intent, the object being to legitimate rite rather than to exegete it. So the *Epistle of Barnabas* begins its testimonia about baptism:

> [11.1] Let us investigate whether the Lord was concerned with giving a revelation beforehand about the water and the Cross. Concerning the water it is written in reference to Israel how they will certainly not accept the baptism which brings the forgiveness of sins, but will build something for themselves.

> [2] For the prophet says, "Be appalled, O heavens, even more, be shocked O earth; for this people have committed two evils: they have forsaken me, the fountain of life, and have dug for themselves cisterns of death. [3] Is my holy mountain Zion a desert rock? For you will be like fluttering birds, like scattered nestlings." [Composite: Jer 2.12-13, Isa 16.1-2][91]

After Christian baptism has been defined by a Judaic "evil twin," the results of Barnabas' archival search is not Rom 6, but the tree planted by the water of Ψ1:

> [6] And again it says in another prophet, "Who does this will be like the tree planted near the water who yields its fruit in due season and whose leaves will never fall, and *all he does* will prosper. [7] Not so the godless, not so; they will be like the dust which the wind blows from the earth. Therefore the godless will not stand in the judgment, nor sinners in the congregation of the righteous. For the Lord knows the way of the righteous, but the way of the godless will perish." [Ψ1.3-6, LXX except for italicized insertion]

Barnabas now briefly interprets:

> [8] Notice how he has marked the water and the cross at the same time. For this means, blessed are those who in the hope of the cross go down into the water, for concerning the reward he says, "in due season"; then, he means, I will pay him. But as for the present, when he says, "The leaves will not fall," he means this: every word which comes from your mouth in faith and love will serve many for conversion and hope.[92]

Wood and water in close proximity are enough to transplant the Christian rite into the OT canon. Rite functions as hermeneutic: Barnabas' investigation threads together testimonia only linked by their congruence to a subtextual narrative about liturgical action and the benefits of the sacrament. Yet how this tree is rooted in the *story* of the cross is never explained.

---

[91] Barn 11.1-3, SUC 2, 168.
[92] Barn 11.6-8, SUC 2, 170.

Generations later, the anonymous Asian paschal homily *In sanctum Pascha* (IP) is also aware of the dangers of the "archival" search. Immediately following the reading of Ex 12, the exegesis is introduced:

> Thus has Holy Scripture ("divine writings") mystically preannounced the sacred celebration. It befalls us now to analyze *accurately* point by point that which has been read, and with the help of your prayers, to penetrate the mysteries hidden in the Scriptures *without destroying the truth by which it was written*, but rather by thinking about the *exact* meaning of the mysteries corresponding to the figures [italics mine].[93]

Though the homilist closely follows Melito's "shadow-fulfillment" schema, there is a decided difference. To insure the transparency of the Pesach narrative to the paschal mystery, the homilist acknowledges both the revealed truth of Ex 12 and the interpretative task.[94] This introduces a tension between text and interpretation absent in the early second century: meaning is still *within* the text and must be unlocked to point to something beyond itself, but that meaning does not exhaust the text. There is correspondence, but not the simple equations of Barn.

The homilist may make this acknowledgment because he knows exactly what he will find. Proof text and actualized prophecy have become a canon of scriptural metaphors, still to be deciphered using mystery as "accurate" key, but fully absorbed into a greater story that can now be told even without typology. With traces in Melito's homily and fully visible in Irenaeus' *Epideixis*, earlier typological exegesis has coalesced into an overarching narrative of the Christ event encompassing both Hebrew and Greek scriptures: early Christianity is furnished not only with a saving event but a history of salvation.[95]

Outside of the later Syriac tradition, which elaborates the search for typology in both testaments into a refined rhetorical art, a general reduction in the number of types accompanies this emerging *historia salutis*. Certain OT narratives, or even individual verses, become more charged with kerygma because of their motival "congruence" with the

---

[93] IP 6, Visoná, Giuseppe, *Pseudo Ippolito, In sanctum Pascha. Studio edizione commento.* SPM 15, 1988, 246. Cf. *Homélies Pascales I. Une Homélie inspiré du traité sur la Paque d'Hippolyte*, ed. Pierre Nautin, SC 27, 129.

[94] A verse-for-verse technique suggests a later date and the influence of Origen and/or Hippolytus.

[95] See Campenhausen, *Heilsgeschichte.*

Christ story or liturgical action, or simply because they had been preached for so long as congruent that they became so in the minds of preacher and congregation. The "archival search" begun in Barnabas has now ended.

4. NT Canon: Drawing the Lines of Trajectory

Serving as brackets around a century or more of exegesis in Asia Minor, Ignatius' opponents, whose method finds a rather dogged application in Barn,[96] and the IP homilist are emblematic of the movement toward a canon of OT interpretation focusing on the Christ event and Christian rite, paralleling, even preceding, a similar movement toward the canon of the NT. The protest of the Antiochene bishop warns that neither the speed with which these traditions coalesced nor the exegesis involved was everywhere the same.

The primacy of OT typology, Christ teaching, and Pauline traditions are still felt in Asia Minor throughout much of the second century. Luke-Acts may be of Asian provenance,[97] but only the second volume becomes a literary model in its country of origins. No apocryphal gospels were produced in Asia Minor,[98] while the list of pseudepigraphic letters (1 Pt, Eph, Col, Past) and acts of various apostles (Peter, Paul) speaks for itself. Compared with the Syrians and the later Copts, whose enthusiasm for "Lives of Jesus" seems endless, this is not a matter of literary taste, but a relative disinterest in the rhetorical potential of Christ narrative to reach theological goals.

Papias of Hierapolis is reluctant to use written gospels and prefers the exegesis of orally transmitted "Words of the Lord."[99] Ignatius' correspondent Polycarp of Smyrna weaves together a cento of citations *inter alia* from 1 Clem, the Pauline and Pastoral epistles, 1 Pet and the Sermon on the Mount, the latter rhymed for mnemonic ease. But of the

[96] Klaus Wengst places Barn among those criticized by Ignatius. See ibid., SUC 2, 115-118; Tradition, 114-118; followed by Berger, Theologiegeschichte, 512-517, in a trajectory he draws to including opponents in the Past and 2 Pet.

[97] Berger, Theologiegeschichte, 697.

[98] M. G. Mara (SC 201, 1973, 215-210) places GosPt in Asia because of similarities she finds in Melito's PP to support her reconstruction of "Quartadecimanism."

[99] Eusebius, EH 3.39.11-13, sees Papias' work as "parables, sayings, and other more fantastic stuff." Papias likely favored Christ teachings, i.e. (oral) narratives *from* Christ over narratives *about* Christ. See Körtner, Ulrich H. J., Papias von Hierapolis. FRLANT 133, 1983, esp. 163-167.

112 NT allusions in Polycarp's two letters to the Philippians,[100] there is no hint of narrative. Without the slightest reference to its place in the passion narrative, Jesus' words to the sleepy apostles at Gethsemane (Mk 14.38, Mt 26.41), are adduced as a general admonition to constant prayer (PolyPhil 7.2).[101] For all the gospel material[102] incorporated into his apologies, it should not be forgotten that Justin Martyr, whose use of typology reaches Baroque proportions in his *Dialogue*,[103] taught in Ephesus for a number of years.

The first mention of a Christian OT canon comes from Melito, who took the trouble to go to Palestine, not merely to visit the "holy places" of the Christ narrative, but to discover what OT books were considered canonical there:

> Since I have traveled to the Orient [i.e. Syria, Palestine] and came to the place where the preachings and deeds took place and have obtained exact information about the books of the old covenant, I impart to you the books as follows. The names are: Genesis, Exodus, Numbers, Leviticus and Deuteronomy; Joshua, Son of Nave, Judges, Ruth, four books of Kings, two Paralipomena [Chronicles], the Psalms of David, Solomon's Proverbs or Wisdom, Ecclesiastes, the Song of Songs, Job, the prophets Isaiah and Jeremiah, the book of the Twelve Prophets, Daniel, Ezekiel, and Ezra. From these writings I shall give excerpts in six books.[104]

These lost *Excerpts* would have catalogued the canon within the canon of the Asian exegetical tradition in a selection of passages read christologically. Among that canonical material, read as primary text about the mystery of Christ, was, of course, the command to observe the Pascha on 14 Nisan, "mystically preannounced" as "hidden mystery." In writers from Asia Minor, then, the rules of liturgical rhetoric

---

[100] Metzger, Bruce M., The Canon of the NT, its Origin, Development and Significance, Oxford 1987, 59-63.

[101] SUC 1, 258 f.

[102] In Justin, events are the second premise of a syllogism: true prophesy – historical event – true kerygma. Christ narrative cannot exist alone, thus 1Apol must include considerable OT material and the LXX translation legend. See Koester, ACG, 376-402, and Blanchard, Sources, 87-95.

[103] "If I, gentlemen," I continued, "were even to list all the rest of the laws of Moses, I could show that they are types, symbols, and allusions to the fate of Christ, the believers in him acknowledged before [the Advent], and also of the deeds of Christ himself." Dial 42.4, Goodspeed, 139.

[104] Eusebius, EH 4.26.13-14. Neither the Greek works of the LXX nor the book of Esther are mentioned. Lam is considered part of Jer, as Neh of Ezra.

are primarily shaped by the LXX read typologically, Christ teaching, and the Pauline corpus, which has been expanded pseudepigraphically by Eph, Col, and the Pastorals. This grammar necessarily structures the way in which narrative material is valued and interpreted in relation to the liturgy.

This is not to say that the four gospels were not emerging as authoritative in second century Asia Minor.[105] Irenaeus, after all, owes a great deal to this tradition, and his exegesis of the Fourth Gospel has a clear precedent in Apollinarios of Hierapolis, who connects the blood and water from Jesus, pierced side to the "double bath" of baptism, spirit and word.[106] Yet beyond this explication of ritual motifs easily read in – or into – John, there is no tendency in the earliest literature from Asia Minor to ritualize NT narrative, a trait Irenaeus shares with his Asian predecessors. In Syria, however, Christ narrative and Christian rite have already begun to interact along mimetic lines beyond the use of OT typology.

Against this Asian background, the importance in the Syrian tradition of ritual mimesis addressed to NT narrative[107] takes on a more definite profile. It will prove no coincidence that of all the provinces of the Great Church, it is Syrians of the third and fourth centuries – the *Didascalia* tradition, Ephrem and Aphrahat[108] – for whom the paschal nature of the Supper has any theological importance. Chrysostom's rhetorical somersaults to deconstruct this reading measures its strength in Antioch as well.[109] Even in the late fourth century Syriac poet Cyrillonas, this tradition is strongly felt:

> The Lamb ate the lamb;
>   Pascha devoured Pascha.
> He ended the institution of his Father
>   and began his own.
> He ended the Law
>   and opened the new covenant of reconciliation.
> Who ever saw such a wondrous meal,
>   to which humankind reclines with its creator?

---

[105] Metzger, Canon, 120-123.

[106] See text below, p. 218.

[107] For image study see Murray, Robert, Symbols of Church and Kingdom. A Study in Early Syriac Tradition, Cambridge, 1977.

[108] See section, "II. A Syrian Counterattack," p. 265 ff. below.

[109] See below, p. 303 ff.

Who ever saw such a sublime meal
in which simple fisherfolk took part with the ocean?[110]

Jesus must perform the paschal rite to fulfill it: the Christian Pascha "devours" Pesach, absorbing its meaning and superseding it. The paschal mystery of the supper and the death and resurrection of Christ are fused with an astonishing literalness that echoes Ignatius: mystery is not *abstracted* from narrative, but *conveyed* through narrative symbols. Ritual is *medium,* not object of kerygmatic discourse. With a glance at the Antiochene eucharistic tradition in Paul and the baptismal mimesis in IgnEph, one suspects a much longer history than the later dates of the *Didascalia*, Ephrem, Aphrahat or even Cyrillonas would indicate.

At this point, lining up a first century apostle, a martyr-bishop from the second, a church order from the third, and three Syriac writers from the fourth may seem like stacking the evidence. Unfortunately, large gaps in our knowledge of regional traditions must either be filled in by a trajectory method[111] or left as insoluble riddles. From Theophilus (ca. 180) to Chrysostom (360), there is nothing from Antioch but silence broken only by faint echoes in Eusebius. Two Persian invasions and forced migration of large numbers of Antiochene Christians to Mesopotamia at mid-third century were also no aids to literary transmission.

Provincial traditions also cannot be plotted out neatly like pins on a map of the Mediterranean basin. Thanks to the Greek language and safe Roman shipping lanes,[112] writers and their writings circulated with remarkable ease. But what remains extant, supplemented by what can be safely retrojected from later texts, suggests that each tradition maintained a particular, though not unique, relationship to both testaments in its paschal practice. Even within one tradition, there could be discussion over the meaning of particular texts for the worship of the church. Otherwise the "exact meaning" for the liturgy "of the mysteries corresponding to the figures" of Ex 12 would never have been cause for dispute.

---

[110] BKV² 6, (Landersdorfer) 1912, 33.

[111] For criticism of this method, see Robinson, Thomas A., The Bauer Thesis Examined. The Geography of Heresy in the Early Christian Church. Lewiston/Queenston (NY) 1988, 140-142, and Sanders, E. P. Paul and Palestinian Judaism, A Comparison of Patterns of Religion. Phila. 1977, 20-24, to whom Robinson refers.

[112] Cf. Irenaeus, AH 4.30.3: "Through them [the Romans] the world has peace and we travel fearlessly on their roads and sail wherever we wish."

III. From Rite to Text: Mimetic Readings East of Antioch

The picture emerging from the early third century Syrian *Didascalia Apostolorum* (DA) is of a Gentile Christian community refounding itself in apostolic tradition and scriptural canon by having the apostles, collectively and individually, do it for them within a pseudepigraphic frame. Hardly a uniquely Syrian development, this search for apostolic roots marks the history of second and third century Gentile Christianity across the Empire and plays a major role in the early paschal controversy. Images projecting from polemic the *Didascalia* aimed at the rhetorical "other" give far less detail, but still produce a rough picture of the various forms of Christianity practiced within the author's milieu.

As a kind of third century Deuteronomy, the DA is designed to erect strong community boundaries by discovering them in the first. Jews who "did not believe in Christ and laid hands upon him" will be forgiven, as will non-believing Gentiles, for "it is against the Son of Man that they blaspheme, by reason of the Cross":

> However, those who blaspheme against the Holy Spirit, those who hastily and in hypocrisy blaspheme against God Almighty, those heretics who receive not his holy scriptures, or receive them ill, in hypocrisy with blasphemy, who with evil words blaspheme against the catholic church which is the receptacle of the Holy Spirit, these are they who, before the judgment to come and before ever they are able to make a defense, are already condemned by Christ.[113]

Though they often lack contour, the "shadows" cast by this rhetoric materialize into Torah-observant Christians, Christian Gnostics, as well as smaller groups of celibate ascetics, some of whose practices are not outside, but very much inside the community. The twenty-sixth chapter, for instance, spends a great deal of rhetorical energy explaining to women that menstruation does not exclude them from the eucharist, and that various water purification rites, whether Judaic or even Mandaean in character, nullify the unique and uniquely forgiving bath of baptism.[114] All of these communities and their practices, the apostle Peter assures, also had "apostolic" ancestors:

[113] DA 24, CSCO 408, 220 f.
[114] DA 26, CSCO 408, 238.6-240.12, esp. 239.22-25. In the letter of Dionysius of Alexandria to Basilides, *excluding* menstruating women from the eucharist is the other issue besides ending the paschal fast.

Indeed, many of them were teaching that a man should not take a wife, and were saying that if a man did not take a wife, this was holiness. And through holiness they glorified opinions of their heresies. Again others of them taught that a man should not eat flesh and said that a man must not eat anything that has a soul in it. Others, however, said that one was bound to withhold from swine only, but might eat those things which the Law pronounces clean, and that he should be circumcised according to the Law. And others again were teaching differently, causing quarrels and disturbing the church.[115]

This sort of rhetoric contrasts sharply with the *Didascalia's* instructions about the deacon's duties before the liturgy:

> But if there comes a person from another congregation, a brother or a sister, let the deacon ask and learn whether she is a wife of a man, or again whether she is a widow, a believer; and whether she is a daughter of the church, or whether she is of one of the heresies; and then let him conduct her and set her in a place that is right for her.[116]

The place for a woman (or man) "of one of the heresies" was not outside the door, but with others of the same station. This is history, not the rhetoric of exclusion. Just as this woman is greeted hospitably, the day-to-day experiences of early Christian congregations were not always dictated by the broadsides written and published by theologians. This obtains as well for literature of a less polemical nature, which seems to cross regional, confessional, and linguistic boundaries with ease.

The ironies of preservation would have it that between Theophilus and the *Didascalia*, Syrian communities moving solidly toward Nicaean orthodoxy are the "shadows" in extant literature. East of Antioch, the *Didascalia's* rhetorical "others" produce a literature of poetry, gospels, and acts inculcating the very rituals and ethics causing "quarrels and disturbing the church" for the *Didascalia's* "Peter." One of these works is the *Acts of Thomas* (ATh), whose more severely unorthodox features were likely expunged by later editors. Orthodox censors would never have bothered if its literary quality and engaging narrative had not made it quite popular in Syriac and Greek with a broad base of Christian readers.

At the same time in East Syria another master storyteller set to work: Tatian, a student of Justin Martyr, who took four (perhaps more)

---

[115] DA 23, CSCO 408, 213.
[116] DA 13, CSCO 408, 132.14-19.

gospels and harmonized them into one continuous narrative. Tatian's severe personal discipline and views on celibacy made him unpopular in the West, but his *Diatessaron* won wide circulation among Syriac-speaking congregations for several centuries.

Each of these works shows ritual mimesis as it moves from rite to text, unfolding the same models already used by Ignatius and the Sibyl. Even if they are only literary inventions, the Sibyl describes the elements, purpose, and meaning of two rituals that could easily be performed, even if they never were. But if a reader had no idea of what was said and done at a baptism, there would be no way of imitating any ritual mentioned, but not described, in the canonical Acts. The plot of ATh is an encratite *Lysistrata* with a tragic denouement: the apostle moves too many wives of too many powerful men to vows of celibacy, finally leading to his martyrdom. Yet there is a liturgical plot just as important when after each conversion baptism is depicted in elaborate – and miraculous – detail. Heavenly voices and other special effects, however, are the only elements of these ritual descriptions that could not be reproduced by following the rubrics in the text. Ritual mimesis has become mimetic literature. Tatian creates no new narrative only in the sense that he holds strictly to the four gospels, but four stories become different by becoming one. In the course of retelling, the Jordan narrative already read by Ignatius as baptismal aetiology becomes not merely an interpretation, but the text itself.

1. Paschal Baptism? Acts of Thomas (Syria, ca. 200[117])

As transparently contemporary as a costume drama, many apocryphal acts project current liturgical practice into an earlier time, making them imminently more accessible to their audiences, but also subtly endowing current piety and practice with "apostolic" origins. Though they rarely depict Christian gatherings (only tourists/pilgrims write about regular worship services), these works often include long prayers, homilies, and liturgical vignettes along with tales of adventure, miraculous deeds, and talking animals who eloquently proclaim the gospel, only to die or run away before they can muddle the plot. Yet the liturgical scenes are not only a prime locus for the miraculous, but are far more responsible for carrying and resolving dramatic action than motifs drawn from popular fiction.

---

[117] Original language: Syriac, Klijn, ATh, 13.

Few of these liturgical set pieces could be strictly called aetiologies, but there is little need for such stories in literature where the earliest Christians worship exactly like contemporaries: the framing itself carries aetiological value. But the texts imitating rite which a variety of scholars are intent upon finding everywhere in the NT now occur in abundance – and with a lack of subtlety matched only by the intricate detective work necessary to find them in the four gospels. This is valid as well for those works written with doctrinal matters closer to the surface – the EpAp, which has no aims at approximating popular literature, or the ATh, which may be read both on the level of popular romance and as deeply symbolic work. Yet in contrast to the first and early second century, a significant change has occurred: narratives about Christians and even Christ cannot be told without recourse to narratives about ritual. Christian worship has become an important narrative structure and integral to the identity of the characters portrayed. If this literature was indeed popular among Christian readers, then this growing role of ritual description as literary sub-genre must reflect a similar increase in the role of liturgical acts in the formation of Christian identity.

In the course of transmission, different readerships would alter liturgical detail to mirror their own practice. In depicting baptism, for instance, the Greek of ATh follows the Western custom of anointing after the bath, while the Syriac maintains the original Syrian practice of anointing before.[118] Rite to text is thus an ongoing dynamic in shaping these traditions.

Although the paschal feast is not mentioned, a baptism scene in the second act in ATh (17-29) may have been influenced by its celebration, or at least read this way by the Greek translator. In India, Thomas meets King Gudnaphar, who, learning of Thomas' architectural skills, commissions the building of a palace. Yet Thomas will begin building the palace in Tishri (autumn) and complete it by Nisan (spring, usual month of Pesach/Pascha). These are not lunar months, but solar months in the Syrian calendar with the same names. No building is attempted during the winter; instead Thomas cares for the poor with the King's money. A palace is splendidly created in heaven, in which the King's brother Gad, having died, wishes to dwell. Gad is raised to life, reports about the heavenly palace, and both royal brothers are converted. They wish to be

---

[118] See Klijn, ATh, ch. 7, Baptism and Eucharist, 54-61, and relevant portions of the commentary.

baptized, and prepare themselves by caring in their own right for the poor. A bath is closed for seven days, and on a Saturday night, the two are baptized amid blazing torches. Jesus himself appears before the baptism, yet the two, not yet baptized, are unable to see him, only hear his voice. After the baptism, however, a beautiful youth appears bearing a single taper. They hear, they believe, they see. A eucharist, and in the Greek version, a short sermon extolling various virtues, is then followed by a meal: "And he spake a blessing over the *bread and the olives*, and gave unto them. *And he himself ate, because the Sunday was dawning*" (Gk. in italics). There is another eucharist later Sunday morning.

The poor suffer more in the winter and perhaps Thomas' unusual construction scheme is designed to assist them. But this heavenly mansion is also to be finished in the spring. The King then imitates this charitable giving to prepare for his baptism. The Greek version has made sure that this baptismal vigil took place on a Saturday night complete with a moral admonition. Did the Greek translator also read the original Syriac story as a *paschal* vigil, following the chronological cue of Nisan? There is, of course, a possibility that the Syriac original had this in mind. According to Ephrem,[119] the winter is a time to prepare for paschal baptism, and Aphrahat also testifies to the practice of baptism on the night of Pascha.[120]

Here a fourth century practice must be retrojected into the early third, a step to be taken with great trepidation, if at all. But if the question is not framed to mirror the later Western practice of baptizing *exclusively* in the paschal night, then there is less danger. That Syrian baptismal theology centered not on the passion narrative but the epiphany at the Jordan would not hamper a paschal baptismal practice: Rom 6 is not the only exegetical path to baptism on or during the only Christian festival. The Pascha celebrated the entire Christ event, not only its culmination. Incarnation/epiphany motifs are prominent until the Pascha becomes the celebration of the Christ narratives of passion and resurrection and Incarnation/ Epiphany become separate feasts at the winter

---

[119] Klijn (ATh, 201) cites from Ephrem's de Virginitate in E. Beck, Le Baptême chez Saint Éphrem, OrSyr 1, 1956, 113-136 (125): October recreat fatigatos a pulvere et sordibus aestatis, pluvia eius lavat, et res eius ungit arbores et fructus earum. Aprilis recreat ieiunantes, ungit baptizat et dealbat; abluit sordes peccati ab animis nostris."

[120] Aphrahat, Demo 12.6, "...that we give the sign and baptism...". Text below, p. 234.

solstice. As this occurs in the course of the fourth and fifth centuries, Syrian writers expand baptismal typology to include further motifs, though baptism during Pascha/Pentecost may have already been a long tradition.

A fragment of a sermon by Severus of Antioch (†538) could offer another understanding of the palace's strange building schedule:

> There are people who are of the opinion that a reason for the eastern location of paradise lies in the fact that those who wish to build temples or houses of God give the rule that the building should be directed toward the rising sun in the month of Nisan, which corresponds with our month April according to the moon, certainly because in that month, the sun rises over the place of paradise. Of these people, some observe the fifteenth of Nisan, because on this day the rays of the sun proceed exactly from the eastern windows [of heaven]; others, however, the fourth, because on this day the sun was created and begun its course.[121]

Despite Severus' even later date, it is tempting to see here the original reason for the completion of the celestial palace in the month of Nisan, and not an allusion to a paschal feast the author did not care to make more explicit. It is both a spatial and temporal cue pointing to the heavenly source of baptismal light.

2. Tatian's Diatessaron[122]

If canonical formation is only movement toward an authoritative holy text, then the gospel harmony of Tatian, which interweaves verses from all four gospels into a seamless whole, moves in the wrong direction. Yet if canon is also the narration of a single holy story, then the *Diatessaron* measures canon far more than Irenaeus' "tetramorph" gospel. Even as Tatian kept as closely as possible to the texts as he received them, blending the four together produces a new work telling a slightly different story. Gethsemane is in one story; soldiers who fall to the ground at the mention of Jesus' name are in another. Yet when these narratives are read in sequence, they take on a different character: the contrast is sharper, the story more poignant, as Jesus turns from human struggle in

---

[121] Text preserved by Moses Bar-Kepha (†903), De paradiso comm., ed. A. Masius, Antverpiae 1569. Cited in: Dölger, Franz, Sol Salutis, LF 4/5, 1925.

[122] A handbook of Tatian scholarship: Petersen, William L. Tatian's Diatesseron. Its Creation, Dissemination, Significance, and History of Scholarship, VigChrS 25, 1994.

private prayer to the last manifestation of divine power before the resurrection. Judging by the harmonies influenced by the *Diatessaron*, Tatian included virtually every narrative detail unique to individual gospels in harmonizing a particular pericope. Each story then becomes more fully descriptive, that is, more mimetic as literature. Time and place of composition – East Syria near the turn of the third century – make the *Diatessaron* a candidate for mimesis of a different kind, where narratives with an aetiological charge are shaped *as text* by their interpretation.

After the martyrdom of his teacher Justin, Tatian left Rome around 172 for his native Syria,[123] where he composed his harmony of the four gospels 'through the four' in his native language. A Greek translation, preserved in a single fragment found at Dura Europos,[124] probably circulated shortly after the work was complete. Tatian's leavetaking of Rome took place under a dark cloud: his rigorist views on fasting, celibacy, and other matters had led to his expulsion from the Roman congregation. In the West, Irenaeus, who also pleads from nature for the appropriateness of four and only four gospels,[125] already regards Tatian as a full-fledged Gnostic. After this initial condemnation, Tatian's reputation among Latin and Greek writers hardly improves with time.

In the East the picture is far sunnier – for the moment. The *Diatessaron* was in continuous liturgical use by Syriac-speaking congregations well into the fifth century. Theodoret of Cyrus, bishop from 423-457 of a small Syrian town two days' distance from Antioch, reports that he confiscated over two hundred copies of the *Diatessaron* and replaced them with the four gospels.[126] Theodoret's contemporary Rabbula of Edessa, noted both for his harshness and his strict orthodoxy, made sure that the

---

[123] Exactly where is unknown. Tatian refers to himself as "Assyrian," (Oratio 42) but so does Lucian of Samosata. The southern coast of Asia Minor, Cilicia and Pisidia, were considered part of Syria. For various proposals, see Petersen, Tatian, 68-72.

[124] Since the verso is blank, this fragment of fourteen lines must have come from a scroll, not a codex. Text and trans., Petersen, Tatian, 197, from original publication of Kraehling, H., A Greek Fragment of Tatian's Diatessaron from Dura, StDoc 3, 1935.

[125] AH 3.11.8: "…there can be no more and no less than four gospels. Since in the world we inhabit there are four cardinal directions and four winds, and the Church has been sown over the whole earth and the gospel is the pillar and foundation of the church and its breath of life, then the Church must according to nature also have four pillars who from all directions breathe out immortality, enlivening humankind."

[126] Theodoret, Haer. fab. comp. I.20, PG 83, 372, trans. Petersen, Tatian, 42.

Diatessaron was also expunged from his province.[127] This decanonization of Tatian's harmony led to its virtual extinction in the East, and of the hundreds of copies in circulation in the fifth century, not one survived.

The *Diatessaron* as a complete work disappeared, leading an underground existence until it emerges in medieval Western vernacular harmonies, its text regularized to the Vulgate and its original sequence – Tatian based his harmony on John – restructured to fit what had become the most important gospel for the church, Matthew. In the West, the noncanonical status of the *Diatessaron* was its salvation. Until the Reformation, there was considerable resistance to translating the Vulgate into vernacular languages, but no such prohibition existed for a gospel harmony. Here, the *Diatessaron* was strictly paraliturgical, furnishing a model for harmonies produced for a burgeoning middle class in Italy, Germany, and the Low Countries who was literate, but not educated in Latin.

Tatian was not the first in Syria to work in such an exhaustive fashion with NT texts. Jerome reports that Theophilus of Antioch gathered the "quattour evangelistarum in unum opus."[128] Since Jerome speaks of the *evangelists* and not the *evangels*, this work was probably not a harmony, but a synopsis preserving the identity of the evangelists and the integrity of each book. Since synopsis is the first step to composing a harmony, Tatian might have used this work as a basis for his own. There are also theories that Justin composed a harmony,[129] but a study of Justin's NT texts suggests that he and his school worked with shorter texts harmonized from the Syn for teaching purposes rather than a full-fledged harmony.[130] While even with his well-developed Logos christology Justin has no place for the Fourth Gospel, Theophilus[131] cites Jn as "inspired scripture" in the same breath as the LXX: Jn had attained canonical status far earlier in Antioch than in Rome.

A harmony is composed of two parts: its text and its sequence. By a collation of principal witnesses the sequence of the *Diatessaron* has been

[127] Canon 43: "The priests and deacons should exercise [due] care that in all the churches a copy of the Euangelion da-Mepharreshe [the Separated] shall be present, and shall be read." Petersen, Tatian, 42 f.
[128] Ep. ad Algasiam (121)6, PL 22, 1020; Petersen, Tatian, 32.
[129] See Petersen, Tatian, 27-29.
[130] Bellinzoni, 141: "...there is absolutely no evidence that Justin ever composed a complete harmony of the synoptic gospels."
[131] Ad Autoclus 2.22.

outlined, revealing the Johannine-Matthean contrast between Eastern and Western traditions.[132] The main focus of *Diatessaron* scholarship has been to recover as many original readings as possible, to trace the subterranean influence of the *Diatessaron* in various gospel mss. and vernacular works, thus to penetrate to a textual level for the four gospels as they circulated in the late second century. What is of interest here, however, is not what Tatian received, but what he passed on.

a) Fire and Light at the Baptism of Jesus

Sibylline Oracles 6 and 7,[133] Justin Martyr,[134] and the otherwise lost *Praedicatio Pauli* cited in PsCyprian *De rebaptismate* 16,[135] all mention a miraculous appearance of fire at the baptism of Jesus. A great light, however, appears in several witnesses of the *Diatessaron*,[136] the so-called *Gospel of the Ebionites* cited by Epiphanius,[137] and two mss. of the Vetus Latina known for Tatianic readings.[138]

Fire and light at the Jordan are often considered variations of a single motif, just as in *Oratio ad Græcos*, Tatian uses fire and light to explain the unity of God and the Logos. Yet H. J. W. Drijvers and G. J. Reinink[139] argue that Tatian transformed an original fire into light by the following scenario: the fire at the baptism of Jesus is a mimetic reading kindled solely by a dramatization of Mt 3.11||Lk 3.16 (baptism with the Holy Spirit and fire) and not by any hypothetical Jewish-Christian gospel or other written or oral source. Its origins lie with the Syrian understanding of gospel narratives of the Jordan baptism as aetiologies for liturgical practice. Tatian learns of the fire motif

---

[132] Leloir, Louis, Le Diatessaron de Tatien, OrSyr 1, 1956, 208-231, 313-334; collation of Arabic, Venetian and Liege (Middle Netherlandic) harmonies, Ephrem's Commentary (Syrian and Armenian) and the Latin of the Fulda Codex, 216-227.

[133] For VII, see above, p. 150 f.; for VI, Kurfess, Weissagungen, 148 f. In the Sibyl, fire is a kind of ordeal Jesus must undergo. Ignatius' reading of Jesus' purifying the water could also have been applied to this tradition.

[134] Dial. 88.3. Fire appears as Jesus enters the water, an action omitted in canonical accounts, but which as liturgical action invites symbolic and narrative interpretation.

[135] CSEL 3.1, 90.

[136] Ephrem's commentary (Leloir: CSCO 145 [Arm 2], 36.10-14); Pepysian Gospel Harmony (Goates: Evangelica Anglica 157, 1922, 10.7-10); see Petersen, Tatian, 14-20.

[137] Pan 30.13.6 GCS 25 (Holl) 350 f., NHS 35, 130.

[138] Ms. a (4 c.): "...lumen ingens circumfulsit de aqua" and ms. g1 (6 c.): "...lumen magnum fulgebat de aqua," both in Itala I. Matthäus (Jülicher), 14.

[139] above, p. 151, n. 58.

from his teacher Justin, transforms it through his own understanding of Johannine light and life as creative manifestations of the Logos[140] into an appearance of light at the baptism, where it finds its way into the later tradition. This assumes that the so-called *Gospel of the Ebionites*, only attested by Epiphanius, is not prior to the *Diatessaron*, but a gospel harmony written, so to speak, in competition with Tatian's work, and that the *Odes of Solomon* stem from the third century.[141]

Great Church and Valentinian traditions in second century Syria both connect chrism with fire/light and the Spirit. In the only passage in the apologetic work of Theophilus of Antioch that could qualify as a liturgical metaphor, light, Spirit, and anointing become the identifying mark of the Christian:

> ...moreover, the air and the whole earth under heaven are also all anointed in some way with light and pneuma. But you do not wish to be anointed with the oil of God? For this is the reason we are called Christians, because we are anointed with the oil of God.[142]

Also of Syrian provenance, the Valentinian *Gospel of Philip* expresses the same sense of baptismal identity with the image of a mirror needing light to produce a reflection:

> Through the holy spirit we are indeed begotten again, but we are begotten through Christ in the two. We are anointed through the spirit. When we were begotten we were united. No one can see himself either in water or in a mirror without light. Nor again can you (sg.) see in light without water or mirror. For this reason it is fitting to baptize in the two, in the light and the water. Now the light is in the chrism.[143]

The motif of purification, however, is signed by fire:

> It is through water and fire that the whole place is purified – the visible by visible, the hidden by the hidden. There are some things hidden through the visible. There is water in water, there is fire in chrism.[144]

---

[140] The two Dutch scholars direct their readers to the Joh character of Tatian's Oratio ad Graecos (esp. c. 5) and to Tatian's use of Jn 1.7-17 as the close of the third chapter of the Diatessaron, Taufe und Licht, 98-100.

[141] Abramowski, Luise, Sprache und Abfassungszeit der Oden Salomos, OrChr 68, 1984, 80-90.

[142] Theophilus of Antioch, Ad Autolycus 1.12, Grant, OECT, 1970, 16.

[143] GPhil 69.4-15, NHLE³ 151.

[144] GPhil 57, NHLE³, 144.

While fire/light may be an accompaniment to baptismal catechesis, none of these sources has placed the sign into the Jordan narrative. Reading the fire tradition as a case of text imitating text, then the transition from fire to light as mimesis addressed to a particularly Joh kerygma, Drijvers and Reinink produce an attractive theory showing how Tatian could have been the first transmitter of this tradition.[145] Since John avoids depicting the actual Jordan baptism, introducing the light motif into a narrative otherwise purely Synoptic, even with extracanonical fire, is an even deeper form of harmonization than interweaving the verses of parallel stories. The real generator of this light, however, is the baptismal rite and discourse about it. Except for the Sibyl's invented ritual, Early Christian initiation did not employ birds in any of its rites. The common association of oil, fire, and light have transferred the symbol of the Spirit to an element of rite, then placed that symbol into the scriptural story of origins.

In later Syrian tradition, fire and light, accompanied by the rays of the sun and worshipping stars, are recombined in the liturgical theology of Severus of Antioch:

> When he rose from the water, the sun inclined his rays, the stars adored the one who sanctifies the flowing waters of the font and all things. From the fire and the wood the waters were set ablaze when the Son of God came and was baptized in the midst of the Jordan. John rose, and as a blessing priest, placed his right hand on the head of the Lord.[146]

Later in the work, Severus mentions the appearance of light:

> He rose from the midst of the water, and his light appeared in the midst of the water, and his light rose over the earth.[147]

John the Baptist is a baptizing priest,[148] while light, as at the Transfiguration, emanates from Christ. The fire occurs when Jesus descends into the water, just as with Justin, but the light spreading over the earth appears as Jesus steps out of the water, and he is its source. The liturgical

---

[145] For this theory in reverse, see Charlesworth, James H., Tatian's Dependence upon Apocryphal Traditions, HeyJ 15, 1974, 5-17; Winkler, Gabriele, Die Licht-Erscheinung bei der Taufe Jesu und der Ursprung des Epiphaniefestes, OChr 78, 1994, 176-229.

[146] De ritibus baptismi liber, cited from the 1572 Antwerp edition of Christophorus Plantinus, 23 f. in Resch, Agrapha, TU 30.3/4, 1906, 75 f. Discussion 73-84.

[147] Plantinus, 88, in Resch, Agrapha, 76.

[148] Plantinus, 71, Resch, Agrapha, 77: "Johannes manum suam imponebat."

action of moving in and out of water already given meaning in Shep-Herm continues to attract narrative. Long after the Jordan narrative had attained its canonical shape, the Syrian tradition still brings the narra-tive into a closer mimetic relationship to actually performed rite, as well as adding miraculous detail, to frame a baptismal story of origins.[149]

b) "Not my feet alone, but my hands, head, and whole body…"[150]

At the footwashing in Jn 13.9, Peter objects, "Lord, not only my feet, but also my hands and my head." The poet Romanos Melodos, whom Petersen shows in his published dissertation[151] is an important Greek witness to the *Diatessaron*, records the following line in his *Hymn on Judas* 33.11:

> Κύριέ μου, εἰ πλύνεις, μή μου τοὺς πόδας μόνον, ἀλλὰ καὶ δέμας ὅλον.[152]
> "My Lord, if you wash [me], then not my feet alone, but also my whole body."

Western witnesses are:
The *Pepysian Harmony* (Middle English, ca 1400):

> "Lorde, nought onelich wasche my feete, bot al the body and the heued"[153]

Vetus Latina, ms. a:

> Dicit ei Simon Petrus: Domine, non tantum pedes sed et manus caput et totum corpus[154]

In these texts, Peter's objection elevates a baptismal allusion to a def-inite sign. Did Tatian compose this narrative as a story of origins? Oddly enough, neither Ephrem nor Aphrahat appear to know this reading, though they would have every reason to use it if they did. Both see the footwashing as a baptismal aetiology close to Jesus' suffering and death,

---

[149] The Gannat Bussame, a Nestorian commentary, citing "Mar Ephrem," (=Aba, student of Ephrem), adds clouds and incense. See Taufe und Licht, 96 f. For Syrian and Armenian liturgical texts influenced by this narrative, see Winkler, Licht, passim.

[150] See Petersen, Tatian, 381-384, or Petersen's earlier addition to Koester, ACG, 427.

[151] Petersen, W. L., The Diatessaron and Ephrem Syrus as Sources of Romanos the Melodist. CSCO 475 [Subs. 74], 1985.

[152] Romanos le Mélode, hymnes IV, SC 128, 1976, (Grosdidier de Matons), 82.

[153] The Pepysian Harmony, ed. M. Goates, 88; named for famed diarist Samuel Pepys because the ms. was once in his possession.

[154] Itala IV (Jülicher), 149.

yet neither mention the "whole body." The Middle English harmony and the Latina ms. could have had a common source, but not one in common with a Greek poet. This agreement can only mean that in Tatian's original, Peter wanted the full bath of baptism.

c) Negative mimesis: "Raising their feasts against me..."

The *Arabic Harmony* presents a reading of Ψ'40(41).9 at Jn 13.18 unique among known *Diatessaron* witnesses:

> "This is not my word for all of you. For I know whom I have chosen. But that the scripture will be fulfilled, 'Who eats bread with me, will raise his *feasts* [Heb., will "make great" the heel] against me.'"[155]

A translation from a Syriac archetype, the *Arabic Harmony* has either preserved an original reading not found in any other *Diatessaron* witness, transforming the OT citation to reflect the paschal frame of Jesus' betrayal, or followed its archetype in doing so. Pesach has become Judas' feast, a weapon "made great" against Jesus by the "Jews." Though Melito had already made much of the "People making merry" while Jesus was humiliated and crucified, he did not link Judas' betrayal specifically to the feast. "Israel," not a lone follower in league with Temple authorities, had betrayed the Christ.

In a secondary redactional level of the *Didascalia*,[156] these motifs are combined, and they are aimed more squarely at Judaic rite. Judas is the archetypal shadow Jew, and the Day of Atonement becomes "mourning" for the death of Christ.[157] Enjoining the Friday fast of Pascha, the *Didascalia* offers a proof text that may lie behind this reading:

> But fast for them again also on the Friday, because on it they crucified me, and in the midst of the feast of their unleavened bread, as it is said of old in David: "In the midst of their festivals they set up their signs, and they knew not" Ψ'63(64).4.[158]

The Arabic reading could easily stem from the same late second-early third century tradition which informs the *Didascalia*. If this version of Tatian's passion narrative was used in liturgical reading, its purpose in

---

[155] Preuschen-Pott, 204.
[156] See below, p. 214.
[157] See below, p. 227 f.
[158] Didascalia 21, CSCO 408, 192.

distinguishing Pascha from its evil "shadow" Pesach would have been quite effective.

d) The Sequence of the Paschal Night

The footwashing and the negative "feasts" occur before Jesus is taken off to die. Yet these narratives present a harmonist with important decisions. Shall Jesus' death occur on or after the paschal feast, and how shall the meal be presented? A connection between the institution narrative and eucharistic celebrations, even for rites that did not include the *Verba*, would also raise the question of Judas' presence at the meal. If the sacrament is an efficacious mystery, then how does it appear when Judas, immediately after partaking of the sacrament, hastens off to betray the Lord?

Ephrem's commentary gives only one important clue: the footwashing occurs before the paschal supper, but nevertheless takes place on the paschal night. Since Ephrem cites very little of Jn 13.1-20, it is mere speculation to ask what Ephrem's text actually looked like. Aphrahat, however, yields more detail. The Persian Sage is convinced that the footwashing occurred on the paschal night, and uses this narrative as a founding story for baptism:

> But Israel was baptized in the sea in the night of Pascha, the day of salvation, and our Savior washed the feet of his disciples in the paschal night, which is the prefiguration of baptism. You should know, my Beloved, that only from this night on our Savior administered the true baptism. For as long as he tarried among his disciples, they were only baptized with the baptism of the priestly law, about which John spoke, "Repent of your sins." And in that night he revealed to them the mystery of baptism of suffering and his death; as the Apostle says, "You are with him through baptism buried in death, and rise with him by the power of God."[159]

By mid-fourth century, it should be no surprise to see Rom 6 incorporated into a baptismal aetiology, here exquisitely interwoven with the footwashing of Jn 13 and an Exodus typology. But what is significant for determining the sequence of the *Diatessaron* is Aphrahat's chronology. The footwashing occurs on the paschal night, along with the supper, and both sacraments are originated on the night in which Christ was

---

[159] Aphrahat. Demonstrationes/Unterweisungen. dÜ, Peter Bruns, FC 5/2, 1991, 308 f.

betrayed. Aphrahat even makes an issue of Pesach-Red Sea as the reverse of both gospel narrative and Christian rite:

> And after he had washed their feet and sat down, then he gave them his body and blood; and not as with Israel, who, after they have eaten the Pascha then were baptized in the cloud and in the sea, as the Apostle says, "Our ancestors were all under the cloud and all went through the sea."[160]

There is no question how Aphrahat reads the chronology of the paschal night. He found this sequence of events in the *Diatessaron*, still in his day the canonical gospel of the Eastern Syrian rite. The paschal night has become in Tatian's harmony a lengthy liturgy with the footwashing understood as baptismal aetiology followed by the meal. Aphrahat is not reading the paschal vigil *into* the *Diatessaron*; it is already there. By incorporating mimetic readings into the text, Tatian has produced the "cultic legend" for Pascha from the passion narratives so sought after by modern scholars.[161]

IV. Observations

As with any act of reading, how references to ritual practice are understood rests finally with the reader – one need only refer to modern discussions about sacramental allusions in Jn 6 as example. For the first readers of ATh, "Nisan" may have meant "paradise" or simply "spring." In the fourth century, readers would have understood the king's charity as a Lenten discipline, a liturgical season that did not yet exist at the time of writing, just as they would understand the temporal frame of the king's baptism as the paschal vigil. There is, of course, a purely practical reason for baptizing in the spring. Even in milder Mediterranean climates, early April would be the first humane time to baptize nude in cold water. North of the Alps it would require a heated bath – or an icepick. It is not surprising that Pentecost remains an "appropriate season" when Christianity spreads to less balmy climes.

---

[160] loc. cit.
[161] There are numerous mimetic readings of the passion narrative: Trocmé, Etienne, Passion as Liturgy, London 1983, the earliest Pascha was a commemoration; the passion narrative is its founding text; also Feneberg, Rupert, Christliche Passafeier und Abendmahl. Eine biblisch-hermeneutische Untersuchung der ntl. Einsetzungsberichte. STANT 27, 1971, esp. 123-138. For critique, see Green, WUNT 2.33, 1988, 192-214.

In the same way, with only two reasonable choices for harmonizing gospel chronology, Tatian may have chosen arbitrarily to place all liturgical action, including the Syn supper and the Joh footwashing, in the paschal night. Other mimetic readings in the *Diatessaron* that alter gospel narrative, however, suggest that the same mimetic constructs that produced light at the Jordan baptism also shaped narrative sequence as Tatian recounted the last days of Jesus' life. Later Syriac writers certainly exploit this convergence, and even in the *Didascalia* the paschal meal stands out against the silence in other regions.

The most obvious conclusion is that Tatian placed such a mimetic reading there for them to find, because he had already found it in Syrian paschal theology. Whether the accent on the eucharist as Pascha is placed in the second century or at the heart of the Synoptic gospels, Tatian's sequence embraces the paschal analog to the Syrian reading of the Jordan baptism: it is the story of origins for liturgical practice, measured by NT canon and constructed by the same mimetic method already applied by Ignatius at the beginning of the second century. If the traditions behind the *Didascalia's* presentation of the meal are not as recent as the week-long fast, then it too, indicates that the aetiological reading of the Synoptic Pesach frame is not a novelty of fourth century Syriac writers.

Why is it that the Syrian tradition insists not only that the meal the night before Jesus' death was a Pesach meal, often even adding the lamb not mentioned in any gospel narrative, but that Jesus ate and drank with his disciples? That this interpretation follows closely the cues of the Syn should not be confused with mere chronology, which may be expanded, compressed, or harmonized as the situation requires. After Hippolytus, Syn chronology is generally adopted in the West, Joh in the East, with a few authors presenting different chronologies in different contexts.[162] If Tertullian's water-bearer/baptism typology is any measure, liturgical mimesis addressed to the Syn meal could have produced such narratives anywhere by mid-fourth century. Both method and NT models

---

[162] Cf. Melito fragment from *Incarnation of Christ*: "His divinity Christ showed through signs in the course of three years after his baptism, but his humanity in the thirty years before his baptism." Preserved by Anastasius Sinaita, Hodegos 3. See this text and lists at Strobel, Kalender, 101-109. Origen makes no definitive conclusion. In Comm. in Mt. 26.2.75, Hom. 32 in Lucam 4.19, De princ. 4.1.4, Ezekiel Hom. 1.4, one year; in Comm. in Mt. 24.15, ser. 40, the Joh three. Hippolytus' calendar is based on a one-year ministry, but he assumes three in Comm. in Daniel 4.3.

were equally available in all regions, yet nowhere else are such stories to be found. Irenaeus finds eating and drinking rhetorically convenient, but his reading of eucharistic texts does not consider anamnesis of Christ's death integral to the sacrament. Except for Sunday celebration, Irenaeus' understanding of the paschal celebration is identical to the broader Asian tradition.

"Eucharistic" readings begin to creep into later paschal homilies such as IP, but only because of the acceptance of the canon, and usually harmonized with the Asian reading of Ex 12 as passion. The institution of the eucharist is a sub-plot of the passion narrative, but not the whole story as it becomes in Syriac writers. For the same reason, Origen must come to grips with a canonical text, but real food has as little place in his banquet of the Logos as real ritual in his paschal metaphors. Since Origen is not concerned for the text's liturgical significance, the paschal frame may remain. The IP homilist, however, has no use for Pesach, and takes pains to show that the Pascha Jesus "desired with a great desire" (Lk 22.15) to eat with his disciples is the "new" eucharist, not the "old" rite of Ex 12. While only a modern exegete can be expected to expound on the meaning of Pesach as Judaic ritual, the allergy to the Pesach frame is still symptomatic. The *Didascalia* redactors wants a non-Judaic Pesach as well, but with meal intact. Syriac readings are fully consistent with what has already been shown here: a strong tendency toward mimetic readings of NT narrative since the days of Ignatius and the Christian Sibyl, shaping Tatian's *Diatessaron*, and overabundant in the *Didascalia.*

One source for this insistence on Jesus' eating with the disciples is thus an unbroken Syrian tradition of ritualization of Christ narrative that does not stop even after the formation of the canon. Second century exegesis across the church had subsumed the rituals of Pesach into kerygmatic narrative. Yet for later Syrian writers, the rites described in Ex 12 do not lose their character as *ritual.* The moment Pesach rites disappeared was at the institution of the eucharist: the Last Supper was a carefully performed ritual at which Jesus as High Priest presided.[163] Without quibbling over the provenance of Mark, the earliest Syrian source depicting the Pesach meal is Matthew. The second is the *Diatessaron,* the third, the *Didascalia.* Somewhere between the gospel and the

---

[163] See Murray, Symbols, 179. Continuity of OT priesthood was assured for the Syriac tradition by John the Baptist or even Simeon.

harmony, between Matthew's ordering the church through words of Jesus and the *Didascalia's* new words of the apostles, there arose an aetiological reading of the Pesach meal narrative for the Syrian paschal feast. The trajectory drawn from Ignatius and the Sibyl would suggest that there are other points on this line that penetrate at least into the early decades of the second century. For the purposes of this study, however, it is only necessary that the *Didascalia*, which cannot say "Pascha" without mentioning Jesus' eating the meal with the disciples, is preserving a tradition at least one generation old, and that theologians in other regions were aware of this reading and reacted to it.

That the Fourth Gospel, whose most striking liturgical feature is its lack of a meal institution narrative, would figure greatly against Antiochene paschal theology is no mystery either. Aphrahat will show that anti-Judaic polemic connected to the Pascha could be effortlessly adopted, even developed, in the Syrian tradition. Yet this tradition would not relinquish the paschal frame of the meal even when it becomes the target of this polemic generously administered by writers in other regions. It is this meal as paschal celebration, indeed, an entire sacramentology fused with scriptural narrative, that is at stake at the Council of Nicaea.

E. The Minor Controversy: Fasting in the Days of Pascha

When the early third century *Apostolic Tradition* turns to the problem of a traveller who did not know when to begin the Pascha, it attempts to provide an answer through the provisions made at Num 9.6-11:

> The Lord spoke to Moses, saying: Speak to the Israelites, saying, Anyone of you or your descendants who is unclean through touching a corpse, or is away on a journey, shall still keep the passover to the Lord. In the second month on the fourteenth day, between the two evenings, they shall keep it ...But if anyone who is clean and is not on a journey, and yet refrains from keeping the passover, shall be cut off from the people for not presenting the Lord's offering at its appointed time, such a one shall bear the consequences for the sin.

To resolve an identical problem in Christian observance, this provision translates:

> In the Pascha, no one may take a meal before the offering is made (i.e., vigil eucharist). For the one who does so is not accounted as having fasted. If one is pregnant or ill and cannot fast two days, because of necessity that person should fast only on the Sabbath, content with bread and water. But if a person was at sea or in some necessity and did not know the day, when he knows it, he should fast after the Fifty (or Fiftieth) Days. *For it is not the Pascha (i.e., Pesach) which we keep*: (only in Copt. and Arm.) the type has passed away so that that of the second month has ceased, and having learned the truth, one need [only] keep the fast.[1]

While this division into two observances may seem perfectly natural, it required a bit of thought and search through the "archives" to find an authoritative solution. This is because the Pascha of the second and third centuries comprised not only the vigil, but a communal fast as much a "work of the people" as the nocturnal liturgy. While a writer may find it necessary to distinguish between fast and liturgy, "Pascha" or "days of Pascha" is often the term used for one or both, and even prepositions such as *in* a period of time or *on* a certain day will not always indicate which is meant. To moderns thinking in discrete liturgical units

---

[1] ApTrad 33, as amended in OAK, 44, from Botte, LQF 39, 78-80. Cf. CQL 44, 58 f.

– Lent, Holy Week, Easter – this use of language seems imprecise, but it merely means that the fast was integral to keeping the Pascha, not strictly preparatory, as if it were a little Lent that grew.

This essential unity is less theological abstraction as experienced reality. A fast is never simple deprivation of food, but a dedicated act of prayer, always accompanied by almsgiving. As the *Didascalia* requires:

> And the gains of your fast of six days offer to the Lord God. However, let those of you whose worldly possession is abounding serve those who are poor and needy and refresh them diligently that the reward of your fast may be received.[2]

As the fast continues, prayers concentrate into the common prayer of worship in a lengthy vigil, where participants, whose physically demanding work followed the rhythm of the sun, deprive themselves of sleep. Second century Christians were "doing the Pascha" as soon as they began the fast, which was broken late in the paschal night with an agape-eucharist. The *Didache's* insistence that Christians not fast on the same days as the Pharisees shows that fasting, its time and duration, was as much a part of religious identity as communal worship: in essence, the *Didache* prohibits inhabiting a common liturgical space.

Sources throughout the second and third centuries suggest that while in some places there is a tendency to extend the fast, there are still marked differences on the regional, communal, and even individual level. Some communities who observed the Wednesday and Friday station days as fasts or half-fasts would be prone to lengthen them, perhaps adding the Thursday as well. Even after the paschal fast is extended to Monday, the Friday and Saturday fast are still considered the most obligatory, probably because it is the older practice. The ApTrad is prepared to shorten this fast only when circumstance or physical condition prohibits the full two-day observance.

As it could fall on any day of the week, the Quartadeciman Pascha would necessarily conflict with the weekly rhythm of stations and the Lord's Day, and it is often assumed – without a great deal of examination – that a one-day fast was common among Quartadeciman communities.[3]

---

[2] DA 21, CSCO 408, 201.21-24.

[3] So Lohse, Passafest, 43-50. See critique, Huber, Passa, 10 f. Epiphanius writes at Pan 50.1.5 of Quartadecimans "who keep the same one day and fast and celebrate the mysteries on the same one day" (NHMS 36, 23), but by then, "Quartadeciman" means Montanist splinter groups, not the Great Church in Asia Minor.

This diversity of choice and custom in the midst of change is a guarantee that while different fasting practices *by themselves* generate no major conflicts, they still produce a great deal of talk about who does what when, for how long, and why. As this discussion progresses, more and more mimetic demands are made on NT narrative, until finally, the *Didascalia* reverses the dynamic to create the perfect aetiology for the paschal fast.

There are enough literary traces to follow this discussion for two centuries as it moves from rite to text and back again. Besides Tertullian's Carthage, there is the Syrian *Gospel of Peter*, ca. 150, a global comment in a letter of Irenaeus around 195, the *Didascalia*, ca. 230, and a letter of Dionysius of Alexandria a decade or so later. While Dionysius' letter intends to end the discussion in Egypt, Aphrahat's paschal treatise of 344/5 shows that a century after the *Didascalia* is published, a community in the Persian Empire is asking the same questions in the same way.

A fragment from a "Gospel of the Hebrews" cited by Jerome also takes part in this discussion, but when and where is anyone's guess. The impossibility of dealing with what Jerome thought he read in a work whose context he may have totally misinterpreted *and* whose translation may be faulty only limits the value of the citation. Somewhere in Egypt, Syria, or Palestine in the first half of the century, a community of Torah-observant Christians was fasting during the Pascha and also seeking to regulate the practice through apostolic example. This search always leads to one particular story about Jesus and fasting, which second century readers were certain was a direct command to fast in the days of Pascha.

I. Carthage, ca. 207 CE

When Tertullian is forced to defend Montanist "innovations," it is because "psychics" opposed to the "pneumatic" Montanists have elevated such differences to the level of community boundary. Not only had the Montanists lengthened the stational fasts past the ninth hour (3 pm), but twice a year observed a Monday-Friday half-fast of xerophagy, "dry eating" of bread and cheese with no fruit juices, meat, or fat. This added severity would hardly have caused the rhetorical border skirmish sounding forth in Tertullian's *De ieiunio* if Carthaginian Christians had not already sharply distinguished between psychic/catholic and pneumatic/Montanist identities. Taking great rhetorical pleasure in depicting the "psychics" as stultified, oversated gluttons with sexual appetites to match,[4] Tertullian has no desire to blur the lines of demarcation.

Helping draw this line on the catholic side are rhetorical tools with which their opponent Tertullian works as a master craftsman – anti-Judaic and anti-Hellenic polemic.[5] Catholics had linked xerophagy to the purification rites of the cults of Apis, Isis and Cybele, while they had negated the "new discipline" with the all-purpose cultic exterminators Isa 58.4 and Gal 4.10.[6] Both rhetorical standbys find a new context, but retain their original function, defining one religious community against another.

In keeping with the "new" method of rubricizing the NT, the catholics had also sought scriptural grounds for breaking the fast at the ninth hour: Acts 3.1, where "Peter and John were going up to the temple at the hour of prayer."[7] At first, this search for apostolic precedence, if undertaken at all, was probably as casual as Tertullian's musings about baptismal types, but when rhetorical situation demanded, its results could be elevated to scriptural commands.

Tertullian deconstructs this use of chronological detail by pointing out that Luke does not mention a fast and tells other stories (Acts 10.9; 2.15) not conducive to such readings. Tertullian even suggests that the ninth hour was a Judaic tradition Peter had retained, and which along with the third and sixth hour still divided the day in the general culture.[8] After "history" neutralizes catholic rhetoric, Tertullian concludes:

> I put this forth only for those who believe they are acting according to Peter's model [ex forma Petri agere], of which they are ignorant, not because we wish to repudiate the ninth hour, which we often observe on Wednesdays and Fridays, but because we must give all the more worthy a reason for those customs observed because of tradition when they do not possess the authority of scripture, until they are confirmed or corrected by heavenly charisma.[9]

---

[4] See De ieiunio 12.3. An imprisoned catechumen is so bloated from provisions brought by "psychics" he cannot make confession. Also 16.8 (CCSL 2, 1275 f.): "Your god is the belly, your temple lungs, your altar rolls of fat, your priest a cook, your holy spirit the smell of burning fat, condiments are your charisms and your prophecies, belching."
[5] At De ieiunio 17.6 f., Tertullian counters with the destruction of the Temple and "showy" Jewish prayers, and pagan cults as demonic imitation of Christian rites, a tactic of Justin. Cf. 2Apol 5.2-5, 1Apol 66.4, and esp. Dial 70.1-3.
[6] De ieiunio 2.4, 6, CCSL 2, 1258.
[7] De ieiunio 2.3, loc. cit.
[8] De ieiunio, 10.2 f., CCSL 2, 1267.
[9] De ieiunio 10.5, CCSL 2, 1267 f.

This unmasks the real dispute: what constitutes authority in the church and who possesses it. Throughout what will become a singularly nasty attack on the catholic majority, there is one fasting aetiology that remains sacred, and which Tertullian even employs for rhetorical advantage – the very one the catholics had accused the Montanists of violating:

> Certainly in the gospel, they claim, are those fastdays determined in which the Bridegroom was taken away, and that these are the only legitimate Christian fastdays, the old Laws and Prophets having been abolished.[10]

Tertullian answers these accusations somewhat later:

> You raise the objection that the ritual customs [sollemnia] of faith are prescribed by scripture and tradition, and that no more observance may be added because innovations are prohibited. Keep to this position if you can! For behold, I accuse you that besides the Pascha, you also fast on other days besides those in which the Bridegroom was taken away...[11]

For both Montanist and catholic, the words of Jesus uttered in a dispute over fasting are an unambiguous command to fast weekly on the station days *and* each year during the days of Pascha, thus not subject to dispute at all. Weekly and yearly rhythm are not fully synchronous with narrative, but they share the same story of origins and can narrate the passion in two catechetical steps. Why do we fast? We fast as our Lord commanded, in the Bridegroom's absence. The aetiological "dialect" would stop here, but an additional search for meaning would turn immediately to absence and presence, cross and resurrection. Tertullian's "imprecision" – here the Pascha is the fast, not the liturgy – also indicates that fast and feast constitute a single observance in the minds of both groups of Carthaginian Christians. They were likely so linked from the very beginning.

In his tactical switch to "real" history, Tertullian is certainly correct about the ninth hour as a time of prayer being a Judaic survival in the Christian cult, and probably correct in deducing its ultimate origins from the rhythm of the day. Yet what of the *paschal* fast? While MPes 10.1 speaks of a half-day fast before the Pesach meal, its prescription has more practical than theological meaning.[12] Celebrants will be hungry for the meal, perhaps providing for the necessary "haste," but skipping

---

[10] De ieiunio, 2.3, CCSL 2, 1258.
[11] De ieiunio, 13.1, CCSL 2, 1271.
[12] Lohse, Passafest, 73 f.

the usual mid-day meal before a banquet is not so much religious motivation as common sense. Jewish fasting practices were also traditionally
anchored more to autumn festivals than spring, while the only fast
enjoined in the OT is the Day of Atonement (Lev 16.29-31, Num 29.7).
Other than a transfer from this observance or a sign of mourning, sup-
plication, or passage not unique to Judaism, the origins of the Christian
paschal fast must be found in the specific Christian celebration, not in
its Jewish matrix.

Merely by its nature as a yearly festival, the paschal liturgy would be
preceded by a fast even in those communities where it did not coincide
with preparation for baptism,[13] because this is what preparation meant in
Late Antiquity, hence the ease with which catholics may make unfavor-
able comparisons to pagan mysteries.[14] The paschal fast obeys a natural
ritual logic not requiring narrative to explain its existence, though as with
any observance, mimesis will seek narrative referents as soon as the practice moves from performed ritual to rhetoric about it. Catechetical traditions tighten the mimetic fit from one generation to the next: today's
"congruence" is tomorrow's story of origins and scriptural command.

Whether as background, subtext, or glaringly on the surface, "absence
of the Bridegroom" as dominical command for the paschal fast has a
voice in almost every conversation about fasting practice, while the negative mimesis of the *Didache* is occasionally heard as a steady drone.
With their particularly one-dimensional view of the relationship between
rite and text, the early third century authors of the *Didascalia* have the
most difficulty acknowledging the Bridegroom aetiology for their purposes. Its geographic spread and long attestation are only part of the
dilemma, for by the time the *Didascalia* traditions were set to writing,
people across the Church were not only connecting this narrative to rite,
but asking exactly how long the Bridegroom was gone.

II. From Rite to Text: The Fasting Apostles

1. Gospel of Peter *(Syria, before 150[15])*

A passion-resurrection narrative discovered in a monastic grave in Upper
Egypt must have been a mere torso when it reached early medieval

---

[13] Lohse, Passafest, 73-75.
[14] Mystery cults often prescribed a short fast, see Burkert, Mysterien, 75-97.
[15] For discussion of provenance, see Brown, Messiah, 1341-1345.

scribes. Beginning after Pilate washes his hands, the fragment ends before a resurrection appearance to Peter, Andrew, and Levi at the Sea of Galilee. A much smaller fragment discovered at Oxyrhynchos shows that the work circulated in Egypt by 200 CE.

Somewhat earlier, Serapion of Antioch writes that Christians in Rhossos (Syrian coast or Cilicia) had been using a Gospel of Peter he had not known until docetic interpretations forced him to write a treatise against it.[16] The *Didascalia* measures how little Serapion accomplished:

> ...Pilate the judge, did not consent to the deeds of their wickedness, but took water and washed his hands and said: "I am innocent of the blood of this man." But the people answered and said, "His blood by upon us, and upon our children." And Herod commanded that he should be crucified, and our Lord suffered for us on the Friday.[17]

Only in GPt does Herod give such a command (1.2), and Pilate is one step closer to sainthood.

Compared to the four canonical accounts, popular story-telling has actualized the narrative in several ways. Jesus is always "the Kyrios," never Jesus, and the "Kyriake," Lord's Day, is mentioned twice (9.35; 12.50).[18] The richness of scriptural allusion, however, has not survived the return to oral forms and back again. Only one reference to the "archives" has withstood the transition:

> But Joseph, the friend of Pilate and of the Lord, had been standing there; and knowing they were about to crucify him, he came before Pilate and requested the body of the Lord for burial... And Herod said, "Brother Pilate, even if no one had requested him, we would have buried him, since indeed Sabbath is dawning. For in the Law it has been written, 'The sun is not to set on one put to death [Dt 21.23].'" And he gave him over to the People before the first day of their feast of Unleavened Bread.[19]

GPt follows Joh chronology, but not Joh theology. Jesus is crucified on 14 Nisan, but an allusion to the paschal lamb is never made:

---

[16] Reported by Eusebius, EH 6.12.2-6, presumably from Serapion's preface.

[17] DA 21, CSCO 408, 199.16-20.

[18] First number is paragraph, the second continuous verse: 4.10 follows 3.9.

[19] GPt 2.3-5, SC 201(M. Mara) 1973, 42; ET, Brown, 1318. The capitalization of "People" is mine, but hardly needs justification.

But a certain one of those wrongdoers reviled them, saying, "We have been made to suffer thus because of the wrong that we have done; but this one, having become Savior of men, what injustice has he done to you?" And having become irritated at him, they ordered that there be no leg-breaking, so that he might die tormented.[20]

Scriptural reference has not just been erased, but reversed by another motivation. Those refusing to break the legs of the executed are not Roman soldiers, but a Jewish mob in the grips of collective paranoia. After the Lord is buried in the "Garden of Joseph,"

> Then the Jews and the elders and the priests, having come to know how much wrong they had done to themselves, began to beat themselves and say, "Woe to our sins. The judgment has approached and the end of Jerusalem." But I with the companions was sorrowful; and having been wounded in spirit, we were in hiding, for we were sought after by them as wrongdoers and as wishing to set fire to the sanctuary. In addition to all these things we were fasting; and we were sitting mourning and weeping night and day until the Sabbath.[21]

The sealed tomb[22] attracts a crowd from "Jerusalem and the surrounding area" (9.34) while "elders" have also camped out to safeguard the tomb (10.38). While Peter and the disciples fast, mourn, and weep, "Jews" and their Roman lackeys hold a shadow paschal vigil around the tomb, daring Jesus to rise from the dead.

The fragment ends with setting the scene for a resurrection appearance along the lines of Jn 21.1-23:

> Now it was the final day of Unleavened Bread; and many went out, returning to their homes since the feast was over. But we twelve (!) disciples of the Lord were weeping and sorrowful; and each one, sorrowful because of what had come to pass, departed to his home. But I, Simon Peter, and my brother Andrew, having taken our nets, went off to the sea. And there was with us Levi of Alphaeus whom the Lord...[23]

"Unleavened Bread" lasts from the death of Jesus on Friday, 14 Nisan, to his appearance in Galilee on the last day of Azyma. The resurrection occurs on the Sunday falling during the festival week.

[20] GPt 4.13 f., SC 201, 46, ET, Brown, 1319.
[21] GPt 7.25-27, SC 201, 52; ET, Brown, 1319.
[22] In the 5 c. Gospel of Gamaliel, the tomb is a holy place (Jerusalem liturgy!) decorated with flowers by Pilate's wife. Van Den Oudenrijn, Marc-Antonius, Gamaliel. Äthiopische Texte zur Pilatusliteratur, SpicFri 4, 1959.
[23] GPt 14.58-60, SC 201, 66; ET, Brown, 1321.

Why do the disciples fast – all twelve of them – *until* the Sabbath? This could, of course, be a similar slip of the pen making Peter observe the Friday station. Yet in narrative time and Hebrew reckoning, if the disciples are fasting until the *break* of Sabbath, they will begin to take food almost immediately after Jesus dies – something remarkable, like David ceasing his fasting and prayers at the death of his first son by Bathsheba (2Sam 12.15-23). Instead, Gentile Christian ritual time measured from sunrise to sunrise may dictate the narrative.

Raymond Brown reads this chronological notice as the Sabbath before the resurrection.[24] The disciples mourn, weep, and fast not just *up to* the Sabbath, but *through* the Sabbath until the Lord's Day: "Unleavened Bread" lasts two days. This may not be *their* Pesach-Mazzot from 14-21 Nisan, but it could reflect instead *our* practice in the author's community. Actual Judaic practice is irrelevant. First century Jewish elders did not break travel restrictions on the Sabbath, a high holy day no less, to subject themselves to corpse contamination at a tomb, but they do so here.

Dominic Crossan[25] sees this Sabbath as the end of Unleavened Bread (21 Nisan) mentioned at 14.58, the initial notice preparing the reader for the lost appearance story.[26] Fasting and mourning in the Bridegroom's absence would be coterminous with a traditional Pesach-Mazzot of seven days. This week-long fast is highly unlikely at mid-second century, but the most probable reading in the third.

The noncanonical detail that Peter and the disciples were fasting and weeping is a clue to early second century Syria paschal fasting practice somewhere north or east of Antioch. Ritual time has affected narrated time in a Christian *Fast* of Unleavened Bread, negatively set off from Judaic ritual, positively modeled by the *forma Petri*. At this stage, even in Syria, this "congruence" is enough. The Bridegroom is gone, and there is fasting in those days, whether every Friday or the fast of Pascha.

---

[24] Brown, Messiah, 1340 f.

[25] Crossan, Dominic, The Cross that Spoke, San Francisco 1988, 23, assigns this narrative to the last of three stages of redaction of his hypothetical "Cross Gospel."

[26] Also Mara, SC 201, 209.

2. *The* Gospel(s?) of the Hebrews *(Egypt, Syria/Palestine? ca. 140)*

Clement, Origen, and Jerome cite a Jewish-Christian writing they term *Gospel of the Hebrews*. It is unlikely that all citations stem from the same work,[27] however reconstructed in relation to an equally reconstructed *Gospel of the Nazarenes*. Frustration over this dilemma directs itself squarely at Jerome, who is particularly inconsistent in his citations and muddies the waters with his theory – later silently dropped – that some work he saw in the library at Caesarea is the Hebrew original of Mt.[28] Whatever its provenance, the work tells a story of origins with an apostolic model:

> Also the Gospel called according to the Hebrews, which I recently translated into Greek and Latin, and which Origen often uses, relates after the resurrection of the Savior: "Now the Lord, after giving the linen cloth to the servant of the priest, went to James and appeared to him (for James had sworn he would not eat bread from that hour in which he had drunk the Lord's cup until he should see him again, risen from among them that sleep)," and again after a little, "'Bring', said the Lord, 'a table and bread'," and immediately it is added, "He took bread and blessed and broke it and gave it to James the Just and said unto him: "My brother, eat your bread, for the Son of Man is risen from among them that sleep."[29]

In the NT, James, leader of the Jerusalem Jewish Christians and sometime opponent of Paul, neither follows Jesus nor partakes of the supper before the crucifixion. Now he does both, and supplants the Magdalene and Peter as first witness of the resurrection. A eucharist with portable table over which the risen Lord presides ends a fast by a model apostle lasting from the supper to the resurrection. Following these rubrics, this community kept a stringent fast longer than twenty-four hours before the paschal vigil – *ex forma Jacobi*. The Bridegroom is absent from the time of his capture. The community vows to fast until his return near dawn on the third day.

---

[27] Klijn places this story in the Egyptian gospel Jerome found cited by Origen. Das Hebräer- und das Nazoräerevangelium, ANRW II,25.5, 3997-4033, summary 4030-3. Pritz, Nazarene, 90-91, claims it for the Syrian/Palestinian Gospel of the Nazarenes.
[28] Around 392, when De viris illustribus was written, Jerome claimed Matthean authorship for the GHeb. These claims disappear about five years later. See Thornton, Timothy C. G., Jerome and the 'Hebrew Gospel according to Matthew', StPat 28, 1993, 118-122.
[29] Jerome, vir. ill. 2. TU 14.1 (ed., E. C. Richardson), 1896, 7 f.

III. Irenaeus: Letter to Victor of Rome, Part One

1. The Background

Since at AH 3.3.2-4 Irenaeus presents the churches of Rome, Smyrna, and Ephesus[30] as exemplars of apostolic tradition, it must have been painful to see a dispute long brewing over paschal observance in the Imperial capital.

To bolster a plea for tolerance, Irenaeus lists a variety of paschal fasting practices whose origins reach back to a shadowy past:

οὐδὲ γὰρ μόνον περὶ τῆς ἡμέρας ἐστὶν ἡ ἀμφιβήτησις, ἀλλὰ καὶ περὶ τοῦ ἔδους αὐτοῦ τῆς νεστείας. οἱ μὲν γὰρ οἴονται μίαν ἡμέραν δεῖν αὐτοὺς νεστεύειν, οἱ δὲ δύο, οἱ δὲ καὶ πλείονας· οἱ δὲ τεσσαράκοντα ὥρας ἡμερινάς τε καὶ νυκτεριανὰς συμμετροῦσιν τὴν ἡμέραν αὐτῶν. καὶ τοιαύτη μεν τοικιλία τῶν ἐπιτηρούντων οὐ νῦν ἐφ' ἡμῶν γεγονυῖα, ἀλλὰ καὶ πολὺ πρότερον ἐπὶ τῶν πρὸ ἡμῶν...[31]

For the controversy is not only about the day, but also about the very form of the fast. For some think it necessary to fast one day, others two, others even more days; and others measure their day as lasting forty hours, day and night. And such variation in the observance did not begin in our time but much earlier, with those before us...

Though the breaking of the fast and not its beginning or duration is at issue,[32] Irenaeus moves the point of contention away from a strict Lord's Day-14 Nisan opposition. While this may seem like a clever diversionary tactic, Tertullian's "imprecision" means that Irenaeus is still focused on dialogue about paschal observance. Some people fast longer than others, some people end the fast earlier than others. Irenaeus is only pointing out a slightly different conversation about time and duration that had never polarized "Two-dayers" and "Forty-hour-ites" into warring camps.

Of the fasts Irenaeus mentions, that of forty hours "day and night" betrays a highly mimetic character. A longer, indefinite period of time in the OT, the number calls to mind the forty days and nights of the flood,

---

[30] "In the same way, the church of Ephesus, founded by Paul, and in which John lived until the time of Trajan, is also a true witness of apostolic tradition." AH 3.3.4, SC 34, 114.

[31] Eusebius, EH 5.24.12-13. GCS 9.1, 494 f.

[32] Campenhausen, Hans, Ostertermin oder Osterfasten? VigChr 28, 1974, 114-138, argues the duration of the fast was the real issue.

the forty years in the wilderness, and already imitative in the NT of these types, the forty-day fast of Jesus after the temptation. Passion chronology and the Bridegroom's absence could also have furnished the primary object of mimesis: from Friday noon to a 3 am eucharist early Sunday morning would yield thirty-nine hours, probably close enough for an aetiology, especially in cultures not enslaved to the clock. Even if this forty-hour fast does not lie behind James' vow in GHeb, this text could do so simply by posing the question of duration. This question, and the whole surrounding discussion, briefly makes an appearance as a supporting argument in Irenaeus' letter.

Irenaeus mentions a variety of practices he must have come to know simply by journeying from Asia to Gaul. When and how did this diversity arise? Given Irenaeus' life history, the myth of an apostolic "Urpraxis" directly inherited from the "Urgemeinde" would have been difficult though not impossible to maintain. The unity and antiquity of apostolic tradition is an effective weapon against Gnostics "innovations."[33]

Yet in another place, Irenaeus describes this unity:

> This message, which it [the church] has received, and this faith, as I have said, sustains the church, although spread over the whole world, with such care, as if it lived in a single house. And it believes in this message as if it had only one soul and one heart, and proclaims, teaches, and passes this message on as if it had only one mouth. For if the languages all over the world are different, the strength [δύναμις] of the tradition is everywhere one and the same.[34]

Irenaeus contrasts the message and its medium, a necessary observation for a grecophone bishop evangelizing the Celts. In his letter, Irenaeus makes a similar contrast:

> [13] καὶ τοιαύτη μὲν ποικιλία τῶν ἐπιτηρεούντων οὐ νῦν ἐφ᾽ ἡμῶν γεγονυῖα, ἀλλὰ καὶ πολὺ πρότερον ἐπὶ τῶν πρὸ ἡμῶν, τῶν παρὰ τὸ ἀκριβές, ὡς εἰκός, κρατούντων τὴν καθ᾽ ἁπλότητα καὶ ἰδιωτισμὸν συνήθειαν εἰς τὸ μετέπειτα πεποιηκ πεποιηκότων των, καὶ οὐδὲν ἔλαττον πάντες οὗτοι εἰρήνευσάν τε καὶ εἰρηνεύομεν πρὸς ἀλλήλους, καὶ ἡ διαφωνία τῆς νηστίας τὴν ὁμόνοιαν τῇ πίστεως συνίστησιν.[35]

> [13]And yet such variation in the observance did not begin in our time but much earlier with those before us, who, without exactness, it seems, passed

---

[33] Brox, N. Introduction to Iren. AH, FC 8/1 1993, 107.
[34] AH 10.2. FC 8/1, 201.
[35] Eusebius, EH 5.24.12-13.GCS 9.1, 494 f.

on a plain and simple custom to posterity. Nevertheless they were all at peace, and we are at peace with one another: the difference in fasting confirms our oneness in the faith.

If "the very form of the fast" is substituted for "language," the arguments are identical. Unity is guaranteed by a common message and faith, not in identical liturgical expressions: the same argument that Paul had used to promote unity among Torah-observant and non-observant Christians in Rome.

2. An Acribious Look at Simplicity and "Idiotism"

The tenor of Irenaeus' characterization of the paschal fast handed on by "those before us" depends upon the meaning, connotation, and relationship of three words in two phrases: παρὰ τὸ ἀκριβές, (accuracy/exactness) and custom (συνήθεια) described as being καθ᾽ ἁπλότητα (simplicity) καὶ ἰδιωτισμόν.

The rare word ἰδιωτισμὸς is a term used by one elite to describe a non-elite. The distinction is between expert and layperson, the trained and the untrained, plain speaking and jargon. The range of connotation runs from a romanticized country innocence through neutral and mildly condescending to accusations of plebeian illiteracy. From Greek the word entered Latin as a special rhetorical term meaning to adopt the common touch for persuasive power, that is, an elite *posing* as a non-elite to achieve a rhetorical goal.

Irenaeus uses the word ἰδιωτισμὸς in one other place in his extant works. He is concerned about a textual variant of Rev 13.18, where the number 666 as symbol of the Antichrist appears as 616. Part of the text is preserved in a Greek, which must be supplemented by the Latin:

οὐκ οἶδα πῶς τινες ἐπακολουθήσαντες ἰδιωτισμῷ καὶ τὸν μέσον ἠθέτησαν ἀριθμὸν τοῦ ὀνόματος, πεντήκοντα ψήφους ὑφελόντες καὶ ἀντὶ τῶν ἓξ δεκάδων μίαν δεκάδα βουλόμενοι ἔναι. Hoc autem arbitror scriptorum peccatum fuisse, ut solet fieri quoniam et per litteras numeri ponuntur, facile littera graeca quae sexaginta enuntiat numerum in iota Graecorum litteram expansa.[36]

I do not see how such who are following "idiotism" have subtracted the number fifty before the six in the ten's column and arrived at 616. But I

---

[36] AH 5.30.1, SC 152, 372 f. The French is identical to Bardy: "certains ont pu se fourvoyer sous l'impulsion d'une opinion particulière."

suspect an error of the scribes, who easily took the Greek letter meaning "sixty" for iota, meaning ten.

Irenaeus continues:

> For some have accepted this without investigation, others have naively [only ἁπλῶς in Gk.; Lat.: simpliciter et idiotice] kept the ten, still others, however, have then dared in their ignorance [quidam autem (et) per ignorantiam] to search for names which possess this false number. Those who have done this simply and without malice, God will forgive.[37]

It may be that Irenaeus is calling these readers rank amateurs in the art of textual criticism. They do not know a variant reading when they see one, such as the important witness to the text of Rev, Codex C, which has the same 616 reading. But an acribious person will note a certain illogic. Put simply, is Irenaeus saying that he cannot see how uneducated persons incapable of performing a simple addition problem produce the sum 616? It is easy to see how such may make errors in mathematics. What Irenaeus cannot see is how anyone following the *plain sense* of the text could make such an error, unless that error were in the text itself, available for a *plain sense* reading. This "simple" and forgivable error does not become "ignorant" until people mistake it for arcane wisdom and seek a name to match the numbers.

This problem comes nearer to solution at the very beginning of AH, where Irenaeus characterizes his own style:

> But since we live among the Celts and for the most part take pains with this barbaric language, you should not seek rhetorical art, which we never learned, nor the power of written expression, in which we have no practice, or beautiful expressions or dialectic, which we do not understand. But what we write to you simply, truly and in plain language (ἁπλῶς, ἀληθῶς, καὶ ἰδιωτικῶς, Lat. simpliciter et vere et idiotice) you will receive with love and allow to grow in you....[38]

This is a rhetorical ἰδιωτισμός: Irenaeus claims the privilege of writing in simple, ordinary language instead of the refinements of Melito or the Atticisms of Clement of Alexandria. But if the two adverbs ἁπλῶς and ἰδιωτικῶς are substantivized and placed in a κατά extended adjective construction, then acribiousness is awarded a simple solution to the

---

[37] AH 5.30.1, SC 152, 372-374.
[38] AH 1 Præf., Harvey, 6.

problem of "idiotism." Irenaeus values simplicity and plain speech more highly than rhetorical art. The use of two of the same terms here and in his letter is not coincidence. Irenaeus feels he is imitating the simple style of the gospels, in which he knows that in a plain reading, there is no concern whatsoever for the duration of a paschal fast.

To support his plea for unity, Irenaeus sets up another contrast: between exactness and simplicity. "Those before us" had a simple practice, but it was not exact. Exactly what? Painstaking exactness must have an object and measure upon which to fix. If this object is not a single "apostolic" practice obscured by tradition, then what might it be? What training or education did "those before us" lack?

Though more physically demanding, a longer fast is not inherently less "simple" or "exact" than a one-day fast. Forty hours is a more exact time linked to narrative, and it seems that the market value of exactness has risen, somehow at the cost of simplicity. Ultimately, Irenaeus is not talking about liturgical praxis, but talking about people talking. He is not making a distinction between "simpler" practices passed on by idiotoi which, for better or worse, the church is stuck with, but one of language: between the rules of an older, simpler liturgical rhetoric, consistently followed in his own works, and a new "exactness," which is complicating everything. Irenaeus is including by reference an entire discourse searching for scriptural and apostolic precedents for liturgical practice.

Much "new style" language about rite is meant to drown out the dissonance between aetiology and "congruence," as well as between tradition and scripture, that Tertullian tries to maintain. The object of "exactness" is NT narrative: a mimetic reading then has a prior claim on "apostolicity" since it is based on "apostolic" writings. Such a reading is simply not a *plain sense* reading in Irenaeus' view. Yet in the paschal controversy, mimetis of NT narrative and appeals to apostolic tradition dictate the entire debate. The Bridegroom is absent. *Our* community fast follows this rule exactly, but we are not sure about *yours*. If this is the type of discourse Irenaeus has in mind, a bishop of Alexandria some seventy years later shares a certain distaste for its implications.

IV. The End of the Trajectory: Dionysius of Alexandria († ca. 265)

Diverging fasting practices continue well into the third century, long after "exact" liturgical mimesis had become the chief means of discourse about the paschal fast. A lengthy discussion of this "exactness" and its limitations occurs between Dionysius, Bishop of Alexandria from 248-264/265, and Basilides, a bishop in the Pentapolis. Dionysius writes:

> You sent to me, my most faithful and learned son, to inquire at what hour one ought to end the fast culminating the Pascha. For you say that some of the brethren maintain one should do so at cockcrow and some at evening. For the brethren at Rome, so they say, await the cockcrow, but concerning those in the Pentapolis you said sooner. And you ask me to set an exact limit and a definite hour, which is both difficult and risky. For it will be acknowledged by all alike that one ought to start the feast and the gladness after the time of our Lord's resurrection, until then humbling our souls with fasting. But by what you have written to me, you have quite soundly and with a good insight into the divine gospels established the fact that nothing definite appears in them about the hour at which he rose. For the evangelists described those that came to the tomb diversely – that is, at different times, and all said that they have found the Lord already risen.

Dionysius wishes very much to end the fast at the very moment of resurrection but by no means before, but after acribious study, he agrees with Basilides that the gospels are ambiguous concerning the exact time. The narrative gap left by diverging chronologies and the empty tomb story must remain intact. Dionysius then makes a decision:

> As things stand thus, we pronounce this decision for those who inquire to exactness at what hour or what half-hour or quarter of an hour they should begin their rejoicing at the resurrection of our Lord from the dead: those who are premature and relax before midnight, though near it, we censure as remiss and wanting in self-restraint; for they drop out of the race just before the end... And those who put off and endure to the furthest and preserve until the fourth watch (i.e. 3-6 am), when our Savior appeared to those who were sailing, "walking on the sea," (Mt 14.25) we shall approve as generous and painstaking. And those midway who stop as they were moved or as they were able, let us not treat altogether severely. For not all continue during the six days of the fast either equally or similarly, but some remain without food until cockcrow on all the days, some on two, or three, or four, and some on none of them.[39]

Dionysius' reply is an interplay of individual piety and endurance, pastoral concern, tradition, and mimesis directed to the gospels. The six-day

[39] CQL 49, 60 f.

fast is tacitly assumed as norm, but is not universally observed. With no "congruence," Dionysius votes for tradition and proper order. Some congregations celebrate the concluding eucharist early. Thinking this a lax innovation, Dionysius then gives an acceptable range: the 3 am conclusion, already witnessed by the EpAp and here linked with a christophany, is the best, but any time after midnight would be satisfactory.

A student of Origen, Dionysius attempts to clarify an obscure scripture by bringing in a similar one, the epiphany on the Sea of Galilee, which only Matthew supplies with a more exact chronology, "in the fourth watch of the night." And like Irenaeus, Dionysius pleads for a certain tolerance, though for different reasons. If Dionysius had been convinced that a mimetic reading of the resurrection accounts could yield the prescription Basilides desired, he certainly would have furnished it. As it stands, the Alexandrian bishop appears quite wearied by persons who demand exactness – acribiously reduced to a fifteen minute tolerance. The Bridegroom is absent. Synchronize your watches.

V. Observations

Much distance has been travelled from the *Gospel of Peter* to Dionysius, even more if late first century texts are taken as starting point. The initial layer of the *Didache* shows no interest in linking the stational fasts to Christ narrative of any kind, but only distinguishing them from those of the "hypocrites." Even if a later redactor added a reference to the words of Jesus, this is enough, just as the meal prayers take a simple narrative of ritual action – people gather – and transform it into a gathering into the Kingdom. There is no lack of mimesis, it is merely directed to a different object, just as Hermas or even Irenaeus can take the simplest narrative possible about baptism – people are bathed – and attach kerygmatic or doctrinal motifs to create a new narrative about rite. This means, of course, that the Christian stational fasts as well as the fast of Pascha were established practices before they were ever directly associated with NT narrative material. The absence of the Bridegroom is not their origin, but the first documented occurrence of ritual mimesis in Syrian sources after the Jordan story of Ignatius and the Sibyl: a word of Jesus read as rubric.

A link to Friday as the day of Jesus' death is the second step, but the identical narrative is used for both the Wednesday station and the paschal fast of whatever duration. In the early second century, Christians would fast for the absent Bridegroom as they might fast for the poor. The reference is to narrative, but not strictly to its sequence: at first the command to fast is understood as a word of Jesus, not mimesis of the passion narrative. Otherwise, the Thursday before Pascha, or in any week for that matter, would have a difficult time explaining itself as a non-fast day. But at this point, no one is asking such a question. Such a command is necessary, as Tertullian points out, because OT prescriptions for fasting have been abrogated by the appearance of Christ.

Though the absence of the Bridegroom lies behind the weeping and fasting apostles in GPt, moderns reading its chronology cannot agree about exactly when and how long the fast occurs. Historically, the earlier the date, the shorter the fast envisioned by the author, though there is always the possibility of a third century "update" to match the longer fast. The original readers would have seen Peter's fast as a mirror of their own, and the author did not need to supply the unnecessary facts moderns most want to know. Yet if *exact duration* were a question originally posed to or by the text, there would be no ambiguity for anyone. The Syrian community behind and immediately in front of GPt fasted because the Bridegroom was absent, and that is all they needed to know.

The question of duration is easier in GHeb, even if Jerome has translated the text not only into Latin, but into the liturgical theology of the fourth century Latin church. Yet whether this text originated in Egypt or the Jewish Christian "Nazarene" community in northern Syria, somewhere, Jewish Christians were engaged in the same search for a fasting aetiology as their Gentile counterparts. This text was designed for them to find.

Irenaeus does not directly engage in the conversation about fasting, but instead briefly reflects on various practices to show Victor that dialogue about liturgical diversity need not lead to division. If rhetoric about the beginning of Pascha ongoing since at least mid-second century has not been divisive, why should rhetoric about its ending? Since Carthaginian Christians are bickering among themselves and not with those of another region, both groups are certain that they are fasting "just like the book says" and can accuse the other side of violating the command. Whether they fast one day, two, or many, Christians in other regions are just as certain they are following the scriptural rubric with the same exactness. This is the origin of the conversation to which

Irenaeus refers. It is one still current in churches of the Patriarchate of Alexandria two generations later.

Dionysius' letter was designed to silence the rhetoric in congregations of the Pentapolis. After all, is the point of the story of Christ's rising from the dead merely to synchronize ritual practice? The fast cannot conform *exactly* to the shape of the canonical gospels. Demanding that the text perform this mimetic task is "difficult and risky," yet Christians in the Pentapolis keep hammering at the text until it obeys. Though Dionysius does not depict where this risk would lead if taken, chances are good that the frightening image he had in mind would look something like the paschal tract of the Syrian *Didascalia*.

VI. Syrian *Didascalia*

As it now encounters the reader, the paschal chapter (21) of the Syrian *Didascalia Apostolorum* (DA) is the product of several stages of editing to address a single concern: regulating the beginning of Pascha. Though it provides more than enough aetiologies for a six-day fast, DA 21 shows minimal interest in the form or content of the vigil and absolutely none in the Pentecost. Was kneeling prohibited during the Fifty Days? Did Christians refrain from the kiss of peace during the fast? These are odd omissions for a church order whose twelfth chapter carefully assigns liturgical roles and proper seating for worship. For DA 21, not Pascha as liturgy, but Pascha as fast is at issue. Allowing narrative tension to remain unresolved, Dionysius transfers the discussion to one of good order and tradition, but the DA perseveres until gospel narrative synchronizes exactly with the fast. Reaching this mimetic goal is expensive: not only does the kerygma of the Pascha disappear, but also the engaging homiletical style and logical composition characteristic of the DA as a whole.

The immediate literary environment only sharpens the contrast. Drawing on homiletic and apologetic traditions, DA 20 makes a natural progression from the resurrection of the dead to martyrdom as ultimate trust in the creative power of God:

> God Almighty raises us up through God our Savior, as he has promised. However, he raises us up from the dead as we are – in this form in which we are now, nevertheless in the great glory of everlasting life, with nothing wanting to us. Indeed, though we be thrown into the depth of the sea, or scattered by the winds like chaff, we are still within the world, and the

whole world itself is enclosed beneath the hand of God. From within his hand therefore will he raise us up, as the Lord our Savior has said: "A hair of your head shall not perish, but in your patience shall you possess your souls" (Lk 21.18 f.).[40]

Old standbys of Christian apologetic make an obligatory appearance: first the Sibyl, then the mythical phoenix of Egypt:

> If thus through a dumb animal God demonstrates to us about the resurrection, how much more ought we – we who believe in the resurrection and in the promise of God, if martyrdom comes to us, as men deemed worthy of all this glory that we should receive an incorruptible crown in the life everlasting – rejoice in the great grace and in the honor and glory of martyrdom for God, and accept it joyfully with all our soul, and to believe in the Lord God who will raise us up in the light of glory.[41]

With rhetorical models like these, the reader is unprepared for the "much confusion of thought and treatment"[42] that swirls through DA 21. This is because the number of voices speaking from the text keep increasing. The homilist and his scriptural citations are joined by an invisible apologist, the apostles speaking collectively, the risen Lord, and a polemicist – all speaking to and about the absence of the Bridegroom, sometimes to and about each other. By the time the chapter concludes, some of these voices have been joined by newer counterparts trying to clarify what the older ones have said, but retaining the same apostolic mask. The text as it exists today is thus as much in dialogue with itself as with the reader.

As if it were a chapter from a Christian Talmud that was never written, DA 21 begins with its "Mishnah" text, the dominical command to fast in the Bridegroom's absence, then strings together interpretive Gamara to modify this command to match a modified practice. A section repeats a thought from the previous one, supplies a contrastive conjunction or some other quickly applied grammatical glue, then goes on to talk about something else. Just as narrative coherence is no requisite for a rabbinical tract, addition and subtraction are the only compositional techniques necessary either for the first authors or later redactors who wish to join the conversation. In this sense, everything

---

[40] DA 20, CSCO 408, 175.15-24.

[41] DA 20, CSCO 408, 181.9-16, (alt.).

[42] Connolly, R. H., Didascalia Apostolorum. The Syriac Version Translated and Accompanied by the Verona Latin Fragments, Oxford 1929, XXXII.

is an "addition" or "interpolation" because there is only a beginning, no middle or end.

A difference in the relationship between rhetoric and history brings this comparison to a dead halt. The Talmud traces its conversations through time by attribution to rabbis of known chronology. The authors of the DA 21 only speak invisibly or behind an apostolic mask, at one point even through the words of the risen Christ. They do so, however, in a decidedly late second century language addressing a third century problem of ritual observance. This means that if source or tradition criticism silences all voices except the initial narrative, nothing is left. Since DA 21 wishes to change the "very form of the fast" as well as its content, then it must also change the way the Bridegroom aetiology is understood.

Grounding the fast in a passion chronology produced solely for its aetiological function is the "red thread" that holds this patchwork of traditions together, leading in two senses to a particularly intricate paschal "code." The DA is a law *code*, not proclamation. Its sole purpose is to be encoded in other speech, just as Epiphanius does in *De Fide* 22.1:

> On the apostle's authority synaxes are set for the fourth day of the week (Wed.), the eve of the Sabbath (Fri.), and the Lord's Day. But we fast till the ninth hour on the fourth day and the eve of the Sabbath, because the Lord was arrested at the beginning of the fourth day (Tues. night!) and crucified on the eve of the Sabbath. And the apostles taught us to keep fasts on these days in fulfillment of the saying, "When the bridegroom is taken from them, that they shall fast in those days.[43]

In Epiphanius' citation, the DA itself is completely invisible, leaving only the mantle of apostolic authority with which it has clothed its ordinances. Epiphanius resizes it to fit not only the fasts, but also the liturgies now held on the station days.

More deeply encoded is a similar aetiology in *De fabrica mundi* of Victorin of Pettau (Ptuj in Slovenia, halfway between Graz and Zagreb), who was martyred in the Diocletian persecutions of 304. This short tract gathers common typologies on the seven days of Creation, expanding with various other groups of four a similar list in Irenaeus' AH 3.11.8 for the "tetramorph" gospel.[44] Victorin writes:

---

[43] Epiphanius, De Fide 22.1, NHMS 36, 662; GCS 37, 522.

[44] Irenaeus' words are used in a large number of Gospel mss. as a preface. Metzger, Canon, 155, n. 18.

Nunc ratio veritatis ostenditur, quare dies IIII. tetras nuncupatur, quare usque ad horam nonam ieiunamus <aut> usque ad vesperum aut superpositio usque in alterum diem fiat.

Irenaeus begins with the four cardinal directions, then the gospels, the cherubim, and the four covenants. Victorin begins with the four elements and seasons, then the cherubim, gospels, rivers of Paradise, "generations" (not covenants) from Adam to Noah, Noah to Abraham, Abraham to Moses, Moses to Christ. But then Victorin adds:

> homo Christus Iesus auctor eorum quae supra memoravimus tetrade ab impiis conprehensus est. itaque ob captivitatem eius tetradem, ob maiestatem operum suorum et <ut> tempora humanitati salubria, frugibus laeta, tempestatibus tranquilla decurrant, ideo <aut> stationem? aut superpositionem facimus.[45]

The aetiology for Friday comes at the appropriate place:

> Adam enimque ad imaginem et similitudinem suam consummavit. idcirco autem prius opera sua consummavit, quam angelos crearet et hominem fabricavit, ne forte adiutores se fuisse falsa dictione adseverarent. hoc quoque die ob passionem domini Iesu Christi aut stationem deo aut ieiunium facimus.[46]

The "absolute independence" of Victorin from the DA, as well as "no reference" to its interpretations was essential to Annie Jaubert's theory of a Qumran survival in the Wednesday station day.[47] Unfortunately, Victorin's commentaries on Matthew and Exodus have not survived to control this chronological datum, but his only other extant work suggests that the roadblocks Jaubert erects are rhetoric, not history. Though Victorin wrote in Latin, he most likely was a native speaker of Greek,[48] thus his less than stellar Latin style and the concern here for "tetra." Continuing the second century Asian millennialist tradition of Papias and Irenaeus, Victorin's *Commentary on the Apocalypse* modifies this older theology with new impulses from Origen.[49] Origen's works were disseminated from Caesarea in the first half of the third century, at the same

---

[45] Victorinus Petavionensis, De fabrica mundi 3, CSEL 49, 4.

[46] Op. cit. 4, CSEL 49, 5.

[47] Jaubert, Annie, La Date de la Céne. Calendrier biblique et liturgie chrétienne, Paris 1957, 90.

[48] Only source about Victorinus is Jerome, De vir. ill. 74, Altaner, 183.

[49] Corti, Carmelo, Il regno millenario in Vittorino di Petovio, Aug 18, 1978, 419-433.

time the original Greek version of the DA was published in northern Syria. Its reworking in the Apostolic Constitutions, as well as early translations, indicates a broad reception. The time frame is the same; the only difference is how quickly the DA could find its way to an eastern Mediterranean port. As for the second point, in a list like this, "reference" is a gap that doesn't exist. Victorin doesn't mention Irenaeus either, and Irenaeus' interpretation of the gospels as the four cardinal winds breathing immortality into the church[50] disappears in a banal list of tetrads. "Interpretations" get lost in the code because Victorin is only interested in the numbers.

Yet to produce this code, the DA must also encode these commands in paschal language, including the strange reading of gospel chronology that echoes in Epiphanius and Victorin. No canonical source claims that Jesus was arrested on a Wednesday. But in the DA, the eve of the fourth day of the week is when the Bridegroom is led away – after eating the paschal meal with his disciples. In the *Didascalia's* scriptural search, "congruence" is not enough, but must give way to the simplistic ritualization of narrative that Tertullian and Dionysius wish to dispel. As a result, acribiousness is the *Didascalia's* most salient feature, for it is the earliest text to depend so heavily upon *mathematics* to make its case.

1. The Shape of Chapter 21[51]

In Harvard Harris 91[52] and allied mss., redactors have made a long but judicious cut only a few sentences after the exhortation.[53] Deleted were four older sections, leaving a newer, smoother flowing addition explaining and expanding, but never completely replacing the original. As if

[50] Text, above n. 125, p. 172.

[51] Dated ca. 230, Bradshaw, Origins, 88. Schwarz, Ostertafel, 104-121, with 7 sections from different traditions/recensions followed by Strobel, Kalender, 325-352, who sees the shorter H (Vööbus: G) ms. tradition is original (edition: Gibson, M.D., The Didascalia Apostolorum in Syriac, London 1903. Vööbus (CSCO 402, 33*-43*) shows H is only a shortened version. Holl, Bruchstück, 209 f., makes two divisions, while Schmidt, TU 43, 649-677) a pleas for the chapter's integrity. G.A.M. Rouwhorst, VigChrS 7.1, favors H[G] to find a "Quartadeciman" layer beneath a Nicaean covering.

[52] Before Vööbus' edition, this ms. was termed "H" for its discoverer, J. Rendel Harris. It has become ms. G, while for Achelis-Flemming and Strobel, it is still H.

[53] TU 25 (Achelis-Flemming), endnote to 105.32, 206. This is followed by mss. EFGIJKN, CSCO 408, 189, n. 92. TF in synopsis of both ms. types in Rouwhorst, VigChrS 7.2, Études, 125-139.

their eyes were on a diminishing supply of parchment,[54] the H-redactors shorten the entire work more drastically toward the end, and there were only five more chapters after the paschal tract had been penned. They did not compose the newer sections, but merely exploited them as commentaries that could replace their objects. While a made-to-order resurrection appearance in glaring conflict with the canonical gospels was dropped, the redactors retained the ordering of "Holy Week" events that collides just as violently with gospel texts. Clarity and brevity, not canon, were the sole criteria.

That there is anything left at all is a sign of generosity. Near the beginning of their work, the H-scribes had copied the later "Commandments from the Writing of Addai the Apostle," a tract not included in another family of important witnesses, but which succinctly originates the then current liturgical week and year as apostolic institutions:

> 3. Again the apostles constituted, that, on the fourth day of the week, there shall be a service, that is to say, qurbana, [eucharist] because on it our Lord revealed to them about His trial, and His sufferings, and His crucifixion, and His death, and His resurrection; and the disciples were in this sorrow.
>
> 4. Again the apostles constituted that on the 'arubta (=parasceve, Friday), at the ninth hour, there shall be a service, because that which had been spoken on the fourth day of the week about the suffering of our Savior was brought to pass on the 'arubta, while the worlds and the creatures trembled, and the luminaries in the heaven were darkened.
>
> …
>
> 6. Again the apostles constituted: observe the day of Epiphany of our Savior, which is the chief of the festivals of the church on the sixth day of January in the long reckoning of the Greeks.
>
> 7. Again the apostles constituted: forty days before the day of the passion of our Savior, you shall fast and then observe the day of the Passion and the day of the Resurrection[55] because our Lord Himself also, the Lord of the festival, fasted forty days, and Moses and Elijah who were imbued with this mystery, they also fasted forty days and then they were made to shine.[56]

What DA 21 accomplishes with a great deal of rhetorical maneuvering – getting from the absent Bridegroom to the weekly and yearly fasts and back to the passion account – DA 3 reaches quite efficiently with the

---

[54] Vööbus, CSCO 402, 37*-39*.
[55] The characteristic Syrian Biduum, documentable to 5 c. See CQL 184 f., n. 'g.'
[56] DA 3, CSCO 402, 37 f.

prophecy-fulfillment motif. With a new aetiology for a more recent practice, the Forty Days, DA 3 also has no need to show that the Bridegroom's absence makes strict logical sense for *both* the stational fasts *and* the fast of Pascha as mimesis of gospel narrative. As the text of DA 21 now stands in the "H" mss. family, the Bridegroom aetiology only does service for the fast of Pascha: DA 21 is now an expanding commentary on DA 3. There was thus no reason to include any of the outdated "confusion of thought and treatment" of DA 21 except respect for an ancient text. Making even more drastic reductions, ms. L leaves only four lines from the entire chapter.[57]

If the "H cut" is shown schematically relative to the whole, then the following chart should reproduce how these redactors read the original material. While there may be still more levels of redaction swimming beneath, here is where the H-redactors invite the modern reader to enter into the stream of tradition.

Except for a section explaining the "three days in the heart of the earth" and two resurrection accounts, each section in the "H cut" finds an equivalent passage with similar purpose and order. Since remaining sections could stand alone without their earlier counterparts, the H-redactors saw no reason for rhetorical doublets.

All prescriptions for fasting in "E" except for the Wednesday and Friday stations are found more concisely in "J." Since this is the point of the whole tract, the original material will have contained a similar passage, probably underlying the prescriptions of "J."

"H" answers "historical" questions about the odd chronology of "C" that would never have arisen without the original. Otherwise, why would an interpolator remove all traces of anti-Judaic rhetoric, then in quite lapidary fashion, count off the days, then the hours, until the resurrection? Yet if "H" could both explain the odd chronology of the original as insidious Jewish intrigue *and* anchor the fast to Monday, then there was no reason to retain the account in "C" or the abstruse exegesis of Zech 8.19 in section "E" set as a resurrection discourse. Though it still contains references to the event, "H" has no *narrative* of the resurrection, a further indication that the material it excised is prior to what remains.

An excurse on the emergence of the Gentile church, "F" struggles with Paul's stance in Rom 11, while "K" engages in a burlesque polemic

---

[57] Ms. Cambridge Add. 2023. Cf. CSCO 401, 41*.

A. Exhortation (CSCO 408, 184.9-188.10)

B. Transition (of sorts) *and Introduction*
And especially in the days of the Pascha, in which all the believers who are in all the world fast as our Lord and teacher said when they asked him…"

Absent Bridegroom (188.13-189.3)
Harmonized citation: Mk 2.18-20, Mt 9.14 f., Lk 5.33-35.[58]
Judas' betrayal: Mt 26.21, Mk 14.18-20

"H Cut"
(189.3-196.16)
Judas' betrayal: Jn 12.35, Mt 26.31
(189.3-8)

C. Passion Chronology I:
Fasting Aetiology (189.9-190.2)
From meal and betrayal Tuesday night, 11 Nisan, daily until crucifixion, Friday afternoon, 14 Nisan.

D. Death-Resurrection (190.2-18)
"Three days in the heart of the earth" Matthean resurrection account (alt.)

E. Stations and Paschal Fast (190.19-192.7)
Resurrection appearance at Levi's house
Zech 8.19: Stational and paschal fast

F. Supercession Excurse (192.21-196.15)
Israel's rejection of Jesus, God's rejection of Israel, and election of the Gentiles

G. Summary and Transition (196.16-21)
Command to fast "in the days of Pascha" And begin when your brethren who are of the People perform the Passover.
For when our Lord and teacher ate the Pascha with us, he was delivered up by Judas after that hour, and immediately we began to be grieved because he was taken from us."

H. Passion Chronology II:
Anti-Judaic Explanation (196.21-198.17)
Judas and Jewish priests plot to kill Jesus, Monday, 10 Nisan (196.21-197.19).
Explanation of "Tuesday night supper" chronology as part of plot (197.19-198.17).

[no equivalent]

J. Paschal Fast and Vigil (198.18-200.5)
Bridegroom aetiology recalled (199.8-15)
Prescriptions for fast and vigil (199.16-200.5)

K. Anti-Judaic Excurse (200.6-201.24)
Friday fast and the "mourning" of the Sabbath (200.6-201.16)
Command to fast on Sabbath of Pascha (201.17-24)

L. Addenda

Paschal Calendar (202.1-5)
Fasting permissible on Lord's Day only from midnight to 3 am at vigil (202.6-13)

[58] Corrected in some mss. See CSCO 408, 188, n. 81.

against Sabbath rituals. H-redactors saw no need for two discourses aimed at the Jews.

Earlier redactors who sought to clarify and complement original material had left cues for their successors to find. They had also considerably increased the anti-Judaic tendency of the chapter, which the H-redactors, by accident or design, further increased by excising older, less strident material.

2. Rhetorical Strategies

When a later scribe wished to summarize the twenty-first chapter for a table of contents, he produced the following outline:

1) Exhorting every Christian to keep himself from all evil and frivolous conversation and from all bad and pagan practice.
2) Concerning the holy fast.
3) Concerning the fourteenth of the passion and crucifixion of our Lord.
4) Concerning the fourteenth of the Pascha of the Jews and concerning the Friday of the passion and the Sabbath of the Gospel and the first day of the resurrection of our Savior.
5) Concerning the mourning of the Sabbath-day of the people of the Jews and concerning the rejoicing of the people of the Christians.[59]

With its reference to the Triduum, the fourth item is a clue that this scribe must be writing no earlier than the end of the fourth century, if not well into the fifth.[60] This does not detract from his ability as a reader, especially since the recension the scribe had before him may have already been revised to include these liturgies. In one family of mss.,[61] for instance, the first vigil of the Syrian Biduum is suddenly instituted by twice substituting "Friday" for "Sabbath." Since in the rest of the chapter there is concern only for a fast, not a liturgy, on this day, this is an "update" not part of the early third century text, but echoes the "apostolic" institution of this liturgy in the Commandments of Addai.

Even without such "updates," later readers could easily appropriate the paschal theology of the DA because it applies the identical historicizing strategy to the Pascha that would eventually unfold into the Triduum. Except for synchronizing the very moment of Christ's resurrection with

[59] CSCO 408, 184, n. 2. Ms. S
[60] Strobel, Kalender, 325 f.
[61] Mss. EFGHIJKN, CSCO 408, 199, n. 230, 231.

the celebration of the vigil eucharist, the DA never applies this strategy to the paschal *liturgy*, but only to the paschal *fast*, each day of the week receiving a particular narrative focus. Just as for Tertullian, both fast and vigil are facets of a single observance, and it would be two centuries or more[62] before anyone could tell that the DA had made the right move too strongly too soon on the wrong ritual practice.

As the scribe was composing the table of contents, he also performed a rudimentary rhetorical analysis: he sees one topic on the paschal fast (2), one on gospel narrative (3), and three contrasting Christian practice with either paganism (1) or Judaism (4,5). Already well at work in the first lines, negative mimesis becomes quite virulent in newer material. Yet even the supercession and the anti-Judaic excurse are tied to the fast. DA 21 leaves no stone unturned – even one hurled at the Jews – in an attempt to find aetiological value.

3. *The Homilist: Exhortation (section "A")*

The opening section of DA 21 is neither anti-Judaic nor even paschal, but uses anti-pagan rhetoric to image proper Christian conduct at a festival. The exhortation begins with an admonition to avoid "words of levity and impurity," strengthening this counsel with Ψ2.10-13 LXX, "Rejoice unto him with trembling." To introduce a series of proof texts[63] against idolatry, the author writes:

> Indeed, a faithful Christian, it says, must not recite the songs of the heathen, nor come near the laws and teachings of foreign assemblies. Indeed, it may happen that through such songs, he will make mention also of the name of idols, which God forbid that it by done by the faithful.[64]

This leads into a warning against swearing by the sun or moon, supported by another series of OT proof texts,[65] concluding with an admonition that neither curses nor the names of idols should come from a believer's mouth, "but blessings and psalms and the dominical and divine scriptures, which are the foundation of the truth of our faith."[66]

---

[62] Cf. Leo the Great, Hom. 49.1, CCSL 138A (Chavasse), 285 =CQL 135: "We do not commemorate single events, rather, we celebrate all of them together."
[63] Jer 5.7, 4.1 f.; Hos 2.17.
[64] CSCO 408, 185.5-10.
[65] Dt 32.21, 4.19; Jer 10.2; Ez 8.16-18.
[66] CSCO 408, 188.8-10.

In the easy syncretism that marks popular religion, astrology, solar piety, and swearing oaths are as much real targets for the "Didascalians" as for Leo the Great and John Chrysostom,[67] or, for that matter, the Hebrew prophets cited in the exhortation. But unless these scriptures were arranged to combat a specific Hellenic festival around the vernal equinox (as Leo is uneasy at the winter solstice), then this scriptural catena has been transferred from somewhere else. While Strobel rightly sees these texts gravitating toward the second and third commandment, most readers will probably not see with him a polemic against the solar paschal reckoning of a heterodox Christian group.[68] If an immediate historical referent must be found, it is not necessary to look beyond the Syrian-born emperor Elagabulus (218-222) and his grandmother Julia Maesa, daughter of the High Priest of Sol Invictus at Emesa. Roman soldiers stationed in Syria were ultimately responsible for promulgating this solar cult in the West, just as Elagabulus established the Syrian cult in the Roman Senate.[69]

The final admonition may suggest this chain of scriptures is even older than this. "Dominical" scriptures, i.e., words of Jesus against the swearing of oaths, are not cited. With a method reminiscent of Barn, a string of OT proof texts from an apologetic tradition has been recruited wholesale to define proper Christian behavior through a negative mask.[70]

4. The First Three Voices and their Echo: Scripture, Apologist, and the Apostles (sections "B" and "G")

With its agenda to lengthen the paschal fast to "Holy Monday," the dilemma the DA faces is immediate. If Christians in the patriarchate of Alexandria are calculating this time period down to the quarter hour, and if Christians in Carthage battle over who is more properly obeying the commandment, then Christians in Syria know that the Bridegroom was not yet gone on Monday. The DA takes great pains to convince them that he was.

Immediately after the exhortation traditional aetiology, the dialogue begins:

[67] See below, p. 297, there n. 20 and 21.
[68] Strobel, Kalender, 328.
[69] Roll, Susan K., Toward the Origins of Christmas, LitCon 5, 1995, 112 f.
[70] DA 13, CSCO 408, 136, uses Hellenic and Judaic piety in an *a fortiori* argument to attend worship: "And in comparison to those who err, what excuse have you?"

And especially in the days of the Pascha, in which all the believers who are in all the world fast as our Lord and teacher said when they asked him: "Why do John's disciples fast, and yours fast not? And he answered and said to them: The sons of the bridechamber cannot fast, as long as the bridegroom is with them; but the days will come when the bridegroom shall be taken away from them, and then they shall fast in those days." *Now by his actions, however, he is with us,* [rest of line cut in H] *but to sight he is remote, because he has ascended to the heights of heaven and seated at the right hand of his Father.*

On this account, when you fast, pray and intercede for those who are lost, as we also did when our Savior suffered. Indeed, while he was yet with us before he suffered, as we were eating the Passover with him, he said to us, "Today, in this night, one of you will betray me." And we said unto him, each one of us, "Is it I, my Lord?" And he answered and said to us, "He who stretches his hand with me into the dish." And Judas Iscariot, who was one of us, rose up and went in order to betray him. [The long H-cut begins here] Then our Lord said to us: "Verily I say unto you, a little while and you will abandon me, for it is written: I will strike the shepherd, and the lambs of his flock shall be scattered," And Judas came with the scribes and with the priests of the people, and delivered up our Lord Jesus.[71]

With a few digressions, the Bridegroom text will control the conversation for the rest of the chapter. Yet the voice that later belongs to the "apologist" interrupts with a theological point that already begins to dissolve the traditional understanding of the text. Christ is always present; therefore his absence is not a proper object of piety. This strategy is immediately reinforced by the "apostles." Before they begin their narration, the idea implicit in the text of fasting *for* the Bridegroom is redirected to fasting for "those who are lost" *when* the Bridegroom is absent. These lost ones, the "apologist" and the risen Christ will assure, are the Jews. In its various guises, the voice calling for a fast "for the Jews" is one of the most insistent in the older section of DA 21. Yet by the time the chapter is over, the only ones depicted as mourning *for* Jesus are the Jews.

Neither "apologist" nor the "apostles" have made an interpolation into an older text, but are voicing a strategy interpolating, as it were, the scriptural aetiology. Modifying duration and content of the traditional reading is the sole purpose for composing the tract.

---

[71] CSCO 408, 288 f., with slight corrections of English grammar.

The H-redactors make their initial incision between two quotations they saw as doublets, so that the text (section "G") reads immediately after the betrayal:

> Therefore, it is required of you, brethren, in the days of the Pascha, to follow closely with (all) diligence and to perform your fast with all care. And begin when your brethren who are of the People perform the Passover. For when our Lord and teacher ate the Passover with us, he was delivered up by Judas after that hour, and immediately we began to be grieved because he was taken from us.[72]

Just as between exhortation and fasting aetiology, the "therefore" is no real transition from the preceding section. Since this section begins the whole conversation over again, the H-redactors had an easy task continuing the chapter as if nothing were missing. Without scriptural elaboration, this summary first accepts the aetiological force of the Bridegroom narrative and commands the fast after the Bridegroom is taken away.

The newer section voices a concern for which the original material had no interest. Why are these new apostolic voices instituting the feast when the People celebrate Pesach-Mazzot? Does the Pascha (the fast) begin *exactly* when the Jewish community begins Pesach (the feast) on 14 Nisan and end on the following Lord's Day? A ritual impossibility, this sort of sliding scale observance is not the "innovation" DA 21 envisions. A later section marks the time less ambiguously: Pascha, now beginning Monday and concluding at the vigil early Sunday morning, is the *week* in which Pesach falls. This is the "old" Antiochene reckoning that comes under attack at the Council of Nicaea, when for rhetorical purposes, the general coincidence of the week-long Pascha with Pesach-Mazzot will become a specific charge of celebrating "with the Jews." Since the cool tone of this newer section does not match the heat of Nicaean debate, these later attacks must only be a distant rumble. This would date this section later in the third century, but not too close to the fourth.

5. *The Apostles Count the Days: Passion Chronology and its First Interpreter (sections "C" and "H")*

Though the Last Supper and betrayal have already been related, in section "C" the narrative backs up to retell the story with days assigned to the events:

[72] CSCO 408, 196.16-21.

Now this was on the fourth day of the week. *[Wed.]*

Indeed, when we had eaten the Passover on the third day of the week *[Tues. night]* in the evening, *[which is really Wed.]* we went out to the Mount of Olives, and in the night they seized our Lord Jesus.

And the next day, *[Wed. day]* which was the fourth of the week, he remained in custody in the house of Caiaphas the high priest. And on the same day the chiefs of the people were assembled and took course against him.

And on the next day again *[Thurs.]*, which was the fifth of the week, they brought him to Pilate the governor. And he remained again in custody with Pilate the night after the fifth day of the week.

But when it dawned on the Friday, "they accused him much" before Pilate. And they could show nothing that was true, but gave false witness against him. And they asked him from Pilate to be put to death. And they crucified him on the same Friday.[73]

Beginning almost every sentence, the *numbers* are more important than the brief narrative that follows. Yet like a mathematical formula, this text is flawlessly consistent. The Bridegroom is absent; Christians fast. Therefore whenever Christians fast, the Bridegroom must be absent. The Syrian preference for gospel events as aetiologies is also unswerving: on Wednesday, the Bridegroom cannot merely be *talking* about being absent as in the Commandments of Addai, but must really be gone.

The point is not narrative sequence, but a synchronicity of rite and story whose exactness has grown since mid-second century. The absent Bridegroom, not the passion narrative, is the primary text. In its striving for a perfect mimetic fit, DA 21 has conflated the aetiology for the paschal fast with the story of origins for the paschal liturgy, the Syn meal. For those who did not yet have a "Maundy Thursday" liturgy to ritualize narrative sequence of the Syn gospels, the violence done to the canonical story is not great, and even could be seen as an improvement. Since two trials are compressed into such a short span, the authors of DA 21 could spread interrogation and trial over two days and have a more plausible story. There are not enough events, however, to reach Monday, which is the ultimate goal. This will take considerable effort – and detailed instruction from the risen Lord. Given the rhetorical task its authors have set for this chronology, however, it is a stunning success.

---

[73] CSCO 408, 189.9-190.2.

An unforeseen measure of this success is the ability still to generate learned discourse, especially since the discovery of the Dead Sea Scrolls. Despite its presence in a third century work, Annie Jaubert sees in this sequence a relic of the 360-day Zadokite solar calendar of Qumran and the book of Jubilees. Since 360 is perfectly divisible by seven, days and dates always remain the same: Pesach would always be celebrated on a Wednesday. This liturgical weight, Jaubert found – though it is in a *yearly* cycle, not a *weekly* one – produced a "predisposition" to Wednesday in early Christianity – "a fundamental continuity between the fixed-day Jewish calendar and the Christian one."[74] If the Christian rhythm of fasting had shifted the Monday-Thursday schedule of the Pharisees, then Christians would fast on Friday and Tuesday, not Wednesday. That Wednesday, as the German *Mittwoch* suggests, is the middle of a week measured from Sunday to Sunday was perhaps too prosaic a point to mention.

This stubbornness of Wednesday to give up its liturgical privilege in a hypothetical transfer from the Essenes was not the point of Jaubert's study, but an exegetical problem that will always plague the acribious – and literal – mind. The disparity between Syn and Joh accounts are finally resolved by the use of different calendars:

> Jesus celebrates Pesach on Tuesday evening, the eve of Pesach according to the ancient priestly calendar.

> Arrest in the night of Tuesday to Wednesday.

> Jesus dies on Friday 14 Nisan, the eve of Pesach according to the official calendar.[75]

Jaubert was not the first to find this sequence of events helpful in tying up loose ends in Jn and the Syn, or even to propose a Judaic source. Epiphanius, one of the strongest witnesses for reception of the DA, can use it to debate those he calls Alogoi (without Logos, also stupid, dumb, irrational) who had rejected the canonicity of the Logos gospel, John:

> Jesus suffered on the thirteenth before the Kalends of April, the Jews meanwhile having skipped one evening, that is, at midnight on the fourteenth of the month. For the Jews came ahead of time and ate the

---

[74] Jaubert, Date, 74 f.
[75] Jaubert, Date, 107.

Passover, as the Gospel says [cf. Mt 26.2] and I have often remarked. They thus ate the Passover two days before its proper eating, that is, they ate it in the evening on the third day of the week, a thing that ought to be done at evening on the fifth day. For on that basis, the fourteenth of the month was the fifth day of the week, (when the Passover should have been eaten].

But Jesus was arrested late on that same third day, which was the night-time of the eleventh of the month, the thirteenth before the Kalends of April. The dawning of the fourth day of the week was the nighttime of the [Jewish] twelfth day of the month, the fifteenth before the Kalends of April. The daytime of the thirteenth day of the month was the fifth day of the week, but the ensuing nighttime was the fourteenth of the month.[76]

How does Epiphanius arrive at this reading? A scribal error here, fudging the numbers there, a calendrical intercalation measured in *hours*… This sort of fun with numbers continues for some time, until Epiphanius finally draws a conclusion:

The Jews were wrong at that time for this reason: not only did they eat the Passover two days early because they were disturbed, but they also added the one day they had skipped, since they were mistaken in every way. But the revelation of the truth has done everything for our salvation with the utmost precision.[77]

Though the Judaic cause is valued differently, the results are the same for Epiphanius and Jaubert: the gospels are "right" and the Jews are somehow "wrong," either because there were two conflicting calendars in use in Jerusalem at the time of Jesus' death, or because the Jews could not calculate the "official" calendar properly in the first place. In each case, conflicting narrated time in the canonical gospels is resolved by projecting a late Christian text wholesale onto first century Jewish time-keeping.

The first to attempt an "historical" explanation of this reordering of events was not Annie Jaubert or even Epiphanius, but the "sub-H" redactor. While the Qumran calendar does not provide an air of mystery, there is reference to the "official" Hebrew calendar "as we count according to the reckoning of the believing Hebrews."[78] These "Hebrews" – not "Jews" – are Jewish Christian communities directly addressed later

---

[76] Pan 51.26.1-3, GCS 31, 295-297; ET: NHMS 36, 57.
[77] Pan 51.27.1, GCS 31, 298, ET: NHMS 36, 59.
[78] CSCO 408, 196.22 f.

in the chapter, while their Torah observance is the object of Barnabas-like polemic in DA 23. The Tuesday supper chronology then finds its solution in two motifs inseparable in the Christian paschal tradition: a christological reading of Ex 12 and anti-Judaic polemic. After setting the meeting of Judas and temple officials on 10 Nisan, the day prescribed at Ex 12.3 to separate the lamb for sacrifice, the redactor explains:

> But because of the crowds of all the people, from every town and from all the villages, who were coming up to the temple to perform the Passover in Jerusalem, the priests and elders devised and commanded and appointed that they should perform the festival immediately, that they might seize him without disturbance. Indeed the people of Jerusalem were occupied with the sacrifice and the eating of the Passover. And moreover, all the people from without had not yet come, because they had deceived them as to the days. That they might be reproved before God of erring greatly in everything, therefore they anticipated the Passover by three days, and performed it on the eleventh of the moon, on the third day of the week. Indeed they said, "because all the people go astray after him, now that we have an opportunity, let us seize him; and then when all the people have come, let us kill him before everyone, that this may be known openly, and all the people turn back from after him."

> And thus in the night when the fourth day of the week dawned, he (namely Judas) delivered up our Lord to them. But they gave the fee to Judas on the tenth of the month, on the second day of the week. On this account they were reckoned by God as though on the second day of the week they had seized him, because on the second of the week, they had devised to seize him and to kill him. And they accomplished their wickedness on the Friday, as Moses had said about the Passover thus: "It shall be kept by you from the tenth to the fourteenth, and then, all Israel shall sacrifice the Passover." (cf. Dt 16.2)[79]

This anti-Judaic rhapsody on an original text completely innocent of such polemic is Epiphanius' source. The meal takes place in "C" on Tuesday night to correspond exactly to the Bridegroom aetiology for the Wednesday station. But the "sub-H" redactor must somehow explain this anomaly against the canonical four. However the numbers add up, they will always lead to an enormous deficit in the "Jewish" column. The truth, revealed or historical, of the canonical four remains inviolate – as does the boundary between Pesach and Pascha.

[79] DA 21, CSCO 408, 197.19-198.18.

Of all the "confusion of thought and treatment" in DA 21, this section and the anti-Judaic discourse soon to follow most resemble the bitter rhetoric at the Council of Nicaea. Eusebius will use a similar scheme to prove to the Antiochenes that Jesus did eat the paschal meal, but that he did not eat it "with the Jews."[80] This paradox is not created by Syn and Joh chronologies, but by the Gentile Christian horror of Judaic ritual and the Jewish identity of Jesus, both unavoidable in a surface reading of the Syn meal account. The original document did not share this horror, and makes a plea that anti-Judaic rhetoric be transformed into something more resembling a Christian ethic.

This accent on Monday, 10 Nisan, is also designed to take up the remainder from Tuesday night to Monday. Another section in the "H-cut" also manages to reach Monday, but not without engaging in the most arcane mathematics in the chapter. The H-redactors saw that the absence of the Bridegroom, at least in intent if not in fact, was established for Monday, so they could dispense with the rest. The aetiology for the Wednesday stational fast given in the Commandments of Addai has simply been transferred to Monday, just as the original document had transferred the aetiology shared with Friday quite consequently to gospel chronology. As for the sub-H redactors, they have ratified their calculation by the highest power possible: "On this account, they were reckoned by God…"

6. The Three Days in the Heart of the Earth
(section "D" and prescription in "J")

As the text reads with the H-cut removed, the more stringent fast on Friday and Saturday is not grounded in a full narrative, but only in a reference found in a general prescription for the fast and vigil in section "J":

> On the Friday, however, and on the Sabbath, fast entirely and taste nothing. You shall assemble together and watch and keep vigil all night with prayers and intercessions, and with the reading of the prophets, and with the gospel and with the psalms with fear and trembling and with assiduous supplication, until the third hour in the night after the Sabbath. And then break your fasts. Indeed, in this way did we also fast, when our Lord suffered, for a testimony of the three days.[81]

---

[80] See below, p. 274 f.
[81] CSCO 408, 199. Cf. Aphrahat, Demo 12.8, text below, p 242 f.

The apostles mourn from the moment of death to the resurrection, which in the canonical accounts they neither witnessed nor knew the exact time. But the prescription in "J" makes a precise calculation of the absence of the Bridegroom that must have been supplied in full in the original text. In the unedited version, the chronology that expanded the trial to two days now calculates the three days to prove Jesus' prophecy:

> He suffered, then, at the sixth hour on Friday. And those hours wherein our Lord was crucified were reckoned a day. And afterwards, again, there was darkness for three hours, and it was reckoned a night. And again from the night hour until evening, three hours a day. And afterwards again, the night of the Sabbath of the Passion. But in the Gospel of Matthew it is thus written: "In the evening of the Sabbath, when the first day of the week, dawned, came Mary and the other Mary, Magdalene, to see the tomb. And there was a great earthquake for angel of the Lord came down and rolled away the stone. And again there was the day of the Sabbath and then three hours of the night after the Sabbath, wherein our Lord slept. And that was fulfilled which he said, "The Son of Man must pass through the heart of the earth three days and three nights" (Mt 12.40).[82]

The moment of resurrection, which Dionysius is understandably reluctant to calculate from the gospels, corresponds *exactly* with the conclusion of the paschal vigil at 3 am.

7. The Risen Lord speaks…and gives a lesson in mathematics (section "E")

If up to this point the original authors have only been tampering with the edges of the Bridegroom aetiology, they now makes a strike at the center. The Syn all set Jesus' fasting "command" at the home of Levi/Matthew.[83] This, curiously enough, is also the setting for the crowning glory of DA 21: a resurrection appearance by Jesus, who, having delivered the command to fast in his absence, returns to make sure there is no misunderstanding of how this command is to be carried out:

> In the night, then, "when the first day of the week dawned on," he appeared to "Mary Magdalene and to Mary the daughter of James." And in the morning of the first day of the week he went in to the house of Levi; and then he appeared also to us ourselves. But he said to us, teaching us; "Are you fasting because of me these days, or do I need it that

---

[82] CSCO 408, 190.2-17.
[83] Mk 2.15-20 || Mt. 9-10-15 || Lk 5.29-35.

you should afflict yourselves? But it is for the sake of your brethren that you have done this."[84]

These are the first words of the risen Christ recorded by DA 21 – no doubting Thomas searching the wounds, no amazed confession of faith, no mysterious meal on a seashore, not even the *Epistola's* revelation of the mysteries of incarnation and birth, but a bland pronouncement of Isa 58.4 f., since the early second century a verse exploited for its ability to negate cult. What Jesus said at Levi's banquet is now annulled by the no longer absent Bridegroom who rises from to dead to lodge a complaint against the fasting practice of his disciples – in the very place where the command was first uttered. More has been lost than an interesting resurrection and recognition scene: mimesis has so overpowered mystery and kerygma that they disappear.

The risen Lord does not immediately embark upon a discourse about fasting for the Jews, but clarifies the new Christian meaning of an OT verse.[85]:

> And do the same in those days when you fast, and on the fourth of the week and on the Friday always. As it is written in Zechariah, "The fourth fast, and the fifth fast." For it is not lawful for you to fast on the first of the week, because it is my resurrection. On this account the first of the week is not counted in the number of the days of the fast of the passion, but they are counted from the second day of the week, and are *five* (sic.) days. Therefore "the fourth fast and the fifth fast and the seventh fast and the tenth fast shall be to those of the house of Israel." [Judah in MT, LXX]. Fast thus from the second day of the week, *six* days entirely, until the night after the Sabbath, and it shall be reckoned to you as a week. "The tenth," however, because the beginning of my name is Yod, in which was made the beginning of the fasts.[86]

This is how the original author gets to Monday. Since "four" is the only number that corresponds without considerable force to actual fasting practice, it could be that only the "fourth fast" was a proof for a Wednesday station fast with no initial relation to paschal practice. But since this verse does such a poor job of producing the desired sum, the author probably stumbled onto it as he was reading Zech 8, a prophecy

---

[84] CSCO 408, 190.19-200.6.
[85] Eduard Schwartz dismissed this section as "absurdes Geschwätz" (absurd chatter): Ostertafeln, 112.
[86] CSCO 408, 191.6-19.

of the restoration of Jerusalem, as a narrative about the church. The fasting commands are the result of a question at Zech 7.3: "Should I mourn and practice abstinence in the fifth month, as I have done for so many years?" The *Didascalia's* Jesus merely appropriates the rubrics. That the numbers count the *month* of the year rather than the day of the week is, of course, irrelevant in the search for types. This search may have provided the cue to reach for the rhetorically more proven Isa 58.4 f., since the prophet's first response (Zech 7.4-6) takes a predictable turn:

> Then the world of the LORD of hosts came to me: Say to all the people of the land and the priests: When you fasted and lamented in the fifth month and in the seventh for these seventy years, was it for me that you fasted? And when you eat and when you drink, do you not eat and drink only for yourselves?

After this the addition gets bizarre. Including the entire citation, the "seventh" can remain for the fast on the Sabbath. But the "fifth" can only be Friday (the sixth day) by counting from Monday, because Sunday as first day in the week doesn't count in this particular addition problem, except, of course, to reach "fourth" for Wednesday. The first time a sum is drawn, the fast lasts five days (after Monday?), the second time, six days (including Monday, the whole point). Rounding out the numbers is the link between the number ten and the first letter of the name of Jesus[87] to arrive at "10 Nisan" as a fasting day. Whatever the number say, they are reckoned as if the fast lasted a week. It is little wonder that H-redactors decided to spare their readers the burden of dealing with this passage, just as sub-H redactors felt called upon to find a much simpler way to arrive at Monday.

8. *Apologist and Polemicist: Supercession and Anti-Judaic Excurses (sections "F" and "K")*

One of the reasons the *Didascalia's* risen Lord may have been intrigued by Zech 8 was not just its cycle of numbered monthly fasts, but their

---

[87] Barn 9.8: For it says, "And Abraham circumcised eighteen and three hundred men. [comb. Gen 17.23; 14.14]. What then was the knowledge given him? Note, that he names the eighteen first. The eighteen: Iota=10, Eta=8. There you have Jesus." Cf. Clem. Alex. Strom. 6.146.7: "And above all the Decalogue, by the letter iota, points to the blessed name and shows that Jesus is the Logos." This interpretation at DA 26, CSCO 408, 224.13-225.6.

content: commemoration of the Babylonian invasion and the destruction of the First Temple. According to 2Kg 25 and its doublet at Jer 52, the walls of Jerusalem were breached in the fourth month, the siege began in the tenth, with the Temple destroyed in the fifth. Gedaliah, the Babylonian-appointed governor with good relations to Israelite prophets (cf. Jer 39.14; 40.13-41) was assassinated in the seventh. Coupled to these fasts is a promise to "the remnant of this people" (Zech 8.6) of the restoration of Jerusalem and the rebuilding of the Temple. The *Didascalia's* risen Lord will assign roles differently, but "mourning for Zion" and *a* restoration of Israel become major motifs in the reorigination of the paschal fast.

After the risen Lord has instituted the fasts, he enjoins the Gentile church to dedicate their prayer and fasting to the forgiveness of the Jews:

> And be constant in fasting during these days always, and especially those who are from the Gentiles. Indeed, because the People were not obedient, I redeemed them [the Gentiles] from blindness and from the error of idols and received them, so that through your fast and of those who are of the Gentiles, and your service during those days, when you pray and intercede for the error and destruction of the People, your prayer and your intercession may be accepted before my Father who is in heaven, as though from one mouth of all the believers who are on the earth, and (that) all they did unto me be forgiven them.[88]

Unlike the later Good Friday Bidding Prayer, where a refusal to pray for the Jews used to be written right into the rubrics, the impression given by these lines spoken by the risen Lord, as well as by the apologetic voice who interprets them, is that they are sincerely spoken. At least since Justin and Melito, the supercession of Israel by the Gentile church, its creation at the expense of the Jewish people, has been a theme inseparable from paschal exegesis. The "Jews" must be removed from Ex 12 to create a story of salvation for Gentile Christians. That is why this section is part of the paschal chapter of the DA, tied as loosely to the whole as the rest.

Though Pascha always means telling this story of origins, the apologist wishes to give it a different reading. The Gentile church is to be a community of prayer, asking that the Jews be forgiven their rejection of Christ and that the punishment meted out by Roman armies – and

[88] CSCO 408, 192.8-17.

homilists like Melito – should cease. As the *Didascalia's* Jesus reoriginates the Gentile church, this intercessory role is its sole reason for existence: the risen Lord places the Gentile church between its own anti-Judaic paschal rhetoric and God.

The apologist remains well within the bounds of that rhetoric. The Temple of Jerusalem was still destroyed as a sign, divine anger still rages against those who murdered the Son of God, but this anger is to be assuaged by the prayers of the Gentile church:

> On account of them, thus, and for the judgment and destruction of the place (of the sanctuary) we are required to fast and to mourn, that we may rejoice and be glad in the world to come, as it is written in Isaiah: "Rejoice all you that mourn over Zion."[89]

The apologist does not reach for the most obvious NT narrative to support this new content for the Christian paschal fast: Lk 23.28, when just before he is crucified, Jesus tells the mourning women following him, "...do not weep for me, but weep for yourselves and your children." Instead, the apologist returns to scriptures long cherished for their messianic readings, Isaiah, and to a text almost completely forgotten in the Gentile church, Rom 11:

> It is required of us, thus, to have pity on them, and to believe and to fast and to pray for them. For when our Lord came to the Jewish people, they did not believe him when he taught them, but allowed his teaching to pass away from their ears. Therefore, because this People did not obey, he received you, the brethren who are of the Gentiles and opened your ears that your heart might hear, as our Lord and Savior himself said through the prophet Isaiah: "I appeared unto those who asked not for me, and I was found of those who sought me not; I said, behold, I am to a people who did not call my name" (Isa 65.1). Now about whom did he speak thus? Was it not about the Gentiles, because of this that they have never known God, and because they were worshipping idols? However when our Lord came to the world and taught you, you believed, those who have believed in him, that God is one. And again those who are worthy, believe, *until the number of those who are to be saved is completed* (cf. Rom 11.25[90]) "a thousand times thousand, and ten thousand times ten thousand," as it is written in David. (Ψ 67(68).18; Dan 7.10).

---

[89] CSCO 408, 193.2-6.

[90] Greek preserved in ApConst: SC 329 (M. Metzger) 260: "πλήρωμα τοῦ ἀριθμοῦ τῶν σῳζομένων γενόμενοι." Vööbus (194, n. 164) directs the reader to 1Clem 2.4, 59.2, but there, there is only the "number of the elect" without any reference to Jews.

Other than Origen's *Commentary on Romans*, section "F" is the only
serious attempt to come to grips with Rom 11 in the third century. The
apologist's image of Judaism is still the paschal "shadow," but it is a radically different image from the one projecting from the two-dimensional
"Jews" of Jn or the paranoid mob of GPt only slightly more demented
than the author's Matthean model. Nor does this voice ring with the tri-
umphalism sounding forth in Barnabas, Justin, and Melito, the very
reaction among Gentile Christians in Rome against which Paul directs a
pointed warning (Rom 11.17-25). This mourning for the Jews can only
be a reaction to the same paschal anti-Judaism that produced Melito's
"oracle" against a Jerusalem that had been rubble for a generation, as
well as the anti-Judaic reading of the *Didascalia's* odd chronology that
the sub-H redactors later append to the original. Theologically, the story
of origins in DA 21 reaches the same goal as Melito – the creation
through Christ of a covenanted people among the Gentiles – but it does
so without rhetorical violence.

Paul's "mystery" was the "hardening" (πώρωσις) that had "come upon
part of Israel, until the full number of the Gentiles has come in (τὸ
πλήρωμα τῶν ἐθνῶν εἰσέλθῃ)" (Rom 11.25). This the DA apologist
describes, but does not assign to divine agency. Since both Latina-Vul-
gate and Syriac text traditions[91] do not speak of "hardness" in this verse,
but "blindness," this "mystery" is likely what the apologist is trying to
explain in a Johannine exegesis of Isa 9.1 f.:

> "Those who sit in darkness" he said about those of the People who later
> believed in our Lord Jesus. Indeed, by reason of the blindness of the People
> a great darkness had surrounded them. Indeed, they saw Jesus, but that he
> is the Christ they did not know. And they did not understand him, not
> from the writings of the prophets nor from his deeds and his healings.
> However, to you, to those of the People who have believed in Jesus, we say:
> "Learn how the Scripture testifies to us and says: 'They have seen a great
> light.'" You then, those who have believed in him, "have seen a great light,"
> Jesus our Lord, and again so shall those see who are yet to believe in him.
>
> But "those that sit in the shadows of death" are you, those who are of the
> Gentiles; for you were in the shadows of death," because you have trusted
> in the worship of idols and did not know God. However, when Jesus
> Christ our Lord and teacher appeared to us, "light has dawned upon you,"
> for you gazed on and trusted the promise of the kingdom everlasting. And
> you have removed yourselves from the customs and manners of the former

[91] Nestle-Aland [26]1979, 430.

error, and no more worship idols as you (once) worshipped them, but have long since believed and been baptized in him, and a "great light has dawned upon you." Thus then, because the People did not obey, they became darkness. But the hearing of your ear, [i.e. obedience], of those who are of the Gentiles, became light. On this account, therefore, pray and intercede for them, and especially in the days of the Pascha, that through your prayers they may be esteemed worthy of forgiveness and may return to our Lord Jesus Christ.[92]

These are the last words of the older material excised by the H-redactors. Without them, the admonition to pray and fast for the Jews now mentioned only peripherally in the edited version takes on the character of the pseudo-prayer of the later Good Friday petitions.

The apologist also tells a story of origins, but unlike Melito's or even Irenaeus' reading of Ex 12, it is a church of two peoples. This is not a new story, but DA 21 is the first time it appears in a paschal context. The prayer is one of conversion and eschatological hope, "so that all Israel will be saved" (Rom 11.26).

One reason the homilist may have gravitated toward Rom 11 is that a similar history, the existence of Gentile and Jewish Christians within one community, has led to similar rhetoric. The "believing Hebrews" are an historical entity, not a rhetorical projection. While the apologist does not disparage their rituals, DA 26 will have more than enough to say, especially about the Sabbath, corpse contamination, and ritual bathing. Here, however, both believing Jews and Gentiles once shared a common darkness, now a common light.

Readers of DA 21 after sub-H redaction did not have to wait for five chapters for this polemic to begin. The H-redactors left untouched a section offered ostensibly as a reason to fast on Friday and the Sabbath. Yet all aetiological value vanishes in a burlesque polemic against Sabbath and Yom Kippur:

> But let us look and see, brethren, that most men in their mourning imitate the Sabbath, and that likewise, those who keep the Sabbath, imitate mourning. Indeed, he who mourns kindles no light nor do the People on the Sabbath, because of the commandment of Moses, for so was it commanded them by him. He that mourns does not wash himself, nor the People on the Sabbath. He that mourns does not furnish a table, nor do the People on the Sabbath, but they furnish and set for themselves the

---

[92] CSCO 408, 195.6-196.15

evening (before), because they have a presentiment of mourning, that they were to lay hands on Jesus. He that mourns does not work, and does not speak, but sits in sadness, (so too) in this way against the People on the Sabbath. Indeed it was said to the people concerning the mourning of the Sabbath thus: "You shall not lift your foot to do (any) work, and you shall speak no word out of your mouth."

Now who testifies that the Sabbath is a mourning for them? The Scripture testifies and says: "At that time shall the people lament, family over against family, the family of the house of Levi apart, and their women apart, the house of Judah apart, and their women apart," (Zech 12.12 f.) even as after the mourning of Christ until now, on the ninth of the month of 'Ab they assemble and read the lamentation of Jeremiah and wail and lament. However, nine signifies Theta, but Theta indicates God. About God therefore they lament, about Christ who suffered – rather on account of God our Savior, about themselves and about their own destruction. Does any man lament, brethren, except he who has mourning?

On this account do you also mourn for them on the day of the Sabbath of the Pascha until the third hour in the night following.[93]

The polemicist shares three features with the apologist and the *Didascalia's* risen Lord: an admonition to "mourn for them," a fondness for Zechariah, and for mathematics. The rest is rhetorical distortion aimed at Jews – and "believing Hebrews." "Mourning for Jesus" becomes completely saturated with a negative image of Judaic practice, whose mimetic origin is explicitly announced in the first line. The reader expects parody, which is amply delivered all the way to the punchline, "Does any man lament, brethren, except he who has mourning?" The rhetorical structure of this "proof," however, is the same as quite serious constructs found in the "Asian" tradition. As Ex 12 foretells the passion or a "shadow" Pesach saves the Gentile church, the Sabbath and the Day of Atonement become a strange pantomime moving to a Christian rhetorical plot – that Moses has written. The theological struggle of the apologist vanishes along with any genuine reason to fast and pray for the Jews.

9. Observations

The "confusion of thought and treatment" of DA 21 is reduced, but not eliminated, by lining out the voices of the original material in the H-cut, then waiting for the replies of later commentators. They do not

---

[93] CSCO 408, 200.21-201.16.

sing in unison, but in a dialogue whose second voice amplifies the anti-Judaism the original tract sought to quieten. This second voice is also far more comfortable with the original reading of the Bridegroom aetiology, only modifying it to match the original concern for a fast "for the Jews" long enough to stay in the conversation. This luxury is likely due to the success of the original in promulgating the week-long fast, now available to bear its share of anti-Judaic polemic constant since mid-second century.

What sub-H redactors had in their hands was never a model of rhetorical composition; their additions do nothing to improve it. This more radical editing would have to wait until 380, when the Antiochene author of the *Apostolic Constitutions* (ApCon), though retaining the immediacy of first person narrative, not only eliminates the strange chronology, but replaces it with a lengthy passion harmony.[94] Jesus still eats the paschal meal – eucharist, not Pesach – but this detail is mentioned only once,[95] and it pales before the harmony's strongly Joh flavor. At the same time, the ApCon makes certain that Judas was *not* at the meal,[96] a question never dictated by narrative, but fears for the efficacy of the sacrament.

Other corrections reflect late fourth century concerns. In the passion harmony, Herod is absent, but in a section based on section "H" of DA 21, the ApCon follows Acts 4.27 in claiming that "Pilate the governor and Herod the king"[97] gave orders for the crucifixion, the author even acting as if the plot against the Messiah of Ψ2.1-2 at Acts 4.25 f. were his own idea. In correcting for historical accuracy, the author probably did not know he was erasing a major motif from a noncanonical gospel. Pilate also takes a step backward from sainthood: he has cowardly listened to a mob and condemned Jesus on conflicting testimony, violating the principles of Roman law, now the legal code of a Christian empire.[98] The apologist also is heard, but only in those sections that laid out proof texts for the election of the Gentiles. The counterpoint to early Christian anti-Judaism is silenced, but so, too, the burlesque polemic on the Sabbath that reduces the apologist's concern for the Jews

---

[94] ApCon 5.14.6-18, SC 329, 250-258.

[95] "Καὶ τῇ πέμπτῃ φαγόντες παρ' αὐτῷ τὸ πάσχα..." ApCon 5.14.6, SC 329, 250.

[96] "'Ιούδα μὴ συμπαρότος ἡμῖν..." ApCon 5.14.7, loc. cit.

[97] ApCon 5.19.5, SC 329, 272

[98] ApCon 5.14.13, SC 329, 254. As noted, Mt 26.60 places the false witnesses before the Sanhedrin.

to parody. The cacophonous voices of DA 21 reduce to a dull background hum. The most important change for paschal observance, however, is the insistence on "exactly" (ἀκριβῶς) observing the equinox as controlling date for finding the paschal full moon.[99] ApCon is not only an update, but a "completely revised and annotated edition" of the *Didascalia* tradition.

Before both sub-H redactors and the ApCon altered its shape, the original document employed a consistent strategy to change form and content of the fast by manipulating the Bridegroom aetiology. As soon as the NT text is cited, its traditional reading is neutralized, but only to be transferred to a week-long observance. DA 21 then bolsters the aetiological force of the Bridegroom narrative with a day by day, then hour by hour rehearsal of the passion to show the exact time the Bridegroom was absent until the resurrection. That moment corresponds exactly to the paschal eucharist and the breaking of the fast. Not only does anamnesis reduce to mere commemoration, but narrative is indistinguishable from rubric. Ritual controls the narrative, not the reverse.

This results in an odd theological contrast. Though the apologist brings a deep reflection about the birth of the Gentile church reminiscent of Rom 11 and its narrative reworking in Lk 21, it is cognitively impossible for any voice speaking in DA 21 to come to the same conclusion as Dionysius: that in the canonical gospels this type of mimesis is simply *not there*.

Nowhere is this strategy more transparent than in the *ex eventu* resurrection appearance at the house of Levi, where the new form and content of the paschal fast become dominical command. If two texts make a parallel and three a genre, then GHeb, EpAp, and DA 21 have created the text type "post-resurrection institutions of paschal observance." Like the liturgical details adding mimetic fullness to various second century gospels and acts, these narratives fill a gap left by NT writers with little concern for cult. Since later readers are certain that the Lord would have instituted the paschal feast had the evangelists cared to record it, they are only too happy to correct the oversight. Liturgical observance is to be founded in Christ narrative, even if narrative is founded solely in the liturgy. In this sense, DA 21 is the best – and worst – example of the Syrian search for scriptural models for ritual praxis.

---

[99] ApCon 5.17.1, SC 329, 266 f.

VII. Aphrahat "the Persian Sage": Demonstration on the Pascha (344/5)

Tracing the Syrian paschal tradition cannot be freed from the *Didascalia's* aetiological entanglement until Syriac writers of the first post-Nicene generation. When this tradition emerges in writers such as Aphrahat and Ephrem, readings of paschal texts have much in common with the "Asian" tradition, except for the one exegetical feature unique to Syria. The paschal meal of the Synoptic gospels is the story of origins for the observance of Pascha. "For on the beginning (i.e. evening) of the fourteenth," Aphrahat writes, "he ate the Pascha with his disciples according to the Law of Israel."[100] If the anti-Judaic contortions of the sub-H redactor of DA 21 are not witness enough, debate at the Council of Nicaea will show that this acknowledgment of the surface meaning of the meal narrative contained in three canonical gospels is a badge of exegetical bravery.

This comfort with the Judaic identity of Jesus of Nazareth is not some Jewish Christian relic preserved in a theological hinterland, but arises from mimetic readings of the Syn gospels that form the exegetical base of Syrian/Syriac liturgical theology. It cannot be assumed that Syriac writers, now no longer within the boundaries of the post-Constantinian Empire, maintain first or second century traditions in some pristine state, or even worse, because of their linguistic kinship with Aramaic, the language of Jesus, represent some delightfully primitive form of early Christianity unsullied by the thought-world of Greece and Rome. The NT is a Greek book reflecting the Hellenistic culture of its day, and so it was received, by a region whose Hellenism has often been romantically underestimated. Those who had any education at all in this region were schooled in Greek rhetoric, just as Koine was the *lingua franca* of trade and commerce.[101]

This bilingualism makes moot the question of when the *Didascalia* began to speak Syriac, or when other Greek literature may have circulated among educated Christians in the Persian Empire. While Connolly was certain that Aphrahat had used a *Syriac* version, Arthur Vööbus is reluctant to date translation earlier than the later fourth century.[102] Even

[100] Demo 12.8, Aphrahat, Demonstrationes/Unterweisungen, dÜ: Peter Bruns, FC 5/2, 1991, 311.
[101] Points especially made in Drijvers, Han J. W., Syrian Christianity and Judaism, in: The Jews among Pagans and Christians in the Roman Empire, London/NY 1992, 124-146.
[102] Connolly, Didascalia Apostolorum, XVII f.; Vööbus, CSCO 402, 27* f.

so, a hundred years is more than enough time for the *Didascalia* to have made its way southeastward in its original Greek, and to cause difficulties for anyone wishing both to follow its "apostolic" prescriptions and square its narrative with the canonical gospels or the *Diatessaron.* Regardless of date, the *Didascalia* can hardly have been translated because of its sudden rediscovery, but because of a steadily growing demand for its "apostolic" teaching among a broader base of Syriac-speaking Christians throughout the fourth century.

1. Strategy, Situation, and Shape

One of the most eloquent renderings of Syriac paschal theology, Aphrahat's Twelfth Demonstration *On the Pascha* (Demo 12) employs the same mimetic strategy as DA 21, yet also draws upon motifs from the common "Asian" tradition. Ex 12, the story of Jesus' death and resurrection, the institution of baptism, eucharist, and the paschal feast are woven into one ritual narrative for the paschal night. Passion chronology provides important structure, but the odd sequence of DA 21 disappears in favor of one with a decided Synoptic/Tatianic character. This sequence is then addressed mimetically to both paschal feast *and* paschal liturgy "from beginning to end." While Aphrahat's exegesis might not have suited Tertullian's taste, it nevertheless maintains a fluid balance between rite proclaiming its kerygma and narrative dictating ritual observance: "rubric" never clashes with "congruence."

While Aphrahat's readers may still have had questions about the paschal calendar, the "Persian sage" dismisses these and other matters of mimetic minutiae with an argument reminiscent of Tertullian's "grace" – and the weariness of Dionysius of Alexandria:

> For if we find here difficulties and only concern ourselves with the fourteenth and not the feast, so could it be our pleasure to celebrate the fourteenth of every month and to mourn on Friday of every week. It is, of course, fitting for us that we do on every day of the week that which is right before the Lord.[103]

Viewed as a whole, however, Aphrahat's treatise does not primarily address problems raised by the paschal debate at the Council of Nicaea, nor does it suddenly reveal its secrets when placed next to other literature emanating from that dispute. The "fourteenth" in this passage is the full

---

[103] Demo 12.8, FC 5/2, 312.

moon of paschal computation, but it is also when the full fast begins on Thursday night according to narrated time in the gospels. At the very beginning, Aphrahat says that Israel "ate the Pascha on the fourteenth of the first month, which is called Nisan, the month of flowers (i.e., spring), in the first month of the year."[104] Though this remark is consistent with the paschal decision at Nicaea, it is also perfectly consistent with the reading of Ex 12 Aphrahat is about to undertake. Demo 12 does not provide a cycle of paschal dates, it makes no overt plea for or against the equinoctial rule, and its overall tone does not suggest a hidden agenda against paschal observances near or far.[105]

Twenty years before, the paschal calendar is the object of a loud and bitter dispute that reverberates past Aphrahat all the way to Epiphanius and Chrysostom. A group of Mesopotamian monastics rail at the new paschal rule as a pagan perversion of apostolic tradition. The Antiochene paschal calendar is marginalized with anti-Judaic polemic that outshouts Barnabas and Melito. If Aphrahat is taking part in this debate, still quite virulent at the Council of Antioch (329),[106] his restraint is too good for this world. Instead, he is writing a community observing a calendar identical to his, thus the difficulty eavesdropping moderns have in reconstructing it. The one passage where this might be possible can thus wait until the major controversy at Nicaea is placed in its full rhetorical context.

Aphrahat's readers did have questions similar to those asked since mid-second century about the fast of Pascha, a practice that affected the lives of ordinary Christians far more than the literary battle raging among bishops and theologians about the finer points of paschal exegesis and the course of sun and moon. When and why does the fast begin, and what does it *mean*? Aphrahat addresses these questions to the same biblical texts in the same mimetic fashion as congregations in the Pentapolis and the *Didascalia's* northern Syria, but with quite

---

[104] Demo 12.1, FC 5/2, 299.

[105] Rouwhorst, VigChrS 7.1, 150-153, sees Aphrahat's anti-Judaism directed at 4 c. Quartadecimans. See also ibid., The Date of Easter in the Twelfth Demonstration of Aphraates, StPat 17, 1982, 1374-1380, where he argues for a celebration only on Fri., a mimetic "fifteenth," a hybrid "between the Quartadeciman Passover and the Easter Sunday observance" (1378).

[106] Canon I, Lauchert, 43, threatens laity with excommunication and clergy with removal from office for celebrating Pascha "with the Jews" (μετὰ τῶν Ἰουδαίων ἐπιτελεῖν τὸ πάσχα) according to the old Antiochene paschal reckoning. For date, see below, n. 12, p. 254.

different results. Thus while the major paschal controversy of Nicaea may lurk beneath Aphrahat's paschal treatise, the minor controversy over the paschal fast marches across the surface. If my reading of Aphrahat is correct, then a major factor in this minor controversy in Aphrahat's community is the reception of DA 21.

Unlike the earlier work, Aphrahat is concerned with the liturgy culminating paschal observance and its content as a christological reading of Ex 12. The Bridegroom aetiology also reduces to subtext. Even though the verse is never cited, "absence" as narrative motivation for the fast controls, but does not completely distort, the retelling of the passion. Instead, Aphrahat is even more consequently "Syrian" in his demand for a dominical model:

> Now understand that whoever is troubled about these days, that on the beginning of the fourteenth our Lord celebrated the Pascha and ate and drank with his disciples, but from the time of the cockcrow on *he no longer ate and drank*, because they had taken him prisoner and had begun holding a trial about him. And as I showed you above, on the fifteenth he was a day and night among the dead. But from us is required that we hold fast to his time, from the beginning to the end: fasting in purity, prayer in truth, praise with zeal and songs as it is becoming; that we give the sign (i.e., chrismation) and baptism, as it is right, that we observe the blessings of the Holy One at the proper time (i.e., eucharistic anaphora), and fulfill all uses of the feast.[107]

This is not only a fast *for* Jesus, but a fast *with* Jesus. "His time" is a full fast from cockcrow Thursday night; the "proper time" is the liturgy culminating in the vigil eucharist. If Aphrahat's readers had approached DA 21 with the same need for dominical example, they might conclude that the strict fast was already to be undertaken on Tuesday night. But one gospel says 13 Nisan, three say 14, all say Thursday, the *Didascalia* says 11, and the *Diatessaron* included all time references and left the reading up to the reader. The Bridegroom is absent. But by whose clock do we measure the time?

After the "confusion of thought and treatment" of DA 21, Aphrahat's Demonstration is a paragon of clear composition, alternating two main objects of exegesis, then providing concluding summaries. The heart of the treatise is a baptismal narrative combining Ex 15 with Jn 13 into a

---

[107] Demo 12.8, FC 5/2, 312.

kerygmatic whole. Peter Bruns has divided the treatise into eight sections,[108] giving a rough outline of literary structure:

1	Ex 12	Paraphrase of Ex 12
2-3	Ex 12	Christian "mystery" contrasted to literal reading and Judaic rituals
4	NT	Passion Chronology (Synoptic/Tatianic) addressed to observance of fast.
5	NT	Three days and three nights (Bridegroom's absence begins after meal)
6	Ex 12	Reprise: Judaic temporary "shadow," Christian eternal reality
	NT	Footwashing as baptismal aetiology, Red Sea as negative type
7	Ex 12	Summary: anti-Judaic polemic
8	NT	Summary: Regulating the fast and liturgy. "Holy Week" chronology. Jesus as model for complete fast from Thursday night. Conclusion: Do not seek dispute, but a pure heart.

After Ex 12 is paraphrased, much as the pericope would be read before a homily, over half of Demo 12 is taken up with a contrast with Judaic paschal rituals as the surface reading of the text. At first this exegesis brings the standard anti-Judaic paschal arguments virtually unchanged since Justin. Yet when Judaic cult has been erased with an array of prophetic scriptures – especially Hos 2.13,[109] the contrast moves to simple supercession, where the Christian "mystery" excels its Judaic counterpart. Interleaved with this thoroughly "Asian" reading are mimetic interpretations of NT material drawn from the canonical gospels. About 35% of rhetorical space is taken up with retelling the passion, yielding "mystery" as well as "history," all pointing to Christian rituals of the Pascha. This, and the accent on ritual as ritual in Ex 12, is the uniquely Syrian component of Aphrahat's treatise.

Just as Aphrahat's anti-Judaic rhetoric follows the rules of a particular tradition, one suspects that the global structure of Demo 12 is also built upon forms well established by mid-fourth century. The genre "paschal treatise" is naturally dictated by larger homiletic and exegetical forms where the mystery of Christ's passion – or in Origen, a narrative of Logos spirituality – is revealed through the images and rituals of Ex 12. Yet neither Aphrahat, Origen, nor any author

---

[108] Syriac text and Latin trans., J. Parisot, PS 1, Paris 1894, divided into 13 sections, followed in TF, Rouwhorst, VigChrS 7.2, 111-121.

[109] "I will abolish their joys and their feasts, their new moons and their sabbath."

of the now lost treatises of the second century will have undertaken this exegesis in a vacuum. The dialogue between Ex 12 and gospel narrative is always matched by one between an acknowledged leader and the needs of a liturgical community, sometimes by one among authors defending their own practices or attacking those of other regions. The occasional nature of such treatises contributed to their disappearance: later readers knew that this literature was not speaking to them.

2. "Asian" Models: Contrast with Judaic Rite and Narrative

As with Melito and Irenaeus, Ex 12 is the story of the emergence of the Gentile church as the true Israel. The christological points so vital to Melito's exegesis, however, are not extracted as "mysteries" as much as they are set in strict parallel in Ephrem's hermeneutical "mirror." Arranging the text in two columns accents this parallel, and it is an interesting exercise to read the series of types in the left column before reading the text as a whole:

But the Pascha of the Jews is 14 Nisan, its night and its day.	And our day of great suffering is Friday, 15 Nisan, its night and its day.
As Israel after the Pascha eats unleavened bread for seven days until the twenty-first of the month,	we celebrate the feast of Unleavened Bread of our Savior
They eat unleavened bread with bitter things,	. and our Savior cast away the bitter cup and took away the whole bitterness of the nations, as he tasted it and did not wish to drink.
The Jews remember their sins from time to time,	and we remember the crucifixion and humiliation of our Savior.
For on the Pascha they escaped the slavery of Pharaoh,	and we are redeemed from the service of Satan on the day of the crucifixion.
They slaughter the lamb from the herds and were saved by its blood from the Destroyer,	and we were redeemed by the blood of the chosen Son from the works of ruin which we have committed.
For them Moses was leader,	and for us Jesus is leader and Savior.
For them Moses parted the sea and led them through,	and our Savior disintegrated hell and broke its gates and he entered and opened them and prepared the way for all those who believed in him.
They were given manna to eat,	and our Lord gave us his body to eat.
For them [Moses] brought forth water from the rock,	and our Savior let the water of life flow from his body.

They were promised the land of the Canaanites as an inheritance,	and to us he promises the land of life to come.
For them Moses raised the bronze serpent so that each person who looked upon it was healed from the bite of the snake,	and for us Jesus was raised, so that we, when we look up to him, are saved from the bite of the snake, who is Satan.
For them Moses erected a temporal tabernacle, so that they might bring sacrifice and food offerings that they might obtain forgiveness from their sins,	and Jesus erected the tabernacle of David which had fallen to ruin, and rose from the dead. And again he spoke to the Jews, "This temple which you see, when you tear it down, I will build it up again in three days." And his disciples understood that he was speaking about his body, which he, when they tore it down, raised it up again in three days. In this tabernacle he promises us life, and in it our sins are forgiven.
Their tabernacle he named a temporal one, for they only used it for a short time,	and ours he calls the temple of the Holy Spirit in eternity.[110]

With only slight variation – the brazen serpent is usually the cross, not resurrection – exegetical traditions little changed since the second century have established each of these interpretations as the surface meaning of the text. What Aphrahat can offer his readers is rhetorical compactness and transparency of form. Drawing motifs from Ex 12 and 15, Aphrahat crafts a coherent narrative of salvation, then tropes it with Christian exegesis. The passion, harrowing of hell, and the resurrection; baptism, eucharist, and the creation of the church – all are narrated in quick succession. But unlike Barnabas' dealing out scripture to "us" and to "them," OT narrative still has a valid Jewish address, and Aphrahat is as much concerned with showing how the two narratives differ as much as they are alike. The serpent "raised" in the desert becomes a sign of resurrection so the entire story of Christian salvation may be narrated without abandoning Exodus-Wilderness typology. The Syrian component comes in the pairing of Judaic ritual with its Christian counterpart to tell not only the kerygma the festival celebrates, but the story of the festival itself: "we celebrate…we remember…we are redeemed." This is not only a theology *about* the liturgy, but a theology *of* and *through* the liturgy.

The consistently ritual approach of Aphrahat is at a loss when it reaches the prescription at Ex 12.9 not to eat the paschal lamb raw or

---

[110] Demo 12.8, FC 5/2, 305-307.

boiled, but cooked in fire. While Origen found the words of scripture cooked in allegorical fires, Aphrahat can only think of the bread of the eucharist, making a rule that certainly was, and never will be, violated:

> This should be thus understood and explained, that the sacrifice which is offered in the community of God is roasted on the fire and one does not boil it, nor is it offered raw.[111]

Second century echoes are stronger in the lengthy anti-Judaic portion of Demo 12. Just as the commandment to consume the paschal lamb in one house (Ex 12.46) and in the Holy City is a polemical point for Justin, Aphrahat is adamant that only the Church, and not the Jews, has the right to celebrate Pascha. Compared to Justin, there is no difference in argument, and Aphrahat even includes a "shadow" Jewish partner:

> Moses prophesied about them, "I will make them jealous by a people that is no people, and through a foolish people I will provoke them." [Dt. 32.21a].

> Now I ask you, learned debater of the People, who does not correctly understand the words of the Law, show me when it has been fulfilled that God made his People jealous with the people that is none and when he provoked them with a foolish people. If you are jealous of the people from the Gentiles, then you fulfill the word that was written. When you conduct the Pesach in everywhere in foreign places, you act against the commandment. This is the reason the bill of divorcement was made up for you. [cf. Jer 12.7-9].

> If you will not be persuaded, listen to the prophet Jeremiah, who said, "I have forsaken my house, I have forsaken my heritage. I have given the beloved of my soul into the hands of her enemies and a colorful bird is my inheritance." [cf. Jer 12.7-9]. What is the colorful bird? I ask you. The colorful bird is the Church of the Gentiles. See how he calls them colorful, because he gathers them from many languages and distant peoples and brings them near.[112]

Aphrahat is following the rules of a long rhetorical tradition: Ex 12 is the story of origins for the "colorful" Gentile church. The jealousy of which Aphrahat accuses his imaginary partner is only a construct to demonstrate the superiority of the exegesis. The reader, not the "shadow,"

---

[111] Demo 12.9, FC 5/2, 307.
[112] Demo 12.4, FC 5/2, 301.

is the one being persuaded, and the "Jews" addressed are the ones who still stubbornly refuse to vanish from Ex 12.

One reason parallels to second century sources seem so fresh in comparison, say, to the Asian IP, is because they probably are. The paschal treatises of the Asian tradition were still circulating in fourth and fifth century Syria just as Irenaeus' AH and *Epideixis*, the latter only extant in an Armenian translation from the Syriac. As many writers in the second century, Irenaeus also wrote a treatise on the Pascha, of which only the briefest citation, and that in an indirect form, is preserved in PsJustin's treatise *Questions and Answers to the Orthodox:*

> Not to kneel on the Lord's Day is a symbol of the resurrection, through which, by the grace of Christ, we were freed from sins and from the death which was killed because of him This custom began in apostolic times, as the blessed Irenaeus, martyr[113] and bishop of Lyon, says in his treatise *On the Pascha*. In it, he also mentions Pentecost, during which we do not kneel, since it is equivalent to the Lord's Day, for the reason mentioned.[114]

Though R. M. Grant[115] considers Theodoret a likely author, Gustave Bardy[116] attributes this work to an unknown Syrian of the fifth century. This is an interesting prospect, for the author has included an "apostolic" prescription for which the *Didascalia* shows no interest. Less subject to speculation is another letter fragment of Irenaeus concerning Sunday celebration of Pascha cited by Severus of Antioch.[117] These few indicators may not point to an Asian renaissance among Syrian authors, but along with Eusebius' history they are a reminder that paschal literature of the second century was still available in the fourth.

3. *"Syrian" Mimesis of Gospel Narrative*

The difference between Syrian and Asian traditions emerges when "old" and "new" Paschas are contrasted, and gospel narrative supplants Ex 12 as holy story:

---

[113] The legendary martyrdom of Irenaeus first appears in Jerome Comm. in Isa. 17.64. Drobner, Lehrbuch 95.

[114] PG 6, 1364-5=Corpus Apol. 3 (Otto), 186-188.

[115] Grant, Fragments, 205.

[116] Bardy, G., art. "Justin" DThC 8.2, 2241.

[117] See below, p. 352.

For Israel was baptized in the middle of the sea, in that paschal night, on the day of salvation. Our Savior washed the feet of his disciples in the paschal night, a symbol for baptism. You should know, my Beloved, that only from this night on, our Savior administered the true baptism. For as long as he tarried among his disciples, they were only baptized with the baptism of the priestly law, about which John spoke, "Repent of your sins." And in that night he revealed to them the mystery of baptism of suffering and his death; as the Apostle says, "You are with him through baptism buried in death, and rise with him by the power of God." Know then, my Beloved, that the baptism of John is not for the forgiveness of sins, but for repentance. The History of the Twelve Apostles reports to us about this, when the disciples asked those who had been called from Israel and from the Gentiles and spoke to them, 'Are you baptized?' and they said, 'We are baptized with the baptism of John,' then they baptized these persons with the true baptism, the mystery of the Passion of our Lord. And also our Savior testifies concerning this, as he speaks to his disciples, "John baptized with water, but you will be baptized with the Holy Spirit." For as our Savior took water and poured it into the washbasin, took an apron and girded his loins with it and began to wash the feet of his disciples, and as he came to Simon Cephas, the latter said to him, "Shall you wash my feet. Never shall you wash my feet." And Jesus said, "If I do not wash you, then you have no part of me." And Simon said, "Then, Lord, wash not only my feet, but also my hands and my head." And Jesus said to him, "Whoever is washed needs only his feet washed." And after he had washed the feet of his disciples, he put his clothes back on, sat down and said to them, "You call me Master and Lord, and that I am; if, then I, your Master and Lord, wash your feet, how much more is it fitting for you that you wash each other's feet?" This example I have given you so that, as I have done, so you should do."[118]

Aphrahat crafts a single story of origins in the paschal night that celebrates "the mystery of baptism of suffering and his death." The footwashing is not only enacted parable with ethical object, but also an institution of the sacrament mirroring that of the supper. The footwashing confirms sign, just as the giving of the Spirit in Acts completes the "baptism of John." Kerygma is not diminished by mimesis any more than this liturgy is "mere" commemoration. The paschal night is a sacramental synthesis of the Christian mystery with its liturgical signs.

When Aphrahat moves to the meal narrative, he acknowledges that there has been much confusion of thought about content and proper observation of the Pascha:

---

[118] Demo 12.10, FC 5/2, 308 f.

But you have heard, beloved, what I have said to you about the Pascha, that its mystery was given to the first People and that its truth today is proclaimed among the nations. For the thoughts of persons foolish and misunderstanding about this great feast day are quite confused about how it should be understood and observed.[119]

Why does this sound like Connolly's assessment of DA 21? Because Aphrahat is likely reacting to the *Didascalia's* strange chronology, its reduction of the passion to adverbs of time, and its wholesale neglect that this story has a message beyond informing the ritually acribious when they should begin a fast. Aphrahat now begins his retelling of the passion:

For our Savior ate the Pascha with his disciples in the usual night of the fourteenth, (i.e., not the *unusual* Tuesday) and for his disciples, changed the prefiguring Pascha into the true Pascha. After Judas had departed from them, he took bread and gave thanks and gave it to his disciples and said to them, "This is my body, take and eat of it all of you. And also over the wine he gave thanks likewise and said to them, "This is my blood of the new covenant, shed for many for the forgiveness of sins. This do in remembrance of me as often as you gather." Before the Lord was taken prisoner, he said these things. And our Lord stood up and left the place where he had celebrated the Pascha and given his body as food and his blood as drink and went to his disciples, where he was taken prisoner. For whoever gives his flesh to eat and his blood to drink is counted as among the dead. Our Lord gave with his own hands his body as food, and before he was crucified, his blood as drink. In the night of the fourteenth he was taken prisoner, and until the sixth hour his trial was held. At the sixth hour they pronounced him guilty, then they led him out and crucified him. While they held his trial, he did not speak and did not give his judges any answer. [cf. Mt. 26.62 f.] For he certainly could have spoken and given answer, and yet for one counted among the dead, it is not possible to speak. From the sixth hour to the ninth there was darkness [Mt. 27.45]. He commended his spirit to the Father in the ninth hour and was among the dead in the night which began the fifteenth, in the night of the Sabbath, and also the whole day with the three hours on Friday. And in the night which began the first day of the week, he arose from the dead at the same time as when he had given his disciples his body and blood.[120]

In contrast to the expansion of DA 21, Aphrahat compresses the story into one to be told in the course of a single night. The "great feast day

---

[119] Demo 12.5, FC 5/2, 302.
[120] Demo 12.5 f., FC 5/2, 302-304.

of Friday" is a Saturday vigil. "Friday" is in the gospel narrative, not in a mimetic ritual, and there is no indication of a dual celebration on Thursday and Saturday nights in the "uses of the feast" Aphrahat describes.[121] The paschal eucharist synchronizes with the hour of the Syn meal *and* the resurrection, the very synchronicity Dionysius cannot find, but which the *Didascalia* is certain coincides with the paschal eucharist. Yet for Aphrahat, the paschal eucharist is not a proleptic celebration of the cross and resurrection, but in the "historic" paschal night, is identical to the mysteries the meal celebrates, a dramatic climax for which the cross is merely the denouement. And for this meal, Judas cannot be permitted a place in the holy rites in the holiest of nights, but only the disciples and the celebrating community. Jesus' giving his flesh and blood as food and drink is the death he willed, proven by his silence before his judges. The crucifixion is merely a consequence of this sovereign decision to give his life. As Ephrem writes:

> The True Lamb knew * that the priests
> and the Levites were unclean * They were not to his stature.
> He himself became for his body * priest and high priest.[122]

While Ephrem's Lamb offers himself to God and Aphrahat's Jesus gives his body and blood to the church, both maintain the absolute sovereignty of Jesus that marks the Joh passion.

When Aphrahat moves to explain the "three days in the heart of the earth," he uses the same rhetorical device as in his anti-Judaic polemic:

> Now show us, Oh wise one, the three days and three nights during which our Savior was among the dead. Behold, we find that it took three hours of Friday and the night of the dawning sabbath and this whole day, and on Sunday night he rose. Then add for me the three days and three nights, where are they?[123]

---

[121] Text above, p. 234. The "great feast day" has been read mimetically. Rouwhorst, Date, sees a Fri. vigil extended to Fri. and Sat. Aphrahat cannot celebrate on Sunday because "the central aspect of the feast is not the Resurrection but the redemptive Passion and Death of Christ..." Similarly Simon, Verus, 370. According to Simon, Pascha was held in the night of 13 Nisan. CQL, 184, n. "g," proposes a vigil Thurs. and Sat. nights. The comment, "The only Church known to have done this is the Syrian...," is puzzling, given Egeria's witness to a Thursday vigil from 7 pm-dawn. Cf. Itinerary 35.1-36.3, CQL 116a.

[122] Ephrem, Azyma 2.2, CSCO 249, 4.

[123] Demo 12.5, FC 5/2, 304.

Although Rouwhorst[124] takes this "wise one" to be none other than the Persian Sage himself, its parallel to the "debater of the People" signals a different address. Either way, Aphrahat is building suspense to tell his readers to expect something unusual:

> Behold, there is only one whole day and one whole night. And yet it happened in truth what our Savior said, "As Jonah, the son of Mathais, was three days and three nights in the belly of the fish, so with the Son of Man also be in the heart of the earth." [Mt 12.40] For from that time on, when he gave his body as food and his blood as drink, are three days and three nights. For it was nighttime, when Judas departed from them, [Jn 13.30] and the eleven disciples ate the body of the Savior and drank his blood. Behold, the night into Friday is the first night, and until the sixth hour when they judged him, it is one day and one night. And the three hours while there was darkness, from the sixth to the ninth hour, and the three hours after the darkness, are already two days and two nights. Let us add then the whole night of the breaking sabbath and the whole day of the sabbath, then our Lord was three days and three nights among the dead, and on the night into Sunday he rose.[125]

The "wise debater of the People" has become a Christian exegete, but one whose mathematics Aphrahat has elegantly altered to count from the Thursday meal, the perfect confirmation that Jesus is counted "among the dead" after offering his body and blood. Aphrahat is addressing DA 21, not to argue with its reading of the darkness at the cross, but to return its mathematical problem to the Syn/Tatianic meal account as the only narrative sequence necessary for explaining the rituals of Pascha. Mimetic "exactness," it would seem, has sacrificed simplicity and the "plain sense" of the text only as Aphrahat must accent Jesus' fasting silence from the moment of capture and – following "idiotism" with far less exactness – set the resurrection simultaneous with breaking the fast. The Friday of the gospels, in which Aphrahat finds cross, meal, and bath, is the scriptural foundation for the paschal fast and the "great feast day" that awaits the resurrection – three days to the minute from the Pesach meal to the eucharist of the paschal vigil. The Bridegroom is absent and returns – in perfect synchrony with a fasting and celebrating community.

---

[124] Rouwhorst, VigChrS 7.2, 116, n. 50.
[125] Demo 12.5, FC 5/2, 304 f.

VIII. A Look Backward…and Forward

Campenhausen's "crisis of the third century" can find no better victim than the *Didascalia's* contorted exegesis of Zech 8.19, or perhaps the paradoxical use and non-use of Num 9.6-11 in the *Didascalia's* Western contemporary, ApTrad. When confronted with a problem of ritual observance, the first impulse is to seek counsel in scriptural authority. When an answer does not issue forth from the cultically mute NT, then there are several alternatives:

(1) A recognized leader may pore through the "archives" and apply any number of time-tested tools – prophetic cultic erasure, typological reading, fulfillment in the Christian cult – to find an answer. This skill was acquired looking at the way earlier exegetes had found kerygma and Christian ritual in the Hebrew scriptures. The "confused thought" of DA 21 speaks loud and clear about the canon, but also shows why early Christian literature does not produce an abundance of such readings.

(2) A second alternative is to make the cultically mute NT speak, or better, to listen carefully as a text is cast into a new situation. The Bridegroom aetiology is one of the oldest and most broadly attested examples of NT mimesis because it could yield motivation for fasting practices just by asking. A "crisis of exactness" results when more is asked of the text than this, but this question is still posed – and elegantly answered – in Aphrahat's treatise almost a century and a half after Carthaginian Christians were certain of the text's meaning.

(3) A third alternative is the one chosen by Dionysius, who, pointing to the failure of the mimetic search, speaks in his own right as bishop of Alexandria. The epiphany on the sea is pointed briefly toward a specific time to end the fast, but this is "congruence," not rubric. Scripture supports the bishop's decision, not the other way around.

(4) Even though the *Didascalia* may have been written by a bishop,[126] the author chooses to amplify his pronouncements not only with the voice of pseudepigraphic apostles, but the risen Lord himself. While one can entertain thoughts about how the first readers may have found the "innovative" fasting story at the house of Levi, it did not suit the taste of either the H-redactors nor the reviser of the ApCon. In essence, this alternative is a non-alternative, or rather alternative (2) run amok.

---

[126] So Brown, Messiah, 1343: "…written by a bishop in Syria ca. 200-225…"

Yet with the same texts and mimetic techniques, Aphrahat crafts a compact ritual narrative that provides grounding in canonical (i.e. Tatianic) narrative for fast, eucharist, and baptism in the paschal night. The comparison is slightly unfair because Aphrahat does not need to originate a fast from Monday, but silently assumes it as traditional practice.

The array of texts dealing with the beginning of Pascha measures not only the growth of mimesis across the Church after the acknowledgment of the two testament canon, but also the consistently mimetic quality of readings emanating from Syrian sources before and after Christ narrative becomes standard speech elsewhere. Even Aphrahat's elegant solution falls on the wrong side of Tertullian's rubric line, while Dionysius already removes the linchpin of Aphrahat's exegesis, the synchrony of paschal eucharist with the moment of resurrection.

The conversation about fasting in the days of Pascha has mainly been a cooperative search – with ever growing exactness – for scriptural authority and content in narratives about rite. The controversy in Carthage was not about the paschal fast, but Montanist practices that exceeded the general practice of the "catholics" and the authority of the bishop. In this context, various verses from Acts are called into duty as liturgical canon: the "hour of prayer" (Acts 3.1) takes on a new meaning for the practice of a self-identified group. That "catholics" need do nothing more than preserve the status quo to obey this rule, while the Montanists are shown to be negligent scofflaws, is the whole point of the exegesis.

When controversy surrounds the end of Pascha rather than its beginning, rhetoric sometimes betrays the mild irritation of Aphrahat and Dionysius, sometimes the rhetorical violence of Carthage, and often the anti-Judaic polemic of the sub-H redactors. Against all of these mimetic voices, Irenaeus makes a plea for unity on other grounds besides liturgical conformity. Controversialists will read the four canonical passion accounts with the same exactness as DA 21, and with the same goal: to imbue liturgical practice, regardless of age and provenance, with the authority of scripture and apostolic tradition.

PART TWO: THE RHETORIC OF DISPUTE

A. INTERLUDE: TRADITIONS MOVING TOWARD CONFLICT

I. Paschal Liturgy and Christian Identity

For the community of readers in "the churches of the east and the west, of the north and the south"[1] summoned by the *Epistola Apostolorum*, the celebration of Pascha is a ritual act so connected to Christian identity that the author not only provides the paschal night with a story of origins and an institution by the risen Lord, but constructs this narrative to mirror the very soteriology he urges upon the reader. Yet in other literature, the paschal feast is not mentioned until the closing decades of the second century. There is, then, an odd literary coincidence with Jewish traditions: the Mishnah tract Pesachim does not find an equivalent in Christian paschal treatises until roughly the same time as these rabbinical traditions were collected and committed to writing.

Reading this absence as history – that the Pascha was not celebrated in enough places to echo in earlier literature – seems ill-advised.[2] There are, after all, remnants of such conversations beginning around 165 in Rome with the discussion of date and day between Polycarp of Smyrna and the Roman bishop Anicetus, the conflict in Asia Minor some twelve years later that generated many of the paschal treatises, and finally ca. 195, the controversy Eusebius calls "a not insignificant dispute." In none of these discussions is observance at issue, but a diversity in practice Irenaeus dates to the first Christian missionaries. This is one bit of rhetoric that may be a valid assessment of history, even if it is only an educated guess. Irenaeus knows that the liturgical traditions in conflict did not happen overnight.

While the first century relationship between exegesis of Pesach-Exodus texts and celebration in the paschal night cannot be completely mapped out, for second century Gentile writers, Ex 12 had already begun to tell

---

[1] EpAp 2(13) only extant in Eth. TU 43, 26.
[2] For Rome: Holl, Bruchstück, 216-218; Talley, Origins, 22-24. See below, p. 338-347.

the story of baptism and the creation of the Gentile Church. Exegesis, community identity, and ritual had fully merged and were attracting other biblical themes, even the red thread in Rahab's window. By the Council of Nicaea in 325, regulating the celebration of Pascha had become an identifying mark of the Great Church as urgent as distancing Arian christology from orthodoxy, so urgent that myth-making about a unified paschal calendar issuing from the Council begins almost as soon as the last bishops leave for home. The importance EpAp ascribes to the paschal feast is now as universal as it wishes its readership.

This, too, is not an overnight development. As the second century draws to a close, the link between Christian rite and Christian identity continues to strengthen. In Acts, Christians often worship and pray, but they are hardly ever shown worshipping and praying. To describe a service at which Paul presided for hours on end, Luke tells in Acts 20 of a room lit by many lamps, Eutychius falling from a window, prayers being said over him, and a final "bread-breaking." But there is not a line from Paul's sermon, no text given for the prayer that resuscitated the sermon-weary victim, and the reader is left with Eutychius as the eucharist is celebrated upstairs. In the *Acts of Paul* a century later, an Ephesian liturgy at which Paul presides is graced by the appearance of an angel, prophecy, and a homily given during the Fifty Days in which Paul tells of his experience on the road to Damascus.[3] This is not merely an increase in mimetic detail: Luke's story is complete with depiction of time, place, a miracle, and even artificial illumination. There are no gaps, except for readers in the later second century and the writers who sought to fill them. Participation in liturgical acts is now depicted as integral to who Christians are and what they believe. In Acts, the liturgical is background for the miraculous; in the *Acts of Paul*, the reverse.

II. The Narrative

In exegetical literature, another comparison to the Mishnah is instructive. While Christian texts are scant, Mishnah Pesachim preserves meticulous rabbinical discussions about the feast of Pesach: the exact time and procedure for removal of leaven, the minimum amount of lamb to be eaten, how far a portion of the lamb may reach outside the ritual

---

[3] NTApo II, 241-243.

boundaries of Jerusalem and what to do should this occur – in short, questions of ritual minutiae likely posed only by the rabbis themselves, an intellectual sport played out within the rituals of the story of origins of the Jewish people and the mystical wholeness of Torah. Since the Exile, this feast, along with circumcision and Sabbath observance, was a hallmark of Jewish identity cast into greater relief after the destruction of the Temple. But where is the Mishnah tract on synagogue worship, a rabbinical "church order"? Again, absence is not historical, but rhetorical. Regular attendance at Sabbath worship was not considered as important a component of religious identity as the study of the Torah.

For Christian writers, the Pesach *texts* and their "historical" rituals provide important vocabulary already before the year 50 CE, are imitated by the Syn meal narratives and more globally in the Fourth Gospel, which not only assigns the Lamb of God immense symbolic value but also incorporates the festival *inclusio* of the Exodus saga into its narrative structure. Written to churches in Asia Minor, the relatively late Revelation is an apotheosis of the Lamb in a celestial liturgy on the "Lord's Day of the Lord." Paschal *observance* may be subtext in these kerygmatic narratives but never quite rises to the surface, nor should it be forced to do so by the eagerly mimetic readings of modern exegetes. The Christian Pascha remains peripheral in extant sources until disagreements arise about its date and day between two important Christian centers, Rome and Ephesus, or more accurately, between the Bishop of Rome and Asian immigrants and their descendants who continue to follow the practice of their homeland for several generations in the imperial city – with the blessings of Asian bishops.

But this is only a prelude to change. At the end of the second century rhetoric about date and content of Pascha is couched in arguments gleaned both from "apostolic tradition" and from mimetic readings of NT narratives by bishops of important sees across the Empire. That this mimetic use of the NT is an innovation often escapes notice, yet except for the brief hints in Ignatius of Antioch, nothing in previous literature anticipates such readings. This allows two preliminary conclusions. I in Rome, a unified paschal observance was desirable, though not attained, already at mid-century. Divergent paschal practice cannot have been the only difference among groups of Christians from all over the Empire living in the capital, but this one difference was seen more and more as divisive, especially with the growing importance of the bishop's role as community leader. Continued immigration of Christians to Rome could only have intensified the problem: divergent practice began to symbolize fracture in the community, a unified practice its integrity. At the end of the century, however, the paschal feast had gained in importance as a marker of Christian identity, and its observance in the Great Church is universal. The bishop of Rome makes another, likely successful, attempt at unified practice, but this time writers from important sees become involved, their participation solicited by Victor himself. It is no longer merely a Roman issue, though here most acutely felt.

At the same time, the gospel canon has begun to shape liturgical theology, but must reflect differing practices. Text can no longer imitate rite, but mimetic interpretation easily leaps over and through canonical "protection," generating secondary texts quite divergent from gospel accounts. As in the gospels, narrative time stretches or compresses, but to match liturgical time: the paschal night or a week-long fast. The text being interpreted is also no longer Ex 12 alone, but the passion narratives of the four gospels as its exegesis. In the first century, the issue was *that* one worships, later in the second, *how* and *when* one worships is becoming just as important. In terms of Christian identity, orthodoxy and orthopraxis are beginning to merge under episcopal leadership.

III. The History

This process is one where rhetoric had to catch up with history. In 150 Justin is still lacing the passion narrative with details from Genesis,[4] and the meal narrative, without paschal frame – is the only NT text he links to rite. In 195 important theologians across the Empire are arguing about the significance of chronology and other details of the passion narratives as they provide aetiologies for liturgical practice. This is not incremental change, but a radical shift in the relationship between text and rite. The "new" canon and the "old" liturgy have begun to measure each other. Irenaeus is caught in between: despite the high value given the gospels in his "rule of faith," not once does he employ this new mutual exegesis of rite and story beyond NT allusions. Instead, taking an active role in the paschal dispute, Irenaeus urges peace on the basis of apostolic tradition.

---

[4] Jesus tied the donkey he rode into Jerusalem to a grapevine (Gen 49.11). Justin, IApol 32.

The liturgy had not waited for authoritative NT texts to proclaim and celebrate the paschal mystery. With a preview at mid-second century, paschal traditions of Rome, Alexandria, the coastal cities of Palestine, Ephesus, Edessa and Antioch begin to converge or collide – with each other and with an emerging authoritative text. This interpretive crucible refines a mimetic language of the liturgy to strengthen claims of apostolic provenance: suddenly "exactness", or its alleged lack in opponents, becomes an important element of liturgical theology, and the legitimacy of liturgical practice becomes a matter of reading the gospels. From this perspective, the paschal controversy appears as a rather hasty scramble for aetiologies in an emergent NT canon for rites that predate its authority. Writers across the Church are faced with conflicting gospel accounts, divergent traditions, and a mimetic liturgical theology that has just emerged as the definitive way of connecting rite and story.

The move toward a more "exact" fit between Christ narrative and Christian rite did not begin or end with a dispute over the day of the Pascha, and the calendar was surely not the only subject matter of paschal treatises written over the course of the second and third centuries. The breadth of paschal thematology already laid out in the NT is enough to widen such a narrow focus, and an elegant christological reading of Ex 12 must have been an irresistible challenge to display rhetorical and exegetical skill. The list of authors also shows a wide scope: Apollinarios of Hierapolis, Melito of Sardis, Clement of Alexandria, Irenaeus, Victor of Rome, Hippolytus, Novatian.[5] Unfortunately, none of these writings has been preserved. As genre they are accessible solely through their last representatives, Origen and Eusebius, the former rescued from an Egyptian trashheap and the latter only partially preserved in the Luke catena of Nicetas of Heraclea. Aphrahat's Twelfth Demonstration is thus the last of its breed, protected from extinction by its context in a larger work.

These works did not disappear all at once, but already in the fourth and fifth centuries, the levels of meaning Christian exegetes could unfold in Ex 12 had come to an end.[6] Photius knows of only three

---

[5] Eus. EH: Melito, 4.26.3; Clem. Alex., 4.26.4; Hip., 4.22. Apol.: ChronPasc PG 92, 80C-D); a single citation from Irenaeus in PsJustin Quaest. 115 (Otto, 3/2, 186-188); Jerome mentions a work by Victor "super questione paschae" whose style was mediocre, vir. ill. 34, and Novatian, "scripset autem de pascha, de sabbato,…" vir. ill. 70.

[6] See Huber, Passa, 2.6, "Das Zurücktreten der Passatypologie," 137-139.

works on the Pascha: a broadside presumably from the Nicean conflict or its aftereffects, and yet another debate about paschal computation between an otherwise unknown Meterodoros and a nameless opponent.[7] Except for the citations in the *Chronicon Paschale*, by the turn of the first Christian millennium the paschal treatises were completely forgotten. The mimetic theology for whose development these documents would have been primary witnesses had become so dominant that the paschal night itself, which celebrated the mystery of salvation more than it commemorated its history, became a mere adjunct to the far more popular services of a dramatic liturgy long appropriated from the Church of the Holy Sepulcher in Jerusalem. Holy Week had become a pilgrimage for which participants did not have to leave home, and its dramatic liturgy was not directed toward the slaying of the lamb and the mysteries of Pesach. In the High Middle Ages, mammoth paschal candles[8] and the exquisite song of the Exsultet could not compensate for loss of meaning in a service now held in the middle of the afternoon. Tradition had absorbed, then forgotten the paschal treatises, because they had nothing more to contribute.

It is a mixed blessing that a residue from these writings could be employed in new rhetorical situations that have nothing to do with the paschal feast. Authors on the wrong side of Chalcedon often took recourse to writings of an earlier period, actualizing an earlier, non-polemicized christology to support their arguments. In these cases it is usually a simple matter to penetrate back to the second century text. The situation is quite different, however, with the most important sources: the *Ecclesiastical History* of Eusebius of Caesarea and the *Chronicon Paschale*. These works were dependent upon sources that by chance or design skew a historical reconstruction either of the rhetoric or the practices involved, and there is always the question of how the author chooses to cite what text and when. These rhetorical texts are thus doubly embedded in rhetoric even before the task of interpretation begins, not to mention further encrustations deposited by two centuries of modern scholarship.

So while chronology may have been a major issue for the *Chronicon*, strict chronological order cannot be followed here. Instead, Nicene and

---

[7] Photius, Biblio. 2.115 f., 86 f.

[8] A paschal candle presented to the church at Echternach (Lux.) by the emperor Maximilian in 1512 weighed 354 lbs. See MacGregor, Alistair J., Fire and Light in the Western Triduum, ACC 71, Collegeville, 1992, 313.

post-Nicene contexts must be penetrated before second and early third
century dialogues may come to light. Texts will remain, as it were, in
situ, but some of the constructs used to craft them will turn out to have
much deeper foundations.[9]

IV. The Surface Layer: The Texts

At the beginning of the fourth century, Eusebius preserves excerpts from
letters from Irenaeus, the bishops of Caesarea and Jerusalem, and Polycrates of Ephesus, all to Victor of Rome. Pierre Nautin has suggested
a Roman provenance for this collection as well as another of the letters
of Dionysius of Corinth. This now joined collection was then sent to
Ephesus, where Polycrates' letter was added along with the letter concerning the Gallic martyrs, then forwarded to Caesarea, where Eusebius
found it along with a letter from his second century predecessor in the
see of Caesarea.[10]
    Whether this convoluted mail route is correct is less important than
pointing out that Eusebius' sources must have come from somewhere,
they are not exhaustive, and the reason for their collection was not likely
compiling primary sources for a history of the paschal controversy.
One way or another, copies of these letters had made their way to the
libraries of Caesarea or Jerusalem. Along with the legendary correspondence between Jesus and King Abgar of Edessa and a very favorable
report about the Christian Gnostic philosopher Bar Daisan, a copy of
another letter had come from Mesopotamian Osrhoëne.
    Half a century later, Epiphanius attempts to come to historical terms
with the paschal rhetoric of Nicaea and also mentions Montanists in Phrygia and Cappadocia who celebrate the Pascha on 25 March, 6 April, or
other fixed days.[11] His *Panarion* (375-8 CE) also gives valuable information

---

[9] The psalm homilies of Asterius come from a later period and are not the work of
a suddenly orthodox Arian Asterius the Sophist (†341) but of an otherwise unknown
Asterius writing, late 4 c. – early 5 c. See Kinzig, Wolfram, In Search of Asterius. Studies on the Authorship of the Homilies on the Psalms, FKDg 47, 1990. This will change
the way one reads Auf der Maur, Hansjörg, Die Osterhomilien des Asterios Sophistes als
Quelle für die Geschichte der Osterfeier, TTSt 19, 1962.
[10] Nautin, Pierre, Lettres et Écrivains Chrétiens des IIe et IIIe siècles. Patristica II,
Paris 1961, 87-91.
[11] See Strobel, Kalender, 223. These groups may be dating from the equinox.

about the Audians, a monastic community originally from Mesopotamia, for whom he has nothing but high praise, except for their teaching on the corporeality of God and their paschal calendar. Safely on the other side of the Euphrates, the Audians refused to go along with the paschal canon of Nicaea, holding firmly to their views even during a four-year sojourn on Cyprus. How they expressed their own identity – non-Roman and morally rigorous – is instructive for the East Syrian tradition, as are, of course, Aphrahat, Ephrem, and the *Cave of Treasures*. The Council of Antioch in 329,[12] as well as a homily of Chrysostom dated to 31 January 387,[13] shows that the Nicene revisions of the paschal calendar were not universally accepted. Yet an anonymous sermon transforming the equinoxes and solstices into kerygma demonstrates that at least one Syrian source had fully adopted equinoctial rhetoric from the West, just in time to urge the Western celebration of Christmas on 25 December in addition to the Eastern observance of Epiphany on 6 January.

Texts preserved by Eusebius and Epiphanius are complemented by the seventh century *Chronicon Paschale*, so called because the preface of the work urges the return to the old nineteen-year Alexandrian paschal cycle with support from patristic citations. The preface cites, in this order: a text from Philo of Alexandria extolling the virtues of the vernal equinox, a lengthy excerpt from a paschal treatise of Peter of Alexandria (bishop, 300-311) also concerning the equinox, an excerpt from a letter of Athanasius to Epiphanius, two short excepts from the paschal treatise of Apollinarios of Hierapolis about 14 Nisan, the same from Hippolytus and Clement of Alexandria, all three defending Joh chronology and vigorously denying that the gospels portray Jesus as having celebrated Pesach the night before his death. Other than the letter from Athanasius, this chain of citations looks suspiciously like a florilegium originally designed for issues no longer current in the Chronicler's day, but tailor-made for Alexandria at the Council of Nicaea. While it is conceivable that the earlier Alexandrian Chronicler had access to ancient works of which the later Constantinopolitan Photius knew nothing, a literary source that had already combined the earlier excerpts would do more to explain this anomaly.

This completes the dossier. There would appear to be a sufficient of texts number to form some sort of picture of the paschal controversies

---

[12] See Huber, Passa, 75 f.
[13] PG 48, 861-872. See Huber, Passa, 77. The year was a worst case scenario.

of 155 (Anicetus-Polycarp), 166/8 (Laodicea), and 195 (Victor-Poly-crates). Yet these texts span several centuries, they cannot all take part in the same dialogue, and almost all have been "pericoped" for another purpose. Writing their history is thus tantamount to reading other people's mail. These texts were not intended to inform the distant future about either the historical or rhetorical situation to which their writers are reacting. The trick, then, is reading into these texts something approximating what was originally not read at all, but nevertheless known and understood by everyone who read them.

B. The Paschal Controversy, 325

"And in a word, as is not unknown to many scholarly persons," Epiphanius writes, "there was a great deal of muddle and tiresomeness whenever trouble was stirred up in the church's teaching on the question of this festival."[1] Unfortunately, much tiresome muddle about who was saying what to whom and why in the paschal controversies is due to scholarly persons. Rhetoric and tradition are paraphrased into history, usually by assuming that letters, paschal treatises, and controversial writings are neutral documents perfectly transparent to their historical situations. All texts dealing with liturgical and calendrical issues generously employ mimetic constructs addressed to scripture and practice. Yet since describing outright the object of these constructs was such an unnecessary rhetorical task, moderns who are not envisioned by these texts as readers are left with the mimetic mirror, but an image that can only be reached by reconstructive methods. If these readers have ever paused to ask themselves why artists' reconstructions of, say, the Second Jerusalem Temple always manage to look like bad sets for *Aida*, then the problem has been defined.

The most compactly distorted example of Nicene paschal rhetoric[2] is a brief notice buried in the *Bibliotheca* of Photius of Constantinople († 891):

> An anonymous book was read, whose title was: "To the Jews, their heretical supporters and the Quartadecimans, who do not celebrate the holy Pascha in the first month according to the Hebrews." This treatment is short, devoid of form and content, but it says that our Lord Jesus Christ did not eat the legal Pascha on Thursday evening. That was not at all the time for it, but on the next day. Since he did not conduct the meal according to the law when he ate, it took place on the next day. He obtained neither lamb, nor unleavened bread, nor anything else observed by those who celebrate the Pascha according to the custom of the Law, but he said he wished to eat his own mystical meal, of which he also gave the disciples bread and cup (cf. Lk 22.15).[3]

[1] Panarion 70. 9.8, GCS 37, 242; NHMS 36, 411.

[2] Strobel, Kalender, 221, n. 1, proposes Victor of Rome as author. Its anti-Judaism points to Nicaea, the contrast between "Hebrews" and "Jews" to Alexandria and allied sees.

[3] Photius. Bibliothéque, II, ed. Henry, Paris 1960, 86.

Jews, Quartadecimans, Hebrews, heretics, mystical meal versus the Law – who and what is this author talking about? How have these rhetorical labels been assigned and why? Yet even before such questions are posed, the work's major thesis, which Photius has succinctly outlined, stands out in bold relief. This work is not an ancient "shadow" of Joachim Jeremias holding forth exegetically about the meal narrative and the pale academic issue of Joh versus Syn chronology. Nor is it ultimately concerned about "Jews" who did not calculate a calendar to set Pesach after the spring equinox every year versus the "Hebrews"(!) who did. The only real-life Jew at issue is Jesus of Nazareth.

Confusion about the role of Asia Minor in the paschal dispute at the Council of Nicaea also muddles rhetoric and history of the controversy in 195, especially its context in the EH of Eusebius. Johannes Quasten[4] points out the political role Eusebius attempted in the Arian conflict between two sharply divided christological positions, a stance that led to his condemnation at the Council of Antioch held shortly before Nicaea.[5] While Eusebius hardly played such a balanced role in the paschal dispute, this might suggest why even earlier, he had been interested in Irenaeus' attempt to mediate between Rome and Asia, and why he omits the equally unhappy outcome. Irenaeus is a model peacemaker, a counterweight to the strife, jealousy and ambition among bishops that Eusebius holds directly responsible for the Diocletian persecutions (EH 8.1.8).

I. Geography and the Global Myth

Despite Louis Duchesne's faulty construct of the paschal controversy 195,[6] the texts he compiled in 1880 to show that the Quartadeciman practice of Asia Minor was not at issue at the Council of Nicaea are incontrovertible.[7] One source, a letter Constantine wrote soon after the

[4] Quasten, Johannes. Patrology III, 310.
[5] See Holland, David Larrimore, Die Synode von Antiochien (324/5) und ihre Bedeutung für Eusebius von Caesarea und das Konzil von Nizäa, ZKG 81, 1970, 163-181.
[6] Duchesne, Louis, La Question de la Pâque au Concile de Nicée. RQH 28, 1880, (5-42) 7: "Les uns pouvaient considérer le moment de la Passion comme le point central de la solennité, les autres attribuer une importance plus grande à la commémoration de la Résurrection." This is identical to Schmidt's "Dort Passah, hier Ostern."
[7] Except for Lohse, Passafest, 17 f. To this, see Huber, Passa, 70, n. 59. See also Kraehling, Carl H., The Jewish Community at Antioch, JBL 51, 1932, 130-160. Here a

Council, may owe more to Eusebius than just its preservation, since Eusebius may have helped compose the letter or retouched it afterward. Such ghost-writing would have been considerably easier were Constantine no longer among the living, which could account for the strong similarities between this letter and Eusebius' paschal treatise.[8]

This actually makes the letter an even more valuable document. Since a major concern of Eusebius' encomium to the first Christian emperor is to show him as unifier of the Church, the letter contains what Eusebius wished Constantine had said at the Council even if he in fact did not. Thus like Eusebius' own treatise, the letter is an excellent summary of the rhetoric that worked at Nicaea. It is also helpful to consider that most readers would have known more about who the disputing parties were and where they lived than about the specific content of an actual paschal decree. What later circulated as this decree may only be a summary of this letter,[9] the first source claiming that Nicaea issued a specific calendar so that Pascha could be celebrated "on one and the same day." Almost immediately, the unified celebration of the paschal feast becomes equated with Nicene orthodoxy.

One characteristic common to many sources is geographic detail. The now regulated celebration of Pascha signs the unity of the church, and to announce the new consensus, opponents are first isolated, explicitly or implicitly, then reintegrated, in catalogues of various lengths of the regions representing the majority. Regardless of its authenticity, the so-called Nicaean "Paschal Decree" sets up an unambiguous opposition:

> Having discussed the problem of the necessity for the whole [church] under heaven to celebrate the Pascha harmoniously, three parts of the world being found in harmony with the Romans and Alexandrians, and only one region, that of the Orient, in disagreement [μόνον κλίμα τῆς ἀνατολῆς ἀμφισβητοῦν], it was decided to relinquish all discussion and contradiction, and the brothers in the Orient [ἐν τῇ ἀνατολῇ] should also

"judaizing" Quartadeciman practice rationalizes Chrysostom's anti-Semitism. Most recently ignored by Brox, Norbert, Tendenzen und Parteilichkeit im Osterfeststreit des zweiten Jahrhunderts, ZKG 83 1972, 291-394; Chupungco, Shaping; Pelikan, Jaroslav, The Two Sees of Peter. in: The Shaping of Christianity in the Second and Third Centuries. Jewish and Christian Self-Definition, Vol. I., Phila. 1980, 57-73. Petersen, William L., Eusebius and the Paschal Controversy. in: Eusebius, Christianity & Judaism, StPBib 42, 1992, 311-325. R. M. Grant's reconstruction upon which Pelikan and Petersen base their arguments is flawed. See below, p. 352, n. 89.

[8] See also Constantine's high praise of Eusebius' paschal treatise, Vita, 3.35.

[9] CQL 162 f.

celebrate as the Romans and Alexandrians and all the rest, so that on one day all may offer up prayers on the holy day of Pascha.[10]

Rome and Alexandria are on one side of the dispute, while the "Orient" is on the other. The "Orient" is not, however, "Anatolia," as the word might suggest. When Melito of Sardis "travelled to the Orient and came to the place where the preachings and deeds took place," he did not stay home.[11] The "Orient" was a common term for the Near and/or Middle East.

In his continuation of Eusebius' EH, Theodoret cites a letter written from the Council to Alexandria:

> We also wish to give you the good news of the accord that has been established concerning our most holy Pascha. Thanks to your prayers, this point has been regulated as have the others. All of our brothers in the East [τῆς ἑῴας] who had not agreed in this with the Romans, with you, and those who have followed your custom from the beginning, will now celebrate the Pascha at the same time as you.[12]

For the paschal question, the letter implies that Alexandria is a higher authority than the Council itself, which has authorized the universal use of Alexandrian computation. Rome, however, continued to use a different method[13] until Leo the Great,[14] finally ceding the determination of the paschal calendar to Alexandria in 455.[15] Even so, other than behind the scenes correspondence between the two sees, it was not until the year 387 that this non-decision had any serious repercussions.

Joseph Schmid concludes that the Council directed Alexandria to determine the proper date of Pascha and forward it to Rome, but that Rome understood the Alexandrian date as non-binding and continued

---

[10] In Pitra, J. B., Spicilegium Solesmense 4, Paris 1858, 541; CQL 53.

[11] Eusebius, EH 4.26.13-14, for text, see p. 163.

[12] Theodoret, EH 1.9.12, GCS 44, 41. Chupungco, Shaping, 48, cites this text to argue that the Quartadecimans were at issue at Nicaea. Other versions of the letter contain the accusation, "with the Jews." See Athanasius Werke 3.1 (Opitz), Berlin-Leipzig 1935, 50.

[13] Rome used an 84-year cycle; Alexandria, 19. Rome did not allow lunae 15, Alexandria rejected lunae 22. The paschal month could begin 5 Mar. at Rome, in Alexandria, 8 Mar. Rome could celebrate on 20 or 21 Mar. If the numbers were "wrong," Rome usually chose a later date. See Duchesne, Question, 40-42.

[14] Schmid, Joseph, Die Osterfestfrage auf dem ersten allgemeinen Konzil von Nicäa. ThStL 13, 1905, 144 f., 92-118.

[15] CQL, 163.

to use its own reckoning. How Alexandria understood its role in realizing the paschal decision may have been more concrete.[16] This ambiguity may have been the compromise that enabled a consensus between Rome and Alexandria without which there could have been no decision at all.[17] Eduard Schwartz, however, holds that the Council simply encouraged a dialogue between Rome and Alexandria that had begun earlier in the fourth century.[18] Since Rome and the far West were underrepresented,[19] the Alexandrians could have acted almost unilaterally, knowing that whatever calendrical differences between Rome and Alexandria would not be as great as those between Antioch and Rome. In either case, Pascha would be celebrated after the full moon of spring, but computational details were left for these two sees to decide.[20] This conclusion receives support from later correspondence between Rome and Alexandria about the paschal date: neither see claims any authority from the Nicene Council.[21]

Centuries later, the *Chronicon* also assumes a unified calendar among the decisions of Nicaea and locates the opposing party in Syria:

> ...after having refuted the folly of Arius and his partisans, they published the symbol of the faith and also established on one accord a definition for the holy and life-giving Pascha, so that the people of Coele-Syria, just as those, in a word, who have conserved intact the apostolic and evangelical word of the orthodox faith, conformed to the ancient usage of the churches of Rome, Alexandria, and the majority of the holy churches of God on the whole earth and also on one accord will celebrate on one and the same day the holy and life-giving Pascha.[22]

---

[16] Eutychios of Alexandria (ca. 935) retrojects canonization of the Alexandrian computus to the 2 c.: "In that time Demetrius, Patriarch of Alexandria, wrote to Gaianos, the Bishop of the Holy City; to Maximos, Patriarch of Antioch; and to Uqtor [Victor], the Patriarch of Rome, concerning the calculation of the Pascha of the Christians and because of the fast and how one can calculate it from the Pascha of the Jews." Annals 172, CSCO 472, 50.

[17] See Huber, Passa, 61-68.

[18] Schwartz, Ostertafeln, 57 f., as early as 313.

[19] Schwartz, Ostertafeln, 121. But Hosius of Cordoba was closes to the Emperor.

[20] Schmidt, Osterfrage, 11, Rome ceded to Alexandria in 333, 345, and 349; Alexandria to Rome in 350, 357, and 360; also 346, Schwarz, Ostertafeln, 26 f.).

[21] Until a letter from Leo to the Emperor about the date for 455: Alexandria is to set the date, but he is certain theirs is wrong. The Emperor is the court of final appeal. Huber calls this "a diplomatic trick," Passa, 66-68. In 417, Rome kept its early date of 25 Mar. Paschasinus tells Leo (PL 54.606) of a font in a remote village that miraculously fills every year before the vigil. In 417, it did not fill until the Alexandrian 22 April. See Schmidt, 12 f.

[22] ChrPasc, PG 92, 84B-C.

That the Council of Nicaea, perhaps *the* fundamental event in Christian self-definition, would not have determined a definitive paschal calendar is not an idea that would have occurred easily to the author of the *Chronicon*, who lists the condemnation of Arius, publication of the Nicene creed, and the paschal decision as terms of that self-definition. Employed here to further the old nineteen-year Alexandrian computation against more modern and accurate interlopers, this same firmly held belief dominates discussion about the paschal calendar all through the Middle Ages.[23] The idea also did not occur easily to Eusebius, who, in fact, is its literary source. This does not require conscious dissembling, only his conviction that the question had found a definitive solution, a not uncommon dynamic in a deliberative body. Since different parties may understand the practical realization of a solution in different ways, a problem can find a "rhetorical" solution that satisfies everyone, but not an "historical" one in actual practice. For those living at the time, the few instances when Rome and Alexandria either potentially or actually celebrated on different dates would appear as acute problems, not a chronic dilemma. It was still a solution that worked.

The geography has now been mapped out. All sources speak of a dispute between Syria/Mesopotamia (the "Orient") and Rome-Alexandria. A problem arises, however, when another important text, a letter from Athanasius, is brought into the picture:

> For the one [i.e., council, of Nicaea] was held on account of the Arian heresy and the question of Pascha, because those in Syria, Cilicia, and Mesopotamia differed from us and they celebrated it at the same time as the Jews. But thanks be to God, that just as there was agreement on the faith, so there was also on the festival.[24]

Athanasius changes neither the map nor the symbolic value of the paschal decision. Syria, Cilicia, and Mesopotamia comprise the Patriarchate of Antioch, and in this Athanasius agrees with the later sources already cited. The problem turns on his comment that this region celebrated "at the same time ($\varkappa\alpha\iota\rho\delta\varsigma$) as the Jews." This comment becomes an extensive tirade in Constantine's letter:

---

[23] Schmid, Osterfrage, Vorwort, VIII-X.
[24] Ep. to African Bishops 2, Athanasiana Syriaca, CSCO 273 (Syr 119), Robert W. Thomson, 1967, 15.

Since it was timely to correct this point so that we do not have any traffic with the People, those murderers of our father and Lord, and further, that the order is appropriate that all churches hold, in the west as in the south and north of the world, as well as some churches in the Orient, thus all of these thought it well, and I myself put it up for consideration, that you would agree that what is unanimously observed in the city of the Romans and in all of Italy and Africa, in Egypt, Spain, Gaul, Britain, Libya, and in all of Greece and in the Asian and Pontian dioceses and in Cilicia: this you should also accept, with the understanding that not only is the number of churches greater in those places named, but also that it is quite seemly when everyone wishes the same thing, which appears to be required by exact calculation and requires no commonality with the accursed Jews.

To summarize the main point: by a unanimous decree it is decided to celebrate the most holy paschal feast on one and the same day, for it is not appropriate that discord should reign in such a holy celebration, and it is better to follow the judgment that there should be no admixture of foreign error and alien godlessness.[25]

Here again, there can be no mistaking the real and rhetorical geography in this, the most ample catalogue dating from the period. Italy, Africa, Spain, Gaul, Britain, Libya, Greece, *Asia*, and Pontus are listed conforming with Rome and Alexandria; Cilicia has appeared in lists of both sides. Yet if rhetoric is mistaken for history, then the absent Syria and Mesopotamia must have been celebrating Pascha "with the Jews" on 14 Nisan as the Asian Quartadecimans two hundred years before. Since this could hardly have been an innovation, then these areas must have been Quartadeciman in the second century as well.[26]

By this point, a warning that anti-Judaic polemic cannot be read as history simply by neutralizing its affect should be superfluous. Athanasius is no more making a calendrical observation than Constantine. Along with other metaphors of alienation, the term "with the Jews" is designed to corner opponents behind a powerful slur learned in the earliest days of the formation of Christian identity.[27] In this permutation,

---

[25] Eusebius, Vita, 3.19, GCS 7, 86 f.

[26] So Lohse, Passafest, 17 f.

[27] For a sampling of rhetoric against the Arians, cf. Ad Ser. 4, CSCO 273, 12; Ad Afros 3, op. cit., 16: "The same is happening to them as then happened to the traitors, the Jews. For just as the latter, when they left the one source of living water, dug for themselves wells unable to hold water (Jer 2.13)...likewise the former, opposing the ecumenical council, have dug for themselves many councils..." In Ad Epict., Arians are paganized: "For their actions are not surprising if they revile what has been written against

the mother church of the Gentile mission and its allied congregations have become mimetic "Jews," juxtaposed in Constantine's letter to "exact calculation." This is the historical cue. The dispute at Nicaea is about the paschal computations of Antioch and "the rest of the world": Alexandria and Rome.

The Quartadeciman world, however, had shrunk considerably by the fourth century. This is why Epiphanius, writing fifty or so years after Nicaea, orders his anti-heretical medicine chest so that the Quartadeciman practice arises *after* the Montanists,[28] who had actualized 14 Nisan to various dates in the first spring month of the Asian solar calendar. These groups are not direct descendants of second century Asian Quartadecimans, but various Montanist sects who had defined themselves against the Asian Great Church by changing the lunar date of Pascha to a solar one, likely directed by a prophetic utterance conveniently making intricate computation superfluous. The practical impetus, however, was probably the growing number of Asian congregations who had moved to Sunday celebration. Montanists were then confronted with either conforming to the new practice, retaining the old, or producing their own "innovation." These groups chose the latter. The historical date of Jesus' death would then seem more accurately reflected in their celebrations, simply because its annual cycle would move to a calendar in general use – and to a mimetic theology that does not appear until the end of the second century.[29]

Not only was the old stronghold of Quartadecimanism not on the opposing side at Nicaea, but Asian bishops were probably some of the strongest supporters of "the West and South," not least because of the Montanist "shadow." This may help explain why Epiphanius discreetly does not mention the *orthodox* Quartadecimans of the second century when he treats the "heresy," even though he is quite familiar with Eusebius' history.[30] The appearance of Cilicia in lists of both groups is

them, just as the heathen also when they hear 'the idols of the gentiles are silver and gold' think that the teaching of the divine cross is foolishness." CSCO 258 (Syr. 115), 55.

[28] "After these two intermingled sects of Phrygians ..., another one, called the sect of the Quartadecimans, appeared in its turn." Pan 30.1.1, NHS 35, 23.

[29] "Montanist" arguments appears in modern proposals for a fixed date. Cf. Doeve, J. W., De Christelijke Paasdatum. Kerk en theologie 27, 1976, 265-275; Adam, Adolf, Ostern alle Jahre anders?, Paderborn 1994. Critics see this move as anti-Semitic. See Adam, 58 f.

[30] "In the time of Polycarp (sic) and Victor the east was at odds with the west and they would not accept letters of commendation from each other." Pan 70.9.8, GCS 37,

another indicator. Tarsus, whose bishop often stepped in when the see of Antioch was vacant or in dispute,[31] was presumably still observing Pascha with Syria, while "some churches in the Orient" had moved their celebrations according to an Alexandrian equinoctial practice now current in Asia.

The only place for anti-Quartadeciman rhetoric to land in the fourth century is against Montanist splinter groups, who, as Epiphanius writes, "do not adhere to the proper order and teaching but to Jewish fables" (Tit 1.14).[32] Given Epiphanius' conflicting dates, chances are good that these groups were involved in a paschal controversy all their own. In the course of the third century, however, the Asian Great Church had begun to celebrate Pascha on Sunday because they could be persuaded by the very Lord's Day theology, and, for that matter, the anti-Judaic polemic, that writers such as Melito helped create.

II. A Syrian Counterattack

Even after the Council of Nicaea, some Christians in Mesopotamia, since mid-third century no longer a part of the Empire, could continue observing an Antiochene paschal reckoning without serious threat of reprisal from across the Euphrates. The Audian monastic community, whether missionizing the Goths after being banished by the Emperor or sojourning on the island of Cyprus after fleeing persecution in Gothia, held tenaciously to the old practice. Epiphanius records a rather delightful bit of Audian polemic lambasting the calendrical innovation of Nicaea:

> For they choose to celebrate the Pascha with the Jews – that is, they contentiously celebrate the Pascha at the same time that the Jews are holding their Festival of Unleavened Bread. And indeed, <it is true> that this used to be the church's custom – even though they tell churchmen a slanderous thing in this regard and say, "You abandoned the fathers' paschal rite in

242; NHMS 36, 411. The confusion of Polycrates with Polycarp shows which story was most memorable: Irenaeus' Polycarp anecdote.

[31] Downey, Glanville, A History of Antioch in Syria from Seleucus to the Arab Conquest, Princeton 1961, 308 f. For a synod in Antioch to discuss the Novatian question, Helenus, Bishop of Tarsus, acting while the see of Antioch was vacant due to the death of Fabian, issued the invitation.

[32] Panarion 50.1.2, GCS 31, Holl 2, 244; NHMS 36, 23.

Constantine's time from deference to the emperor, and changed the day to suit the emperor." And some, again, declare with a contentiousness of their own, "You changed the Pascha to Constantine's *Genesia*."[33]

As Holl pointed out,[34] the Audians may have actually accused the Council of presenting the calendrical change as a *gift* to Constantine, not setting the Pascha on the emperor's *Genesia*, which, after all, was celebrated on 25 July. But why cloud such splendid rhetoric with the drabness of history? Such "exactness" may not have been as important to the Audians as distancing themselves from the head of a foreign government interfering, as they would see it, in a strictly ecclesiastical matter. The Audians are saying that Pascha celebrated in the West had been degraded to a secular, if not a pagan, holiday.

While Epiphanius concedes that the Antiochene paschal reckoning was "the former custom of the church," he also feels compelled to explain the rhetorical slur "with the Jews" to mean exactly what the *Didascalia* instructs it readers in the early third century:

> Wherever, then, the fourteenth of the Pascha may fall, observe it in this way. Indeed, neither the month nor the day corresponds in time every year, but it is changed. When therefore that People performs the Pesach, do you fast. And be careful to complete your vigil within their feast of Unleavened Bread.[35]

Epiphanius is far enough away from the rhetorical situation of Nicaea to feel a certain inexactness in the term "with the Jews," but close enough to know what it meant – and to use it himself against the Audians. His juxtaposition of the "former custom" to "with the Jews" is as telling as that of Constantine's "exact calculation" and "community with the Jews." A "former custom" had been improved by "exact calculation." But unlike the earlier controversy, apostolicity cannot number among those arguments supporting Alexandria and Rome. Only Epiphanius' Audians can say, "You abandoned the fathers' paschal rite..." This is the reason for the high temperature of anti-Judaic polemic over the paschal calendar at the Council of Nicaea: it must be applied with considerable pressure to neutralize a legitimate claim of prior *Christian* tradition not to be given up easily for Western "innovations."

---

[33] Pan 70.8.11-9.4, GCS 37, 241; NHMS 36, 410 f. 'Passover' changed to 'Pascha.'
[34] Holl, Bruchstück, 241.
[35] DA 21, CSCO 408, 202.

III. The Day and its Meaning in the Syriac Tradition

The prime reference for paschal celebration in any region of the Church is the death and resurrection of Christ, but how that historical reference is defined may, as in the four gospels, differs in its relationship to Pesach and Ex 12. Conflicting narratives may be resolved by accenting their convergence: Jesus died on a Friday. Twenty years after the Council, Aphrahat begins by acknowledging Syn chronology:

> Indeed the Pascha of the Jews is the fourteenth day, its night and its day; but our great day of the passion is the day of the Parasceve, the fifteenth day, its night and its day.[36]

The nonpolemical version of this distancing from 14 Nisan is simply the ritualization of Syn narrative, but in the context of Nicaean debate, it could dismiss any hint of celebrating "with the Jews" from the minds of Aphrahat's readers. By accenting Syn chronology, Aphrahat is saying that his community's celebration encompasses the entire mystery and its narrated time in the gospels. Yet however Syriac sources read the dates, they invariably tell the same story: the institution of the eucharist is the founding narrative for the paschal feast.

Aphrahat puts forth his own calendrical rule reminiscent of the *Didascalia*, except for one major provision:

> So that you are persuaded and may persuade the brothers who belong to your community who find difficulties with the time of the Pascha, I wish to write to you the following: for those of healthy understanding it is not difficult to comprehend. If it occurs that the day of Pascha and the Passion of our Savior [historical date of the death of Christ] falls on a Sunday, then we must celebrate it [i.e., week of fasting] according to Law on Monday, so that the whole week of the feast is celebrated with his Passion and with his unleavened bread. For onto the Pascha follows the seven days of Unleavened Bread until the twenty-first. And if the Passion falls on another day, on a weekday, then we do not have to make any trouble about it. Our great feast day however is Friday [lit., the "evening," i.e., of the Sabbath].[37]

The ease of comprehension Aphrahat offers readers of "healthy understanding" does not extend to their modern counterparts. Though

---

[36] Aphrahat, Demo 12.8, FC 5/2, 303.
[37] Aphrahat, Demo 12.8, FC 5/2, 305.

this passage is in an occasional writing making direct reference to "difficulties," van Goudoever argues that Aphrahat presents an

> ideal calendar in which the fourteenth day of the month "Passover" falls on a Sunday; in such an ideal calendar the seven days of Unleavened Bread could be celebrated from its beginning to its end (i.e. from the fourteenth to the twenty-first day). So both the Didascalia and Aphraates speak about an ideal calendar.[38]

G. A. M. Rouwhorst reconstructs a concrete situation where this "ideal" would translate into practice. He sees a permissive move: a christianized "Azyma" *following* Pascha, the opposite of the later Old Syriac lectionary he cites, which refers to Holy Week as "Unleavened Bread." Those being persuaded are Quartadecimans whom Aphrahat allows to celebrate Azyma if and only if 14 Nisan falls on a Sunday.[39]

In Schwartz's table of paschal dates abstracted from Athanasius' epistles, between 346-373, the fourteenth of the moon falls six times on a Sunday.[40] By the Alexandrian rule, whose earliest lunar date was the fifteenth, Pascha would then be moved to the following Sunday, where the moon would be twenty-one days old. In 346, the year following Aphrahat's treatise, the Alexandrian paschal date of 23 March was too early for Rome, which would neither permit Pascha on the fifteenth of the moon nor before the Roman equinox, 25 March. The full moon then looked less full to Athanasius, and Pascha was transferred to the Roman date of 30 March, which was counted the twenty-first, though in fact it was a day older. The numbers were bent, but Pascha was celebrated on "on one and the same day."[41]

Rather than permitting hypothetical Quartadecimans to observe a sporadic, ritually impossible rhythm for a practice that otherwise has no documented evidence, the transfer of the fourteenth to the twenty-first sounds far more like Aphrahat answering a question about Alexandrian paschal computation for those who would never receive a helpful letter from Athanasius. Aphrahat does so, however, completely within the grammar of Syrian paschal language – no equinox, no moon tables, no calculation – only biblical narrative. This translation, reinforced by the

---

[38] Goudoever, Biblical Calendars, 178.
[39] Rouwhorst, Date Aphraates, 1378.
[40] Schwartz, Ostertafeln, 24 f. Years: 346, 349, 353, 360, 363, 373. For the rest of the century, table, op. cit., 185 f., 377, 380, 383, 387 (!), 397.
[41] Schwartz, Ostertafeln, 26 f.

anti-Judaism sounding forth in Constantine and Athanasius, is the very strategy that wins the "Orient" to the equinoctial rule.

"The day of Pascha and the Passion of our Savior" is the anchor date for paschal reckoning, the paschal full moon, *XIV lunae* in the moon charts. If this day falls on a Sunday, then the entire paschal observance from fast to eucharist is moved to the following Monday. The addition of OT paschal passages as aetiologies means that Aphrahat has suddenly switched chronologies from his "great feast day," 15 Nisan. The date is now 14 Nisan by the Hebrew calendar, another cue that Aphrahat is thinking in liturgical and calendrical, rather than historical time.[42] Ex 12 and the duration of Mazzot are only enlisted as an "old" style aetiology for the week of fasting. This is "congruence," the *Didascalia* is rubric.

Unlike Tertullian, Aphrahat may read Johannine but always think Synoptic. The earliest lunar date for Pascha by this reckoning is the Alexandrian 15 Nisan, but the "great feast day" remains. Otherwise, as Aphrahat point out, if the full moon of the fourteenth falls on any other day of the week, Pascha will be the Sunday falling within the seven days of Unleavened Bread – by a Christian reading of scripture, not in reference to an actual Jewish celebration. The scriptural rubric for the transference is 14-21 Nisan as a christianized Pesach-Mazzot. Yet by this reckoning, an exact convergence of these dates with Pascha and its fast is impossible – except, of course, rhetorically.

Just as Aphrahat switches to the fourteenth of the moon to speak of the calendar, a commitment to 14 or 15 Nisan is also a rhetorical, not a fixed datum of the Syriac tradition. As any other authors, Syriac writers may choose the day that suits their rhetorical purpose. Since Tatian had joined John's footwashing and meal with the Syn account of the Pesach into one ritual event, the difference between 14 and 15 Nisan is not a major issue until the *Diatessaron* is supplanted by the four gospels. Even then it is likely that as a logical solution for disparate canonical accounts, i.e., as a hermeneutical structure now a part of the act of reading, Tatian's sequence long outlived the liturgical use of his harmony. Tatian's narrative time, however, was no more inviolable than that of the "Gospel of the Separate" when it came to reflecting the liturgical time of paschal celebrations. As Rouwhorst[43] points out, when Ephrem's *Commentary on the Diatessaron* attempts to square the chronology of

---

[42] CQL, 184, n. 'f.'
[43] Rouwhorst, Date, 1379, n. 1.

the last days of Jesus' life, it resolves the contradictions by accenting Jn 18.28: the Pharisees' reluctance to cross the threshold of the Praetorium – on 14 Nisan.

Chronology can be shaped by rhetorical situation as much as the reverse. An accent on Friday, 15 Nisan, may once have had a polemical "twin" as a distancing maneuver from Ex 12 – and thus the Asian Quartadeciman tradition – to mirror a thoroughly eucharistic Pascha. Now, however, it enables the Syriac tradition to harmonize not only the gospel accounts and the new Alexandrian computation, but also to absorb Asian readings of the lamb typology. This comes through even clearer in Ephrem's third *Hymn on the Crucifixion*:

> On the fourteenth the paschal lamb was slain –
> toward evening, as it is written.
> Beforehand it was written down, a pledge for him,
> that even his time would be prophesied by him.
> The time of the true lamb's slaying
> teaches us how fulfilled (it is).
> On the fifteenth he was slain – on the day
> when both sun and moon were full.
>
> Refrain: Praised be the one who proclaims his symbols!
>
> Blessed are you also, final evening!
> For in you the evening of Egypt was fulfilled.
> In your time our Lord ate the little Pascha
> and became himself the great Pascha.
> Pascha was mixed with Pascha,
> Feast bound to feast;
> a Pascha that passes away, and another that does not pass away;
> symbol and fulfillment.[44]

The full moon still shines on 15 Nisan, but the meal is the Pesach in the Upper Room where Jesus washed the disciples "in the basin, which is the symbol of unity."[45]

In contrast, the *Cave of Treasures* may place Jesus' death on 14 Nisan, but the paschal meal is still observed:

> [9] He ate the Pascha at the house of Nicodemus, the brother of Joseph, who was from Ramtha; he was imprisoned in the house of Annas and was

---

[44] Ephrem, Crucif. 3,1-2, CSCO 249, 40.
[45] Ephrem, Crucif. 3.8, CSCO 249, 41.

beaten with a reed at the house of Caiaphas. [10] He was taken by the soldiers and beaten with a whip in the pretorium of Pilate.

[11] Friday, in the first month of Nisan, the fourteenth of the moon, he suffered physically for us. [12] In the first hour [of Friday], God formed Adam from the dust and in the first hour of Friday, the Messiah received the spittle of the cursed children of those who crucified him.[46]

This section is followed by an hour by hour correlation of the death of Christ and the salvation of Adam culminating with the descensus:

> [30] At the ninth hour of Friday, Adam descended to the earth below, then to the heights of paradise. And at the ninth hour of Friday, the Messiah descended to the regions beneath the earth after the heights of the cross to those who sleep in the dust.[47]

Narrative time is both compressed and expanded. Everything occurs on 14 Nisan, but there is an hour-by-hour account of this day. This mimetic construct recapitulates the Fall exactly in reverse, yielding Aphrahat's "great feast day" of Friday. The *Cave of Treasures* has furnished a "liturgy of the hours"[48] for its cultic narrative.

In all these texts, not the *date*, but the *day* and what occurs is the determining factor. What is important for the Syrian tradition is that Jesus ate the meal, here with certain gospel motifs tightened for a better narrative: Nicodemus and Joseph of Arimathea are brothers, and it was Nicodemus' home where the paschal meal was held. There are no narrative gaps remaining, no character unresolved. The mimetic fit between rite and text is tightest of all.

If Syrian bishops at Nicaea were to be won over to the equinoctial rule, then it would have be to translated into the highly mimetic language of Syrian liturgical theology: the course of the sun and moon, the first month according to the zodiac, is the wrong code. For the equinox, Romans and Alexandrians had long prepared such mimetic narratives to provide their computation with kerygmatic content as well as legitimacy through the NT canon. This leaves only one major difference between Syria and "the rest of the world" – the supreme importance assigned to the Pesach meal of Jesus of Nazareth.

---

[46] CavTreas 48.1-30, CSCO 487, 153 (Western ms.)

[47] CavTreas 48.30, loc. cit.

[48] This at least partially occurs in later Syriac liturgy. See Thekeparampil, Jacob, Adam-Christus in den Passionssedre und in der Schatzhöhle, OCA 221, 1983, 323-332.

272 THE ANTENICENE PASCHA

IV. Eusebius' *On the Paschal Solemnities*

Eusebius' paschal treatise Περὶ τῆς τοῦ Πάσχα ἑορτῆς (PH) shows that "the rest of the world" was not content merely to press for the observance of the equinox as calendrical limit but also attacked the Syrian mimetic reading of Syn/Tatianic meal narratives. What is most instructive about Eusebius' work, however, is his occasional attempt to absorb and restate the Antiochene position, a diplomatic move that some in Antioch may have remembered when they later wished to elect Eusebius as their bishop.

The tactic enabling Eusebius' concessions is a time-honored technique: the anti-Judaic polemic common to all paschal traditions. Eusebius includes a report of the Council more than reminiscent of Constantine's letter, including the "birds of a feather" argument:

> 8 But after the God-favored emperor took his place in the middle of the holy Synod, there ensued a lively discussion as soon as the controversy concerning Pascha came up for debate. Three quarters of the assembly of bishops of the whole earth, who were of a different opinion, won the upper hand over the representatives of the Orient. The people of the North joined with those of the South and the West, after they had unanimously gathered against the Orientals who defended the old practice. The Orientals, however, finally acquiesced, and thus came the one feast of Christ. They left the murderers of the Lord to be joined to the like-minded (in faith), for Nature draws like to like.[49]

From this casually dropped bit of anti-Judaism aimed at the "old practice," Eusebius immediately moves to deconstruct a mimetic reading of the Syn meal narrative. The same "Orientals" are the target:

> Someone might say, however, that it is written, "On the first day of Unleavened Bread the disciples came and said to the Savior, 'Where do you wish for us to prepare the Passover?" [Mt 26.17]. But he sent them to a certain man, commanding and having them tell him, "I will celebrate the Passover with you." [Mt 26.18 f.] We counter such a person with the fact that this was no fundamental commandment, but rather an historical representation of the events of that time when the Savior suffered. For it is one thing to relate a past event and quite another to make a law and to leave those coming after a commandment.[50]

---

[49] Eusebius, PH 8, PG 24, 701D-703A.
[50] Eusebius, PH 8, PG 24, 703A.

Of all texts from the period, this is the clearest restatement of the Antiochene position and its clearest refutation: Origen's "Ebionites" now have a more definite address. "Someone" had defended the Antiochene paschal "command" with the canonicity of the Syn meal narratives. This Eusebius admits, but he then counters liturgical mimesis with literary mimesis: the Pesach meal of Jesus depicted in the Syn is historical narrative, not a scriptural rubric to be imitated. What Jesus instituted was a new observance, the eucharist, and this was the Pascha he desired:

> [9] But at the time of his suffering, the Savior did not celebrate the Pascha with the Jews. For at the time when they are accustomed to slaughter the lambs, he did not conduct his own Pascha with his disciples. They did so on Friday as the Savior suffered, which is why they did not go into the pretorium, but Pilate came out to them. He himself reclined at table with his disciples a whole day before on Thursday. As he ate with them, he said, "I have desired with a great desire to eat this Pascha with you." Do you thus see that the Savior did not eat the Pascha with the Jews? Since this meal was of a new kind and contradicted the traditional way and Jewish custom, he urgently added, "I have desired with a great desire to eat this Pascha with you before I suffer." These were old and outdated customs he followed when he ate with the Jews. These were not the object of his desire, but rather the new mysteries of his New Covenant, which he left as inheritance to his disciples.[51]

After this discussion of conflicting gospel narratives, Eusebius enlists an argument well ensconced in Syrian tradition, modifying it slightly, but still maintaining its bizarre contours. Gospel chronology is harmonized by adding an extra day at the house of Caiaphas, but then resolved to its original discord: there were two meals on two different days. The meal in John is the "true" Pascha. If there is a discrepancy, a paradox, an inconsistency, then there can only be one group at fault – the "Jews." Eusebius begins with a statement whose illogic is amazing:

> [10] However, he himself ate the Pascha with his disciples. He celebrated the feast before he suffered and not together with the Jews.

Admitting that Jesus ate the paschal meal at all is a major concession to the Syrian tradition. Eusebius then restates this tradition, relieving it of its "Jewish" taint:

---

[51] Eusebius, PH 9, PG 24, 703B.

After he had celebrated in the evening, the high priest together with the betrayer laid hands on him. But they did not eat the Pascha on that evening themselves so that they had time for him. As soon as they had captured him, they led him away to the house of Caiaphas and there remained for the entire night. When it became day, they gathered and held a trial. Then they arose and with the crowd led him to Pilate. Then, however, as it is written, they did not go into the Praetorium, so as not to enter under a Greek roof and, as they believed, become unclean. Those most egregiously unclean wanted to remain pure to be able to eat the Pascha on the coming evening. They who strain for gnats have swallowed a camel. They whose souls were made unclean through the murder of the Lord feared uncleanness. But those who on the day of suffering ate the cursed Pascha of their own souls, commended the saving blood not to their benefit, but to their condemnation [1 Cor 11.29!]. Our Savior celebrated the feast which he desired, not then, but he dined with his disciples a day before.[52]

The crowning glory of this harmonized chronology comes by incorporating a variant of the Alexandrian equinoctial myth: while ancient "Hebrews" always celebrated after the equinox, since the death of Christ and the Fall or Jerusalem, "Jews" had become mentally deranged and unable to calculate the calendar properly. For Eusebius, it would seem, even the "Hebrews" were in error – from the very beginning. The feast they did celebrate is a "shadow" eucharist bringing condemnation according to 1Cor 11.29. This, of course, is a message for the Antiochene "Jews." They must cross the Gentile threshold and leave the unclean, gnat-straining, camel-gulping, self-condemning "Jews" to peer inside. This polemic is then read into the gospel narratives themselves:

> [12] I say that the Jews were deluded from the very beginning about the truth, which is why they persecuted the truth and drove the Word of Life away. The Holy Gospels demonstrate this quite openly. They do not testify that on that day on which the Pascha (lamb) is slain, as Luke mentions, they ate the customary Pascha. That occurred on the following day, which was the second day of Unleavened Bread, the fifteenth of the moon, on which our Savior was condemned by Pilate and they did not go into the Praetorium. Thus they did not eat it according to the Law on the first day of Unleavened Bread which they were obliged to do, for otherwise they would have kept the Pascha with the Savior, but even then consumed with their treacherous plan against our Savior, blinded by their evil, they fell

[52] Eusebius, PH 10, PG 24, 703D-705A.

into error concerning this truth. We, however, celebrate the same mystery throughout the entire year, commemorating on every Friday the holy suffering by a fast, which first the apostles held, after the Bridegroom was taken from them [Mk 2.19]. On each Lord's Day we are made alive through the sacred body of his saving Pascha and our souls sealed with his precious blood.[53]

So Jesus of Nazareth actually celebrated Pesach after all, but the "Jews," consumed with treachery, intercalated a day. Nevertheless, these "Jews" were considerate enough to resolve for all time the issue of conflicting Syn and Joh chronology. As a parting shot, Eusebius repeats his previous argument setting the meal narrative against its paschal frame. Pesach can become a story of origins for the eucharist only by its negation, but the connection of the eucharist to Pascha is still maintained. Eusebius' rhetoric has accomplished one thing: it has maintained every connection to the Syn meal narratives cherished in Syrian tradition, but by stressing its eucharistic character, frees it from an annual cycle. Eusebius' understanding of the Friday fast day, stressing the "Absent Bridegroom" aetiology for the paschal fast, had already been generalized to the weekly fast day in the *Didascalia*, just as the sub-H redactors had composed an anti-Judaic rhapsody on the "Tuesday night supper" chronology. This too would have resonated with the Syrian bishops. Yet even if such minor convergences could hardly have won the day, if Eusebius and others could get the Syrian side to agree to scapegoat the rhetorical "Jews" at Nicaea instead of taking the role themselves, the battle for the equinox was more than half won.

V. The Art of Persuasion

1. Selling the Equinox

Syriac writers show how they could maintain the essentials of their paschal theology despite Western attacks. All identifying marks of the Christian liturgy – baptism, eucharist, and Pascha – still find their stories of origins in the night before Jesus' death. The paschal night is the paradigm for all Christian liturgy and the story of origins for the Church and its apostolic ministry. Yet one argument with only the

---

[53] Eusebius, PH 12, PG 24, 705CD.

briefest mention in Eusebius' treatise was perhaps the very one enabling the final acquiescence of Syrian bishops. From the Audians' point of view, the equinox looked at best like a theologically neutral solar date, at worst like a pagan celebration of civic religion. With the "historical" Pesach of Syn/Tatianic narratives elevated to stories of origins for all essential ritual action of the Church, dating the Pascha from the course of the sun must have seemed like a blasphemous secularization. At the beginning of deliberations at Nicaea, this likely represents the most extreme Antiochene position. But unlike the Audians, Syrian bishops whose sees were on the Roman side of the Euphrates had much more contact with Western traditions and far more at stake than this group of uncompromising monastics. The initial "hard-line" represented by the Audians may have been softened well before Nicaea, thus making change less traumatic for those who had considerably more investment in the unity of the Church.

The ultimate cure for the Nicaean trauma may have been quite simple: in the West, the vernal equinox according to the Julian calendar, 25 March,[54] had been equated, calendrically and historically, with the day Jesus was crucified. As Eusebius reports from Constantine's letter, the "Jewish" calculation could be supplanted by "a truer order, which we have preserved from the day of the passion until the present."[55] Armed with tables of numbers, complicated lunar charts, and "exact calculation" from NT chronology, scholars could convince the "Orient" of the historical value of the new calendar and at the most crucial point, the ultimate anchor for the paschal celebration, elegantly substitute the equinox for the day Jesus died.

a) Hebrew Timekeeping[56]

Both historically and rhetorically, the Nicaean dispute over determining the date of Pascha is a dispute over Christian versions of Hebrew timekeeping. Accused of celebrating "with the Jews," the patriarchate of Antioch had not instituted the rule that Pascha should be celebrated on

---

[54] See Loi, Vicenzo, Il 25 Marzo data pasquale e la chronologia giovannea della passione in età patristica. EL 85, 1971, 51-69.

[55] Eusebius, Vita 3.18, GCS 7, 85.

[56] Following abstracted from Herr, M. D., The Calendar, CRI 1/2, 833-864; Ginzel, F. K., Handbuch der mathematischen und technischen Chronologie. Das Zeitrechnungswesen der Völker, Vol. II (1911), Die Juden, 1-115. See also Strobel, Kalender, 430-440.

the first Sunday after the first full moon after the vernal equinox. First emerging in third century Alexandria, this calendrical variant uses a solar date as control but still maintains the lunisolar character of the ancient Hebrew calendar. Since the equinox is the only feature distinguishing the Alexandrian reckoning from the "Jewish" one, this solar date must be loaded with as much theological meaning as possible, while the opposing practice is stripped of its Christian identity.

The usual method of ferreting out the history behind this conflict has been to follow Nicaean rhetorical cues and search out the history of the Hebrew calendar in the first three centuries of the common era – or simply to create one. "Dependence on the Jews for the date of Easter," Roger Beckwith maintains, "would be likely to originate in a place where this was least embarrassing."[57] This place, according to Beckwith, was Antioch. Since Beckwith stresses the lack of calculation in the Hebrew calendar, i.e., the academic translation of Judaic calendrical depravity, these three centuries of dependence would have been alleviated by watching the skies, counting to 29 or 30, and tossing in an extra month when Pascha threatened to fall in the dead of winter.

Another victim of the Qumran craze, Venance Grumel[58] proposed in 1960 that the mysterious change behind Christian accusations of mathematical depravity was the transfer from a solar calendar *in general use* among Jewish communities to lunar reckoning.[59] While texts from Nicaea are read as accurate history, not a single text from the Mishnah, Talmud, or any other Judaic source is cited to support this claim. This was a wise move, for there are none.

Since for their Gentile readers Jewish writers may occasionally equate Hebrew months with a solar equivalent in the Julian calendar, Eduard Schwartz was convinced that the dispute arose because Jewish communities whose calendars early Christians had adopted had simply dropped ancient biblical reckoning and given biblical names to different solar months according to calendars in use in their regions.[60] A list of March full moons labelled "Jewish" in a document from the Council of Sardica

---

[57] The Origin of the Festivals Easter and Whitsun, SL 13, 1979, (1-20) 17.

[58] Grumel, Venance, Le problèm de la date pascale aux IIIᵉ et IVᵉ siècles. L'origin du conflit: le nouveau cadre du comput juif. RB 18, 1960, 163-178.

[59] To this point see Herr, Calendar, 834.

[60] I can only regard Talley's hypothesis (Origins, 8 f.) that the Great Church of Asia Minor, not just later Montanists, transferred Pascha to 6 April by the solar calendar, as a crumbly amalgam of Schwartz's idea with Strobel's Qumran holdovers.

(342 CE)[61] becomes the key to open the mysteries of the paschal dispute. Palestinian Jews used the Tyrian calendar, setting Nisan to the month of Xandikos (18 April-18 May), while Antioch used the month Dystros (1-31 March),[62] though the following month (=April) was named "Nisan." Such a hypothesis also enables Schwartz to take literally the "Great Sabbath" on which Polycarp was martyred to be the Sabbath before Pesach, since Asian Jews, he claims, had set the *Asian* month of Xandikos (21 February-23 March) equal to Nisan.[63] To set up these equations, Schwartz must completely ignore the cultic and calendrical role of New Moon festivals in Judaism, but he does not stop there. The perpetual Hebrew calendar of the late fourth century, which thus would have represented an inexplicable return to a more biblical lunar reckoning, was a rabbinical response to Christian criticism at Nicaea. Never one to mince words, Schwartz concludes with a particularly mimetic image:

> Here it is acutely obvious how the Jewish calendar-improvers wanted to confront the accusation by a church ruled by the Alexandrian cycle that the Jews could no longer celebrate their own Pascha at the right time…Let them be proud of their work; they only forgot that it was the hated opponent from whom they copied the principle. The improved calendar is just like the synagogues, which painfully avoid all Christian emblems but betray immediately to every observer that with more or less lack of taste, they imitate some kind of Christian style of architecture.[64]

Though Schwartz follows Duchesne concerning who and what was at stake at Nicaea, it is hardly surprising that Schwartz reads almost every anti-Judaic polemic as objective historical truth, even citing medieval *Islamic* anti-Judaic polemic with obvious approval.[65] Thus while his study of Christian paschal calendars may still be of value, what Schwartz says about Hebrew timekeeping may only be used in a history of anti-Semitism among German intellectuals at the turn of the century.

[61] Schwartz, Ostertafeln, 121-125.
[62] See table, Schwartz, Ostertafeln, 149.
[63] Schwartz, Ostertafeln, 125-138.
[64] Schwartz, Ostertafeln, 160.
[65] Al Birini (ca. 1000 CE) argued that the complicated rules that make sure the eves of major festivals do not fall on the Sabbath result because Jews do not want to give up two workdays, as Schwartz sees it, the chance of profit. Schwartz, Ostertafeln, 157.

Assumptions about the nature of Hebrew timekeeping that ignore its cultic nature are aided by a general lack of historical sources concerning how both Palestinian and Diaspora Jews reckoned their months and feasts. Yet what sources are available are often misinterpreted for the sole purpose of rationalizing the Christian rhetoric at Nicaea. With Timothy Thornton,[66] the first assumption that must be challenged is that there was a single unitary Hebrew calendar promulgated by a single authority recognized by all Diaspora Jews at a time when early Christianity would have adopted this reckoning for its paschal feast.

aa. The Month and the New Moon

As all measures of time in the ancient Middle East except the Egyptian,[67] the Hebrew calendar originally measured the month based upon observable lunation, the span of time from the sighting of the new crescent moon through its four quarters until its resighting to hail the beginning of a new month. The new crescent, however, is only visible for a brief time after sunset, the moon remaining invisible the rest of the night. The period of lunar darkness after the moon's disappearance until the new crescent may vary from one to four days at Middle Eastern latitudes, depending upon when the true new moon, the astronomical conjunction of earth and moon, actually occurs. Because of varying speeds of earth and moon due to their gravitational relation to each other and to the sun, a lunation may vary in duration, a lunar month having 29 or 30 days.

Beyond the seven-day rhythm of the sabbath, the basic unit of the Hebrew calendar was the month, whose inaugural day, the sighting of the new crescent, was accompanied by ritual acts unique in the ancient world. With the conservatism that marks virtually all ritual practice, these rites would remain stable even as calendrical knowledge might have been absorbed from Babylon or Egypt, especially as they involved community participation in sighting the elusive new crescent. Thus

---

[66] See Thornton, Timothy C. G., Problematical Passovers. Difficulties for Diaspora Jews and Early Christians in determining Passover Dates during the First Three Centuries A.D., StPat 20, 1989, 402-408.

[67] The Egyptian year was a "vague" (i.e. wandering, as in *vagabond*) solar year of 365 days: 12 x 30-day months + 5 epagomenal days. It "wandered" because of the $1/4$ day discrepancy to the true solar year and therefore moves backward one day every four years. Ginzel, Vol. I,159. The first intercalary year was 29 BCE., op. cit., 227.

while the weekly and yearly cycles of Hebrew timekeeping were modified as they were adopted into Christianity, the monthly cycle with its
"moongazing" could become an easy object of anti-Judaic polemic.[68]
The Talmud records a hallowing ritual for first century Palestine.
Witnesses, for whom banquets were prepared to insure their eager
attendance, gathered for the hallowing of the new moon in a large
courtyard in Jerusalem called Beth Yazeq, and R. Gamaliel the Elder
ordered that they be permitted to walk within two thousand cubits on
the Sabbath. There was a brief liturgy: the chief of the court would say,
"It is hallowed," which was repeated twice again by the people.[69] This
liturgical archaism could lead to inevitable conflicts between "science"
and "religion":

> Once the heavens were covered with clouds and the likeness of the moon
> had been seen on the twenty-ninth of the month. The public wished to
> declare the new moon, and the court wanted to hallow it, but R. Gamaliel
> said to them: "I have it on the authority of my father's father that the
> renewal of the month takes place after not less than 29 $^1/_2$ days." On that
> day the mother of ben Zaza died, and Rabban Gamaliel made a great
> funeral oration over her, not because she had merited it, but so that the
> public should know that the court had not hallowed the month.[70]

The hallowing of the month was tied to creation and human observation, both of which could vary according to latitude and weather conditions. General knowledge of the mean synodical month could only be
used as a control – for clouds or an eager public – but no method could
predict when and if the crescent would actually be sighted. This also
means that if Diaspora communities observed similar rituals, until the
promulgation of the perpetual calendar in the latter fourth century, any
date in Hebrew timekeeping would only have a *regional* significance. In
Palestine, 14 Nisan could vary one, even three days from the same date

---

[68] A sampler: "And do not worship him according to the way of the Jews. ..., for
they serve angels and archangels, the month and the moon. And if the moon does not
shine, then they do not celebrate the so-called first Sabbath, nor do they celebrate the
New Moon, the Feast of Unleavened Bread, the Feast (of Tabernacles), or the Great Day
(of Atonement)." Preaching of Peter, cited, Strom 6.41.2 f., GCS 52, 452. Identical
argument in Aristides, Apol 14.4, Goodspeed, 18 f. "That their trepidations about food
... and their hypocrisy with fasts and new moons are ridiculous and of no worth, you
do not, I think, need first to learn from me." Ep Diog 4.1, SUC 2, 316 f.
[69] RH 23b, Goldschmidt 3, 355.
[70] RH 25a, Goldschmidt 3, 361.

in Egypt or Rome, though their determination from the new crescent variously observed in each locale was identical. There was, then, no one single Hebrew calendar, but several local ones, all permutations of a time reckoning designed not for millions strewn from Gaul to Persia, but for a tightly-knit tribal group in the hill country of Palestine.[71]

bb. The Year and its Intercalation

A lunar "year" is a fiction attempting to harmonize the smaller basic unit of the month to the solar cycle, or alternately to the sidereal year of certain stars, that is, the rising again at the same point in the sky of an easily observed constellation after the earth has made a complete orbit around the sun. Either method requires the periodic addition of a thirteenth month, the only intercalation possible in a truly lunar calendar, if this "year" and its festivals are to remain synchronous with the observable seasons. Thus a non-intercalary year will contain 354-355 days, an intercalary year 384-385.

A method of intercalation is not a matter of higher mathematics, but simple arithmetic, which, with a bit of extra practice, any ancient shopkeeper could master. How many lunar years can be contained in how many solar years with the least possible remainder? The larger the number of years, the less significant the remainder and the less often a calendar would have to be adjusted. Large numbers, however, could be cumbersome, and even Babylon, the calendrical giant of the ancient world, worked first with an eight-year, then a nineteen-year cycle.[72]

The calendrical cycle is also only as accurate as the values placed into the problem: the lunar cycle and the length of the solar year, which our shopkeeper, other than noticing the regularity of the seasons and the phases of the moon, neither knew nor needed to know. Taxes would become due at regular times, market days had their own rhythm, and feasts and other observances were determined by calendars set by religious authorities. But if our shopkeeper were given knowledge of the Julian solar calendar of 365 days and its intercalation every four years, and had observed that the lunar cycle is sometimes 29 days, sometimes 30, then he could have produced a calendar with the same general accuracy as anyone else in the ancient world. This mathematical acumen,

[71] Thornton, Passovers, 402 f.

[72] Van der Vyver, A., L'Évolution du Comput Alexandrin et Romain du IIIe au Ve Siècle, RHE 52, 1957, (5-25) 5.

however, would not necessarily elevate our shopkeeper to a recognized timekeeper for an entire religious community.

As the Nicaean conflict shows, a religious or civic calendar is far less a question of accurate calculation than social contract. After the destruction of Jerusalem calendrical matters were decided for a time in Babylonia instead of Palestine, and there is a report that while imprisoned, R. Aqiba (d. 137 CE) felt called upon to disclose the calendar for the next three years.[73] The calendar was solely in the hand of respected authorities, and there was an established means of intercalation, though which is unknown.[74] A number of measures mentioned in the Talmud assured that both remained so. Intercalation was not to be published earlier than six months in advance, and the whole point of the anecdote about R. Aqiba is to show that his disclosure was not to set a precedent.[75] A letter from Palestine to Mesopotamia indicates a last minute announcement in late winter.[76] To proclaim the beginning of a new month, the Mishnah also mentions a series of torch signals across the mountaintops of Judaea, but this method was abandoned in favor of a system of messengers, it claims, because of Samaritan sabotage.[77]

Torches, letters, and messengers would only be required for those who acknowledged the authority of the Palestinian rabbis, and the Mishnah's mountain fires may give a fair indication of their influence in the early second century. In Rome, Egypt, or Asia Minor, torches could not be seen, and letters and messengers might not arrive in time to determine the date of festivals. These measures were inadequate for the

---

[73] San 12a, Goldschmidt 7, 39. "The Rabbis taught: It is not permitted to intercalate the following year in the course of the previous year, also not three years in a row. R. Simon said, 'Once R. Aqiba intercalated three years in a row when he was locked in prison.' He was answered, 'Is this supposed to be a precedent? The court met together and determined intercalation for each year at the proper time.'" This was an unusual move because Aqiba was to be executed.

[74] Presumably the Babylonian 19-year cycle with 7 intercalary years, but there was discussion about which years in the cycle to intercalate. See Strobel, Kalender, 434 f. Also Segal, J. B., Intercalation and the Hebrew Calendar, VT 7, 1957, 250-307.

[75] San 12a, Goldschmidt 7, 38.

[76] Cf. San 2.6: "To our brethren the exiles in Babylonia and those in Media, and to all the other exiles of Israel: May your peace be great. We beg to inform you that the doves are still tender and the lambs too young and the crops not yet ripe. To me *and my colleagues* it seems right to add thirty days to this year." This text is repeated twice, the second time with the italicized words to indicate collegial humility recently acquired. Talley, Origins, 7, infers from this text that intercalation was strictly "ad hoc."

[77] RH 22b, Goldschmidt 3, 352 f.

wider Diaspora, but there is also no indication that they were either sought or attempted. After the destruction of the Temple and the end of pilgrimage festivals so overworked by Christian exegetes, even approximate synchrony with Palestine was far less urgent. Yet the first contract in Hebrew timekeeping was with the Creator and the markers of time, the sun and moon. If the lunisolar year were intercalated differently in various regions, then Pesach could in some years be more than one lunar month apart. The feast was thus far more easily adaptable to changing conditions than the method used to fix its date.

Similar to R. Gamaliel's funeral oration, the Talmud shows that mathematics and ritual could lead to other curious juxtapositions of language. The tract *Sanhedrin* preserves "primitive" discussions about natural phenomena to guide intercalation – ripeness of grain, bad weather to prevent pilgrims already underway from reaching Jerusalem, etc.,[78] as well as "scientific" debate about how many days of Nisan – 14, 16, and a minority view for 20 days – may cross the equinox and whether the day of the equinox belongs to the season just ending or just beginning. There is also discussion over the role of the autumnal equinox and the fall festivals, and whether a single day might be intercalated in Nisan to keep Pesach-Mazzot in the vernal quarter of the year.[79] This is hardly the discourse of people depending solely upon empirical observation to determine their yearly calendar, but it at least indicates that in the fourth century another religious community calculating a lunisolar calendar is conflicted about the role of the equinox and traditions of timekeeping.

There is no information about when second and third century rabbis might have set the Tequfa ("change" = equinox or solstice) of Nisan equivalent to contemporary solar calendars. Two facts, however, are certain. After the destruction of the Temple, the Hebrew calendar in Palestine moved the first month from Nisan to Tishri (autumn), though Nisan remained the New Year for "feasts and kings."[80] Since no harvest could be undertaken before the end of Unleavened Bread, it is more important to the Talmud that in a famine year intercalation be delayed.[81]

This ancient rule balancing human need with astronomy and the inviolability of Torah points out an essential fact: the cardinal role of the

---

[78] San 11ab, Goldschmidt 7, 35-37.
[79] San 13ab, Goldschmidt 7, 41-43.
[80] Herr, Calendar, 844 f. Cf. Rosh haShanah 1,1 (=RH 1a, Goldschmidt 3, 291).
[81] San 11b-12a, Goldschmidt 7, 37 f.

equinox in paschal computation is a Christian issue, not a Judaic one. As much as equinoxes and solstices may figure in rituals of many cultures, they do not have an independent, universally recognized value, least of all for a religious community that moves to a lunar rhythm. Until rhetoric changes its significance, the equinox is an astronomical phenomenon and nothing more. This control is difficult to maintain against rhetorical torrents in which a "Jewish" calendar appears to be at issue, while the historical context is a dispute among major Christian sees about the date of a Christian festival calculated independently from any Jewish authority. Beckwith's "dependence" on Jewish timekeepers disappeared with the dissolution of the social contract with Judaic authority – except the canon of Hebrew scriptures and the dates recorded in the NT. Bishops of Antioch had not sent out spies to lurk about local synagogues to find out when to celebrate Pascha, as much as opposing rhetoric would like to give that impression.

b) The Christian Recensions

With or without the equinox as control, Christian recensions of the ancient Hebrew calendar are designed to find but one single lunar date, whose equivalent is 14 Nisan. Beginning with the year 222, Hippolytus' calendar is engraved in two columns on the base of his "statue"[82]: in the first is the day 14 Nisan/full moon, in the second, the day Pascha will fall.[83] It allows the celebration of Pascha on 20 March, five days before the accepted Roman date of the vernal equinox,[84] and the 16-year cycle he proposes would already be three days out of phase with the moon by its first completion. Though the latter is due to ignoring Julian leap years and working with an inaccurate length of a lunar month, the former is due to using not the equinox, but the March 18 entrance of the sun into Aries as the earliest that the full moon could fall.[85] This provides a *terminus post quem* for the equinoctial rule in Rome, but not independent Christian calculation. A letter from Caesarea to Rome[86] attests calendrical discussions between Alexandria and Caesarea at the

---

[82] The "statue" of Hippolytus was actually of a female figure "restored" during the Renaissance. Speculation about this statue makes up the bulk of Brent, Hippolytus.
[83] Brent, Hippolytus, 65 f., proposes that the difference each year between the fourteenth of the moon and Sunday marked the paschal fast, a ritual impossibility.
[84] Duchesne, Question, 18 f.
[85] Schwartz, Ostertafeln 29-35.
[86] Text below, p. 326.

end of the second century, not likely a new topic even then. That Hippolytus' calendar was engraved in stone, however, indicates the continued significance in Rome of a unified celebration of the paschal feast.

A method of calculation designed to predict the full moon can also determine the lunar calendar of years past, including the year Jesus was crucified. Pointing out that much later calendars often took a calculated date of Jesus' death as the first year of whatever cycle was chosen, August Strobel determined that while Hippolytus' calendar was inaccurate, the dates Hippolytus calculated both for the death (Friday, 25 March, 29 CE) and *birth* of Jesus (Wednesday, 2 April, 2 BCE), both 14 Nisan, were astronomically correct for the years assumed.[87] The calendar sacrifices accuracy for theologizing the solar year, turning the cosmic order into kerygma. The total of 31 years, the "about thirty" of Lk 3.23 and the Syn one-year ministry after the baptism, meshes perfectly with the natural order, though not with Hippolytus' other use of Joh chronology. Incarnation and cross are linked to Pascha, and as vernal equinox, the 25 March date was irresistible for the light and solar imagery it could generate. This is a calendar designed more for exegesis than predicting the full moon.

Around 230, roughly the same time the *Didascalia* is urging its readers to observe the Sunday in Unleavened Bread, Dionysius of Alexandria insists on a paschal celebration after the equinox (EH 7.20.1). Even Origen casually mentions the equinox and problems of date when he discusses the "Passover of the Jews" of Jn 2.13.[88] In both Jewish and Christian writers, the role of the equinox thus emanates from Egypt: a land that for millennia had used a strictly solar calendar, and whose cloudless skies had long furthered the science of astronomy. In the first half of the second century, the Alexandrian Claudius Ptolemaeus discovered the exact lunar cycle. In the Latin West, a derivative of the 25 March date in the anonymous *De Pascha computus* (243) sets the equinox on Wednesday 25 March, the fourth day of creation when sun and moon were formed, Jesus' death then falling on Friday 27 March, the day of Adam's creation. Schwartz is probably correct in assuming that the numbers came before the narrative, not the other way around.[89]

[87] Strobel, Kalender, 124.
[88] Text, above, p. 109.
[89] Schwartz, Ostertafeln, 39.

The equinox thus began to bear heavy theological and historical value, not directly polemic in character, but not oblivious to the meaning this date held in pagan cults. In his paschal treatise, Eusebius preserves some of the arguments used to further the equinoctial rule:

> This time of celebration brought destruction to the Egyptians who loved demons but to the Hebrews who were keeping a feast to God [note: proto-Christian "Hebrews" not the "Jews"], deliverance from evil things. This was that very time of year which had been kept [τετηρημένος] since the beginning for the creation of the universe, the time when the earth germinated, in which the lights [φωστῆρες, sun and moon] came to be, when heaven and earth were made and all that is in them. In this season the Savior of the whole world accomplished the mystery of his own feast, and the great light illumined the world with the rays of true belief, and the season seemed to embrace the birth of the world.[90]

This hymn to the glories of spring is impossible, at least in theory, if Pascha is still celebrated before the equinox in the winter quarter, spring's first day in the "beginning of years" and "first month" of Ex 12. But if there were Syrian bishops at Nicaea who cherished the traditions behind the *Cave of Treasures* with its Adam christology turned into a Good Friday "liturgy of the hours," then such cosmic metaphors in favor of the equinox might have met with some approval. The deciding factors, however, were an argument from history and a weakened ability to think in terms of lunar years. It would be inappropriate to remember the death of Christ before the solar date upon which it occurred. Pascha must come after the equinox and after the fourteenth of the moon.

3. Bargaining over the Equinox

a) Athanasius and Epiphanius, Epiphanius and the Audians

Along with excerpts from second century writers, the *Chronicon* cites extended passages from a paschal treatise by Peter of Alexandria and a letter from an elderly Athanasius telling Epiphanius quite bluntly to quit meddling into the paschal question and concentrate instead on the peace of the church.[91] Despite Athanasius' gruff answer, Epiphanius' detailed argument against the dwindling Audian monastics goes to some lengths

---

[90] Eusebius, PH 3, PG 24, 697A.
[91] ChrPasc, PG 92, 76CD.

to present their position before displaying the requisite rhetorical skill to refute it. Since the preceding chapter of the *Panarion* dispenses with the Arians, the Audians will allow Epiphanius to complete his retelling of the Council of Nicaea.

Under the title *Diataxis*, Epiphanius cites what is commonly held to be an otherwise unknown recension[92] of the *Didascalia*:

> When they feast, mourn ye for them with fasting, for they crucified Christ on the day of the feast. And when they mourn on the Day of Unleavened Bread and eat with bitter herbs, then feast ye.[93]

Since these lines are not present in any extant version, it is often assumed that Epiphanius is not citing verbatim, but only giving the sense. The lengthy exposition of the Tuesday supper chronology, however, as well as other allusions in this chapter, shows that Epiphanius knew a form of the *Didascalia* much the same as extant mss. This text is also closely allied with two sentences at the end of DA 21:

> When therefore that People performs the Pesach, do you fast. And be careful to complete your vigil within their feast of Unleavened Bread.[94]

What has happened to this text on its way to the *Panarion*? The "sense" has been reduced to the first "feast-fast" opposition, which has attained rhetorical balance, expansive detail, and a negative "exactness" not found in the original. Negative mimesis approaches parody, but with loss of content. What is missing is any "apostolic" instruction to celebrate Pascha on the Sunday during Mazzot, the very practice the Audians are defending, but which Epiphanius supplies in another argument against them:

> But from the very words that are said there, their contradiction will be evident. For they (DA apostles) say that the vigil should be held half way through the Days of Unleavened Bread. But by the church's dating, this cannot always be done.[95]

Even though DA 21 does not mention "bitter herbs," every other feature in this "troped" version could be inspired by the "very words" of the sub-H redactors. Has their bombastic parody of Sabbath rituals as "mourning" influenced Epiphanius' recall? There is another possibility.

[92] Schwarz, Ostertafeln, 104-121, an earlier, Quartadeciman recension.
[93] Epiphanius, Pan 70.11.3, NHMS 36, 413.
[94] DA 21, CSCO 408, 202.
[95] Pan 70.12.4, GCS 37, 245; NHMS 36, 414.

"It is uncertain, however," Frank Williams notes in his translation, "whether he is using an Audian written source, or retailing scraps of conversation and debate."[96]

Another citation attributed to the Audians' *Diataxis* is far less difficult to judge:

> Reckon ye not, but celebrate when your brethren of the circumcision do; celebrate with them... Even though they are in error, let it not concern you.[97]

With an aversion to mathematics[98] hardly characteristic of the DA, "exact" ritual parody has progressed to ritual solidarity. Yet no redactional level of DA 21 uses the word "circumcision." The reiteration of "celebrate with them" also betrays the same oral quality of virtually all of the *Panarion*, which comprises material dashed off in shorthand and later transcribed by a certain Anatolius "with much labor and the utmost good will."[99]

After making a plea to "the fathers' tradition" bolstered by anti-pagan polemic, the Audians have suddenly turned to say, "Yes! We celebrate with the erroneous Jews, just like you say we do! And we don't care!" This polemicized version of the *Didascalia's* instructions so blatantly reflects the attacks on the Syrian tradition that it cannot have come from the Audians themselves. While they may have railed at moon charts and calculation just as Aphrahat translates them elegantly into gospel narrative, no proponent of the Antiochene calendar would ever have turned Alexandrian fantasies about the calendrical depravity of the Jews into a positive statement and defended it. What stood in the *Diataxis* was nothing more than sub-H summary statement: "And begin when your brethren who are of the People perform the Passover,"[100] in other words, "Celebrate with them." The rest is rhetorical echo. While

---

[96] NHMS 36, 402, n. 1.

[97] Epiphanius, Pan 70.10.2, 6, GCS 37, 242 f.; NHMS 36, 412.

[98] In the Apology, Melanchthon discusses this passage at length, "...after the Council of Nicaea, certain nations held tenaciously to the custom of using the Jewish time. But as the words of this decree show, the apostles did not want to impose an ordinance on the churches." M. summarizes Epiphanius' refutation, but adds a new twist: "The apostles wisely admonished the reader neither to destroy evangelical liberty nor to impose a necessity upon consciences, since they tell him not to be bothered even if there has been a mistake in calculations." Apology, ad art. 7, 8; Tappert, 176 f.

[99] De Fide.25.3, GCS 37, 526; NHMS 36, 665.

[100] DA 21, CSCO 408, 196.

such an argument was unnecessary for the Audians, Epiphanius wants to rehearse the entire Nicaean debate about the paschal calendar, impossible without a convenient "shadow." The *Diataxis* is Epiphanius' Trypho.

Unlike Justin's conversation with an urbane Hellenistic Jew, real debates between Epiphanius and the Audians are not mere speculation. The monk-bishop reports that after a persecution in Gothia (Crimea, Ukraine), Audian refugees sojourned on Cyprus before returning to their monasteries in the Taurus mountains and Palestine. There may still be Audians, he says, in Syria and Mesopotamia, though "greatly reduced in number."[101] Both parties will have argued from the *Diataxis* (*Didascalia*), which had canonical status for both. Why should the words have changed to match the interpretation? If intelligent authors can argue endlessly *from the text* whether Judas was present at the supper, if Epiphanius can transfer Irenaeus' bath anecdote to "Ebion" for rhetorical effect, then he can present what he would have liked the Audians to have said about the *Diataxis* as a direct citation. Epiphanius is certain to win the rhetorical replay of Nicaea because this "citation," like Justin's Trypho, provides the proper impetus for rhetorical display.

It becomes painfully obvious that this new "redaction" of the *Didascalia* is a rhetorical construct of Epiphanius when he uses this text to neutralize the argument the Audians really made: "apostolicity." The brethren *of* the circumcision, Epiphanius explains, are not Jews *in* the circumcision, but the apostles *from* the circumcision.[102] He then attempts an historical reconstruction in which the first Christian community in Jerusalem celebrated the Pascha on the Sunday after 14 Nisan. But after 135, confusion reigned, "occasioning ridicule every year,"[103] until in Constantine's time a harmonious solution was found:

> But the Audians were not aware of the apostle's intent and the intent of the passage in the Diataxis, and thought that the Pascha should be celebrated with the Jews. And there were altogether fifteen bishops from the circumcision. And at that time, when the circumcised bishops were consecrated at Jerusalem, it was essential that the whole world follow and celebrate with them, so that there would be one concord and agreement, the celebration of one festival. Hence their diligence in bringing people's minds into accord with the church.

[101] Pan 70.15.5 f., GCS 37, 248 f., NHMS 36, 417 f.
[102] loc. cit.
[103] Epiphanius, Pan 70.9.7, GCS 37, 242; NHMS 36, 411.

But since the festival could not be celebrated in this way for such a long time, a correction for harmony's sake was made in Constantine's time by God's good pleasure.[104]

This is the furthest any author goes in acknowledging the antiquity of the Antiochene practice. Epiphanius' point is not calendrical, but one of ecclesiastical order, the passive voice barely avoiding equating Nicaea with the Twelve. This "history" is pure fantasy, of course, but it is Epiphanius' attempt to historicize "apostolic" rhetoric in such a way that apostolicity could become outdated.

This is much further than Epiphanius' uncooperative correspondent Athanasius is prepared to go:

> Just as you fought along [in the battle] and rejoiced along with [the peace], in the same way you should stop finding fault and rather pray that henceforth the church may be permitted to establish peace, that the heretics will cease their baleful divisions and that those contentious persons who relish quarrels under the pretext of the saving Pascha – but first and foremost out of the sheer love of dispute – stop their controversy. For they appear to be of us, boasting to be called Christians, but they rival the treacherous Jews. Yet how may their defense be quickly refuted? As it is written: *On the first day of Unleavened Bread, when one must sacrifice the Pascha (lamb)* [Lk 22.7] But it has happened well that now according to Scripture: *they have always erred in their hearts.* [Ψ'94(95).10][105]

This is probably the baldest statement of Nicaean anti-Judaism, and the most transparent to its rhetorical function, ever uttered against the Antiochene paschal calendar. Athanasius' opponents appear Christian, but they are in truth "treacherous Jews." The fragment is not, however, as transparent to its historical situation. Though the text employs a construct identical to that of Eusebius' paschal treatise, the strength of its language leads a group of French scholars to suggest that Athanasius is railing at the Meletians, and the "battle" and "peace" are that of the Synod of Alexandria in 362,[106] which recognized Paulinus of Antioch as rightful bishop. This did not bring "peace," but yet more "battles" in Antioch: another group gathered loyally behind Meletius, who after various exiles and other troubles alleviated by the demise of two

[104] Epiphanius, Pan 70.10.3-5, GCS 37, 243; NHMS 36, 412.
[105] ChrPasc, PG 92, 76CD.
[106] See Beauchamp, J. et. al., Temp et Histoire I: Le Prologue de la Chronique Pascale. TrMem 7, 1979, (223-301), n. 36, 237 f.

emperors,[107] finally became bishop of Antioch, in which office he ordained John Chrysostom as deacon. Meletius died during the Council of Constantinople in 381. In his paschal letter of 367, Athanasius attacks the Meletians using quite familiar methods:

> And after them [i.e., Jews who denied Christ] are the heretics with whom the miserable Meletians are mixed. Denying him, they abandon the fountain of life and wander in waterless regions [Jer 2.13, anti-Judaic standard]. For this reason their assembly is a bread of sorrows, even if they hypocritically speak of the Pascha because of human vanity, for they are evilly disposed toward the truth, so that everyone who sees such a gathering applies to them what is written, "Why do the nations conspire and the peoples plot in vain?" [Ψ2.1] For the Jews assembled in the manner of Pontius Pilate, the Arians and the Meletians in the manner of Herod, not to celebrate the feast, but to blaspheme the Lord with the words, "What is truth?" [Jn 18.38] and then "Take him, crucify him, give us Barabbas!" [Lk 23.18], so that the plea for Barabbas actually is, "The son of God is a creature!" and "There was a time when he was not!" Thus it is no surprise that they remain dead in their disbelief, tied to their evil thoughts, just as the Egyptians remained bound to their chariots [Ex 14.25].

> We, however, wish again to celebrate the feast according to the traditions of the fathers, for we have the Holy Scriptures. They are sufficient for us to instruct completely. If we read attentively and carefully, then we will be like the tree that grows on the water's edge, which brings forth fruit in due season, whose leaves will never fall [Ψ1.3].[108]

As in standard anti-Judaic paschal polemic, Arians and Meletians lose the right to celebrate Pascha. Between the contrast of Jer 2.13 and Ψ1 by which Barn already defined the Christian community against the Jews, Athanasius manages to vilify the "Jewish" Meletians by making the Jews the "raging heathens" of Ψ2, only to return to the Exodus saga to drown them with the Egyptians. Athanasius completes this community definition with a complete list of the OT and NT canon. The rhetorical function of both negative mimesis and canonical list is identical.

What is missing from this barrage is any hint of the *calendrical* anti-Judaism in the letter to Epiphanius. Since the Meletian schism arose after both Nicaea and the Council of Antioch, which sharpened prohibitions

---

[107] Schwartz, Eduard, Zur Geschichte des Athanasius, Gesammelte Schriften 3, Berlin 1959, 36-54.

[108] Athanasius, PascEp 39 [367], Athanase, Lettres festales, (ed. Th. Lefort), TF: CSCO 151 (Copt. 20), 33 f., Coptic: CSCO 150 (Copt. 19), 17.

against the old computation, the Meletians did not likely retain the old computation as a distinctive mark of group identity – as the Novatians did. In the first excerpt, Athanasius can dismiss the "protopaschites" with mere reference to the scriptural arguments. The rhetoric of the epistle, however, is a transfer of anti-Judaism dictated by the genre "paschal epistle." Its polemic is more severe because these pseudo-Christians, as Athanasius sees them, are celebrating on "one and the same day" as he.

b) Anatolius of Laodicea

Proponents of the calculation auspiciously forbidden by Epiphanius' *Diataxis* had already begun to appropriate such anti-Judaic polemic in the third century. Ancient proto-Christian "Hebrews" had calculated Pesach using the equinox as a calendrical limit but "Jews" did not. This is the reason for the bizarre juxtaposition of lushly poetic praises of spring[109] and condemnations of the mathematical depravity of the Jews found in many of these passages.

Such rhetoric begins neither with anti-Judaic polemic nor its odd distinction between "Jews" and "Hebrews,"[110] but with an appeal to an equinoctial rule bolstered by appeals to Alexandrian Jewish literature:

> We thus maintain that those who place the first month in this last twelfth of the year [before the vernal equinox] and in this way calculate the four-teenth day of the Pascha have committed a neither small nor insignificant error. This does not, however, come from us. The ancient Jews before Christ knew this and it was exactly observed by them.[111]

This is followed by a list of Hellenistic Jewish authors before and after the turn of the era, all of whom, Anatolius maintains, held that Pesach could not be celebrated before the vernal equinox:

> I know that from these men numerous other reasons, partly proof from probability, partly decisive proof, were presented with which they attempted

---

[109] For non-polemical use of this imagery, see Chupuncgo, Anscar, The Cosmic Elements of the Christian Passover, StAn 72, 1977, and its revision, Shaping, 1992, esp. 21-36; and an older study, Michels, Thomas OSB, Das Frühjahrssymbol im österlicher Liturgie, Rede und Dichtung des christlichen Altertums, JLW 6, 1926, 1-15.

[110] Harvey, Graham, The True Israel. Uses of the Names Jew, Hebrew and Israel in Ancient Jewish and Early Christian Literature, AGAJU 35, 1996. "Hebrew," always associated with Abraham, was a "good Jew;" "Jew" could carry negative connotations.

[111] Anatolius, Paschal Canon frag., EH 7.32.15 f., GCS 9.2, 722. Enoch proposes a variant of the Qumran calendar.

to demonstrate that the feast of Pesach and Unleavened Bread must take place in every case after the equinox [μετ᾽ ἰσηερίαν]. Yet I refrain from demanding such excess of proof from those for whom the veil lying upon the Law of Moses has been taken away and who now with unveiled face view Christ and Christ's teaching and suffering as in a mirror. But that the first month with the Hebrews comes around the equinox [περὶ ἰσημερίαν] is also seen in the teachings of the Book of Enoch.[112]

Though no works remain from other authors save "Enoch," Anatolius' claim can be checked by Philo's *Questions and Answers on Exodus,* where Philo exegetes Ex 12.2:

> Accordingly, it is quite appropriate to calculate the cycle of the months from the vernal equinox. For this month is as much the "first" as "the beginning." These are mutually explanatory, because it is said that this month is the first in order and strength; similarly the time proceeding from the vernal equinox appears as the first in order and strength as the head of a living animal. Thus the astronomers have given it such a name, because the Ram (Aries) is the beginning of the zodiac, because it is in it [this sign] that the sun appears, producing the vernal equinox...
>
> That it [Ex 12.2] presupposes that the vernal equinox is the beginning of the cycle of months is clear, when one considers the notions of time contained in the rites and traditions of various peoples.[113]

If this passage is read with the necessary "exactness," then Philo infers that the *new moon* of Nisan is controlled either by the entrance of the sun into Aries or the vernal equinox a few days after. The full moon of Pesach would never fall in the month of March, but on some date on or after 1 April. "Strength" and "firstness" proceed from the equinoctial "head" but these qualities also emanate from that period of time between the sun's entrance into Aries, which Philo also characterizes with a birth image, and the equinox itself. Does the gestation period for this birth extend to days *before* the sun's entrance into Aries? Or is Philo simply adopting this astronomical birth for the Hebrew month of Nisan, without quibbling over how long this month takes to give birth to the equinox?

This is not the question Philo wishes to answer, but a much more interesting one about the beginnings of the world and the Pesach-Mazzot feast:

---

[112] op. cit., EH 7.32.19, GCS 9.2, 724 f.
[113] QuæstEx 1.1, Œvres 43C, 59 f.

So in this way it [this beginning] took place for the benefit of humankind, to whom God entrusted the beginnings of customs, so that they might find everything immediately perfect and perfectly created.

Philo continues:

But all do not compute the months and years in the same manner. Some compute one way and others another; some according to the sun, some according to the moon. That is because the founders of divine feasts have expressed different views on the subject of the beginning of years and attributed different beginnings to the revolutions of the seasons to correspond to the beginnings of the cycles. That is why it is said, "This month is for you the beginning," determining a clear and precise way the distinct number of the seasons, so that because of their association with the Egyptians, it forbids them to imitate or to be led astray by the customs of the surrounding culture. For it wishes that this season should be the beginning of creation for the world and the beginning of months and years for the human race.[114]

Read with the same "exactness," Philo now appears to advocate that the equinox control the "divine feast" of Pesach-Mazzot. But there is a rhetorical address to Philo's calendrical musings that Anatolius may have missed. Philo's precision disappears to talk about the "clear and precise" way in which the cycle of four *seasons* are ordered in the year, and that some peoples use a solar, others a lunar calendar. There are no seasons in a lunar calendar, only phases of the moon, but a lunisolar calendar may begin in a certain season. This is hardly news to his readers, who would be familiar with the old Roman year beginning 1 March, various Egyptian festal calendars following a lunar cycle, and the Hebrew lunisolar calendar. Perhaps they knew of the Athenian lunar calendar as well, or various reckonings of other peoples. The calendrical contrast Philo wants to make, however, is with the one his immediate readers know the best: the Egyptian fixed solar calendar that began on 1 Thoth, 29 August, the same contrast that he makes in a more general way when he speaks of the Mazzot festival in *Spec Leg*. "For it seems to me," Philo writes, "that the autumnal equinox is to the vernal as a servant to a queen."[115] Philo's interest lies in "firstness," not a precise "beginning," and in making sure his readers know that the Egyptian calendar they use daily is not in harmony with the will of the Creator. Ex 12.2 is thus a

[114] op. cit., 63.
[115] QuæstEx 1.1, Œvres 43C, 61.

prophetic boundary set long ago between Jew and Egyptian to insure that no false imitation might result.

This is "congruence," not "rubric." Philo is not making an "exact" paschal computation, but speaking about various types of timekeeping in a cosmic scheme. The "exactness" of Ex 12.2 reduces to a rather vague hymn to spring, but expands into a speculative narrative about Gen 1. Perhaps the sun's entrance into Aries or the equinox figured into computation of the first month of a lunisolar year, but *exactly* how these dates might have been applied cannot be deduced from this text.

This, of course, is of no interest to Anatolius, who reads Philo's rhetoric only for its mathematics. For if there were no historical continuity between the Alexandrian paschal computation and earlier Alexandrian Jews, or in the usual parlance, "Hebrews," Anatolius assumes it anyway. Anatolius set the equinox on 19 March, six days earlier that the Roman date of 25 March, then 21 March. But he is just as confident that the ancient "Hebrews" had this day in mind as other Christian authors were for their calculations. Thus the change is not an innovation, but the restoration of the calendar's pristine state before "Jewish" derangement. With a higher rhetorical temperature, contemporary Jews could then be labelled alternatively apostate or insane.

c) Peter of Alexandria-Trikentios

Like Anatolius, the *Chronicon*'s florilegium is concerned with one point: that the equinoctial date has a pre-Christian history, even support from the Hebrew scriptures, and, indeed, as long a history as possible: a scramble for rootedness familiar from other contexts. An extensive excerpt from the *Peri Pascha* of Peter of Alexandria (ca. 300) present this view, then restates in summary form the main points of another work with which the author disagrees. Peter begins where Anatolius left off:

> As it is written, "This month shall be the first for you and the beginning of the months of the months of the year." As soon as the sun has come into the month of harvest, the lights show forth stronger and more brilliant. The day lengthens and extends, the night, however, withdraws and becomes short. The new, rising grain is thoroughly cleansed and gathered into barns. Yet not only this, but also the many fruit trees grow and begin to grow fruit. Then many and various fruits are gathered in one after another, as finally the grape is harvested in its time, as the Lawgiver says, "And the days were days of spring, the firstfruits of the vine" [Num 13.21]. This was the time he had sent those who scouted out the land and brought

the giant grape on a pole and also pomegranates and figs. For at that time, as it says, the Creator and Demiurgos of the world, our eternal God, created everything which he, as is well known, enumerated: [Gen 1.11] "The earth shall bring forth growing plants. It shall produce seed according to its kind, and fruitbearing trees, whose seed according to its kind is over the earth." And then God added, "And it came to pass and it was very good."

God showed the Hebrews the month that had been determined as the first, which we know to have been observed by the Jews until the conquest of Jerusalem, because this is especially transmitted by the Hebrews. Yet after the conquest this was looked upon with ridicule from a certain hardness against this month which to us, who rightly and truly observe it, has been transmitted. In this respect according to the words of ..., who says, ...(we have no?) doubt concerning the proper day of our holy feast, which *the elect have obtained, but the rest were hardened,* just as Scripture says. [Rom 11.7].

While Anatolius was content merely to appropriate the "ancient Hebrews" of Hellenistic Judaism in support of the equinoctial rule, Peter arranges images of burgeoning springtime growth, links them to the Creation story, and addresses them to the new method of computation. The "mystery" of Rom 11 resolves into "Jewish," not "Hebrew," depravity, and a divine guarantee that Christians may calculate with confidence. But the mimetic construct Peter uses is hardly a novelty. Biblical texts are harvested as proof for a Christian practice read as their true meaning, contrasted with "Jews" who have refused this revelation in the same way as they remain unconvinced of prophetic proof of Jesus as Messiah and Son of God. "Jews" have lost the right to the first month of the ancient biblical calendar by their hardness of heart. The equinox has been rhetorically equated with the person and message of Christ, and the paschal calendar tells the same story of divine rejection of the Jews as the paschal feast.

Bringing his initial argument to a close, Peter then includes an excerpt from a certain Trikentios, who has a different reading of both rhetoric and history of the Hebrew calendar:

[Peter writes:] For it is contemporaries [Jews] who, out of ignorance, celebrate it before the equinox in such a negligent and erroneous way, also because they do this year after year, as you yourself have written:

That the Jews are in error when they often celebrate their own Pesach according to the course of the moon in Phamenoth (25 February-26 March),

or every three years because of the intercalary month, in Pharmuthi
(27 March-25 April), is of no concern to us. For we wish to do nothing
but to conduct the anamnesis of his passion, and that at the appointed
time [χαιρός] transmitted to us by eyewitnesses [Lk 1.2], before the Egyptians believed. For now is not the first time that they observe the days of
the moon and by necessity celebrate Pesach two times in Phamenoth and
one time every three years in Pharmuthi: it is obvious that they have
always done so, from the beginning and before the *parousia* of Christ. This
is why God reproves them through the voice of the prophet: and I say,
"They are a people whose hearts go astray"...Therefore in my anger I
swore, "They shall not enter my rest." [Ψ'94(95). 10 f.].

Peter then refutes Trikentios' point:

In this moment, as you see, you have exposed a massive lie, not only
against humankind but against God. For first of all, the Jews never committed this error because they were together with those who from the
beginning were *eyewitnesses and servants* [of the word, Lk 1.2]; much less
from the beginning before the parousia of Christ. For it is not because of
the commandment of Pesach that God reproaches them that their hearts
go astray, as you have written, but because of the sum of their disobedi-
ence, especially because of their horrible and perverse deeds when he saw
them returning to idolatries and fornications.[116]

   While Peter baptizes proto-Christian "Hebrews," he transforms
"Jews" after the death of Christ into sex-possessed pagans. Yet the point
of contention between Peter and Trikentios is not whether the "Jews"
are in error, but which ones, for how long, and why. At stake are the
Hellenistic Jewish patriarchs of the Alexandrian paschal computation
whom Anatolius had already ushered into heavenly bliss. Were they correct and only contemporary Jews wrong, as Peter maintains? The
ancients, Trikentios argues, were as "erroneous" as all who have ever followed the Hebrew lunar calendar, at least in the region with which he
is familiar. The Jews had not fallen away from some cosmic order
now revealed to Christians, but simply continued to calculate with the
same method as before. But this is irrelevant, because Trikentios believes
that his own practice has apostolic precedence "before the Egyptians
believed." It is of no concern when the Jews celebrate "their own
Pesach," nor does Trikentios wish the Christian calendar to refer to the
"erroneous" Hebrew calendar in any way.

---

[116] ChrPasc 73D-76A.

It is often assumed that Trikentios is a proponent of the Antiochene computation[117] and that he is identical to the Crescentius whom Epiphanius reports corresponded with Alexander of Alexandria about the paschal calendar.[118] His off-hand remark about Egypt[119] means that he must come from a city prominent in the NT. Yet there are several problems with assigning this rhetoric to Antioch. Besides the delightful – and anachronistic – irony of an Alexandrian correcting an Antiochene with a literal interpretation of Ψ94(95).10 f., after the smoke clears, Trikentios represents not a position opposing Peter but an extreme version of the same view. Is Trikentios saying that even though the Jews have never calculated properly he and his community will stubbornly continue to celebrate "with the Jews," this after providing scriptural proof for their eternal error? Trikentios is attacking the exegetical underpinnings of the Alexandrian calendar, not the numbers. He and his community celebrate Pascha with Alexandria, but Trikentios does not care to do so with the proto-Christian "Hebrews." Peter is afraid that if the Hebrew calendar is "wrong" from the beginning, then there is no way to find the proper day to remember the passion. But the Alexandrian discovery of ancient computation had already taken care of this "error." Thus the defense of the "eye-witnesses": if Jews at the time of Christ calculated improperly, then the date of Jesus death is no longer recoverable for use in a paschal calendar.

The most obvious match to Trikentios is not Ephrem or Aphrahat, who remain within the bounds of second century anti-Judaism, or even Chrysostom. Rather it is Eusebius, bishop of Caesarea, with traditions "direct from the apostles" whose predecessor in the paschal controversy 195 had also exchanged letters with Alexandria about the paschal calendar. The story of Cornelius in Acts 10 already appears in Origen[120] as

---

[117] Holl, Bruchstück, 220 f.; CQL 160 f. Strobel, Kalender, 207, garners Trikentios for the lunar Quartadecimans, while appropriating the greater portion of Peter's treatise, including the "hymn to Spring" and the mention of "in the same week" for Trikentios.

[118] Epiphanius, Pan 70.9.9, GCS 37, 242. Duchesne, Question, 31, n. 1; Huber, Passa, 63, n. 12. In a millennium, scholars will be sure that Monet and Manet were the same artist.

[119] This remark would have been difficult if Trikentios had known the legendary founding of the Alexandrian church by Mark. See Smith, Morton, Clement of Alexandria and a Secret Gospel of Mark, Cambridge (US), 1973. At EH 2.16.1, Eusebius makes little use of this legend because Philo's Therapeutæ had more interesting possibilities, including episcopal authority (EH 2.17.23). See Grant, Eusebius, 52.

[120] Origen, Hom. num. 11.3, GCS 30 (Origenes 7), 80.

a founding narrative for the Gentile church of Caesarea, while Acts also gives a certain unintended priority to this city over Antioch, which, after all, only appears in the next chapter. With obvious pride, Eusebius follows the same Lucan order in his presentation at EH 2.3.3.[121] There may even be a echo of Ψ'94(95) in the second century letter: the Palestinian bishops are concerned that those not following their paschal reckoning "err in their spirits" (πλανῶσιν ἑαυτῶν τὰς ψυχὰς), while the "Jews" of Trikentios and Athanasius "err in their hearts" (πλανῶνται τῇ καρδίᾳ). Eusebius also insists that the Jews had "erred from the beginning."

Trikentios' urging that the anamnesis of Christ's passion[122] be paramount over other concerns does, however, have a certain parallel in the final paragraph of Aphrahat's *Demonstration*, when the Persian Sage, somewhat irritated with those who only worry about the "fourteenth," tries to point the discussion back to the celebration of Pascha rather than all the chatter about it. If Trikentios writes from Caesarea, Jerusalem, or any other Palestinian city, then his setting of priorities is not an embittered determination to remain with a calendar whose error he admits, but a plea to recognize the real issue: celebrating the Pascha, coupled with Aphrahat's same symptoms of battle fatigue. The Jews celebrate "their own Pesach" and the Christians celebrate theirs not by reference to a lunar year, but to a full moon after a solar date, both determined by their own – theologically and mathematically flawless – calculation.

4. Buying the Equinox: De solstitiis *and PseudoIgnatius*

While the equinox originally had no theological, biblical, or historical value whatsoever, Roman and Alexandrian exegesis shows that what is not there may be created by a few simple equations enriched by tradition and a bit of poetry. At the end of his book on the feast of the Epiphany, Bernard Botte published a Latin homily entitled *On the Solstices and Equinoxes*,[123] which preserves a reading of the Annunciation where the greeting angel says to Mary, "Peace to you,"[124] a variant only

---

[121] EH 2.3.3, GCS 9.1, 112 f.

[122] According to his Easter-Pascha dichotomy, Schmidt (TU 43, 614) holds Trikentios to be Asian.

[123] Botte, Bernard, Les Origines de la Noël et de l'Épiphanie. Étude Historique. TEL 1, 1932 (repr. 1961), 88-105.

[124] "Pax tecum quae invenisiti gratiam apud deum..." Lk 1.28, var. De solst., 208 f.

found in Syrian sources. Other NT citations had been normalized to North African Latina models. Botte then suggested a Syrian provenance for the sermon,[125] confirmed on further linguistic grounds by Hieronymus Engberding.[126]

The sermon is later than Nicaea, but it shows the Syrian reception of some of the arguments Eusebius preserves. The strategy of the sermon is both calendrical and cosmic: the Roman date of the vernal equinox, 25 March, is equated with the historical date of the *conception* and the death of Christ. The sermon opens with a "scientific" argument:

> I do not know, brothers, whether anyone before the birth of Christ dared to comprehend or determine the course of the hours of the days and nights by which the solstices and equinoxes could be known, as glorious Job was told in the midst of his sufferings, "And tell me, do you know the course of the sun and moon?"[127] – those two lights which we see were both instituted to constitute day and night. If a great man such as he, enduring his martyrdom, is contradicted in such a way, who among mortals could it have been, who, compared to this glorious and excellent man, would have impudently dared to know – except for the Lord himself, the Creator and Divider of Light and Night, who is called the Sun of Righteousness by the prophets, who illumined the world, who became flesh for those of flesh, mortal for mortals. He appeared as a mortal and was able to defeat death in his [im]mortality.[128] For this reason the heavenly powers cry aloud, "Death, where is your sting? Death, where is your victory?" [1Cor 15.55] Saying this, they gave witness that Christ would conquer death...For he is our light and the true light that came into this world, illuminating our hearts.

This moves immediately to "exegetical" anti-Judaism:

> For not even Moses or the prophets were told of his advent or his passion, though, indeed, the time of his conception and birth were revealed. About this the Lord said to the Jews, "You search the scriptures in which you

---

[125] Botte, Origines, 89-91.

[126] In line 118, the sermon uses a transliterated Syrian word for the Feast of Tabernacles, then the Greek, "*metellitum* sine scaenophegiam." Botte, Origines, 96. See Engberding, Hieronymus, Der 25. Dezember als Tag der Feier der Geburt des Herrn, ALW 2, 1952, 25-43. Results summarized Talley, Origins, 92 f.

[127] Cf. Job 38.19-20: "Where is the way to the dwelling of light, and where is the place of darkness, that you may take it to its territory and that you may discern the paths to its home?" Botte suggests this chapter generally, Origines, 93, n. 1.

[128] Mss. ABE have "immortality."

believe you have eternal life; these same are those which witness to me [Jn 5.39]." And again he said, "You hypocrites! The signs of the heavens and earth you know how to interpret, why can you not interpret the current time?"[Mt 16.14][129]

This argument is no longer being used to make the equinox palatable to the Antiochene tradition, but to demonstrate the perfect cosmic harmony of another feast day being adopted in the East. The feast of the Nativity of the Baptist contradated to the summer solstice corresponds to the Western celebration of the birth of Christ, not on 6 January as in the East, but 25 December. This turns the course of the seasons and the changing length of daylight into mimesis of the Baptist's prophecy at Jn 3.30: "He must increase, but I must decrease."

Ephrem's *Commentary on the Diatessaron* suggests that the homilist had only to modify an existing tradition to fit the new liturgical calendar:

> Elizabeth conceived in the month of Sahmi, [third month of Armenian calendar, roughly October], the time when Zachariah had completed the days of his service of the ministry. The annunciation was made to Mary on the tenth of the month of Areg, just as [it was made] to Zechariah on the tenth day of the month of Hori, Behold it is her sixth month. But the Law prescribes that on the tenth day of the month of Areg the [paschal] lamb is to be closed up. According to the same computation the Lamb of truth was closed up in the womb of the virgin at the time when the light was reigning. In this way he showed that he had come to cover Adam's nudity. He was born on the sixth day of the month of Kaloc, [Ced 9=Jan 7], according to Greek computation, at the time when the light begins to conquer, to show that Satan was condemned and that Adam had conquered in him who conquers everything.[130]

On the Solstices presents the ultimate argument from nature that Pascha can neither be celebrated before the historical date according to the solar calendar nor before the lengthening of daylight after the vernal equinox. Ephrem's narrative is made far more precise by coinciding with the quarter points of the year. Nevertheless, other than the first canon from the Council of Antioch, no other Syrian author acknowledges the equinoctial rule until the Syrian *Apostolic Constitutions* around 380.[131]

---

[129] De solst. 1-10, Botte, 93.

[130] Ephrem, Commentary on the Diatesseron §29, Saint Ephrem's Commentary on Tatian's Diatessaron, McCarthy, Carmel, trans., ed., JSS.Sup 2, 1993, 57.

[131] CQL, 187, n. 'o.'

This historical fact may have soon been obscured by a bit of forged rhetoric: the letters of PsIgnatius, which have such strong contacts with the ApConst that Marcel Metzger and others suspect common authorship.[132] After a rather tedious explication of the Holy Trinity and the baptismal rite, PsIgnatius' letter to the "Philippians" turns to the Forty Days and Pascha before closing:

> [13.3] Do not dishonor the feasts: do not disdain the true Quadragesima – for it contains an imitation of the Lord's "way of life" (μίμησιν γὰρ περιέχει τῆς τοῦ κυρίου πολιτείας) – do not despise the Week of the Passion, fast on the fourth day and the Parasceve, offering what remains to the poor. If anyone fasts on the Lord's Day and the Sabbath, save the one Sabbath (i.e., of the Pascha), that one is a Christ-murderer (χριστοκτόνος)...
>
> [14.2] I direct the bishops and presbyters in the Lord, whoever performs the Pascha with the Jews (μετὰ Ἰυδαίων) and adopts the sign of their feast (τὰ σύμβολα τῆς ἑορτῆς αὐτῶν), is in fellowship with those who killed the Lord and his apostles.[133]

Circulating in late fourth century Syria,[134] this forgery not only exponentially increases the already high level of Nicaean anti-Judaism, but condemns the Antiochene practice through the most revered figure in Syrian Christianity. Yet even for PsIgnatius, there is no connection between the two paschal controversies. Otherwise, he would not have bothered with the word "symbol" and would have forged a letter not to Philippi, but to an Asian congregation. That this letter was regarded as genuine testifies to how short a memory oral history can have: the Forty Days is now as ancient and "apostolic" as the *Liber Pontificalis* will think it to be.

5. Enforcing the Bargain: Homilies of the Year 387

In the year 387,[135] the full moon rose on Friday, 19 March, and the old Antiochene reckoning had set Pascha for the following Sunday, 21 March, the equinox that bore so much theological weight for the Alexandrians. For those who kept the "former custom," the synchronicity of full moon and Friday must have seemed particularly auspicious. Yet

---

[132] SC 320, 54-62.
[133] PsIgnatius Phil 13.3, 14.2, Opera Patrum Apostolicorum II, 120 f.
[134] Fischer, SUC 1, 112.
[135] See paschal calendar for 387 in Homélies Pascales III. Une Homélie Anatolienne sur la date de Pâques en l'an 387. SC 48 (F. Floëri, P. Nautin), 1957, 32-34.

that year, the heavens were not conducive to a paschal feast celebrated "everywhere on the same day." Since the full moon had not passed through the equinox, Alexandrians looked to the next full moon, which by their calculation fell a day later than the Roman, on Sunday, 18 April. Since the moon must be fifteen days old on the Sunday of Pascha, the Alexandrian rule moved the feast a week later to the latest date possible, 25 April.[136]

Four times over the past thirty years, Rome had given up an early paschal date for a later one set by Alexandria,[137] but under the Roman calendar, 25 April was four days beyond the limit set for the paschal lunar month.[138] A Roman paschal table for that year gives a choice of two dates: either the Antiochene date of 21 March or 18 April. Though no source indicates which date was chosen, since in 346 Rome did not celebrate Pascha on 25 March because the equinox had not passed,[139] the April date would seem almost assured.[140] Asian Montanists who observed a dominical Pascha would celebrate on 11 April, the Sunday after the fourteenth day of the first Asian month of spring (6 April). Some Novatians and others who distanced themselves from Nicaea would observe the old Antiochene date. If the Hebrew perpetual calendar were already in use in Antioch by 387, Pesach was celebrated on the night of 18 April. Historically, then, the only Christians who celebrated that year "with the Jews" may have been Rome and the West.[141]

a) Chrysostom's Homily against the "Protopaschites"

On 31 January 387,[142] John Chrysostom mounted the bema of Antioch's great octagonal church and delivered a sermon against those who

[136] Still the latest possible date, which occurred in 1943 and will again in 2038. Chupungco, Shaping, 46.

[137] 368: Rome set 23 Mar., celebrated 20 Apr.; 371: 20 Mar., celebrated 17 Apr.; 379, 24 Mar., celebrated 21 Apr. But in 373 Rome celebrated for no apparent reason on 24 Mar., Alexandria on 31 Mar. Schwarz, Ostertafeln, 52.

[138] The dies natalis of the City of Rome, 21 April, may have set the limit. See Grumel, Le problèm, 167.

[139] Chupungco, Shaping, 44.

[140] A letter supposedly from Ambrose (Ep. 23, PL 16, 1075) announcing that Æmilia will celebrate with Alexandria in 387 is a later forgery. See Schwarz, Ostertafeln, 54 f.

[141] Chupungco, Shaping, 46.

[142] This was already Tillemont's conjecture. For calculation, see Schatkin, Margaret, St. John Chrysostom's Homily on the Protopaschites: Introduction and Translation, OCA 195, 1973, (167-186) 171.

would soon observe the Forty Days by the old Antiochene reckoning. Unlike the other seven in a series of the most rabidly anti-Judaic homilies of the patristic age, this homily is not directed at the Jews or even those who join in Jewish holidays, but Christians in Antioch who still wish to celebrate Pascha "with the Jews."[143] Other than a few of the now ancient arguments against Jewish rights to celebrate Pesach, the majority of the sermon is a plea for unity under the aegis of the Nicaean patriarchs:

> What do you say? If your brother has something against you, you are not allowed to go to the offering before you have been reconciled to him. Yet when the whole church and so many fathers [of Nicene Council] are against you, you stubbornly hold to your plan, without giving up this unmodern inappropriate dissension, to come to the heavenly mysteries. How could you in this state of mind still celebrate the Pascha [eucharist]?[144]

Unless Chrysostom is depriving these Christians of the right to the eucharist as he does the Jews of the right to celebrate Pesach, this argument from Mt 5 only makes sense if the "protopaschites" addressed were in communion with the bishop. In view of the stern measures of the Council of Antioch in 329, which defrocked "protopaschite" clergy and excommunicated laity,[145] the main target of Chrysostom's sermon is not a stubborn group of anti-Nicaean holdovers, but a second and third generation "neoprotopaschite" backlash against the late date of Pascha in 387.

The "former custom" thus still had its adherents and its defenders, but the majority of them gathered in groups no longer in communion with the bishop: Novatians, and a splinter group from the latter, the Sabbatians. The Novatians had decreed that the date of Pascha was no reason for division,[146] but Sabbatios, as Socrates writes,[147] used the differing date as a pretext for forming a sect to fulfill his ambition to become a bishop. This pretext is likely only rhetoric, but historically, these are the groups with whom the "protopaschites" would be celebrating the

---

[143] See Wilken, John, Chrysostom and the Jews, Rhetoric and Reality in the Late Fourth Century, Berkeley 1983, but backwards: Wilken provides a Simonian interpretation before analyzing the rhetoric, which he shows to be both conventional and distorting.

[144] Chrysostom, AdvJud 3.6, PG 48, 870. For the non-polemical version, see either version of a Maundy Thursday sermon, De prod. Judae 1(2).6, PG 49, 381 f. (390 f.).

[145] Lauchert, 43.

[146] Huber, Passa, 79 f.

[147] Socrates, EH 7.5.2-4, GCS NF 1, 350 f.

paschal feast, thus the rhetorical need to concentrate on Nicaean unity and the peace of the church.

Against images of discord gleaned from 1Cor, Chrysostom hurls an image used centuries earlier by a bishop of Antioch:

> For this reason the father [bishop] is accustomed, when he enters, not to climb this throne before he has prayed for peace for all of you, and when he rises, he does not begins his address to you before he has given peace to all. And when the priests wish to bless, then they first of all ask for peace for you and thus begin their benediction. Also the deacon, when he bids to pray with the others, begins with the angel's prayer for peace. Also the psalm verse introducing the reading is full of peace, and the one who dismisses you from the assembly prays for you in the words, "Go in peace." It is not possible to say or do anything without peace...With peace I do not mean a friendly greeting or what we wish each other in a common meal, but the love of peace according to God, which comes from spiritual unity, which now many are prepared to destroy, attempting with their outdated, inappropriate rivalry to negate our celebration and make the celebration of the Jews more meaningful, as they hold these to be more trustworthy teachers the their own [council] fathers and believe the murderers of Christ concerning the Passion. What could be more paradoxical than this?[148]

As homilist, Chrysostom argues from liturgical action more than any other preacher of his century, so much that it is possible to form an accurate picture of the liturgies of both Antioch and Constantinople while he served there.[149]

"Believing the murderers of Christ concerning the Passion" translates into "outdated [ἄκαιρος]"[150] Antiochene paschal reckoning. As elsewhere in his anti-Judaic tirades, Chrysostom's rhetoric betrays a particular shrillness, in this sermon because the paschal decision of Nicaea is still being ignored after fifty years and about to be again by members of his own congregation. By 387, for instance, the "former practice" had been degraded to "a stupid (ἄλογος) habit":

> But what is their clever rationale when we hold this before them? "You, didn't you also keep this fast earlier?" they say. It isn't your place to say that

---

[148] AdvJud 3, loc. cit.

[149] See van de Paverd, Frans, Zur Geschichte der Messliturgie in Antiocheia und Konstantinopel gegen Ende des Vierten Jahrhunderts. Analyse der Quellen bei Johannes Chrysostomos, OCA 187, 1970.

[150] See Malkowski, J. L., The Element of ἄκαιρος in John Chrysostom's Anti-Jewish Polemic, StPat 12.1, 1975, 222-231.

to me, but it is more fitting when I say to you that, yes, we did fast in this way at an earlier time; nevertheless we found that a date valid for all was more important.[151]

Chrysostom's strategy is to move the argument from one date against another to the issue of Church unity. "Days, months, and times" are easily negated with Gal 4.10, while Phil 3.5,7 is drawn in to show that Paul could distance himself from Jewish practice for the sake of Christ. Identifying with Paul and distancing themselves from the "Jewish" practice of the old paschal reckoning is the escape Chrysostom plans for his opponents. This is followed by an appeal to Nicaea:

> Three hundred fathers or more came together in Bithynia and set this into law. And all this you disdain? You make one thing out of two: either you judge their ignorance, since they would not have had any exact knowledge, or their cowardice, since they would have had this, but pretended not to know it and thus betrayed the truth. If you then do not hold fast to what they decreed, this is a matter of course. Yet that they showed much intelligence and bravery at that time is revealed by all the events. For their intelligence was shown by the officially formulated creed, which not only closed the mouths of the heretics but like an unassailable wall repelled all of their attacks. Bravery was shown during the persecution only shortly ended and the war against the churches.[152]

"Exact knowledge" in calendrical matters is joined to doctrine, and Athanasius' link between orthodoxy and orthopraxis could not be stronger. Chrysostom clinches this *tertium non datur* argument with a polemic unchanged since mid-second century:

> Or do you believe that the Jews are more clever than the fathers who came from every place, and this, when they have fallen away from the paternal way and do not celebrate a festival? For with them there is no Feast of Unleavened Bread, also no Pascha – for I just heard many say[153] that Pascha takes place at the same time as Unleavened Bread – with them there is no Feast of Unleavened Bread. Hear the Lawgiver, as he says, "You shall not celebrate Pascha in any of your cities which the Lord your God gives you, but only at the place where his name is called" [Dt 16.5 f.].[154]

---

[151] Chrysostom, AdvJud 3.3, PG 48, 864.
[152] Chrysostom, AdvJud 3.3, PG 48, 865.
[153] Perhaps "protopaschite" hecklers in the congregation.
[154] Chrysostom, AdvJud 3.3, PG 48, 865 f.

Jews are also blind and deaf [Isa 42.19], they sacrificed their children to demons [Ψ104(105).37], and they have utterly abandoned God [Dt 32.18]. These three choice scriptures were also included in the barrage Justin launched against his "shadow" Trypho when the latter dared – conveniently – to question Justin's exegesis of cult-critical prophecy.[155] They are now meant to silence another rhetorical, but historically real, opponent. For Chrysostom, "place" is crucial to his argument. The second Pesach rule for the ritually unclean or for travellers is adduced to show that God values place over time, in Chrysostom's translation, the common liturgy of the orthodox over a "Jewish" date.

Jesus, however, celebrated the Pascha with his disciples not to set a precedent, but to show the "shadow" quality of Pesach. Christ could not have instituted "days and months" because of Gal 4.10: the eucharist has supplanted Jewish rites, and the common meal is not bound to any day or time. Origen's strange juxtaposition of the meal account as eucharistic versus paschal aetiology, which Eusebius had already adopted, reappears:

> Pascha and Lent are not the same thing: the Pascha is one thing, Lent another. For Lent comes once a year, but the Pascha three times a week, sometimes even four, or as often as we wish.[156] For the Pascha is not fasting but the offering of the sacrifice which takes place in every synaxis. And that is so, listen to Paul, who says, "Our Pascha was sacrificed for us, namely Christ" and "As often as you eat this bread and drink this cup, you proclaim the death of the Lord." [1 Cor 11.26]. Hence, as often as you approach with a clean conscience, you celebrate Pascha – not whenever you fast, but whenever you partake of that sacrifice. For "as often as you eat this bread and drink this cup, you proclaim the death of the Lord." For the offering made today and the one carried out yesterday and the one everyday is one and the same sacrifice happening that day of

[155] Dial 27.1-38.1, Goodspeed, 120-124. Impetus for this tirade against the Judaic cult is: "Why in your explanations do you choose from the words of the prophet so arbitrarily and pass over God's explicit command to observe the Sabbath? For through Isaiah it is said…(verses 13-14 cited in full)." See above, p. 55, n. 115.

[156] An odd parallel: "Christ means to say: 'I institute a Passover or Supper for you, which you shall enjoy not just on this one evening of the year, but frequently, whenever and wherever you will, according to everyone's opportunity and need, being bound to no special place or time' (although the pope afterward perverted it and turned it back into a Jewish feast)." Luther, Large Catechism 5, Tappert, 452. The target is the decision of the Fourth Lateran Council (1215) to require Easter communion.

the week. The former is not holier than the latter, and the latter is not less worthy than the former; rather they are one and the same, equally awe-inspiring and salvific.[157]

The argument is quite similar to Origen's: a mimetic reading of the meal account as Pascha could only serve for a yearly observance and thus is internally inconsistent. Yet Chrysostom is not deconstructing the paschal feast as much as he is forcibly removing the Pesach frame of the supper. This aspect of the meal narrative only comes into play against the "protopaschites" to eliminate any institution associated with a specific day. In fact, Chrysostom deconstructs any aetiology, rubric, or liturgical custom that crosses his path so that there is nothing left but his central argument:

> Thus since what is complete has come to pass, we also do not wish to rush back to an earlier time and observe days, times, and years, but we wish everywhere to follow the church with care by preferring love and peace to all else. For even if the church is in error, then it receives not so much praise for its common observance of the day than blame for this discord and division.

> Now I have no argument for the determination of the day, for not even God has one, as we have shown, as I have used so many words. Yet one thing I ask of you, that we do everything in peace and unity so that when we fast and the whole people and the priests speak common prayer for the world, you do not stay home drunk. Consider that that is the influence of the devil and that it is not one, not two, not three sins, but many more. He removes you from the flock, arranges it that you condemn many fathers, he thrusts you into contentiousness, pushes you toward the Jews, sets you up as a stumbling block to your own people and strangers. Yet these are not the only transgressions, for great harm could result if during these fastdays you do not partake of the enjoyment of Scriptures, the assemblies, the blessing, or common prayer, but rather pass the whole time with a bad conscience, in fear and trembling that you could be found out as a foreigner or stranger, when it is proper to celebrate everything together with the church – with openness, joy, confidence and every freedom.[158]

Gone are arguments from history, scripture, and the phases of the moon, but the lines of Christian identity could not be more clearly

---

[157] Chrysostom, Adv. Jud. 3.4, PG 48, 867, trans. slightly altered from CQL 77 f.
[158] Chrysostom, AdvJud 3.6, PG 48, 870 f.

drawn. All that remains is the unity of the Church in common worship. The "neoprotopaschites" would damage this unity because they listen both to "Jews" and demons, the two great mimetic shadows of second century polemic.

b) Pseudo-Chrysostom's Seventh "Little Trumpet"

The calendrical arguments Chrysostom chooses not to employ appear in full regalia in the last of a collection of seven homilies, τὰ σαλπίγ-για,[159] which later circulated under his name. Because of its meticulous explanation of the late Alexandrian date for Pascha, the mention of three consecutive paschal dates, its use of the Asian calendar, and a notice about the fast beginning "in the next week,"[160] the sermon may be dated with confidence to Asia Minor[161] during the week of 28 February-7 March 387.[162] The homily seeks to answer a question that, in view of the extreme tardiness of Pascha and the sensible Montanist solution to dispense with elaborate calculation, must have been posed often in that year:

> We have heard many ask, "The Nativity of the Savior is celebrated on a fixed day (occurring, as everyone knows, on the eighth of the kalends of January according to the Roman calendar),[163] similarly the Theophany (celebrated also on a fixed day, the thirteenth of the fourth month according to the Asian calendar); also when we observe the memorials of the martyrs, we observe their anamnesis on a fixed day. Why is it then that the reasoning is not the same with Pascha?" But the mystery of Pascha does not depend upon a single day or a single event, but upon several appointed times which we shall reflectively gather together about this subject, imparting their theoretical explanations.[164]

---

[159] Except for hom. 4-5, the collection appears as Homélies Pascales I, II, and III: SC 27, P. Nautin, 1950 (hom. 6, also psHippolytus IP); SC 36, P. Nautin, 1953 (hom. 1-3); and SC 48, F. Floëri-P. Nautin, 1957 (hom. 7). Hom. 4 and 5 summarized SC 36, 31 f. The title derives from a genuine homily, AdvJud 2, PG 48, 843 ff. (polemicizes against the shofar), which gave the name σάλπιγγες to another collection. See SC 27, 17.

[160] SC 48, 171.

[161] The Asian calendar was used in Bithynia, western Cyprus, and perhaps Cappadocia. See SC 48, 81-83.

[162] SC 48, 18-26.

[163] Only the date of the Nativity is given in the Roman calendar, a remnant of foreignness, though "everyone knows" about it. SC 48, 112.

[164] Hom 387 3, SC 48, 113.

The homilist takes great pains to explain the theological significance of the rules of the Alexandrian computation: the equinox, the full moon, and the Three Days. Since all three must converge to celebrate the Pascha, in 387 the church must wait until the night of 24 April to observe the feast. Other groups – Jews, Quartadecimans, Montanists, Novatians – only have a part of the truth. The Jews do not observe a fixed date (i.e. of the solar calendar), but unlike the "Hebrew sages" before the death of Christ whom Anatolius had canonized, they have fallen into error by not observing the equinox. At "hour zero" of creation, light and darkness were in perfect balance. Thus nothing could exist before the equinox, much less a paschal date.[165] The Quartadeciman "heresy," to which the homilist devotes all of one sentence, not only suffers from the same error as the Jews with whom they celebrate, but does not observe the Three Days which "harmonize with the τέλος of the mystery."[166] The Three Days are not yet the liturgical Triduum, but narrated time in the gospels. Demons have caused Montanists to observe the fourteenth of a solar month, but not the moon. Novatians "appear to imitate" more closely the practice of the church, observing the Three Days, but they too ignore the equinox and the Nicaean decision for unity.[167]

Of far greater interest is the highly mimetic argument explaining the ultimate rightness of the Alexandrian calendar.

> [38] Because of all of this, Christ observed [ἐτήρησεν] the primordial times appointed for the new Passion; and thus we too observe all the times to demonstrate the mystical reasons, attending to the imitation [τὸ μίμημα]. For the Savior, bringing to completion the true Pascha to free all humankind from the punishment impending above them, as fitting the true Pascha, brought together all of the times corresponding exactly to the week of creation, in order to accomplish exactly its recapitulation [ἵνα τὴν ἀνακεφαλαίωσιν ἀκριβῶς ἐκτελέσειεν]. But because the dates do not always converge, we perform an imitation of the true Pascha: we combine as closely as possible the imitation of the pertinent times, yet abandon the temporal exactness of the prototypic Pascha of the Savior [τῷ πρωτοτύπῳ πάσχα τοῦ σωτῆρος].

> [39] Also, the Only Begotten was sacrificed a single time for all and fulfilled the Œkonomia. A lamb is no longer sacrificed. But the Savior, prior to the

[165] Hom 387 19-22, SC 48 129 f.
[166] Hom 387 5, SC 48, 115.
[167] Hom 387 8 f., SC 48, 118.

passion, took bread and a chalice as imitation of the lordly sacrifice, his own body and blood, and over each with ineffable epicleses, commanded to perform the Pascha with these types. Thus imitating the times, we follow as closely as possible this imitation, bringing together the pertinent times: the equinox, the fourteenth of the moon, and the Three Days – the fourteenth according to the week [of creation], the same way the Three Days, but the equinox because of the time of the Pascha.[168]

The very strategy that Chrysostom cannot use against a Syrian opponent is explained serenely in an Asian homily. As the eucharist celebrated many times is mimesis of the one sacrifice of Christ, sacramental elements are types given as mimesis of Christ's body and blood, instituted for ritual imitation in the Church's worship. The paschal calendar imitates this mimesis by prescribing in series the kairoi whose conjunction at the passion was as unique as the event itself. The "acribiousness" of Christ, who consciously chose the proper moment for his death on the "prototypic" Pascha to recapitulate the first week of creation, cannot be imitated with the same exactness. But the Alexandrian calendar attempts an approximation by having both the fourteenth of the moon and the Three Days pass through the equinox. Such a heavy concentration of mimesis and related words is a rarity in the fourth century, but the homilist's strategy is to explain the divergence between type and mimesis as much as their correspondence. In the year 387 the mirrors are much further apart than ever before or ever will be again in the hearers' lifetime.

VI. Summary

Antiochene paschal calculation is not the only issue driving Nicaean rhetoric, but a much deeper one about the identity of the Church and Jesus of Nazareth. Whether Jesus died on 14 or 15 Nisan is only a corollary to the real question: did Jesus celebrate a Pesach meal "with the Jews" according to the Law of Moses, i.e., a Jew observing Jewish law, the night before his death? This is how opponents first framed the question, then soundly negated it, perhaps one reason why the paschal and Arian conflicts are invariably linked: the paschal question also had important christological implications. Unlike the dispute couched in

---

[168] Hom 387.38 f., SC 48, 149 f.

philosophical categories about the nature of the Trinity, paschal rhetoric remained encoded in exegetical arguments and their anti-Judaic accompaniment.

From the Antiochene perspective, at stake is a paschal theology fused to the eucharist – with pre-Pauline roots, gospel witness in Mark, Matthew, and Luke, elevated to a story of origins by Tatian's *Diatessaron*, defended by the *Didascalia*, and still active in Syriac authors well past Nicaea. For Aphrahat the paschal night furnishes a story of origins for baptism as well as a commissioning of the apostles through their own "completed" baptism. In the "historical" paschal night, Jesus washed the feet of the disciples and he ate and drank with them, and that meal was the Pesach of Ex 12. The date of the meal cannot be placed in opposition to that of the crucifixion because the meal *is* the cross.

In the year 387, two homilies approach the same problem with different strategies. The Asian homily spins out Alexandrian calendrical mimesis into perfect imitation of date, time, and event, even finding a place for the unique *kairos* of the meal. This transformation of subtextual strategy into surface rhetoric is necessary because the old Antiochene date actually corresponded to historical events much better than the latest possible Alexandrian date. Taking cues from the Nicaean deconstruction of the Syrian paschal aetiology, Chrysostom pits the timeless eucharist against the now "untimely" Antiochene calendar. Yet "protopaschites" were not a continuous community of Nicaean hold-outs, but a new group who objected to the extremely late date of Pascha. This would alleviate Huber's[169] charge that the paschal canon of the Synod of Antioch met with considerable resistance and that Athanasius "probably exaggerated" in his letter *De synodis* when he said that the Syrians had conformed. That Athanasius does not mention Mesopotamia and Cilicia also does not mean, as Huber claims, that these regions retained the old computation. These suppositions are only transition so that Chrysostom's sermon forms the denouement of an historical narrative. The sermon makes more historical sense as an insignificant epilogue: the stubborn rebellion Huber imagines is nothing more than grumbling from the back pews.

Yet Aphrahat shows that the adoption of the equinoctial rule need not change a single tenet of Syrian tradition, the Alexandrian limit of

---

[169] Huber, Passa, 76 f.

the fifteenth of the moon easily absorbed into the "great feast day." An older typology for Unleavened Bread as the week of fasting can be employed to explain the transference of Pascha when the fourteenth of the moon falls on a Sunday. Though its full form is the work of the author, this argument would not have been possible had proponents of the new rule not been able to make the same translation into biblical narrative before and during the Council of Nicaea. In Council debate the meal rite also comes under attack because this particularly Syrian form of NT mimesis was foreign to the common paschal tradition and looked far too "Ebionite" for Alexandrians with Origenist tastes in exegesis. Syrian liturgical theology and its calendar were no more "Jewish" than the equinoctial rule was "pagan," but this is the language of polemical separation, not history. Both of these strategies – calendar as cosmic and historical mimesis and removal of the Pesach frame from the Syn meal – have longer histories. Anti-Judaic arguments have the longest history of all. "Jews" are "wrong," "not like us:" the rhetorical "other."

What method of computation was the target for the anti-Judaic polemic at Nicaea? The "fourteenth," Jewish night of 14-15 Nisan or Christian XIV lunae, is still today either the full moon of March or April. "For if we always celebrate on the Jewish date," Epiphanius writes, "we shall sometimes celebrate after the equinox, as they often do, and we too; and again, we shall sometimes celebrate before the equinox, as they do when they celebrate alone."[170] Historically then, the whole Church often celebrated "with the Jews" on the Sunday after Pesach, but sometimes only the Patriarchate of Antioch chose March – probably why a list of these lunar dates is labelled "Jewish" at the Council of Sardica.[171] There are thus at least six variations on Hebrew timekeeping in use in the early fourth century: Antiochene, Roman, Alexandrian, the solar Montanist, and whatever intercalary method or methods were used by Jewish and Samaritan communities. Trying to find the answers to specifically Christian dilemmas in the latter, however, is a dead end.

Instead of an entire year of festivals, Christian recensions only needed rules to determine when to choose which full moon, as well as some means of predicting them far enough in advance to draw up a list of paschal dates. None of these tasks requires mathematical skills beyond

---

[170] Pan 70.11.5, GCS 37, 244; NHMS 36, 414.
[171] See above, n. 61, p. 278.

addition and subtraction: finding a simple eight or nineteen-year cycle would not have taxed the faculties of the well-educated. Yet even if Christian communities were as calendrically inept as their rhetoric presents the "Jews," such information could have easily been procured – with utmost discretion – from another favorite target of early Christian polemic: an astrologer.[172] Accuracy, however, is only a second desideratum after a calendar is generally recognized as a social contract within a self-identified group.

Aphrahat's switch to an "old style" typology suggests another reason for celebrating "with the Jews": an equally "old style" paschal computation governed by the sun's 18 March entrance into Aries – the solar date mentioned tantalizingly by Philo and used in Hippolytus' calendar[173] – *and* "the fourteenth" as permissible lunar date. The latter rule, though not the former, would present Columba and his Irish monks with major difficulties when they moved southward in the seventh century. The label "Quartadeciman" was dusted off once more for a divergent paschal practice.[174] This does not reveal some hidden connection between seventh century Ireland and third century Antioch or anywhere else, but reference to the same biblical texts actualized into a calendar, "just like the Bible says," in an island country isolated from the rest of Europe for centuries. Long before Columba's dispute with Gregory, Rome and Alexandria were not in agreement either over the equinox (25 or 21 March) or the age of the moon (16 or 15 days) on the Sunday of Pascha. Yet both could be united against an older Antiochene computation that set paschal limits earlier than either. This might lie hidden in Anatolius' conjunctions:

> Yet the sun appears on 26 Phamenoth (=22 March) mentioned before *not only* in the first sign [of the zodiac], *but also* as already having passed through it by four days.[175]

If this hypothetical calendar used 18 March as limit for the *fourteenth of the moon*, then in the year 303, Antioch could have celebrated Pascha

---

[172] So Schwartz, Ostertafeln, 30: Hippolytus found the first full moon of his computation "wohl mit Hülfe eines *Chaldaeus.*"

[173] See text, above, p. 293.

[174] Lohse, Passafest, 131-134, Joh and Syn chronology used in the dispute means historical continuity with 2 c. Quartadecimans, especially since the Irish rule was labelled "Quartadeciman."

[175] Eh 7.32.15, GCS 9.2, 722.

on 21 March, the full moon having occurred on Friday 19 March. From the Chronograph of 354, a Roman date of 18 April is historically secure.[176] This is a case similar to the fateful year of 387: Rome would celebrate on 18 April, Alexandria a week later, while the "protopaschites" and various splinter groups celebrate on 21 March. However, if the 18 March date, or even the Alexandrian equinox, were used as limit for the *Pascha itself*, the moon being 14-21 days old, then two other cases arise when Antioch would have celebrated earlier than Rome and Alexandria, who would celebrate *together* on 18 April. According to the Chronograph, in 314, a full moon fell on Wednesday 17 March, again yielding an Antiochene date of 21 March. In the year of the Nicaean Council 325, a full moon occurred on Monday 15 March, with Antioch hypothetically celebrating again on 21 March.

These dates of 21 March versus 18 April (or in 387, 25 April) are purely mathematical coincidences dictated by the inevitable reoccurrence of Sunday on the same date, the day and week of the March full moon, and Roman and Alexandrian computation. That Rome and Alexandria celebrated Pascha on 18 April while Antioch may possibly have observed on 21 March – in the same year that these sees battle bitterly over a paschal calendar as a sign of united orthodoxy – may be a coincidence of another kind. This is pure guesswork, nothing more, but I would suggest that the place to look for the history of this calendrical dispute is, appropriately enough, the calendar. The answer must lie somewhere in these "387-type" years, not in sterilizing Nicaean polemic into the history of Judaism.

The first pleas for the equinox issue from early third century Alexandria. In support, Peter defends Anatolius' Hebrew patriarchs against Trikentios' deconstruction of the Alexandrian calendrical myth. Was an equinoctial rule observed by the Egyptian Diaspora in the first century or even earlier, only to disappear with the demise of Hellenistic Jewish culture? Anatolius was convinced he knew the answer, but contemporary Jews did not seem to obey this rule. Alexandrian calendrical speculation could find an explanation for this anomaly only through the filter of Gentile Christian anti-Judaism, which also rushes to defend the historicity of both Syn and Joh gospel accounts. At the same time, Alexandria easily found a proto-Christian "Hebrew" in Philo, regardless of what the first section of his *Questions and Answers on Exodus* may

---

[176] Cf. table, Schwartz, Ostertafeln, 46 f.

have meant for its original readers. More important for the history of the Nicaean conflict, however, was that such continuity had the force of historical truth for the Patriarchate of Alexandria.

Alexandria successfully convinced enough Syrian bishops its paschal computation was historically correct. Those not persuaded by chronology, lunar charts, and images of spring and creation were then barraged with anti-Judaic polemic while an attempt was made to restate the rule in Syrian paschal language. Antioch could only understand this as a signal that Alexandria and Rome were not prepared to negotiate. For these two sees were not only convinced that their calendar was perfect mimesis of the cosmic order and biblical history, but a restoration of a divine ordinance perverted by the "Jews." Eusebius offers solutions that appealed to all sides, redirecting anti-Judaic polemic to its original target, the "Jews" of the gospels. Besides this more aggressive tactic, Alexandria and Rome may have used different constructs – cosmos or kairos – to mirror their computations, but both were united on one point: the equinox or a date thereafter was the historical date of Jesus' death and thus the only one suitable as an anchor date for the calendar. This required retrojecting the equinoctial rule to the time of Christ; for safety's sake, even earlier. Only Christians and their pre-Christian twins could properly fulfill the paschal command of Ex 12, while contemporary Jews could not.

De solstitiis shows that this type of synchronicity could be absorbed by the Syrian tradition, curiously enough, in order to inculcate another Western date, the celebration of the Nativity on 25 December, the 25 March date no longer as with Hippolytus the birth, but the conception of Christ. For all the rhetoric versus history questions raised by this conflict, the forged Ignatius has a ready answer by making the new paschal computation a concern for the real one.

In exegesis of Christ narrative toward liturgy or calendar, few writers employ anything resembling modern "exactness." Chronological elements may be separated or combined. As in Irenaeus, where a three-year "Johannine" ministry suddenly sports a "Synoptic" meal, Syrian writers may adopt 14 or 15 Nisan without any change in their paschal theology. Aphrahat and the *Didascalia* may compress or expand narrative time to reflect liturgical time. Though no Western author save Origen has any use for the paschal frame of the meal, the Paschal *Computus* of 253 uses the Syn date as a chronological base. The shape of these retellings of the passion narrative depends solely upon their objects. "Chronology" measured either by year, day, date, or hour was never in itself an issue but only a motif interpreted mimetically toward a particular "message," whether that message was to proclaim the mystery of the paschal night or to demonstrate the correctness of a paschal computation.

Excavation of the rhetorical ruins of Nicaea has required some reconstruction, but the foundations are secure. Though Caesarea's long contact with Alexandria and an Origenist background place Eusebius in the Alexandrian camp, his paschal treatise reflects rhetoric that won the day. Far from taking an position opposed to Alexandria and Rome, Asian bishops were in agreement with these two sees against the paschal computation of Antioch. Contrasting rhetorical strategies of the two homilies of 387 offers the best proof: Chrysostom still presses for the unity of the church, the Asian Anonymous may serenely point to the paschal date as mimesis of gospel events. The Antiochene presbyter is still deconstructing the meal aetiology, while the Asian, unlike second century predecessors, has adopted it.

These findings may alleviate Eusebius of some charges of revisionism but give rise to others. He cannot be accused of slanting a narrative about the Quartadeciman controversy against the original parties, since they were configured differently at the end of the second century around an issue which was not that of Nicaea. With this, the excavation may now uncover Eusebius' presentation of the earlier controversy in his *Church History*.

C. The Quartadeciman Question, ca. 195

I. Reading Eusebius' Reading of the Paschal Controversy: The Battle over Apostolic Tradition

The most generous source of information about the second century Pascha is Eusebius, whose EH brings texts arising from three controversies about paschal observance. Only the last – between Asia Minor and "the rest of the world" – is presented in historical context. The first is signaled by a reference to Irenaeus' letter to Victor immediately before Eusebius cites from AH 3.3.4 about Polycarp's apostolic roots (including the bath story) and from the story of his martyrdom:

> He [Polycarp] spent time in Rome and discussed with Anicetus the controversy over the day of Pascha, as Irenaeus reports.[1]

For a discussion in Laodicea ca. 166, there is only a single witness, a citation of the preface of another work on the Pascha by Melito of Sardis. After a list of Melito's works, Eusebius begins a series of five excerpts with the paschal treatise:

> In Περὶ Πάσχα, he indicates at the beginning the time when he wrote it in these words: "Under Servillius Paulus, [correct: L. Sergius Paulus[2]] proconsul of Asia, at the time when Sagaris was martyred, there was a considerable dispute about the Pascha, which fell according to season in those days, and this was written.[3]

Eusebius next offers a helpful cross-reference:

> Clement of Alexandria mentions this work in his own Περὶ Πάσχα, whose composition he says was occasioned by Melito's work.[4]

---

[1] EH 4.14.2, GCS 9.1, 332.
[2] Rufinus has "Sergius Paulus," thinking of Acts 13.7. There was an L. Sergius who was proconsul of Asia around 164-166. Eusèbe de Césarée. Histoire Ecclésiastique, G. Bardy, Livres I-IV. SC 31, 209, n. 13.
[3] EH 4.26.3, GCS 9.1, 382; CQL 25.
[4] EH 4.26.4, loc. cit.

This is followed by three excerpts from Melito's *Apology*, one from the *Eclogae*, and Eusebius' typical closure:

καὶ τὰ μὲν τοῦ Μελίτωνος τοσαῦτα.

So much for that of Melito.

This should remind the reader more of Photius' library notes than anything resembling Josephus or Herodotos. All that is missing is Photius' ubiquitous introduction, "A book was read... (Ἀνεγνώσθη βιβλίον)" and a short comment about the style. Eusebius only brings an incipit. If Melito had introduced his work in some other way, no one would ever know that such a discussion took place. It is important to Eusebius *that* Melito wrote such a work and when, but why is of no consequence. For Melito, however, rhetoric and history surrounding his paschal treatise were important enough to begin with their description.

In chapters 23-25 of his fifth book, Eusebius excerpts three letters, all to Victor, Bishop of Rome: the one from Irenaeus, another from Polycrates, Bishop of Ephesus, and the third from a meeting jointly chaired by Narcissus of Aelia Capitolina (Jerusalem) and Theophilus of Caesarea. These three letters, and others mentioned but not cited, were archived in the libraries to which Eusebius had easy access: in Caesarea under his care, and that of Jerusalem founded by Alexander, pupil of Origen, and others of Origen's school (EH 4.20.1).[5] Begun by Eusebius' teacher Pamphilius, the library at Caesarea was greatly enriched when Origen moved there from Alexandria, and its holdings had been catalogued by Eusebius himself (EH 6.32.3; 36.3). This task likely gave Eusebius the idea that he had the makings of a book. The origins of these two libraries also account for the Alexandrian slant of Eusebius' history, the heightened role of Origen, and the contents of the letter archive, Eusebius' only source for these chapters.

The time of writing, shown by the Syriac translation to be before the final redaction of the EH, may even date a decade or more earlier.[6] Yet diverging calendars were not overnight problems suddenly demanding attention at Nicaea. How are the two conflicts different? How the same?

---

[5] Grant, Eusebius, 41, 83.

[6] Grant, 10-11. Syriac version (5 c.) along with ms. tradition BDM, reflects the edition of 325, after Constantine's defeat of Licinius but before the Council of Nicaea. Books 1-6 probably completed much earlier. Grant, 14. For other theories, see Gödecke, Monika, Geschichte als Mythos. Eusebs "Kirchengeschichte," EHS 23.307, 1987, 20 f.

Modern historians would draw parallels from previous controversies to their own time, as Irenaeus does, or at least give sufficient background information, scarcely better known in the fourth century than today, to evaluate the letters cited. Eusebius does none of this.

As frustrating as this may be, it is quite consistent with Eusebius' self-understanding as an anthologist rather than interpreter of events. He outlines the plan of his work at the very beginning:

> As many items, then, as we consider useful for the proposed subject out of what they have occasionally been mentioned, collecting them and anthologizing the appropriate sayings of the earlier writers themselves as from an intellectual meadow,[7] we shall endeavor to organize through historical treatment, eager to preserve the successions from the especially distinguished apostles of our Savior in the prominent churches that are still remembered even now.[8]

Grazing in Eusebius' meadow may leave a bitter taste, the "historical treatment" hardly sweetening the intellectual task, but it can scarcely be claimed that Eusebius' sections on both Melito and the paschal controversy do not perfectly accord with this plan. The focus of Eusebius' anthology is first on persons (earlier writers, especially distinguished apostles), not events and their significance, then the succession of apostolic authority "in the prominent churches." As virtually every introduction of this kind, Eusebius' plan is really no plan at all, but a summary written after the work was complete in which the author functions as most informed reader and bids others to follow.[9] This is what Eusebius thinks his book is about and how he directs the reader to view it.

Eusebius' directive also explains why all citations from the controversy 195 speak the language of apostolicity. Not one passage about "chronology" is cited, nor is there any trace of exegetical conflict, even though at Nicaea Eusebius was more than willing to debate about both. Unlike the *Chronicon*, the EH is not interested in this issue, but in the people involved and their writings. Thus the selection of texts in the *Chronicon* and the EH is complementary for modern readers, but mutually exclusive for the authors who selected them.

---

[7] This image literalizing the metaphor in "anthology" (flower bouquet) taken from Clem., Strom 1.11.2, also appears at Eusebius' Ecl. proph. 1.1. Grant, Eusebius, 26 f.

[8] EH 1.1.4, GCS 9.1, 8. Grant's translation, above note.

[9] The preface is from a second edition. Grant, Eusebius, 33-35.

One earlier text may clue how Eusebius understood the context of the letters he found in Caesarea. There is an allusion to the paschal question discussed between Rome and Ephesus addressed to the major ritual controversy of the third century, heretical baptism, in a letter ca. 256 from Firmilian of Cappadocian Caesarea to Cyprian:

> That the Romans do not observe in every way that which has been handed down from the beginning, and that they attempt in vain to take shelter behind the authority of the apostles, can also be seen in that some differences clearly exist concerning their paschal celebration and many other divine mysteries, and that [in Rome], not everything is observed in the same way as in Jerusalem, just as in most of the other provinces a great deal varies according to place and people. Nevertheless there was never any departure from the peace and unity of the church.[10]

Except for the usual practices varying a great deal "according to place and people," the chief difference between mid-third century Rome and Jerusalem may only have been Rome's paschal computation versus the Alexandrian reckoning followed by Jerusalem and coastal Palestine at least since the late second century.[11] But there is an echo of an earlier controversy in which a bishop of Rome was deeply involved. Firmilian's conclusion is so similar to that of Irenaeus' letter to Victor that it may be considered an indirect citation. It also is the earliest source to suggest the outcome: peace, by whatever means, was preserved.

For Firmilian, the earlier paschal controversy is paradigmatic for a current conflict. The target is Stephen, Bishop of Rome, who favored tolerance toward heretical baptisms, a stance opposed by Cyprian and Firmilian. That a controversy between Rome and an Eastern[12] province is remembered as a story of a Roman bishop who overestimates the

---

[10] Cyprian, Ep. 75.6, CSEL 3.2, 819.

[11] See below, p. 326. Brox, Parteilichkeit, 315, assumes a Quartadeciman Firmilian using Jerusalem to bolster apostolicity. With close ties to Palestine, Firmilian also attended a synod at Antioch over Novatian at which no Asian bishop was present. Harnack, Adolf, Die Mission und Ausbreitung des Christentums in den ersten drei Jahrhunderten, Leipzig ⁴1924, 664.

[12] The Great Schism becomes the reality of which the paschal controversy was the "shadow." This is Pelikan's "Two Sees," while Petersen uses the anachronistic term "caesaropapism" for the Nicaean conflict. (For these essays see n. 8, p. 161). Harvey heard the "the first note of discord...sounded between the Churches of the East and of the West, that, however varied in character and object, has never to the present day been resolved in a cordial harmony." (Harvey I, clix f.)

apostolicity of his see gives some major directives for Eusebius' treatment some sixty years later, with one important change consistent with the "plan" of his work. *The entire section on the paschal controversy is not about the paschal controversy at all.* It is Eusebius' story about an eirenic Irenaeus who sues for peace amid liturgical diversity, at the same time soundly lecturing Victor in a fashion Cyprian and Firmilian would very much like to have adopted toward Stephen. Eusebius' "historical treatment" of the paschal controversy is structured just like his section on Melito: an anecdote about Irenaeus troped with excerpts of letters, prefaced by a brief summary and bibliographical notes. In telling an Irenaeus story, Eusebius has also framed the dispute not as the clash of scriptural exegesis or liturgical symbols, but of episcopal power and its icons. The hero Irenaeus requires an anti-hero, and this role is played quite well by an invisible Victor of Rome.

Perhaps reclassifying the genre of this section will relieve scholars of the burden of assuming either an omniscient Eusebius suppressing information to support some hidden agenda or a rankly stupid Eusebius who has misconstrued the letters he read. Second century paschal literature may not have been extant in numerous mss. across the Empire, but like Firmilian, others had access to the same works. "History," though not its "treatment," could not have been subject to gross manipulation. Usually, however, both of these Eusebioi are two sides of the same figure, the malevolently prophetic Eusebius who spent considerable time fashioning this chapter toward the sole object of confounding modern theories. Eusebius is not writing for readers who want detailed information about a now irrelevant controversy over the day of Pascha two hundred years before, but for those who wish to connect to the heroes of a glorious Christian tradition Eusebius is constructing for them.

For Eusebius' first readers, this connection must have been almost instantaneous, because the images he draws of first and second century tradition always manage to look like the ideal church of the fourth. Other than numerical gain and geographic spread, and that usually with miraculous swiftness,[13] development through time of any facet of Christian thought or practice is a concept utterly alien to Eusebius' work. Thus when he finds various letters about the paschal controversy, he

---

[13] Inspired by Luke's of Pentecost, Eusebius writes, "In all cities and villages there at once arose churches attended by thousands, full like barns." EH 2.3.2, GCS 9.1, 112.

reads them as if they had come from some Nicaea-by-mail whose tabulated results were binding on all parties.[14]

Viewed apart from their "historical treatment," however, these letters have more in common with 1 Clem than the synodical decrees of a later age.[15] Those who write Victor are concerned with the unity of the Roman community, though various writers may have different ideas of how this unity is to be maintained. It should also be noted that Victor, having requested the opinions of other bishops across the Empire, shows an initial reluctance to act unilaterally that runs completely counter to the image produced by Eusebius' shaping of the material.

1. First and Last: Eusebius' Introduction and the Letter from Caesarea

Eusebius introduces his three excepts with the briefest of "historical treatments," then lists the letters archived in the Caesarean library:

> At that time a not insignificant controversy arose because all the dioceses of Asia thought it right, as by a very ancient tradition [ὡς ἐκ παραδόσεως ἀρχαιοτέρας], to observe for the feast of the Savior's Pascha the fourteenth day of the moon, on which the Jews had been commanded to kill the lamb. Thus it was necessary to finish the fast on that day, whatever day of the week it might be. Yet it was not the custom to celebrate in this manner in the churches throughout the rest of the world, for from apostolic tradition [ἐκ ἀποστολικῆς παραδόσεως] they kept the custom which still exists that it is not right to finish the fast on any day save that of the resurrection of our Savior.
>
> Many meetings and conferences with bishops were held on this point, and all unanimously formulated in their letters the doctrine of the church for those in every country that the mystery of the Lord's resurrection from the dead could be celebrated on no day save Sunday, [ἐν ἄλλῃ ποτὲ τῆς κυριακῆς 'εμέρα τὸ τῆς ἐκ νεκρῶν ἀναστάσεως ἐπιτελοῖτο τοῦ κυρίου μυστήριον] and that on that day alone we should celebrate the end of the paschal fast.
>
> There is still extant a writing of those who were convened in Palestine, over whom presided Theophilus, bishop of the diocese of Caesarea, and Narcissus, bishop of Jerusalem; and there is similarly another from those in

---

[14] Eusebius presents "the Church of the second century governed by a well organised body of bishops, the ideal so widely spread among Eastern prelates of the fourth century." Zernov, N., Eusebius and the Paschal Controversy, CQR 116, 1933, (24-41) 34.

[15] Zernov, 36-38. See also Andresen, Carl, Zum Formular frühchristlicher Gemeindebriefe, ZNW 56, 1965, 233-259, esp. 252 to end.

Rome on the same controversy, which gives Victor as bishop; and there is one from the bishops of Pontus over whom Palmas presided as the oldest; and of the dioceses of Gaul, of which Irenaeus was bishop; and yet others of those in Osrhoëne and the cities there; and a private letter of Bacchyllus, the bishop of the church of Corinth; and of very many more who expressed one and the same opinion and judgment, and gave the same vote.[16]

The facts: proconsular Asia and contiguous areas had maintained the "very ancient" night of 14-15 Nisan as the night of Pascha, while Alexandria, Edessa (Osrhoëne), Palestine and – as it becomes clear from the letters Eusebius cites – a majority of Roman Christians celebrated the feast on an "apostolic" Sunday, a practice "which still exists." That the "mystery of the Lord's resurrection from the dead" should "be celebrated on no day save Sunday" is, of course, anachronistic,[17] but it is a construct no more remarkable than the "Good Friday-Easter" dichotomy of Duchesne and Schmidt, who as all readers came to these texts with a prior understanding of what motifs constituted "Easter" in the second or any other century. Since there are no second century "Easter" texts extant from the West for comparison, this directive to contrast the anamnesis of the resurrection to the Quartadeciman practice must have been the seed from which this minimal pair grew. Presenting the Quartadeciman practice as defective also explains why it no longer exists in the early fourth century except perhaps in a few marginal communities. "Apostolic" practices survive. If they do not, they are not apostolic, but "very ancient."

For Eusebius, that Pascha was celebrated on the Lord's Day from the very beginning is a belief no text could challenge, and he read with great approval the claims of apostolicity made by Palestinian bishops even if he chose not to cite them. This is also no more unusual than the assumption in Harvey's day that Irenaeus was really talking about the Forty Days instead of a forty-hour fast.[18] Rufinus reads this "apostolic" view of a single practice right into his translation,[19] just as the *Liber Pontificalis* pushes the origins of Lent back to the early second century.

---

[16] EH 5.23.3, GCS 9.1, 488 f.

[17] Mohrmann, Christine, Le conflit pascal au IIe siècle. Note philologique. VigChr 16, 1962, (154-171) 158 f.

[18] Harvey II, 474. The text includes a period after "forty," just as Rufinus read it, but there, n. 6, Harvey connects the forty-hour fast with the absence of the Bridegroom.

[19] 41, 70 n. 17. Divergent fasting practice falls away from a single apostolic norm "…qui non simpliciter, *quod ab initio traditum est,* tenentes in alium morem vel per neglegentiam vel per imperitiam postmodum decidere." GCS 9.1, 494.

326 THE ANTENICENE PASCHA

Eusebius reads that portion of Irenaeus' letter about the fast as discussing not its varying duration but the time and day the fast ended, a conclusion reducing Irenaeus' argument to a simple equation of "14 Nisan" to "end of fast." Irenaeus' actual equation is more algebraic: *tolerated* diversity of fasting practice = x diversity of paschal date, with ample clues to Victor on how this equation is to be solved.

To finish the entire section, the letter from Jerusalem-Caesarea that Eusebius mentions first shows that his home turf was on the "right" side of the conflict. The Asian practice is "very ancient," the Roman "apostolic," but the Caesarean paschal tradition, Eusebius proudly reports, "is direct from the apostles":

> 25.1 However, those in the region of Palestine – Narcissus and Theophilus, whom we have just mentioned, and Cassius, bishop of the church at Tyre, Clarus of the one in Ptolomais, and those assembled with them – put into writing most of the elements of the tradition about the Pascha which had come to them directly from the apostles, and at the end of the document they appended this (which I quote exactly):

> Try to have copies of our letter distributed to every diocese, so that we may not be responsible for those who recklessly lead their own souls astray. We inform you that also in Alexandria they celebrate on the very same day as we do; for letters travel from us to them and from them to us, so that we keep the holy day in harmony and at the same time.[20]

Local patriotism and a direct line to the apostles (likely drawn from apostolic writings in new mimetic readings) could not force Eusebius to cite more of this letter. Why? Because it would add nothing to the narrative about Irenaeus. Bishops of coastal Palestine and Aelia have written to Rome about their use of an Alexandrian paschal computation. If this is the custom in Caesarea, it is little wonder that Eusebius thinks it should be the custom everywhere, a point he may have made at Nicaea by citing this letter – against Rome, not Antioch. On the other hand, "former customs" or "very ancient" practices can lose their claim to apostolicity by rhetorical fiat. In this, the paschal controversies of 325 and 195 are identical, just as Eusebius understands the conflict to be between one province and "the rest of the world." Letters arising from the conflict are read as the conflict itself. The local importance for Rome, whose bishop in Eusebius' day had long since determined

---

[20] EH 5.25, GCS 9.1, 496.

the paschal date for congregations from Corinth to Spain, gets lost in the mail.

The Irenaean "plot" has determined what will *not* appear in this section; fourth century categories have dictated how the letters were originally read. Yet Eusebius chose the other two excerpts not for their exemplary nature, richness of information, clarity, or even rhetorical vigor. They were selected because their authors chanced upon an argument that produced something Eusebius loves dearly: lists. Lists of bishops, apostles, martyrs, any important Christian figures showing the living link to Jesus and the apostles abound in the EH, as Eusebius is "eager to preserve the successions from the especially distinguished apostles of our Savior in the prominent churches." There is no information in this introductory section that Eusebius could not have gleaned solely from the letters themselves, or even from the excerpts. Eusebius has manipulated the texts, but not to tell a different story about paschal observance. His "historical treatment" is a catalogue entry prefaced by a brief introduction giving just enough information to evaluate the role of Irenaeus.

2. Letter from Polycrates of Ephesus

The foil for Irenaeus' approach to peacemaking is provided by a scathing letter from Polycrates of Ephesus putting Victor in a singularly poor light:

> These [bishops listed] issued the single definition which was given above; but the bishops in Asia were led by Polycrates in insisting that it was necessary to keep the custom which had been handed down to them of old. Polycrates himself in a document which he addressed to Victor and to the church of Rome, expounds the tradition which had come to him as follows:

> "Therefore we keep the day undeviatingly, neither adding nor taking away, for in Asia great luminaries (στοιχεῖα) sleep, and they will rise on the day of the coming of the Lord, when he shall come with glory from heaven and seek out all the saints. Such were Philip of the twelve apostles, and two of his daughters who grew old as virgins, who sleep in Hierapolis, and another daughter of his, who lived in the Holy Spirit, rests at Ephesus. Moreover, there is also John, who lay on the Lord's breast, who was a priest wearing the breastplate, and a martyr, and teacher. He sleeps at Ephesus. And there is also Polycarp at Smyrna, both bishop and martyr, and Thraseas, both bishop and martyr, from Eumenaea, who sleeps in Smyrna. And why should I speak of Sagaris, bishop and martyr, who sleeps at

Laodicaea, and Papirius, too, the blessed,[21] and Melito the eunuch, who lived entirely in the Holy Spirit, who lies in Sardis, waiting for the judgment[22] from heaven when he will rise from the dead? All these kept [Οὗτοι πάντες ἐτήρσαν] the fourteenth day of the Pascha according to the gospel, never swerving, but following according to the rule of the faith. And I also, Polycrates, the least of you all, live according to the tradition of my kinsmen, and some of them have I followed. For seven of my family were bishops and I am the eighth,[23] and my kinsmen always kept the day when the People put away the leaven. Therefore, brethren, I who have lived sixty-five years in the Lord and conversed with brethren from every country, and have studied all Holy Scripture, am not afraid of threats, for they who were greater than I have said, "It is better to obey God rather than human beings" [Acts 5.29].

He continues about the bishops who when he wrote were with him and shared his opinion, and says thus:

"And I could mention the bishops who are present whom you required me to summon, and I did so. If I should write their names they would be many multitudes; and they, knowing my feeble humanity, agreed with the letter, knowing that not in vain is my head grey, but that I have ever lived in Christ Jesus.[24]

Polycrates' communion of Asian saints – resting, lying, sleeping, waiting, and very *present* – imbues the Quartadeciman practice with the power of the eschaton, transforming the usual euphemisms for death into a powerful testimony for the Asian practice. Asians will follow this apostolic witness, Polycrates implies, until the end of time. Polycrates' list of "stars," followed by the non-list of multitudinous bishops, comes at the very end of the letter, the last paragraph before some formulaic closure. Eusebius found this passage interesting because letters to a Nicaea-by-mail should bear more than one signature. In context, however, Polycrates implies that one bishop of Ephesus is enough to neutralize one bishop of Rome plus several Italic colleagues.[25] And if all the stars of

---

[21] Rufinus took μακάριον to be the name of another "star."

[22] Mohrmann, 157 f.

[23] Bishops within the same extended family were also quite common in Mesopotamia, Armenia, Spain, and the Nile Valley. "Under the hereditary system one might not get the best man for the job, but at least his election was not likely to lead to street fights." Chadwick, Henry, The Church of the Third Century in the West, 7.

[24] EH 5.24.7, GCS 9.1, 492.

[25] Protocol would require the signature of a number of bishops to respond in kind to a synodical letter bearing more than one signature. Andresen, Formular, 254 f.

Asia cannot outshine the martyr cult of Peter and Paul, the words of Peter from Acts 5.29 should at least give Victor pause.

The "therefore" at the beginning of the citation must refer to other proofs for the legitimacy of the Asian practice Eusebius chose not to quote. An excerpt from Apollinarios of Hierapolis in the *Chronicon* will gives some clues as to what these may have been. In many translations, however, an additional "καὶ" is added so the first sentence reads: "Also in Asia…"[26] implying that Victor had laid claim to the "stars" of Rome, Peter and Paul, if not specifically for the dominical practice, then at least for the authority of the Roman church. The former is the view of the later historians Socrates and Sozomen,[27] who, basing their sections concerning the paschal controversy on this passage, simply supply the argument. While this second καὶ is not part of the original text, it is not needed to make the inference. Polycrates mentions only those "stars" *buried* in Asia Minor, not those, such as Paul, who had worked there, or "Peter," who addressed a letter to Asian congregations. Polycrates could have easily brought forward these arguments, but it is rhetorically more astute to play the game by Victor's rules and still win.

Continuing this mirroring technique, another conjecture might be that these στοιχεῖα are an ironic wordplay against Victor's citation of Gal 4.10 (or its twin Col 2.20), where Paul rails against the Galatians for wanting to gaze at nonmetaphoric stars to determine the Hebrew calendar. This would be a much easier inference were there other traces of an anti-Judaic or anti-Judaizing argument reflected in the excerpt. But in what remains of the letter, there are none, and Eusebius would hardly have been the one to have removed them. Compared with the anti-Judaism of Nicaea, the second century controversy has a surprise in store. As much as a paschal celebration on 14 Nisan may seem quintessentially "Jewish" to modern scholars, no contemporary text preserved by either Eusebius or the *Chronicon* employs an anti-Judaic argument against the Asian practice. Historically, the Asians celebrated Pascha on the same day as the Jews, but not "with the Jews" in opposing rhetoric. This is not the case, however, when in the next generation the Quartadeciman practice becomes more and more associated with Montanists and other schismatics, becoming in the process not only "more ancient," but heretical.

---

[26] Lohse, Passafest, 114. Two καὶ's are a variant reading at EH 3.31.3, GCS 9.1, 264.
[27] Sozomen, EH 9.19.1, GCS 50, 330.

What Polycrates' letter does not reflect is what must have been Victor's major argument: a plea to celebrate the Pascha on the Lord's Day, supported by scripture and apostolic tradition. Yet Polycrates could scarcely be expected to attack a Lord's Day theology cherished by Romans and Asians alike. Apostolic practice, Johannine chronology, and a christological reading of Ex 12 are thus the only means to defend the paschal date, which is why Polycrates must imbue his catalogue of "stars" with as much rhetorical power as possible.

Past these suggestions, there is no point in further attempting to mirror Polycrates' letter to find what Victor might have written. Polycrates invokes the "rule of faith," his knowledge of the gospel and all scripture, his correspondence with theologians in other regions, his family of bishops, his age and grey hair, and the "multitude" of bishops whose names he will not bother to append. This barrage nicely furthers the Irenaen plot Eusebius has in mind.

3. Irenaeus' Letter to Victor, Part Two

a) Eusebius and the Texts

Eusebius continues his "historical treatment," now arranged as background for his Irenaeus story, with Victor's quite predictable reaction:

> Upon this, Victor, who presided in Rome, immediately tried to cut off from the common unity the churches of all Asia, together with the adjacent churches, on grounds of heterodoxy, and he wrote letters announcing that all the Christians there were absolutely excommunicated.[28]

This is as close Eusebius comes to letting Victor speak for himself. Yet even if Eusebius had found several letters from Victor, citing even one of them would only have delayed the plot Eusebius wishes to speed along. After the long excerpt from Polycrates, a summary must suffice. As Eusebius shapes the narrative, Victor is the antagonist the reader only sees in rhetorical mirrors: a threatening presence, alternately rash, presumptuous, narrow-minded, and disrespectful of his elders, in short, in dire need of correction. Yet Polycrates is as immovable as Victor. This elicits a response:

> But not all bishops were pleased by this, so they issued counter-requests to him to consider the cause of peace and unity and love towards his neighbors.

---

[28] EH 5.24.9, GCS 9.1, 494.

Their words are extant, sharply rebuking Victor. Among these too Irenaeus, writing as head in the name of the brothers in Gaul, though he says that the mystery of the Lord's resurrection should be observed only on the Lord's Day, nevertheless exhorts Victor in an appropriate fashion not to excommunicate whole churches of God for following a tradition of ancient custom, and many other things, continuing as follows:

"For the discussion is not only about the day, but also about the very form of the fast; for some think that they ought to fast one day, others two, others even more, some count their day as forty hours, day and night. And such variation of observance [ποικίλια τῶν ἐπιτηροῦντων] did not begin in our own time, but much earlier, in the days of those before us, who, it would seem, disregarding exactness, maintained a plain and simple practice, establishing it for the future, and nonetheless all these lived in peace, and we also live in peace with one another and the disagreement in the fast confirms our agreement in the faith."

He adds to this a narrative which I may suitably quote, running as follows:

"Among these too were the presbyters before Soter, who presided over the church of which you are now the leader, I mean [λέγομεν] Anicetus and Pius and Telesphorus and Xystus. They did not themselves observe, nor did they enjoin it on those who followed them, and though they did not observe they were nevertheless at peace with those from the congregations which it was observed when they came to them, although to observe was more objectionable to those who did not [καίτοι μᾶλλον ἐναντίον ἦν τὸ τηρεῖν τοῖς μὴ τηροῦσιν].[29] And no one was ever rejected for this reason, but the presbyters before you who did not observe sent the eucharist to those from other congregations who did;[30] and when the blessed Polycarp was staying in Rome in the time of Anicetus, though they disagreed a little about some other things as well, they immediately made peace, having no wish for strife between them on this matter. For neither was Anicetus able to persuade Polycarp not to observe, since he had always done so in company with John the disciple of our Lord and the other apostles with whom he had associated; nor did Polycarp persuade Anicetus to observe, for he said that he ought to keep the custom of those who were presbyters before him. And under these circumstances they communicated with each other, and in the church Anicetus yielded the celebration of the eucharist

---

[29] See below, p. 347 f.

[30] This may be the first attestation of the "frumentum": a portion of bread from the bishop's celebration sent to the *tituli* as a sign of unity. Cf. Innocent I, Ep. ad Decennium 5.

to Polycarp, obviously out of respect, and they parted from each other in peace, for the peace of the whole church was kept both by those who observed and by those who did not."

Adding the moral of the story, Eusebius now brings his narrative to a close:

And Irenaeus, who deserved his name, making a plea for peace in this way, gave exhortations of this kind for the peace of the church and served as its ambassador, for in letters he discussed the various views on the issue which had been raised, not only with Victor but also with many other leaders of churches.[31]

With this happy ending, the antagonistic force of Victor of Rome has been neutralized by Irenaeus, who imitates the eirenic etymology of his name not only with the Roman bishop, but with "many other leaders of churches." The Irenaeus anecdote that frames a Polycarp anecdote wins the reader. But there is no more mention of the "various views on the issue." Were there more than two? What about the other letters criticizing Victor in an *inappropriate* fashion? From whom? Was Irenaeus successful? Did Victor withdraw excommunication? What of the Asians in Rome? And what of the Asians in *Asia*? Some – but by no means all – of the answers to these questions may be deduced from Eusebius and other sources, but they lie totally outside this section of the EH. These are questions Eusebius did not believe his readers would ask, and he moves immediately from this brief encomium to another catalogue entry: a listing by title of Irenaeus' works. Except as a name in citations Eusebius makes from works of Hippolytus and Clement of Alexandria, i.e., more lists, this is the last mention of Irenaeus in the entire EH. So much for Irenaeus.[32]

By this point it should be fairly obvious that as much as Eusebius reads the second century as the fourth, he did not write a short *roman à clé* about the paschal dispute in his own day. For if he did so, he was utterly alone: no extant source concerning the Nicaean debate even hints at the earlier controversy. Irenaeus' solution was not adopted by Victor, just as at Nicaea neither Rome, Alexandria, nor the Bishop of Caesarea was prepared to permit the diversity for which Irenaeus so

---

[31] EH 5.24.9-17, GCS 9.1, 494 f.

[32] Actually, Eusebius' closing is a bit longer: "These are the writings of Irenaeus which have come to our knowledge." EH 5.26, GCS 9.1, 498.

eloquently pleads. Perhaps some Syrian bishop made an appeal to the earlier controversy as Firmilian did seventy-five years earlier, but for extant sources, all stemming from the Roman-Alexandrian "winners," the earlier controversy did not exist.[33] If lines between second and fourth century controversies must be drawn, then in Eusebius' mind they far more likely connect Irenaeus and Eusebius – in the other conflict at Nicaea. Eusebius urgently wished to see his part in the Arian dispute as eirenic/Irenean – a peacekeeping role that failed as miserably as that of the earlier Bishop of Lyon.

Thus if Eusebius edited this section after the Council's decision, as Brox, Grant, Petersen, et. al. maintain, he did so with a subtlety bordering on the invisible. Eusebius praises a solution diametrically opposed to his paschal treatise. "Apostolic" diversity did not win at Nicaea, but an "apostolic" uniformity Eusebius helped to achieve. Uniformity also won the day in second century Rome, encouraged by a letter from Eusebius' predecessor in Caesarea. The easiest "Nicaean" revision would have been to cite more of this letter with traditions "direct from the apostles." An excerpt, however brief, from the letter(s) of Victor would also have given the Roman bishop as ancestor of the Nicaean majority a human face to counter the distorted images refracting from the letters of Polycrates and Irenaeus. But that would have changed the narrative into something else.

b) The Second Century Level

Because this fragment is the only source that might yield information about the earliest paschal practice in Rome, usually with all post-Reformation associations intact, it has been subject to a type of microcriticism usually reserved for biblical texts. Microcritics also assume that the parties to this dispute had full knowledge of the earliest history of paschal observance, which, while not explicit in the texts, may be extracted by a variety of methods.

Irenaeus harkens back to mid-century for an anecdote about Polycarp, the human bridge to the apostolic age. Polycrates also invokes the Smyrnan martyr-bishop, whom he must have known personally. He enlists as well seven bishops in his family who had celebrated Pascha

---

[33] The Syriac *History of the Council of Nicaea* does not even mention the paschal question. See, or rather don't bother seeing, Braun, O., ed., trans., De Sancta Nicaena Synodo, Münster 1905 (dÜ).

"when the People put away the leaven." Not all Basils and Gregories, some members of this episcopal septet must have come from a previous generation, if not two. If Polycrates is 65 around 195, then he was born around 130. Perhaps Onesimus, the bishop of Ephesus "indescribable in love"[34] who visited Ignatius, also numbers among these seven. With the even more elderly Polycarp as proponent of the Quartadeciman practice, the Asian Pascha is documented at least to the final decades of the first century. At that point Polycrates' history begins to take on a legendary quality as it moves toward the apostolic age. In this, he is no different from leaders of other major centers who read the NT as closely as possible for stories of origins for their sees. But thanks to the providential longevity of two Asian bishops, also traditionally assumed for the composite figure of John the Apostle/Evangelist/Presbyter/Divine,[35] Smyrna and Ephesus have less time to cover with legends.

Late second century writers, however, yield little information about the earliest Christian communities between the Acts of the Apostles and the "apostolic Fathers." Other than Hegisippus, who supplied Eusebius with narratives about the early Jerusalem church, they often seem to compress the century between the martyrdoms of Paul and Polycarp as if it did not exist. In the same way, Jewish Christianity hardly exists for second century Gentile authors, and Judaic roots of Christianity, except in apologetic literature, are deeply buried. These rhetorical silences are connected. They are muted even more as background for lists of bishops or teachers leading directly to the apostolic age. It thus requires a major conceptual leap to assume that either Victor or Irenaeus knew anything at all of the earliest paschal practice in Rome or anywhere else, and it would be generations before the *Liber Pontificalis* discovers Hermas' angelic revelation. Yet even if Irenaeus' knowledge of Christian origins approached omniscience, the question is whether Irenaeus' "history" may be read in a way other than he intended rhetorically.

Modern scholars are correct in pointing out that the apostolic icons of Rome are not in the text. *But they are very much present in the minds of both the author and the recipient of the letter.* Irenaeus does not invoke the tombs of Peter and Paul or any of the rhetoric of the dominical party because he is writing to its leader. Why reinforce Victor in what

---

[34] Ignatius, Eph 1.1, SUC 1, 142.

[35] Irenaeus, AH 3.3.4, cited Eus., EH 3.23.4, with corroborating testimony from Clem. Alex. John was supposed to have still been alive during the reign of Trajan (98-117).

he already thinks, when there is all the more reason to downplay it? Instead, Irenaeus switches codes: rather than apostolic rhetoric, he gives instead a bit of real history, a list of bishops, unpretentiously called presbyters,[36] who had maintained peace within the Roman community without demanding a unified practice. This history is then reinforced by a moral tale. Not only did a bishop like Victor not break fellowship with anyone either in Rome or Ephesus, but had "sent the eucharist to other [i.e. Quartadeciman] churches" in Rome, even yielding the most visible sign of his office, presiding at the eucharistic table, to a visiting Asian bishop.[37]

This anecdote is not meant to inform Victor – or eavesdropping moderns – of a relatively recent history Victor already knows and moderns are desperate to find out, or a more remote history unknown to either, but to persuade Victor to relinquish his hard-line position by placing him in the narrative. Irenaeus *is* writing a *roman à clé*. Anicetus is Victor. "The custom of those who were presbyters before him" (Anicetus), "who presided over the church of which you are now the leader" (Victor), is not just a particular way of celebrating Pascha, but a way of preserving the peace of the community. This is something Irenaeus knows. He does not know when, how, or whether various congregations in Rome celebrated the paschal feast in the apostolic age.

c) The List

During a visit to Rome in the 170's, the Palestinian Hegesippus testifies to interest in demonstrating unbroken continuity of apostolic teaching through a list of names reaching at least as early as Anicetus,[38] and the first traces of a Jerusalem list appear to be contemporary with Hegesippus' visit.[39] Irenaeus, signaling his list as somewhat of an afterthought by the verb λέγομεν, uses a partial list of Roman bishops whose full

---

[36] Irenaeus often uses this archaic terminology. See Mohrmann, Note, 160 f.

[37] DA 13 regulates this ritual of deference: "And if it be a bishop (i.e., who comes to visit), let him sit with the bishop .... And you, O bishop, tell him that he preach to your people. And when you offer the oblation, let him speak. But if he is wise and gives the honor to you, and does not wish to offer, yet let him speak over the cup." CSCO 408, 133.3-10. By this measure, Polycarp was either unwise or shown greater deference.

[38] EH 4.22.3, GCS 9.1, 370, makes no sense as preserved, as succession (διαδοχή) alone, not a list or determination of its existence, is the object of the verb ἐποιησάμην.

[39] Grant, Eusebius, 51.

336 THE ANTENICENE PASCHA

number, including Peter and Paul, had appeared some decade earlier in his antiheretical work. This list, compared to the one Irenaeus gives in his letter to Victor, is what has produced such an academic puzzle.

Since such lists often appear in tandem with an argument against a heretic whose pedigree cannot possibly reach back to the apostolic age, this rhetorical situation, coupled with the rise of the monarchial episcopate and the sheer passage of time, is likely identical to their history. Yet it is a decidedly *oral* history, and in the second century, the only history available. The original intent is historical, though not chronological.[40] "There was no interest originally in individual persons," Theodor Klauser wrote, "even less for the time in which these men lived. The list only had value as a whole, to the degree that it demonstrated a connection of contemporary teaching with the apostles."[41]

The list of Jerusalem bishops, fifteen each before and after the fall of Jerusalem to the time of Narcissus, had not been "chronologized" even in Eusebius' day. Since there was a legend that Simeon, son of Clopas, had been martyred as bishop at the ripe age of 120,[42] Eusebius was hard-pressed to make sense of the list from James the Just to 135. "About the years of the bishops in Jerusalem" Eusebius writes, "I have been unable to find any written report, but according to tradition, they lived only a short time."[43] Yet more than any other, the Jerusalem list witnesses to the rhetorical power of conjunctions to span historical and cultural discontinuity. The congregation of Aelia Capitolina (Jerusalem) was less than 35 years old when Hegesippus wrote, yet found itself surrounded by very historic geography. The bishops' list is designed to resolve this paradox.

Of all the lists, that of Rome likely preserves more "real" history than others. "From the middle of the second century on," Harnack wrote, "they are trustworthy, but even before this they are not worthless."[44] Yet before Eleutherius, even late second century authors could not verify the information. Irenaeus, for instance, links the name of Linus, the first

[40] Discussion of lists for Jerusalem, Antioch, and Rome, Grant, Eusebius, 45-59. Caspar, E., Die älteste römische Bischofsliste, Berlin 1926, alters Harnack's, conjecture of an early episcopal chronicle. The earliest names may not be those of bishops, but still those considered the "bearers of apostolic tradition." Caspar, 256.

[41] Klauser, Theodor, Die Anfänge der römischen Bischofsliste, JbAC.Eb 3, 1974, (121-138) 133, (=BZThS 8, 1931, 193-213).

[42] EH 3.32.1-5, GCS 9.1, 266 f.

[43] EH 4.5.1, GCS 9.1, 304.

[44] Harnack, Adolf, Über die Herkunft der 48 (47) ersten Päpste, SPAW[PH] 37, 1904, (1004-1062) 1046, n. 1.

name of the Roman list, to 2Tim 4.21.[45] The mysterious Anecletus, who appears as the second bishop of Rome, may be actualized from Titus 1.7,[46] but the name, while rare, does have inscriptional attestation, especially for slaves.[47] In later centuries, specific dates and other information, even country of origin and father's name, were then supplied by whatever means of conjecture or fantasy available.

Is Irenaeus' short list in his letter to Victor of the same genre? The division at "those before Soter" occurs elsewhere. The death of this bishop forms the division between Eusebius' books four and five, though otherwise, Eusebius uses the reigns of Roman emperors as well as the succession of bishops as markers of time. In his "apostolic" list, Irenaeus makes a break in the line of Roman bishops, this time at Anicetus and Soter:

> Clement was followed by Evaristus, and Evaristus by Alexander. The sixth bishop after the apostles was thus Xystus, after him Telesphorus, the glorious martyr, then Hyginus, Pius, Anicetus. After Anicetus was followed by Soter, now Eleutherius as twelfth successor of the apostles holds the office of bishop. In this order and succession, the ecclesiastical apostolic tradition and the preaching of truth has come to us.[48]

In his antiheretical work, Irenaeus is prepared to encode the Roman bishop's list with the very attributes – apostolicity, purity of teaching, etc. – that Victor had likely used in his letter to Ephesus. But except for knowing that Telesphorus was martyred, Irenaeus produces nothing more than a list of names framed to accent its value as continuous ordered tradition. The twelfth bishop after the time of the Twelve, a number reached only by omitting Peter and Paul, is an artful way of reinforcing the connection, prepared by a division at the sixth bishop. At the same time, Irenaeus, who as presbyter had brought letters from Gaul to Rome,[49] knew Eleutherius personally: the remote past starts with Soter.[50] For Eusebius, this could be nothing more than a literary convenience, but what of Irenaeus?

---

[45] An onomastic obsession is the hallmark of the tritoPauline Pastorals. See Kirkland, Alastair, The Beginnings of Christianity in the Lycus Valley, Neotest 29, 1995, (109-124) 118-120.

[46] Abramowski, Luise, Irenaeus, Adv haer. III.3.2...and...3.3, JTS 28, 1977, 101-104. Ἀνέγκλητος means "blameless, irreproachable."

[47] Caspar, loc. cit.

[48] AH 3.3.3, cited EH 5.6.4-5.

[49] EH 5.4.2, GCS 9.1, 434.

[50] Holl, Bruchstück, 217.

Karl Holl, and after him Wolfgang Huber,[51] interprets this watershed event as the first paschal feast ever celebrated in Rome. Yet Holl's idea that an anachronistically monolithic "Rome" did not celebrate the Pascha until Soter's time has no foundation except by reading Irenaeus' "rhetorical" list against the "historical" one. Holl does this to counter Duchesne's equally indefensible conclusion that the earliest "pope" listed, Xystus, had introduced Sunday observance across the Empire.[52] Both the French and the German scholar begin with the assumption of a single unitary "apostolic" Quartadeciman practice that then moved to the more Christian Sunday, and both are certain that Irenaeus' list gives information about when this move occurred. The Catholic maintains that Rome originated Sunday Pascha; the Lutheran counters with a Gentile Jerusalem practice after 135. This, of course, is the same problem the authors of the *Liber Pontificalis* sought to solve: how to flesh out liturgical history from the bare bones of a list of bishops.

For Thomas Talley, Holl's solution explains why Irenaeus "reports no similar claim to apostolic tradition on Anicetus' part, if in Irenaeus' mind, Anicetus was speaking in defense of a tradition of the Sunday Pascha with apostolic roots."[53] That Irenaeus' letter is not a neutral historical document, but a highly rhetorical letter to the bishop of Rome should answer this objection. Irenaeus' lists cannot be compared because each has a specific rhetorical objective which has shaped the text. The Asian lists says, "This is an apostolic practice," which, the Roman list says, "was tolerated among Roman congregations." Repeating the Roman list with apostolicity intact – as in AH – would have said, "Apostles at war." If Talley is correct, Polycrates would need no list at all, only recent memory, and the "custom of those who were presbyters before him" that Anicetus felt he ought to keep would have been a non-custom. Couching the Anicetus-Polycarp anecdote as defense and attack is exactly what Irenaeus wishes to avoid.

Perhaps the most remarkable tenet of Holl's thesis is its appeal to the most patently ahistorical bishops' list of the Antenicene period, that of Jerusalem, by reinterpreting a comment in Epiphanius' *Panarion* that has only one purpose: to rationalize the paschal decision of Nicaea. Unlike Sozomen, who thinks the rhetoric of both Quartadeciman and

---

[51] Holl, Bruchstück, 218. Huber, Passa, 56-61.
[52] Duchesne, 7. Hall, S. G., The Origins of Easter, StPatr 15, 1984, 554-567, attempts a synthesis: Soter was the first to introduce dominical celebration.
[53] Talley, Origins, 23.

dominical parties has no support from apostolic tradition, Epiphanius is certain that the apostles had ordained one way of celebrating the Pascha. Dominical Pascha is apostolic. Therefore the apostles must have observed it. The original custom that could not be maintained was not the Quartadeciman Pascha, which Epiphanius never acknowledges as ever having existed except in Montanist groups, but the Antiochene paschal reckoning. Holl has read Epiphanius and given modern "historical" values to terms such as "with the Jews" and "apostolic" to which Nicaean rhetoric had assigned different meanings.

Moreover, a congregation in a city resettled after a crushing military defeat such as Corinth, Carthage, or Aelia would not likely decide that this cataclysm was best met with liturgical innovation, which for some reason was then eagerly awaited by more established sees for adoption. If Aelia celebrated Pascha on Sunday after 135 CE, it did so because Caesarea and other sees on the Palestinian coast had not only supplied many of the new residents, but in the case of Caesarea, episcopal oversight still in force even after the Council of Nicaea established the patriarchate of Jerusalem. Talley's[54] adoption of this theory is even more paradoxical given his approval of La Piana's study on the evolution of the Roman monarchial episcopacy from an earlier presbyteral organization. If there was no centralized authority until mid-second century who felt called upon to unify paschal observance for all Roman Christians, what authority in the first half of the century was able to keep those from other regions from celebrating the feast or teaching the "Romans" to do so?

Reading is an acquired skill, and along the paper trail behind Holl's and Talley's conclusions are an army of unquoted footnotes, all marching to their various drummers, all the way back to the French historian Tillemont at the beginning of the eighteenth century. As Lohse discovered, Tillemont did not merely content himself with repeating the findings of ancient historians.[55] The Quartadeciman tradition was a Jewish heresy found in those regions – Asia Minor, Syria, and Mesopotamia – with large Jewish Christian populations. The celebration of Pascha on 14 Nisan was a permissive move by the apostles, who celebrated Pascha on the Lord's Day, this being the apostolic practice.[56] Since the Pope

[54] Talley, Origins, 22 f.; so also Hamman, A., Valeur et signification des reseignements liturgiques de Justin, StPat 13.2 (=TU 116), 364-374.
[55] See Lohse, Passafest, 21 f.
[56] Lohse cites to Tillemont, t. 3, 104.

(Victor) in conjunction with bishops in Italy and across the church (proto-cardinals and archbishops) had condemned the Asian practice, then there must have been something doctrinally *wrong* with it. Familiar dichotomies are drawn – Jewish-Christian, East-West, heresy-orthodoxy – which, with or without the claim of Syrian celebration on 14 Nisan, still shape the dialogue. All of these minimal pairs are still capable of producing a great deal of rhetoric superficially more interesting than a disagreement over the day or date of Pascha. Texts from the paschal controversy achieve a kind of historical transcendence where they may symbolize many other conflicts, regardless of when or why they occurred.

Tillemont's thoroughly Western view attains a kind of overripe perfection in an article by a USAmerican Catholic scholar, Charles L. Souvay, CM.[57] The practice common to Rome, Palestine, and Alexandria is dutifully and falsely characterized after Eusebius as a πάσχα ἀναστάσιμον, while Asia Minor kept a πάσχα σταυρώσιμον, the Greek always giving the impression that this was a second century distinction.[58] "As a consequence," Souvay writes, "the former were rejoicing in the Lord whilst everywhere else their brethren were afflicting their souls" [45].[59] There were many immigrants to Rome, Souvay notes. "As foreigners in our American cities they flocked together," [45] but those from Asia were not "always the cream of the Christian fold":

> Rome seems to have been the mecca of heresiarchs of every ilk; and it is well known that Asia produced a plentiful crop of them; these naturally in the Eternal City cast their nets first among their Christian fellow-countrymen whom they met in their own religious assemblies, their *national Churches,* we might say. [46]

After the reader is prepared to regard Quartadecimans as foreigners huddled in ethnic ghettoes subject to sedition from abroad, Victor of Rome is characterized:

> Pope Victor gauged the situation exactly. He was an African, that is a Latin, with the Latin turn of mind for law, administration and order, and

[57] Souvay, Charles L. The Paschal Controversy under Pope Victor I. CQH 15 (NS 9) 1929-30, 43-62. Further citations in text.

[58] This error still being shown: Cabié, Robert, A Propos de la "Question Pascale": Quelle Pratique opposait-on à celle des Quartodecimans? EO 11, 1994, (101-106) 105 f.

[59] A transfer from Eusebius (and "Constantine"), Vita 3.5, 3.18, where joy and affliction refer to different times of the paschal fast. Irenaeus, of course, argues *from*, not *against* diversity of fasting practices.

a natural aversion for the hair-splitting and the mischief-laden dilatory compromises which are the pride of the eastern intellect. [52]

While the "foreign-native" construct may be of more recent vintage, this catalogue of xenophobic clichés has its roots in the Great Schism. I have always harbored a suspicion that this Latin love of law and order would never be drawn with such sharp lines if the Latin language had definite articles like modern vernaculars and had it not for centuries been taught with such grammatical precision by persons of little imagination. But none of these constructs, fortunately, has anything to do with Talley's conclusion. Souvay's highly rhetorical coda is where it begins:

A local friction became by the sheer force of uncontrollable circumstances a problem of the Church universal, and forced Victor to interfere with the customs of a whole group of Christian communities in Asia. About one hundred years before, Clement had already done so by his famous letter to the Corinthians. But after these one hundred years what a difference! Rome has actually become the center of the life of the Church: Rome is in correspondence with all the churches throughout the empire; to Rome letters are sent from abroad with the request that they be communicated to all. Yet more: Rome now holds a position and wields a power which are acknowledged abroad: for Victor writes to the provinces, requesting the holding of synods; and everywhere synods are convened; he threatens and then fulminates excommunication from the Church universal; bishops, to be true, express doubts about the opportuneness of this measure, but not one of them denies his right to do so, or thinks the Bishop of Rome has overstepped the limits of this right and assumed an authority hitherto unknown. What matters that the sentence was recalled? It is the principle that counts; and this principle is acknowledged on all sides. Christianity is no longer a loose aggregate of local communities: it is truly the Church Catholic, Apostolic – and ROMAN. Rome is the head with which, as Irenaeus then affirms in a well-known passage, "on account of its greater authority, must agree every church in which was ever maintained the tradition derived from the Apostles."[60] And the Bishop of Rome is the head of the universal Church, for, as Duchesne pointedly remarks after narrating the facts rehearsed above: "How are we to speak, if we are not allowed to call by the title of head of the Church him who wields such a power?"[61] We may not say with Renan: "The Papacy was born"; for the Papacy was born more than one hundred and sixty years before in the plain of Caesarea Philippi; but we may declare – and that is what he meant: – "The Papacy had reached man's estate." [61 f.]

[60] AH 3.3.2.
[61] Souvay refers to Duchesne, Églises Séparées, 144.

After this symphonic praise of the papacy, it is difficult to recall that the image of Victor projecting from the fifth book of the EH does not leap tall buildings in a single bound. So much for Eusebius. Yet as the citations suggest, Souvay's dialogue is with French Catholic historians, thus a citation at the very beginning of his article of Tillemont. Turning the "recall" of excommunication into a "principle" is aimed at those who suggest that since Asia Minor remained in fellowship with the church catholic (cf. Firmilian), Irenaeus, Gallicized into a local hero, must have persuaded Victor to withdraw his threat:[62]

> How from these most clear words can some historians, perhaps with more zeal for the spotlessness of a pope's escutcheon than for the artless candor of truth, extract with a slight of hand the conclusion that "the pope threatened excommunication against those who followed the Asiatic practice, but the Bishops (sic) of Gaul, especially St. Irenaeus prevented a rupture?" [57]

This rhetorical question is posed to a citation from the *Histoire de l'Église,* a French translation of the noted Trier historian F. X. Kraus,[63] who had elevated Irenaeus' role higher than Souvay was willing. Trier is ancient Augusta Treverorum in Gaul, and like many French historians, Kraus had a special interest in the role of Irenaeus. This conversation is also not important to Talley or Holl. But whenever an apologetic hymn was being sung about "Pope" Victor, albeit usually with less coloratura, Lutherans were listening.

A reaction from the other side of the Reformation requires only the voice of Hugo Koch, whose article written in 1914 was the first time that Irenaeus' bishops' list was unequivocal proof that Rome before Soter did not celebrate Pascha.[64] Lutheran footnotes to the paschal controversies do not go back to Tillemont, but to the Augsburg Confession,[65] which recruits Irenaeus' peacemaking effort for diversity in rite and ceremony, and to the Apology, where Melanchthon[66] agrees with

---

[62] Still Gustave Bardy's view, SC 41.2, 71, n. 21.

[63] Paris, ⁴1898, I, 205.

[64] Koch, Hugo, Pascha in der ältesten Kirche, ZwissTh NF 20, 1914, 289-313. Further citations in text.

[65] "The ancient Fathers maintained such liberty with respect to outward ceremonies, for in the East they kept Easter at a time different from that in Rome. When some regarded this difference as divisive of the church, they were admonished by others that it was not necessary to maintain uniformity in such customs. Irenaeus said, 'Disagreement in fasting does not destroy unity in faith.'" CA 26, Tappert, 70.

[66] See above, p. 288 n. 98.

Epiphanius about the Audians: harmony and "evangelical freedom" in matters liturgical are by far the more desirable good.

Beginning with an examination of Tertullian's "imprecision," Koch notes that such nomenclature does not point to a Triduum or Biduum [289-293] as many scholars had proposed, but only to fast and vigil. There was no "Good Friday" liturgy in Carthage. This correct deduction is obtained by a method that Koch will transfer to Irenaeus' letter. Koch takes Tertullian's arguments about the paschal fast, sets them against various hypotheses about liturgies observed in Carthage read into the text, then negates them. Only the fast remains. This will function equally well for liturgies that are not read into, but in Irenaeus' letter. Since Tertullian speaks more of the fast than the liturgy, Koch concludes that in the West, the fast was the more important ritual component [293]. The Montanist versus catholic history behind the greater rhetorical space Tertullian devotes to the fast does not hinder Koch from making the transfer.

The "Good Friday-Easter" dichotomy is not derived directly from Eusebius, but from a letter preserved in Cyprian's correspondence from the Roman Celerinus to the North African Lucius, which speaks of "dies laetitiae Paschae."[67] Thus in Rome, Pascha was a "day of joy" [297]. If this is the case at mid-third century, then also in the second. Days of fasting are not joyous days, as anyone can see in Tertullian's works.

Moving to the disagreement between Polycarp and Anicetus, Koch sees the difference between "those who observe" and "those who do not" to be greater then than when Irenaeus is writing. With Holl, Talley reads the same way. "Why," Talley asks, "does Irenaeus say that the Quartadeciman practice was 'more opposed' to the practice of Victor's predecessors from Xystus through Anicetus ... than it was in the situation confronting Victor?"[68] But this isn't what Irenaeus says:

...καίτοι μᾶλλον ἐναντίον ἦν τὸ τηρεῖν τοῖς μὴ τηροῦσιν.

...although more contrary/opposed/(quite literally) "in your face" was the observing to those not observing.

In context, Irenaeus does not say that the difference *then* was greater than *now*, and it would have been awkward to make such an aside in the middle of his "historical" example. Practices of different times are not

---

[67] Cyprian, Ep. 21.2, CSEL 3.2, 530.
[68] Talley, Origins, 21.

being compared, but attitudes. The contrast here is between Quartadecimans and those who fast until the paschal eucharist on Sunday, the
same situation then as now. It is perhaps *objectionable* when different
congregations observe different customs, but under normal circumstances, feasting is *more objectionable* to a fasting person than fasting to
one who feasts. Even so, no one was rejected *then*, and they should not
be *now*. The adverb μᾶλλον modifies the opposition in reference to the
attitude of non-observers. Observance (of the Quartadeciman date and
its earlier fast) was more objectionable to Sunday "non-observers" (than
non-observance was to observers).

After rehearsing the variety of fasting practices, Koch notes:

> And there were, Irenaeus may have continued, those who do not keep any
> paschal fast. And to those actually belonged the Roman bishops up to
> Soter (Anicetus, Pius, Hyginus, Telesphorus, and Xystus), who did not
> themselves keep a paschal fast and yet got along with those from other
> churches in which a paschal fast was held, although "observing" was more
> opposed to "those who did not observe." [300].

Here, we have not yet reached Holl and Talley, but Theodor Zahn,[69]
along with a scholarly interpolation into Irenaeus' letter for which there
is no room. "No fast" is not an option in Irenaeus' list any more than
"no liturgy": the "very form" of the fast now includes an invisible, non-
existent variant. The essential unity of Pascha as fast and Pascha as
liturgy is momentarily dissolved. Now returning to the ground prepared
by his North African texts, Koch reunites them:

> Under Anicetus the difference was much greater than under Victor
> because the Roman church did not hold a paschal fast at all, they did not
> celebrate Pascha at all. [301]

This is the end of the trail, and also where Holl and Talley arrive. But
to see why this particular trek was undertaken in the first place, the
surrounding landscape still needs to be described. Now addressing the
later second century controversy, Koch points out that Polycrates celebrates 14 Nisan "according to the *written* gospel" [306]. After reviewing
the findings of various scholars, Koch finds that the Asians are really
commemorating the institution of the eucharist with a liturgy, to which
the Romans are opposing a recently instituted fast with neither eucharist

---

[69] Zahn, Theodor, FGNK 4, 1891, 286-303.

nor liturgy, all projected from Tertullian's Montanists [307 f.]. Koch could not know Melito's sermon, which is completely devoid of eucharistic references, but there is also not a single text until Origen and the *Didascalia* where the Pesach frame of the supper is acknowledged in a non-polemical setting, much less placed at the center of a liturgy. Yet in Koch's mind, Rome is leading a battle against the sacrament and the Words of Institution enshrined in the paschal night. Although their practice also differs from other provinces who celebrate on Sunday, the Romans joined the common movement against the Asians to achieve some political agenda. Further, since there is no second καὶ in Polycrates' letter, Victor not only did not call forth the Roman icons Peter and Paul, but he couldn't even if he so desired. This dual ancestry was only later contrived to counter the impressive pedigree of Ephesus [311]. Nevertheless,

> [i]n the paschal controversy it was impossible for it [the Roman church] to call on Peter and Paul, even if this appeal were already well known, since in Rome, as Irenaeus knew, there was absolutely no paschal celebration until Bishop Soter.

> "Πειθαρχεῖν δεῖ θεῷ μᾶλλον ἢ ἀνθρώποις" This is the first time in the history of the church that this word, which was first directed against the orders of a similarly "divinely instituted" Jewish hierarchy, were set against Roman claims. [311]

With the briefest hint of anti-Judaic polemic now aimed at the Council of Trent, the scholarly mask begins to fall. The authority of Rome rested solely in its agreement with the rest of the churches *against Asia*, and Polycrates is hardly acknowledging "canonical obedience" to Rome. The strong need to show Roman bishops as hopeless losers forces Koch to reread the conflict between Cyprian and Stephen over heretical baptisms. That Asia Minor congregations later remained in the Great Church as much as Cyprian's Carthage represents a "loss" for Rome. A composite of the early "papacy" comes into focus:

> The domineering Bishop Victor of Rome took the first test of strength and – was defeated, as in the third century Bishop Stephen was defeated in the second test of strength against Cyprian and the Asians. The ἀποκόπτειν περᾶται of Eusebius (EH V, 23) tells of the first defeat of Rome. [312]

Koch then concludes his article:

> The behavior of the bishops in the paschal controversy is proof of how little communion with Rome meant communion with the whole church

or a rejection by Rome an excommunication from the church catholic; how little a Roman claim was valid for the whole church as canon law; how little bishops saw in a Roman decision a res iudicata, how little they renounced an independent investigation and decision of an ecclesiastical question. In the whole of Christian antiquity, there was no "Roma locuta, causa finita," also not for Augustine, to whom the idea of this sentence is often attributed. [313]

It does not requires Solomonic wisdom, or even Jonathan Smith's *Drudgery Divine*, to discern that the rhetorical codas of both Souvay and Koch also have something to do with the way they do their schoolroom Greek and Latin in the body of their articles. Eusebius' Irenaeus story becomes a Pope story, with disastrous results. Even though a more ecumenical spirit has mostly put an end to such naked displays of confessionalism, the constructs used to reach these mutually exclusive narratives live on. That several Catholic scholars have adopted Holl's position – all of them French representatives of Souvay's bête noire, Gallic historians (and liturgiologists)[70] – does not detract from "the artless candor of truth." Had Irenaeus' letter been written to a bishop of some other city, it would never have been subjected to such acribious scrutiny, nor its grammar and rhetoric dissected as far beyond "idiotism" as a dead language could allow.

The first time this text proved that Rome, unlike the "rest of the world," did not celebrate Pascha until Soter, it had been thrown against Tertullian and a third century letter from Rome to show the unity of fast and liturgy and the "joyous" character of the Roman Pascha. Fastdays are not joyous days. Therefore Romans did not fast in the days of Pascha. If they did not fast, they also did not celebrate the liturgy. But then in Victor's time they fasted, but with no liturgy. When Holl picks up the argument to use against Duchesne, bishops' lists had already been read as liturgical history. This has a certain naive charm in the *Liber Pontificalis*, but not here. All of these leaps in logic are prodded by a Protestant reaction to Catholic apologetics: the sum of any calculation of fast and liturgy will always come out zero. Rome, not Asia, is deficient, and since this cannot take the form of orthodoxy, orthopraxis must take its place. Constructs deriving from other conversations – from USAmerican paranoia of recent immigrants, Gallic patriotism, rhapsodic loyalty to the

---

[70] Richard, Marcel, La question pascal au IIe siècle, OrSyr 6, 1961, 212-221; also Hamman, Valeur et signification, and most recently: Cabié, Question Pascale.

papacy, the Great Schism, the Reformation – have found their way into this text and directed the act of reading. The text will always say *something* when forced to take part in these dialogues, but this type of mimesis overpowers Irenaeus' rhetoric with centuries of noise.

The reason for the differences in Irenaeus' lists is rhetorical purpose: to establish a pattern just long enough to impress the last number in the series. Earlier presbyter/bishops had accepted "observers" with a tolerant hospitality that Victor should emulate. "Those who came to them" may once have come from Asia Minor, but for generations they have lived next door. Christians "Asian rite" were not successful in placing one of their own upon the bishop's throne, but they had not been marginalized from the beginning by an indigenous "Roman" community of which they were historically, though with Victor not rhetorically, a part.

Perhaps in Anicetus' day, there was a discrete community of Asian Quartadecimans with such cohesiveness that they remained a distinct group in the two generations or so until Victor. But what social forces would have kept them that way among Christians, also Greek-speaking, as "foreign" as they, in an urban population up to 90% of non-Latin origin?[71] Except for their religion, which could often be hidden, and economic or social status, which could not, neither race, language, nor land of origin would have been impediments to life in the imperial capital. Souvay silently assumes a Latin majority in the Roman church, who then inexplicably retained Greek as their liturgical language until the fourth century.[72] In short, this community was catholic long before it was Roman.[73] Irenaeus is attempting to maintain this catholicity – and its inherent diversity – as marker of communal identity.

d) Observing and Not Observing

Irenaeus uses a word for "observing" (τηρεῖν) with no direct object, which has led to an academic fixation over what object may be implied:

---

[71] Polomé, Edgar C., The Linguistic Situation in the Western Provinces of the Roman Empire, ANRW 2.29.2, 1983, (509-553) 510.

[72] Klauser, Theodor, Der Übergang der römischen Kirche von der griechischen zur lateinischen Liturgiesprache. Studi e Testi 121, 1946, 467-482 (=JbAC Eb 3, 1974, 184-194); Lampe, 117-119.

[73] "It is not an exaggeration to say that the Church of Rome became very early the great laboratory of Christian and ecclesiastical policy." La Piana, George, The Roman Church at the End of the Second Century. HThR 18, 1925, (201-277).

the feast of Pascha itself,[74] the paschal fast,[75] the 14 of Nisan,[76] or more generally "the day."[77] Since Polycrates uses the same term with the object "the fourteenth," Christine Mohrmann, arguing that this word is also something that Irenaeus brought with him from Asia Minor, finds no correspondence in Hellenic sources referring to ritual. Even in Christian authors, the usual term for "keeping" the Pascha, she discovered, is "doing" it: ἀγεῖν τὸν πάσχα.

Except that the word comes from a "Jewish" milieu, Mohrmann does not draw any conclusions from her comparison to NT texts. Yet these occurrences point to literature either composed in Asia Minor or anciently held to have been: Jn (8.51 f., 9.16, 14.23, 14.15, 15.10), 1 Jn (2.3-5, 3.22 f., 5.3), Rev (12.17, 3.10, 14.12), Acts 15.5, 1 Tim 6.14. The attestation in other NT works is sparse: James 2.10, Mt 19.17, Mk 7.9. The direct objects are rarely Judaic ritual such as the Sabbath (Jn 9.16), but rather the Law or the new commandments of Jesus. Second century examples come from Barn 10.11, where the δικαιώματα, precepts of righteousness, i.e., commandments, of Christ are to be observed. For the Roman Hermas, fasting and good works are also "observed."

Mohrmann neglects an important usage in Justin, disguised as his rhetorical "shadow" Trypho:

> I also know that your teachings in the so-called gospel are so sublime and great that I believe no one can follow them, for I have read them with interest. But we cannot understand that you, although you wish to be God-fearing and believe in an election before the rest of the world, still do not withdraw and live apart from the Gentiles and that you do not observe either the feasts or Sabbath... [μήτε τὰς ἑορτὰς νήτε τὰ σάββατα τηρεῖν][78]

Since the first half of Justin's dialogue is concerned with a rite-by-rite destruction of Judaic ritual in Judaic scripture, it is no wonder that Brox could say that even in Irenaeus' letter the word "takes on a polemic color."[79] If so, Irenaeus' letter would be the last place to find it, and the

---

[74] Text above, p. 330.

[75] So Campenhausen, Osterfasten? The "very form" would then be formless.

[76] Mohrmann and "the rest of the world." See CQL, Intro., 10.

[77] Richard, Marcel, La Lettre de Saint Irénée au Pape Victor, ZNW 56, 1965, 260-282.

[78] Dial 10.2 f., Goodspeed, 101.

[79] Brox, Tendenzen, 306.

"new commandments" of Christ would be "observed" with some other verb. In the late second century the word *may* have become specific to paschal observance, but this narrowing is not necessary to understanding its use, and may even obscure the kind of conversation that gave rise to such vocabulary.

There is, after all, a certain illogic to match the ellipsed accusative. Unless one agrees with Talley, Holl, et. al., no one could accuse the Romans of "not keeping," since they "keep" Pascha, but on Sunday. The disagreement is about ritual observance, but the language of dispute employs a different and, as Mohrmann suggests, a more ancient grammar. If so, then the verb also recalls when Ex 12 and its christological reading were successfully being employed to further the observance – *on this one point of ritual law*. For the implied direct object of τηρεῖν is more properly Ex 12.18 according to the letter understood as "new commandment," the festival according to its reading as "mystery."[80] Thus it is a word pointing not just to a particular practice or day, but to a whole constellation of possible objects orbiting about the canon.

This, of course, is Polycrates' main argument. The same canonical status of Ex 12 in Melito's homily drives Polycrates' unmistakable use of canonical language: the day is observed neither "adding nor taking away," Polycrates has "studied all the scriptures," the practice is "according to the gospel" and the "rule of faith," and he closes with "It is better to obey God rather than human beings." Can there be any question of where this divine command is found?

Somewhere behind this word lies a confrontation between, say, the Asia Minor Deutero-Paul of Colossians and one of the ancestors of Polycrates. When they spoke of shadows and truth, there would be much agreement. Yet the direct object of the verb τηρεῖν would have been the object of considerable dispute. This was the first paschal controversy of all, for which this single word may be the only literary witness.

4. The Geography

Eusebius' geography only refers to the letters he examined, the "very many more" taken on the usual Eusebian scale of hyperbole to mean

---

[80] Hippolytus uses τηρεῖν negatively with the object "letter of the Law." See below, p. 368 f. This is probably what Victor understood, regardless of what Irenaeus meant.

"several."[81] While these other letters may have been helpful to a history of the paschal controversy, this was not the history Eusebius was writing. As at Nicaea, the Quartadeciman practice is positioned against "the rest of the world" for which no more examples are necessary.

Pontus. Though part of the Asia Minor peninsula, Pontus is a thin coastal plain separated from the mainland by high mountains. Roman roads linked Amastris to the principal cities of Asia Minor, and a major route from Tarsus to Sinope gave cartographers the idea that Asia Minor was narrower there.[82] Sunday Pascha could have travelled the same way. Yet Pontus was linked to the world primarily by sea, and Marcion, a shipping magnate born in Sinope, made his way not to Ephesus or Antioch, but to Rome. Sinope also enjoyed Roman citizenship long before Severus extended its privileges across the Empire.[83] Pontus was a strategic area for Roman attack against Persia, and veterans were often settled in the region. Dionysius of Corinth had been in correspondence with congregations in Pontus and in one letter mentions Palmas by name. Had the communities first established in this region celebrated Pascha on 14-15 Nisan, earlier letters from Corinth and new arrivals from the West may have persuaded them to transfer the feast to Sunday.

Gaul. From Eusebius' geography introduction, it is generally assumed that paschal practice in Gaul was uniformly dominical. Yet Irenaeus' letter speaks on behalf of congregations in at least two cities, Lyon and Vienne, both having close ties to Asia and Phrygia, to whom the letter concerning the martyrs of 177 CE was addressed. The whole point of Irenaeus' letter is that divergent paschal practices *in themselves* do not have to lead to division. With the wrenching experience of persecution still fresh, Christians in Gaul hardly needed liturgical uniformity to be cemented into a cohesive community. Why, after all, should Asian immigrants to Gaul have given up their practice so easily when those who chose to live in Rome did not? What sounds in Irenaeus' letter to Victor may be the collective voice of both dominical and Quartadeciman congregations who are quarreling neither with each other nor with Irenaeus as bishop.

In the race to point out Eusebius' revisionism, Norbert Brox follows Lohse in characterizing Eusebius' summary of Irenaeus' view of

---

[81] Grant, 25 f.

[82] Charlesworth, M. P., Trade-Routes and Commerce of the Roman Empire, Cambridge 1924 (repr. Hildesheim, 1961) 83. Tarsus was Syrian, not Asian.

[83] Harnack, Verbreitung, 756, n. 3.

Sunday observance as "highly inaccurate and tendentious."[84] No letter from Lugdunum would have so enthusiastically put forward a
practice adopted only when Irenaeus travelled to the West. Pier Franco
Beatrice[85] goes even further as he transforms Irenaeus and the *entire*
province of Gaul into Quartadecimans. Reading Irenaeus' rhetorical use
of the paschal meal against docetic christologies as paschal manifesto,
Beatrice assumes that the meal must mean Syn chronology, and Syn
chronology means Quartadeciman practice. The passage hardly permits such a reading:

> When he had then raised Lazarus from the dead (Jn 11.1-44) and the
> Pharisees pursued, he went to the city of Ephraim (Jn 11.47-54). From
> there "he went to Bethany six days before the feast of Pascha" (Jn 12.1), as
> it is written in Scripture. From Bethany he went to Jerusalem (Jn 12.12),
> ate the Passover, and suffered on the next day. Should they who brag that
> they know everything not know that the month in which the paschal feast
> is celebrated and in which the Lord suffered is not the twelfth, but rather
> the first, then they may discover this in Moses. It is therefore wrong when
> they declare the one year and the twelfth month, and they must either
> condemn their explanation or the gospel. At any rate, how should the
> Lord have only preached a single year?[86]

Only lightly harmonized to the Syn, the three Passovers of the
Fourth Gospel are put forward solely to counter the twelve aeons of
Valentinian cosmogony signed in the one-year ministry. If Valentinian theologians had found instead some significance in three Passovers,
then Irenaeus would have argued the reverse, but the meal would have
remained. Unless the paschal controversy so consumed Irenaeus' thoughts
that he is involuntarily engaging in this conversation instead of the one
with Gnostics and Valentinians, to which he devotes a work in five
books written over a long period and where this passage is found, then
the accent must lie on *manducans* pascha, not manducans *pascha*. Irenaeus mentions Jesus' eating the lamb, not because of the paschal frame
of the Syn supper, but because a docetic Christ would not have taken
food at any meal. So, too, Irenaeus reports that Jesus drank wine at the
wedding at Cana, and when he rehearses the words of institution, he

---

[84] Brox, Tendenzen, 299.
[85] Beatrice, Pier Franco, La lavanda dei piedi. Contributo alla storia delle antiche
liturgie cristiane, BEL.S 28, 1983, 37-40, 45-56.
[86] AH 2.22.3, SC 294, 219 f. "...et manducans pascha et sequenti die passus."

adds a similar motif, "...after giving thanks, he took the cup, *drank from it*, gave it to his disciples...".[87]

This passage is Synoptic, but the time frame is just as irrelevant to Irenaeus' presentation of the eucharist as Jesus' eating to his paschal theology.

Objections to Eusebius' summary, mild or extreme, evaporate if a fragment generally available since Harvey's edition is considered genuine. Ascribed to a letter of Irenaeus "to a certain Alexandrian," the text is preserved in the Syriac of Severus of Antioch (†538). Since Severus is an especially good witness to Irenaeus' writings, bringing 22 genuine fragments from AH, this ascription is not to be dismissed easily.

With slight variation in wording, the identical text made its way into an Arabic codex. Somewhere in the course of tradition, what was originally something like "in ancient times, bishop of Lugdunum, hearer of Polycarp, disciple of the apostles" was transformed into "Archaeus, after the disciples of the Lord, Bishop of Liptis,"[88] a city in North Africa suddenly presenting an apostolic pedigree by jumbling a few consonants and taking the Greek word for "old" as a personal name.

SYRIAC	ARABIC
From Irenaeus, Bishop of Lyon, who was a contemporary of the disciples of the apostle, Polycarp, Bishop of Smyrna and martyr, and thus worthy to be held in high regard, wrote to an Alexandrian[89] of the necessity of celebrating the Feast of the Resurrection on the first day of the week. He wrote in the following way:	*From Archaeos, who after the disciples of the Lord was bishop in the city of Leptis in Africa:* The Pascha should be celebrated on the Lord's Day,
For then in truth there will be a universal joy fully realized for all those who believe in life, and in each person are made firm the mystery of the	for it was then the joy of the church catholic was accomplished and each person destined to eternal life. For on that day, the mystery of the resurrection,

---

[87] AH 5.33.1, SC 153, 404-406. Cf. Epid 53. The curds and honey of Isa 7.14 ff. sign the incarnation.

[88] See Jordan, Hermann, Wer war Archaeus? ZNW 13, 1912, 157-160.

[89] The younger Grant sees this letter supporting dominical practice in Alexandria: The Fragments of the Greek Apologists and Irenaeus, in: Biblical and Patristic Studies (Mem Casey) Freiburg 1963, (179-234) 202. Grant now holds Alexandria was Quartadeciman. Apollinarios was not. Apologists, 90.

resurrection, undying hope, and the first fruits of the resurrection, when the Lord defeated death, the enemy of humankind, and that he and his flesh, raised from the dead, would die no more. Made incorruptible, mixed with the spirit and glorified, our Lord offered it (flesh) to the Father.[90]

of unchangeable hope, and of inheriting the kingdom was established. At this time, the Lord triumphed over humanity's enemy, death, having revived his body, which will never die any more but with the spirit continues on unchangeable. This is the body, enveloped in glory, which he offered to the Father when the gates of heaven opened to him.[91]

As the introductions to both versions show, texts cut out of context often unravel around the edges and become somewhat permeable: the color of the new context begins to bleed into the fabric of the original. Here the more protected center remains a tight interweaving of Lord's Day, resurrection, and ascension motifs. The Lord's Day is *the* holy day on which Christ rose and ascended into heaven, a day when the eschatological promises of joy, resurrection, and hope for eternal life are both accomplished historically and celebrated weekly in the church's worship. The victorious ascension of Christ in the flesh as the gates of heaven open for the King of Glory is remembrance, hope for the future of every believer, and made present to all in the paschal night.

This excerpt was brought into the christological discussions issuing from the Council of Chalcedon (451). This context is of more interest here because in the Syriac version, a typically Irenaean "mixture"[92] of Christ's divinity and humanity is being actualized to bolster a monophysite position. On the other hand, the Arabic version has preserved a more transparent allusion to the gates opening for the king of glory of Ψ'23(24).7, 9, which Irenaeus connects to the ascension at Epid 84 and AH 4.33.13.

None of this new coloration can turn Irenaeus into a monophysite any more than Pfaff's forgeries turned Irenaeus into an eighteenth century German Pietist[93] or Harvey's footnotes could transform him into

---

[90] Syriac Fragment 26, Harvey II, 456.

[91] Codex Vatican. arabic. 101, in Mai, Spic. Rom. III, 1840, 707; Latin trans.: Jordan, Archaeus, 157 f., OAK 31, 58 f., CQL 31, 51.

[92] See de Jong, Johannes Petrus, Der ursprüngliche Sinn von Epiklese und Mischungritus nach der Eucharistielehre des heiligen Irenäus, ALW 9, 1965, 28-47.

[93] Harnack, Die Pfaff'schen Irenäus-Fragmente als Fälschung nachgewiesen, TU 20.3, 1900, 1-69.

a nineteenth century Anglican opponent of transubstantiation.[94] Yet sometime before Chalcedon, this text had already been actualized to reflect the "heavenly sacrifice" so dear to the heart of Theodore of Mopsuestia,[95] or perhaps even by later Arians who had in turn actualized Theodore's theology to mirror their own. Note, for instance the similarities to an Arian fragment exegeting Eph 4.12:

> He ascended, then, with the *body* to his Father where he been before, and as the acceptable sacrifice, he offered his *body* to our Father, receiving his seat at the right hand, from thence he shall come again in glory and power to judge the living and the dead and give to each according to his works.[96]

In an explanation of recapitulation through the incarnation of Christ, Irenaeus also alludes to Eph 4, in a sentence that rivals its deuteropauline model in lack of "idiotism":

> This is the reason why "the Lord has given us a sign" "in the depths and in the heights" without humanity (homo=ἀνθρόπος) having "demanded" it [Is 7.14, 11 f.], for as it could hope to behold a virgin conceive and bear a son, and to behold in him the "God with us," – who descended to the earth [Eph 4.9 f.], who searched for the lost sheep [Lk 15.4-6], which was, of course, of his own fashioning, and "ascended to the heights," to offer and commend to his Father the humanity he had found again, he himself having risen as firstfuits from the dead [1 Cor 15.20], – so that as the head, the rest of the body of humankind who, after the determined time of damnation for its disobedience, had received life, joined and knit together in every ligament [Eph 4.15] through the act of God, just as every member has its particular and proper place on the body, for as there are many mansions with the Father, so there are many members of the body.[97]

A generation after Irenaeus, Hippolytus offers a slightly different version of the same Ephesian motif, that at Christ's ascension, he "brought humanity as a gift to God"[98] as fulfillment of the offering of the new grain to usher in the harvest at Lev 23.15-21.[99]

---

[94] The sparse notes of Harvey's 1857 edition (II, 205-209) become thick proving Irenaeus thought of the eucharist as a 19 c. Anglican – without the sacrifice of the mass.

[95] See Bruns, Peter, Den Menschen mit dem Himmel Verbinden. Eine Studie zu den katechetischen Homilien des Theodor von Mopsuestia, CSCO 549 (Subs. 89), 1995, 359-370.

[96] Arian Frg. 21, CCSL 87, 261.

[97] AH 3.19.3.3, SC 34, 336 f.

[98] "...καὶ τὸν ἄνθρωπον δῶρον τῷ θεῷ προσενέγκας..." Full text below, p. 369 f.

[99] Even more explicit in a fragment of the paschal treatise by Clement of Alexandria preserved in the Chronicon Paschale. For text, see below, p. 366.

Harnack termed the motifs of this letter fragment "gängig" (common, run of the mill).[100] Compared to what? For a rhetorical history of the Pascha, Irenaeus' letter to an Alexandrian is extremely valuable, for it is the only text from the second century to give any sense of why Pascha should be celebrated on the Lord's Day, rather than why it should or should not be observed on 14 Nisan. With ample support from the NT and new mimetic readings for Lord's Day texts, such arguments were often and vigorously made, especially in the letters Eusebius cites or mentions. Yet since fourth century readers would have found such rhetoric as "gängig" as Harnack, it has disappeared with the rest of second century paschal literature. These very arguments, however, must have been the ones to persuade Christians "Asian rite," including Irenaeus, to abandon the full moon for the Lord's Day.

Antioch and Edessa. The most glaring absence, and puzzling presence, concern Western and Eastern Syrian traditions. Antioch, one of the four "apostolic" sees, is not mentioned at all, while, a letter had come from Osrhoëne "and the churches there," though no bishop is named. Walter Bauer[101] claims that Antioch had no influence at the time over congregations in its vicinity, the churches of Syria uniting under Jerusalem and Caesarea. Completely opposite to this view, Jaroslav Pelikan holds with R. M. Grant that the "real" conflict was between Rome and Antioch, the "two sees of Peter," and Eusebius had suppressed information concerning a Quartadeciman Antioch still at issue at Nicaea.[102]

The most plausible reason for the omission of Antioch without calling upon the deviousness of Eusebius is that in the archives he researched, no letter had been preserved from or to Maximinus, bishop after about 188. Since another voice from "the rest of the world" is unnecessary for what Eusebius has in mind, he did not bother to obtain this information if he did not already know it. This only means a copy of such a letter did not make its way either to Alexandria, Caesarea, or Aelia, and Rome had not sent a copy to any of these cities. Another possibility is that no letter was ever written. The see may have been vacant between Maximinus and Serapion, who assumed the office before the turn of the third century.

---

[100] Harnack, Geschichte der frühchristlichen Litteratur I, Leipzig 1893, 776, n. 14.
[101] Bauer, Walter, Rechtgläubigkeit und Ketzerei im ältesten Christentum, BHT 10, ²1964, 28. A more accurate view, Harnack, Verbreitung, 663.
[102] As in Pelikan, Two Sees.

As for Antioch, during the Persian invasion and the forced immigration of large numbers of Christians to Mesopotamia, including Bishop Demetrianus, in the year 256, and again in 260,[103] the first thing on everyone's mind was not likely preserving the episcopal archives for posterity. This major break in the history of Christian Antioch is another fact in which Eusebius shows no interest, but it does give Ephrem and Aphrahat clearer theological antecedents than might otherwise be found in early Syriac Christianity.

Osrhoëne, on the other hand, Bauer theorized, should not be in the list at all. A heavily Jewish-Christian area,[104] if Christians were in Edessa in 195,[105] they would have been Quartadeciman, and they would not have had a bishop. Bauer,[106] followed by Rouwhorst, points out that Rufinus did not include the notice about Osrhoëne in his Latin translation. The conclusion: Osrhoëne was not listed in the early manuscript Rufinus had at his disposal but was a "linguistically clumsy addition of a later hand, who missed Edessa and the surrounding region" in Eusebius' list.[107] Why the sudden concern of clumsy editors for a region no longer part of the Roman Empire? Clumsy though they were, these interpolators were both swift and thorough, since every extant Greek ms. of Eusebius' work contains the notice. In the Syrian translation, Mesopotamia is listed, but Pontus is missing.[108] That the one is significant and the other meaningless depends, of course, on who is reading the text and why. Rufinus' mangling of the translation of Irenaeus' discussion of fasting practice does not inspire trust; his appearing in tandem with Walter Bauer does nothing to alter this impression.

Bauer was a master of the argument from and of silence,[109] and when it was not there, as in the case of Eusebius' list of letters, it was created.

<hr/>

[103] Downey, Antioch, 309: "...the Persians were careful to take the leader of the Christian community so that he might reconcile his people to their fate and keep order among them."
[104] So Barnard. L. W., The Origins and Emergence of the Church in Edessa during the First Two Centuries A. D., VigChr 22, 1968, 161-175.
[105] The grave inscription of Aberkios (Phrygian, end of 2 c.) mentions crossing the Euphrates (Nisibis) and finding "brothers" there.
[106] Bauer, Rechtgläubigkeit, 14. Harnack, Verbreitung, 680, has no difficulties with the mention of Osrhoene.
[107] Bauer, loc. cit. Cf. Rouwhorst, Nisibe. VigChrS 7.1, 130.
[108] See German translation by Nestle, TU 21 (NF 6), 1901, 208. Palmas is mentioned.
[109] "Is it a coincidence that all these areas (e.g., Egypt, Syria-Antioch, Edessa) remain untouched by the paschal controversy and see no reason to take a position, or does this not show their disinterest in questions which move 'the church'?" Bauer, Rechtgläubigkeit, 79.

Since the first chapter on Edessa is the flagship of Bauer's thesis of ubiquitous "heresy" before "orthodoxy," he takes pains to break Edessa's connection to Antioch, to downplay Antioch's second century role as a major see, and generally to isolate Edessa from the mainstreams of Hellenistic culture. Antioch's lessened role is easily understandable, Bauer asserts, in view of the "intellectual mediocrity" of Theophilus and the "helpless position" of Serapion in his confrontation with the *Gospel of Peter*.[110] Few inscriptions in Greek are found, Bauer notes,[111] and since Chrysostom does not once mention Edessa, this is proof positive for how loose the connections still were between the two cities,[112] which, after all, lay a good 300 km apart.[113]

What Bauer does not mention is that these 300 km stretched across one of the oldest and most lucrative caravan routes of the ancient world, the "silk road." There was no direct route from Jerusalem through the desert, and anyone travelling to Edessa had to pass through Antioch to get there; beyond lay the riches of Persia, India, and the Far East. Drijvers[114] has also addressed the myth of the "Jewishness" and the supposedly pristine Semitic nature of Edessan Christianity.[115] Called the "Athens of the East" because of its famous school,[116] Edessa was no stranger to Hellenistic culture and language, and Christian impulses likely came quite early from Antioch.

As far as bishops "in Osrhoëne and the cities there" are concerned, if Eusebius has no qualms about turning Philo's Therapeutae into Christians celebrating the paschal vigil,[117] then it would require far less for Eusebius to transform names of which he knew nothing – missionaries, presbyters, or other ecclesiastical leaders – into authorities speaking for a unified practice in a unified church east of Antioch. This may be Eusebius' reading of the letter's context, but it does not impinge upon

---

[110] Bauer, Rechtgläubigkeit, 23.

[111] Bauer, Rechtgläubigkeit, 6.

[112] Bauer, Rechtgläubigkeit, 24.

[113] loc. cit.

[114] Drijvers, Syrian Christianity, esp. 128 f., 138 f.

[115] A view popularized by Arthur Vööbus.

[116] Drijvers, Syrian Christianity, 126. Every extant Christian work written between Antioch and Edessa in 2-3 c. is known in a Greek and a Syriac version.

[117] EH 2.17.21, GCS 9.1, 152. An Alexandrian borrowing, since Caesarea is mentioned in the NT. Since Philo also mentions "services" (διακονίαι) and "oversight" (ἐπισκοπή), Eusebius sees "the first proclaimers of the evangelical teaching and the original customs handed down by the apostles." EH 2.17.23 f., 152.

the existence of the letter itself. Whatever this notice means as ecclesiology, the text must stand as written. At the end of the second century a – not the – Christian community in Osrhoëne with ties to the West celebrated the Pascha on the Lord's Day.

II. Exegetical Conflict: Early Texts in the *Chronicon Paschale* and Other Sources

In the previous chapter, I suggested that after citing more recent sources – the letter from Athanasius to Epiphanius and a dialogue in the paschal treatise of Peter of Alexandria – the author of the *Chronicon Paschale* made use of a patristic florilegium gathered by the Alexandrian side for the Nicaean calendrical debate against Antioch. The *Chronicon* wishes to appropriate the "global decision" and authority of Nicaea for its own chronological and calendrical concerns and finds these excerpts tailor-made for the purpose. Complementing this florilegium, two texts from Hippolytus not found in the *Chronicon* exhaust the literature available for a history of the second century paschal controversy.

Noting that these fragments cannot be neatly arranged along Quartadeciman and dominical lines, Cyril Richardson poses the "riddle":

> We know that it (the controversy in Laodicea) had to do with the observance of Easter, and we know that notable Romans, Asiatics, and Alexandrines engaged in it and were all united in vigorously espousing the Johannine chronology. A curious situation indeed. At the very moment of the conflict between West and East on how to celebrate Easter and when to terminate the fast, we find the leading theologians of East and West alone immersed in a heated debate on Easter and concurring in pressing John's dating of the Passion. Can we make sense of this anomaly?[118]

Wolfgang Huber attempts to solve the riddle in a novel way. As much as his study brought needed correction to Lohse's findings, Pascha as eschatological idea is still so attractive that he must remove Melito of Sardis from the Quartadeciman camp.[119] This odd conjecture receives a

---

[118] Richardson, Cyril C., A New Solution to the Quartodeciman Riddle. JTS.NS 24, 1973, (74-83) 75.

[119] Huber, Passa, 31-45.

major assist by assuming as Richardson that chronology is the foundational issue in paschal disputes:

> If the defense of Johannine chronology was the chief content of a work directed against Melito, [i.e. by Clement of Alexandria], then Melito must have put forward Synoptic chronology; he thus stood on the side of those against whom Apollinarios of Hierapolis had polemicized. But since the Quartadeciman paschal celebration was bound to the observance of Johannine chronology, then Melito was no Quartadeciman; instead, he attacked in his work the Quartadeciman Pascha at one of its foundations, namely, the question of chronology.[120]

Following the directives of the *Chronicon*, this chain of conditionals also shows an understandable reluctance to look beneath chronology for reasons why sentient adults should be arguing about the menu of the Last Supper. But since the first "if" must be answered in the negative, the rest of the chain falls apart.

Richardson goes on to postulate a missing clue to the riddle: a group of Asian Quartadecimans who found exegetical support in Synoptic chronology and the paschal frame of the supper. The Passover meal "smacked of Judaism"[121] and so was countered with Johannine chronology by a group who wished to transform the festival into a commemoration of Christ the Protomartyr imitative of the observance proposed at the end of the *Martyrdom of Polycarp*.

Except for Richardson's novel suggestion of the role of MartPoly, a missing third link in the brief Laodicean chain of rhetoric is an inevitable result of collating the evidence. In this, Richardson has a nineteenth century predecessor with a particularly literal slant on what might have "smacked of Judaism" in a second Quartadeciman group. In 1848, K. L. Weitzel came to the following conclusion:

> In the final analysis everything resolves into an opposition between Judaism and Christianism, between a mixed-Jewish and a purely Christian significance of the paschal celebration. The one side had abandoned the type, which of course was no longer performed by the Lord in the year of his death; the other still maintains it, finding support in the last act of the Lord. As a result, the one side, as will be shown later, apparently even retained the lamb, and thus the Jewish form of the meal, which the other had completely cast off. For a chronological reason lying

[120] Huber, Passa, 40 f.
[121] art. cit. 84.

ultimately at the beginning of Christian history, the one side kept the fourteenth as a date, because here the type and its fulfillment converged; the other, because the object of celebration was simultaneously a continuation and expansion of the meal linked to this day in Mosaic Law, thus a purely legal reason, since for the Jewish element the νόμος was still valid. We thus have before us a division in the Quartadeciman camp: two groups of proponents of the fourteenth, catholic and Ebionite, not church standing against church, but the chief representatives of the church against an isolated party.[122]

Because of its unswerving consistency, this text attains a kind of perfection rare in contemporary scholarship. All rhetoric up to the Nicaean controversy – its anti-Judaism, its battle against the eucharistic Pascha, Origen's accusation of "Ebionism," the progress from Jewish "mixture" to "pure" Christianity, a "Christian" Rome and Alexandria triumphing over a rhetorically isolated "Jewish" Antioch – has not only been read as pure history, but read right back into the second century conflict, including a ritual meal of lamb.

Oddly enough, using Laodicea as the dumping ground for this rhetoric rescues Polycrates, Melito, and Apollinarios from every taint of Judaizing. The "pure" Quartadeciman Pascha may then embody major tenets of Pauline and Johannine theology in an observance perfectly mirroring the liturgical ideals of Friedrich Schleiermacher:[123]

> We cannot fail to recognize that we have here [in the dominical Pascha] the originally apostolic and strictly traditional festival type, which, as it determines the aesthetic character of the Christian paschal moments totally according to the personal feelings of the Twelve, has not yet been elevated to the universal understanding of the death of Jesus in its dogmatic, soteriological aspect as reconciling death and as the initial point of the transfiguration of Jesus, and thus not to an expression of this understanding in its festal observance.
>
> It is quite different, however, with the church of Asia Minor. Its chief founders Paul and John have elevated themselves to a universal, more free dogmatic position; this predominates in these two, – also in John, who

---

[122] Weitzel, K. L., Die christliche Passafeier der drei ersten Jahrhunderte. Zugleich ein Beitrag zur Geschichte des Urchristenthums und zur Evangelienkritik, Pforzheim, 1848. A Christian lamb dinner also served in Greenslade S. L., Schism in the Early Church (Cadbury Lectures, 1949-50), London 1953, 100 f.

[123] See Albrecht, Christoph, Schleiermachers Liturgik, Theorie und Praxis bei Schleiermacher und ihre geistesgeschichtlichen Zusammenhänge, VEGL 13, 1963.

certainly not without reason entered the Pauline mission field. Personal feelings have been intimately joined in his free spirit with more general, dogmatic views. From the original Christian events of which he was a witness, a richer faith, a thoroughly formed Christian consciousness [christliches Bewußtsein] was developed, which lies before us in his gospel and first epistle, just as the sharply developed Christian consciousness of his fellow apostle in Asia in the Pauline letters. The church of Asia Minor also is based on this more free and general dogmatic understanding. Thus for this church the commemorative week of those saving events was not only to be a complete imitation [Nachbild] of personal sentiments originally awakened in the apostles, and as such a form of consciousness already present at that time, but much more the image [Abbild] of that religious idea given voice in those events, an expression of that meaning which those events had for the salvation of humankind and the transfiguration of the person Jesus.[124]

This remarkable interpretation contrasting pietistic imitation of grieving apostles with that of a sublime religious idea to further "Christian consciousness" stems from Weitzel's understanding that the West was more concerned with the fast as mourning Christ's death. The East was concerned with the proper historical date, 14 Nisan, but had risen from such specificity to the universal religious idea – in short, Eusebius' Good Friday-Easter dichotomy translated into nineteenth century Protestant discourse. This high praise for a feast without a trace of Justin's "carnality" is also designed to rescue the apostolic authorship of the Fourth Gospel, whose "Quartadeciman" chronology had been attacked by F. Chr. Baur and other Liberal Protestant theologians of the Tübingen school.[125] As counterploy, Weitzel has shown that the Quartadeciman Pascha was the ultimate Liberal Protestant festival.

Similarly echoing the avid interest in eschatology of Protestant theology in post-war Germany,[126] Strobel also finds a third party to the Laodicean dispute.[127] They are *solar* Quartadecimans, a practice attested only for fourth century Montanists.[128] Discarding the lunar calendar, these groups celebrated according to the Asian calendar either on the fourteenth day of the first spring month or the fourteenth day after the

---

[124] Weitzel, Passafeier, 81 f.
[125] For overview of 19 c. Protestant scholarship, see Lohse, 21-26.
[126] See above, p. 111 f.
[127] Strobel, Kalender, esp. 389-392.
[128] Sozomen, EH 7.18.12-14, GCS 50, 329 f.

equinox, that is, either 25 March or 6 April, or the Sunday following. But Strobel claims a much longer history:

> We maintain that along side the lunar Quartadeciman celebration, which with a claim of the oldest apostolic tradition is scientifically demonstrable in the second century, there was also a Christian solar Quartadecimanism, equal in importance and probably tradition, whose origins are also to be sought in the Oriental church, perhaps even in a distinct heterodox Jewish milieu.[129]

These groups, whom Strobel obviously does not limit to the Montanists, calculated the Pascha by the Asian recension of the Roman solar calendar and at the same time were heavily influenced by that ubiquitous cultural force, the calendar of Qumran.[130] These solar groups were the target of polemic that falls outside a two-party scheme, and in Strobel's eyes, their shadow reaches into almost every source relevant to paschal disputes other than Eusebius' letter fragments and the EpAp, which Strobel reads as a lunar Quartadeciman text.[131] All texts dealing with the equinox, even those of Anatolius' Hebrew worthies,[132] are really talking about the Essene calendar, and the Quartadeciman practice, abandoned by Asia before Nicaea, had mysteriously spread to Syria and Mesopotamia.[133] Since this new twist to Jaubert's theory is convenient to Thomas Talley's understanding of the origins of the Christmas-Epiphany festivals as "contradated" six months away from either 25 March or 6 April, it is no surprise that the USAmerican scholar has adopted most of Strobel's views.[134]

Richardson is correct that there was a third party involved in paschal questions from the end of the second century to Nicaea, but not the "Synoptic" Quartadecimans he projects from the rhetoric, not Huber's Synoptic Melito, and not the Jewish ritual survivalists whose lamb dinner sullied Weitzel's "pure" Christianity. Nor are they the solar Quartadecimans

---

[129] Strobel, Kalender, 352.
[130] Strobel, Kalender, 449: The 2-3 c. Christian tendency to a fixed Easter date was probably "spurred on or encouraged by the older example of the Jewish Essenes."
[131] Strobel, Kalender, 288 f. The section on "The Montanist Question," (167-224) is answered by recruiting the Paschal Computus of psCyprian Clem. Alex. Strom 1.145.1-146.4 (only a Gnostic?, 189), and Trikentios, with additions from Peter by giving the formulaic φησίν a personal subject (202, n. 1,2,3).
[132] Strobel, Kalender, 211-213.
[133] Strobel, Kalender, 389-392.
[134] Talley, Origins, 6-8.

reworking the Qumran calendar whom Strobel reconstructs as the magic key. The third party to the dispute is the *Chronicon's* rhetorical shadow that Eusebius and most everyone after him has omitted: the see of Antioch and its reading of the Syn meal narrative.

Even though the issue is always the *time* of paschal celebration, the language of debate is not "chronology" or calendrics as the *Chronicon* has cast the dispute, but whether Jesus of Nazareth ate the Pesach meal as the Synoptics, the *Diatessaron*, and the *Didascalia* depict. When this must be admitted because of the canonical status of the gospels, then the question moves to whether the meal narrative may legitimately be used as an aetiology for the paschal feast. The Fourth Gospel is given an important role in these disputes, not because of its sublimely transcendent "Christian consciousness," but because it is the sole canonical gospel with two important characteristics: it has no institution narrative and it sets the date of Jesus' death to 14 Nisan. This leads to identical proof texts for completely different purposes. As Origen removes the Antiochene reading to substitute his own Philonian διάβασις to the spiritual life, so Apollinarios of Hierapolis and Hippolytus: the Asian because of Quartadeciman investment in 14 Nisan as the day when the mystery of Pesach was fulfilled on the cross, the Roman because of an equal investment in 14 Nisan as both birthday and death day of Christ in a cosmic scheme.

1. Apollinarios of Hierapolis

Chronologically, the first witness the *Chronicon* summons is Apollinarios of Hierapolis, a contemporary of Melito of Sardis not listed among the stars of Asia. Perhaps Apollinarios was as long-lived as Polycrates and thus could not yet be promoted to stellar status. Serapion of Antioch, who died in 212, writes of Apollinarios as "most blessed,"[135] so he cannot have lived much longer than the turn of the third century. Cantalamessa[136] maintains that the work was occasioned along with Melito's treatise by the discussion around 166 in Laodicea. Chronology and geography are conducive to such a theory, and Apollinarios as bishop of a nearby city was certainly a participant along with Melito and unnamed others.

---

[135] EH 5.19.2, GCS 9.1, 480.
[136] CQL 141, note b., See also L'Omelia, 75.

The first excerpt begins by restating the exegetical argument of the opposing side:

> There are some, however, who because of ignorance stir up disputes about these things, yet what they do may be excused, since ignorance does not deserve blame but rather requires instruction. They say that the Lord ate the sheep with his disciples on the fourteenth and suffered on the great day of Unleavened Bread, and they explain Matthew's words according to their interpretation. Yet their opinion is contrary to the Law, and according to them, the gospels contradict one another.[137]

To follow the *Chronicon's* directive and treat this passage as dealing solely with chronology, one must read straight through the main point of Apollinarios' opponents: "They say that the Lord *ate the sheep* with his disciples." If this meal is the Pesach, then it naturally takes place on 14 Nisan, at least until gospel chronology gains such remarkable elasticity in the third and fourth centuries. The date, however, is purely incidental to the meal. Matthew's passion narrative is being used as an aetiology for the Pascha, and the meal is of vital importance. The opponents whose position Apollinarios has restated are not those from the West who celebrate Pascha on the Lord's Day, but those in the "Orient" who also observe the Pascha on Sunday: Antioch.

With this brief citation the chief difference between Nicaea and earlier controversies comes to the fore: an incredible lack of civility in the fourth century. After the standard claim that opponents are in it only for the fight, Apollinarios takes a very reasoned approach, pointing out that this view is merely a faulty exegesis he is only too happy to correct, primarily by removing the supper from the Quartadeciman date. If Pascha is passion, it cannot be Pesach, at least not by the calendar. His argument is first "historical" or legal: either the Joh meal on 13 Nisan is not Pesach or, as Cantalamessa suggests, Apollinarios alludes to a prohibition of executions on the day of a feast.[138] Then comes both a logical and a confessional argument: the gospels cannot contradict one another. How Apollinarios further extracts himself from this exegetical corner is not cited.

The second excerpt is a hymn to 14 Nisan as Pascha:

> The fourteenth is the true Pascha of the Lord, the great sacrifice: the Son of God instead of the lamb; the one bound who bound the strong one [cf.

---

[137] Apollinarios, ChrPasc PG 92, 80D-81A.
[138] CQL 141, n. 'c.'

Mt 12.29]; the one judged, "judge of the living and the dead" [Acts 10.42]; handed over to sinners to be crucified; raised upon the horns (sic) of the unicorn; whose sacred side was pierced; who poured out of his side the double cleansing, water and blood [Jn 19.34], Word and Spirit; and who was buried on the day of the Pascha with the stone placed over the tomb.[139]

In this passage, NT material has taken over the foreground from the Pesach institution narrative: Jn 19.34 has the force of a baptismal aetiology in harmony with the earliest ritual interpretation of Ex 12. This use of the NT, as well as the rhetorical vigor of the passage, would have naturally appealed to a fourth century compiler. Yet the concentration of NT allusions indicates a position closer to Irenaeus than Melito – and to the NT-based arguments of Apollinarios' opponents. Otherwise, Apollinarios is firmly within the Asian tradition: the Pascha of the Lord is the cross. Apollinarios is not arguing against Quartadecimanism solar or lunar,[140] but supporting 14 Nisan against the Antiochene tradition. If these fragments accurately reflect the controversy at Laodicea, then the issue was shoring up the Asian tradition against dominical Syrians stirring up "disputes over these things" either present at the meeting or extending their influence into Asia Minor.

2. Clement of Alexandria

Of all the now lost paschal treatises, perhaps the most mourned should be that of Clement of Alexandria, not because of any quality of this writer-philosopher, but because of the nature of his work, as Eusebius reports:

> And in his book *On the Pascha*, he acknowledges that he was constrained by his companions to transmit to posterity in writing traditions that he happened to hear from the early presbyters; there he mentions Melito and Irenaeus and some others whose explanations he has also set down.[141]

This is Eusebius' summary of Clement's preface, which included a standard "command performance" to write the book. Given Clement's great joy in lengthy citation, this work if extant could have neatly outlined the paschal theology of the second century. Though the two

---

[139] Apollinarios, ChrPasc, loc. cit.
[140] So Lohse, 20, n. 1; Grant, Apologists, 90.
[141] EH 6.13.9. GCS 9.2, 548.

excerpts in the *Chronicon* bring a similar deconstruction of the Pesach frame of the meal narrative as in Apollinarios, no opponent is immediately visible on the horizon of the text:

> In the celebrations of previous years, the Lord ate the paschal victim sacrificed by the Jews. But after he preached, being himself the Pascha, the lamb of God, led like a sheep to the slaughter, he immediately taught his disciples the mystery of the type, on the thirteenth, the day on which they asked him, "Where do you wish us to prepare for you to eat the Pascha?" [Mt 26.17]. On this day, you must know, occurred both the sanctification of the unleavened bread and the preparation of the feast. Thus John records that suitably on this day the disciples had their feet washed by the Lord as a preparation. The passion of our Savior took place on the following day, himself being the paschal victim offered in pleasing sacrifice by the Jews.[142]

Further proofs from John are brought in the second excerpt:

> This is why on the fourteenth, the day on which he suffered, the high priests and scribes, having brought him to Pilate early in the morning, "did not enter the pretorium so that they might not be defiled but might eat the Pascha" [Jn 18.28] unhindered in the evening. All the Scriptures harmonize and the Gospels concord with this precise reckoning of the days. The resurrection too testifies: he rose on the third day, which was the first of the weeks of the harvest and the day on which the priest was commanded by the Law to offer the sheaf [Lev 23.10-11].

Clement grants that Jesus celebrated the Pesach according to Law before his public ministry, but the meal the night before he died was an enacted parable of Ex 12 as passion narrative a day before the actual event. This is an extension of the "shadow-reality" construct explaining the Pesach frame of the meal, which Clement extends to the "sanctification of the unleavened bread": the "preparation" was the footwashing. This enacted parable was in answer to the disciples' request for preparation for the Pascha at Mt 26.17, whose unambiguous literal sense invariably requires a side-stepping exegesis to maintain the historicity of both accounts. The institution of the eucharist was the "mystery of the type," but it was not revealed in a Pesach meal. The only connection between the eucharist and Ex 12 is that both are mysteries signing the death of Christ. The cultic nature of the institution narrative

---

[142] ChrPasc, Pref., PG 92, 82 BC.

is maintained, even with a baptismal connection through Jn 13, but it has been removed from both the date and rituals of Pesach. Even if this is done with the utmost civility, the Syrian reading is shown to be directed toward the wrong "mystery."

Further extending the Pesach ritual as passion narrative, Clement finds a place for the waving of the new sheaf of grain of Lev 23 to signal the harvest of the firstfuits of the dead. "All the scriptures harmonize and the Gospels concord" because OT texts have been read more closely into the gospels than in the Asian tradition. Clement attempts to excel the Asians at their own exegetical game. His close reading yields an aetiology for Sunday, the day after the Sabbath, which is designated in Lev 23 for the omer ceremony. A plea for Sunday celebration to reflect this "harmony" probably did not wait long in Clement's exegesis.

3. Hippolytus of Rome

Hippolytus may not have been born when the debate at Laodicea took place and was likely still too young to be heard in the paschal controversy 195. Even if the issues did not disappear immediately, Hippolytus learns the language of paschal controversy secondhand. There are two different practices addressed in fragments of Hippolytus' works. The *Chronicon's* compiler excerpted this text set against an aetiological reading of the meal:

> I see, therefore, that the matter is controversial. For he says, Christ kept the Pascha on that precise day, then died; therefore I too must do exactly as the Lord did. But he errs, not recognizing that at the time when Christ died, he did not eat the legal Pascha. For he himself was the Pascha which had been foretold and which was fulfilled on the day set for it.[143]

Being and eating the Pascha are mutually exclusive, but Hippolytus has restated his opponent's argument in all its "precise" and "exact" mimesis of the Syn meal narrative, the same tactic Apollinarios uses. Although this convergence between a second century Asian and a later Roman is the source of the "Quartadeciman riddle," rhetoric, not history, has generated the likeness. "That precise day" is the false cue which has brought a second Quartadeciman, or better, "Quintadeciman" group into existence, whether Weitzel's "isolated group" of low Christian

---

[143] ChrPasc, Pref., PG 92, 80C.

consciousness or the shadowy reflection cast by Strobel's solar Quartadecimans. This "precision," however, is exegetical, not liturgical. It is impossible that Hippolytus and Apollinarios were participating in the same dispute with the same people at the same time. Hippolytus was not at Laodicea, and his argument is not with a major see or even with someone he considers orthodox.

The compiler cuts the text so there is no antecedent for the pronoun, but not out of carelessness. A reference to the original historical context of any of the *Chronicon* excerpts would detract from their status as theological absolutes handed down "from those before us." Since Hippolytus' text stems from the *Syntagma*, a lost anti-heretical work, this pronoun could refer to anyone from Syria/Mesopotamia beginning with Tatian, but an unsavory name would have deflected the excerpt from its new address: Antioch of the fourth century.

Again, what contrasts these earlier passages with later refutations of Antiochene paschal theology is their reasonable tone and a lack of anti-Judaic polemic. While the usual convention accuses opponents of mere contentiousness, for Hippolytus, the "matter" is controversial. Apollinarios' offer of instruction may be patronizing, Clement, as usual, is pedantic, but all exegetical arguments sound like politely negative reviews of Jeremias' *Eucharistic Words of Jesus*. Even in the early third century, this dispute is still an inner-Christian discussion without any attempt at polarizing Antioch into mimetic "Jews." Calendrical reform is still in its infancy, the "former custom" is in many places still observed, and Hippolytus' calendar offers only a small improvement. Moreover, if third century authors were to assign the "Jewish" role in the earlier controversy, it would be given to the Quartadecimans:

> [1] Certain others, however, of a contentious nature, of knowledge ignorant [ἰδιῶται τὴν γνῶσιν], and above all out for a quarrel, argue that one must observe the Pascha on the fourteenth day of the first month [Ex 12.18] according to the provision of the Law, on whichever day it might fall. They are thinking of that saying in the Law, cursed is the one who does not observe as prescribed.[144] But they do not notice that the Law was given to the Jews, who would suspend/kill [ἀναιρεῖν] the true Pascha, which then came to the Gentiles and was understood with faith and now is not kept [τηρούμενον] according to the letter [of the Law]. [2] They hold to this one commandment but ignore what the Apostle said, "I testify to

---

[144] Cf. curse for not observing Pesach, Num 9.13; the entire Law, Dt 27.26.

all who circumcise themselves that they are obliged to fulfill the entire Law"[Gal 5.3]. Otherwise they are in concord with everything the apostles handed on to the church.[145]

Hippolytus' last line blunts the rhetorical power of what in his day must have been the standard array of anti-Quartadeciman arguments, all dealing with a point of OT law. Hippolytus can only change the forms in which this argumentation is cast, one of which is now decidedly anti-Judaic. After the usual epithets of quarrelsomeness and ignorance, Hippolytus argues against the aetiological, or in his view, inconsistently legalistic, use of Ex 12, a commandment now properly understood in the Gentile church and thus not observed (τηρεῖν!) according to the letter, except by Quartadecimans. The Roman has taken the Asian canonical term and the myth of origins of the Gentile church always read in Ex 12 and turned them against the Quartadeciman practice. Barnabas' charismatic gnosis, in which the Quartadecimans are uneducated ἰδιῶται, has met Justin's argument of Jewish literalism. None of this will have been original to Hippolytus. The pun on "ἀναιρεῖν," however, is likely Hippolytus' own. By "suspending" the true Pascha on the cross, Jews have also "suspended" the true paschal observance.

Hippolytus' wordplay is much more subtle than his use of Gal 5.3, which rhetorically circumcises the Quartadeciman practice and places it firmly on the wrong side of a "faith-letter" exegesis of the Hebrew scriptures. This parting volley is prepared by a mock Quartadeciman anxiety over the divine curse hanging over anyone who does not obey the law. Otherwise, Hippolytus' is in full concord with Asian paschal tradition: the supercession of Pesach by Pascha, the reading of Ex 12 as passion narrative, and in a much milder form, Asian anti-Judaism, now turned against the Asians themselves.

This concord rings out quite loudly in a citation in Theodoret's Eranistes, attributed to Hippolytus' treatise on Elkinah and Hannah:

> Therefore there were three seasons [καιροὶ] in the year "pretyped" [προε-τυποῦντο] toward the Savior, so that he might fulfill the mysteries prophesied about him: Pascha, to show that it was he himself that would be sacrificed as a lamb and shown to be the true Pascha, as the Apostle says, "Our Pascha is sacrificed for us: Christ" the God; Pentekoste, to "presign"

---

[145] Hippolytus, Refutatio 8.18.1-2, GCS 26.

[προσημήνῃ] the kingdom of heaven, as he as the first ascended to heaven and brought humanity as a gift to God. [καὶ τὸν ἄνθρωπον δῶρον τῷ θεῷ προσενέγκας]¹⁴⁶

Though the excerpt breaks off before the third season, Georg Kretschmar¹⁴⁷ maintains that since Hippolytus is arguing from Ex 23.14,17, the third καιρός must have been the Feast of Tabernacles. With the ultimate harvest, the three festivals would then become stations in an allegory of salvation history. Yet characteristic of the new way of reading NT material for its aetiological value, 1 Cor 5.7 is not only a concise kerygmatic statement, but also a rubric, the first evidence of a long use of this scripture as proclamation, content, and commandment to celebrate the Pascha.¹⁴⁸ This "rubrical" mimesis may also not be original to Hippolytus, but it will not be much older.

A connection between the Pentecost and "first fruits" of the dead¹⁴⁹ figures in three writers observing Pascha on the Lord's Day: Hippolytus, Clement, and Irenaeus. Since Clement and Hippolytus place this motif within a Joh chronology, the offering of first fruits is not used as an aetiology for a *Day* of Pentecost in mimesis of Acts, but of the Joh ascension on the Sunday of the resurrection, with Christ bearing, according to Irenaeus and Hippolytus, humanity as a gift to God. The appearance of this motif in polemical contexts searches out an aetiology for dominical observance in the same exegetical territory appropriated by the Quartadecimans: OT cultic prescriptions first read christologically, then as aetiologies for liturgical practice.

This argument does not mean that the resurrection was a motif lacking in Quartadeciman paschal theology, but in their all-important text, Ex 12. Instead, using the same shadow-fulfillment hermeneutic for Lev 23.9-12 as second century Asians use for Ex 12, the "first fruits" typology addresses that motif to Sunday as the beginning of the Fifty Days:¹⁵⁰

¹⁴⁶ Hippolytus, In Elcanam et Annam (frag. in Theodoret, Eranistes) PG 83, 173A; GCS 1, 122; CQL 47, 78, omits the disturbing ὁ θεὸς.
¹⁴⁷ Kretschmar, Georg, Christliches Passa im 2. Jahrhundert und die Ausbildung der christlichen Theologie, RSR 60, 1972, (287-323) 307.
¹⁴⁸ Nine times in the paschal epistles of Athanasius. See index, CSCO 151, 117.
¹⁴⁹ Cf. 1Cor 15.23. J. van Goudoever, The Celebration of the Resurrection in the New Testament, StEv 3.2, 1964 (=TU 88), 254-259, find this aetiology in the NT.
¹⁵⁰ For of the Jewish debate concerning when the Fifty Days were to be counted, see Rordorf, Willy, Zum Ursprung des Osterfestes am Sonntag, ThZ 18, 1962, 167-189.

The LORD spoke to Moses: Speak to the people of Israel and say to them: When you enter the land that I am giving you and you reap its harvest, you shall bring the sheaf of the first fruits of your harvest to the priest. He shall raise the sheaf before the LORD, that you may find acceptance; on the day after the sabbath the priest shall raise it.

A mimetic reading of the new harvest did not arise solely as a Sunday foil to the Asian reading of Ex 12, but it likely helped persuade Asian bishops that Sunday observance was not only in harmony with "the rest of the world," but with a "spiritual" understanding of the scriptures far better than "observing" the letter in a single chapter. This vestigial smudge of Jewish nomism, Hippolytus implies, inappropriate to the otherwise impeccable Christian identity of apostolic churches, may be erased, and the chasm between law and gospel overcome, by transferring Pascha by at most six days to the following Lord's Day.

The rhetorical matrix underlying these fragments engenders not one dialogue, but several throughout the second and early third centuries about paschal theology and observance. Hippolytus echoes the dispute over "τὸ τηρεῖν" between Ephesus and Rome, reproducing this argument with an anti-Judaic twist. The Asian practice and its understanding of canon is at issue. But there is another dialogue between Ex 12 and the meal rite where Sunday Quartadecimans of Rome/Alexandria argue with Sunday "Quintadecimans" from Syria – about the Judaism of Jesus of Nazareth. Day or date is not at issue, but differing mimetic narratives directed toward the same practice. Apollinarios, however, is a liturgical Quartadeciman using the same arguments against Syrian paschal theology as it moves along the southern coast of Asia Minor toward the Quartadeciman heartland. The Bishop of Hierapolis is thus the first witness for what will become at Nicaea a particularly harsh anti-Judaic strategy against Antioch. In the dominical Quartadecimans Irenaeus, Clement, and Hippolytus, the sheaf typology is "old style" mimesis designed to negate the "very ancient custom" of Asia Minor. This rhetorical grid is not complete because no writer of the Asian Great Church could possibly attack Sunday observance without giving up the orthodox identity Hippolytus assures them. Any of these dialogues take on a more pointed edge when they are transferred to heterodox proponents of otherwise orthodox paschal theologies.

Perhaps others will choose to solve the "Quartadeciman riddle" differently. This solution, however, has the advantage of neither inventing theological and liturgical modes on flimsy or no evidence nor bolstering their existence by constant appeals to Eusebius' malice or stupidity. It also assumes that one of the major provinces of early Christianity and its most important see were not silent in paschal disputes before Nicaea just because Eusebius the anthologist did not include a letter from Antioch he may never have seen or may never have existed in the first place.

III. On the Margins or at the Center? Pseudo-Tertullian's Blastus and the Homily In sanctum Pascha

Reconstructions of early paschal disputes often include two texts this study has yet to give any "historical treatment." A cryptic note about a schismatic in second century Rome is so marginal it can only add or subtract a detail from the historical narrative. Yet whether the homily *In sanctum Pascha* (IP) lies closer to the center of the second century debate not only has important repercussions for dating and provenance, but is illustrative of the way texts may shed their contexts and gain new ones on their way to becoming rhetorical tools – in polemic and in scholarly prose.

1. Blastus in Eusebius and Pseudo-Tertullian

In a fragmentary third century[151] work falsely ascribed to Tertullian, a certain Blastus makes a brief appearance after Tatian and various Montanists:

> Besides these, Blastus adds himself to all of these, who wants secretly to introduce Judaism. Pascha, he says, may not be celebrated except according to the Law of Moses on the fourteenth of the month [of Nisan/April?].[152] Who does not know that the grace of the gospel is made empty if Christ is reduced to the Law?[153]

The "Jewish" role Hippolytus assigns the Quartadeciman practice becomes blatant in this text, written by an unknown author against an all but unknown heretic, whose "crypto-Judaism" consists of a divergent paschal practice. This suggests two alternatives. (1) The work was a later third century cabinet of heretical horrors written when Great

---

[151] CQL, 194. Altaner, 136, suggests Victorinus translated PsTert. into Latin.
[152] Finding a lacuna in the text, Kroymann adds "Nisan" or "April" after "month." This could also simply be "first."
[153] CCSL 2, 1410.

Church writers no longer needed to muffle their polemic against a mori-
bund Quartadeciman practice,[154] or (2) the work reflects second century
polemic against Blastus, who because of other divergences not reflected
in this passage, was cornered behind his "Jewish" paschal practice more
tightly than the orthodox. Whatever the case, this may be one of the
first instances where a full-blown anti-Judaic rhetoric is transferred to the
Quartadeciman practice. By the time these lines were written, Blastus is
dead and his following likely dissolved: even Epiphanius' compendious
work is silent about a "Blastian" heresy. Thus he may dismissed in a few
sentences. A full-fledged anti-Judaic argument is also economical. Hippolytus' anti-nomian argument had to apply thought.

A common assumption makes Blastus a native of Asia Minor or
Phrygia,[155] yet Eusebius' "historical treatment" does not strictly allow
such a finding:

> Again the enemy of the Church of God, who bears a deadly hatred of the
> good and loves evil and who can let no opportunity pass by to hound
> humankind, stirred up heresies against the church. Some like poisonous
> snakes slithered about Asia and Phrygia and praised Montanus as the Par-
> aclete and his devotees Priscilla and Maximilla as the prophetesses of Mon-
> tanus. The others rose up in Rome. At their head stood Florinus, who had
> laid down the ecclesiastical office of presbyter and beside him Blastus, who
> in the same way had fallen away. These had turned away many from the
> church and drawn them to themselves.[156]

As in Pseudo-Tertullian, this mention in Eusebius immediately follows
a condemnation of Tatian, but only because Tatian, the Valentinian Florinus, and Blastus were active in Rome at the same time that Montanism
"slithered" about in Asia Minor. Chronology is clear from Eusebius, but
not Blastus' theological position or provenance. He may have been
Asian or Phrygian, as all the other "foreign agitators" in this paragraph,
but he need not be. The commonly employed "lumping" technique,[157]
where heretical groups become an undifferentiated, and in Eusebius'
eyes, clearly Satanic, mass of evil, is yet again at work.

---

[154] Following E. Schwarz, Huber considers this stronger anti-Judaism may be the
result of a later 3 or 4 c. redactor. Passa, 73, n. 72.

[155] CQL 194, note a.

[156] EH 5.14 f., GCS 9.1, 458.

[157] This heretical "lump" did not lack as much differentiation as commonly held. It
did not include Valentinian as full-fledged Gnostics. See Edwards, M. E., Gnostics and
Valentinians in the Church Fathers, JTS NS 40, 1989, 26-47.

Later in the fifth book, Eusebius notes that Irenaeus wrote a treatise entitled *To Blastus concerning the Schism*.[158] There is no citation from this work to complement the extensive excerpt from Irenaeus' work written against Florinus, *Concerning the Ogdoad*.[159] The reason? Irenaeus knew the older Florinus personally:

> For when I was still a boy, I saw you in lower Asia with Polycarp. You had a glorious position at the imperial court and sought to gain Polycarp's favor...
>
> I can testify before God that if that blessed apostolic presbyter had heard such false doctrines, he would have cried aloud, stopped his ears and according to his usual custom cried out, "O great God, for such times you have preserved me, that I should experience such as this!"[160]

What may gleaned from this narrative is that Irenaeus did not have a made-to-order Polycarp story to admonish Blastus as he had Florinus and Victor, and that Eusebius, if he had read Irenaeus' treatise, did not find anything else there that would add to the Irenaen plot of the paschal controversy. Quartadeciman practice that had been long observed in Rome does not need to be introduced, nor would Irenaeus have written an entire treatise merely to correct Blastus' paschal calendar, for which Irenaeus otherwise pleads tolerance. Blastus also does not have to number among Souvay's foreign agitators in Rome. His equally Quartadeciman grandparents could have been born there.

Though these unknowns make a definite identification impossible, certain possibilities can be eliminated. Blastus is not the heretical antecedent of the missing pronoun in Hippolytus' *Syntagma* since the argument there is against the ritualization of the meal narrative, not Ex 12.[161] "Schisma" in the title of Irenaeus' work, coupled with a stronger anti-Judaism otherwise not used against the Quartadecimans in Rome or Ephesus, also indicates that the calendar was not the only issue involved, though this is the only factor mentioned in Pseudo-Tertullian. By this point, divergent paschal practice, as "apostolic" as it may have been historically, has become heretical.

Allen Brent[162] believes that these two texts are enough to confirm "our identification of him as the Quartodeciman representative in Rome, despite Eusebius' garbled account." Instead, this confirms our suspicion

---

[158] EH 5.20.1, GCS 9.1, 480.
[159] EH 5.20.4-8, GCS 9.1, 482 f.
[160] EH 5.20.5-6, 7.
[161] See above, p. 367. Considered as a possibility in CQL, 157, note 'a.'
[162] Brent, *Hippolytus*, 66.

that modern historians are as eager to historicize anti-Judaic polemic as ancient historians were to write it themselves. While N. Zernov[163] and Marcel Richard[164] argue that the schism of Blastus was the impetus behind Victor's letterwriting campaign that unleashed the controversy of 195, August Strobel[165] turns Blastus into the earliest representative of the Montanist solar Quartadeciman observance, reading the heretical "lump" as a positive identification. This scholar points to Tertullian's defense of Montanist "innovations" in *De ieiunio* 14.2-3, where Tertullian's opponents made use of Paul's condemnation of "days and months and seasons and years" in Gal 4.10.[166]

This testifies to anti-Judaizing polemic against Montanists some twenty years after Blastus was active in Rome. Yet polemic addressed to the Montanist calendrical "update" couches it as a violation of actualized OT law rather than a "Jewish" practice.[167] Nowhere does Tertullian suggest that the Montanist conventicle celebrated Pascha on a day different from the rest of Christian Carthage: an "innovative" paschal calendar in nowhere on the horizon in *De ieiunio*.

One reason Blastus is forced into the role of Quartadeciman ringleader is the need still to present the Asian practice in Rome as somehow *doctrinally* deficient. Why else should a differing day of paschal celebration lead to such conflict? The issue in Rome in 165 was the same as in Carthage in 207: episcopal authority to determine ritual practice. For this to occur, Quartadecimans in Rome need not have been "more opposed" even than Montanists and catholics were in Carthage. All that is required is a group identifying with a particular practice against a majority, or for a majority to label a minority with the distinctive practice, like the term "Quartadeciman" itself.

2. In sanctum Pascha

In the homily *In sanctum Pascha* (IP), eucharistic motifs, Origenist or otherwise, perform important rhetorical, structural, and theological

---

[163] Zernov, Eusebius, 35: Since the Roman majority failed to convince the Quartodecimans, "...under the leadership of Blastus, temporarily separated themselves from the rest of the Roman community."

[164] Richard, question pascale, 198 f. Blastus' opposition "...provoked Victor's decision to instigate a large inquiry..."

[165] Strobel, Kalender, 216-220.

[166] De ieiunio 14.2-3, CCSL 2, 1272 f.

[167] Text below, p. 404 f.

functions.[168] Not only does the homily as it is spoken in the assembly become a paschal meal feasting on the Word, but the entire œkonomia of Christ is the "festive table." This role given the eucharist is a novelty for the Asian tradition not found in Melito's homily (PP), or, for that matter, any other witness of the Asian tradition of paschal exegesis: the sacrament discovered in Ex 12 is always blood as baptismal seal, not the meal as eucharist. The IP homilist explores both,[169] at one point explaining the mimetic relationship between shadow, reality, and sign:

> [36] *Which is the Pascha, the Pascha of the Lord* [Ex 12.11]: Can the Spirit proclaim more clearly than this that the Pascha is not a type, not a tale, not a shadow, but truly the Pascha of the Lord?

> [37] *The blood as a sign* [Ex 12.13]: a sign, that is, of the future reality, first prefiguration of the true Spirit, an imitation of the great anointing.

> [38] *"I will see the blood and I will protect you"*: You, O Jesus, have truly protected us from a terrible ruin; you have extended your fatherly hands (on the cross), having caused divine blood to be spilled out on the ground with your care for Humankind; you have covered us with fatherly wings; you have removed from us the menace of your scorn and in exchange have given us from on high the firstfruits of reconciliation.[170]

Though he will do so later, the homilist has not yet connected the blood and water streaming from Jesus' wounded side to baptism, but chrismation has been linked securely to the cross as mimesis. The Christian kerygma, the homilist points out, is not mimesis, being neither type, narrative, or shadow, but is the reality to which both the paschal blood of Ex 12 *and* chrismation point. The "great anointing" is the cross, not ritual, but Christian initiation is the place where the spiritual benefits of this death are conferred. This passage not only reflects the most traditional paschal motif in early Christian exegesis, but reflects *upon* it theologically. Once the mimetic relationship has been fixed, it can in turn become the object of discourse, a move not taken in earlier tradition, which is concerned with establishing the relationship in the first place.

---

[168] See above, p. 117.
[169] Cf. IP 15.1 f. The apotropaic power of baptism is stronger than in PP.
[170] IP 36-38, SC 27, 159 f.

a) The Mystic Song

Another comparison to Melito shows a further reworking of tradition. Like PP, the homily divides into two sections: a typological exegesis of Ex 12, in IP verse by verse, and a proclamation of the mystery of Christ from incarnation to ascension. But beyond this generic similarity common to virtually all Ex 12-based homilies, the likeness stops. The ambiguity between old and new, transitory and eternal, that structures the first sections of PP has become part of the IP homilist's exegesis and is simply declaimed.[171] The rhetorical highpoints of IP also have a completely different character: they are not dramatic, but lyric, coming in five hymnic passages of various lengths. The sermon ends with a reference to the Song of Miriam and Moses so strong it may be read as a rubric:

> Raise above us today your prize and grant us to sing with Moses the hymn of victory, for yours is the glory and the power, from age to age. Amen.[172]

The homily begins, however, with a hymn to light that Cantalamessa[173] sees as a precursor, both in genre and content, of the later *laudes ceres*:

> Lo, the sacred rays of the light of Christ are shining, the pure flames of the pure Spirit have risen and the heavenly treasures of glory and divinity have been opened.

> The great black night is swallowed up; by this light the somber shadows have been dispersed, and the tragic shade of death has itself been covered with darkness.

> Life penetrates all things, everything is filled with perfect light and the dawn of dawns fills the universe.

> For the one who is before the morning star and all the lights of heaven, Christ, the immortal, the great, the immense, shines above all things greater than the sun.

> For this one great, eternal, luminous day without sunset is instituted among all of us who believe in him:

---

[171] Cf. IP 2, SC 27, 119 f.; IP 9 f., 135-139. At 9.1, the Law is in a Philonian sense the "mystic imitation of the heavenly way of life" (μίμημα μυστικὸν τῆς ἐν οὐρανῷ πολιτείας).

[172] Cantalamessa, IP 63, SC 27, 191.

[173] L'Omelia, 96-108.

the mystic Pascha, celebrated in figure under the Law, accomplished in the reality of Christ, miraculous Pascha, wonder of divine strength, work of his power, true memorial feast of eternity.[174]

One ancient source of this light imagery is the moon of 14 Nisan, which as all full moons, rises at sunset so the sky is never truly dark. Yet once this hymn to light becomes a song to the *lumen christi*, the moon can wane by the Sunday following, but the song remains.

After Ex 12 as figure for the true reality of Christ is briefly introduced, another hymnic section is an exultant elaboration of the pathetic fallacy: all creation, the heavens, angels, archangels, the stars, air, the water of the sea, the land, "and the spirit of every human being celebrates, brought to life by the resurrection in a new regeneration."[175] Here, too, is the reason why the Song of the Three Young Men[176] is later sung at the paschal vigil, if not already by the homilist's time.

Later in the homily, the author returns to images of nature and spring, recalling earlier Jewish speculation on the Pesach:

The explanation which circulates privately among the Hebrews says that this is the time in which God, Maker and Artisan of the Universe, created all things and which was like the first flower of creation and the ornament of the world when the Creator admired the splendid work of art moving harmoniously according to God's Reason. This is based on the favorable conjunction of the stars, on the mildness of the season, on the regularity of the sun, of the rising of the full moon, on the rising of seed, on the growth of plants, on the sprouting of the rich florescence of the trees and on the birth of lambs in the flock.

For all the earth is recovered in green, the trees flower immediately to give birth to their fruits.

When the farmer, loosening the yoke from the plow, lets the neighing team rest, and having cast the divine seed in the earth, waits from on high the springs of heaven to open.

When the shepherd milks from the flock the white milk and the beekeepers gather the sweet honeycombs from the hives; when the happy sailor places his trust in the sea and faces the green wave, expecting gain from his art.

---

[174] IP 1.1-3, SC 27, 117 f.
[175] IP 3, SC 27, 121.
[176] Greek additions to Daniel, inserted between 3.23-4, vv. 29-68.

This regularity of all elements, this harmony of the universe, this – it may be said – good fortune is the prime and beginning of the universe, the beginning of the year cheered by the sweetness of the climate. I do not refuse to believe in this explanation. However, I believe firmly that it is because of the spiritual feast of Pascha that it has received the name of "first', the head and absolute sovereign of all time and every epoch, this month of Pascha, in which took place and in which is celebrated a great mystery.[177]

The IP homilist has begun to speak the "Egyptian" paschal dialect, augmented with a few stock images of spring. Pascha is a harmonious sign of rebirth and the beginning of the year. The praises of Philo for the full moon and the joys of spring are "privately circulated" because they are not contained in scripture as hymns to the paschal feast. This accent on the cosmos takes part in the same discourse as more arcane calendrical speculation, which attempts to match mathematics to cosmic mimesis – here in its decidedly non-polemical form. As far as extant sources may allow a conclusion, this type of timeless harmony emerges as a content of the paschal feast in Christian authors of the third century, not the second.

Perhaps the starkest contrast to Melito, the coda of the sermon is a hymn to Christ as Pascha, which reprises virtually every paschal motif employed in the homily:

O, mystical founding of the feast (χορηγία)[178]
 O spiritual celebration!
 O, holy Pascha!
From the heavens you descend to the earth
 and from the earth again you rise to heaven!
O holy joining of all things!
 O solemnity of all Creation!
 O joyous hymn of the universe,
his honor, celebration, and delight!
Through you dark Death has been destroyed
 and life is diffused through all things.
The gates of heaven are opened:
 God has appeared as human.
For you the gates of Hell have been ripped off their hinges
 and the iron chains have rusted away. [Ψ106(107).16]

[177] IP 17.2 f., SC 27, 145-149.
[178] A χορηγός was a patron who funded a public feast. Cantalamessa, L'Omelia, 375.

The people beneath the earth are raised from the dead [Mt 27.52-53],
   having received the good news,
   and from the heavenly ranks
   a chorus is formed reaching to the earth.
O divine Pascha!
You have united us spiritually with God,
   that the heavens could not close again.
For you the great wedding hall is filled;
   all clothed in wedding garments [Mt 22.10-11]
   no one is cast out because of the lack of a nuptial garment.
O Pascha,
   light from the new torch,
   splendor of the virginal torch (δαδουχία)[179]!
Through you the lamps of the spirit do not extinguish,
but the spiritual fire of grace divinely transcends all,
food for the body,
   from the Spirit
   and from the ointment of Christ.[180]

Those who fast in the Bridegroom's absence now know that he has returned for the nuptial feast. If it is remembered that the ultimate origins of this passage lie in a single typological equation of Christ and the paschal lamb of 1Cor 5.7, the remarkable generative power of this first occurrence of Christian exegesis of Ex 12, which may not even reflect an actual liturgical celebration, emerges with particular clarity. Each hymnic section of IP, and indeed the entire homily, is a reflection of what and how this equation bears meaning. As in Origen, Christ *is* the Pascha, but for the IP homilist, that embodiment is the paschal night itself. IP strives for the most complete mimesis possible between narrative, mystery, and cosmos.

At the same time, "mystery" has become even more associated with ritual, much as in Clement's parody of Hellenic initiation:

Oh how truly holy are the mysteries, oh, how pure the light! I am illumined by the light of torches [δαδουχοῦμαι] to see the heavens and God...

I will salve you with the ointment of faith, freeing you from all that is transitory, and will show you uncovered the image of righteousness, in which you may rise to God...[181]

---

[179] On the Eleusian background, see Cantalamessa, L'Omelia, 104-106.
[180] IP 62, SC 27, 189 f.
[181] Protr 120.1,5; GCS 58, 84 f.

...and in a Greek inscription that Peter Lampe reconstructs as marking liturgical space for Valentinians meeting in a villa on the Via Latina:

> Fellow brothers (συνάδελφοι) of the bridal chambers celebrate with torches the baths for me, They hunger for banquets in our rooms (δόμοισι), Lauding the Father and praising the Son; O may there be flowing of the only spring and of the truth in that very place/time (ἔνθα).[182]

Lit by the same Eleusian torches that shed a paschal light in IP, Clement's mystery sounds like baptism only because he speaks the language of initiation, but the sacred bath of the Valentinian inscription is entirely missing. Yet in IP, the torches are also holy because they illuminate holy actions in the paschal night. Their Hellenic "mystery" may be absorbed.

The evocative power of this association is also the reason why Clement is the first Christian writer to use the adjectival form μυστικός or adverbial μυστικῶς with any regularity.[183] This is a strategy followed by the IP homilist, who uses these forms nine times.[184] The usage of these terms and the nominal form from which they derive still centers on Ignatius' "loud-shouting mysteries" of incarnation and cross and the "mysteries" of scripture, now including details of the passion narrative, which receive a point-by-point exegesis like the ritual features of Ex 12. At IP 7.1, the "types, symbols, and mysteries" of OT narrative come to completion in us" through a term drawn directly from Hellenic cults: ἐν ἡμῖν δὲ πνευματικῶς τελεσιουργούμενα.[185]

Now the homilist sees with Apollinarios baptism in the blood and water streaming from Christ's side:

> Then having drunk the vinegar and gall of the soldier, he, in exchange, let flow for us the sweet fount from his side. For wishing to destroy the work of the woman and counterpoised to she who in the beginning came from the rib, that bearer of death, see how he opens in himself his sacred rib

---

[182] Lampe, Peter, An Early Christian Inscription in the Musei Capitolini, StTh 49, 1995, (79-92) 80.

[183] Marsh, H. G., The use of ΜΥΣΤΗΡΙΟΝ in the Writings of Clement of Alexandria with Special Reference to his Sacramental Doctrine, JTS 37, 1936, 64-80.

[184] The *mystic* Pascha (IP 1.2); *mystic* blood of the lamb (9.1); Law prepared for a *mysterious* plan of salvation (10.1) and is a "*mysterious* imitation of a heavenly way of life" (9.1); the *mystic* sheep (20); Zech 6.2 (LXX-"dawn") points "most *mysteriously*" to Christ (45.4); Adam was brought to life by the "*mystic* breath of the Father" (47.2).

[185] IP 7.1, SC 27, 133.

from which gush sacred blood and water, the initiations to the spiritual and mystical wedding, sings of adoption and of regeneration. For it is written, "He will baptize you in the Holy Spirit and with fire." [Mt 3.11] "In the Spirit" suggests the water, the fire indicates the blood.[186]

Blood and water has transformed Christ into the New Adam, who gives birth to the church through baptism, the initiation to the nuptial feast of the eucharist. This is an aspect of the Pascha to which the IP homilist gives particular attention.

b) The Feast

Apart from the more general question "What is the Pascha?", the relatively minor place IP has for rhetorical suspense is taken up by why at Lk 22.15, Jesus did not eat the Pascha, though he had "desired with a desire" to do so:

> This is the Pascha which Jesus desired to suffer for us. Through his suffering he has liberated us from suffering [and/or, through his Passion he has liberated us from passions][187]; with his death he has vanquished death, and by means of visible food he has given us immortal life. This was the saving desire of Jesus, this his purely spiritualized love, to show his disciples figure by figure and then, however, in its place, to give them his sacred body: "Take and eat, this is my body. Take and drink, this is my blood, the new covenant, which is given for many for the remission of sins." Thus the [Pascha] was not eaten which he desired, but rather he suffered it, in order to liberate us from suffering through our eating it.
>
> Thus he supplanted wood with the wood and in place of the perverse hand stretched out impiously in the beginning [for forbidden fruit] he faithfully let his pure hand be nailed [to the cross], and shows true life hanging [from the tree].
>
> You, O Israel, you have not been able to eat of it, but we, provided with an indestructible spiritual knowledge, we eat of it, and eating, we do not die.[188]

The concluding anti-Judaic comment signals the traditional discomfort with the paschal frame of the supper, but it seems especially gratuitous

---

[186] IP 53.3-4, SC 27, 181.

[187] "τοῦτο ἦν τὸ πάσχα ὃ ἐπεθύμησεν ὑπὲρ ἡμῶν ὁ Ἰησοῦς παθεῖν· πάθει πάθους ἠλευθέρωσε καὶ θανάτῳ θάνατον ἐνίκησε…"

[188] IP 49 f., SC 27, 175 f.

in this homily, which follows closely Melito's exegesis – except his tirade against the murderers of God. Second century arguments have become institutionalized. Yet despite its milder form, anti-Judaism performs the same function and has the same rhetorical address as in PP: the Jews of the "old" dispensation who have now been replaced by Gentile Christians as surely as the pure spirituality of the eucharist has supplanted the "carnality" of the Pesach meal. The trees of Eden, whose fruit brought death to Adam, have found their redeeming types in the tree of the cross, which brings life and indestructible knowledge. The eucharistic bread and wine are fruits brought forth by the saving wood. From this harvest, the Jews are excluded.

This aspect of supercession becomes quite transparent when the homilist reacts to the "anti-Gentilism" of Jesus' encounter with the Canaanite woman:

> The blood is put on the doorposts as on the Church with its two posts [Ex 12.7] like its two peoples. The Savior does not deny that he was sent in the first place to you, O Israel. For he says, "I am not sent to you, but to the last sheep of the house of Israel." [Mt 15.24] I however like a little dog sit at the table of others; I can not eat the bread, but like a parasite at the table of others, I pick up the fallen crumbs. But from the moment when you did not recognized the manna which comes from heaven, the bread is given to me because I have believed and from a dog as I was, here I am now, become a son.[189]

None of these types is new, but the connection between the two *lentils* and two peoples, Jews and Gentiles, is not expressed exactly in this way anywhere else. Since Irenaeus finds the same meaning in the daughters of Lot,[190] it can be assumed that this exegesis was generally available for anything occurring in pairs. Adam as antetype of Christ, the wood of the cross, and the creation narrative have all been combined before, but not with the same stress of motifs. As in Aphrahat, rhetorical art may arrange typologies so that various "likenesses" tell a slightly varied version of the same kerygmatic story. Anti-Judaism, regardless of the large or small rhetorical space given to it by various authors, invariably performs the same rhetorical functions. Here it contrasts the chosenness of Gentile Christianity with the rejection of the Jews and the pure spirituality of the eucharist.

[189] IP 25, SC 27, 153 f.
[190] At AH 4.31.1-3, SC 100/2, 788, See above, n. 87, p. 47.

In Origen's paschal treatise, Jn 6 and the "table of the word" play a vital role in shaping the exegesis, but in IP, the eucharist is unambiguously a ritual act – and with the words of institution included in the text, unambiguously Synoptic. The two meanings of "pathos" as suffering and passion are maintained simultaneously, which enables the IP homilist to remain true to the Asian Pascha=passion typology, the now canonical meal narrative, and to the Alexandrian motif of Pascha as freedom from passion. Even with the influence from Origen apparent in other passages, this latter motif may be less an Egyptian echo than it reflects the general vocabulary of Christian homiletics in Late Antiquity. Passion and desire can be impulses of evil and death, as in Adam's impure hand stretched out for godlike power. Eros becomes spiritualized (ἔρος πνευματικώτατος) and a love that saves from death. The slight discomfort with Jesus' "desire," emphasized by Luke with a cognate dative (ἐπιθυμία ἐπεθύμησα), has likely been heightened by numerous other sermons warning the congregation of the dangers of human passion. The homilist must unload the term before he can turn it into a vehicle for the gospel. The eucharist soon to be celebrated is where this desire is now fulfilled.

Another rhetorical echo requires far less speculation – the idolatrous "zoo" of Egyptian deities abhorrent to Jewish and Christian authors alike:

> Egypt, large and gloomy, is the image of the dark and deep straying away. From there, in fact, came the first rising of error: calves, fish, birds, wild beasts and every other species of animal were worshipped and honored as a divinity. But when vengeful wrath was revealed from heaven and great anger was poured out upon all the earth, then the error of superstition and idolatry would be the first to be smitten. For it is written, "I will make war against all the gods of the Egyptians, I, the Lord." [Ex 12.12][191]

But why were only the firstborn struck down? "The plague struck all the firstborn," the homilist explains, "for those who claimed for themselves the right of age were also for a greater time in the service of idols."[192] This odd take on the plagues of Egypt stems from a rhetorical filter: other, more hortatory sermons the homilist has preached against Hellenic religion.

---

[191] IP 12, SC 27, 139 f. The animal form of Egyptian deities was a frequent target of anti-pagan polemic. Cf. early 2 c. *Preachings of Peter*, Strom 6.40.1 f.; Philo, above, p. 88.
[192] IP 13, SC 27, 140.

The IP homilist's redeeming of "desire" and condemning the eldest of idolatrous siblings is enough to show that sermons do not take place in a rhetorical or an historical vacuum, even when the latter is far less transparent. Does the homilist also echo the paschal controversy when he exegetes Lk 22.15, as Raniero Cantalmessa claims?[193] If this homily were not extant and someone such as the compiler of the *Chronicon* had excerpted this sole eucharistic text and set it beside similar statements of Hippolytus and Apollinarios, then there would be no question that it would tell the same story: an exegetical dispute concerning the paschal meal and gospel chronology as it relates to the celebration of Pascha.

This is Cantalamessa's method, as he combines this text, those in the *Chronicon*, and even the passage in Irenaeus' AH where Jesus eats.[194] Cantalamessa acknowledges the danger of including texts without specific reference to the paschal controversies of Rome or Laodicea, but this is soon dismissed by globalizing the problem. "It is perhaps not exact," Cantalamessa writes, "to make the dispute of Laodicea of 164-166 the sole matrix of a question which agitated the minds of almost all of Christianity in the second century."[195] With this move, it is little wonder that Cantalamessa can see both Irenaeus and the IP homilist as echoing this exegetical argument. So virtually *all* of Christendom was concerned in the second century with whether Jesus died on 14 or 15 Nisan?

Such a view seemed so absurd to Walter Bauer that he could not believe that the incipit of Melito's paschal treatise, which mentions the martyrdom of Sagaris and the Laodicean dispute in the same breath, could possibly have been written by Melito himself:

> But what should one think of a Christianity over whom a sword hangs, that is so endangered it must offer up its bishop as a blood sacrifice, then, since the martyrdom fell in the days of Easter, allows itself to be drawn into a hefty row over the proper paschal celebration, instead of standing together shoulder to shoulder against the common enemy![196]

---

[193] Cantalamessa, L'Omelia, 67. IP 49 is "uno dei testi fondamentali" for Quartadeciman provenance.

[194] Cantalamessa, L'Omelia, 74. "Irenaeus, in fact, appears to hold the same position combated by Apollinarios, Clement, and Hippolytus, since he affirms that Christ *ate the Pascha* and died the following day."

[195] L'Omelia, 74.

[196] Bauer, Rechtgläubigkeit, 156.

The history of this and all the other paschal controversies lies hidden in the rhetoric – and somewhere between Bauer's absurdity and Cantalamessa's burning exegetical problem. The connection of paschal and eucharistic motifs with martyrdom as the ultimate *imitatio christi* is well attested since Luke portrayed James' death during Pesach, but Melito does not make Sagaris' death *cause* the paschal dispute as Bauer thinks. Even so, what Bauer offers is a sobering reality check: troubled by the negative connotations of the word, the homilist is far more concerned with the "desire" of Jesus to eat the Pascha than whether he did or not. Since Luke never really gives an answer, the IP homilist then may fill this hermeneutical gap with the entire content of the gospel. In this global rhetorical strategy, there is no room for paschal controversy.

IP takes part in several dialogues in second and third century Christianity – with the superseded "Jews" of scripture, with pagan culture and its "mysteries," with calendrical speculation – but only for the original hearers at the paschal vigil, not in dispute with others. In fact, since IP is not aimed even obliquely at other paschal theologies, it offers a reasonable control for the "lambless" rhetoric of Hippolytus, Clement, and Apollinarios before it was transformed by controversy. So too the hymns to spring and the cosmic significance of Pascha are not aimed at other paschal computations, but are found in their original rhetorical situation: preaching in the paschal night. The sun turned dark at the cross. Now the universe sings. Second and third century theologians did not always fight about the Pascha. Cantalamessa's "agitation" would have to pause at least long enough for them to celebrate it.

Except for the unbroken bones of the lamb presaging the resurrection in Jn,[197] Ex 12 does not yield a motif to sign Jesus' rising from the dead. Thus Melito must drop the typology for the coda of his sermon and speak in the first person as the risen Lord, while the Alexandrians move the accent to the passage through the Red Sea. The IP homilist finds this motif in the eucharist, which he sees as Pascha and anamnesis of the passion, but not Pesach. The eucharist is mimesis of the cross, but through its kerygma "proclaiming Christ's death" and eternal life, not as it imitates the rituals of Ex 12. The homilist reads the "historic" meal of the gospels in the same way. Jesus could not eat the meal until the sign was fulfilled:

---

[197] Cf. IP 30, SC 27, 157: "Thou shalt not break any of its bones. [Ex 12.10], because the Resurrection was manifest in the body. For it says, "Put your finger in the wound in my side, and know that a ghost does not have flesh and bone." [Jn 20.27]

it was, as Hippolytus says, not the proper *kairos*. In IP, this *kairos* is now – in the paschal eucharist. Yet even with the "great feast day" of Friday, Aphrahat reads the same significance into Jesus' performing the rites of Pesach, the cross an unfolding, even mimesis, of Jesus giving his body and blood. The dispute resolves, then, to one of mimetic objects: for the "Johannines," Ex 12 as text; for the "Synoptic" Syrians, Ex 12 as ritual. But this dispute does not lie on the rhetorical horizon of this text.

Dating anonymous texts is "difficult and risky" because they must always be considered derivative imitations of the few extant authors available for comparison. Yet without allusion to persons, places, and events that moderns can place within an historical framework, both time and place are rhetorical constructs that may not correspond to historical realities. Sometimes, this is not especially important. If IP were preached anywhere in the Empire, it is still within the "Asian" paschal tradition. Yet regardless of author, IP cannot be the single source of so much innovation. Eucharistic motifs, the developed allegorical exegesis also reflecting upon the hermeneutical act, the greater role of now canonical passion narratives, the developed use of Hellenic mystery language, even the adverbial and adjectival forms of "mystery" – all are signs of a theological conversation with beginnings in the second century, but when taken together pull the homily further and further into the third. Perhaps more than any other example of paschal rhetoric, IP is most transparent to its rhetorical history, but refuses to reveals clues to its historical situation: another, yet unplanned, aspect of the homilist's paschal mystery.

D. CONCLUSION: FINDING THE HISTORY

It is somehow "congruent" to end a discussion of the second century Pascha with two texts that yield more questions than answers. Except for those who simply juxtapose the texts to create narrative, showing why the theological stance of Blastus can never be reconstructed is far less problematic than showing how it can. In the same way, the paschal controversies can be of little use in dating IP, the homilist having far more to say about the Pascha than rehearsing a learned dispute that may have meant little to his first hearers. Yet in controversial writings, this historical opaqueness often seems the sole rhetorical purpose: to assign value and identity to what in other contexts may seem utterly trivial, to focus complicated historical realities into sharply outlined symbols, and to generate icons with enough rhetorical power to assure group loyalty and devastate the rhetoric of opponents. Whether Jesus of Nazareth ate lamb the night before his death has no currency in modern scholarly discourse, which prefers the scientific and comfortably polysyllabic world of "chronology." But this translation must elevate the auxiliary detail of 14/15 Nisan to a *status confessionis*, all the while ignoring the complete seriousness with which early Christianity spoke the language of types, especially as "new style" mimesis conflicts with the "old" at the end of the second century.

By the same token, despite various attempts to pour theological content into the Roman-Ephesian dispute – passion versus resurrection, eschaton versus history, "Jewish" versus "Christian," foreign heresy versus domestic goodness, or even Weitzel's "Christian consciousness" – the disappointing news is that these second century "stars," who in other contexts may shimmer with theological brilliance, really were talking about whether Pascha should be celebrated on the Lord's Day, no more, but also no less. While the Constantinian change may have imbued Nicaean rhetoric with the air of imperial politics, this dispute also concerned a matter of timing: the role of the equinox in paschal computation, a measure of united orthodoxy far easier to comprehend than the array of christologies converging toward the other controversy at Nicaea.

For all the differences between the Asian, Alexandrian, and Antiochene "dialects," the language of both paschal disputes repeats familiar modes of establishing Christian identity. At the end of Klaus Berger's exhaustive *Theologiegeschichte des Urchristentums*, the author concludes:

> The history of theology of the first century CE presents itself as an uninterrupted dialogue [Auseinandersetzung] concerning the problem of how Judaic Christianity was to be. All authors of the NT were apparently Jewish Christians; only with Ignatius of Antioch does Gentile Christianity come on the scene. The controversy in the NT is thus not whether Christianity will have a Jewish-Christian coloration (which it will always have), but to what degree Judaic regulations are individually valid. If that is the case, then the central problem of the first century is not a defense against Gnosis, mystery religions, the cult of the caesars, etc.[1]

Geographically, this intra-Christian dialogue took place in and between two major centers: Ephesus and Antioch, with Rome and Alexandria appearing at first only on the periphery. By the late second- early third century, minor players have definitely moved to the majors, and the themes Berger lists have become the central problems that they were not in the first. The most important difference, however, is that Jervell's "mighty minority" of Jewish Christians has disappeared from the dialogue. Gentile authors are still talking *among themselves* about "how Judaic Christianity was to be" in the same language, but in new situations, after ritual boundaries – Sabbath, circumcision, dietary laws, table fellowship – had already been firmly drawn. Yet all along, the question was not how much certain leaders or communities – James, Paul, Jewish Christians, "Judaizers" in Galatia – would determine Christian rite and practice, but, as Berger suggests, "to what degree Judaic regulations are individually valid." The primary dialogue is with the power and influence of the Hebrew scriptures.

Later literature still bears traces of this *Auseinandersetzung* well into the third century. Even with all the rhetoric allegorizing, spiritualizing, or simply abolishing the Judaic cult, Christian authors still perform various operations on ritual texts, not only to transform them into kerygma, but to order the worship of the church. The author of the ApTrad turns to Num 9.6-11 for an answer to a delay of Pascha because of an identical situation, just as the *Didascalia* attempts, rather desperately, to invest the paschal fast with the authority of Zech 8.19, also an answer to a direct inquiry about a fasting rule (Zech 7.3). The point is not that these exegetes have to manipulate these verses beyond recognition to obtain the desired results, but that they turn to them in the first place.

---

[1] Berger, Theologiegeschichte, 718.

When all the rhetorical smoke clears, paschal disputes ultimately revolve around Num 28.16 and its parallels: "On the fourteenth day of the first month there shall be a Passover offering to the Lord." While Rome, Ephesus, and others quarrel over the fourteenth, the Nicaean debate is concerned with "firstness" – in a Christian recension of Hebrew lunar timekeeping with the vernal equinox as intercalary control. A dispassionate view of such controversies requires a much finer calibration of "Jewishness" than the rhetoric would imply. It is measured first in days, then weeks, yet even with the equinox, by the full moon of Ex 12.

The counterpoint to calendrical "exactness" is a mimetic language that can bend time and its measures into many shapes. As their narration becomes more and more connected to paschal ritual, the last events of Jesus' life are rearranged to provide scriptural grounding for a paschal fast, as in the *Didascalia* and Aphrahat, or for the sub-H redactors, Eusebius, and Epiphanius, to remove the Christian holy meal and its institution from its "Jewish" paschal frame. The non-polemical, catechetical version of such rhetoric seeks the perfect mimetic fit with kerygmatic motifs so that rite and text are mutually reinforcing. Yet the same need to turn to a common language of authority that leads to Num or Zech also seeks rubrics in NT narrative to legitimate or defend liturgical practice.

Just as Protean is the image of the "Jew" projecting from Christian paschal rhetoric. While this image may attain a sort of tragic nobility in first layer of the *Didascalia*, there is no dispute over the depravity of the Jews except between Peter and Trikentios, where the question is which Jews were "in error" and when. Jews beg for judgment and destruction in GPt and do not believe even as eyewitnesses of the resurrection; the razing of Jerusalem is proof of Jesus' divine vindication for Melito. Other examples of the Judaic "shadow" need not be reviewed, except once more to point out the main reason for the vehemence of anti-Judaism at the Council of Nicaea. In this paschal controversy, anti-Judaism is not a measure of Antioch's continuity "with the Jews," but with an ancient Christian paschal computation that must be incessantly labelled a Judaic perversion to loosen a Christian bond to its own tradition. The bitter irony of this polemic lies at its source: Alexandria's imagined continuity with proto-Christian "Hebrews," who are used to support the equinoctial rule and to condemn the calendrical madness of their descendants.

Modern reconstructions of the Antenicene Pascha thus ultimately stand or fall on their reading of Nicaean anti-Judaism. If "with the Jews" and other rhetorical constructs are read as history, then every text from Paul to Chrysostom takes on a completely different cast, yielding a narrative something like this:

> Until the Council of Nicaea, the Christians of these countries [i.e., the "Orient"] were Quartadeciman. In the night of 14/15 Nisan, the date of the Jewish Pesach, they observed and celebrated a kind of anti-Pesach. They fasted and prayed for the deicide Jews as long as these were eating the paschal meal. Beginning with the moment when the Jews had ended the meal and begun to observe the days of Azyma, the Christians broke their anti-Judaic fast and celebrated an agape and a eucharist. It may be supposed that, according to their Quartadeciman Pascha, just as Melito these Christians especially commemorated the passion and death of the Lord, his descent and victory over Sheol and his return, but not primarily his resurrection and rising from the tomb.[2]

This is Gerard Rouwhorst's conclusion to his study of Ephrem's paschal hymns, but it has a very familiar ring to it. After commenting on the role of the Last Supper narrative as the supposed difference between Syrian and Asian Quartadecimanism, Rouwhorst continues:

> Quite soon after the Council of Nicaea a large number of Christians conformed to the decisions reached at this council on the subject of paschal celebration. They abandoned their Quartadeciman tradition and transferred their Pascha to the Friday and Saturday after the fourteenth day of the paschal month.[3]

As it exactly reproduces much paschal anti-Judaism and mimetic narrative as liturgical practice, this narrative is best termed "rhetoric as rubric." Except for the Easter-Good Friday dichotomy originating in a reading of Eusebius – discarded, by the way, by every other modern scholar but Rouwhorst – each component has been projected from the rhetoric of DA 21 and Epiphanius' *Diataxis*. "They fast, we feast" was printed in red. It was exactly observed. Aphrahat "great feast day of Friday" is a rubric initiating a christianized Azyma.

Oddly enough, there really is such an anti-Pascha still being celebrated by a small religious group in the Middle East. In the Asurijah festival of

---

[2] Rouwhorst, VigChr 7.1, 191 f.
[3] op. cit., 192.

the Mandaeans, the only Gnostic sect still surviving in small numbers in Iraq, anti-Judaic rhetoric becomes ritual act. Held near the vernal equinox, the festival consists of a sacred meal commemorating the Egyptians drowned in the Red Sea, whom the Mandaeans consider ancestors along with John the Baptist.[4] Whatever its history, this festival is a "shadow" Pesach not merely part of a polemic narrative, but of a liturgical calendar.

Interest in the Mandaeans has waned considerably, but once their literature was the Qumran and Nag Hammadi darlings of their day. Richard Reitzenstein[5] wanted desperately to read the Mandaean claim of Baptist ancestry as history: Mandaean lustrations were the direct ancestor of Christian baptism, and the group provided a missing link in a grand scheme of the evolution of Indo-European religion from Persia. This, of course, was nonsense. The connection to John the Baptist was invented, and their literature set to parchment, to convince Islamic rulers that the Mandaeans were also an ancient "People of the Book" like Judaism and Christianity, and thus should be tolerated, unlike indigenous cults.[6] It must have worked.

The Antenicene Pascha bears no resemblance to the anti-Pesach of the Mandaeans, but until revisions in the twentieth century, such negative mimesis was not entirely mute. In a pseudo-prayer for the Jews,[7] now revised in the Roman liturgy to a prayer based solidly on Rom 11, anti-Judaic polemic became ritual act in Good Friday liturgies.[8] This

---

[4] Rudolph, Kurt, Die Mandäer, Bd. II, Der Kult, FRLANT 75, 1961, 333.

[5] Reitzenstein, Richard, Die Vorgeschichte der christlichen Taufe. Mit Beiträgen von Luise Troje, Leipzig/Berlin 1929; also ibid., Das iranische Erlösungsmysterium, Bonn 1921.

[6] See Rudolph's first volume: Die Mandäer, Bd. I: Prolegomena: Das Mandäerproblem, FRLANT 74, 1960.

[7] Amalarius of Metz explains, De eccl. off., PL 105, 1027: "We bend the knee for all prayers to show through gesture spiritual humility, except for the prayer for the *perfidious* Jews. For when they bent the knee before Christ (cf. Mt 27.29, but only mocking soldiers), they perverted a good custom, since they did this in ridicule." The word *perfidus* (unbelieving) now has its more negative meaning. See Schreckenberg, Heinz, Die christlichen Adversus-Judaeos-Texts und ihr literarisches und historisches Umfeld (1. -11. Jh.), EHS 23.172, 1982, 501 f.

[8] On the question of the Improperia unleashed by Werner, Eric, Melito of Sardes, first poet of Deicide, HUCA 37, 1966, 191-210, see Drumbl, Johann, Die Improperien in der Lateinischen Liturgie, ALW 15, 1973, 68-100; Schütz, Werner, "Was habe ich dir getan, mein Volk?" Die Wurzeln der Karfreitagsimproperien in der alten Kirche, JLH 13, 1968, 1-38. Willa, J. A., LThK 5, 1996, 441 f.: "Calling to mind the biblical-

negative mimesis, however, no more explains the origin and content of the Antenicene Pascha than Reitzenstein's historicization of Mandaean apologetics produces the history of Christian baptism.

Christians of the late second century, and a goodly number in the late twentieth, would counter Reitzenstein's claims with the historico-confessional category of "apostolicity." Yet the rhetoric of both paschal controversies would have had a completely different shape were apostolicity not a construct that could create its own history. From its beginnings as mere names ordered into episcopal lists around 170, the paschal controversy of 195 is that creation in progress, and Eusebius' EH a witness to its success. The legends of Mark's founding the Alexandrian church, Victor's appropriation of Peter and Paul, and Polycrates' adorning John with the High Priest's πέταλον are all of the same rhetorical genre. As historical icons, such lists and legends could explain both the church's geographic and cultural diversity as well as its essential unity in the *regula fidei* under growing episcopal leadership. In the city of Rome, Christians from all over the Empire lived out this diversity in microcosm. Perhaps this is the reason not one apostolic missionary – Mark, John, or Thomas – but two, Peter to the Jews and Paul to the Gentiles, were needed as unifying symbols. Nor did Nicaea see the end of such traditions: as "New Rome," Constantinople would fortuitously discover that its church had been founded by Andrew, who, after all, was called as disciple before his younger brother Peter. Whether legend or fact, tradition is a process of continuous actualization, a living view of a social institution that forgets differences and elevates convergences to the timeless now. As in the texts pericoped in the *Chronicon*, this invariably requires a certain tampering with the original context to shift old texts into a new historical situation. Otherwise, the past is condemned to eternal irrelevance, but the future, i.e., readers of a later age, may not be able to follow every rhetorical transfer.

That second century literature is not especially transparent to anything moderns might call liturgical history is not by chance, but design. Jewish Christianity furnished many rituals and prayers, but no ancestors of choice, and Justin's bare toleration of Torah-observant Christians[9]

prophetic and liturgical character of penitence of the Improperia prohibits today, in contrast to the ancient Church (e.g., Melito, Byzantine Troparia), misinterpretations hostile to the Jews."

[9] Cf. Dial 45.2-47.2. Justin is prepared to let Jewish Christians follow Mosaic laws consonant with "natural" (i.e., "cultless") law.

indicates how quickly rhetoric could transform apostolic history into communal amnesia. Just as Eusebius could only see the fourth century church in second century documents, the second century church was in the process of redefining itself by the characters and action in the NT, simultaneously recasting these narratives as it had the LXX into a Gentile Christian mold. Yet despite the radical changes from the apostolic age, Irenaeus shows that novelty was hardly a cherished quality in either practice or doctrine, and whatever apostolic roots could be found were unearthed as icons of tradition and orthodoxy. Stepping into the breach, rhetoric could substitute for history: when apostolic origins could not be historically claimed, they could just as easily be spoken into existence. Perhaps the true novelty was that they were now imminently desirable.

This interplay among apostolic authority, authoritative apostolic writings, and apostolic sees is not merely a phenomenon of liturgical history, but for Georg Kretschmar represents a threshold for the entire Christian tradition:

> The church of the late second and third centuries cannot be understood as the organic continuation of the various forms of Christianity in the second century, but rather came about by a decisive harkening back to the apostolic gospel as norm of church unity in the gathering around the canon of the NT. Viewed historically, this means that in the course of a few generations one among many directions in Christianity became dominant in most, and then finally all areas of the Church and eliminated all others as heresy. Something similar must have played itself out in the history of Christian worship. Apparently at the same time, orders originally kept in a few congregations or areas began to dominate in certain areas of the church and to edge out everything else, in the same way claiming apostolic origin.[10]

What part did the paschal feast play in this Darwinian reconfiguration around apostolicity as the definition of what is Christian? The trait "ritual conformity" could remain recessive in early Christian literature because in small housechurches with 50-60 members it would likely be fairly dominant anyway, and the confession "christianus/a sum" in any language probably took care of any differences from one community to another.[11]

---

[10] Kretschmar, Georg, Die Geschichte des Taufgottesdienstes in der alten Kirche. Leitourgia 5, 1964-66, (1-346), 7.

[11] Cf. the rules of Christian hospitality at Did 12.1-5.

The Corinthian correspondence of Paul and Clement of Rome shows
that a sense of authority strengthened by personal relationships was no
guarantee that things would always run smoothly. Yet with steady geographic and numerical growth, the environment in which this conforming trait becomes a chief means of identification had radically changed.
If ritual is becoming a way to identify with literary characters in the
apocryphal acts, then it is performing the same social function for a
growing religious movement. Catechesis that has loaded ritual acts with
apostolic tradition and scriptural origins then takes on a polemical edge
when the rhetoric of apostolic uniformity meets historical diversity of
practice. Harkening back to a visit of Polycarp to Rome and pleading
for a different reading of apostolicity, Irenaeus' letter to Victor attempts
to reverse the process, but this nostalgic rhetoric falls short of its purpose. That purpose did not include outlining historical events unknown
to either the writer or the recipient. No second century text may be
forced to reveal the origin of the paschal feast because along with much
of the Judaic heritage in Christianity, it had been selectively forgotten.

Where, then, besides outside the rhetorical purview of these texts, lie
the origins of the second century Pascha? Unless all appearances deceive,
there was no higher authority in the late first century who could have
either prohibited or instituted a feast "from above" against the custom
of individual or closely allied communities. The *Didache*, ritually close
to Judaic patterns but firm in its Christian identity, has a limited though
definite liturgical program it wishes to see instituted among its congregations, but there is no mention of a paschal feast. Yet whatever the
paschal practice of the *Didache*'s communities, ritual continuity from
the Jewish Pesach must have occurred primarily "from below": first, by
Jewish Christians inviting Gentiles with whom they otherwise shared
table fellowship to the paschal meal, then from one community to
another as the feast began to carry more and more Christian content.

In this continuity, Marcel Simon sees yet another instance of the
"attractiveness" of Judaic ritual in early Christianity. The paschal controversy was indicative of the strong attachment to local practices, "[b]ut
it reveals in the Oriental provinces still another character: the persistent
prestige of synagogal practices and norms in the eyes of certain believers."[12]
Since one of the major pillars of Simon's reconstruction of Jewish-Christian relations is Chrysostom's polemic against participating in Jewish

[12] Simon, Verus Israel, 362.

festivals,[13] it is curious that he did not see the Quartadeciman practice in the same fashion. At least Melito knew that those who heard his homily on the night of 14 Nisan were not at home sipping wine and reading the *Haggadah*.

Once again, Simon's reversal of anti-Judaic rhetoric into positive history is difficult to square with historical facts. What surfaces in second century Gentile authors is name and story, day and time,[14] and a sense of history that scarcely penetrates beyond living memory. Other customs, such as the removal of leaven, the special dishes of the Seder, and even more oddly, the Hallel psalms,[15] have disappeared. If Pesach is a genetic ancestor in the evolution of the second century Pascha, why did these rituals become extinct?

Unlike the Corinthian practice of baptizing for the dead,[16] most "prestigious" ritual customs do not usually vanish without leaving some rhetorical trace, which may have been another reason why Weitzel tried so desperately to find this rhetoric in Apollinarios. The *Didache* enlists anti-Judaism and the words of Jesus to anathematize the fast days of the "hypocrites," but the Christian Sh'ma threads its way through five centuries.[17] In Tertullian's day, Carthaginian Christians still observe the "Noachian" dietary laws agreed upon at the Apostolic Council (Acts 15.20), just as Christians in Gaul the generation before.[18] Yet there are no longer powerful Jewish Christian "pillars" to placate.[19] Chrysostom attempts to strip the synagogue of ritual efficacy for those who swear oaths before the Torah scroll,[20] while Leo the Great harangues against a

---

[13] See ibid., La polémique anti-juive de S. Jean Chrysostome et le mouvement judaisant d'Antioche, 4, 1936, 403-421.

[14] Casel, Art und Sinn, 4.

[15] Huber, Passa, 6-8, attempts to connect 4 and 5 c. use of Ψ117(118) the 2 c. Two groups mining the OT for liturgical material require no other connector.

[16] Tertullian has no idea what the practice could have meant, and reinterprets it as baptism of that which is subject to death, the body. See AdvMarc 5.10.1, CCSL 1, 692.

[17] Cf. 1 Tim 2.5. Twice-daily praying of the Sh'ma was already widely practiced before the destruction of the Temple, Bradshaw, Origins, 18-21. For a late "Christianized" Sh'ma in the Antioch area, see Kretschmar, Georg, Die Bedeutung der Liturgiegeschichte für die Frage nach der Kontinuität des Judenchristentums in nachapostolischer Zeit, in: Aspects du Judéo-Christianisme. Paris 1965, 113-137.

[18] Cf. Eusebius, EH 5.1.26. A tortured servant asks how Lyonnaise Christians could devour children when prohibited from consuming the blood of dumb animals.

[19] Tertullian, Apol 9.14 f., CCSL 1, 104.

[20] John Chrysostom, AdvJud 1.3.4-6, PG 48 847 f. Cf. his catechesis against swearing oaths without reference to the synagogue, Instructions 9.36-46, 10.1-4, 18-29.

sunrise prayer that smacks of paganism.[21] This is ritual continuity, with or without rhetoric.

The relationship of Pascha to Pesach turns out to be much like that of the Syn meal rite: the frame is there, but the picture has changed. In extant literature there are no rhetorical traces of banning the Seder dishes or silencing the psalms. Melito uses the bitter herbs as allegorical polemic because they are in the text, not the ritual life of his congregation, and there was no place for parsley in the passion narrative. The paschal fast that Irenaeus so artfully exploits did not grow organically from Judaic practice as if the half-day fast attested in rabbinical sources were some sort of ritual zygote. Further, the meal is an agape-eucharist for the whole community, not family units, held in the early morning hours[22] and the story a thorough christological reading of Ex 12 – in a homily, not a haggadic accompaniment to the meal. For the majority of Christian communities, the day is not 14 Nisan but the Sunday following, though the service remains the nocturnal vigil the EpAp describes. By whatever process, "attractive" Pesach rituals and "synagogal norms" have been suppressed in favor of established Christian liturgical forms.

But were these "synagogal norms" ever really there in the first place? Early in the second century, there may have been some, perhaps even many communities that did not celebrate the paschal feast, observance or non-observance not a feature from region to region, but from one congregation to another, even within the same city. Ritual continuity from Christians "Jewish rite" to Gentile converts is historically plausible, though not demonstrable, in Corinth at mid-first century, and there are many other cities where the "dividing wall of hostility" was low enough for other Judaic practices to cross over. Otherwise, Berger's Jewish-Christian "coloration" would be far paler than it is. Although Gentile Christian rhetoric eagerly rebuilt this wall within a few generations, the paschal feast, tied one way or another to a lunar date in the Hebrew calendar, is documented from Edessa to Lugdunum by the end of the second century. The point of transfer can thus not lie beyond the closing decades of the first, nor must it be too specifically localized to

---

[21] Leo, Sermo 27(26), In Nat. Dom. 7.4, PL 54, 218 f. See Dölger, Franz Josef, Sol Salutis, LF 4/5, 1925, 2-5.

[22] The prohibition at MPes 10.9 of the Pesach feast lasting past midnight is often taken to mean that this was a custom everywhere observed, and the Christian paschal fast was *designed* to outlast Pesach by three hours, e.g. Huber, Passa, 9 f.; Talley, Origins, 6. Why, then, the prohibition?

one region. But where is the missing link between this hypothetical Christian Pesach and the second century Pascha? Kretschmar's take on natural selection in the liturgy would suggest that if there were such a link, it had gone the way of the Neanderthal well before the end of the second century. An impulse from Judaic ritual is thus the first, but not the most crucial step in the shaping of Pascha. After an initial transfer, paschal observance was generated and sustained by that canonical text which all along had prescribed meal and story as anamnesis of salvation in a nocturnal ritual, now read – and ritualized – in a new context: Ex 12.

Historical narratives which suppose unbroken ritual continuity with Judaism for the second century Pascha thus betray a certain inaccuracy, regardless of the earlier negative, now positive value placed on the Jewish matrix of Christianity. Wherever and whenever it emerges, the canonical trajectory is intent not upon reoriginating these rituals into a Christian feast, but transforming ritual narrative into kerygma. This abundantly attested rhetoric points toward one historical conclusion: a christianized Pesach, with some or all rituals intact, did not survive into the second century except perhaps in isolated Jewish-Christian groups for whose ritual life there are almost no literary remains.

There have, of course, been attempts to derive Pascha from Christianity's other gene pool, its Hellenistic environment. The most radical proposal is a history of religions "parallel" drawn by Anton Baumstark:

> As the Gnostic Epiphany vigil cannot be separated from the nocturnal celebration of the birth of Aeon, so in a more broadly focused view of the history of religions, the Pannychis of the Hilaria cannot be separated from the cultic nightwatch, which along with the preparatory fast was the second major component of the Christian paschal celebration. And this component was certainly already present when the two controversies – concerning much more than just the calendrical question of its day – threatened to open a chasm between Rome and the Orient, represented by the traditions of the old Asia Minor congregations.[23]

To flesh out this story of origins, Baumstark commented on the rough temporal convergence of the two observances (Hilaria=25 March), the motifs of the death and resurrection of a god, and the ritual use of

---

[23] Baumstark, Nocturna Laus, LQF 32, 1957, 28.

light. If used aetiologically, the gospels would have yielded "at the most" a cultic commemoration in the early morning hours, not an extended vigil.[24] For Baumstark, neither the Jewish matrix of Christianity nor Ex 12 figure into the genetic makeup of the "mother of all vigils."

Odo Casel read the earliest sources much too carefully to present the second century Pascha as a reoriginated pagan feast, but he did note the increase of mystery vocabulary in the next century and beyond. Assuming paschal baptism as an early and universal practice,[25] Casel can then point out an "external resemblance" to the nocturnal initiation of various mystery cults:

> [The Church], however, did not overlook the similarity of religious type and expression that concern us here, and thus used the symbolic language of type in order to make the nature of its own cult more or less comprehensible to the people of its day and to be able to express itself in language.[26]

Casel does not use the current buzzword "inculturation," but that is the point he is trying to make. Beyond establishing parallels painfully reminiscent of Plutarch's "ritual pattern," all this means is that a communal nocturnal vigil held in the spring, with or without baptism and culminating in a meal rite, is a ritual form that for all differences in content, affect, and promised efficacy, would generally be recognized as "religion" by Gentile converts in Late Antiquity intelligent enough not to expect incestuous orgies and the blood of infants.

Yet for all the parallels to pagan mysteries Casel draws, for the IP homilist, "mystery" is kerygmatic narrative, not mimetic rite, and Christ alone is myste and mystagogue:

> This is what the Pascha is: a hymn of praise of all beings, sent into the world by the will of the Father, divine dawning of Christ on earth, eternal solemnity of the angels and archangels, immortal life of the whole world, mortal price for death, incorruptible food for Humankind, heavenly spirit of all things, sacred initiation of the earth and of the heavens, which prophesied mysteries ancient and new, contemplated with earthly eyes, yet understood only in heaven.

---

[24] Baumstark, 28 f.

[25] Baumstark (30) did not assume this, more likely because of his "law" that the liturgy always moves from simple to complex.

[26] Casel, Art und Sinn, 65.

For this reason, joined to the one who was initiated into mysteries old and new through a sacred knowledge (προσκυρούμενοι τοῖς τὰ καινὰ καὶ παλαιὰ μετὰ γνώσεως ἱερᾶς μεμυνμένοις), we have wished to explain in few words what this universal feast of Pascha is.[27]

Pascha is something else, a hybrid form suitable for the "third people" of the ancient world, but neither the Hilaria nor a direct line to Pesach rituals explains its genesis. Justin and others may rail at the Jews for observing a feast now precluded outside of Jerusalem because Christians did not really celebrate it either. The only true mimesis of Ex 12 is its Christian mystery, the sacrificial death of the Lamb. In this sense, Melito's homily is not some permutation of the Pesach Haggadah as some have proposed,[28] but a narrative demonstrating how Christ alone performs and fulfills the rituals of Ex 12.

Asian rhetoric thus gives one answer to the historical question. The strongest connection of Pascha to Pesach, indeed the only one, is Ex 12, a text that all Gentile authors of the second century are certain was never written with "carnal" Jewish rituals in mind. The paschal controversies, and thus their history, are not about ritual continuity or the relative "Jewishness" of this or that practice, but about the Christian ritualization of Ex 12 and how important Christian centers across the Empire construed liturgical mimesis differently toward this text. The true carrier of the paschal tradition is an act of reading that continued to discover layers of meaning in Ex 12 far beyond the relatively few allusions in the NT. This depth was measured by the greatest "congruence" of all: the importance of Pesach to Judaic sacred narrative, ritual, and identity, and the death of Jesus of Nazareth. A story of the creation of a covenant people through a saving act of God, Ex 12 also commands the remembrance of both in an anamnetic meal rite in the spring of every year. The death of Jesus during Pesach-Mazzot had insured that this text and its rituals would not only narrate the passion but also tell the story of baptism and the creation of the People of God from the Gentiles. For the Synoptic evangelists and the Syrian paschal tradition, Ex 12 could

---

[27] IP 3.3-4.1, SC 27, 121 f.

[28] More baldly by Frank Cross, JTS ns 11, 1960, 162 f., at Hall, Stuart G., Melito in the Light of the Passover Haggadah, JTS ns 22, 1971, 29-46, restricts "haggadism" to the second half. Carried to the absurd by Angerstorfer, Ingeborg, Melito und das Judentum, Regensburg 1985, using texts as late as the 15 c. Melito's relationship to Judaism is then termed ambivalent "ambivalent" (232).

also generate narratives about the Christian meal rite. As Christian authors view Ex 12 as a narrative frame for stories about Christ and the Church, the paschal night provides a liturgical space for these stories to be told. In this sense, Ephrem's paschal hymn with its vanishing Pesach rituals is the most revealing text of all for the history of the second century Pascha.

If this is the case, then the question of how the thoroughly Christian Sunday seduced Pascha away from the not so thoroughly Christian 14 Nisan must be recast, not in terms of historical priority, but in terms of hermeneutic. While the paschal controversy 195 can be framed as the weekly liturgical cycle at loggerheads with the yearly cycle of an important Christian center, the amount of scholarly energy expended to adduce forces leading to the change is a tribute to the power of Asian rhetoric still to persuade its readers. Polycrates' constellation of Asian stars has lost none of its luminous power, Apollinarios' hymn to 14 Nisan still sings, the mere addition of the ages of two Asian bishops renders the claim of apostolicity historically plausible. Yet without the weight of canon and apostolic tradition, both still in a state of rhetorical flux at the end of the century, the practical problem of moving a liturgical observance based upon a "spiritual" reading of Ex 12 to the eve of the chief day of Christian worship hardly seems insurmountable, at least for those for whom 14 Nisan had not been elevated to a primary marker of religious identity. After all, it was not Asian Christians themselves, nor even their immediate opponents at the end of the second century, who coined the term "Quartadeciman." Nor would this change necessarily be limited to Gentile communities: with a bit of imagination even the "Hellenists" Luke gathers around Stephen would make likely candidates for the move. But regardless of where and by whom this transformation took place, there are far too many possibilities in the interplay of ritual, the Christian "spiritual" hermeneutic of scripture, and religious identity simply to label as Hippolytus does 14 Nisan as "Jewish" legalism and the Sunday after as "Gentile" grace. With Asia Minor as a major center for the development of OT canon and typology in the second century, it is far easier to ferret out the reasons why this region did *not* make the transition than why the "rest of the world" seems to have transferred the festival so much earlier, or even celebrated Pascha on the Lord's Day from the beginning. This means that outside proconsular Asia, the Quartadeciman Pascha need not be historically prior to the Sunday observance, as much as an evolutionary narrative offers an easy substitute for historical unknowns. Such narratives may be appropriate for explaining the origin, say, of flying squirrels, but not of a cultural phenomenon whose continuation depends upon ritual action and speech.

When he moved to Lugdunum, Irenaeus apparently made the change with ease, because for him the issue was the day Pascha was celebrated, not any grave theological deficiencies of the Asian practice. His letter "to an Alexandrian," along with the Omer typology in Hippolytus and Clement, are the only rhetorical traces of an argument that may have tipped the balance toward the Lord's Day, which had no explicit scriptural aetiology, instead of the paschal full moon, which did. But such Sunday typologies would be more strongly drawn and have broader attestation had the practice been derived mimetically from these texts,[29] rather than offering "congruent" scriptural support for the day of Pascha already long observed. Tradition has also skewed the balance, because later readers – Eusebius and the author of the *Chronicon* among them – would find arguments based upon a Lord's Day theology as lackluster as Harnack did. Asian leaders would also never have admitted that their practice fell on the wrong side of the law-gospel question, nor was this necessary, since Hippolytus' accusation of legalism is the application of a Pauline construct to an issue where it scarcely applies.[30] But a wish to remain in harmony with the rest of the church, coupled with an appealing typology that could more fully reflect both gospel narrative and a "spiritual" reading of the rites of Unleavened Bread, must have been able to neutralize Asia's investment in 14 Nisan. With the emergence of the NT canon and the "new" style of liturgical mimesis, how long could Asian homilists continue to treat the passion narrative as Melito did only as an auxiliary story? Homilists in the vein of Melito and Apollinarios would discover that their entire tradition could remain intact even if the moon were not quite so full and the OT date had fallen up to six days before. The IP homilist is the best example of how the Asian tradition could absorb motifs both from other regions and the NT canon. It would be difficult to term this hymnic work an impoverishment.

---

[29] So Rordorf, Ursprung.
[30] Cf. Shepherd, Massey H., The Paschal Liturgy and the Apocalypse. ESW 6, London 1960, 14: "However apostolic the Quartadeciman observance may have been in origin… it was rightly suspected … as a Judaizing practice. For it tied the celebration of the redemptive event within the time-framework of the old Law. The judgment of Hippolytus … was just…" For a far more balanced view of Rev, see Thompson, Leonard, Cult and Eschatology in the Apocalypse of John, JRel 49, 1969, 330-350.

With the lengthening of the paschal fast and a deep reluctance to fast on the Lord's Day, dominical Pascha would not only be a sign of unity with other sees, but far more convenient. The rest is probably less a matter of liturgical history than ecclesiastical politics. As the third century progressed, the cost of maintaining a paschal practice at odds with the rest of the church would simply have been too high. The Montanist "shadow" would offer additional incentive not to become one of "them," but to remain one of "us." As much as scholars enjoy presenting this controversy as some symbolic foretaste of the Great Schism, the Great Church in Asia understood the cost and chose to conform. "Be concerned for unity," Ignatius had written Polycarp, "beyond which there is nothing of value."[31] Barraged with anti-Judaic rhetoric that makes Barnabas seem the quintessence of reason, the see of Antioch would learn this well at the Council of Nicaea.

In his letter to Cyprian, Firmilian shows that there was still some living memory of the Quartadeciman controversy at mid-third century, though his contrast is between Rome and Jerusalem, not Rome and Ephesus, an indirect tribute, one might add, to the "apostolic" rhetoric of the Gentile Christians of Aelia Capitolina and Caesarea to which Eusebius alludes. Yet by the later fourth century neither Epiphanius nor PsChrysostom gives the slightest hint that Asian congregations had ever celebrated Pascha differently from the "rest of the world." This, too, is a contributing factor to Eusebius' structuring the Quartadeciman controversy as a story about Irenaeus. By this point, Asia Minor had completely distanced itself from its former practice, and Eusebius shows no antiquarian interest in the Christian past.

What could not be totally forgotten, even by Chrysostom, is that the Antiochene reckoning was older than the equinoctial rule. Thus Pseudo-Pionius in his *Life of Polycarp* can fantasize about Paul's paschal sojourn in Ephesus as did the author of the *Acts of Paul*:

> Paul then, entering his (i.e., Strataeas, brother of Timothy) house and gathering together the faithful there, spoke to them about the Pascha and Pentecost, reminding them of the New Covenant of the offering of bread and the cup; how they should certainly perform it during the days of Azyma, but to hold fast to the new mystery of passion and resurrection. For the Apostle clearly teaches that we should perform it neither outside the time of Azyma, as do the heretics, especially the Phrygians,

---

[31] τῆς ἑνώσεως φρόντιζε, ἧς οὐδὲν ἄμεινον. IgnPoly 1.2, SUC 1, 216.

nor necessarily on the fourteenth, since he names not the fourteenth, but Azyma, Pascha, and Pentecost, confirming the gospel.[32]

The same reasoning laid out in the Asian Anonymous of 387 does not mean Asian provenance any more than Polycarp remained a local saint, a tradition Irenaeus already exploits two hundred years before. The Syrian eucharistic aetiology and the old Antiochene rule of celebrating "with the Jews" on the Sunday in Azyma "confirming the gospel" are apostolic practices reinforced, not founded, by Paul. As a consequence, the Montanist "shadow" and its fourth century calendrical innovations are projected into apostolic times, but this is a small price to pay for a new Polycarp anecdote about paschal practice. Yet unless PsPionius wishes for some inexplicable reason to show Polycarp as directly disobeying a rule "manifestly" (φαίνεται) laid down by Paul himself, the author has no knowledge that Smyrna and its "star" ever celebrated Pascha on 14 Nisan. As in PsChrysostom, there is a token accusation that the Quartadeciman practice is an incomplete interpretation of the "new mystery," but this rhetoric has survived longer than the memory of its original context.

Along with the "eucharistic" Pascha found nowhere else, the real clue to the provenance of PsPionius is the provenance he assigns Polycarp: as a young man, the martyred bishop of Smyrna was a slave brought to Asia Minor from the Ἀνατολή, the Syrian "Orient."[33] The false Pionius knows as little about the earliest paschal controversy as the false Ignatius, but like the Audians, he remembers "the fathers' paschal rite." The Montanist "Phrygians" are the reason why the Asian Great Church did not keep the memory of the Quartadeciman practice alive.

Lined up with the indirect connection between Pesach and the eucharist in IP and Asian 387, these echoes of Syrian paschal theology suggest another possibility. Outside the gospels, the first connection of Pesach to Christian ritual is to baptism: a faint allusion in Barn, a testimonia source in Justin, and a major theme in Melito. Even the tiny snippet from Apollinarios' paschal treatise alludes to this rite, and Irenaeus has no use for the paschal frame of the supper except as proof of Jesus' nourishing a non-docetic body. Even if Barn were not written in Asia Minor, this mimetic understanding of the blood rite of Ex 12

---

[32] PsPionius, Life of Polycarp 2, The Apostolic Fathers II,3, J. B. Lightfoot, [2]1889, 434.

[33] TU 43B, 718-725.

is a fixed component of the Asian tradition, which had no place for
the paschal nature of the eucharist, either historically as the Pesach meal
of Jesus, or rhetorically in its preaching. This connection, important
enough for the Synoptic gospels to rearrange chronological sequence
and for the Fourth Gospel to negate it, is a theological motif that along
with the rituals of Pesach did not make the transfer from Jewish Christianity to the Gentile church – finally to emerge in the region that likely
gave rise to the motif in the first place, Syria. "Polycarp" did not bring
this paschal theology to Asia, but someone did. Eucharistic motifs,
despite Apollinarios' rhetoric, enter the stream of Asian paschal tradition. His heightened use of NT narrative shows how this was inevitable,
even if the initial impulse did not come directly from Syria, but from an
encounter with an emerging two testament canon.

Yet even if every canonical gospel were written in Syria, and even if
the Syn evangelists, as Feneberg[34] theorizes, wrote their meal narratives
as aetiologies for a first century Christian paschal observance, this same
encounter, not an unbroken tradition *ab initio,* is also the origin of the
Syrian "eucharistic" Pascha. For if this understanding of the meal rite
narrative had been carried along with the Antiochene Gentile mission,
much less by Paul and others, then the hybrid form of IP would have
been reached far sooner, and Antioch would never have had to hear the
strange attacks on the paschal frame of the supper that it did at Nicaea.
Instead, the meal aetiology comes to light in that region which first creates a liturgical theology with Christ narrative as object, sometime
before the *Didascalia,* but after the *Didache.* This mimesis addressed to
any rite exists nowhere before Ignatius of Antioch. Mimesis is present
in all ritual narratives, but it is directed to the OT canon, kerygmatic or
doctrinal motifs, not stories about Jesus. While one could muse about
how Ignatius understood the "archival" Ex 12 and its relation to the
Syn, it would be a reasonably safe conjecture that the paschal analogue
to the Syrian reading of the Jordan narrative arose at least by the next
generation.

Could the real Ignatius, who admonishes the Magnesians to "live
according to the Kyriake" (Mag 9.1) have celebrated Pascha on the
"archival" 14 Nisan? PsIgnatius certainly didn't think so when he
decided to doctor the genuine letters and compose a few of his own.
This reading leads to another conjecture. Berger's major players in the

[34] See above, n. 162, p. 180.

first century were Ephesus and Antioch. For Pascha on the Lord's Day, this leaves only one choice, but the matter is not quite as simple as that. Behind the earliest paschal celebrations were Jewish and Gentile Christians on the local and regional levels engaged in their own "Apostolic Councils" about the meaning and performance of ritual acts – in scenes much like the one PsPionius concocts for Paul and the Smyrnans. These conversations cannot be reconstructed as easily as PsPionius would have liked, but both topic and language are known – the same discussion over Judaic ritual in the writings of the NT that repeats itself, with new associations, in the second century. As all conversation about ritual, these dialogues will have employed mimetic constructs, but not a single one directed toward the Christ narrative of the gospels. Otherwise, the total absence of "new style" mimesis in 1 and 2 Clement, Hermas, Barnabas, the *Didache*, Justin Martyr, and even Irenaeus would be very difficult to explain. Yet the apotheosis of the Lamb in a mysterious letter sent to seven churches of Asia may provide a clue. In the night of nights, these churches had ritualized Ex 12 with their own form of "exactness": the text that continued to yield its exegetical treasures of the suffering Lamb contained a rubric simple to perform.

The dialogue in Antioch may have taken on a different shape, and a different decision reached on how and when to celebrate the Pascha. What the "rest of the world" may have received from the Antiochene mission early enough to fade from living memory was the celebration of the Pascha on the Lord's Day, a practice more "Christian" only because it takes its cue from the chief day of worship rather than the equally Christian interpretation of Ex 12 still current in second century Asia Minor. For all the effort to find the perfect minimal pair – Good Friday-Easter, Jewish-Christian, law-gospel, paschal lamb-Omer, etc. – "Sunday" and "14 Nisan" really do not reduce well to any of them, because they are more than positional variants along an artificial line. Each represents a different configuration of mystery, kerygma, and mimetic motifs that cannot be forced into one dimension. It is true that Sunday as anamnesis of the resurrection has a higher relief in Ignatius than in Barnabas or even Justin, but all that remains of Melito's treatise on the Lord's Day is the title. Even this is enough to indicate that Asia Minor was not "Sunday-deficient," but "Ex 12 rich." This, I think, was what Irenaeus was trying to say with his Polycarp story. The two paschal languages and the traditions behind them only become deficient when they attempt a stringently "opposing" comparison. Anicetus and Polycarp really had nothing to say to one another until they learned a different language beyond apostolic ancestry, scriptural exegesis, or episcopal power, and spoke of peace.

If Sunday Pascha was the Syrian solution at some series of lesser "Apostolic Councils" passed on by "those before us," this was not the case either with the "eucharistic" Pascha or the particular form of mimesis that produced it. Here, there is no artificial comparison, but a simple test of how various writers perform the same task on the same material. Even if authors were not trying to create works of great beauty but persuasive power, Barnabas' typological readings cannot reach the standard set by Clement of Rome, Justin, Irenaeus, or even the Shepherd of Hermas. In the same way, Aphrahat and Ephrem have no equals. Within a decade or so of each other, Tertullian, one of the most rhetorically brilliant writers of the Latin West, dabbles in NT mimesis and produces a water-bearing man, while the *Didascalia* already has the feel of an epigone. Long after Aphrahat crafts his perfectly synchronous reading of Jn 13, Severus of Antioch still returns to the Jordan narrative first told by Ignatius. At the end of the second century, when the Syrian reading only functions as rhetorical "shadow," the paschal controversy shows how writers in other provinces could speak "rubric" when it came time to appeal to the NT canon. In other contexts Irenaeus, Tertullian, or even Epiphanius could use the meal narrative momentarily for rhetorical advantage. Yet sometime between the death of Ignatius and mid-second century, I suspect Syrian theologians had begun to speak this way all the time.

Other regions resisted both Synoptic "chronology" and the Antiochene aetiological reading because their theologians harmonized the array of scriptures – first Ex 12, then the passion narratives – differently toward the Pascha and the eucharist. In the heat of controversy much nuance melts away, leaving certain key interpretations as the bare bones of contention. Was Jesus' longing to celebrate the Pesach with his disciples unfulfilled until he gave his body and blood to a new community, now struggling to articulate how the eucharist signs cross and resurrection? And was this fulfillment of Ex 12 not realized until the resurrection promised this continued presence? Yet beneath the rhetoric, and often glaringly on its surface, is the deep discomfort with the Jewish identity of Jesus of Nazareth and the true history of Christianity. The Savior of the nations could not have historically performed a Jewish ritual whose sole purpose was to sign the greater story in which the meal narrative was imbedded. This too is an attempt to come to grips with the deepest rhetorical structure of the Pesach narrative: to proclaim and celebrate, in ritual and narrative, the creation of a covenant People of God.

> *For all types had dwelled in the Holy of Holies*
> *waiting on the All-fulfilling One.*
> *The symbols were seen by the true Lamb;*
> *they ripped the curtain and came out to meet him.*
> *They all rest upon him, for they all had proclaimed only him,*
> *and they came and sat down before him.*
> *In him the symbols and types were fulfilled,*
> *as he himself spoke the seal:*
> *"It is finished."*
> Ephrem Syrus, Azyma 6.11-14, CSCO 249, 12.

E. BIBLIOGRAPHY

Translations of canonical and deuterocanonical writings taken from the New Revised Standard Version. The New Oxford Annotated Bible with the Apocrypha. An Ecumenical Study Bible. Completely Revised and Enlarged. Edited by Bruce M. Metzger and Roland E. Murphy. New York, 1991. NRSV copyright by Division of Christian Education of the National Council of Churches of Christ in the USA, 1989.

1. Primary Sources, Editions, Translations

a) Christian Literature

Amalarius of Metz. De ecclesiasticis officiis. PL 105, 985-1242.

Anonymous Asian, 387. Homélies Pascales III. Une Homélie Anatolienne sur la date de Pâques en l'an 387. SC 48, F. Floëri, P. Nautin, 1957.

Aphrahat, the Persian Sage. Demonstrations. Demonstrationes/Unterweisungen. dÜ, Peter Bruns, FC 5/2, 1991.

Apostolic Constitutions. Les Constitutions Apostolique. Tome I, Livres I et II. Intro., trad., et notes par Marcel Metzger. SC 320, 1985.
   Les Constitutions Apostolique. Tome II, Livres III-VI, Intro., trad., et notes par Marcel Metzger. SC 329, 1986.

Arian Frg. 21, CCSL 87, 261.

Aristides of Athens. Apology. Goodspeed, Edgar J. Die ältesten Apologeten. Texte mit kurzen Einleitungen. Göttingen 1914 (= Goodspeed), 2-23. Frühchristliche Apologeten und Märtyrerakten I. Die Apologie des Philosophen Aristides von Athen. Übers. von Dr. Kaspar Julius. BKV² 12, 1913.

Athanasius of Alexandria. Werke 3.1 Hg., Hans-Georg Opitz, Berlin-Leipzig 1935.
   Athanasiana Syriaca I. 1. De incarnatione, 2. Epistola ad Epictetum, CSCO 258 (Syr. 115), 1965.
   Athanasiana Syriaca II, Homily on Matthew XII 32 (Epistola ad Serapionem IV §8-23), 2. Epistola ad Afros, trans., Robert W. Thomson, CSCO 273 (Syr. 119), 1967.
   Athanasiana Syriaca III. De incarnatione contra Arianos; Contra Apollinarium I; De cruce et passione; Quod unus sit Christus; De incarnatione Dei Verbi; Ad Jovianum, trans. Robert W. Thomson, CSCO 325 (Syr. 143), 1972.

Paschal Epistles. Athanase, Lettres festales, (ed. Th. Lefort), TF: CSCO
   151 (Copt. 20), CSCO 150 (Copt. 19).

Paschal Epistle 1, PG 26, 1360B-1366D.

Paschal Epistles. Osterfestbriefe des Apa Athanasios. Aus dem Koptischen
   übersetzt und erläutert von Pius Merendino OSB, Düsseldorf 1965.

Augustine of Hippo. Ennarratione in Ps. CI-CL, CCSL 40, 1956.

Barnabas, Epistle of. Schriften des Urchristentums, zweiter Teil. Didache
   (Apostellehre), Barnabasbrief, zweiter Klemensbrief, Schrift an Diognet.
   Eingeleitet, herausgegeben, übertragen und erläutert von Klaus Wengst.
   Darmstadt, 1984. (=SUC 2), 138-195.

Cave of Treasures. La Caverne des Trésors. Les Deux Recensions Syriaques,
   trad. Su-Min Ri, CSCO 487 (Syr 208), 1987.

Chronicon Paschale. PG 92, Paris, 1860. (= ed. L. Dindorf, Bonn 1832).

Clement of Alexandria. Excerpts from Theodotus. Extraits de Théodote, ed.,
   trad., F. Sagnard SC 23, 1948.

   Protreptikos. GCS 58.

   Stromata 1-6. GCS (Clemens Alexandrinus II), hg. O. Stählin, 3. durchg.
      Aufl. von U. Treu, Berlin 1985.

   Stromata 7-8, hg. v. O. Stählin, in 2. Auf. neuhg. von L. Früchtel, 4. Auf. mit
      Nachträgen von U. Treu, GCS (Clemens Alexandrinus III), Berlin 1970.

   Stromateis. Übers. O. Stählin. BKV^2 17, 19, 20, 1934-7.

Conciliar Documents and Histories. Die Kanones der wichtigen Altkirchlichen
   Concilien nebst den Apostolischen Kanones. Hg. Fr. Lauchert. (=Samm-
   lung ausgewählter kirch- und dogmengeschichtlicher Quellenschriften,
   R. 1, H. 2) Freiburg/Leipzig 1896.

   Syriac History of the Council of Nicaea. Braun, O. De Sancta Nicaena
      Synodo, Münster 1905.

Cyprian of Carthage. Testimonia. Ad Quir (Test), CSEL 3.1, ed. G. Hartel,
   Vienna 1868.

   Epistles. CSEL 3.2, ed. G. Hartel, Vienna 1871.

Cyril of Jerusalem. Mystagogical Homilies. St. Cyril of Jerusalem's Lectures on
   the Christian Sacraments (= Texts for Students 51), ed., F. L. Cross, London 1966.

Cyrillonas. Poems. Sämtliche Gedichte, in: Ausgewählte Schriften der
   Syrischen Dichter, hg. P. S. Landersdorfer, BKV^2 6, 1912.

Didache. (Apostellehre), SUC 2, 66-91.

Didascalia Apostolorum. Didascalia Apostolorum. The Syriac Version Translated and Accompanied by the Verona Latin Fragments, ed., trans., R. H.
   Connolly, Oxford 1929.

   Die älteste Quellen des orientalischen Kirchenrechts, zweites Buch. Die
      Syrische Didaskalia, übers. und erkl. von Hans Achelis und Johannes
      Flemming, TU 25.2, 1904.

Vööbus, Arthur. Ed. and Trans. The Didascalia Apostolorum in Syriac I. Chapters I-X. CSCO 401 (Syriac), 402 (ET) = Script. Syri 175, 176. The Didascalia Apostolorum in Syriac II. Chapters XI-XXVI, CSCO 407 (Syriac), 408 (ET) = Script. Syri 179, 180, Louvain 1979.

Dionysius of Alexandria. Canonical Epistle (to Basilides). Dionysius von Alexandrien. Das erhaltene Werk. Eing., übers. und mit Anm. vers. von Wolfgang A. Bienert, BGL 2, 1972, 54-58.

Ephrem Syrus. Paschal Hymns. Des heiligen Ephraem des Syrers Paschahymnen (De Azymis, de Crucifixione, de Resurrectione) CSCO 249 (Syr 109), 1964.

　Paschal Hymns. Rouwhorst, G. A. M. Les Hymnes Pascales d'Ephrem de Nisibe II, Textes, VigChrS 7.2, 1989.

　Saint Ephrem's Commentary on Tatian's Diatessaron. Trans., ed., Carmel McCarthy, JSS.Sup 2, 1993.

Epiphanius of Cyprus (Salamis). Panarion. Epiphanius (Ancoratus und Panarion), hgg. Karl Holl, Haer. 1-33, GCS 25 (Epiphanius 1), Leipzig 1915.

　Haer. 34-64, GCS 31 (Epiphanius 2), Leipzig 1922.

　Haer. 65-80, GCS 37 (Epiphanius 3), Leipzig, 1933.

　De Fide. GCS 37, 496-526.

　Panarion. The Panarion of Epiphanius of Salamis. Trans. Frank Williams. Book 1 (1-46), NHS 35, 1987.

　Books 2-3 (47-80; De Fide), NHMS 36, 1994.

Epistula Apostolorum. Carl Schmidt and Isaak Wajnberg. Gespräche Jesu mit seinen Jüngern nach der Auferstehung. TU 43, 1919.

　Guerrier, Louis and Sylvain Grébaut. Le testament en Galilée de notre-Seigneur Jésus-Christ. PO 9.3, 1913, 141-236.

Eusebius of Caesarea. Die Kirchengesichte des Eusebius, aus dem Syrischen übersetzt von Eberhard Nestle, TU NF 5.2, 1901.

　Eusebius Werke, Bd. 2. Die Kirchengeschichte, hg. von Eduard Schwarz, die lateinische Übersetzung des Rufinus bearbeitet von Theodor Mommsen. GCS 9 Eusebius II/1-3, Leipzig 1903-1909.

　Kirchengeschichte (EH) Hrsg. und eingeleitet von Heinrich Kraft. Übersetzung von Philipp Haeuser (=BKV², 1932) neu durchgesehen von Hans Arnim Gärtner. Darmstadt 1967.

　Eusèbe de Césarée, Histoire Ecclésiatique, Livres V-VII, ed., Gustave Bardy, SC 41, 1955.

　On the Paschal Solemnities, PG 24, 1857, 693-706.

Vita Constantini. Über das Leben Constantins, Constantins Rede an die Heilige Versammlung, Tricennatsrede an Constantin, hg. Ivar A. Heikel, GCS 7 (Eusebius 1), Leipzig 1902, 1-148.

Eutychios of Alexandria. Annals, CSCO 472 (Arab. 45), ed. Michael Breydy, 1985.

Hermas, Shepherd of. Der Hirt des Hermas. Hg. Molly Whittaker, GCS 48, Berlin ²1967.

Hippolytus of Rome. In Elcanam et Annam (fragment in Theodoret, Eranistes) PG 83, 173A; GCS 1, Hippolytus 1, (Achelis), 1897, 122, CQL No. 47, 78.

Refutatio omnium haeresium, GCS 26 (Hippolytus 3) Wendland, Leipzig 1916.

Pseudo-Hippolytus. Homélies Pascales I. Une Homélie inspiré du traité sur la Paque d'Hippolyte, ed. Pierre Nautin, SC 27, 1950.

Visonà, Giuseppe, Pseudo Ippolito, In sanctum Pascha, studio, edizione, commento, SPM 15, 1988.

Honorius Augustudenensis, Gemma Animae, PL 172.

Ignatius of Antioch, Epistles. Die Sieben Ignatius-Briefe. SUC 1, 142-225.

Pseudo-Ignatius. Epistles. Funk, F. X., Opera Patrum Apostolicorum II, Tübingen 1881.

Irenaeus of Lyon. Irénée de Lyon, Contre les Hérésies. Book 1: (A. Rousseau, L. Doutreleau) SC 263-264, Paris 1979; Book 2: (Rousseau, Doutreleau) SC 293-294, Paris 1982; Book 3: (Rousseau, Doutreleau) SC 210-211, Paris 1974; Book 4: (A. Rousseau with B. Hemmerdinger, L. Doutreleau, Ch. Mercier) SC 100/1, 2, Paris 1965; Book 5: (Rousseau, Doutreleau, Mercier) SC 152-153, Paris 1969.

Adversus Haereses. 2 Bde. Übers. E. Klebba. BKV² 3-4, 1912.

Gegen die Heresien. Hg., übers. Norbert Brox, FC 8/1 1993.

Epideixis. Des Heiligen Irenäus Schrift zum Erweise der apostolischen Verkündigung (ΕΙΣ ΕΠΙΔΕΙΞΙΝ ΤΟΥ ΑΠΟΣΤΟΛΙΚΟΥ ΚΗΡΥΓΜΑΤΟΣ), ed., trans. Karapet Ter-Mekerttschian and Erwand Ter-Minassiantz, TU 31/1, 1907.

Des Heiligen Irenäus Schrift zum Erweis der apostolischen Verkündigung. Aus dem Armenischen übers. v. Dr. Simon Weber, BKV² 4, 1912.

Fragments. Jordan, Hermann, Armenische Irenaeusfragmente mit deutscher Übersetzung nach Dr. W. Lüdtke, TU 36/3, 1913.

Jerome. De Viris Illustribus. TU 14.1, ed., E. C. Richardson, 1896.

Commentary on Matthew, CCSL 77, 1969.

John Chrysostom. Orationes VIII adversus Iudaeos, PG 48, 1859, 843-942.

Acht Reden gegen Juden. Eingeleit. u. erläutert v. Rudolf Brändle, übers. v. Verena Jegher-Bucher, BGL 41, 1995.

Schatkin, Margaret. St. John Chrysostom's Homily on the Protopaschites: Introduction and Translation, OCA 195, 1973, 167-186.

Justin Martyr, Apologies: I = Goodspeed 26-77, II (Appendix) = Goodspeed 78-89; Dialogue with Tryphon the Jew, Goodspeed, 90-265.

Apologies. Frühchristliche Apologeten und Märtyrerakten I. Die beiden Apologien Justins des Märtyrers. Übers. von Dr. Gerhard Rauschen. BKV² 12, 1913.

Dialog with Tryphon. Des Heiligen Philosophen und Märtyrers Justinus Dialog mit dem Juden Tryphon. Übers. u. mit einer Einl. von Dr. Philipp Haeuser. BKV² 33, 1917.

Leo Magnus. De Quadragesima XI, Sermo 49, PL 54, 1846, 301B-306C.

In Nativitate Domini VII, Sermo 27(26), PL 54, 1846, 216C-221C.

Melito of Sardis. Paschal Homily. Bonner, Campbell, The homily on the Passion by Melito Bishop of Sardis and some Fragments of the Apocryphal Ezekiel, StDoc, 1940.

Hall, Stuart G. Melito of Sardis and Fragments, OECT, 1971.

Oracula Sybillina. Kurfess, Alfons, Sybillische Weissagungen, Berlin, 1951.

Oracula Sybillina. A New Translation and Introduction by J. J. Collins, in: Old Testament Pseudepigrapha OTPseud I, ed. James H. Charlesworth, 317-429.

Origen. Commentary on Matthew, GCS 38 (Origines 11), hg. Erich Klostermann, Leipzig, 1933.

Homilies on Jeremiah. GCS 6 (Origenes 3), hg. Erich Klostermann, Leipzig 1901, 169; CQL No. 42.

Homilies on Joshua. Homilien zum Hexateuch in Rufins Übersetzung, zweiter Teil, Die Homilien zu Numeri Josua und Judices, GCS 30 (Origenes 7), hg. W. A. Baehrens, 1921.

Homilies on Numbers, GCS 30 (Origenes 7), hg., W. A. Baehrens, Leipzig 1921.

Commentary on John. GCS 10 (Origines 4), hg. E. Preuschen, 1903.

Commentary on John. Origène. Commentaire sur St. Jean. Ed., Cécile Blanc. Livres 1-5, SC 120, Livres 6 et 10, SC 157, 1970; Livre 13, SC 222, 1975; Livres 19-20, SC 290, 1982; Livres 38 et 32, SC 385, 1992.

Commentary on Romans. FC 2, hgg. u. übers., Theresa Heither, 1994.

On the Pascha. Daly, Robert J. Origen. Treatise on the Passover and Dialogue of Origen with Heraclides and his Fellow Bishops on the Father, the Son, and the Soul, ACW 54, 1992.

On the Pascha. Origène. Sur la Pâque, O. Guéraud, P. Nautin, ed., ChrAnt 2, 1979.

Peter, Gospel of. ed., M. G. Mara, SC 201, 1973.

Photius of Constantinople. Biblioteca. Bibliothéque, II (84-155), Text etabli et trad. René Henry, Soc. d'Edition Les Belles Lettres (Collection byzantine), Paris 1960.

Pseudo-Pionius. Life of Polycarp, The Apostolic Fathers II,3, J. B. Lightfoot, ²1889.

Polycarp of Smyrna. Epistles. Die beiden Polykarp-Briefe. SUC 1, 246-265.
Romanos Melodos. Romanos le Mélode, hymnes IV, ed., Grosdidier de Matons, SC 128, 1967.
Socrates. Church History, GCS NF 1, hgg. v. Günther Chr. Hansen, Berlin 1995.
Sozomen. Church History, GCS 50, Bidez-Hansen, Berlin 1960.
Tatian. Diatessaron (witness). Pepysian Gospel Harmony, ed., Goates, Evangelica Anglica 157, 1922.
    Diatessaron (witness). Tatians Diatessaron. Aus dem Arabischen übers. von Erwin Preuschen, mit einer einleitenden Abh. und textkrit. Anm., hg. von August Pott, Heidelberg 1926.
    Oratio ad Graecos. Goodspeed, 266-305.
Tertullian. Quinti Septimi Florentis Tertulliani Opera. Pars I, Opera Catholica, Adv. Marcionem; Pars II, Opera Montanistica, CCL 1-2, Turnholt 1954.
    Tertullians private und katechetische Schriften. Neu übers. mit Lebensabriß und Einleitungen versehen von K. A. Heinrich Kellner, BKV² 7 (Tertullian 1), 1912.
    Tertullians apologetische, dogmatische und montanistische Schriften. Übers. und mit Einleitungen versehen von Dr. K. A. Heinrich Kellner, durchg. und hsg. von Dr. Gerhard Esser, BKV² 24 (Tertullian 2), 1915.
Theodore of Mopsuestia. Commentary of Theodore of Mopsuestia on the Lord's Prayer and on the Sacraments of Baptism and the Eucharist; ed., trans, A. Mingana; WSt 6, 1933.
Theodoret. Church History, GCS 44, Parmentier-Scheidweiler, Berlin ²1954.
Theophilus of Antioch. Ad Autolycum. R. M. Grant, OECT, 1970.
Timothy Aelurus. Against Chalcedon. ed. Ebied, R.Y. and L. R. Wickham, in: After Chalcedon. Studies in Theology and Church History (FS A. Van Roey) =OLA 18, 1985, 116-166.
Traditio Apostolica. ed. B. Botte, LQF 39, ⁵1989.
Victorinus Petavionensis. De fabrica mundi, ed., J. Haussleiter, CSEL 49, 1916.

b) Judaic Literature

Haggadah. Roth, Cecil, Haggadah, London (n.d.)
Josephus. Against Apion. Eng. trans. by Henry St. John Thackeray. LCL 186 (Josephus I), Cambridge, MA; London ⁵1987.
    Jewish Antiquities. Books XII-XIV. Eng. trans. by Ralph Marcus. LCL 365 (Josephus VII), Cambridge, MA; London ⁷1986.
    The Jewish War. Books IV-VII. Eng. trans. by Henry St. John Thackeray. LCL 210 (Josephus III), Cambridge, MA; London ⁵1979.
Jubilees. Das Buch der Jubiläen. Übers., Hrsg. Klaus Berger, JShrZ II/3, Gütersloh 1981.

Mishna Pesachim. Neusner, Jacob. A History of the Mishnaic Law of
    Appointed Times, Part Two, Erubin, Pesachim, SJLA 34, Leiden 1981
Mishnah Pesachim. Beer, G., Pesachim (Ostern). Text, Übersetzung und Erk-
    lärung. Nebst einem textkritischen Anhang. Mischna II,3. Gießen 1912.
Philo of Alexandria. Die Werke in deutscher Übersetzung, ed. L. Cohn, I.
    Heinemann, M. Adler, W. Theiler, 7 vols. Berlin.
    Opera quæ supersunt. ed. L. Cohn, P. Wendland, 6 vols. Berlin 1896-
        1915.
Quaestiones et Solutiones in Exodum I et II e versione armeniaca et fragmenta
    graeca. Intr., Trad., et Notes par Abraham Terian. Les Œvres de Philon
    d'Alexandrie 34C, Paris 1992.
Qumran. Die Texte aus Qumran, Hebräisch und Deutsch, mit masoretischer
    Punktation, Übersetzung, Einführung und Anm. hg. E. Lohse, Darmstadt
    1964.
Talmud, Babylonian. Der Babylonische Talmud mit Einschluss der vollstaendi-
    gen Misnah, Ed. Lazarus Goldschmidt, 9 vols., Haag 1933.

c) Valentinian and Gnostic Literature

Gospel of Mary. Die Gnostischen Schriften des Koptischen Papyrus Berolinen-
    sis 8502, hg., übers., u. bearb. v. Walter C. Till, TU 60, 1955, 62-79.
Herakleon. Fragment. (Origen, Comm. John) GCS 10, 190 f.
Nag Hammadi Library in English, third revised edition, James Robinson, ed.
    Leiden 1988.
Ptolemy. Letter to Flora. ed., trans., Gilles Quispel SC 24, 1954, ²1966.
Theodotus. See Clement of Alexandria, Extracts.
Three-formed Protennoia. Die Dreigestaltige Protennoia, ed. and trans. by
    Gisene Schenke. Nag-Hammadi-Codex XIII. TU 132, 1984.

d) Hellenic Literature

Anthology. Whittaker, Molly, Jews and Christians: Graeco-Roman Views,
    CCWJCW 6, 1984.
Plato. Republic. Platon. ΠΟΛΙΤΕΙΑ. Der Staat. Bearbeitet von Dietrich Kurz.
    gr. Text von Émile Chambry, dÜ von Friedrich Schleiermacher, =Werke,
    Bd. 4, Darmstadt 1971.
Pliny the Younger. Epistles. C. Plini Caecili Secvundi Epistvlarvm Libri
    Decem, ed. R.A.B. Mynors, SCBO, ²1968.
Plutarch. De Iside et Osiride. Ed., intro., and trans. J. Gwyn Griffiths. Cam-
    bridge 1970.
    Questiones Conviviales. Moralia VIII. LCL 424, ed., trans., Paul A.
        Clement and Herbert B. Hoffleit, 1969.

Tacitus. Histories. Cornelii Taciti Libri qui supersunt. Quartum recognovit Carolus Halm. Tomus posterior historias et libros minores continens. Lipsiae 1889.

2. Secondary Literature

Anonymous. Etwas von der Liturgie, besonders der Chürsächsisch-Evangelischen. Halle 1778.

Abramowski, Luise. Sprache und Abfassungszeit der Oden Salomos. OrChr 68, 1984, 80-90.

— Irenaeus, Adv. haer. II.3.2... and... 3.3. JTS 28, 1977, 101-104.

Adam, Adolf. Ostern alle Jahre anders?, Paderborn 1994.

Albrecht, Christoph. Schleiermachers Liturgik, Theorie und Praxis bei Schleiermacher und ihre geistesgeschichtlichen Zusammenhänge, VEGL 13, 1963.

Altaner, Berthold and Alfred Stuiber. Patrologie: Leben, Schriften und Lehre der Kirchenväter., Freiburg [8]1978.

Andresen, Carl. Zum Formular frühchristlicher Gemeindebriefe, ZNW 56, 1965, 233-259.

Angerstorfer, Ingeborg. Melito und das Judentum. Regensburg 1985.

Audet, Jean-Paul. L'hypothèse des Testimonia, RB 70, 1963, 381-405.

Auerbach, Erich, Mimesis. Dargestellte Wirklichkeit in der abendländischen Literatur (=Sammlung DALP 90), Bern/München [3]1946.

Auf der Maur, Hansjörg. Die Osterhomilien des Asterios Sophistes as Quelle für die Geschichte der Osterfeier, TTSt 19, 1962.

Aune, David Edward. The Cultic Setting of Realized Eschatology in Early Christianity. NT.S 28, 1972.

Bärsch, Jürgen. Das Dramatische im Gottesdienst. Liturgiewissenschaftliche Aspekte zum Phänomen der Osterfeiern und Osterspiele im Mittelalter, LJ 46, 1996, 41-66.

Bar-On, Shimon. Zur literarkritischen Analyse von Ex 12,21-27, ZAW 107, 1995, 18-31.

Barbel, Josef. Christos Angelos, Theoph. 3, 1941.

Bardy, Gustave. Cérinthe. RB 30, 1921, 344-373.

Barnard, Leslie W. In Defence of Pseudo-Pionius' Account of Saint Polycarp's Martyrdom, in: Kyriakon (FS Johannes Quasten) I, 1970,192-204

— The Epistle of Barnabas – A Paschal Homily? VigChr 15, 1961, 8-22

— The Origins and Emergence of the Church in Edessa during the First Two Centuries A. D. VigChr 22, 1968, 161-175.

Bauer, Walter. Rechtgläubigkeit und Ketzerei im ältesten Christentum, BhTh 10, [2]1964.

Baumstark, Anton. Nocturna Laus, LQF 32, 1957.

Baus, Karl. Das Nachwirken des Origenes in der Osterfrömmigkeit des Ambrosius, RQ 49, 1954, 21-55.

Beatrice, Pier Franco. La lavanda dei piedi. Contributo alla storia delle antiche liturgie cristiane. BEL.S 28, 1983.

Beauchamp, J. et. al., Temp et Histoire I: Le Prologue de la Chronique Pascale. TrMem 7, 1979, 223-301.

Beck, Edmund. Le Baptème chez Saint Éphrem, OrSyr 1, 1956, 113-136.

Beckwith, Roger. The Origin of the Festivals Easter and Whitsun, SL 13, 1979, 1-20.

Bellinzoni, A.J. The Sayings of Jesus in the Writings of Justin Martyr. NT.S 17, 1967, 136-138.

Berger, Klaus. Manna, Mehl und Sauerteig. Korn und Brot im Alltag der frühen Christen, Stuttgart 1993.

— Theologiegeschichte des Urchristentums, UTB, 1994.

Bernard, L. W. The Use of Testimonies in the Early Church and in the Epistle of Barnabas, in Studies in the Apostolic Fathers and their Backgrounds, Oxford, 1966, 109-135.

Bertrand, Daniel Alain. Le baptême de Jésus. BGBE 14, 1973.

Betz, Hans Dieter. Der Galaterbrief, (=dÜ Galatians, Phila. 1979) München 1988.

Betz, Johannes. Die Eucharistie als Gottes Milch in frühchristlicher Sicht, ZKTh 106, 1984, 1-26; 167-185.

— Die Eucharistie in der Zeit der griechischen Väter, Bd. 1/1, Die Actualpräzenz der Person und des Heilswerkes Jesu im Abendmahl nach der Vorephesinischen griechischen Patristik, Freiburg (D), 1955.

Blanchard, Yves-Marie. Aux sources du canon, le témoignage de'Irénée, CogFid 175, 1993.

Blöningen, Christoph. Der griechische Ursprung der jüdisch-hellenistischen Allegorese und ihre Rezeption in der alexandrinischen Patristik, EHS 14/59, 1992.

Bokser, Baruch. The Origins of the Seder. Berkeley/Los Angeles 1984.

Bonz, Marianne P. Differing Approaches to Religious Benefaction: The Late Third-Century Acquisition of the Sardis Synagogue. HThR 86, 1993, 139-54.

— The Jewish Community of Ancient Sardis: A Reassessment of its Rise to Prominence. HSCP 93, 1990, 342-259.

Botte, Bernard. Les Origines de la Noël et de l'Épiphanie. Étude Historique. TEL 1, 1932 (repr. 1961)

Bradshaw, Paul. The Search for Origins of Christian Worship, London 1992.

Braulik, Georg, Pascha–von der alttestamentlichen Feier zum neutestamentlichen Fest, BiKi 36, 1981, 159-165.

Brent, Allen. Hippolytus and the Roman Church in the Third Century. Communities in Tension before the Emergence of a Monarch-Bishop, VigChrS 31, 1995.

Brightman, Frank Edward, ed., trans. Liturgies Eastern and Western. Vol. I, Eastern Liturgies. Oxford 1896.

Brown, Raymond E. The Death of the Messiah. London/NY 1994.

Brox, Norbert. Tendenzen und Parteilichkeit im Osterfeststreit des zweiten Jahrhunderts, ZKG 83 1972, 291-394.

Bruns, Peter. Den Menschen mit dem Himmel Verbinden. Eine Studie zu den katechetischen Homilien des Theodor von Mopsuestia, CSCO 549 (Subs. 89), 1995.

Buckley, Jorunn Jacobsen, A Cult-Mystery in the Gospel of Philip, JBL 99, 1980, 569-581.

van de Bunt, Annewies. Milk and Honey in the Theology of Clement of Alexandria, in: Fides Sacramenti, Sacramentum Fidei (FS=Smulders), Assen 1981,27-39.

Burkert, Walter. Antike Mysterien, München 1990.

Buschmann, Gerd, Martyrium Polycarpi, Eine formkritische Studie, BZNW 70, 1994.

Cabié, Robert, A Propos de la "Question Pascale": Quelle Pratique opposait-on à celle des Quartodecimans? EO 11, 1994, 101-106.

Cacitti, Remo, Grande Sabato. Il contesto pasquale quartodecimano nella formazione della teologia del martirio. SPMed 19, 1994.

Campenhausen, Hans Frhr. von. Bearbeitungen und Interpolationen des Polykarpmartyriums. in Aus der Frühzeit des Christentums, Tübingen 1963, 253-301 = SHAW.PH 2, 1957/3)

— Ostertermin oder Osterfasten? VigChr 28, 1974, 114-138.

— Die Entstehung der Heilsgeschichte, in: Urchristliches and Altchristliches, Tübingen 1979, 20-62 (= Saec 21, 1970, 189-212).

— Das AT als Bibel der Kirche. Vom Ausgang des Urchristentums bis zur Entstehung des NT.s, in: idem., Aus der Frühzeit des Christentums. Studien zur Kirchengeschichte des ersten und zweiten Jahrhunderts, Tübingen 1963, 152-196

— Die Entstehung der christlichen Bibel, BHT 39, 1968

— Ostertermin oder Osterfasten? Zum Verständnis des Irenäusbriefs an Viktor (Euseb. Hist. Eccl. 5,24,12-17), VigChr 28, 1974, 114-118.

Cancik, Hubert, Das jüdische Fest, ThQ 150, 1970, 335-348.

Cantalamessa, Raniero, L'Omelia "In S. Pascha" dello Pseudo-Ippolito di Roma. Richerche sulla teologia dell' Asia Minore nella seconda metà del II secolo, PUCSC 3.16, Milan 1967.

— Easter in the Early Church. An Anthology of Jewish and Early Christian Texts. Selected, annotated, and introduced by Raniero Cantalamessa. Revised and Augmented by the Author. Newly Translated from the Sources and Edited with Further Annotations by James M. Quigley, SJ, and Joseph T. Lienhard, SJ. Collegeville, MN (USA) 1993 = ET Cantalamessa, Raniero, La Pasqua nella Chiesa Antica (=Traditio Cristiana), Torino 1978.

Casel, Odo. Art und Sin der ältesten christlichen Osterfeier, JLW 14, 1938, 1-78.

Caspar, E. Die älteste römische Bischofsliste, Berlin 1926.

Chadwick, Henry, The Church of the Third Century in the West, in: The Roman West in the Third Century, in: The Roman West in the Third Century (A. King, M. Henig, eds.) Oxford 1981, 5-13. (=ibid., Heresy and Orthodoxy in the Early Church, article XIV, Hampshire/Brookfield VT [orig. num. retained.])

Charlesworth, James H. Tatian's Dependence upon Apocryphal Traditions, HeyJ 15, 1974, 5-17.

Charlesworth, M. P. Trade-Routes and Commerce of the Roman Empire, Cambridge 1924 (repr. Hildesheim, 1961).

Chevallier, Max-Alain. L'apologie du baptême d'eau à la fin du premier siècle: Introduction secondaire de l'étiologie dans les recits du baptême de Jésus, NTS 32, 1986, 528-543.

Childs, Brevard, Exodus. A Commentary, OTL, London 1974.

Chilton, Bruce. A Feast of Meanings, NT.S 72, 1994.

Christiansen, Irmgard. Die Technit der allegorischen Auslegungswissenschaft bei Philon von Alexandrien. BGBH 7, 1969.

Chupungco, Anscar, The Cosmic Elements of the Christian Passover, StAn 72, 1977.

— Shaping the Easter Feast. NPM Studies in Church Music and Liturgy, Washington DC 1992.

Conzelmann, Hans. Bemerkungen zum Martyrdom Polykarps. NAWG.PH, 1978, 41-58.

Cornelius, E. M. The Relevance of Ancient Rhetoric to Rhetorical Criticism, Neotest 28, 1994, 457-467.

Corti, Carmelo. Il regno millenario in Vittorino di Petovio, Aug 18, 1978, 419-433.

Countryman, L. Wm. Tertullian and the Regula Fidei, SecCent 2, 1982, 208-227.

Crawford, John S. Multiculturalism at Sardis. BAR 22, no. 5, 1996, 38-47.

Cross, Frank. Rev.: B. Lohse's edition of Melito, Leiden 1958. JTS ns 11, 1960, 162 f.

Crossan, Dominic. The Cross that Spoke, San Francisco 1988.

Daniélou, Jean. Daniélou, J., Traversée de la mer Rouge et baptême aus premiers siècles, RSR 33, 1946, 402-430.

Daxelmüller, Christoph, Der Untergrund der Frömmigkeit. Zur Geschichte und Pathologie religiöser Bräuche, Saec 47, 1996, 136-157.

de Jong, Johannes Petrus, Der ursprüngliche Sinn von Epiklese und Mischungritus nach der Eucharistielehre des heiligen Irenäus, ALW 9, 1965, 28-47.

Decock, Paul B. The Reading of Sacred Texts in the Context of Early Christianity. Neotest 27, 1993, 263-282.

Dehandschutter, Boudewijn, Martyrium Polycarpi. Een literairkritische studie. BETL 52, 1979

Dix, Gregory. Shape of the Liturgy, London ²1945.

Doeve, J. W. De Christelijke Paasdatum. Kerk en theologie 27, 1976, 265-275.

Dölger, Franz, Sol Salutis, LF 4/5, 1925.

Downey, Glanville. A History of Antioch in Syria from Seleucus to the Arab Conquest. Princeton 1961.

Draper, Jonathan A., Christian Self-Definition against the "Hypocrites" in Didache 9-10, SBL 1992 Seminar Papers, Atlanta 1992, 362-377.

Drijvers H.J.W., and G. J. Reinink, Taufe und Licht. Tatian, Ebionäerevangelium und Thomasakten, in: Text and Testimony, FS Klijn, Leiden 1988, 91-110.

Drijvers, Han J. W. Syrian Christianity and Judaism, in: The Jews among Pagans and Christians in the Roman Empire (J. Lieu, J. North, T. Rajak, eds. London/NY 1992, 124-146.

Drobner, Hubertus. Lehrbuch der Patrologie. Freiburg, Basel, Wien, 1994.

Drumbl, Johann. Die Improperien in der Lateinischen Liturgie. ALW 15, 1973, 68-100.

Duchesne, Louis. La Question de la Pâque au Concile de Nicée. RQH 28, 1880, 5-42.

Edwards, M. E. Gnostics and Valentinians in the Church Fathers, JTS NS 40, 1989, 26-47.

Engberding, Hieronymus. Der 25. Dezember als Tag der Feier der Geburt des Herrn, ALW 2, 1952, 25-43.

Engnell, Ivan, Pæsah-Massot and the Problem of 'Patternism'. OrSuec 1, 1952, 39-50.

Epp, Eldon Jay. The Theological Tendency of Codex Bezae Catabrigiensis in Acts. SNTS.MS 3, 1966.

Erlemann, Kurt. Naherwartung und Parusieverzögerung im NT. TANZ 17, 1995, 393 f.

Farkasfalvy, D. Theology of Scripture in St. Irenaeus. RevBen 78, 1968, 319-333.

Fascher, Karl. THbNT VII, I, 1 Kor¹, ⁴1988.

Feldmeier, Reinhard. Die Christen als Fremde. WUNT 64, 1992.

Feneberg, Rupert. Christliche Passafeier und Abendmahl. Eine biblisch-hermeneutische Untersuchung der ntl. Einsetzungsberichte. STANT 27, 1971.

Finley, I. M. Myth, Memory, and History, History and Theory 5, 1965, 281-302.

Fitzmyer, Jos. A. The Use of Explicit OT Quotations in Qumran Literature and the NT, NTS 7, 1960/1, 296-333.

Füglister, Notker, Die Heilsbedeutung des Pascha. SANT 8, 1963, 33.
Gager, John G. The Origins of Anti-Semitism. Attitudes Toward Judaism in Pagan and Christian Antiquity, NY 1985.
Ginzel, F. K. Handbuch der mathematischen und technischen Chronologie. Das Zeitrechnungswesen der Völker. Vol. II (1911), Die Juden.
Girard, René. The Scapegoat, trans. Yvonne Freccero, Baltimore 1986.
Gödecke, Monika, Geschichte als Mythos. Eusebs "Kirchengeschichte," EHS 23.307, 1987.
Goodenough, Erwin, By Light, Light: The Mystic Gospel of Hellenistic Judaism. New Haven 1935.
Goppelt, Leonhard. Typos, Die typologische Deutung des AT.s im Neuen. Gütersloh 1939.
van Goudoever J. The Celebration of the Resurrection in the New Testament. StEv 3.2, 1964 [=TU 88], 254-259.
— Biblical Calendars, Leiden ²1961.
Grant, Robert M. Eusebius as Church Historian. Oxford 1980.
— Greek Apologists of the Second Century. London 1988.
— The Fragments of the Greek Apologists and Irenaeus, in Biblical and Patristic Studies (Mem: Casey) Freiburg 1963, 179-234.
Green, Joel B. The Death of Jesus. WUNT 2.33, 1988.
Greenslade S. L. Schism in the Early Church (Cadbury Lectures, 1949-50), London 1953.
Grelot, Pierre. Les Juifs dans l'Évangile selon Jean. Enquête historique et réflexion théologique. RB 35, 1995.
Grillmeier, Aloys. Christ in Christian Tradition, London ²1975.
— Das "Gebet zu Jesus" und das "Jesus-Gebet": Eine Neue Quelle zum "Jesus-Gebet" aus dem Weißen Kloster, in: After Chalcedon. Studies in Theology and Church History (=OLA 18, FS A. Van Roey), 1985, 187-202.
Grossi, V. Regula veritatis e narratio battesimale in sant'Ireneo, Aug 12, 1972, 437-463.
Grünwaldt, Klaus. Exil und Identität. Beschneidung, Passa und Sabbat in der Priesterschrift. BBB 85, 1992.
Grumel, Venance. Le problèm de la date pascale aux IIIe et IVe siècles. L'origin du conflit: le nouveau cadre du comput juif. REB 18, 1960, 163-178.
Gry, Louis. La date de la Parousie d'après l'Epistola Apostolorum, RB 49, 1940, 86-97.
Gutmann, Joseph. Early Synagogue and Jewish Catacomb Art and its Relation to Christian Art, ANRW II.21.2, 1984, 1313-1342.
Halbe, Jörn. Erwägungen zu Ursprung und Wesen des Massotfestes. ZAW 87, 1975, 324-346.
Hamman, A. Valeur et signification des reseignements liturgiques de Justin, StPat 13.2 (=TU 116), 364-374.

Harvey, Graham. The True Israel. Uses of the Names Jew, Hebrew and Israel in Ancient Jewish and Early Christian Literature, AGAJU 35, 1996.

Hall, Stuart G. Melito in the Light of the Passover Haggadah. JTS, NS 22, 1971, 29-46.

— The Origins of Easter. StPatr 15, 1984, 554-567.

Hardison, O. B. Christian Rite and Christian Drama in the Middle Ages. Essays in the Origins and Early History of Modern Drama, Baltimore 1965.

Harnack, Adolf (von). Die Chronologie der altchristlichen Litteratur 1, Leipzig 1897.

— Die Mission und Ausbreitung des Christentums in den ersten drei Jahrhunderten, Leipzig ⁴1924.

— Die Pfaff'schen Irenäus-Fragmente als Fälschung nachgewiesen, TU 20.3, 1900, 1-69.

— Über die Herkunft der 48 (47) ersten Päpste, SKPAW 37, 1904, 1004-1062.

Heither, Theresia. Translatio Religionis, Die Paulusdeutung des Origenes, BBKg 16, 1990, 31-34.

Helderman, Jan. Die Anapausis im Evangelium Veritatis, NHS 18, 1984.

Henniger, Joseph. Les Fêtes de printemps chez les Sémites et la Pâque Israélite, Paris 1975

— Über Frühingsfeste bei den Semiten. In: In Verbo Tuo. FS Missionspriesterseminars St. Augustin bei Siegburg. Siegburg 1963, 375-398.

Henscheid, Eckhard. Dummdeutsch, Stuttgart 1993 (Reclam 8865).

Herr, M. D. The Calendar. CRI 1/2, 833-864.

Hills, Julian. Proverbs as Sayings of Jesus in the Epistula Apostolorum, Semeia 49, 1990. 7-34.

— Tradition and Composition in the Epistula Apostolorum. HDR 24, Minneapolis 1990.

Hodgson, Robert Jr., The Testimony Hypothesis, JBL 98, 1979, 361-378.

van den Hoek, Annewies. Clement of Alexandria and His Use of Philo in the *Stromateis*. An Early Christian Reshaping of a Jewish model, VigChrS 3, 1988.

Holland, David Larrimore. Die Synode von Antiochien (324/5) und ihre Bedeutung für Eusebius von Caesarea und das Konzil von Nizäa, ZKG 81, 1970, 163-181.

Hopkins, Clark (ed. Goldman, Bernard), The Discovery of Dura-Europos, New Haven/London 1979.

Hornschuh, Michael. Studien zur Epistula Apostolorum. PTS 5, 1965.

Howard, George. Paul: Crisis in Galatia. SNTS.MS 35,²1990.

Howard, J.K. "Christ Our Passover": A Study of the Passover-Exodus Theme in 1 Corinthians. EvQ 41, 1969, 97-108.

Huber, Wolfgang. Passa und Ostern. Untersuchungen zur Osterfeier der alten Kirche. BZNW 35, 1969.

Hvalvik, Reidar. The Struggle for Scripture and Covenant. The Purpose of the Epistle of Barnabas and Jewish-Christian Competition in the Second Century, WUNT 2.82, 1996.

Jacques, Francis. Von den Sprachspielen zu den "Textspielen." Con (Dt) 31, 1995, 178-192.

James, E. O. Christian Myth and Rituals. London 1937.

Jasper, Ronald Claud, and G.J. Cuming. Prayers of the Eucharist: Early and Reformed. NY ³1987.

Jaubert, Annie La Date de la Céne. Calendrier biblique et liturgie chrêtienne. Paris 1957.

Jeremias, Joachim, Die Passahfeier der Samariter und ihre Bedeutung für das Verständnis der alttestamentlichen Passahüberlieferung, BZAW 59, 1932.

— Abendmahlworte Jesu, Göttingen, ⁴1967.

Jervell, Jacob. The Mighty Minority. StTh 34, 1980, 13-38.

Jeske, Richard. The Rock was Christ: The Ecclesiology of 1 Corinthians 10. in: Kirche (FS Günther Bornkamm 75). Tübingen 1980. 245-255.

Jordan, Hermann. Wer war Archaeus? ZNW 13, 1912, 157-160.

Jossua, Jean-Pierre. Le Salut Incarnation ou Mystère Pascal. Chez les Pères de l'Église de saint Iréné à Léon le Grand. CogFid 28, 1968.

Joubert, S. J. A Bone of Contention in Recent Scholarship: The 'Birkat Ha-Minim' and the Separation of Church and Synagogue in the First Century AD. Neotest. 27, 1993, 351-363.

Juel, Donald. Messianic Exegesis. Christological Interpretation of the OT in Early Christianity, Phila. 1988.

Katz, Steven T. Issues in the Separation of Judaism and Christianity after 70 CE: A Reconsideration. JBL 103, 1984, 43-76.

Kee, H. C. The Transformation of the Synagogue after 70 CE: Its Import for Early Christianity, NTS 36, 1990, 1-14.

Keel, Othmar. Erwägungen zum Sitz im Leben des vormosaischen Pascha und zur Etymologie von פסה. ZAW 84, 1972, 414-434.

Kelly, J. N. D. Early Christian Creeds. London ²1960.

Kinzig, Wolfram. In Search of Asterius. Studies on the Authorship of the Homilies on the Psalms, FKD 47, 1990.

Kirkland, Alastair. The Beginnings of Christianity in the Lycus Valley, Neotest 29, 1995, 109-124.

Klauser, Theodor. Der Übergang der römischen Kirche von der griechischen zur lateinischen Liturgiesprache. Studi e Testi 121, 1946, 467-482 (=JbAC Eb 3, 1974, 184-194).

— Die Anfänge der römischen Bischofsliste. JbAC.Eb 3, 1974, 121-138 (=BZThS 8, 1931, 193-213).

Klijn, A. F. J. Das Hebräer- und das Nazoräerevangelium, ANRW II,25.5, 3997-4033.
— Jewish Christianity in Egypt. Roots 161-175.
Knowles, Michael P. "The Rock, His Work is Perfect": Unusual Imagery for God in Dt 32. VT 39, 1989, 307-322.
Koch, Dietrich-Alex. Die Schrift als Zeuge des Evangeliums, BHT 69, 1986.
Koch, Hugo. Pascha in der ältesten Kirche. ZwissTh NF 20, 1914, 289-313.
Koester, Helmut. Ancient Christian Gospels. Their History and Development. London/Philadelphia 1990.
— Dialog und Spruchüberlieferung in den gnostischen Texten von Nag Hammadi. EvTh 39, 1979, 532-556.
— Einführung in das Neue Testament im Rahmen der Religionsgeschichte und Kulturgeschichte der hellenistischen und römischen Welt. Berlin 1980.
— History and Cult in the Gospel of John and in Ignatius of Antioch. JThCh 1, 1969, 111-123 (= Geschichte und Kultus im Johannesevangelium und bei Ignatius von Antiochien, ZThK 54, 1957, 56-69).
— The History-of-Religions School, Gnosis, and Gospel of John, StTh 40, 1986, 115-136.
— Jesus' Presence in the Early Church. CrSt 15, 1994, 541-557.
Kohata, Fujiko, Jahwist und Priesterschrift in Exodus 3-14, BZAW 166, 1986.
Körtner, Ulrich H. J. Papias von Hierapolis. Ein Beitrag zur Geschichte des frühen Christentums. FRLANT 133, 1983.
Kraabel, Alf Thomas. Paganism and Judaism: The Sardis Evidence. In: Paganisme, Judaïsme, Christianisme. Influences et affrontements dans le monde antique. (FS Simon, A. Benoît, M. Philonenko, C. Vogel, eds.) Paris 1978, 13-33.
Kraehling, Carl H. The Jewish Community at Antioch, JBL 51, 1932, 130-160.
— A Greek Fragment of Tatian's Diatessaron from Dura, Studies and Documents 3, London 1935.
Kraft, Robert. "Ezra" Materials in Judaism and Christianity ARNW II 19.1, 119-136.
Kraus, Hans-Joachim, Gottesdienst in Israel, München ²1962.
Kretschmar, Georg, Die Bedeutung der Liturgiegeschichte für die Frage nach der Kontinuität des Judenchristentums in nachapostolischer Zeit, in: Aspects du Judéo-Christianisme. Colloque de Strasbourg 23-25 avril 1964. Paris 1965, 113-137.
— Christliches Passa im 2. Jahrhundert und die Ausbildung der christlichen Theologie, RSR 60, 1972, 287-323.
— Die Geschichte des Taufgottesdienstes in der alten Kirche. Leitourgia 5, 1964-66, 1-346.

Kutsch, Ernst. Erwägungen zur Geschichte der Passafeier und des Massotfestes. ZThK 55, 1958, 1-35.

La Piana, George. The Roman Church at the End of the Second Century. HThR 18, 1925, 201-277.

Laaf, Peter. Die Pascha-Feier Israels, BBB 36, 1970.

Lampe, Peter. An Early Christian Inscription in the Musei Capitolini. StTh 49, 1995, 79-92.

— Die stadtrömischen Christen in den ersten beiden Jahrhunderten. Untersuchungen zur Sozialgeschichte. WUNT 2.18. Tübingen 1987.

Leloir, Louis. Le Diatessaron de Tatien, OrSyr 1, 1956, 208-231, 313-334.

Leon-Dufour, Xavier. Abendmahl und Abschiedsrede im NT, Stuttgart 1983 (= Le partage du pain eucharistique selon le NT, Paris 1982).

Lies, Lothar. Wort und Eucharistie bei Origenes. Zur Spiritualisierungstendenz des Eucharistieverständnisses. InThSt 1, 1978.

Lietzmann, Hans. Ein liturgisches Bruchstück des 2. Jh.s ZNW 54, 1912, 56-61 (=Kleine Schriften III, TU 47, 43-47).

— Messe und Herrenmahl. Eine Studie zur Geschichte der Liturgie, AKG 8, ³1955.

Lohse, Bernhard. Das Passafest der Quartodezimaner, BFChrT 2/54, 1953.

Loi, Vicenzo. Il 25 Marzo data pasquale e la chronologia giovannea della passione in età patristica. EL 85, 1971, 51-69.

Lundberg, Per. La typologie baptismale dans l'ancienne église. ASNU 10, 1942, 116-135.

Luther, Martin. Lecture on Hebrews 1517-1518, WA 57.

Lyons, Campbell N. D. From Persuasion to Subversion: A Review of Past and Current Trends in Defining Rhetoric. Neotest 28, 1994, 429-456.

MacGregor, Alistair J. Fire and Light in the Western Triduum, ACC 71, Collegeville, 1992.

Mack, Burton L. Philo Judaeus and Exegetical Traditions in Alexandria, ANRW II.21.1, 1984, 227-271.

Maertens, Thierry. Heidnisch-jüdische Wurzeln der christlichen Feste (dÜ=C'est fête en l'honneur de Yahvé) Mainz 1965.

Malkowski, J. L. The Element of ἄκαιρος in John Chrysostom's Anti-Jewish Polemic, StPat 12.1, 1975, 222-231.

Marsh, H. G. The use of ΜΥΣΤΗΡΙΟΝ in the Writings of Clement of Alexandria with Special Reference to his Sacramental Doctrine. JTS 37, 1936, 64-80.

Martyn, J. Louis, A Law-Observant Mission to Gentiles: The Background of Galatians, SJT 38, 1985, 307-324.

Mazza, Enrico. Mystagogy. A Theology of Liturgy in the Patristic Age. NY 1989.

McKay, Heather A. Sabbath and Synagogue. RGRW 122, 1994.

Metzger, Bruce M. The Canon of the NT, its Origin, Development and Significance, Oxford 1987.

Meyers, Eric M. Early Judaism and Christianity in the Light of Archaeology. BA 51/2 (June 1988) 69-79.

Michels, Thomas OSB, Das Frühjahrssymbol im österlicher Liturgie, Rede und Dichtung des christlichen Altertums, JLW 6, 1926, 1-15.

Mohrmann, Christine. Le conflit pascal au IIe siècle. Note philologique. VigChr 16, 1962, 154-171.

— Note sur l'homélie pascale VI de la collection Pseudo-Chrysostomienne dite "des petites trompettes," in: Mélanges en l'honneur de Mgr. M. Andrieu, Strasbourg 1956, 351-360.

Molland, Einar, The Heretics Combatted by Ignatius of Antioch, JEH, 5, 1954, 1-6.

Muir, Lynnette. Biblical Drama of Medieval Europe. Oxford 1995.

Murphy-O'Connor, Jerome. St. Paul's Corinth. Texts and Archaeology. Good News Studies 6, Wilmington (DE) 1983.

Murray, Robert. Symbols of Church and Kingdom. A Study in Early Syriac Tradition, Cambridge, ^2 1977.

Nautin, Pierre, Lettres et Écrivains Chrétiens des IIe et IIIe siècles. Patristica II, Paris 1961.

Niebuhr, Karl-Wilhelm. «Judentum» und «Christentum» bei Paulus und Ignatius von Antiochien, ZNW 85, 1994, 218-233.

Niederwimmer, Kurt. Der Didachist und seine Quellen, in: The Didache in Context. Essays on its Text, History, and Transmission (ed. Jefford, Clayton N.), NT.S 77, 1995, 15-36.

Norris, F. W. Melito's Motivation. AThR 68, 1986, 16-24.

Nygren, Anders. Agape and Eros, trans. Philip S. Watson, Chicago 1982 (=repr. Philadelphia 1953).

Orr, Wm. F., and James Arthur Walther, 1 Cor AB 32, 1976.

Van Den Oudenrijn, Marc-Antonius, OP. Gamaliel. Äthiopische Texte zur Pilatusliteratur, SpicFrib 4, 1959.

Pagels, Elaine H., The Johannine Gospel in Gnostic Exegesis, SBL.MS 17, 1973,78-82.

— Mystery of Marriage in the Gospel of Philip. in: The Future of Early Christianity (FS: Koester) Minneapolis 1991, 442-454.

— A Valentinian Interpretation of Baptism and Eucharist. HThR 65, 1972, 153-169.

Paverd, Frans van de. Zur Geschichte der Messliturgie in Antiocheia und Konstantinopel gegen Ende des Vierten Jahrhunderts. Analyse der Quellen bei Johannes Chrysostomos, OCA 187, 1970.

Pearson, Birger A. Earliest Christianity in Egypt: Some Observations, Roots, 132-157.

— Philo and Gnosticism, ANRW II.21.1, 1984, 295-342.

Pedersen, Johannes. Passahfest und Passahlegende, ZAW 52 (NF 11), 1934, 161-175.

Pelikan, Jaroslav. The Two Sees of Peter. in: The Shaping of Christianity in the Second and Third Centuries. Jewish and Christian Self-Definition, Vol. I. E. P. Sanders, ed., Philadelphia 1980, 57-73.

Perkins, Pheme, Gnosticism and the NT, Minneapolis 1993.

Petersen, William L. The Diatessaron and Ephrem Syrus as Sources of Romanos the Melodist. CSCO 475 [Subs. 74], 1985.

— Eusebius and the Paschal Controversy. in: Eusebius, Christianity, & Judaism (ed. Attridge, H.W., G. Hata) StPBib 42, 1992, 311-325.

— Tatian's Diatesseron. Its Creation, Dissemination, Significance, and History of Scholarship. VigChrS 25, 1994.

Peterson, Erik. Εἷς θεός, Epigraphische, formgeschichtliche und religions-geschichtliche Untersuchungen, FRANT, NF 24, 1926.

— Jüdisches und christliches Morgengebet in Syrien, ZKT 58, 1934, 110-113.

Petraglio, Renzo. Le interpolazioni cristiane del Salterio greco, Aug 28, 1988, 89-109.

Pfitzner, Victor. Cultic Narrative and Eucharistic Proclamation in First Corinthians, LThJ 25, 1991, 15-25.

Polomé, Edgar C. The Liguistic Situation in the Western Provinces of the Roman Empire. ANRW 2.29.2, 1983, 509-553.

Pratzner, Ferdinand. Messe und Kreuzesopfer. Die Krise der sakramentalen Idee bei Luther und in der mittelalterlichen Scholastik. WBT 29, 1970.

Preiss, Th. La mystique de l'imitation du Christ et de l'unité chez Ignace d'Antioche. RHPhR 18, 1938, 197-241.

Pritz, Ray A. Nazarene Jewish Christianity. From the End of the NT Period until its Disappearance in the Fourth Century, Jerusalem/Leiden 1988.

Procter, Everett. Christian Controversy in Alexandria, AmUSt VII/172, 1995, 69 f.

Quasten, Josef. Patrology III. The Golden Age of Greek Patristic Literature from the Council of Nicaea to the Council of Chalcedon. Utrecht. 1963.

Radl, Walter, Befreiung aus dem Gefängnis. Die Darstellung eines biblischen Grundthemas in Apg 12, BZ NF 27, 1983, 81-96.

Reicke, Bo. Diakonie, Festfreude und Zelos. In Verbindung mit der altchristlichen Agapenfeier. Uppsala Universitets Årsskrift 1951:5. AUU. Uppsala/Wiesbaden 1951.

Reitzenstein, Richard. Die Vorgeschichte der christlichen Taufe. Mit Beiträge von Luise Troje. Leipzig/Berlin 1929.

— Das iranische Erlösungsmysterium, Bonn 1921.

Renckens, Han. Le Chant de la Diaspora. Théologie et mélodie. In: Fides Sacramenti, Sacramentum Fidei (FS=P. Smulders), Assen 1981, 1-8.

Rengstorf, Karl Heinrich and Siegfried von Kortzfleisch, Kirche und Synagoge: Handbuch von Christen und Juden, vol. 1, Stuttgart 1968.

Resch, Agrapha, TU 30.3/4, 1906.

Reventlow, Epochen der Bibelauslegung, Bd. I. Vom AT bis Origenes, München 1990.

Richard, Marcel. La Lettre de Saint Irénée au Pape Victor. ZNW 56, 1965,260-282.

— La question pascale au IIe siècle. OrSyr 6, 1961, 179-212.

Richardson, Cyril C. A New Solution to the Quartodeciman Riddle. JTS.NS 24, 1973, 74-83.

Ricœur, Paul. Zeit und Erzählung, Bd. I. Zeit und historische Erzählung, München, 1988 (=dÜ, Temps et récit, tome I, Paris 1983).

Riedweg, Christoph. Mysterienterminologie bei Platon, Philon und Klemens von Alexandrien, UALG 26, 1987.

Robinson, Thomas A. The Bauer Thesis Examined. The Geography of Heresy in the Early Christian Church. Lewiston/Queenston (NY) 1988.

Roll, Susan K. Toward the Origins of Christmas, LitCon 5, 1995.

Rordorf, Willy. Der Sonntag. Geschichte des Ruhe- und Gottesdiensttages im ältesten Christentum. ATANT 43, 1962.

— Zum Ursprung des Osterfestes am Sonntag. ThZ 18, 1962, 167-189.

Ross, J. M. The Extra Words in Acts 18.22, NovTest 34, 1992, 247-249.

Rost, Leonhard. Weidewechsel und altisraelitischer Festkalender. ZDPV 66, 1943, 205-216.

Rouwhorst, G[erard] A. M. The Date of Easter in the Twelfth Demonstration of Aphraates, StPat 17, 1982, 1374-1380.

— La célébration de l'eucharistie selon les Actes de Thomas, in Omnes Circumadstantes (FS Wegman, C. Caspers, M. Schneiders, eds.), Kampen 1990, 51-77.

— Les Hymnes Pascales d'Ephrem de Nisibe I, Étude, VigChrS 7.1, 1989.

Rudolf, Kurt. Die Mandäer, Bd. I, Prolegomena: Das Mandäerproblem, FRLANT 74, 1960.

— Die Mandäer, Bd. II. Der Kult. FRLANT 75, 1961.

Ruether, Rosemary Radford. Faith and Fratricide: The Theological Roots of Anti-Semitism, NY 1974.

Runia, David T. Philo in Early Christian Literature. A Survey. CRI III,3, 1993.

Sagnard, François Marie-Mattaeus. La Gnose Valentinienne et la Témoignage de Saint Irénée. EPhM 36, 1947.

Salzman, Jorg Christian. Lehren und Ermahnen. Zur Geschichte des christlichen Wortgottes-dienstes in den ersten drei Jahrhunderten, WUNT 2/59, 1994.

Sanders, E. P. Paul and Palestinian Judaism, A Comparison of Patterns of Religion. Phila. 1977, 20-24.

Sandmel, S. Philo Judaeus: An Introduction to the Man, his Writings, and his Significance, ANRW II.21.1, 1984, 3-46.

Schenk, W. Der Kolosserbrief in der neueren Forschung (1945-1985), ANRW 2.25.4, 3327-3364.

Schille, Gottfried. Das Leiden des Herrn. ZTK, 52, 1955, 161-205.

Schmid, Joseph. Die Osterfestfrage auf dem ersten allgemeinen Konzil von Nicäa. ThStL 13, Vienna 1905.

Schmidt-Lauber, Hans-Christoph. Die Bedeutung der "Lima"-Liturgie für die ökumenische Bewegung, LJ 35, 1985, 131-147.

Schmitt, Rainer. Exodus und Passah. Ihr Zusammenhang im AT, OBO 7, 1975.

Schrage, Wolfgang, 1 Kor¹, EKK 7/1, 1991.

Schreckenberg, Heinz. Die christlichen Adversus-Judaeos-Texts und ihr literarisches und historisches Umfeld (1. -11. Jh.), EHS 23.172, 1982

Schulz, Siegfried. Die Decke des Moses, ZNW 49, 1958, 1-30.

Schüssler Fiorenza, Elisabeth. Rhetorical Situation and historical Reconstruction in 1 Cor. NTS 33, 1987, 386-403.

Schültz, Werner. "Was habe ich dir getan, mein Volk?" Die Wurzeln der Karfreitagsimproperien in der alten Kiche. JLH 13, 1968, 1-38.

— Zur Geschichte des Athanasins. Gesammelte Schriften 3, Berlin 1959, 36-54.

Schwartz, Eduard. Christliche und jüdische Ostertafeln. AGWG^PH NF 8.6, 1905, 149.

Scicolone, Ildebrando, ed., La Celebrazione del Triduo Pasquale, Anamnesis e Mimesis. Atti del III Congresso Internazionale di Liturgia, Roma, Pontificio Istituto Liturgico, 9-3 Maggio, 1988, StAns 102 (=AnLit 14), Rome 1990.

Scott, R. B. Y. Meteorological Phenomena and Terminology in the Old Testament. ZAW 64, NF 23, 1952, 11-25.

Seeliger, Hans-Reinhard. Gemeinsamkeiten in der antijüdischen und antichristlichen Polemik in der Antike, in: Christlicher Antijudaismus und jüdischer Antipaganismus, (H. Frohnhofen, ed.) HThSt 3, 1990, 88-94.

Segal, J[udah]. B. Intercalation and the Hebrew Calendar, VT 7, 1957, 250-307.

— The Hebrew Passover from the Earliest Times to A. D. 70. LOrS 12, 1963.

Segelberg, E., The Baptismal Rite according to some of the Coptic-Gnostic Texts of Nag-Hammadi. StPatr 5, 1962, 117-128.

Seters, John Van. The Place of the Yahwist in the History of Passover and Massot, ZAW 95, 1983, 167-182.

Shepherd, Massey H. The Paschal Liturgy and the Apocalypse. ECW 6, London 1960.

Simon, Marcel. La polémique anti-juive de S. Jean Chrysostome et le mouvement judaisant d'Antioche, AIPHO 4, 1936, 403-421.

— Verus Israel, Étude sur les relations entre Chretiens et Juifs dans l'Empire romain (135-425). BEFAR 166, Paris 1948.

Skarsaune, Oskar. The Proof from Prophesy. A study in Justin Martyr's Proof-Text Tradition: Text-type, Provenance, Theological Profile. NT.S 61, 1987.

Smallwood, E. Mary. The Jews Under Roman Rule. From Pompey to Diocletian. SJLA 20, 1976.

Smith, Jonathan Z. Drudgery Divine. On the Comparison of Early Christianities and the Religions of Antiquity. JLCR (SOAS), 1988.

Smith, Morton, Clement of Alexandria and a Secret Gospel of Mark, Cambridge (US), 1973.

Souvay, Charles L. The Paschal Controversy under Pope Victor I. CHQ 15 (NS 9) 1929-30, 43-62.

Staats, Reinhold, Die törischten Jungfrauen von Mt 25 in gnostischer und antignostischer Sicht, in: Christentum und Gnosis (ed. W. Elstester) BZNW 37, 1969, 98-115.

Stendebach, F. J. Das Verbot des Knochenzerbrechens bei den Semiten, BZ NF 17, 1973, 29-38.

Sterling, Gregory E. Wisdom among the Perfect: Creation Traditions in Alexandrian Judaism and Corinthian Christianity. NovTest 37, 1995, 355-384.

Stommel, Eduard. «Begraben mit Christus» (Röm 6.4) und der Taufritus. RQ 49, 1954, 1-20.

Streeter, B. H. The Four Gospels, London/NY [2/11]1964.

Strobel, August. Passa-Symbolik und Passa-Wunder in Act. XII. 3ff. NTS 4, 1957-58, 210-215.

— Ursprung und Geschichte des frühchristlichen Osterkalenders, TU 121, 1977.

— ZBK 1 Kor, 1989.

Stuckenbruck Loren T. Angel Veneration and Christology, A Study in Early Judaism and in the Christology of the Apocalypse of John, WUNT 2.70, 1995.

Stuhlhofer, Franz. Der Gebrauch der Bibel von Jesus bis Euseb. Wuppertal 1988.

Sumney, Jerry L. Those Who "Ignorantly Deny Him": The Opponents of Ignatius of Antioch. JECS 1, 1993, 345-365.

Swartley, W. M. The Imitatio Christi in the Ignatian Letters, VigChr 27, 1979, 81-103.

Sykes, Alistair Stewart. Melito's Anti-Judaism. JECS 5, 1997, 271-283.

Taft, Robert. Historicism Revisited. SL 14, 1982, 97-109.

— In the Bridegroom's Absence. The Paschal Triduum in the Byzantine Church, StAns 102 (=AnLit 14), 1990, 71-97.

— The Liturgy of the Great Church: An Initial Synthesis of Structure and Interpretation on the Eve of Iconoclasm, DOP 34/35, 1980-81, 45-75.

— The Origins of the Liturgical Year. New York, [2]1991.

Talley, Thomas. From Berakah to Eucharistia: A Reopening Question. Wor 50, 1976, 115-137.

— The Origins of the Liturgical Year. New York, [2]1991.

Tappert, Theodore G., trans., ed. The Book of Concord. The Confessions of the Evangelical Lutheran Church. In collarboration with Jaroslav Pelikan, Robert H. Fischer, Arthur C. Piepkorn, Phila. [15]1983.

Taqizadeh, S. H., The Iranian Festivals Adopted by the Christians and Condemned by the Jews. BSOS 10, 1940-42, 623-693.

Taylor, Joan E. Christians and the Holy Places. The myth of Jewish-Christian origins, Oxford 1993.

Taylor, Miriam S. Anti-Judaism & Early Christian Identity. A Critique of the Scholarly Consensus. StPBib 46, 1995.

Tcherikover, V. The Decline of the Jewish Diaspora in Egypt During the Roman Period. JJS 14, 1963, 1-32.

Theißen, Gerd, Die Starken und Schwachen in Korinth, Soziologische Analyse eines theologischen Streites. Studien zur Soziologie des Urchristentums, WUNT 19, [3]1989, 272-289 (=EvTh 35, 1975, 155-172).

— Soziale Schichtung in der korinthischen Gemeinde, Ein Beitrag zur Soziologie des hellenistischen Urchristentums, in: Studien zur Soziologie des Urchristentums, WUNT 19, [3]1989, 231-271 (=ZNW 65, 1974, 232-272).

Thekeparampil, Jacob. Adam-Christus in den Passionssedre und in der Schatzhöhle, OCA 221, 1983, 323-332.

Thompson, Leonard. Cult and Eschatology in the Apocalypse of John, JRel 49, 1969, 330-350.

Thornton, Timothy C. G. Jerome and the 'Hebrew Gospel according to Matthew', StPat 28, 1993, 118-122.

— Jewish New Moon Festivals, Gal 4.3-11 and Col 2.16, JTS NS 40, 1989, 97-100.

— Problematical Passovers. Difficulties for Diaspora Jews and Early Christians in determining Passover Dates during the First Three Centuries A.D. StPat 20, 1989, 402-408.

Tortorelli, Kevin M. The *Ars Poetica* of Horace as a point of reference for reading Irenaeus, VC 27, 1990, 333-338.

Trebilco, Paul. Jewish Communities in Asia Minor, SNTS.MS 69, 1991.

Trocmé, Etienne. Passion as Liturgy, London 1983.

Turner, Victor W. The Ritual Process, London 1974.

Vanovermeier, Pedro. Livre que Jésus-Christ a révélé à ses disciples, unpub. Diss. Institute catholique de Paris, 1962.

Vielhauer, Philip. Paulus und die Kephaspartei in Korinth. NTS 21, 1974-75, 341-352.

Van der Vyver, A. L'Évolution du Comput Alexandrin et Romain du IIIe au Ve Siècle. RHE 52, 1957, 5-25.

Wambacq, B. N. Les Massot. Bib 61, 1980, 31-54.

Wehr, Lothar. Arznei der Unsterblichkeit. Die Eucharistie bei Ignatius von Antiochien und im Johannesevangelium. NTA, NF 18, 1987.

Weimar, Peter. Zum Problem der Entstehungsgeschichte von Ex 12.1-14. ZAW 107, 1995, 1-17.

Weitzel, K. L. Die Christliche Passafeier der drei ersten Jahrhunderte. Zugleich ein Beitrag zur Geschichte des Urchristenthums und zur Evangelienkritik, Pforzheim 1848.

Weitzmann Kurt, and Herbert L. Kessler. The Frescoes of the Dura Synagogue and Christian Art. DOS 28, Washington DC, 1990.

Wellesz, E. J. Melito's Homily on the Passion: An Investigation into the Sources of Byzantine Hymnography. JThS 44, 1943, 41-57.

Wengst, Klaus. Tradition und Theologie des Barnabasbriefes. AKG 42, 1971, 105-118.

Werner, Eric. Melito of Sardes, first poet of Deicide. HUCA 37, 1966, 191-210.

White, James F. Introduction to Christian Worship. Revised Edition. Nashville 1990

Wifstrand, A. The Homily of Melito on the Passion. VigChr 2, 1948, 201-223.

Wilken, John, Chrysostom and the Jews, Rhetoric and Reality in the Late Fourth Century, Berkeley 1983.

Wilson, S. G. Passover, Easter, and Anti-Judaism: Melito of Sardis and Others. in: Neusner, J.; Fredrichs, E. S., eds., To See Ourselves as Others See Us: Christians, Jews, "Others" in Late Antiquity, Chico CA, 1985, 337-355.

Winkler, Gabriele. Die Licht-Erscheinung bei der Taufe Jesu und der Ursprung des Epiphaniefestes, OChr 78, 1994, 176-229.

— Zur frühchristlichen Tauftradition in Syrien und Armenien unter Einbezug der Taufe Jesu. OkSt 27, 1978, 281-306.

Winslow, D. F. Melito of Sardis' Christology. StPatr 17/2, 1982, 765-776.

Winston, David. Philo's Ethical Theory. ANRW II.21.1, 372-416.

Winter, Paul. On the Trial of Jesus. StJud 1, Berlin 1961.

Wiseman, James. Corinth and Rome I: 228 BC-AD 267. ANRW II.7.1, 1979, 438-548.

Zahn, Theodor, Forschungen zur Geschichte des neutestamentlichen Kanons und der altchristlichen Literatur 4, Erlangen/Leipzig 1891.

Zernov, N. Eusebius and the Paschal Controversy. CQR 116, 1933, 24-41.

PRINTED ON PERMANENT PAPER • IMPRIME SUR PAPIER PERMANENT • GEDRUKT OP DUURZAAM PAPIER - ISO 9706

ORIENTALISTE, KLEIN DALENSTRAAT 42, B-3020 HERENT